ARCHIE BROWN

The Rise and Fall of Communism

D0315260

VINTAGE BOOKS
London

Published by Vintage 2010

2 4 6 8 10 9 7 5 3 1

First published in Great Britain in 2009 by
The Bodley Head

Vintage
Random House, 20 Vauxhall Bridge Road,
London SW1V 2SA

www.vintage-books.co.uk

Addresses for companies within The Random House Group Limited can be
found at: www.randomhouse.co.uk/offices.htm

The Random House Group Limited Reg. No. 954009

A CIP catalogue record for this book
is available from the British Library

ISBN 9781845950675

The Random House Group Limited supports The Forest Stewardship
Council (FSC), the leading international forest certification organisation. All
our titles that are printed on Greenpeace approved FSC certified paper carry
the FSC logo. Our paper procurement policy can be found at
www.rbooks.co.uk/environment

Typeset in Dante MT by Palimpsest Book Production Limited,
Grangemouth, Stirlingshire

Printed and bound in Great Britain by
CPI Cox & Wyman, Reading RG1 8EX

Contents

To
Susan and Alex,
Douglas and Tamara
and
to my grandchildren
Isobel and Martha,
Nikolas and Alina

The sixteen Communist countries in 1980

(See inset map on facing page for Eastern Europe detail)

0   1000   2000   3000   4000 miles

Equatorial scale

A Note on Names

There is no completely consistent way of rendering people's names in a book such as this. In languages with a different alphabet from that used in English, there is more than one transliteration system – for example, from Russian and from Chinese. In the Russian case, I have used a simplified version of the standard British system, adopted also by a number of North American journals. That means, for example, Trotsky, rather than Trotskiy (or the Library of Congress variant, which would be Trotskii). I have also favoured familiarity in the use of names. Thus, Trotsky's first name in Russia was Lev, but he is better known in the outside world as Leon, and that is the form I adopt. I do not use the Russian soft sign in the text. What in strict transliteration would be Zinov'ev I render, as is more usual in English, Zinoviev. But when citing books or articles (and their authors) in Russian in the endnotes, as distinct from the main body of the book, I do aim to transliterate precisely. When a Russian author has published a book or article in English, I use the spelling of his or her name adopted by that author.

In the case of Chinese names, I have generally used the pinyin system, adopted by most China scholars now – to take the obvious example, Mao Zedong rather than Mao Tse-tung. But here again I have made concessions to familiarity. Since Chiang Kai-shek was dead long before the old Wade-Giles system was abandoned by China specialists, his name appears in that familiar form. For similar reasons I have used Kuomintang, rather than Guomindang. (The former and older rendering of the name of the movement established by Sun Yat-sen in 1919 is still used in Taiwan.)

Names which are written in the English alphabet, but with the addition of diacritical marks, such as, for example, the Slovak Alexander Dubček, or the Hungarian János Kádár, are used in precisely that way in the book. There are, however, people who have become better known in the anglicized version of their names – especially monarchs such as Tsar Nicholas II of Russia or King Paul of Yugoslavia – and those are the forms I have used. Similarly, there are some Russians with the first name Aleksandr, such as Solzhenitsyn and Yakovlev, whose first name is usually rendered in English as Alexander, and for the sake of familiarity I have followed that practice. Stalin's first name is the equivalent of the English-language Joseph. Again, there is no one correct use. Stalin was a Georgian, and a strict transliteration of his name from Georgian would be Ioseb. In Russian it became Iosif. In English it is sometimes rendered as Josif, and that is the form I prefer – making clear that it is the equivalent of Joseph, but not anglicizing it so completely.

The naming of places can be no less problematical than what to call people. The capital city of Ukraine is correctly transliterated from Ukrainian as Kyiv, but in Russia it is called Kiev, and long ago that was the way in which it entered the English language. I have not changed that familiar usage. To those who object, I would point out that Russians are quite relaxed about the fact that we call their capital city Moscow, not Moskva (which it is in Russian). Similarly, we call the Czech capital Prague, rather than Praha which it is in the Czech Republic. And the English, who have been at odds with the French over many matters and many centuries, do not hold it against their near neighbours that they call the English (and British) capital Londres. During most of the Soviet period the pre-revolutionary Russian capital of St Petersburg, renamed Petrograd from 1914 to 1924, was called Leningrad, and it is now St Petersburg (though not the capital) once again. I usually refer to it by its name at the time in question.

A bigger issue is raised by my use of 'Eastern Europe'. Some of the countries which were designated as being in Eastern Europe – a term in common use, especially after they became Communist states – were located in central Europe. Thus, Eastern Europe, as distinct from eastern Europe, is more of a political than a geographical designation. That is why I use a capital letter in 'Eastern'. Given that this *was* a political description, the term became ambiguous and misleading from the moment Communist regimes collapsed in Europe. Its meaning was, however, clear enough under Communism, and it is with that period I am concerned in this volume. The Communist era comes up to the present day in several countries, but none of them are located in Europe.

Communist parties in Eastern Europe had different names at different times, such as the Polish United Workers' Party (PUWP). While sometimes using their official designation, I also use the generic term of Communist party when writing about them, employing a lower-case 'p' when that was not the official title. The capital 'C' is used for Communist states and parties. Lower-case 'communism' refers to the stateless society of the future which was supposedly to be the ultimate stage of social development.

Sources cited are listed in the endnotes. The first name as well as surname of an author is given on his or her first mention in the notes to each chapter. Other bibliographical details of a book, article, or archival document are also provided in full on their first mention in the chapter endnotes and abbreviated in the remainder of that chapter.

Glossary and Abbreviations

Agitprop – Agitation and Propaganda
ANC – African National Congress
apparat – apparatus, bureaucracy
apparatchik – bureaucrat, full-time official (especially of Communist
   Party)
BBC – British Broadcasting Corporation
BCP – Bulgarian Communist Party
blat – pull, influence through reciprocal favours (Russia)
BSP – Bulgarian Socialist Party
Bund – Jewish socialist organization
CC – Central Committee
CCP – Chinese Communist Party
Cheka – All-Russian Extraordinary Commission for Combating
   Counter-Revolution and Sabotage (December 1917–22)
CIA – Central Intelligence Agency (USA)
Cominform – Communist Information Bureau (1947–56)
Comintern – Communist International (1919–43)
CPGB – Communist Party of Great Britain
CPI – Communist Party of India
CPI (M) – Communist Party of India (Marxist)
CPR – Chinese People's Republic
CPRF – Communist Party of the Russian Federation
CPSA – Communist Party of South Africa
CPSU – Communist Party of Soviet Union
CPUSA – Communist Party of the USA
CPV – Communist Party of Vietnam
CPY – Communist Party of Yugoslavia (to 1952)
CSCE – Conference on Security and Co-operation in Europe
CWIHB – Cold War International History Bulletin
DPA – Democratic Party of Albania

DRV – Democratic Republic of Vietnam
FNLA – National Front for the Liberation of Angola
FRG – Federal Republic of Germany
GDP – Gross Domestic Product
GDR – German Democratic Republic
glasnost – openness, transparency
Glavlit – state censorship (USSR)
Gosplan – State Planning Committee (USSR)
guanxi – connections, networking, reciprocal exchange of favours
  (China)
ID – International Department (CC of CPSU)
ILO – International Labour Organization
IMEMO – Institute of World Economy and International Relations
  (Moscow)
INF – Intermediate-range Nuclear Forces
Iskra – The Spark (newspaper and organization founded by Lenin)
JCP – Japanese Communist Party
KAN – Club of Non-Party Activists (Czechoslovakia, 1968)
KGB – Committee of State Security (USSR)
Komsomol – Young Communist League (USSR)
KOR – Workers' Defence Committee (Poland)
KPD – Communist Party of Germany
Kuomintang (also known as Guomindang) – Chinese Nationalist Party
LCY – League of Communists (Yugoslavia – after 1952)
MAD – Mutally Assured Destruction
MAKN – Mongolian People's Revolutionary Party
MGB – Ministry of State Security (USSR, 1946–53)
MKS – Inter-Factory Strike Committee (in Poland)
MPLA – Popular Movement for the Liberation of Angola
MVD – Ministry of Internal Affairs (USSR)
MSZMP – Hungarian Socialist Workers' Party
NEM – New Economic Mechanism (Hungary)
NEP – New Economic Policy (of Lenin in 1920s)
NKVD – People's Commissariat of Internal Affairs (name of Soviet
  security police during worst years of the purges)
nomenklatura – Communist system of appointments; also used to refer
  to people appointed to high positions by this system as an especially
  privileged social stratum
Novy mir – New World (Russian monthly literary journal)
NSA – National Security Archive (Washington DC)

OGPU – name of Soviet security organs before they became NKVD

Okhrana – pre-revolutionary Russian secret police

ORI – Integrated Revolutionary Organization (name of Cuban Communist party, 1961–65)

PCC – Cuban Communist Party

PCE – Spanish Communist Party

PCF – French Communist Party

PCI – Italian Communist Party

PDPA – People's Democratic Party of Afghanistan

perestroika – reconstruction (or restructuring)

PKI – Communist Party of Indonesia

PLA – People's Liberation Army (China)

Politburo – Political Bureau of Central Committee of Communist parties (the highest collective policy-making body in Communist states)

POUM – Worker Party of Marxist Unification (Spain)

PSP – Popular Socialist Party (early name of Cuban Communist party)

PUWP – Polish United Workers' Party

RFE – Radio Free Europe

RL – Radio Liberty

RSDLP – Russian Social Democratic Labour Party (forerunner of CPSU).

RSFSR – Russian Soviet Federative Socialist Republic (Russian republic of USSR)

Sovnarkom – Council of People's Commissars (name of Soviet government – became Council of Ministers from 1946)

sovnarkhozy – regional economic councils (Khrushchev era, USSR)

SPD – Social Democratic Party (Germany)

SRs – Socialist Revolutionaries (a Russian political party, 1902–22)

svyazi – connections (Russia)

UDF – Union of Democratic Forces (Bulgaria)

UN – United Nations

USSR – Union of Soviet Socialist Republics

vozhd' – leader and guide, with strongly positive connotation (Russia)

Introduction

'Have you ever met a Communist?' The question was put to me by the editor of my home-town Scottish newspaper where I worked as a teenage reporter in the mid-1950s. This was prior to National Service in the army and before I went to university, which led to a career switch to academia. The answer to the question was, 'No, I can't say I have.' The implication behind the question, soon to become clear, was: do you realize how different from us these people are – and how dangerous?

In fact, I probably had met a Communist by that time. The teacher of my French class at school in 1952–53 was widely rumoured (I think correctly) to be a Communist – one consequence, no doubt, of his studies in France where Communist ideas in the early post-war years were much more popular than in Britain. Except in his presence, he was invariably known to his pupils as 'Wee Joe'. And though he was indeed small, his first name was not Joseph. The 'Joe' referred to Josif Stalin, so closely was Communism associated in those years with the Soviet dictator.

In the years since then I have met and talked with hundreds of Communists – especially in the former Soviet Union, but also throughout Eastern Europe and in China. They included some of the small British contingent. Oddly, the first Communist I got to know to any extent was in the army – a soldier who later went AWOL. He told me that not even a small corner shop could be left in private ownership, for it would be like a cancerous cell that would spread throughout the body politic. (This was in 1957. For all I know, that youthful Communist may now be a retired businessman.)

What became clear, however, when I began the serious study of Communist systems some years later, was how little it revealed about a particular person to be told that the individual was a Communist. Joining a Communist party when it was an underground organization within a conservative authoritarian or a fascist state was different from joining a Communist party in a democracy. It was very different again from joining the party within an established Communist state where that organization had a monopoly of political power. Membership then aided career advancement and was a precondition for holding almost all of the higher positions within the society, even when these were not overtly political.

Ruling Communist parties did not try to enrol the entire population as members. The ranks of the obedient followers always had to be much larger than those of the party faithful. These were mass parties but also selective ones. As a general rule, in Communist countries, about one in ten of the adult working population was a member. They belonged to a 'vanguard party', exercising what became known as the 'leading role' (a euphemism for monopoly of power) within a Communist state. People's motives for joining varied according to time, place, and personality. In countries in which Communists ruled, the ranks of the party were dramatically increased immediately after the successful seizure of power. Revolutionaries by firm, often fanatical, conviction were soon outnumbered by those who leapt on the Communist bandwagon once it had rolled into governmental office. These members' reasons for joining the now ruling party were generally quite different from those which led people into a persecuted and illegal party with its risks of exile, imprisonment or death.

In the Soviet Union during the Second World War, joining the party was for many recruits just another aspect of patriotism at a time when loyalty to the regime went hand in hand with loyalty to a motherland under mortal threat. In the relatively tranquil years, by Soviet standards, when Leonid Brezhnev headed the Soviet Communist Party – between 1964 and 1982 – acquiring a party membership card was much more commonly related to career advancement. It was a fact of life that in all Communist countries ambitious people tended to join the ruling party. It is one reason why in the first two decades since 1989, former Communists have continued to be quite disproportionately well represented in high positions, including the top political offices, in many of the post-Communist states.

My professional interest in Communist systems began in the early 1960s when I was an undergraduate and graduate student at the London School of Economics. By 1964 I was lecturing on Soviet politics at Glasgow University, and before the end of the sixties I had launched a course there called 'The Comparative Study of Communist States'. (Throughout the 1970s and 1980s I taught a similar course with a different title at Oxford.) The subject of 'Comparative Communism' which emerged in the late 1960s within the study of politics was both a recognition that Communist states had enough in common to be grouped together as a quite distinctive type among the world's political and economic systems and an acknowledgement that there were differences among them sufficiently great to require analysis and explanation.

Over a period of forty years I visited many of the Communist states while they still were (or are) under Communist rule, and the people I met there ranged from dissidents to members of the party's Central Committee. The majority of those with whom I spoke fell into neither of those two categories. Many were party members, many were not. It is helpful, when coming to write a book like this, to have had a variety of experiences – from warm friendships and cultural enrichment to secret police surveillance and time-wasting bureaucracy – in these countries while they still had Communist systems. It is no less of an advantage, however, to be writing now that most of these states are no longer under Communist rule. Many archival materials have become available – including minutes of Politburo sessions and transcripts of meetings between Communist leaders from different countries – which were beyond the dreams of scholars a few decades ago. People who were leading political figures in Communist states can be interviewed and numerous revealing memoirs have been published.

Communist systems had a number of essential things in common, in spite of the many peculiarities which distinguished one country from another. There remain at least *some* common features among the five remaining Communist states – China, Cuba, Laos, North Korea and Vietnam – although the differences between, for example, China and North Korea are enormous. It is important to examine those features that make it meaningful to call a system Communist, although that is not my starting point in this book, since history should preferably be written forwards, not backwards. First of all, in Part I, I look at the origins and development of the idea of Communism and then what it meant in practice up to the outbreak of the Second World War. That occupies the first five chapters. I turn to the question of what we mean by a Communist system only in Chapter 6.

The greater part of the book is naturally concerned with the post-Second World War period, for until then there was only one major Communist state – the USSR (and one minor one, in terms of population and influence, Mongolia). The very fact that the Soviet Union, the revolutionary successor to Imperial Russia, was the first country to establish a Communist political and economic system meant that it profoundly influenced the organization of subsequent Communist states, even in cases where the regime had not been placed in power by Soviet force of arms. Although I pay attention to non-ruling Communist parties and to the reasons why some people were drawn to these parties even within democracies, my main concern is with countries which were under Communist rule. By the late 1970s there were sixteen of them. Although there *were* never more than that number of fully fledged Communist states, there *are* thirty-six states which have at one time been under Communist rule. That seeming contradiction is explained by

the fact that three Communist countries which had federal constitutions –
the Soviet Union, Yugoslavia and Czechoslovakia – split into their component
parts after the Communist system, which had held them together, ceased
to exist. In the Soviet case alone, one state became fifteen.

The sixteen countries which by my criteria count as having been
Communist for a significant period of time are the same sixteen which
were regarded as 'socialist' – as the only ruling parties to belong to the
international Communist movement – by the Soviet leadership as the 1980s
drew to an end.[1] (By the end of 1989, or early 1990, half of these countries
had *ceased* to have Communist systems.) In alphabetical order the sixteen
are: Albania, Bulgaria, Cambodia (Kampuchea), China, Cuba,
Czechoslovakia, the German Democratic Republic (East Germany),
Hungary, North Korea, Laos, Mongolia, Poland, Romania, the Soviet
Union, Vietnam, and Yugoslavia.

A major task of this volume is to provide a reliable account of, and
fresh information on, the rise and fall of Communism and on the individuals who played the most crucial roles in these tumultuous events.
The book, though, sets out to be more than a narrative history of
Communism. While addressing also a number of other big issues, it aims
especially to provide an interpretation of (1) how and why Communists
came to power; (2) how they were able, in a variety of countries on
different continents, to hold on to power for so long; and (3) what brought
about the dismantling or collapse of Communist systems. To answer those
questions involves paying attention both to the internal workings of
Communist party-states and to the different societies in which they operated. Communism was a far more successful and longer-lived movement
than any of its totalitarian or authoritarian rivals. Its appeal to many intelligent, highly educated, and comfortably-off people as well as to the
socially and economically deprived calls for explanation. So does its structure of power, which contributed so greatly to its longevity. Communist
rule in Russia survived for over seventy years. Even today, the most
populous country in the world, China, is regarded as a Communist state,
and in some (though not all) respects it still is.

The book is divided into five parts. As already noted, the origins and
development of Communism are discussed in Part 1. This section takes the
story of Communism from its founders, Karl Marx and Friedrich Engels
(with a brief look at pre-Marxian 'communists'), to the outbreak of the
Second World War. That war had a different starting year in different countries – as late as June 1941 in the case of the Soviet Union. This opening
section sees the Bolsheviks coming to power, the formation of the
Communist International, and the evolution of the Soviet system under

Lenin and Stalin. It also examines the scope and limitations of Communism outside the Soviet Union and the tensions in Europe between Communists and social democrats. Part 2 is concerned with the years between the Second World War and the death of Stalin – a period in which Communism took off beyond the boundaries of the Soviet Union. In particular, it looks at the establishment of Communist systems throughout Eastern Europe and in China. It is in this section that particular attention is paid to the broader issue of the appeals of Communism. The third part deals with Communism in the quarter of a century, broadly speaking, after the death of Stalin, a time of highly contradictory trends. The system was still expanding, and gaining adherents in the 'Third World', although few countries in Asia (as compared with the Communist takeover of Eastern Europe) and none in Africa acquired Communist systems. Yet, at the same time 'revisionism', reformism and even revolution (in Hungary) – not to mention the Sino-Soviet split – were posing a greater challenge to Soviet orthodoxy than had existed hitherto.

The fourth section, entitled 'Pluralizing Pressures', is concerned mainly with the period from the mid- and late-1970s to the mid-1980s when the problems facing the international Communist movement intensified, ranging from the aftermath of the 'Eurocommunism' of major non-ruling parties to, more significantly, the rise of Solidarity in Poland and the adoption of radical economic reform in China. It is a time to which many commentators trace the downfall of Communism, drawing attention to such disparate factors as the decline in the rate of economic growth, Soviet failure to keep pace with the technological revolution, the election of a Polish pope, and the policies of President Ronald Reagan. How important these factors were, and whether any of them was in reality more fundamental than other less noticed factors, is a major theme of Part 5.

In that final section, I address a number of big questions. Karl Marx argued that capitalism contained the seeds of its own destruction. Did this turn out to be truer of Communist systems, with, paradoxically, the positive achievements, no less than the failures and injustices of Communism, contributing to the growth of disillusionment with the system? Given the interlinkage between the political systems of east-central Europe and that of the Soviet Union, from where did the decisive influence flow at different times during the period of the fall of Communism? How important was influence from the West and how much did the spread of ideas from one Communist state to another matter? How much did differences and divisions behind the monolithic façades which Communist parties presented to their own peoples and the outside world have to do with the dramatic end of Communism in Europe and its modification in China? And, given that – due especially to the huge population of China – more than a fifth of the world's population still live under Communist rule, how do we explain the resilience of those Communist states which still exist? These are but some of the big issues tackled in the chapters which follow.

PART ONE

ORIGINS AND DEVELOPMENT

I

The Idea of Communism

'A spectre is haunting Europe – the spectre of communism.' When Karl Marx began his *Manifesto of the Communist Party* of 1848 with these famous words, he – and his co-author, Friedrich Engels – could have had no inkling of the way in which Communism would take off in the twentieth century. It became not merely a spectre but a living reality. And not just in Europe, but for hundreds of millions of people spread across the globe – in places very different from those where Marx expected proletarian revolutions to occur. Communist systems were established in two predominantly peasant societies – the largest country in the world, Imperial Russia, which became the Soviet Union, and in the state with the largest population, China. Why and how Communism spread, what kind of system it became, how it varied over time and across space, and why and how it came to an end in Europe, where it began, are the central themes of this book.

Marx's claim was an exaggeration when he made it in the middle of the nineteenth century. By the middle of the twentieth century it had become almost an understatement. That is not to say that the 'Communism' which held sway in so many countries bore much resemblance to anything Marx had envisaged. There was a wide gulf between the original theory and the subsequent practice of Communist rule. Karl Marx sincerely believed that under communism – the future society of his imagination which he saw as an inevitable, and ultimate, stage of human development – people would live more freely than ever before. Yet 'his vision of the universal liberation of humankind' did not include any safeguards for individual liberty.[1] Marx would have hated to be described as a moralist, since he saw himself as a Communist who was elaborating a theory of scientific socialism. Yet many of his formulations were nothing like as 'scientific' as he made out. One of his most rigorous critics on that account, Karl Popper, pays tribute to the moral basis of much of Marx's indictment of nineteenth-century capitalism. As Popper observes, under the slogan of 'equal and free competition for all', child labour in conditions of immense suffering had been 'tolerated, and sometimes even defended, not only by professional economists but also by churchmen'. Accordingly, 'Marx's burning protest against these crimes', says Popper, 'will secure him forever a place among the liberators of mankind.'[2] Those who took power in the twentieth century, both using and misusing Marx's ideas, turned out, however, to be anything but liberators. Marxist theory, as interpreted by Vladimir Lenin and subsequently refashioned by Josif Stalin in Russia and by Mao Zedong in China, became a rationalization for ruthless single-party dictatorship.

During most of the twentieth century Communism was the world's dominant international political movement. People reacted to it in different ways – as a source of hope for a radiant future or as the greatest threat on the face of the earth. By the middle decades of the last century there were Communist governments not only in a string of Soviet satellite states in Europe but also in Latin America and Asia. Communism held sway in what became the 'Second World'. The 'First World' – headed by the United States and its main European allies – was to engage in prolonged struggle with the international Communist movement for influence in the 'Third World'.

Even in countries with strong democratic traditions, among them the United States and Great Britain, many intellectuals were drawn for a time to Communism. In France and Italy, in particular, Communist parties became significant political forces – far stronger than they were in Britain and America. The French and Italian parties had substantial popular as well as intellectual support, together with significant parliamentary representation. After Communist systems had been put in place not just in Eastern Europe and Asia but in Cuba, too, it seemed to some at one point as if the system would triumph also in Africa. The global rivalry between the West and the Communist bloc led to prolonged tension and the Cold War. At times that came close to 'hot war' – most notably during the Cuban missile crisis of 1962.

The rise of Communism, even more than the rise of fascism, was the most important political phenomenon of the first half of the twentieth century. For Communism turned out to be a much stronger, and longer-lasting, movement – and political religion – than fascism. That is why by far the most significant political event of the later part of the century was the end of Communism in Europe – and its effective demise as an international movement. The decline, which preceded the fall, occurred over several decades, even though these were highly contradictory years which saw also Communist advances. It was *after* the Soviet leader Nikita Khrushchev had exposed some of the crimes of Stalin in 1956 that Communism had its singular success on the American continent – in Cuba – and that its Asian reach expanded to embrace the whole of Vietnam.

It is worth noting at the outset that Communist parties did not call their own systems 'Communist' but, rather, 'socialist'. For them, 'communism' was to be a later stage in the development of society – the ultimate stage – in which the institutions of the state would have 'withered away' and would have been replaced by a harmonious, self-administering society. Throughout the book – to reiterate an important distinction – I use 'communism' when referring to that fanciful future utopia (and 'communism' also for other non-Marxist utopias), but 'Communism', with a capital 'C', when discussing actual Communist systems.

Early Communists

While Marx and, later, Lenin were overwhelmingly the most important theorists of Communism – in Lenin's case, a key practitioner as well – the idea of communism did not originate with Karl Marx. Many different, and idealistic, notions of communism had come into existence centuries earlier. Most of these forerunners of both Communism and socialism had little or nothing in common with the practice of twentieth-century Communist regimes (or with those few such systems which survive into the twenty-first century) other than a belief in a future utopia, one more sincerely held by 'communists' from the fourteenth to the nineteenth centuries than by most Communist Party leaders in the second half of the twentieth century. Yet there were also millennial sects, attracted to a primitive communism, which foreshadowed Communist, even Stalinist, regimes in the the degree of their intolerance and their commitment to violent repression of their perceived enemies.

In medieval times social reformers looked back to the early Christians as examples of people who held everything in common. The prominent German historian Max Beer argued that even if it 'may fairly be doubted whether positive communistic institutions really existed amongst the primitive Christian communities . . . there cannot be any doubt that common possessions were looked upon by many of the first Christians as an ideal to be aimed at'.[3] Indeed, according to the Acts of the Apostles, the disciples of Jesus 'were of one heart and of one soul: neither said any of them that ought of the things which he possessed was his own; but they had all things common'.[4] In the second half of the fourth century, St Ambrose, the Bishop of Milan (the mentor of St Augustine), declared: 'Nature has poured forth all things for all men, to be held in common. For God commanded all things to be produced so that food should be common to all, and that the earth should be a common possession of all. Nature, therefore, created a common right, but use and habit created private right . . .'[5]

Many fourteenth-century Christian theologians, among them the English church reformer John Wycliffe, assumed that the earliest form of human society was one of 'innocence and communism'.[6] Indeed, on occasion Wycliffe contended that 'all good things of God *ought* to be in common' (emphasis added).[7] He cautiously qualified this, however, by saying that in practical life there was no alternative to acquiescing with inequalities and injustices and leaving wealth and power in the hands of those who had done nothing to deserve it.[8] It was around the year 1380, Norman Cohn has argued, that people moved beyond thinking of a society 'without distinction of status or wealth simply as a Golden Age irrecoverably lost in the distant past' and began to think of it as something to be realized in the near future.[9] Only a minority, however, challenged the monarchs and feudal lords and tried to create – or, as they saw it, 'recreate' – a communist society which would combine freedom for all with broad equality. One such person was the revolutionary priest John Ball, who years before the Peasants' Revolt of 1381 in England had occupied himself 'inflaming the peasantry against the lords temporal and spiritual'.[10] Ball was regarded as an instigator of that major revolt, for which he was executed in the same year. An extract from one of the speeches, said to have been delivered by him, exemplifies his radical, but religiously based, egalitarianism:

> Things cannot go well in England, nor ever will, until all goods are held in common, and until there will be neither serfs nor gentlemen, and we shall all be equal. For what reason have they, whom we call lords, got the best of us? How did they deserve it? Why do they keep us in bondage? If we all descended from one father and one mother, Adam and Eve, how can they assert or prove that they are more masters than ourselves? Except perhaps that they make us work and produce for them to spend![11]

Ball put the same point still more pithily in the verse attributed to him:

> When Adam delved and Eve span,
> Who was then the gentleman?[12]

Ball had his revolutionary counterparts in continental Europe. Especially in Bohemia and Germany, these movements were more intense and, in some of their manifestations, more extreme than in England. In early fifteenth-century Bohemia, Jan Hus was a reformer rather than a revolutionary. Like Wycliffe, he attacked corruption within the Church and insisted that when papal decrees contradicted 'the law of Christ as expressed in the Scriptures', Christians should not obey them. Arguing that the papacy was a human, not divine, institution, and that Christ was the head of the Church, he was excommunicated in 1412 and burnt as a heretic in 1415. Outrage in Bohemia at Hus's execution turned unrest into 'a national reformation' – a century before Luther – and led to the creation of a Hussite movement, one manifestation of which was a popular rising in Prague in 1419.[13] An extreme offshoot of the Hussites, known as the Taborites, practised a form of communism in anticipation of the imminent Second Coming of Christ. Thousands of peasants in Bohemia and Moravia sold their belongings and paid the proceeds into communal chests.[14] The principle that 'all people must hold everything in common, and nobody must possess anything of his own' was somewhat undermined by the practice whereby 'the Taborite revolutionaries were so preoccupied with common ownership that they altogether ignored the need to produce'.[15]

In the early sixteenth century, revolutionaries writing and preaching in German were among the most severe in the treatment they advocated for enemies of their imagined egalitarian social order. One such person, whose real name is unknown, but whom historians have called 'the Revolutionary of the Upper Rhine', argued that the road to the millennium led through massacre and terror. He forecast that 2,300 clerics would be killed each day in a bloodbath that would continue for four and a half years. There were limits to his revolutionary zeal, for he did not advocate doing away with the emperor. He did, however, favour the abolition of private property, writing: 'What a lot of harm springs from self-seeking! . . . It is necessary therefore that all property shall become one single property, then there will indeed be one shepherd and one sheepfold.'[16] A more erudite advocate of a new social order, to be achieved by violent means, was Thomas Müntzer, whose active proselytizing began a decade or so later than that of the Revolutionary of the Upper Rhine. He was to earn the approval in the nineteenth century of Friedrich Engels, who wrote: 'The mystics of the Middle Ages who dreamed of the coming millennium were already conscious of the injustice of class antagonisms. On the threshold of modern history, three hundred and fifty years ago, Thomas Müntzer proclaimed it to the world.'[17] Müntzer did his utmost to stir up the peasantry against the nobility and the ecclesiastical establishment. It was not, obviously, his belief in an imminent Second Coming that appealed to some nineteenth-century revolutionaries, including Engels, but his commitment to class war. Müntzer played a part in encouraging peasant insurrection in sixteenth-century Germany in rhetoric which was violent and uncompromising. Thus, in a letter, urging his followers to attack 'the godless scoundrels' who represented Church and state, he wrote:

Now go at them, and at them, and at them! It is time. The scoundrels are as
dispirited as dogs . . . It is very, very necessary, beyond measure necessary . . .
Take no notice of the lamentations of the godless! They will beg you in such
a friendly way, and whine and cry like children. Don't be moved to pity . . .
Stir people up in villages and towns, and most of all the miners and other
good fellows who will be good at the job. We must sleep no more! . . . Get
this letter to the miners.[18]

After leading an ill-equipped peasant army – which was instantly routed –
against forces marshalled by German princes, Müntzer was captured,
tortured, and beheaded in 1525.

On an altogether higher level, intellectually and in its humanity, was the
work of Sir Thomas More. One of the most intriguing early portrayals of
an imagined communist society is to be found in More's *Utopia*, published
in 1516.[19] With this book, he gave a name to the entire genre of utopian
fiction, of which several thousand examples saw the light of day over the
next five hundred years.[20] More himself eventually suffered the same fate
as John Ball (and Müntzer) – he was executed, although, unlike Ball, not
primarily for anything he wrote or said. In contrast also to Ball, he had risen
high in English society, holding the important rank of lord chancellor. He
was beheaded because he did not endorse Henry VIII's decision to appoint
himself the supreme head of the Church in England, thereby supplanting
the pope. More did not openly oppose the king. He was put to death principally for opinions he did not make public, his very silence becoming a
'political crime'.[21]

Yet More's *Utopia* would, on the face of it, appear to be more subversive
of the hierarchy largely taken for granted in medieval Europe than his silence
over the king's extension of his powers. The narrator in his story says:
'. . . I'm quite convinced that you'll never get a fair distribution of goods,
or a satisfactory organization of human life, until you abolish private property altogether. So long as it exists, the vast majority of the human race,
and the vastly superior part of it, will inevitably go on labouring under a
burden of poverty, hardship, and worry.' The book is written in the form
of a dialogue, and More provides his own objection to that statement, saying:
'I don't believe you'd ever have a reasonable standard of living under a
communist system. There'd always tend to be shortages, because nobody
would work hard enough.'[22] He evidently harboured some doubts about his
utopia, but he weights the argument in favour of the society of his imagination and against that in which he lived, putting into the mouth of the
principal character in his story the following words:

In fact, when I consider any social system that prevails in the modern world, I can't, so help me God, see it as anything but a conspiracy of the rich to advance their own interests under the pretext of organizing society. They think up all sorts of tricks and dodges, first for keeping safe their ill-gotten gains, and then for exploiting the poor by buying their labour as cheaply as possible.[23]

Concluding his book, More reflects on what the 'traveller' has told him about how things are organized in the country called Utopia, and says: '. . . I freely admit that there are many features of the Utopian Republic which I should like – though I hardly expect – to see adopted in Europe.'[24]

Another notable utopia, a little less than a century after More's work, was produced by the Italian Dominican monk Tommasso Campanella, whose La Città del sole (The City of the Sun) was published in 1602. Campanella was in frequent trouble with the authorities and this work was written while he was enduring a twenty-seven-year sentence as a prisoner of the Spanish Inquisition. Campanella sees the family as the main obstacle to the creation of a communistic state, and holds that parents for the most part educate their children wrongly and that the state must, therefore, be responsible for their education. He stresses the dignity of work, although in his city of the sun, working hours have been reduced to four a day, with much of the rest of the time devoted to 'learning joyously'.[25]

The eighteenth-century Enlightenment – with its secularization, embrace of science, and belief in progress – paved the way for a different manner of thinking about the society of the future.[26] This had both evolutionary and revolutionary manifestations. Prefiguring in important respects the thought of Marx, though much less dogmatically, Montesquieu and Turgot in France and such major figures of the Scottish Enlightenment as Adam Smith, John Millar and Adam Ferguson elaborated a theory of stages of development of society which, they argued, provided the key to understanding the evolution of society. It was the economic base, society's mode of subsistence – specifically, the four stages of development from hunting to pasturage to agriculture (with the acquisition of property in the form of land) and, finally, commerce – which went a long way towards explaining the form of government and the ideas prevailing in each epoch.[27] Marx read these authors and others who developed a sociological understanding of the development of law and property, but his theory of stages – outlined later in the chapter – differed significantly from them.

The French Revolution of 1789 gave rise to a more radical mode of thought than that of Smith or Turgot, concerned less with detached analysis of society than with changing it through direct action. All subsequent revolutionaries, including Marx and Lenin, paid close attention to the French Revolution which from its beginning was seen as 'an epochal event which completely transformed the social and political identity of the civilized world'.[28] In its variant that bore the greatest family relationship to Communism, it was known as Babouvism, after its leader, Gracchus Babeuf. For the Babouvists equality was the supreme value, and they were ready to embrace 'a period of dictatorship in the general interest for as long as might be necessary to destroy or disarm the enemies of equality'.[29] In contrast with Babeuf, the French theorist the Comte de Saint-Simon was no believer in equality, but he has some claim to be regarded as the 'founder of modern theoretical socialism, conceived not merely as an ideal but as the outcome of a historical process'.[30] Saint-Simon believed that free economic competition produced poverty and crises and that society was moving inexorably to a stage when its affairs would be planned in accordance with social needs. He was resolutely opposed to violence and held that the most educated section of society would become convinced of the necessity of the development of more rational administration, based upon the application of science, and that other social groups would be won over to an appreciation of such a development.[31] Although Saint-Simon's was the first form of socialism to which the young Karl Marx was introduced – by his future father-in-law, Ludwig von Westphalen – Marx was later to pour scorn on Saint-Simon's followers on account of their utopianism, commitment to peaceful change and trust in the possibility of class cooperation rather than the inevitability of class struggle.[32]

Charles Fourier and Pierre-Joseph Proudhon were also significant figures in the development of nineteenth-century socialist thought. Fourier wished to retain private property, but he envisaged work in the future being carried out by co-operatives, government being reduced to economic administration, a single language being used by all humankind, and people's personalities liberated from the form of 'slavery' which he attributed to hired labour.[33] Both Fourier and Proudhon were read by Marx and also strongly attacked by him. Indeed, Marx devoted an entire book which he entitled *The Poverty of Philosophy* to a critique of Proudhon's work, *The Philosophy of Poverty*. Proudhon is famously associated with the slogan, 'Property is theft', though the wording was not original to him, having already been used on the eve of the French Revolution. Although an inconsistent and utopian thinker, Proudhon thought of himself as a systematic analyst and he was the first person to use the expression 'scientific socialism'. He believed that social harmony was the natural state of affairs and that it was the existing economic system that prevented its flourishing. He was not, for the most part, an advocate of revolutionary struggle, since he supposed that the realization of his ideals should appeal to all, given that they would be 'no more than the fulfilment of human destiny'.[34]

The nineteenth century saw many attempts to think about how society might be organized on a co-operative or, in some instances, communist basis. A French 'utopian socialist', Étienne Cabet, who was born in 1788, is credited by the *Oxford English Dictionary* with being the first person to use the actual term 'communism' (*communisme*), in 1840. In that year he published under a pseudonym his *Voyage en Icarie*. The Icaria of his imagination is an egalitarian community in which there is neither private property nor money and in which all goods are held in common. Cabet was opposed to violent revolution and his communism was inspired by Christianity. As such, it is hardly surprising that it had made no impact on Karl Marx, but Cabet's writings did enjoy a degree of popularity in France. He spent some time in Britain and in 1849 emigrated to the United States where he died (in St Louis) in 1856.[35] In his seven years in America he established several communist settlements – in Missouri, Iowa and California. The one at Cloverdale, California, survived until 1895.

One of the utopian socialists who was treated most seriously in his own lifetime was Robert Owen, a man who significantly influenced Cabet. Owen, who was born in 1771 and died in 1858, was an entrepreneur as well as a political thinker and educationist. A Welshman by origin, he took over a mill at New Lanark in Scotland which became in the second decade of the nineteenth century a model factory. A believer in the perfectibility of human beings if they were given the right environment and education, Owen provided schools at New Lanark which were advanced and enlightened for their time. The factory workers were also paid better, and worked shorter hours in far better conditions, than almost all their competitors. What helped to give Owen credibility in the wider world was that the factory was also for a time an outstanding commercial success, although – or because – large sums were constantly being spent on new amenities for the workforce.[36]

At that time Owen was still a paternalist employer, albeit a highly unusual one, but his ideas became more utopian, as well as impulsive, over time. He made more than one attempt to set up a co-operative commune, of which the most famous was at New Harmony in the United States. The Rappite Community at Harmony in Indiana, close to the Illinois border, had been set up by a group of around a thousand German settlers, mainly peasant farmers, led by a preacher, George Rapp, who had emigrated to the United States for the sake of religious freedom. In 1825 Robert Owen established a community there which he promptly named New Harmony. Owen's status at that time was such that, on his way to Indiana, he had meetings with the current American president, James Monroe, the president-elect, John Quincy Adams, and three former presidents no less illustrious than John Adams, Thomas Jefferson and James Madison.

While the founding of New Harmony was the point at which Owen embraced a form of communism or communitarianism, 1825 was also, as even a very sympathetic biographer observes, the year when his business sense and, indeed, his common sense 'appear to have entirely deserted him'.[37] Owen – who was described by the liberal Victorian writer Harriet Martineau as 'always palpably right in his descriptions of human misery' but 'always thinking he had proved a thing when he had only asserted it in the force of his own conviction'[38] – aspired to have complete equality of income in New Harmony, with all residents enjoying similar food, clothing and education. The self-governing community, however, found it very difficult to manage themselves and after a few weeks of trying, they called on Owen, who had soon departed from his creation, to come back for a year to sort things out. He duly returned, but unfortunately, 'Owen's autocracy . . . proved no more effective than communist democracy.'[39] After several unsuccessful reor-ganizations of New Harmony, which had become more discordant than harmonious, Owen abandoned the project in 1827.[40]

Marx and Engels

For inspiring the development of the Communist movement, Karl Marx, needless to say, stands far apart from all other nineteenth-century radicals other than his close friend and collaborator, Friedrich Engels.[41] Both men were born and brought up in Germany and both spent much of their adult life in Britain, Marx in London, Engels in Manchester. Marx came from a long line of rabbis, but his Jewish businessman father, who converted to Lutheran Christianity, was a lawyer and also the owner of several vineyards. Marx had a comfortable bourgeois upbringing in the town of Trier in the Rhineland where he was born on 5 May 1818. He later studied at the univer-sities of Bonn and Berlin. During his London years, he never had a salaried job, but spent a vast amount of time in the Reading Room of the British Museum. He was a prolific writer, both as a journalist and as the author of polemical and theoretical books. The most influential advocate of proletarian revolution in world history married in 1843 a woman of aristocratic back-ground, Jenny von Westphalen, whose father, Baron Ludwig von Westphalen, was from the Prussian aristocracy on his father's side and the Scottish nobility on his mother's.[42] Marx and his wife were frequently impoverished, and the material conditions in which they lived in London contributed to the early deaths of three of their six children.[43] On many occasions the survivors kept going thanks only to the beneficence of Engels or to pawning Jenny's family silver.[44] Although Marx's most important political activism took the form of his writings, he played at times a notable part in an organization founded in 1864 as the International Working Men's Association, later known as the First International. Most of the leading members were, indeed, manual workers, but they embraced a wide variety of viewpoints in addition to what would become known as 'Marxism', including Proudhonism and anarchism. Marx died in London on 17 March 1883 and was buried, in the presence of only eleven mourners, in Highgate Cemetery (which was to become a place of pilgrimage for visiting Communist dignitaries in the twentieth century).

Engels, who was born in Barmen, near Düsseldorf, on 28 November 1820, came from a Prussian Protestant family and a wealthier background than that of Marx. His father owned a textile factory in Barmen and was the co-owner of a cotton mill in Manchester. The young Engels did not have the opportunity to go to university, for his father insisted that he enter the family business straight from school at the age of sixteen. Although Engels thus had his formal education cut short, he more than made up for it with voracious reading. He rebelled against both the religious and the political orthodoxy of his parents, and following a year of military service, he had an important meeting in Cologne with Moses Hess, the person 'who had perhaps the best claim to have introduced communist ideas into Germany'.[45] According to Hess, 'Engels, who was revolutionary to the core when he met me, left as a passionate Communist.'[46] Before going to Manchester in 1842 to help run the family business as his day job, and to collect material that would be useful in the revolutionary struggle as his vocation, Engels had his first meeting with Marx, who was initially unimpressed. When, however, Engels began to supply articles about working-class life in Manchester for the radical newspaper which Marx was editing at the time in Cologne, the relationship blossomed.[47]

The successful collaboration between Marx and Engels began when they met again, this time in Paris in 1844, and the following year Engels published his important book, *The Condition of the Working Class in England*. In some respects Engels was much less bourgeois in his personal life than was Marx; in other ways, he led a more upper-middle-class life. On his first visit to Manchester in 1842 he became the lover of a largely uneducated young Irishwoman of proletarian origin, Mary Burns, and they were later to live together for years until Mary's sudden death in 1864, after which her place was taken by her sister Lizzie.[48] Engels also, however, maintained a separate residence in Manchester, at which he entertained a wide variety of professional people. His recreations included fox-hunting, and he frequently rode with the Cheshire hunt.[49] Engels outlived Marx by twelve years and he spent that time elaborating Marx's ideas, including the mammoth task of compiling the second and third volumes of *Capital*, which Marx had left in note form, having published only the first volume of this landmark work (more famous than read) during his lifetime.[50]

Between 1840 and the Russian Revolution of 1917 – especially in the nineteenth century – the terms 'socialism' and 'communism' were often used more or less interchangeably. Marx, however, made it clear that the Communists espoused a revolutionary brand of socialism, and he was dismissive of the utopian socialists and earlier 'communists' who did not see what he and Engels believed was not only the necessity, but also the inevitability, of proletarian revolution. In one of the most resonant sentences in their most widely read work, the *Communist Manifesto*,* Marx and Engels wrote: 'The history of all hitherto existing society is the history of class struggles.'[51] Four years after the publication of the *Manifesto*, Marx put in a letter what he thought was original in that work: 'What I did that was new was to prove (1) that the *existence of classes* is only bound up with particular, historic phases in the development of production; (2) that the class struggle necessarily leads to the *dictatorship of the proletariat*; and (3) that this dictatorship itself only constitutes the transition to the *abolition of all classes* and to a classless society.'[52] He had, of course, 'proved' nothing of the kind. Along with careful historical study and an impressive grasp of the social science of the day, to which he added original insights of his own, Marx had a strong capacity for wishful thinking and even the utopianism which he scorned in others. Neither in the *Communist Manifesto* nor elsewhere did he address the question of the political and legal institutions which should be formed following the revolution. These things, apparently, would take care of themselves.

In his *Critique of the Gotha Programme*, written in 1875, Marx attacked the document which had emerged from a conference at Gotha in that year which had seen the coming-together of two German proletarian parties to form the Social Democratic Workers' Party. The programme adopted at the

---

* The impact of the *Communist Manifesto* was modest in 1848. The revolutionary turmoil of that year occurred quite independently of it. Yet this short book, with its resounding phraseology, was increasingly influential in the last three decades of the nineteenth century and in the years leading up to the First World War. During that time translations of it came thick and fast. By choosing the term 'Communist' for this, their most famous joint production, Marx and Engels helped to ensure that would become the name of the movement they founded. The book's claim to be enunciating a scientific form of socialism, combined with its brevity and readability, guaranteed its impact would long outlive its principal author.

congress attempted to address the question of how socialism could be introduced into a state democratically, but for Marx's taste this 'old familiar democratic litany' was nothing like revolutionary enough. The authors of the Gotha Programme had failed to realize that 'between capitalist and communist society' what was required was *the revolutionary dictatorship of the proletariat*', although, as usual, Marx left totally unclear what that might mean in institutional terms.[53] In the *Critique*, he distinguished between a lower and higher phase of 'communist society'.[54] In the first phase there would be inequalities, but given that such a society had only just emerged 'after prolonged birth pangs from capitalist society', these defects were inevitable. In the higher phase of communist society the division of labour would be overcome, the distinction between mental and physical work would vanish, the springs of co-operative wealth would flow more abundantly and the communist principle would be established: 'From each according to his ability, to each according to his needs!'[55]

Marx's understanding of the stages of human development was different from that of his eighteenth-century precursors mentioned earlier in this chapter – precursors only in the sense that they linked the development of institutions and ideas to the property relations and means of subsistence prevailing in different historical epochs. Marx shared their view that the first stage in human development consisted of a kind of primitive communism. The main stages which followed, as he saw it, were those of ancient society, which depended on slave labour; feudal society, in which production relied on serf labour; and bourgeois (or capitalist) society, in which wage labourers were exploited by the capitalist class.[56] (He also identified what he called an Asiatic mode of production, in which there was an absence of private property and where the need to organize irrigation led to a centralized state and 'oriental despotism'.) It was Marx's firm, but fanciful, belief that 'the bourgeois relations of production are the last antagonistic form of the social process of production . . . The productive forces developing in the womb of bourgeois society create the material conditions for the solution of that antagonism. This social formation brings, therefore, the prehistory of human society to a close.'[57]

In his Preface to the English edition of the *Communist Manifesto* of 1888, Engels (writing alone, since Marx had died five years earlier) explained why he and Marx had called it 'Communist' rather than 'Socialist'. The latter term, he said, was associated in 1847 with 'adherents of the various Utopian systems: Owenites in England, Fourierists in France' or with 'multifarious social quacks' who professed to address all manner of social grievances 'without any danger to capital and profit'. Socialism, Engels says, was in 1847 a middle-class movement, but Communism was a working-class movement. Socialism, in continental Europe, had become respectable; Communism was not respectable.[58] Essentially, the commitment of Marx and Lenin to the cause of proletarian revolution was what made them describe their manifesto as Communist.

Engels gives Marx the lion's share of the credit for their joint production, saying that the fundamental proposition – the nucleus of the work – belongs to him. That central proposition sets out much of the essence of Marxism both as a way of understanding history and as an exhortation to the working class to act out its preordained revolutionary role, so it is worth citing how Engels puts the central idea in one sentence (even though it is a monumentally long sentence):

> . . . in every historical epoch, the prevailing mode of economic production and exchange, and the social organization necessarily following from it, form the basis upon which is built up, and from which alone can be explained, the political and intellectual history of that epoch; that consequently the whole history of mankind (since the dissolution of primitive tribal society, holding land in common ownership) has been a history of class struggles, contests between exploiting and exploited, ruling and oppressed classes; that the history of these class struggles forms a series of evolutions in which, nowadays, a stage has been reached where the exploited and oppressed class – the proletariat – cannot attain its emancipation from the sway of the exploiting and ruling class – the bourgeoisie – without, at the same time, and once and for all, emancipating society at large from all exploitation, oppression, class distinctions and class struggles.[59]

Marx and Engels wrote many more abstruse books than the *Communist Manifesto*, and while there was almost invariably a polemical element, they were generally bolstered by substantial research. Marx was a prodigious reader across several disciplines, and since he was living in Britain during the greater part of his writing career, he also drew upon the primary sources that were to hand, such as the 'Blue Books' containing the results of official inquiries authorized by Parliament or the Privy Council and the Hansard reports of parliamentary debates. The bibliography of Volume I of *Capital* includes a remarkable range of parliamentary and statistical reports.[60] As part of his explanation in his 'Preface to the First German Edition' of *Capital* of why so many of his examples are drawn from the country in which he was living, Marx wrote: 'The social statistics of Germany and the rest of Continental Europe are, in comparison with those of England, wretchedly compiled.'[61]

While Marx and Engels devoted most of their attention to social conditions and their economic determinants, a century later some intellectuals in Communist countries who wished to get away from ideological dogma and analyze real political life would cite as important precedents *The Eighteenth Brumaire of Louis Bonaparte* (Marx's short book on the coming to power of Napoleon III in France, in which he examines the relationship between class and state power) and *The Civil War in France* (on the Paris Commune of 1870).[62] In these works Marx paid special attention to the political 'superstructure' as distinct from the economic 'base' which was his more general concern.

Marx's thought was crucially influenced by time and place. Doubtless, given the same disposition and character, he would have been a radical had he lived in the eighteenth century, but his thought would have been different from what it became, living when and where he did. Marx's analysis, its various intellectual antecedents notwithstanding, was a product of the later stages of the Industrial Revolution and the intensive development of European capitalism. The existence of a large industrial workforce was a precondition for what was to become known as 'Marxism'. That social group, or class as Marx saw it, both constituted a principal subject of his investigations and embodied his hopes for the future. And it was in Britain, where Marx lived much of his adult life, that industrialization in the middle of the nineteenth century was most advanced.

Marx was a great original thinker who drew inspiration from many sources. He was less influenced by previous socialist writers than by German Hegelian philosophy and British political economy, of which school Adam Smith was the founder and pre-eminent thinker. Marx, though, drew very different conclusions from those of either Hegel or Smith. From Hegel, he took a terminology which often obscured, rather than illuminated, his meaning. One central idea was that of the dialectic. For Hegel this meant 'the development of the spirit' which came through 'the conflict and reconciliation of opposites'.[63] Hegel described the process which gave birth to its opposite as the thesis; the opposite he labelled the antithesis; and the phase when the opposites were reconciled he called the synthesis.[64] Marx transposed Hegel's 'development of the spirit' into a materialist interpretation of history. He took over also Hegel's ambiguous term 'contradictions' to describe growing incompatibilities in each of the historical epochs he identified between the institutional relationships and the changing forces of production. Marx believed that from Hegel he had taken the 'rational kernel' to be found in the 'mystical shell'.[65] His conviction that the proletariat will become not only stronger but also more revolutionary as the capitalist system develops turned out, however, to be an article of misplaced faith. Moreover, as David McLellan observes, in 'looking to the development of the productive forces to bring about the changes he envisaged', Marx showed little awareness of 'the intrinsic value of the natural world' or of the fact that natural resources are not inexhaustible.[66] He was, of course, far from alone in that respect. For most of the following century, Western industrial corporations were only slightly less culpable than their Communist bureaucratic equivalents in their reckless disregard for the natural environment.

Marx was not only a theorist of revolutionary change but a revolutionary by temperament. Even though his theory suggested that highly developed industry and a lengthy period of capitalism were twin necessities before any given society would be ripe for a workers' revolution, he was eager to see revolution wherever it might occur. Many revolutionaries in Russia thought that the traditional peasant commune in that country might provide a short cut to socialism and communism, and the last thing they wanted was a lengthy period of capitalist dominion. Some of them, attracted to Marx's teaching but worried by its implications, appealed to him for advice and elucidation. One such person was Vera Zasulich, to whom Marx sent a brief and ambivalent reply in 1881 after composing three lengthy drafts (which he did not send, but which survived in his personal archive).[67] The most encouraging part of his reply for Zasulich was that when he wrote about the 'historical inevitability' of capitalist development, he was expressly limiting the generalization 'to the countries of Western Europe'.[68]

In their Preface to the Russian edition of the *Communist Manifesto* of 1882, Marx and Engels went further. They left as an open question whether it would be possible to 'pass directly to the higher form of communist common ownership' from the traditional Russian peasant commune or whether it must 'first pass through the same process of dissolution as constitutes the historical evolution of the West'. They concluded that, provided the Russian Revolution became 'the signal for a proletarian revolution in the West', then the 'present Russian common ownership of the land' might, indeed, 'serve as the starting point for a communist development'.[69] Marx was encouraged by the fact that Russian radicals seemed to be more serious in their revolutionary commitment than their counterparts in the countries he knew best, Britain and Germany, but he, and especially Engels, linked the ultimate success of their endeavour to a Russian revolution triggering proletarian revolution in the West.[70]

Marx, in spite of his belief in 'inevitabilities', was far from being as mechanistic in his interpretation of history as many of his disciples became. He was also well aware that revolutionaries, attempting to build a new social order, were never starting with a blank sheet. In a passage that referred to the revolutionary unrest in Europe in 1848 and, more specifically, to the coming to power of Louis Napoleon (who declared himself emperor as

Napoleon III) in France in 1851, but which has resonance also for the coming
to power of Communists in Russia almost seven decades later, Marx wrote:
'Men make their own history, but they do not make it just as they please;
they do not make it under circumstances chosen by themselves, but under
circumstances directly encountered, given and transmitted from the past.
The tradition of all the dead generations weighs like a nightmare on the
brain of the living.'[71]

2

Communism and Socialism – the Early Years

Communism and socialism had some common roots, and initially shared a belief in the need to introduce universal public ownership of the means of production. However, a fundamental division emerged between those who supported revolution and those who favoured evolutionary change. In the first category were people prepared to countenance violence in the pursuit of their goals, in the second those who espoused a peaceful path to a socialist society. Yet since means affect ends, over time the goals themselves changed. Communists who favoured the violent overthrow of capitalism went on to justify the use of severe coercion to repress internal critics of the system they had created. And socialists who preferred an evolutionary approach gradually ceased to believe that they could build an entirely new system that would replace capitalism. By the middle of the twentieth century, electorally successful socialist parties in Western Europe had accepted a 'mixed economy', with public and private ownership co-existing. Throughout the second half of the twentieth century socialism came to be associated more with the welfare state, and with step-by-step improvements in the living conditions of the majority of citizens, than with an entirely new social order.

Among the revolutionaries themselves, there were many divisions from the outset. There was major tension throughout much of the second half of the nineteenth century between Communists and anarchists. Marx and his followers envisaged an eventual withering-away of the state, in the course of which all coercive institutions would somehow disappear and people would administer things for themselves without the need for state authority. But the anarchists did not believe that this would be the end result of applying Marx's doctrine. They were, moreover, impatient to destroy the state right away. This clash of doctrine was made all the sharper by personal antagonism between Karl Marx, on the one hand, and the leading advocate of anarchism, Mikhail Bakunin, on the other. Like most revolutionary theorists, Bakunin was not of proletarian origin. Unlike Marx and Engels, though, with their bourgeois German backgrounds, he came from an aristocratic Russian family, and he harboured strong anti-German sentiments. In 1848 and 1849, years of revolutionary turmoil, Bakunin enthusiastically chased around Europe, doing his best to catch the latest revolution and help it succeed. His anti-German sentiments doubtless owed something to the years he spent in German prisons after the 1849 uprising in Dresden in which he participated was quelled (although when he was eventually handed over to the Russian authorities, he found that the conditions in the Peter and Paul fortress in St Petersburg were still more disagreeable).[1] More fundamentally, for Bakunin − as for another notable representative of the nineteenth-century Russian intelligentsia, the socialist and populist theorist Alexander Herzen (himself half-German) − the stereotype of a German was of a person who worshipped the state.[2] For an anarchist, what could be worse?

Bakunin's doctrine revolved around the idea of 'freedom'. The word 'state' stood for 'all the evil which must be banished from the world'.[3] Bakunin supposed that solidarity came naturally to people, making them capable, when freed from the fetters of the state, of self-sacrifice and an ability to organize themselves in small autonomous communes, in which each person would have absolute freedom. He sought equality as well as freedom, and so one of his immediate objectives was to abolish rights of inheritance.[4] Although Bakunin's own goals were utopian in the extreme, he made some telling criticisms of Marx's project. He pointed to the incompatibility between Marx's belief in the need for a centrally organized economy and his notion of the eventual disappearance of the state with its political functions. Bakunin questioned how centralized economic power could exist without political coercion, and he was, perhaps, the first, as Leszek Kołakowski puts it, 'to infer Leninism from Marxism'.[5] He scorned the Marxists' claim that 'only a dictatorship, their own, of course, can bring the people freedom', continuing: 'we reply that a dictatorship can have no other aim than to perpetuate itself, and that it can engender nothing but slavery in the people subjected to it. Freedom can be created only by freedom, that is by a rising of the whole people and by the free organization of the working masses from below.'[6]

Even among the followers of Karl Marx, doctrinal differences quickly emerged, and some of the fiercest ideological arguments of the late nineteenth century − still more in the twentieth − were between different schools of Marxism. The First International, whose founding congress in London in 1864 Marx had attended (he was elected to its General Council), split in several different directions and was formally disbanded in 1876. The Second International (known also as the Socialist International) was founded in Paris in 1889. The year and the location had symbolic significance − this was the hundredth anniversary of the French Revolution. The International was composed of national political parties and trade unions, many of whose members had been influenced by Marxist teaching. From the outset, however, there was a tension between socialists who believed in the importance of parliamentary means and those for whom revolutionary class struggle was a higher priority.

Engels, unlike Marx, was still alive and was present at the inaugural meeting. Russian revolutionaries were active members of the Second International, and among those who attended the 1889 Paris gathering was Georgy Plekhanov, the most influential Russian Marxist theorist of the last decades of the nineteenth century. The delegates were a very diverse group. From Britain they included the writer, artist and romantic socialist William Morris, and the man who has the strongest claim to be regarded as the founder of the British Labour Party, Keir Hardie. There were, in fact, two socialist conferences held in Paris at that time – one Marxist and the other non-Marxist, known as 'possibilist', meaning more pragmatic. Keir Hardie managed to attend both. Shortly before the Paris meetings, Hardie told Engels in a letter that the British 'are a very solid people, very practical, and not given to chasing bubbles'.[7] In Paris he annoyed William Morris as well as the revolutionary Marxists by declaring that 'no person in England believed in other than peaceful methods to achieve the amelioration of conditions'.[8] A number of the delegates – even at the Marxist meeting of the Second International – were supportive of class struggle but opposed to violence, basing their socialism on ethical, partly Christian, foundations at least as much as on Marx. Keir Hardie, who had left school at the age of eight and from the ages of ten to twenty-three had worked in coal mines, was a case in point. His socialism was an eclectic mixture, owing much to the poetry of Robert Burns, religious mysticism and an intuitive feel for 'the gradualist, peaceful evolution of British society, however pugnaciously he might champion the workers' cause'.[9] To the British political establishment, Hardie seemed an extremist (not least as a result of his attacks in Parliament on the monarchy); for the revolutionary Lenin, he epitomized 'opportunism'.[10]

The co-founders of the German Social Democratic Party, August Bebel and Wilhelm Liebknecht, were also active participants in the Second International. Their party, by the time of the founding congress, was well on the way to being the most successful of the socialist parties in the nineteenth century. In the imperial German elections of 1890, the Social Democrats won almost 20 per cent of the votes. France was represented by two prominent Marxists, Edouard Vaillant and Jules Guesde, who generally favoured a parliamentary road to socialism, although they believed that revolution was desirable under certain circumstances. Apart from Marx, a major influence on both of them had been the French socialist theorist Louis Blanc, who, following the failure of the revolutions of 1848, had spent a prolonged exile in Britain, returning to France in 1870. (He died seven years before the establishment of the Second International.) From Spain came Pablo Iglesias, a man who had spent his childhood in a foundling home but went on to become a major trade union leader and one of the founders of the Spanish Socialist Party. As Communists and socialists increasingly diverged in the first decades of the twentieth century, Iglesias was to play a major role in putting the Spanish party on the path of democratic socialism. Although all who took part in this Second International had been influenced to a greater or lesser extent by Marxism, they were, it is evident, a far from homogeneous group.

Prior to the success of the Bolshevik revolution in 1917, the dividing lines between socialists and Communists were less clear-cut than they were to become. To an extent, both were united by a class analysis of politics, although even among Marxists there were great differences between those who saw the industrial working class as people who would develop a socialist consciousness on the basis of their own experience, leading them to take power themselves in the interests of the majority of the population, and those who believed that this consciousness would not develop spontaneously. The latter held that the necessary ideas would have to be brought to the workers from outside their ranks – by intellectuals armed with Marx's supposedly scientific, and certainly revolutionary, theory. The very notion of thinking in terms of class was a development of the nineteenth century, and Marx himself was hugely influential in encouraging growing numbers of people across Europe to see the basic dividing lines in society in terms of class conflict. Although Marx believed that ideas were to a large extent a side-effect of economic change, the impact of his own thinking was, paradoxically, a prime example of the independent significance of ideas. His doctrine, after all, turned out to make the most decisive difference in Russia, which was far from being the most industrially developed country of Europe.

In politics, actions and beliefs are in large measure dependent on, and partly constituted by, concepts. Moreover, notwithstanding the adage that deeds speak louder than words, in political life words are also deeds. Language 'is an arena of political action'.[11] As Donald Sassoon has aptly put it:

> By thinking of the working class as a political class, ascribing to it a specific politics and rejecting the vaguer categories ('the poor') of earlier reformers, the pioneers of socialism thus virtually 'invented' the working class. Those who define, create. 'Democratic' politics, that is, modern mass politics, is a battlefield in which the most important move is that which decides what the battle is about, what the issue is. To be able to define the contending parties,

name them and thus establish where the barricades should go up, or where the trenches should be dug, gives one a powerful and at times decisive advantage.[12]

Lenin and the Origins of Russian Communism

One person who was very conscious of the validity of that argument, even though he would not have couched it in those terms, was Vladimir Lenin, a crucially important figure in the development of Communism and the principal founder of the Soviet Union. Too young to attend the 1889 founding meeting of the Second International (he first travelled abroad from Russia in 1895), Lenin nevertheless played a significant part in the International and an overwhelmingly important role in the revolutionary movement of his own country. His real name was Ulyanov, but in the course of underground struggle against the tsarist authorities, he had adopted a number of pseudonyms. 'Lenin' was the one which stuck. He was of mixed ethnic origin, including Russian, Jewish, German, Swedish and Kalmyk – not so very unusual in the multinational Russian empire, as the first of his biographers to gain access to the relevant Russian and Soviet archives, Dmitri Volkogonov, pointed out.[13] What gave these origins potential significance was that a national chauvinism, from which Lenin himself was free, gained ground in Stalin's Soviet Union, and Lenin's mixed descent became a closely guarded state secret. When his elder sister, Anna, suggested in a letter to Stalin in 1932 that it might be a good idea to publicize the fact that Lenin's great-grandfather, Moishe Blank, was a Jew, since this could 'help combat anti-semitism', she met with a categorical refusal and a stern warning to keep such knowledge to herself.[14] If the desire to spread this information about Lenin had been expressed by someone other than his sister, that might well have been deemed a capital offence. For misdemeanours less serious than breaking a state secret (and, more often than not, wholly imaginary crimes), hundreds of thousands of Stalin's future victims met their deaths.

Lenin's maternal grandfather changed his first name from Srul to Alexander, converted to orthodox Christianity, and was thus able to enter medical school in St Petersburg.[15] As Dr Alexander Blank, he became a respected figure in Russian society and, following his change of religion, was not affected by the state-supported anti-semitism. His wife, Lenin's maternal grandmother, was German by nationality and Lutheran by religion. Lenin's parents, Ilya Nikolaevich Ulyanov and Maria Alexandrovna Ulyanova, avoided political activity, were opposed to revolutionary violence, but supportive of reform. They approved of the innovations of Alexander

II in the 1860s (which had included not only the abolition of serfdom but also significant local government and legal reform). However, given the moderation of his parents' opinions, Lenin certainly did not acquire his political views from them.[16] What he did inherit was sharp intelligence. In addition, he imbibed in the home environment a demanding work ethic and a high value placed upon study and self-improvement.

The future Lenin – Vladimir Ilich Ulyanov – was born in 1870 on 22 April, and died relatively young on 21 January 1924. In Stalin's Soviet Union, the anniversary of Lenin's death was commemorated, although the cult of Lenin in those years was on a minor scale compared to the adulation orchestrated for Stalin himself. From 1955 onwards, Lenin's birthday, rather than the date of his death, became the day which was marked throughout the Soviet Union. Nikita Khrushchev announced that 'it is now more appropriate to commemorate V.I. Lenin not on the day of his death, which leaves an imprint of mourning and sorrow, but on the day of his birth – 22 April, making this date a holiday that will better correspond to the whole spirit of Leninism as an eternally alive, life-affirming teaching'.[17] Among other things, this anniversary was marked by a prestigious and comprehensively reported lecture delivered by a prominent member of the political elite. In addition to paying homage to Lenin, the speaker ostensibly applied Lenin's ideas to the problems of the day.[18]

In his early years Lenin had a comfortable enough life. His father was a school teacher who became, in turn, a school inspector and then director of schools for the province. He won the esteem of the Russian state authorities and received a variety of decorations, ending up with the rank of state counsellor, which meant that he had entered the Russian nobility. Since that was hereditary, the noble rank passed also to his son, Vladimir. Lenin's class origins were, however, not covered up by Soviet historians in the way that his ethnic origins were. The young Ulyanov received an exacting, albeit somewhat narrow, academic education at a local Simbirsk school, where the headmaster, by an irony of history, was Fedor Kerensky, the father of Alexander Kerensky, prime minister of the provisional government of Russia when it was overthrown by Lenin and the Bolsheviks in November 1917. Lenin's tranquil childhood ended with the death in 1886 of his father, aged fifty-three (the same age as Lenin was when *he* died). Lenin was just fifteen at the time of his father's death, but shortly after his seventeenth birthday, there was to be a death in the family of greater resonance for his future career as a professional revolutionary – that of his older brother, Alexander, in 1887. A natural sciences student at St Petersburg University, Alexander Ulyanov had become involved not only in a revolutionary group but also in a plan to assassinate the tsar, Alexander III. The entire group was arrested.

Those who, at their March 1887 trial, pleaded to the tsar for clemency had their death sentences commuted to hard labour. Those who refused to beg for forgiveness – Alexander Ulyanov among them – were hanged on 8 May 1887. The hardening of Lenin's opposition to the tsarist regime may be dated from then; he first became involved in revolutionary political circles in the year following his brother's execution.[19] It was, however, 1889 at the earliest that he became a Marxist and much later before he went on to develop his own particular brand of Marxism.[20]

Marx's *Capital* was first published in Russia in 1872, getting past the censorship because it was considered too dull to have much of an impact. It may have been sufficiently hard-going to influence no more than a minority. However, minorities can be important in politics, especially a sizeable minority of revolutionaries in an oppressive, authoritarian (but not totalitarian) regime. A boring title could also camouflage dangerous contents and be a useful way of getting a subversive book past the tsarist censors. This was the device of the leading Russian Marxist theorist, Georgy Plekhanov, whose *On the Question of Developing a Monist View of History* was published, under the pseudonym of N. Beltov, in 1895.[21] Plekhanov had already become a major influence on Lenin, not least through his insistence in most of his major writings on the imperative need for those with an understanding of the theory and practice of socialism to bring their knowledge to the working class.[22] Nevertheless, though he co-operated with Lenin in the early years of the twentieth century, he continued, unlike Lenin, to hold the orthodox Marxist view that a fairly lengthy period of bourgeois government, following a bourgeois revolution, would be necessary before a socialist revolution could take place. He naturally supported the first of Russia's two revolutions of 1917 – which overthrew tsarism – but was strongly opposed to the Bolshevik revolution less than nine months later. (Plekhanov died the following year.)

Lenin was influenced in his early days not only by orthodox Marxism but by the revolutionary populist views of Petr Tkachev. Populism was a movement of radical intellectuals which emerged in Russia during the 1860s. Its adherents believed that the peasant communes could provide Russia with a means of achieving socialism without going through the stage of capitalism. Tkachev, one of the most extreme of the populists, was in favour of a revolutionary minority seizing state power. Having read Marx selectively and taken what he wanted from Marx's ideas, Tkachev attacked Engels for his lack of revolutionary fervour and reluctance to countenance socialist revolution in Russia until the condition of 'advanced economic development of bourgeois society had been met'.[23] Lenin approved of Tkachev's emphasis on the vital role which should be played by a small circle of revolutionaries. And although he rejected the arbitrariness of the terrorism practised by the Narodnaya Volya (People's Will) group, on whom Tkachev's views had a significant impact, he was far from opposed to the use of terror per se. Lenin was critical of Plekhanov's lack of sympathy both for Tkachev and for the People's Will movement itself. Nikolay Volsky, a revolutionary who got to know Lenin well when they were both in exile in Geneva (he is better known under his pseudonym of Valentinov), reports Lenin telling him in 1904: 'Plekhanov's attitude to Tkachev is wrong. In his day, Tkachev was a great revolutionary, *a real Jacobin*, who had a great influence on the most active section of the People's Will.'[24]

Even Plekhanov, with his much more critical view of Narodnaya Volya, wrote in 1884:

> First of all, we by no means deny the important role of the terrorist struggle in the present emancipation movement. It has grown naturally from the social and political conditions under which we are placed, and it must just as naturally promote a change for the better. But in itself so-called terror only destroys the forces of government and does little to further the conscious organiza-tion of its opponents. The terrorist struggle does not widen our revolutionary movement's sphere of influence; on the contrary, it reduces it to heroic actions by small partisan groups.[25]

Lenin's attitude to terror was much less equivocal. Vasily Starkov, an engin-eer and a member of a St Petersburg Marxist group which Lenin, aged twenty-three at the time, joined in 1893, said that Lenin heatedly defended the use of terror in ways which to those 'brought up on the articles of Plekhanov which sharply criticized the program and tactics, based on terror, of the Narodnaya Volya . . . appeared heretical'.[26] For Lenin, the ends justi-fied the means. Starkov summarized Lenin's view thus: 'The main thing is ends, and every means of struggle, including terror, is good or bad depending on whether, in the given circumstances, it conduces to the attainment of those ends or, on the contrary, diverts from them.'[27]

A huge impact was made on Lenin, emotionally as much as intellectu-ally, by the writings of an older Russian revolutionary, Nikolay Chernyshevsky – in particular, by his *What is to be Done?*. Although, in Isaiah Berlin's words, that novel was 'grotesque as a work of art', it was also remarkably influential.[28] The son of an Orthodox priest, Chernyshevsky himself suffered long years of exile for his political views, but remained unyielding in his devotion to the cause of revolution and the creation of a co-operative socialist commonwealth. The hero of his novel was the kind of utterly dedicated 'new man' – morally serious, and impervious to hardship or to any distractions from the good of the cause – who provided an inspiring example for young Russian revolutionary opponents of the tsarist autocracy. No one, Berlin observes, did more than Chernyshevsky to sharpen the distinction between 'us' and 'them'.[29] There was no place for neutrality or timidity in the revolutionary struggle. Although Lenin was not especially prone to hero-worship, he was a devoted admirer of Chernyshevsky.[30]

One day in Geneva in 1904, Volsky (Valentinov) made the mistake of referring in Lenin's presence to Chernyshevsky as 'untalented' and 'crude'.[31] Lenin responded furiously, describing Chernyshevsky as 'the greatest and most talented representative of socialism before Marx', and went on:

> I declare that it is impermissible to call *What is to be Done?* crude and untalented. Hundreds of people became revolutionaries under its influence. Could this have happened if Chernyshevsky had been untalented and crude? My brother, for example, was captivated by him, and so was I. He *completely transformed my outlook.* When did you read *What is to be Done?* . . . Chernyshevsky's novel is too complex and full of ideas to be understood and appreciated at an early age. I myself started to read it when I was 14. I think this was a completely useless and superficial reading of the book. But, after the execution of my brother, I started to read it properly, as I knew that it had been one of his favourite books. I spent not days but several weeks reading it. Only then did I understand its depth. This novel provides inspiration for a lifetime: untalented books don't have such an influence.[32]

Given the oppressive character of the tsarist Russian state, its low level of industrialization in the nineteenth century, and – for both these reasons – the weakness of any working-class movement as compared with Britain, Germany or France, it is not altogether surprising that a number of Russian revolutionaries laid emphasis on the role of 'social democrats', as they called themselves, from outside the proletarian ranks in bringing revolutionary socialist enlightenment to the workers. The term 'social democracy' at the end of the nineteenth century and in the early twentieth did not yet demarcate democratic socialists from Communists. 'Social Democrats' embraced in the Russia of those years, as well as in the rest of Europe, socialists and trade unionists of very different hues. When the forerunner of the Communist Party of the Soviet Union was founded in 1898, it bore the name of Russian Social Democratic Labour Party (RSDLP). Lenin missed its inauguration. As a result of his revolutionary activities, he had been arrested in late 1895 and spent the remainder of the decade in prison or Siberian exile. During that time he completed a lengthy book, *The Development of Capitalism in Russia*, which he published under the pseudonym, Vladimir Ilyin in 1899. Siberian exile in the late tsarist period did not prevent him from receiving a supply of books, paper and pencils. It was a far milder punishment than that to which dissidents throughout most of the Soviet era were subjected.

During his exile, Lenin had thought about producing an underground newspaper which would be a platform for his strongly held views. On his release from exile in 1900, he launched such a publication with the co-operation of Julius Martov and Alexander Potresov. Called *Iskra* (The Spark), this newspaper became not only Lenin's propaganda tool but also his organizational base, one he used to seek control of the RSDLP both personally and ideologically. Among the most central elements of Lenin's contribution to revolutionary thought – which found expression in *Iskra* – were his emphasis on the need for a highly disciplined party and his implacable opposition to spontaneity, whether in the realm of ideas or action, in the revolutionary movement. He was dedicated to the principle of disciplined organization, although the reality – in his lifetime, as distinct from what happened subsequently in the Soviet Union and the international Communist movement – frequently fell far short of his aims. An inveterate polemicist, Lenin mercilessly berated those who did not share his view of the need for a party of a new type, which would be centrally controlled, strictly disciplined, and would imbue workers with a revolutionary socialist consciousness. Workers, left to their own devices, he argued, would develop only a 'trade union consciousness'. As he put it in his important political tract, *What is to be Done?* (the title consciously echoing that of Chernyshevsky),[33] published in 1902: 'The spontaneous labour movement by itself is capable of creating (and inevitably creates) only trade unionism, and trade-unionist politics of the working class is precisely bourgeois politics of the working class.'[34] The workers needed professional revolutionaries to give them a theoretical understanding, one that would persuade them that their true interests could be served only by destroying capitalism. What was required was abolition of their position as hired labour, not the trade union aim of getting a better deal from their employers.

Bolsheviks and Mensheviks

A decisive moment in the history of the Russian revolutionary movement came in 1903 at the Second Congress of the RSDLP. There was no question of holding that in Russia, where the tsarist secret police, the Okhrana, would have had a field day rounding up the usual suspects. It had been planned to hold the Congress in Brussels, but word passed by the Okhrana to the Belgian police put a stop to that.[35] Hasty arrangements were made to move the Congress to London, where Lenin had to swallow his distaste for any form of religion, and especially for the Christian socialism which he regarded as an oxymoron, when the site found for the Congress turned out to be a Congregationalist chapel. The Congress witnessed a variety of splits – including within the ranks of the *Iskra* group – between what Lenin called the 'hards' and the 'softs'. With some justice, he saw himself as the number-one 'hard'. The 'softs' included his co-founders of *Iskra*, Martov and Potresov; the most notable Russian woman revolutionary of that time, Vera Zasulich, notwithstanding the fact that in 1878 she had shot and wounded the police chief of St Petersburg; and an especially eloquent Marxist who had turned up in London the previous year to introduce himself to Lenin, having just escaped from his own Siberian exile, Leon Trotsky.[36] Later Trotsky was to write: 'One can say of Lenin and Martov that, even before the split, even before the congress, Lenin was "hard" and Martov "soft". And they both knew it.'[37]

The Congress had begun with fifty-seven delegates, of whom only forty-three had voting rights. Lenin could not initially command a majority among them and lost a vote on the wording of the party rules. He was able to dominate the proceedings only after seven of the delegates walked out. They were the five delegates from the Jewish socialist organization the Bund, and two representatives of 'Economism', people whose main emphasis was on improving the economic situation of the workers, a viewpoint Lenin despised. The members of the Bund wanted to preserve their autonomy in all matters relating to the Jewish proletariat, but the Congress had insisted that they must be brought under central control – in effect, control by the *Iskra* group, which itself included many revolutionaries of Jewish origin, among them Martov (originally Tsederbaum); Trotsky, whose real name was Bronstein; Pavel Akselrod, whose continuing political evolution made him a severe critic of the dictatorial tendencies implicit in Lenin's idea of a rigidly centralized party ·controlled by professional revolutionaries; and Nikolay Bauman, a close ally of Lenin who was beaten to death by a mob in St Petersburg in 1905.[38]

The walkout by the Bundists and the 'Economists' worked entirely to Lenin's advantage, for he could now win a majority of votes in the Congress. He was able to push through his own policies, organizational demands, and choices of personnel. Thus, for example, he made sure that the Central Committee of the party would be small and that it would be dominated by the 'hards'. As many writers have noted, however, Lenin's tactical skill was nowhere more evident than in his invention at this congress of the terms Bolsheviks and Mensheviks. He had no sooner got his majority than he named his group the Bolsheviki (the Majorityites, from the Russian word for majority, *bol'shinstvo*) and his opponents the Mensheviki (the Minorityites). As Bertram Wolfe wrote of Lenin some sixty years ago:

> Though but yesterday he had been in a minority, and, more often than not would be in the minority in the future, he would never relinquish the psychological advantage of that name . . . What pride it could give to his caucus, no matter how it might dwindle, always to call itself 'Majorityites'. What conviction, what an air of . . . democratic, majority sanction, it would give in appealing to the rank and file and the non-party masses.[39]

However, as Wolfe added, Lenin's tactical astuteness was matched by the extraordinary political ineptitude of those who found themselves in a temporary minority within the party and who thereupon accepted the name of Mensheviks, by which they permanently became known.[40] The Mensheviks, however – and Martov, most notably – were much more committed to democratic advance for its own sake than was Lenin (or, for that matter, Trotsky). For the Bolsheviks, political democracy had 'mainly instrumental value, as enabling workers more effectively to fight for socialism'.[41]

Lenin pressed on with his demand for a centralized party which he and like-minded allies could control, although some of those who had supported him at the Second Congress of the RSDLP soon repented of that decision and began to oppose him. He devoted over two hundred pages of a polemical pamphlet, published in 1904, to the minutiae of party organization. Called *One Step Forward, Two Steps Back*, it hammered home his obsessive belief that in the 'struggle for power the proletariat has no other weapon but organization'.[42] Rounding on his critics, Lenin wrote:

> One step forward, two steps back . . . It happens in the lives of individuals, and it happens in the history of nations and in the development of parties. It would be the most criminal cowardice to doubt even for a moment the inevitable and complete triumph of the principles of revolutionary Social-Democracy, of proletarian organization and Party discipline.[43]

West European Alternatives

With the establishment of the Bolshevik faction within the RSDLP, the rifts within the Second International and between Bolshevism and evolutionary socialism became wider. In Germany, where social democracy, in the broad sense of the term, was stronger than in Russia, there were also vital doctrinal battles taking place. The most important long-term challenge to what became Leninism, and, indeed, to the arguments of Marx and Engels, emanated from Eduard Bernstein. He had himself been schooled in Marxism and was sufficiently close to Engels to have been appointed by the latter both as the executor of his estate and as his joint literary executor, along with another notable socialist theorist, Karl Kautsky. Bernstein had spent twenty years in London – in exile from his native Berlin – and had been much influenced by the gradualist philosophy of the British Fabian socialists. Within the European Marxist camp he was the first great 'revisionist'. That term – used as one of extreme disparagement by Lenin and by his Soviet successors up until the mid-1980s – sat oddly with Marxism's claim to scientific status, since science involves a constant readiness to revise theory which no longer accords with observable facts. Bernstein, for his part, did not disdain the revisionist label which had been attached to him and his ideas by more orthodox Marxists.[44]

Bernstein's most important book, *Die Voraussetzungen des Sozialismus und die Aufgaben der Sozialdemokratie* (*The Postulates of Socialism and the Lessons of Social Democracy*), had a big impact when it was published in Germany in 1899. It had already gone through nine German editions by the time it appeared in English in 1909 with the catchier title of *Evolutionary Socialism*. Charles Darwin's great work on biological evolution, *The Origin of Species*, first published in 1859, indirectly influenced the thinking of many socialists, strengthening their belief in a parallel evolution of society. (Marx himself had wished to dedicate the second volume of *Capital* to Darwin, but Darwin declined the honour.)[45] Bernstein writes approvingly of how in England 'social democracy' (which he says he is using in the broad sense of 'the whole independent socialist movement')[46] had moved from being a 'Utopian, revolutionary sect, as Engels represented it to be, to the party of political reform which we now know'.[47] He continues:

> No socialist capable of thinking, dreams to-day in England of an imminent victory for socialism by means of a violent revolution – none dreams of a quick conquest of Parliament by a revolutionary proletariat. But they rely more and more on work in the municipalities and other self-governing bodies. The early contempt for the trade union movement has been given up; a closer sympathy has been won for it and, here and there also, for the co-operative movement.[48]

Bernstein combined realism and idealism. His case for an evolutionary socialism was both a pragmatic and a moral one. He detected the utopianism which was present in Marx, however much the latter inveighed against utopian socialists. Just as Lenin had succeeded in attaching the pejorative label of Menshevik to his intra-party opponents, so – much earlier – Marx had succeeded in establishing in the minds of many that his brand of socialist thought was scientific and his predecessors were utopians (although by no means all of them were). Bernstein did not accept this distinction which Marx sought to impose, observing: 'We have to take working men as they are. And they are neither so universally pauperized as was set out in the *Communist Manifesto*, nor so free from prejudices and weaknesses as their courtiers wish to make us believe.'[49] Bernstein is probably most famous for saying that the movement was everything to him and what was usually called 'the final aim of socialism' was nothing. That was not only because, as he noted, 'I have not been able to read to the end any picture of the future' but also because, in his judgement, 'a greater security for lasting success lies in a steady advance than in the possibilities offered by a catastrophic crash'.[50]

Bernstein argued, furthermore, that it was time to give up using the phrase 'the dictatorship of the proletariat', since representatives of social democracy, through their electoral and parliamentary work, were directly influencing legislation, and these activities were 'inconsistent with a dictatorship'.[51] He was vehemently attacked for his departures from orthodox Marxist doctrine, not only by Lenin but by leading participants in the German social democratic movement, most notably by the Polish-born revolutionary Rosa Luxemburg, who was a prominent member of the Second International and active not only in Poland but especially in Germany. Karl Kautsky, who was of Czech parentage but lived most of his life in Germany, also attacked Bernstein, but from a more centrist position than that of the fiery Luxemburg. Kautsky had at one time been a Marxist theorist much admired by Lenin, although as early as 1893 he had displayed a more sympathetic attitude to parliamentarism, writing that 'a genuine parliamentary regime can be just as good an instrument for the dictatorship of the proletariat as it is an instrument for the dictatorship of the bourgeoisie'.[52] Later not only Kautsky, but also the more radical Luxemburg, who had scathingly attacked Bernstein for his notion of evolutionary socialism, were to point to the dictatorial implications of the seizure of power in Russia by Lenin and the Bolsheviks. That event and the revolutions and world war which preceded it are the theme of the next chapter.

3

The Russian Revolutions
and Civil War

Not every delegate to the Second Congress of the Russian Social Democratic Labour Party, discussed in the previous chapter, was prepared to be classified by Lenin as either a Menshevik or a Bolshevik. A revolutionary who did not fit neatly into one camp or the other was Leon Trotsky. While closer to, and identified with, the Mensheviks after the split of 1903, Trotsky did not actually join them. He maintained good relations with individual Mensheviks, but between 1903 and 1917 he was 'a revolutionary without a revolutionary base'.[1] He laid particular emphasis on the need for the Russian proletariat to make common cause with the more numerous proletariat of western Europe and to have their support. He also favoured compressing to a minimum the period separating a 'bourgeois revolution' from socialist revolution. By 1917, he felt that Lenin had come round to his view on these two major issues, and he joined forces with the Bolsheviks. Although, in his few years in power, following the Bolshevik revolution, Trotsky was at least as authoritarian as his colleagues, he had been an early observer of the dangers inherent in Lenin's model of party organization, writing in 1904: 'Lenin's methods lead to this: the party organization first substitutes itself for the party as a whole; then the Central Committee substitutes itself for the organization; and finally a single "dictator" substitutes himself for the Central Committee . . .'[2] Against that, Lenin's insistence on 'the importance of centralization, strict discipline and ideological unity within the party' made some sense for a political party operating as an underground organization in a police state.[3] When, however, even fifty or sixty years after the Communists had come to power, Soviet politicians invoked Lenin in support of their strictly disciplined, rigidly hierarchical party, the implication that Lenin would have wished or expected such a form of organization to prevail for so long was dubious.

Nevertheless, it is hardly fanciful to discern here what political scientists call 'path dependency', a pattern of acceptance of earlier institutional choices, albeit ones made in different circumstances and under different constraints. There was a logic of development whereby the centralized Bolshevik party (with the leadership often operating in secrecy) introduced its own distinctive brand of still more authoritarian rule once it had supplanted the old regime and itself occupied the offices of state.[4] It was not only numerous later scholars but also many of Lenin's contemporaries, among them disenchanted former comrades, who viewed Lenin's antipathy to 'looser mass organizations allowing greater diversity and spontaneity' as not just a matter of expediency and tactical necessity but as reflecting an authoritarian mindset.[5] One such contemporary, Nikolay Volsky, who had joined the Bolsheviks and had become devoted to Lenin, broke with him because he could no longer stand his intolerance and intemperance when they were discussing philosophical views of which Lenin disapproved.[6] The Mensheviks, from 1903 onwards, pointed to the dangers of dictatorship inherent in Lenin's utter certainty of his own correctness taken together with his insistence on disciplined obedience within the Bolshevik group. Lenin's intolerance was evident long before he became the first leader of the Soviet Union. Indeed, in the last two or three years of his life he was more open to doubts than he had been throughout his whole career as a professional revolutionary.[7]

The Bolsheviks and Mensheviks were far from being the only warring factions in the Russian revolutionary movement in the first two decades of the twentieth century. The party which enjoyed most support among the Russian peasantry – who constituted over 80 per cent of the population – was the Socialist Revolutionary Party, known simply as the SRs. They emerged in the 1890s as an offshoot of the Russian populist movement. Their leader and principal theorist was Viktor Chernov, who argued that the peasantry must form the 'main army' for the revolution, even if the proletariat were to be in the vanguard. Chernov was not a Marxist. He wanted to avoid the coming of capitalism in Russia. Like his populist forerunners of the 1860s and 1870s, he believed that the peasant commune could form a bridge to socialism in Russia. The Marxists, on the contrary, argued about the extent to which capitalism had already arrived in that country.

The 1905 Revolution and the Last Years of Tsarist Russia

The first of three revolutions which culminated in the Bolshevik takeover in late 1917 occurred against a background of appalling social conditions in the Russian cities, poverty in the countryside, and a lack of basic political rights and freedoms. In the last decades of the nineteenth century, quite a rapid industrialization was getting under way in Russia, notwithstanding the numerical dominance of the peasantry. The abolition of serfdom (a form of slavery) in 1861 involved too many concessions to the landowners – who were to be deprived of their property in the form of people but kept their land – for it to be a satisfactory settlement for the peasantry.[8] It did, however, mean that peasants could now leave the countryside and seek work in the towns as industry developed. Thus there emerged a first-generation industrial proletariat, albeit a small proportion of the total population – a social group disorientated by the move from rural poverty to city squalor.

An economic depression, which began in 1899, provided further grounds for discontent in the expanding ranks of the workers, and there were major (although localized) strikes in several Russian cities in the early years of the twentieth century.[9] In addition to these domestic problems, in 1904–05 Russia was fighting an unsuccessful war with Japan. Its failure in this conflict came as a great shock to the political elite no less than to the population as a whole. They had regarded themselves as a great European power and, by definition, superior economically and militarily to any Asian state. Although both sides were to blame for the outbreak of the war, the Japanese had turned out to be more efficient in the conduct of it. The war ended with Japan securing more of the imperial spoils. It damaged the reputation of the tsar, Nicholas II, and deepened the sense of political crisis in Russia.[10]

One curious element in the Russian political struggle was what was known as 'police socialism'. This was a movement encouraged by some officials, partly as a result of their recognition of genuine popular grievances, and partly to steal the thunder of the Revolutionaries. But, paradoxically, it was a march led by the rather mysterious police socialist leader, a priest named Father Georgy Gapon, which triggered the 1905 Russian Revolution. In early January 1905 some 120,000 workers were on strike in St Petersburg and Gapon took up their cause. In a petition to the tsar they asked for 'justice and protection', saying that they were impoverished, oppressed, over-burdened and treated contemptuously.[11] Gapon led a vast unarmed procession – many of the marchers drawn from the ranks of the striking workers – in the direction of the Winter Palace to hand over their petition. The march – which took place on 9 January, according to the Julian calendar used in Russia until 1918 (and still used by the Orthodox Church), 22 January according to the modern calendar – was entirely peaceful until the procession was fired upon by troops instructed to prevent them from reaching the palace. The tsar himself had been sufficiently unconcerned about the impending protest to have left St Petersburg for the weekend. That day became known as 'Bloody Sunday'. Apart from the deaths of many of the marchers, other peaceful demonstrators were massacred in different parts of the city. It was rumoured at the time that thousands had died. The real figures – approximately 200 dead and 800 wounded – were bad enough.[12]

This was the beginning of the end for the autocracy. The tsar's reputation never fully recovered from Bloody Sunday. Many who had formerly looked up to Nicholas II now held him responsible for the cold-blooded murder of his innocent subjects. The event set in motion a year of revolutionary turmoil. Throughout 1905 there were daily strikes and demonstrations and looting of landlords' homes. The SRs succeeded in killing the tsar's uncle, the Grand Duke Sergey, who had made himself especially unpopular as an advocate of repression. Pressure on the government came from many quarters – from trade unions, from a peasant union which was formed in the middle of 1905 at the instigation of the SRs, and also from the professional classes, who were demanding some participation in government. Thus, there was liberal as well as revolutionary pressure. One source of the former was the zemstvos, the local government authorities which had been set up by Alexander II as part of the Great Reforms of the 1860s. With so many forces ranged against the autocracy in 1905, there was still a vital difference from 1917. In 1905 the great part of the army stood firmly on the side of the authorities. In 1917 the army was in disarray and open revolt.

The continuous strikes of 1905 culminated in a general strike – the first of its kind – in October. Faced by this, the government made concessions, urged upon Nicholas II by his prime minister, Count Sergey Witte, a moderate conservative. The tsar issued what became known as his 'October Manifesto', which granted personal liberty to the population at large and proposed elections for a national duma on the basis of a wide suffrage. Even in principle, this new assembly was to be a good deal less than a parliament. It could 'participate' in supervising the legality of legislation introduced by the tsar and his ministers but it did not have clear legislative supremacy. And neither the tsar nor his government was responsible to it. The Manifesto was a contradictory document and it reflected confusion in Nicholas's own mind. The tsar thought he had safeguarded the unlimited autocracy, although the Manifesto did include a promise that no law would take effect without the approval of the Duma. The word 'Duma' is derived from the Russian verb 'to think', but there was an evident lack of clear thought in its institutional design.

Between the elections to the first Duma in 1906 and 1917 there were four dumas, although they represented a narrowing, rather than a widening, of the suffrage. Increasing control by the authorities over the composition of this legislative assembly accordingly reduced the number of radical critics in the last two Dumas. Even in 1905, the tsar's October Manifesto did not satisfy Russia's emerging liberals, and it was treated with contempt by the revolutionaries. The day after the promulgation of the Manifesto, tens of thousands of people gathered in front of St Petersburg University, aroused, in Trotsky's words, 'by the struggle and intoxicated with the joy of their first victory'.[13] Trotsky adds: 'I shouted to them from the balcony not to trust an incomplete victory; that the enemy was stubborn, that there were traps ahead; I tore the Tsar's manifesto into pieces and scattered them to the winds.'[14]

Trotsky was to play a leading role in a quite different institution which emerged in 1905 and was to have later political resonance. This was the formation of the first soviet. Although 'soviet' is simply the Russian word for council, it acquired from the outset a revolutionary connotation from its origins as a strike committee in St Petersburg and by its full title, the Soviet of Workers' Deputies. After the arrest of the Soviet's first president, a 'presidium' was elected, with Trotsky at the head of it. He became the main driving and intellectual force of the Soviet, an organization which was to be skilfully revived in 1917. Trotsky was also formulating at this time his theory of 'permanent revolution'. In part, this was his view, already alluded to, that the 'bourgeois' and 'socialist' revolutions would interact with each other and that it would be necessary to lose no time after the former before pressing on with the latter. Moreover, in the Russia of 1905, he argued, it was 'the strikes of the workers that for the first time brought Tsarism to its knees' and this led him to draw optimistic conclusions about the West. If 'the young proletariat of Russia could be so formidable, how mighty the revolutionary power of the proletariat of the more advanced countries could be!'[15]

When, however, Petr Stolypin was appointed Minister of the Interior in 1906 and, while keeping that post, became Chairman of the Council of Ministers (or prime minister) the following year, the revolutionaries found they were up against a more formidable opponent than most of the tsarist appointees. Stolypin stepped up the forcible repression, closing down radical newspapers and arresting (in some cases executing) tens of thousands of opponents of the regime. He combined this, however, with a policy of implementing reforms. In particular, he instituted an important land reform designed to turn the peasant into something more like the farmer of western Europe. The policy involved breaking up the old village commune, known as the *obshchina* or *mir*, which had since the 1861 abolition of serfdom collectively owned the land the peasants worked. The aim was to carry through an enclosure movement and create individual peasant land ownership. The reform worried a number of revolutionaries, Lenin among them. They did not believe that it could prevent revolution from ultimately taking place, but they feared it might postpone it by decades. The belated reform, however, was less successful than liberals hoped and revolutionaries feared. The country gentry were mainly opposed to it and did their best to undermine it. The peasants themselves were not initially eager to accept the risks of farming on their own account, thereby losing the shared resources (even if at times it meant shared misery) provided by the commune. Moreover, they did not trust the source or the motives behind this renewed 'emancipation'. Stolypin in the end had the support only of a narrow band of liberal conservatives. His reforms went too far for traditionalists, his willingness to disband the Duma and change the electoral system in order to get a more compliant assembly antagonized the liberals, and the revolutionaries had good cause to regard him as an implacable enemy.

Stolypin was almost assassinated in 1906 – in the attempt on his life several people were killed and two of his children were injured. Although 1906 and 1907 were considered a relatively quiet time, in comparison with 1905, assassinations of officials by the revolutionaries continued on a large scale. Numerous bank robberies took place, some of them led by Ioseb Djugashvili, in order to pay for the upkeep of the revolutionary movement.[16] This Georgian Bolshevik, who had studied in a religious seminary (until his expulsion from it in 1899), was to become better known as Stalin, the name he began using in late 1912. Lenin himself sanctioned a number of the raids and regarded them as a legitimate part of the struggle with tsarism. As his wife Nadezhda Krupskaya put it: 'the Bolsheviks thought it permissible to seize tsarist treasure and allowed expropriations'. The Mensheviks, in contrast, were strongly opposed to bank robberies.[17]

In 1911 Stolypin was eventually assassinated, a fate which he had assumed would be his from the time he became Chairman of the Council of Ministers.[18] The person who shot him – in a theatre in Kiev at a celebratory performance attended by the tsar – had both Socialist Revolutionary and police associations. It has remained unclear for which side he was acting on this occasion, although some of the evidence points in the direction of disaffected members of the tsarist secret police. It was the head of the Kiev Okhrana who gave the killer, Dmitry Bogrov, the ticket for the Kiev opera house on the fateful day. Bogrov was subsequently hanged without a public trial.[19]

Liberal reformism in Russia between 1905 and 1917 was represented mainly by the Constitutional Democrats, a political party popularly known as the Kadets, and by a still more moderate liberal party, the Octobrists, so called to indicate their support for the tsar's 1905 October Manifesto. Apart from liberalism and revolutionary socialism, these were years in which a powerful current of nationalism, xenophobia and anti-semitism also came to the fore. There were pogroms of Jews and, as a result, large-scale Jewish emigration from the Russian Empire to Western Europe and North America. Discrimination against Jews was nothing new in Russia and other parts of the Empire, including especially Ukraine. It is one reason why Jews were

so very well represented in the leading ranks of the revolutionary parties –
not so much the SRs with their populist origins but both the Mensheviks
(in particular) and the Bolsheviks.

In the forefront of persecution of the Jews was the nationalist Union of
the Russian People, or the Black Hundreds, as Russian democrats called
them. It was formed in 1905 with the blessing of Nicholas II in order to
mobilize the mass of the people against revolutionaries and radical
reformers.[20] Many of the Black Hundreds themselves regarded the tsar as
too weak and hesitant in his efforts to suppress the revolutionaries. Anyone
who was regarded as a democrat and an opponent of the autocracy was
liable to be beaten up by the Black Hundreds, but Jews in particular, were
singled out. Several thousand were murdered in the course of 1905 – 800 in
Odessa alone. By the end of 1906 the Union of the Russian People had
around 300,000 members.[21] Some of the demagogic and anti-semitic organizations formed in Russia between the beginning of the twentieth century
and 1917 looked remarkably like prototypes of the fascist movements which
flourished elsewhere in Europe in the 1920s and 1930s. It would be naïve to
assume that the only conceivable alternative to socialist or Communist revolution in 1917 was a gradually developing liberal democracy. Liberals had
far less support not only than the revolutionaries but also than the bigots
from the opposite side of the political spectrum. An entirely possible alternative to the victory of the Communists was the development of an
extremely right-wing nationalist regime.

The growing crisis in Russian society was brought to a head by the
outbreak of the First World War. Lenin and many of the revolutionaries
declared that this was an imperialist war and would have nothing to do with
it. However, the advent of war split the socialist movement throughout
Europe. Some of its leading representatives (such as Eduard Bernstein in
Germany and Keir Hardie in Britain) opposed it on pacifist grounds, others
primarily on the political grounds that it was imperialist, but many rallied
to the defence of their particular motherland. Any known Bolsheviks who
remained in Russia, including members of the Duma, were arrested following
Russia's entry into the war in alliance with France and Britain against
Germany and Austria-Hungary.[22] Russian Marxists were split on whether or
not to support Russia's war effort. Lenin and Trotsky were prominent among
the 'defeatists', not only opposing the war on principle but also believing
that it presented a great opportunity. They were convinced that a Russian
defeat would hasten the success of revolution. Plekhanov, on the contrary,
believed that the cause of socialism would be advanced by the victory of
Russia and its allies. In reality the legitimacy of the regime was by now
sufficiently weak that when the army suffered major setbacks, Russians as

a whole did not rally behind the state authorities and defence of the motherland in the way they had when attacked by Napoleon and the French
army in 1812, or as they were to do in the Second World War under the
onslaught of Hitler's Germany. Incompetence in the conduct of the war,
vast human losses, and dwindling confidence in the authorities made the
tsarist regime more vulnerable than ever before.[23]

Nicholas II's wife Alexandra was the granddaughter of the British queen
Victoria, whom she revered, but mainly German by ethnic origin. As a
result, doubts were – quite wrongly – cast on her commitment to the Russian
cause. A more major concern among some of the tsar's ministers as well
as courtiers was the influence exerted over the empress by Grigory Rasputin.
A charismatic and bisexual Siberian peasant, he had been associated with a
sect which engaged in sexual orgies, intermingled with religious revelations.
It was the influence Rasputin was believed to wield which, however, most
agitated his rivals for the tsar's attention. He was held by some – particularly the Empress Alexandra – to possess mystical powers. Rasputin won
the trust of Nicholas, and still more of his wife, through his apparent ability
to stop the bleeding of their haemophiliac son and heir to the throne, Alexei,
at a time when the medical profession was quite unable to help.

Rasputin's impact increased during the First World War, especially during
the periods when the tsar was away from the capital at the front. The fact
that his advice was so readily accepted by Alexandra – who in turn wielded
profound influence over her husband – outraged many in the court and government. Rasputin was murdered in December 1916 by a group which included
the tsar's first cousin, the Grand Duke Dmitry, and an ultra-conservative Duma
deputy, V.M. Purishkevich. Even the murder added to the legendary status of
Rasputin. A heavy drinker at the best of times, he downed several glasses of
poisoned wine and ate some cyanide-laced cake without any obvious ill-effects.
One of the conspirators, Prince Felix Yusupov, after an hour of impatient
waiting for Rasputin to expire, shot him with a pistol and, assuming he was
now dead, briefly left the room. By the time he returned, Rasputin was making
his way through the courtyard snow in the direction of the embankment of
the River Neva. Two more shots finally killed him and his weighted body
was subsequently dumped in the Neva.[24]

The 1917 Revolutions

The removal of Rasputin did nothing, however, to save the old regime. By
the second half of 1916 and early 1917, the crucial factor was increasing dis-
affection in the Russian army. These 'peasants in uniform', as Lenin called

them, were sick of the war. When soldiers were brought in to suppress a strike in Petrograd (as St Petersburg had been renamed in 1914) in October 1916, they fired at the police instead of at the workers. Well over a million Russian soldiers were killed in the First World War, more than four million were wounded, and some two and a half million were taken prisoner.[25] Bolshevik promises of peace and land had much popular resonance in 1917, but the revolution which ended over three hundred years of the Romanov dynasty (founded in 1613) came as a complete surprise to most Marxist revolutionaries. Three of the most famous of them, Nikolay Bukharin, Leon Trotsky and the one woman who was to become a prominent member of the first Bolshevik government, Alexandra Kollontai, were all in New York on the eve of the February revolution.[26] Like almost all of the leading Bolsheviks, Lenin, too, was living abroad at the time. In a sparsely attended lecture he delivered in Zurich in January 1917, commemorating the twelfth anniversary of the 1905 revolution, he clearly had no inkling that revolution in Russia was imminent, although he had no doubt that it would eventually occur. He said: 'We old folks may not live to see the decisive battles of the coming revolution.'[27] Lenin was at that time aged forty-seven.

On 12 March, according to the modern calendar – 27 February on the Julian calendar – the first of the two revolutions of 1917 took place. The tsar was as surprised as was Lenin. On 7 March he had written to his wife from the front: 'I greatly miss my half-hourly game of patience every evening. I shall take up dominoes again in my spare time.'[28] On the eve of the decisive day of what was to become known as the February Revolution, almost all the factories in Petrograd were on strike, there was widespread looting, and mutiny was spreading throughout the garrisons stationed in the Russian capital.[29] The climax came when the Duma attempted to take power into its own hands and formed a committee which became the nucleus of a provisional government. Simultaneously, a Soviet of Workers' Deputies was formed in Petrograd, modelling itself on the institution which had sprung to life briefly in 1905. Between them the Duma and the Soviet took command. The Soviet, realising that a large part of the army was behind them, renamed itself the Soviet of Workers' and Soldiers' Deputies. Most of the ministers in the pre-existing government were arrested, and when the tsar tried to return to Petrograd, his train was diverted. Nicholas II abdicated on 15 March. He was persuaded by senior generals that the Duma had taken control and that there were serious doubts about the loyalty of the Petrograd garrisons, should they be asked to come to his defence. The throne was offered to Grand Duke Mikhail, who had supported the February Revolution. He had the good sense to decline it. Yet he was refused permission by Lenin to emigrate and was shot by a group of Bolsheviks in June 1918. A month later

Nicholas II, the Empress Alexandra, their four young daughters and still younger haemophiliac son were brutally killed in Ekaterinburg in the Urals, where they had been kept under house arrest. The decision to exterminate the entire family was taken by the top leadership of the Bolsheviks, including Lenin.[30]

The Bolsheviks, however, had played no part in the drama which put an end to the Romanov dynasty. The Mensheviks, some of whom were active in the Petrograd Soviet, and Socialist Revolutionaries played a small part in that February Revolution. More important was the spontaneous unrest, together with the efforts of liberals in the Duma to force out the tsar and introduce efficient government. In the succinct judgement of one of the leading historians of twentieth-century Russia, Sheila Fitzpatrick, 'the autocracy collapsed in the face of popular demonstrations and the withdrawal of elite support for the regime'.[31] The fact that the army was not prepared to defend that regime was ultimately the decisive factor in bringing to an end monarchical rule in Russia.

Lenin was able to re-enter Russia courtesy only of the German authorities, who were delighted to facilitate the return from Switzerland of someone who would cause trouble in the enemy camp and who was opposed to Russian participation in the war. The idea of getting back to their homeland by train, with the connivance of the German High Command (and in a sealed carriage), had been Martov's. Lenin, for his part, was happy that some Mensheviks as well as Bolsheviks should take this route back to Russia, since it meant that the Mensheviks would not subsequently be able to use collaboration with the Germans as a stick with which to beat him and his supporters.[32] Lenin and the group of returning revolutionaries arrived at the Finland Station in Petrograd shortly before midnight on 3 April 1917. He had busied himself during the journey writing a document which he was to call his 'April Theses'. These did not openly call for the overthrow of the recently established Provisional Government, but they implicitly rejected the orthodox Marxist idea that there should be a lengthy period of bourgeois rule before the society would be ready for socialist revolution. And on his arrival in Petrograd, when he addressed a crowd of several thousand from the roof of an armoured car supplied by local Bolsheviks, Lenin's message was that no support should be offered to the Provisional Government and that the task of genuine socialists was to bring down capitalism in Russia and throughout Europe.[33]

The Provisional Government of Russia in 1917 was headed first by Prince Georgy Lvov, a member of the Kadet party, and from July by Alexander Kerensky, a moderate socialist politically and somewhat histrionic temperamentally. Under both its leaders the Provisional Government failed in three main ways. First, it carried on with the war at a time of great war-weariness. While Germany and its allies were by now losing the war, the progress of Russia's allies was obscured by the success of Bolshevik propaganda. Second, the government failed to disband the private army – the Red Guard – which the Bolsheviks had quickly set up. Third, it failed to deal with the land problem. The peasants were clamouring for more land, and some of them forcibly seized land belonging to large landowners. The Provisional Government insisted that they could take no action on this problem until a Constituent Assembly had been formed, and they delayed the convening of such an assembly, adding to public impatience. A Congress of Soviets was held in June 1917, and shortly afterwards the Petrograd Soviet issued its Order No. 1, aimed at the armed forces. It instructed the soldiers to obey the Provisional Government only if their orders did not conflict with those of the Soviet. This was clearly an executive act of the kind which only a government should have the right to take. However, the Soviets were speedily acquiring power without responsibility while the Provisional Government, which had responsibility, was rapidly losing power.

The period was accurately described as one of 'dual power', and as such, it neither could nor did last. It had nothing in common with an agreed separation of powers but meant that there were two bodies vying for full power within the one state. More than seventy years later, as the Soviet state was coming to an end – in 1991 – a form of dual power (with the Russian president and legislature pitted against the Soviet president and legislature) once again played an important part in bringing about the collapse of a regime. In the latter case, however, there was nothing like as acute an ideological divide as in the year in which Communist rule was born. In 1917 Lenin and Trotsky, the two key figures in the overthrow of the Provisional Government, decided that the soviets, which were increasing in both numbers and popular support, would be a suitable instrument of the next revolution. Besides their slogan, 'All Power to the Soviets', the Bolsheviks promised 'freedom, bread, and peace'. They did not actually wish all power to be in the hands of the soviets until they controlled the soviets, but they made progress in that direction throughout the year. The Socialist Revolutionaries (SRs) remained the most popular party with the peasantry, but the Bolsheviks were the better organized.

That is not to say that the Bolshevik party in this year of revolutions operated in anything like the disciplined way that Lenin had advocated in *What is to be Done?*. Too much emphasis can be, and has been, placed on Bolshevik organization as an explanation of their success in 1917. Strict party discipline was to come later, but this was a time of great expansion in party numbers and much open disagreement within the leadership, including on the crucial question of whether the Bolsheviks should seize power by force.[34] A stark example of the lack of unity of the Bolsheviks came in July 1917, when a crowd of sailors from the port of Kronstadt, along with soldiers and workers from Petrograd factories, took part in a massive street demonstration under the banner of 'All Power to the Soviets' with the intention of bringing down the Provisional Government.

From Lenin's standpoint, this was dangerous and premature. It led to the arrest of a number of Bolsheviks, as well as of Trotsky (who did not formally join the Bolshevik party until early October). Orders were issued for Lenin's arrest, and since rumours were now being spread that he was a German agent, he decided to seek safety in Finland. The left-wing insurrection of the 'July Days' was followed in August by an attempt from the opposite end of the political spectrum to seize control. General Lavr Kornilov attempted to lead his troops to Petrograd to suppress the soviets and the danger, as he saw it, of socialist revolution. He believed that Kerensky would welcome such assistance. Kerensky's response, while initially ambivalent, was ultimately hostile, and in any event, railwaymen obstructed and diverted the troop trains. Kornilov was arrested, though he later took part in the civil war against the Bolsheviks, being killed in battle in 1918.

The Bolsheviks, although far from united in 1917, were organizationally stronger than the SRs and much more ruthless than the Mensheviks. Their intransigent insistence on condemning compromise with the Provisional Government and 'willingness to seize power in the name of the proletarian revolution' caught the mood of the urban workers and of disaffected soldiers and sailors.[35] Lenin and Trotsky succeeded in winning great influence over the Petrograd and other soviets. On 12 October, according to the old calendar, Trotsky took command of the Military Revolutionary Committee of the Petrograd Soviet and on 25 October (7 November according to the modern calendar) the Bolsheviks seized power in Petrograd. Bolshevik troops took over public buildings and arrested ministers of the Provisional Government. Kerensky escaped and lived on until 1970, mainly in the United States.

Although 7 November entered history as the day of the successful Bolshevik revolution, in many respects it was more of a coup than a revolution. It supplanted the regime that had been established as a result of the earlier (February) revolution, which had initially commanded widespread support. At the time they seized power, the Bolsheviks were not the most popular party in Russia. This was made abundantly clear by elections for the Constituent Assembly, which were held in December 1917. The Bolsheviks had earlier in the year supported, for propaganda purposes, the holding of these elections, and they allowed them to go ahead. The SRs won 299 seats compared with the Bolsheviks' 168. Of the other parties, the Left SRs with

39, the Mensheviks with 18, and the Kadets with 17 were the largest.[36] When the Constituent Assembly opened on 18 January the Bolsheviks broke it up. Its first day was also its last. In Lenin's words: 'The dispersal of the Constituent Assembly by the Soviet regime is the full and open liquidation of formal democracy in the name of the revolutionary dictatorship.'[37]

Bolshevik Power and the Civil War

One of the most respected figures in the international Marxist movement, Karl Kautsky, who in his youth had known Marx and Engels personally, wrote a book in 1918 entitled *The Dictatorship of the Proletariat*, arguing that Lenin's 'revolutionary dictatorship' was far removed from what Marx had in mind when he used the phrase (and very infrequently) 'the dictatorship of the proletariat'. Marx, Kautsky wrote, had not meant by this 'a form of government'.[38] Having come later than socialists such as Bernstein to an understanding of where Lenin's ideas were leading, Kautsky now insisted:

> The proletarian class struggle, as a struggle of the masses, presupposes democracy ... Masses cannot be organised secretly, and above all, a secret organisation cannot be a democratic one. It always leads to the dictatorship of a single man, or of a small knot of leaders. The ordinary members can only become instruments for carrying out orders. Such a method may be rendered necessary for an oppressed class in the absence of democracy, but it would not promote the self-government and independence of the masses. Rather would it further the Messiah-consciousness of leaders, and their dictatorial habits.[39]

Kautsky also observed that 'quite properly' the Bolsheviks had stopped calling themselves Social Democrats, and now 'described themselves as Communists'.[40] Lenin was outraged by Kautsky's sober analysis of the un-democratic character of the Bolshevik revolution. Even though he had already assumed the reins of government, he devoted time to writing a vitriolic reply, *The Proletarian Revolution and the Renegade Kautsky*, in which invective substituted for reasoned argument. As Kautsky had noted, the Bolsheviks began calling themselves Communist in 1918. From that time onwards the gulf between socialists who accepted the principles of democracy and Communists who rationalized dictatorship in the name of the class power of the proletariat grew ever wider.

Although the Bolsheviks had taken power surprisingly easily, holding on to it over the next few years was much harder. Immediately after the October

Revolution, a government was formed called the Council of People's Commissars (or Sovnarkom in its Russian acronym). Lenin presided over it. Trotsky become the commissar for foreign affairs, and Stalin was appointed commissar for nationalities. Its first acts were to issue a Peace Decree and a Land Decree. The former called on the governments of all the peoples still at war to begin immediate negotiations for a peace without annexation of territory. This proposal met with no response, but with its army first demoralized and then disbanded, Russia was in no position to carry on the fight. Trotsky announced in February 1918 that the war with Germany was over and that the Russian army was to be demobilized. Later in the month the army was re-formed as the Red Army – the Workers' and Peasants' Army – but its first task was to deal with enemies within the state rather than engage in a European war. The Germans had responded to Trotsky's declaration by ordering their troops to advance into Russia, and so in early March 1918 the Soviet government was forced to accept very unfavourable peace terms, involving significant loss of territory which had belonged to the Russian Empire, and sign the Treaty of Brest-Litovsk. Nevertheless, the widespread demand for an end to the war had been met.

The Land Decree also responded to at least a substantial body of peasant opinion. It abolished private ownership of the land and established, in principle, joint ownership of it by those who worked in agriculture. However, class war ensued in the countryside, as poor peasants, with Bolshevik encouragement, turned against the richer peasants. The peasantry as a whole, however, resisted attempts by the revolutionary government to take away, in compulsory requisitions, the food they had produced. In the civil war which broke out in Russia in the middle of 1918, the peasants sometimes supported the Red Army and sometimes the White Army, but the cruelty of both sides rapidly alienated them. The Bolsheviks had originally supposed that their army could be composed largely of volunteers, especially workers. This soon proved inadequate, and so they instituted compulsory call-up. On Trotsky's initiative, they also recruited officers from the former Imperial army, but put alongside them armed Bolshevik commissars to ensure they remembered which side they were fighting on.

The Whites were a disparate army of anti-Bolsheviks, who naturally included also Imperial army officers, although among their keenest volunteers were Cossacks, who had centuries ago succeeded in escaping from serfdom by settling in empty land in southern Russia. Many of them fought to prevent the Bolsheviks from encroaching on the territory which they freely farmed. Given the social composition of Russia at the time, it is hardly surprising that most of the soldiers on both sides were from the peasantry. While most factory workers supported the Bolsheviks, the peasants were deeply ambivalent about the civil war. Those who could keep out of the conflict did so. Sometimes they would welcome the arrival of the Whites, only to find that they wished to restore the old system of landlordism, whereupon the peasants would co-operate with the Reds to drive them out. What they wanted, as some of them put it, was neither a Red nor a White, but a Green government, by which they meant one that would safeguard the distinctive interests of the rural communities.

Within Russia the anti-Bolshevik forces were reinforced by foreign help, especially from the Czechs. Small British forces were landed, partly to prevent military equipment which had been provided for the former Russian government falling into Bolshevik hands. Winston Churchill was keen to launch an all-out offensive against the new Soviet regime, but David Lloyd George, the British prime minister at the time, identified the new government with the Russian people as a whole and took the view that nobody could defeat Russia on Russian soil. The identification of the Bolsheviks with Russia was an oversimplification, since Russia remained deeply divided, although Lloyd George's scepticism about the practicality of Western military intervention was no doubt justified.

Once British forces had been landed in Russia, small contingents were also sent by France, the United States, Italy, Canada and Japan.[41] They, perhaps, helped to delay the defeat of the Whites, but did not play a decisive role. The one element in the foreign intervention which was significant for a time was the Czech Legion. Some 40,000 Czechs – who had come to fight against Austria, since their goal was an independent state and the defeat, therefore, of the Austro-Hungarian Empire – were in Russia at the time of the Bolshevik revolution. The change of regime in Russia put a stop to their participation in the European war, and as they journeyed through Russia they found themselves in conflict at times with the Red Army. The Czechs had superior training and equipment and won a number of victories in these skirmishes before they returned to their homeland. In contrast, the British and other troops which had been sent to Russia to combat the Bolsheviks were too few to have a bearing on the ultimate outcome, although the foreign intervention in the civil war was given great prominence in later Soviet historiography.

As early as December 1917 the Bolsheviks created a new organization called the All-Russian Extraordinary Commission for Fighting Counter-Revolution and Sabotage, better known in its abbreviated Russian form as the Cheka. Headed by Felix Dzerzhinsky, a revolutionary of Polish noble extraction, it became the main instrument of the Red Terror. It was, in effect, the successor to the tsarist political police, the Okhrana, albeit in a more ruthless variant. The Cheka was many times larger than its tsarist predecessor, and in the years of its existence while Lenin was still alive it killed some 140,000 people.[42] It became a feared instrument of mass arrests and a pitiless killing machine in its subsequent incarnations as the OGPU and especially NKVD. In the final form it took in the Soviet era, by then more politically restrained, it was known as the KGB. The Cheka was intended to be a temporary organization, dealing with the 'extraordinary' situation which faced the Bolsheviks as they tried to hold on to power in the immediate aftermath of revolution. However, like many a supposedly temporary institution, it survived and prospered under its various different names until the end of the Soviet Union – and, arguably, even beyond. Throughout the Communist period the political police liked to refer to themselves as 'Chekists', since this gave them a certain revolutionary elan, even when they were acting in the 1970s in defence of an ageing, conservative political elite.

The civil war ended in 1922 with the Bolsheviks triumphant. Leon Trotsky, as the war commissar, had been both efficient and ruthless and the Cheka had also played its violent part. Bolshevik organization was superior to that of the Whites. Lenin led the government and Stalin was playing an increasingly important part in the Communist Party organization, the Bolsheviks having renamed themselves the Communist Party in 1919 (although 'Bolshevik' was retained in brackets until 1952). Yet force and organization alone did not produce the victory of the Reds in the civil war. Although there was still at this stage open argument within the party, the Bolsheviks possessed a more coherent ideology than the Whites. The latter not only failed to win over the peasant majority in the country, they also produced neither an outstanding leader nor a unifying idea.

4

'Building Socialism':
Russia and the Soviet Union, 1917–40

During August and September of 1917, Lenin had used his time in Finland to write a book, *The State and Revolution*, which he failed to finish. In a November postscript to the first edition, he wrote that his work 'was "interrupted" by a political crisis – the eve of the October Revolution of 1917', adding that it was 'more pleasant and useful to go through the "experience of the revolution" than to write about it'.[1] Compared with what was to follow the Bolshevik seizure of power, the work seems remote from reality. Yet Lenin was happy for it to be published even after Bolshevik rule had begun. It is reasonable to regard it as part of his belief system, rather than as dissemblance for tactical reasons, since it had no immediate relevance to the task of holding on to power.

It is clear that Lenin believed not only in the dictatorship of the proletariat – although, Kautsky suggested, in a different sense from that of Marx – but also in the eventual withering-away of the state. Even as he denies being a utopian, Lenin offers evidence of the utopianism which accompanied his ruthlessness, writing that 'only communism makes the state absolutely unnecessary, for there is *nobody* to be suppressed – "nobody" in the sense of a *class* . . .'.[2] He accepted that individual people would be guilty of 'excesses', but no special apparatus of suppression would be needed to deal with them. This would be done 'by the armed people itself'. Moreover, it was 'the exploitation of the masses, their want and their poverty' which was the cause of 'excesses'. With the removal of that cause, 'excesses will inevitably begin to *"wither away"*'.[3] Where Marx had spoken of a first, or lower, phase of communist society, Lenin prefers to call the first stage 'socialism' and the later stage 'communism'.[4] In this later stage, freedom will be combined with equality and the distinction between mental and physical labour will disappear – along with the state. 'So long as the state exists', writes Lenin, 'there is no freedom. When there will be freedom, there will be no state.'[5]

Lenin's *The State and Revolution* has often been hailed as evidence of a libertarian or democratic Lenin and contrasted with the Lenin of *What is to be Done?*, with its emphasis on hierarchy and discipline within the revolutionary party. It has been used in support of the contention that he was a 'revolutionary humanist' and by those who wish to distance him from the way the Soviet system developed after his death.[6] It has been contrastingly assessed as 'the crowning achievement of Lenin's political thought in the latter period of his life'[7] and as 'the most simple-minded and improbable of all famous political pamphlets'.[8] The more essential point is that even in this work of reflection on the state, with its apparent support for a fuller and more libertarian democracy than had hitherto been seen on earth, Lenin rejected any kind of political pluralism. He was oblivious to the fact that freedoms depend on institutions capable of defending them. *The State and Revolution* added to the doctrinal foundations of what became a highly authoritarian (and later totalitarian) regime. As A.J. Polan justly observed: 'The central absence in Lenin's politics is that of a theory of political institutions . . . Lenin's state form is one-dimensional. It allows no distances, no spaces, no appeals, no checks, no balances, no processes, no delays, no interrogations and, above all, no distribution of power.'[9]

This rejection of institutions which would underpin accountability, individual freedoms and political pluralism became a common feature of Communist systems. Yet the ideas and utopian goals of the Communists exerted on their adherents a powerful attraction. The coming to power of the Bolsheviks in the Russia of 1917 was not only a matter of their willingness to use force against the Provisional Government. It was not simply a result of economic hardship, still less something which had been economically determined. Nor was it just a matter of the tactical skills and willpower of Lenin and Trotsky, important though they were. It was, in addition to all these things, a victory of ideas – of the idea that capitalism was doomed, the belief that the proletariat was destined to supplant the bourgeoisie as the ruling class, and that it would proceed to build socialism before merging into a classless, self-administering society bearing the name of 'communism'. For a significant proportion of young workers, as well as intellectuals, this was an inspiring doctrine. Those who embraced it found it easy to dismiss the kind of parliamentary and judicial institutions needed to safeguard political freedoms as the mere optical illusions of 'bourgeois democracy'.

The short-lived and somewhat anarchic democracy inaugurated by the February Revolution might well, given the discontent within Russian society, have led to change with a revolutionary dimension even in the absence of Lenin and Trotsky. If the election to the Constituent Assembly, in which the Bolsheviks received only a quarter of the votes, had been allowed to stand, a non-Communist socialist government would have emerged. Its ideas would, however, have been different from those which, after Lenin's death, were to become known as Marxism-Leninism. Lenin's own ideas did not remain static, and in his last years he had to modify some of them in the light of circumstances. Yet even when he made a major retreat on economic policy in an attempt to mollify the country's largest social group, the peasantry, he not only stepped up the repression of political opponents but pejoratively labelled dissent within the Communist Party as opposition, and at the Tenth Congress of that party in March 1921 declared that it was time 'to put the lid' on it.[10]

The March congress followed almost immediately after the Kronstadt Revolt, an uprising by sailors in the naval base which had been in the vanguard of Bolshevik militancy in 1917. The protesters' desires in 1921 were essentially democratic and not at all, as much Bolshevik propaganda against them suggested, in favour of restoration of the old regime. The main demands of the Kronstadt sailors were for the immediate re-election of soviets by secret ballot, for freedom of speech and assembly, for free trade unions, for equal rations for all, and for peasants to be allowed to do as they pleased with the land, 'provided that they use no hired labour'.[11] Lenin, in a moment of frankness at the March 1921 congress, went so far as to admit that the Kronstadt rebels 'do not want the White Guards, and they do not want our power either'.[12] He was also increasingly concerned by groupings within the Communist Party which questioned the way things were going, such as the Workers' Opposition, led by Alexander Shlyapnikov. The latter was not quite an organized faction, but those who belonged to this group wanted trade unions and their worker representatives to be in control of industry. They were met with the rebuff that only the Communist Party could be in the vanguard of the proletariat, for otherwise the 'working masses' would fail to resist 'petty bourgeois waverings' and fall prey to 'their trade-union prejudices'.[13] Dissent on major policy was essentially classified as factionalism or opposition. Organized factions were discerned where they barely existed and a resolution on 'party unity' delegitimized intra-party dissent, although it was not until the 1930s that it was to be equated with treason.[14]

Lenin, NEP, and the Rise of Stalin

A political tightening of the screws at the Tenth Congress was, however, accompanied by economic liberalization. The attempt made soon after the Bolshevik revolution to nationalize all industry and deny peasants the right to trade had been disastrous. There was famine in many parts of the country and growing unrest. Accordingly, Lenin unveiled the New Economic Policy – subsequently known as NEP – at the March 1921 congress. In May of that year the decree which had earlier nationalized all small-scale industry was revoked. The Party held on to the 'commanding heights' of the economy – large-scale industry, banking, and foreign trade – but, in a retreat of major proportions, it now introduced what was 'a form of mixed economy, with an overwhelmingly private agriculture, plus legalized private trade and small-scale private manufacturing'.[15] In the course of the 1920s the economy revived, with agriculture in particular benefiting from the new freedoms. However, those who profiteered from the partial restoration of small-scale capitalism became known as Nepmen and were widely resented.

The year 1922 was an especially significant one. In April, Josif Stalin was chosen, with Lenin's full approval, to occupy the new post of General Secretary of the Communist Party. This did not seem such a momentous event at the time, but Stalin thereby became the only person to be a member of all three of the party's leading executive bodies: the Political Bureau, or Politburo; the Organizational Bureau, or Orgburo; and the Secretariat. The Orgburo was merged with the Secretariat in 1952, but what mattered is that from 1922 Stalin headed the general staff of the party, leading both the Orgburo and Secretariat. Since the Politburo, in which Lenin was the most authoritative member, was, in principle, a higher organ, and since much policy was made in the Sovnarkom, chaired by Lenin, it was not immediately obvious in 1922 what great potential levers of power were being placed in Stalin's hands. Nevertheless, power had already been moving from Sovnarkom to party organs. The author of the major study of Sovnarkom's first five years observes that 'by 1921 the Central Committee and its inner organs were well on the way to becoming the true government of the Soviet Republic, while the hierarchy of party officials was emerging as the key instrument of rule throughout the country'.[16]

The potential the General Secretaryship offered was given a still greater chance of becoming reality when in May 1922 Lenin suffered a stroke. This was the second of three events with immense long-term consequences to occur in that same year, Stalin's accession to the post of General Secretary having been the first. Lenin resumed his duties in the autumn, and by the end of the year he had became so critical of Stalin's high-handedness that he concluded it had been a mistake to put the substantial powers of the General Secretaryship into the Georgian's hands. He was not against those powers as such, but against Stalin continuing to wield them.[17] Lenin was not, however, able to achieve his desired outcome – to remove Stalin as General Secretary. His health had become too weak and a further stroke in March 1923 effectively ended his political career. He died in January 1924. With Lenin out of the way, Stalin spent the rest of the 1920s discrediting his rivals (many of whom had underestimated both his ability and his ambition) and consolidating power.

Although Trotsky had played a more important role than Stalin in 1917 and in the civil war, during which time the two men had often clashed, he was notable among those who made the mistake of overlooking Stalin's intelligence and political skills, as well as underestimating the significance of the power base Stalin had acquired in the form of the Secretariat.[18]

The third event of great long-term importance to occur in 1922 came at the end of the year, when the four republics then under Communist rule, namely the Russian republic, Ukraine, Belorussia, and Transcaucasia, came together to form the Union of Soviet Socialist Republics – the USSR, or the Soviet Union as it became more generally known. The name was deliberately coined to avoid mentioning any particular nationality, since the idea behind it was that other countries would gradually become part of this new socialist entity. It was established as a federation, although throughout almost the whole of the Soviet era this was a highly centralized state which was far from meeting the criteria normally associated with federalism. Nevertheless, within that formal federation which, in Stalin's words, was to be 'national in form, socialist in content', new possibilities for the flourishing of national cultures and languages were opened up.[19]

This last development was of long-term significance. Prior to 1917 in, for example, the important case of Ukraine, Russian had been the language in which literacy was taught – to the extent it *was* taught, for in 1920 only 24 per cent of the Ukrainian population was literate.[20] In spite of shortage of textbooks and other difficulties, that changed in the 1920s. By 1927, 76 per cent of pupils in the Ukrainian republic were attending Ukrainian-language schools.[21] Some of the many languages spoken in the USSR were only given written form in the first decade after the civil war. Soviet policy, especially from 1922–23 onwards, was to recognize numerous national territories in which one or other of the many different nationalities in the country predominated, and to train and promote into leadership positions people who belonged to the local nationality. At the same time they took steps to establish the local language as the official language in that territory.[22] Both measures had important long-term consequences. Although there was to be a substantial reversal of the 1920s policy of 'indigenization' from the early 1930s until at least Stalin's death, the Communist state, both by promoting the spread of education and by embedding national structures in its institutional framework from the 1922 constitution onwards, had sown the first seeds of its ultimate destruction.

Stalin had earlier been commissar for nationalities within Lenin's government, and he regarded himself, and was so regarded by others, as a specialist on the national question. Over time, however, his views developed in a direction close to Russian chauvinism. As noted earlier, Stalin was a Georgian whose original name was Djugashvili, the name Stalin being just one of his pre-revolutionary pseudonyms, derived from the Russian word for steel (*stal'*). He became an admirer of the strongest and harshest of tsars, those who had both ruled with an iron fist and expanded Russian territory, especially Ivan the Terrible and Peter the Great. In other respects, too, Stalin departed from Lenin's ideas and practices. Unlike Lenin – who had been very ready to employ the weapon of terror against opponents of the Bolshevik revolution but was content to out-argue his intra-party opponents – Stalin, by the time he felt sufficiently powerful in the mid-1930s, used terror against his fellow Bolsheviks. He also subsequently allowed a cult of his personality to be carried to extreme lengths. This even involved, by the later 1930s, people leaping to their feet at public meetings and conferences whenever his name was mentioned. It was, said Nikita Khrushchev – Stalin's successor as Soviet leader – 'a sort of physical culture we all engaged in'.[23] Unlike Peter the Great, who at the end of the seventeenth and beginning of the eighteenth centuries sought advanced ideas in Europe, Stalin in his later years encouraged the propagation of an absurd version of Russian history in which almost every major scientific invention, normally attributed (as orthodox Marxists would expect) to more economically and educationally advanced countries, turned out to have been anticipated by a Russian.

For most of the 1920s, however, Stalin was an orthodox enough Leninist. While Lenin had been sufficiently pragmatic to place a lot of post-revolutionary power in the hands of the new government, Sovnarkom, as distinct from the Communist Party, few Marxists prior to 1917 had accorded a greater role in principle to a disciplined, revolutionary party than Lenin himself. Thus, for the party to emerge as a more powerful instrument of rule than the government (in the Soviet sense of that term), as it did in the course of the 1920s, was scarcely at odds with the Bolshevik tradition. What became a Communist Party dictatorship was not called that by the leaders of the USSR. They described their rule both as 'Soviet power' and as a 'dictatorship of the proletariat'. They also increasingly claimed, especially from the time of the adoption of the 'Stalin Constitution' in 1936, that the regime was democratic.

None of these three ascriptions made much sense. The soviets were of some consequence in the revolutionary year of 1917, but even then it was the Bolshevik *party* which seized power in November. Thereafter, the soviets were never the principal organs of political power. For the first few post-revolutionary years the ministries (or commissariats, as they were then known) were arguably even more important than the party leadership in political decision-making, but that had changed by 1921. In subsequent years it became especially clear that the Communist Party leadership had a superior power and authority to that of Sovnarkom (which in 1946 became the Council of Ministers).

The 'dictatorship of the proletariat' was also a misnomer. The proletariat as a whole could not dictate. It was the Communist Party which did this in the name of the proletariat. The party leadership simply assumed that they represented the will of the workers – or, at least, their 'real will', if only they recognized where their true interests lay – and substituted itself for the actual proletariat. For a 'dictatorship of the proletariat' to be compatible with even a minimal notion of democracy, one would have to assume, first, that the proletariat constituted an absolute majority of the population, which in the USSR of the 1920s was far from being the case (in 1926 urban dwellers made up only 18 per cent of the population), and, second, that within the proletariat itself there were no real and persistent differences of opinion, something which has never been true in Russia or anywhere else. The notion of unity of opinion within any working class, however sociologically defined, is scarcely less fanciful than the idea that a universal consensus would be achieved in the communist society of the future.[24]

Stalin's Revolution

The concessions made to the peasantry by the New Economic Policy were not popular with many rank-and-file Communists. Stalin staked out from the mid-1920s two major positions which he made his own. The first was the possibility of 'Socialism in One Country'. That is to say, he argued that even without revolution in advanced industrial countries, the USSR could thrive independently. This gave him a political weapon with which to attack Trotsky, whose internationalism could be represented as a lack of patriotism. Stalin's line went down well with party workers who disliked Trotsky's emphasis on the necessity of Communists taking power in other major European countries.[25] Stalin's second, and closely linked, emphasis was on the paramount importance of speedy industrialization, to be accompanied by the forcible collectivization of agriculture. Between 1928 and 1932, some twelve million people, mainly young men, left the villages.[26] Some were sent into forced labour for having resisted collectivization, or were arrrested as kulaks, the name given to the richer peasants. 'Kulak' was, however, so loosely defined that anyone opposing the compulsory incorporation of their village, along with other villages, into a single vast collective farm could be put into that category. Other peasants voluntarily migrated to the towns and the developing industry.

Stalin advocated indiscriminate war against the kulaks and ruthless collectivization – until peasant resistance forced him into making a tactical retreat. In many areas the peasants chose to kill their farm animals rather than have them collectivized. There were also, in the first three months of 1930 alone, more than 1,600 cases of armed resistance.[27] In November 1929 Stalin said: 'We have gone from a policy of *limiting* the exploiting tendencies of the kulak to a policy of *eliminating* the kulak as a class.' By the beginning of March 1930, he was already taking a different line, writing an article for the main Communist Party newspaper, *Pravda*, in which he said that some comrades, in their pursuit of collectivization, had become 'dizzy with success'. He hypocritically complained that they had inappropriately used force, rather than allowing the peasants a choice, in the creation of collective farms.[28]

Forced collectivization and massive upheaval in the countryside had dire consequences. Millions of peasants were uprooted and at least 63,000 'heads of households' had been imprisoned or executed by the end of 1930. Well over a million 'kulaks' were deported between 1929 and the beginning of 1932.[29] Collectivization proceeded more rapidly in Ukraine than in the Russian republic, and when famine struck, as a result of state requisitions of grain and the turmoil in the countryside, this hit Ukraine especially hard. By the summer of 1933, some five million people had died. Corpses lay beside the roads and there were cases of cannibalism. Famine severely hit the North Caucasus and Kazakhstan as well as Ukraine, and it was the direct result of policies pursued by Moscow – the combination of compulsory collectivization and the seizure of grain by the central authorities to feed the towns, and even to export grain, while people in the Soviet countryside were starving.[30]

The radicalization of policy was accompanied by the General Secretary's consolidation of his power. At Stalin's behest, Trotsky was sent into internal exile in the Soviet Union in 1927 and expelled from the country in 1928. He lived the rest of his life abroad, penning eloquent critiques of what he called 'the Revolution Betrayed' and 'the Stalin School of Falsification'.[31] Although much of what he wrote about the Soviet Union was true, he got some prophecies badly wrong. For example, he believed in the late 1930s that if the Soviet Union were to be involved in major war, this would lead to the overthrow of Stalin's regime, whereas in reality the Second World War strengthened the Stalinist political order. While Stalin had much more to think about than Trotsky, out of sight for him never meant out of mind. With the help of his spies, he closely monitored the activities of his defeated rival throughout his various foreign travels. The Soviet secret police succeeded in penetrating Trotsky's entourage in Mexico in 1940, and one of their assassins killed him with a blow from an ice-pick.

Stalin had earlier been supported in the New Economic Policy stage of concessions to the peasantry by one of the other major figures in the Bolshevik leadership, Nikolay Bukharin, who was, however, a much more genuine enthusiast for NEP. Lenin had viewed this change of course as a strategic retreat, not just a tactical one – something, accordingly, that would need to last for several decades. Bukharin shared this view. With his will-ingness to tolerate concessions to private enterprise, Bukharin was regarded by the late 1920s as being on the 'right' of the party. He had been Stalin's ally in the fight against Trotsky, who headed the 'left opposition'. Stalin, in contrast, had managed to portray himself during much of the 1920s as a centrist, and having defeated the 'left', he turned on the 'right'.

This involved a fundamental shift of policy, not just the settling of scores with potential rivals. So radical were the changes that they have been vari-ously described as a 'revolution from above', 'Stalin's revolution', 'the second revolution', or (by *not* conflating the February and October revolutions of 1917) the 'third revolution'. Simultaneously with dramatic change in the economy, there was a 'cultural revolution', involving massive upheaval in the professions and a clear-out of students and teachers of bourgeois origins from higher educational institutions.[32] The end of the 1920s saw not only the abandonment of NEP, and the start of the forcible collectivization of agriculture, but also, in 1928, the introduction of the First Five-Year Plan, geared to speeding up dramatically Russia's industrialization. Stalin had no difficulty in reducing the influence of his erstwhile ally, Bukharin, who was removed from the Politburo in 1929. Although Bukharin kept a tenuous position within the Central Committee of the party until the mid-1930s, in 1937 Stalin had him arrested and then, following a show trial, executed in 1938. For later reformist Communists, including some in the mid-1980s, Bukharin became a symbol of a non-Stalinist way of 'building socialism'.[33] Although personally honest and courageous, Bukharin had, however, helped to construct the highly authoritarian system which made Bolshevik power (that turned into Stalin's power) uncheckable.

In a much-quoted speech in 1931, Stalin, after referring to the USSR as 'our socialist fatherland', spoke of the need 'to develop a genuine Bolshevik tempo in building up its socialist economy', for 'those who fall behind get beaten' and 'we refuse to be beaten!' He declared: 'We are fifty or a hundred years behind the advanced countries. We must make good this distance in ten years. Either we do it or we shall go under.'[34] Since Stalin's reference to making up the leeway of half a century or even a century in ten years came precisely a decade before the Soviet Union was attacked by Nazi Germany in 1941, it has often been lauded as a tribute to his foresight. Ten years hence the USSR did indeed have the industrial base which could provide for a vast armaments industry and the wherewithal to prevail in a desperate and protracted war against Germany.

The price paid for the industrialization, however, was horrendous. And Stalin was not as far-sighted as his Communist admirers throughout the world believed. He credulously entered into a pact with Hitler in 1939 which he did not expect Hitler to breach in a surprise attack, as he did in June 1941. The Soviet Union's unpreparedness for war had been greatly exacerbated by Stalin's purges. For some reason he trusted Hitler more than he trusted many of the senior officers who had fought in the Red Army during the civil war. In the late 1930s he killed off a high proportion of the Soviet army officer corps. Thus the Soviet Union suffered heavier losses in the earliest stages of the war on the Russian front than would have occurred if their army had been properly prepared and professionally led.

Social Transformation and Political Repression

Enormous political and social changes differentiated the Soviet Union in the 1930s from the 1920s. In the course of the twenties, Stalin, through skilful appeal to the party rank and file, as well as use of the resources of the Secretariat, defeated his potential rivals in the Communist Party politically. In the later 1930s, he destroyed them physically. More will be said shortly about the scale of the bloodletting, but the regime survived not only through the ruthless deployment of terror against enemies, whether real or imagined. It prevailed also because it seemed to be holding out hope of a better future, making people believe that history was on its side. It was, furthermore, consolidated because even in the short run there were many winners as well as losers.

The Communists in power undertook a massive educational programme. At the time of the outbreak of the First World War less than 40 per cent of the population of the Russian Empire was literate. By 1926 this had risen to just over 50 per cent, although there were great discrepancies between urban and rural areas and between men and women. Two-thirds of women in the countryside, where the bulk of the population still lived in the mid-1920s, were illiterate.[35] The beginning of the 1930s saw a still greater emphasis than in the twenties placed upon raising literacy levels. The years children spent at school were extended and adult literacy classes expanded. Whereas in 1926 only 39 per cent of females and 73 per cent of males in rural Russia could read and write, that figure by 1939, according to the official Soviet sources (possibly inflated, although by how much cannot be ascertained), had become 79 per cent for women and 95 per cent for men.[36] There were huge differences in the 1920s in the levels of literacy from one nationality to another. Russians had 45 per cent literacy at that time, but at the other end of the scale were the Kirgiz, Uzbeks, Chechens, Turkmen and Tajiks who all had literacy rates below 5 per cent of the population. There was, in other words, an enormous east–west divide within the country, as well as a gender division.[37]

The Communist Party was concerned to create, along with an industrialized society, its own new elite by promoting workers and peasants and educating them and their children. In this they succeeded. The Soviet Union had seven leaders in seven decades, and only the first was from an educated professional background. Lenin's father, as noted in Chapter 2, made such a successful career in tsarist Russia that he was promoted to the ranks of the nobility. Stalin was the son of a drunken cobbler who for a time worked on his own account and later in a shoe factory. Of the five remaining Soviet leaders – Nikita Khrushchev, Leonid Brezhnev, Yury Andropov, Konstantin Chernenko and Mikhail Gorbachev – all but Andropov (who was the son of a white-collar railway employee) came from peasant or worker families.[38] Countless thousands of officials of similar origins occupied posts at all levels of the party hierarchy.

More broadly, peasants became workers and many workers became managers. The children of workers and, to a somewhat lesser extent, peasants were given possibilities on a hitherto unimagined scale to go into higher education and become professionals in a variety of occupations – as engineers, architects, doctors, and many other specializations. The massive industrialization drive alone was responsible for much of this social mobility – modernization on the Stalinist model. The most appalling aspects of Stalinism also contributed in their own way to social mobility. The purging of hundreds of thousands of people (many killed, others sent to labour camps) produced an equivalent number of job vacancies. As a much higher proportion of intellectuals and white-collar workers than of manual workers were swept away by the purges, the promotion prospects of the new beneficiaries of Soviet education were correspondingly improved.

Alexander Zinoviev, who won a reputation as a scholar in the field of formal logic, and then much wider fame as a writer of a devastatingly witty satirical account of Soviet politics and society, *The Yawning Heights* (the publication of which in the West, during the Brezhnev years, led to his dismissal from academic work and his subsequent emigration to Germany), has described what happened in his own family:

Before the Revolution 80 per cent, if not 90 per cent of the Russian population were peasants living at subsistence level at the bottom of the social pyramid. They lived miserable lives, only an iota above the level of serfs. The Revolution did produce changes. Take my own family, who were peasants. As a result of the collectivization of agriculture my parents lost everything they had. But my elder brother eventually rose to be a factory manager; the next one to him in age made it to the rank of colonel; three of my other brothers qualified as engineers; and I became a professor at Moscow University. At the same time millions of Russian peasants were given a formal education and some became professional men and women.[39]

In spite of the appalling suffering which had been inflicted on the peasantry, many of the beneficiaries of rapid social mobility, including Zinoviev himself, came to the conclusion that it had all been worthwhile. There were those who drew a less lucky ticket in the lottery of life under Stalin and took a different view. Such was the success, however, in building an image of Stalin as a strict but just paternal figure that vast numbers of his victims, awaiting execution or doing forced labour in the camps, believed that he would inter vene on their behalf if only he knew how unfairly they had been treated. A majority blamed neither Stalin nor the system, viewing their fate as a malfunctioning of the system rather than as a feature of the system itself.

The sheer numbers who were victims of state terror in the 1930s greatly exceeded those of the 1920s. In the distinctive 'show trials' the victims were beaten into reciting a script that had been prepared by the political police, admitting to crimes they could not have imagined, still less committed. These were an invention of the era of 'high Stalinism' – the period from the mid-1930s until Stalin's death. By that time even a hint of opposition to his policies by members of the ruling Communist Party led to imprisonment and, usually, execution. Although the idea of murdering his party comrades would have been unthinkable for Lenin, it was he who was instrumental in setting in motion the ruthless killing machine which Stalin 'creatively developed'.

A meeting of Sovnarkom, presided over by Lenin in December 1917, had established the Cheka. There was not even a decree setting up this ancestor of the NKVD and the KGB. Thus, strictly speaking, it did not have a legal basis, but that did not inhibit its functioning. The prime movers in establishing this political and punitive police arm of the state were Lenin himself and the Polish revolutionary who became the first head of the Cheka, Felix Dzerzhinsky.[40] Lenin's willingness to use violence ruthlessly is illustrated in a letter he sent to Vyacheslav Molotov, later to become one of Stalin's closest allies, chairman of Sovnarkom and Soviet foreign minister. Writing on 19 March 1922, Lenin declared: 'The more representatives of the reactionary clergy and the reactionary bourgeoisie we succeed . . . in killing the better.

We must right now teach this public [such a lesson] that for several decades they will not even dare to dream about any resistance.'[41] Even so, Lenin's use of terror was much more selective than that of Stalin, and it was directed at opponents of the Bolshevik revolution, not (as was the case with tens of thousands of Stalin's victims) supporters of it.[42]

The earliest trial of people who had actually co-operated with the Soviet authorities was of engineers of 'bourgeois' origin who, in what became known as the Shakhty Trial, were found guilty in 1928 of sabotage. More than fifty engineers and technicians working in the Donetsk basin (Donbass) of Ukraine were accused of sabotage. The trial saw the launch of an orchestrated campaign against 'wreckers', even though most of the evidence of deliberate sabotage by the Shakhty accused was flimsy. Those who confessed did so under duress. Five of the Shakhty defendants were executed in July 1928, and a majority of the others were imprisoned. A few were released.[43] Compared with the period between 1928 and 1931, the three or four years which followed, between 1932 and the first part of 1936, were something of a breathing space before the Great Purges of 1937–38.

WOMEN IN SOVIET SOCIETY

Among the many social transformations which occurred in this period of Soviet history, one of the greatest was in the position of women. This was far from being the unalloyed liberation of women proclaimed by Soviet propaganda, but one of the early acts of the Bolsheviks in power was to place women on an equal legal footing with men. While women were brought into the industrial and professional workforce in the Soviet Union to a far greater extent than in pre-revolutionary Russia, the majority of them, who were peasants, had long played an important part in the rural economy – taking part in mowing, raking and hay-baling as well as tending the vegetable garden – in addition to assuming virtually all the household tasks, including those of childcare.[44] Yet whether married or unmarried, a woman had no rights of inheritance apart from her dowry and some domestic utensils, so long as a male relative lived (although in some regions exceptions were made for widows).[45] Changing the legal framework helped, only slowly and extremely partially, to alter deeply rooted social attitudes.

In the earliest years of Communist rule, religious control over marriage and divorce was swept away, only civil marriage was recognized, and divorce was made easy and inexpensive. Abortion was legalized in 1920, although it was viewed not as an integral part of the liberation of women, but as a necessary and temporary evil. State-sanctioned abortion was required in order to reduce the high incidence of mortality associated with illegal abortions.[46] Women under Soviet rule were not only given the right to paid work, they were also expected to join the workforce, and the great majority of them did so. In the period up to the outbreak of war (in wartime the conditions became devastatingly worse), women in the Soviet Union had not only the notorious double burden of full-time work in the factory, fields, or office, combined (far more often than not) with full responsibility for the domestic household. They had to do this in the absence of the kind of labour-saving devices which were increasingly available to their Western counterparts, all the while coping with the queues and shortages which were part and parcel of the Soviet economy. This was not simply because the USSR had a command, rather than market, economy, but because the political priorities of the planners lay in the sphere of heavy and defence industry, with a concomitant underdevelopment of the service sector and of consumer goods production.[47] On the positive side, the rapid improvement in educational opportunities for women, noted earlier in this chapter, enabled a significant minority to achieve professional qualifications and career opportunities which were open to few before 1917. Others, however, found themselves undertaking heavy physical labour of a kind which, in the urban environment at least, had previously not been carried out by women.

In the 1930s, further legal as well as social changes occurred in the position of women in Soviet society. Stalin, paradoxically – in the light of his notable contribution to reducing the number of Soviet citizens through executions – became concerned about insufficient population size. Living conditions were such – the extremely cramped communal apartments in the towns, taken in conjunction with women's double burden – that it was extraordinarily difficult for urban dwellers to have large families. Soviet officialdom decided that the answer to the problem was to make divorce more difficult, abortion illegal, and to celebrate the family as an institution. A June 1936 decree outlawed abortion except when there were strong medical reasons for it, and in November of the same year the exceptions became subject to more stringent criteria. These measures were accompanied by an extensive propaganda campaign on the dangers of abortion, with no reference to the still greater risks of termination of pregnancy by illegal abortionists. Financial inducements were offered for large families, the bonuses being especially high for each child in addition to ten in the family. The beneficiaries of this state largesse were overwhelmingly peasants rather than city dwellers. The latter, however, benefited from an extension of nurseries and paediatric clinics as part of the pro-natalist drive.[48] In the Soviet mass media there was a new emphasis on the sanctity of the family. As David L. Hoffmann has noted: 'By the mid-1930s, Soviet officials' perceptions of the family had evolved. Not only did they see strong families as a means to maximize the birth rate but they had come to believe that the family could instill Soviet values and discipline in children, and thereby serve as an instrument of the state.'[49]

While the Soviet policies intended to promote a higher birth rate had something in common with pro-natalist policies in other countries, they also had some distinguishing features. Women were encouraged to continue to work during pregnancy and to return to work after giving birth. The Politburo in 1936 approved a decree which made it a criminal offence to refuse work to a pregnant woman or to lower her pay during pregnancy. And 'at no time during the campaign to bolster the family did Soviet officials suggest that a woman's place was in the home'.[50]

Cultural policy changed in many ways during the 1930s, including visual representations of women. The muscular, plainly dressed women portrayed in posters and the mass media during the First Five-Year Plan gave way in films and newspapers to pictures of women which emphasized femininity.[51] More generally, the 1930s saw some rehabilitation of aspects of bourgeois life, among them ballroom dancing. Whereas the 1920s had produced more impressive 'high culture', the years 1932–36 saw an expansion of popular culture. Folklore, often pseudo-folklore, was officially encouraged, although minus its religious ingredients. By way of contrast, this was also the 'red jazz age', when Western as well as Soviet bands visited many cities.[52] In spite of the doctrine of 'socialist realism' which was supposed to permeate all art – and which in practice meant exposing the degradation of capitalism, glorifying Soviet life, and maintaining an obligatory optimism about the society's future – some popular mass art existed throughout the Soviet period. There was a great expansion in the number of cinemas in the Soviet Union in the 1930s, but as the decade went on the most popular foreign films were seen less and less. The turning point came in 1936, when repression was stepped up. Soviet mass culture became more thoroughly 'folklorized' and foreign imports more deeply suspect.[53] Soviet citizens were also presented with an artistically enhanced and sanitized version of their own post-revolutionary experience. As the historian of the Soviet cinema Richard Taylor has noted, however, audiences in the USSR between the two world wars preferred Charlie Chaplin, Buster Keaton, Douglas Fairbanks and Mary Pickford 'to tractors and the history of what was, after all, supposed to be their Revolution. In other words they preferred escapism to realism, however unreal that realism might in fact have been.'[54]

Stalin's Personal Dictatorship

In a number of respects, at the end of the 1920s and especially after the early 1930s, there was a great leap backwards as well as forwards.[55] The celebration of the official date of Stalin's fiftieth birthday – 21 December 1929 – saw the launch of what was later to be called 'the cult of personality'. While this helped to bolster Stalin's inordinate power, he believed it also suited the Russian psyche. A case can be made that it was, at least, in keeping with a strong Russian tradition. The revolutions of 1917 had 'in rapid succession ousted both tsar and God, those age-old supports and foci of devotion'.[56] With the death of Lenin, followed rapidly by the removal from power and subsequent exile of Trotsky, the regime was deprived of its most inspirational, albeit highly authoritarian, leaders. It was not willing to resort to democracy as a basis of its legitimacy, since that would have led to electoral rejection and the defeat of the Leninist project, as interpreted by Stalin. Accordingly, as the British historian John Gooding put it:

> . . . the regime under Stalin took the unBolshevik but deeply Russian course of restoring the charismatic element. So successfully did Stalin do this that by the late 1930s much of the population had become abjectly dependent upon him. Lenin's aim of genuine mass support and a real bonding between people and rulers was thus achieved, yet it was achieved by means that had nothing whatever to do with socialism or the Bolsheviks' original ambitions.[57]

The Seventeenth Congress of the Communist Party, held at the beginning of 1934, was called 'the Congress of Victors'. The internal enemies had, apparently, been defeated, collectivization of agriculture had been accomplished, and rapid industrialization was well under way. The mood changed with the assassination of Sergei Kirov, the head of the Communist Party in Leningrad (the name given to the former capital, St Petersburg – renamed Petrograd during the First World War – after Lenin's death). Kirov's shooting in December 1934 led to a wave of arrests. There has been speculation that Stalin himself was responsible for ordering his assassination, both because he may have feared him as a potential rival and as an excuse to launch a new wave of terror. No evidence for Stalin's complicity (strongly hinted at by Nikita Khrushchev in his speech to the Twentieth Congress of the Soviet Communist Party in 1956) has, however, been adduced, even following the partial opening of the Soviet archives at the end of the 1980s and in the 1990s. Certainly, however, Stalin took full advantage of the atmosphere created by

Kirov's assassination to settle many scores. Some of the most prominent old Bolsheviks, who had crossed swords with him in the 1920s and earlier, among them Grigory Zinoviev and Lev Kamenev, were arrested and imprisoned, although they had no connection whatsoever with Kirov's death. They were both executed in 1936.

The old Bolshevik Zinoviev was no relation of the writer Alexander Zinoviev, whose positive account of his family's ascent on the Soviet professional ladder has already been cited. The latter's characteristically Russian name was his own, but both Grigory Zinoviev and Kamenev had changed their Jewish surnames to Russian ones. Although Stalin's suspicion of Jews was to become more overt in the post-Second World War years, even in the 1930s Jewish origins were not a recommendation in his eyes. Kamenev had made matters much worse both by marrying Trotsky's sister and by then oscillating in the dispute between Stalin and Trotsky. In the earlier 1920s he had supported Stalin against Trotsky, but later in the decade he became closer to the 'left opposition'. He was three times expelled from the Communist Party and on the first two occasions subsequently readmitted. When he was expelled for the last time in 1934, this was the prelude to his arrest in 1935 and execution the following year.

Stalin's personal power had been increasing throughout the first half of the 1930s, but it was with the mass purges between 1936 and 1938 that the last vestiges of oligarchical rule gave way to personal dictatorship. As the Russian historian (and senior researcher at the Russian state archives) Oleg Khlevniuk has observed:

> The thesis of the decisive role of the 'Great Terror' in the consolidation of Stalin's personal dictatorship has long been accepted in the historiography and new documents completely confirm it. Relying on the punitive organs, Stalin had several members of the Politburo executed and subordinated his remaining colleagues with threats of violence to them and their families . . . Younger leaders brought into the Politburo by Stalin were raised . . . in a different tradition, the essence of which was personal loyalty to [Stalin] . . . In this new order, key political decisions were Stalin's exclusive prerogative. The Politburo as a collective organ ceased to function, and was replaced by meetings of Stalin and certain colleagues . . .[58]

'Socialism', Stalinist-style

The mid-1930s saw the emergence of what became known as the Stakhanovite movement. Alexey Stakhanov, a miner, was said to have 'hewed 102 tons of coal in a single six-hour stint in August 1935', fourteen times higher than the norm established by the mine's managers.[59] The authorities immediately encouraged others to emulate such labour feats and thus hasten the development of the economy. While some workers were inspired by patriotism or the 'building of socialism' to make such attempts, there was a large element of subterfuge involved in most Stakhanovite achievements. Stalin claimed that the Stakhanovite movement was an expression of 'socialist competition of a new type', differing from the old because it was based on new technology.[60] These exemplary workers, however, required the co-operation of the management to produce maximally favourable conditions, not to mention statistical inflation of their output. And those who achieved the accolade of Stakhanovite naturally made other workers seem laggards by comparison. The Stakhanovites were also given special privileges, such as access to scarce goods. As a result, the praise bestowed on them in the Soviet press was not matched by popularity among fellow workers. This is illustrated by the 1930s story about a deaf old woman who joined a queue in Russia, not knowing what it was for. That was a common practice in Russia throughout virtually the whole of the Soviet period. Most goods and foodstuffs were in short supply, so a long queue was a sign that something had just become available. People often enquired what they were standing in line for only after they had joined the queue. In this case the old woman asked 'What are they giving out?', to which someone answered, 'A slap in the face.' The deaf newcomer in the queue enquired, 'To everyone, or just Stakhanovites?'[61] (Even in Stalin's time, though on a less widespread scale than in the Khrushchev and Brezhnev periods, Soviet citizens told political jokes. There were, indeed, jokes about political jokes, such as the response to the question: 'Who are the bravest people in the world?' The answer was: 'The Russians, for every fourth person is an informer, and still they tell political jokes.' In reality, the proportion of informers was not as high as one in four, but high enough to make a report to the political police all too grim a possibility during the 1930s and 1940s.)

An event which produced an enormous fanfare of self-congratulation in the Soviet Union, and congratulations also from many credulous foreigners, was the adoption of a new Soviet constitution in 1936. This was actually the third constitution – the previous ones were promulgated in 1918 and 1924 – and on paper it was the most democratic. The 1918 constitution had, for example, disenfranchised undesirable elements such as clergymen of all denominations and people who employed hired labour for profit. By 1936 there were far fewer of the former and none of the latter in existence, and in the new constitution, no one was disenfranchised. That was, however, of absolutely no consequence, since the elections for soviets had but a single candidate. Stalin, in his speech of 25 November 1936 introducing the constitution, contrasted it with the constitutions of bourgeois countries which were purely formal and sometimes contained restrictions based on gender or property. Lauding the new constitution as more democratic than any hitherto seen, Stalin said that it provided 'not only democratic freedoms' but also the 'material means' for realising them. 'It is understandable', he added, 'that the democratism of the draft of the new Constitution is not "ordinary" and "universally recognized" democratism in general, but *socialist* democratism [emphasis in the original].'[62]

In fact, the superficially democratic constitution had many reservations and ways of constraining the rights of citizens, quite apart from the qualification implied by Stalin's understanding of 'socialist', should anyone dare to appeal to the constitution against the dictatorial state. The very first article stated: 'The Union of Soviet Socialist Republics is a socialist state of workers and peasants.' That immediately put the intelligentsia, who were regarded in Soviet ideology as a distinctive social stratum, but not a class, at something of a disadvantage. Article 125 began: 'In conformity with the interests of the toilers, and in order to strengthen the socialist system, citizens of the USSR shall be guaranteed (a) freedom of speech; (b) freedom of the press; (c) freedom of assembly, including the holding of mass meetings; (d) freedom of street processions and demonstrations.' Not one of these freedoms existed in reality, and admirers of Stalin's constitution and the supposed bestowal of such freedoms missed the qualification in the introduction to the article. Should anyone wish to assert those freedoms, who would decide whether they were in conformity 'with the interests of the toilers' or whether their actions were designed 'to strengthen the socialist system'? The answer, of course, was the Communist Party leadership and the political police who did Stalin's bidding.

Stalin's speech introducing the 1936 constitution was, nevertheless, an important one. It was in that oration that, for the first time, he declared unambiguously that the Soviet Union had become a socialist state. Until that point they had been 'building socialism'. Stalin, whose didactic style included much intentional repetition for rhetorical and pedagogical effect, declared: 'Our Soviet society has already succeeded in bringing about socialism in the main; it has created a socialist structure, that is to say it has realized what Marxists call either the first or lower phase of communism. It means we have already in essence accomplished the first phase of communism, socialism.'[63]

In terms of Soviet self-perceptions and ideology, it was a significant moment when it was decided that 'socialism' had 'in the main' been built. In objective reality, though, it was about as meaningful as the claim that Soviet society had also by 1936 become democratic. (I have more to say later in the book – in Chapter 6 – about why it is greatly preferable to call this system Communist, not socialist). What became immediately obvious was that the 1936 Soviet constitution did not herald an era of respect for human rights, democracy or freedom. In fact, the two years which followed were those of the Great Purge, when arrests and executions reached a new intensity and when the revolution devoured both its fathers and its children – old Bolsheviks who had been Stalin's comrades-in-arms in the late tsarist period and the civil war, and people who had joined the Communist Party when it was already in power and had been rapidly promoted to senior positions in party and state institutions.

When, for the first time, a Soviet leader drew attention to some of the crimes of Stalin, it was not surprising that the focus should be on 1937–38, for these were the years when the full force of the terror was turned against members of the Communist Party, including very notable ones. The person who broke the taboo on criticising Stalin was Khrushchev, and more will be said in a later chapter about the Twentieth Party Congress in 1956 at which he did so. Far more peasants than party workers were imprisoned or killed at Stalin's behest in the 1930s, and earlier many priests and 'bourgeois' opponents of the Communists met the same fate. These were passed over in silence by Khrushchev when he drew attention to some of Stalin's crimes. The seniority within the system of many of the people executed in the second half of the 1930s was, however, remarkable. Because those who appeared in court confessed to various plots, with each person's story generally corroborated by other defendants in accordance with the pre-rehearsed script, their guilt was assumed by many Western ambassadors and journalists – notwithstanding the fact that old Bolsheviks were confessing to such outlandish crimes as having been German, British or Japanese spies. The ranks of the gullible included the American ambassador to Moscow, Joseph E. Davies, who wrote: 'The extraordinary testimony of Krestinsky, Bukharin, and the rest would appear to indicate that the Kremlin's fears were well justified . . . But the government acted with great vigor and speed. The Red Army generals were shot and the whole party organization was purged and thoroughly cleansed.'[64]

Khrushchev himself had a differentiated view of the legitimacy of violence in the course of building socialism and communism, and what most shocked him was the deaths of dedicated Communists. His party audience was even more shocked than he (who knew so much more) when he told them that 'of the 139 members and candidates of the party's Central Committee who were elected at the 17th Congress [in 1934], 98 persons, i.e. 70 per cent, were arrested and shot (mostly in 1937–1938)'.[65] The same fate, Khrushchev added, was met by a majority of delegates to that congress (which he reminded his audience had been called the Congress of Victors). Of the 1,966 delegates, 1,108 were arrested on charges of counterrevolutionary crimes.[66] Given that Khrushchev was himself addressing the delegates to a party congress (the Twentieth), it is hardly surprising that the official report records that his revelation met with 'Indignation in the hall'.[67]

There has been much controversy about the numbers of those imprisoned and killed at various times in the Stalin years, but the opening of the archives has led to some convergence towards a middle (but still horrific) figure, some millions fewer than the earlier highest estimates and some millions more than the estimates of those who downplayed the scale of Stalin's terror. Ronald Suny, the editor of a recent major volume on twentieth-century Russian history, suggests that the 'total number of lives destroyed by the Stalinist regime in the 1930s is closer to 10–11 million than the 20–30 million estimated earlier'.[68] Anne Applebaum, the author of a detailed study of political prisoners in the Soviet Union, arrives at a figure of 28.7 million forced labourers over the whole Soviet period. She includes in that number the 'special exiles', such as 'kulaks' and particular nationalities, among them the Tatars and Volga Germans, who were deported during World War Two. Applebaum notes that a figure of around 786,000 political executions between 1934 and 1953 is now quite widely accepted, although her own view is that the true figure is probably significantly higher than that number.[69] The Russian non-governmental organization Memorial, dedicated to investigating the cases of repression in the Soviet period, more recently came up with the figure of 1.7 million people arrested in 1937–38 alone, of whom, they say, at least 818,000 were shot.[70]

Some of the earlier purges were a logical consequence of the choice of the Soviet leadership not to embrace what Stalin called 'ordinary democratism' or 'universally recognized democratism' but to impose their will, and many harsh policies, on the population by dictatorial fiat. Other purges, including those of party workers and of the officer corps of the Red Army, went well beyond the logic of Communist rule. Stalin was both a true believer in the strand of Leninism he had himself developed and a disordered personality who, as Lenin had recognized too late, should never have had great power placed in his hands. As Stalin grew older, he became increasingly paranoid. However, his pre-revolutionary experience had provided a rational element in the distrust he was later to harbour. As a Bolshevik revolutionary activist, he had failed to spot that one of his colleagues whom he trusted, Roman Malinovsky, was an agent of the tsarist secret police, the Okhrana. For that blind spot he subsequently overcompensated spectacularly. Chronic suspicion, a love of power (behind a façade of modesty), and bloodthirsty vindictiveness became ever more prominent features of Stalin's personality. Stalinism thus became a distinctive form of Communism, one whose excesses had devastating consequences for Soviet society and whose extremes incorporated much more than was required to maintain a Communist Party in power.

5

International Communism
between the Two World Wars

The task for Britain, said its prime minister, David Lloyd George, in November 1918, was to create 'a fit country for heroes to live in'. Soldiers returning from the horrors of the trenches of the First World War found that no European country lived up to this level of aspiration. Workers, who had been quiescent during the war, became increasingly restless in its aftermath. At almost no time in the twentieth century did revolution in the West seem even a remote possibility. The main exception was the period between 1918 and 1920.[1] For a significant number of industrial workers, especially those mobilized in trade unions, the Russian Revolution was an inspiration, raising hopes that society could be rebuilt on new foundations. Manual workers formed the largest social group in developed Western countries, and one natural outcome of the war was an enhanced interest in the world beyond national boundaries. In welcoming the overthrow of tsarism and approving the fall of the Russian Empire, even politically conscious workers were, however, vague about the realities of the Bolshevik revolution. Although romanticized as the working class taking power into its own hands, this had been a seizure of power by professional revolutionaries who were a minority not only in Russian society but even among Russian socialists. Yet what was subsequently in the Soviet Union to be called 'Great October' could be regarded, and by many was initially regarded, as the first serious attempt, on the landscape of an entire country, to build socialism.

The Bolsheviks, for their part, had hoped, and initially expected, that their revolution would trigger a series of revolutions further west in Europe. No other lastingly successful Communist takeover, in fact, took place in Europe until after World War Two. However, in 1921 a Soviet protectorate was established by the Red Army in Mongolia – a country lying between Russia and China, greater in size than France, Germany, Italy and Britain put together, but with a population no bigger than Jamaica's. As the Mongolian People's Republic, this became in 1924 the world's second Communist state.[2] It was, though, essentially a Soviet satellite and, as such, a forerunner, in its relationship with Moscow, of a number of states that were to be established after World War Two as a result of the success of the Soviet army.

Immediately after the First World War there was revolutionary turmoil in Germany, whose fate mattered much more for the Communist project than that of Outer Mongolia. Ever since the 1870s there had been tensions within the social democratic movement in Germany between its reformist and revolutionary wings. The war had added to the strains and the Bolshevik revolution meant that every party of the left had to define where it stood in relation to that ostensible attempt to build a socialist state.[3] This became all the more salient an issue with the creation in 1919 of the Third International, or Comintern, to which more attention will be paid later in this chapter.

The German social democratic movement, the largest in Europe, split three ways at the end of the First World War. The most substantial part retained the name of the German Social Democratic Party (SPD). A more radical group established the Independent Social Democratic Party (USPD), while those committed to revolution formed the Spartacus League, of which the highly educated militant Rosa Luxemburg and Karl Liebknecht were the most prominent leaders. It was formally established on 11 November 1918, two days after Luxemburg had been released from prison and one day after a predominantly socialist government had taken office in Germany. The Spartacists, who were made up of skilled manual workers, intellectuals, and white-collar workers, changed their name to that of the German Communist Party (KPD) at a founding congress, held from 30 December 1918 to 1 January 1919.[4]

Revolutionary uprisings had taken place in different parts of Germany in November 1918. The Emperor Wilhelm II was forced to abdicate and the two moderate socialist parties seized the initiative and became major partners, alongside other democratic parties, in the coalition government which was formed following elections in January 1919. Prominent army generals, alarmed by the possibility of a Soviet-style revolution in Germany, transferred their allegiance from the emperor to the new government, offering their help in maintaining order and suppressing revolution. Shortly before the elections, when a spontaneous rising in Berlin came under the control of Communist leaders, the government, already dominated by the SPD and USPD, called on the support of paramilitary groups of demobilized soldiers to put down the revolt by force. They did so brutally, in the process assassinating both Luxemberg and Liebknecht on 15 January. The later inability of Communists and social democrats to co-operate when faced by the rise of fascism, although largely determined by policy emanating from Moscow, had an added bitterness in Germany which owed much to the suppression of the Spartacists and the deaths of two of their most revered leaders.[5] Throughout February, March and April 1919 there was unrest in Germany, with the Communists reacting to what they saw as 'White terror' in January. For a period of just under a month in April a Soviet republic was even established in Bavaria. But it too was suppressed.[6]

Apart from their local and temporary successes in Germany, Communists succeeded also in seizing power in Hungary, establishing the Hungarian Soviet Republic, which lasted for 133 days in 1919. The end of the war and the loss of Hungarian territory, following the defeat of the Austro-Hungarian Empire, had led in 1918 to a largely bloodless revolution against Hungary's traditional aristocratic rulers and the formation of a government, including socialists, headed by a liberal member of the nobility, Count Mihály Károlyi, who was prepared to introduce democracy to Hungary. A number of Hungarian socialists had been among the half-million prisoners of war in Russia, and they included a politically significant minority who converted to Communism in the Russia of 1917 and 1918.[7] Among them was the Hungarian Jew Bela Kun, who was arrested by the Károlyist–socialist government and charged with conspiracy against public order and incitement to riot.[8]

When Kun was released from prison, those who rallied to his cause cut across class boundaries. Numerous Hungarian patriots, resentful of the loss of territory at the end of the war, as well as radicalized workers and intellectuals welcomed the Communists' coming to power. Most of the socialist leadership agreed in March 1919 to a merger of their party with the Communists. The middle-class support which the Communists briefly enjoyed was based on the assumption that the new leadership was going to defend Hungarian borders against the encroachment of the victorious allies, while the peasantry hoped for land distribution. In fact, the Communists quickly alienated the first group by attacking symbols of Hungarian nationhood, confiscating Church property, and allowing priests to continue to function only if they used their pulpits to express support for the government. All classes of Hungarian society came to resent the extreme anticlericalism of the new regime as well as the fact that thirty-two of the Kun government's forty-five commissars were Jewish.[9] Bela Kun's radical measures included taking into public ownership industrial enterprises employing more than twenty-five people. The peasants were rapidly disillusioned by the Communists' land policy – in particular, their intention to move as rapidly as possible to the collectivization of agriculture and in the meantime to nationalize all landholdings of over one hundred acres.[10]

The Bela Kun government had a brief respite when it attempted to link the spread of its brand of socialism with the reconquest of territory that had formerly belonged to the Hungarian part of the Austro-Hungarian Empire. Its army conquered two thirds of Slovakia. There they were welcomed by the large Hungarian minority, though not by the Slovaks. An attempted coup against the Hungarian Soviet Republic on 24 June 1919 failed, prompting Kun to declare a dictatorship of the proletariat and to step up the use of terror against 'internal enemies'.[11] A military offensive against Romanians occupying formerly Hungarian territory was unsuccessful, and opinion began to swing strongly against the Kun regime. The old ruling elite of Hungary reasserted itself, enjoying now widespread lower-middle-class and unskilled worker support, and the Hungarian Soviet Republic disappeared as suddenly as it had arisen.[12] Kun fled to Austria, where he was interned. On his release in 1920 he emigrated to Russia and remained there until his death. The Soviet Union in the 1930s was an even more dangerous place for foreign Communists than a conservative authoritarian regime, of the kind which was to be established in Hungary. Like many revolutionaries who sought refuge in the USSR, Kun became a victim of the Great Purge. He was arrested in 1937 and killed in 1939.

While many Communists took pride in the fact that a Communist government had been established, however briefly, in a European country which did not have a border with Russia, the short-lived regime was highly damaging for the development of Hungarian democracy. As Joseph Rothschild observed:

> . . . a final tragedy of the Kun episode was that, by the manner of its rise and fall, it appeared to discredit by association the Károly experiment that had preceded and given birth to it, and hence allowed the counterrevolutionary white regime that followed it to equate liberalism with Communism. Social and political democratization could thus be resisted henceforth as allegedly treasonable to the Hungarian way of life.[13]

The end of the First World War saw the re-creation of Poland, which had been part of the Russian Empire, as an independent state. War between Soviet Russia and Poland in 1919–20 has been interpreted as an attempt both 'to recreate that Empire in socialist guise, and to spread the Revolution to the advanced countries of Europe'.[14] For Lenin, the latter desire was the more important, but optimism about the forces of history being on his side blinded him to political realities in other countries. The Red Army, facing tough resistance from the Poles, was in disarray by the summer of 1920, and Lenin realized that to attempt to continue the fight would endanger the Soviet regime itself. In September of that year the Russian government conceded victory to the Poles, offering them 'as much territory on the borderlands as they cared to take, on the one condition that a halt to the fighting was called within ten days'.[15] In that same month, Karl Radek, a Polish Jewish Communist renowned for sharp wit combined with serious knowledge of Europe, was sarcastic about Lenin allowing himself to be governed by revolutionary optimism, remarking: 'Now comrade Lenin is demonstrating a new method of information gathering: not knowing what is going on in a given country, he sends an army there.'[16] (Lenin was not, of course, the first or the last politician to make that mistake.) A failed attempt at revolution by the German Communists in 1921 was a further setback for the Bolshevik leadership, as was the suppression of Communist-inspired uprisings in Saxony and Hamburg during the German hyper-inflation of 1923.

The Comintern

Radek (who had joined the Bolshevik Party in 1917) was active both in Russia and in Germany. While under arrest in Germany in 1919, following the failure of the German Communists' insurrection in January of that year, he was elected *in absentia* to the Central Committee of the Russian Communist Party. He was a natural choice to become, in March 1920, a secretary of, and a leading figure in, the Third International. That organization had been formed at a congress held in Moscow exactly one year earlier. It was to become better known as the Communist International, or Comintern. Not all delegates believed that the time was ripe for the creation of this body. The sole delegate from the German Communist Party, Hugo Eberlein, objected that 'Real Communist parties exist in only a few countries, and most of these were created only in the last few weeks.'[17] Nevertheless, the Bolsheviks were determined to press ahead with the creation of a new organization which would simultaneously further revolution worldwide and enhance the security of Soviet Russia. That these Communist desiderata did not necessarily go together was to become increasingly plain over the years, and when there was a conflict, the Comintern normally had to place the interests of the Soviet Union ahead of the aspirations of any other section of the international Communist movement.[18] There was also a tension *within* the Soviet government between their desire to support revolution elsewhere and their need to have a working relationship with the governments of other countries. This was manifested as early as 1921, when the Commissar for Foreign Affairs, Georgy Chicherin, wrote to Party Secretary Vyacheslav Molotov saying: 'I do not understand why, thanks to the Comintern, we have to fall out with Afghanistan, Persia and China.'[19]

The Comintern was a much more serious political organization than the First or Second Socialist Internationals precisely because it had a major state power at its centre. Yet that was a weakness as well as a strength, given that Communist parties would often have fared better in their own countries had they not had to bend to the will of Moscow. It did, however, make for unity of action. Lenin produced nineteen (later twenty-one) conditions for membership of the Third International for its Second Congress held in August 1919. The essence of them, in the words of Donald Sassoon, was: 'expel all reformists and centrists, accept the discipline which the new international organization will demand, support the Soviet Republic, be prepared for illegal political work and call yourselves communists'.[20] Ironically, one of the two conditions added to Lenin's original nineteen came from an Italian Communist, Amadeo Bordiga, and it had the effect of strengthening still further the centralized, disciplined nature of the movement.[21] The addition was that any party members who opposed the enumerated conditions should be expelled from the Communist Party. The irony lay in the fact that in later years the Italian Communist Party (PCI) – which after the Second World War was (along with the French) one of the two largest Communist parties in western Europe – turned out to be among the least orthodox within the international Communist movement.

From 1919 onwards the distinction between Communists and non-Communist socialists was clearer than ever before, though the degree of hostility between them varied over time, partly in response to the policies of the Comintern. The staff of the Comintern were mainly Russian and even most of the foreign Communists who were to play a prominent role in it – among them the Finn Otto Kuusinen, the Hungarian Mátyás Rákosi, the Bulgarian Georgi Dimitrov, and the Italian Palmiro Togliatti – were long-term residents in the Soviet Union. Two of them – Kuusinen and Togliatti – were in the post-Stalin era to display some capacity for innovative thought. Their views had been close to Bukharin's in the 1920s,[22] but both were loyal Stalinists throughout the 1930s and 1940s. There were five distinct periods in the life of the Comintern between its foundation in 1919 and the Soviet Union's entry into the Second World War in 1941. They very closely reflected changes in Soviet domestic policy, and illustrate the extent to which the Comintern became an instrument of the Kremlin leadership, with strict limits on its autonomy.

THE 'RED WAVE'

The first period, known also as the 'Red Wave', lasted from 1919 to 1923. The earliest head of the Comintern was Grigory Zinoviev, who by the mid-1920s was in sharp disagreement with Stalin. (The danger of such a course of action became fully clear only in the 1930s. In Zinoviev's case, it eventuated in his arrest in 1935, followed by a show trial, and execution in 1936.) By 1923 it was evident that Communists were not about to come to power in any European country apart from the European republics of the Soviet Union, where their hegemony was now being strengthened. (The USSR – the Union of Soviet Socialist Republics – had been formed on 30 December 1922.) A reassessment of foreign policy – to parallel the New Economic Policy – was required. As a result of the Bolsheviks' seizure of power in 1917, Soviet Russia had been excluded from the Paris peace talks of 1919, but for a time it looked as if an agreement might be reached between the new Soviet state and the western European powers when they met at Genoa in 1922. Lenin, however, was unwilling to accept the terms on offer and instructed the Soviet Commissar for Foreign Affairs not to underwrite the Treaty of Versailles' territorial arrangements. Instead Chicherin was urged to secure a separate agreement with Germany (which, along with the other defeated powers, had been excluded from participation in the post-war settlement). Some of the ground had been prepared before the Genoa conference began, and Chicherin, continuing to work discreetly, reached agreement with the German delegation. Just one week into the Genoa conference, the Soviet delegation signed the Rapallo Treaty, the basis of which was 'a mutual repudiation of debts and claims, the granting of unconditional recognition, the promise of expanded economic relations and continuation of their surreptitious military ties'.[23] As Carole Fink has observed: 'The Soviet Union subsequently employed the Rapallo model to conclude bilateral agreements with individual Western governments. But, from a multinational perspective Genoa also became a model of failure, because neither side in 1922 was willing or able to desist from exploiting the other's weakness.'[24]

'THE PARTIAL STABILIZATION OF CAPITALISM'

The second period of Comintern's history was that which they termed 'the partial stabilization of capitalism'. In major pronouncements in April 1924, Stalin not only attacked Trotsky's notion of 'permanent revolution' and made the case for 'socialism in one country' but also recognized the failure of revolution elsewhere – Germany, in particular. Accordingly, he held, the Soviet state had to accept a temporary accommodation between Communism and capitalism. The doctrine of 'peaceful co-existence' (a concept earlier enunciated by Lenin) became the foreign policy counterpart of 'socialism in one country'.[25] There was, as a result, some improvement in state-to-state relations, even though the Comintern retained the long-term goal of Communist takeover in western Europe. The minority Labour government in Britain, headed by Ramsay MacDonald, officially recognized the Soviet Union in 1924. Benito Mussolini, a former socialist turned fascist, had hoped that Italy would initiate the breaking of the isolation of the Bolshevik state, but Britain, with the encouragement of the Soviet author-ities, got in first. Other countries – with the major exception of the United States – followed quite rapidly. The USA delayed its recognition of the Soviet Union longer than any other major state, not doing so until November 1933.

THE 'THIRD PERIOD' – 'CLASS AGAINST CLASS'

If throughout most of the 1920s there had been a desire within the Soviet leadership – for tactical reasons and especially in the light of their economic difficulties – for rapprochement with the West, this altered with a change of Comintern policy that coincided with the end of NEP in the Soviet Union. The Comintern's 'Third Period', or that of 'Class against Class', began in 1928. Already, in December 1927, Stalin had spoken of a 'new revo-lutionary upsurge', and at the Sixth World Congress of the Comintern in the summer of 1928 'right deviationists' were identified by him as the prin-cipal threat to the Communist movement. Communists went on the offensive against social democrats.[26] Communist parties throughout the world were expected *not* to co-operate with non-Communist socialists. In Germany, which had at the time the largest Communist Party in western Europe, this was an especially fateful decision.

Parties of major states, even when they were relatively unimportant in the context of the domestic politics of their countries, such as those of the United States and Britain, were forced to remove party officials thought to be lukewarm at best about the new Comintern line. The British comrades did this rather reluctantly. Dmitry Manuilsky, the son of a Ukrainian Orthodox priest who had become a leading figure in the Comintern and acted as an overseer of Western European Communist parties, made clear his dissatisfaction. The British Communist Party, he said in 1928, had not learned that in a revolution 'it will perhaps be necessary to chop some heads off'. Whereas 'the German comrades' were adept at organizing a purge – 'they attack the least deviation' – the party in Britain seemed like 'a society of great friends'.[27] Nevertheless, among those removed from high positions within the CPGB were some of the most popular party officials – notably Tom Bell, J.R. Campbell, Arthur Horner and Albert Inkpin – and the result of toeing the Moscow line was loss of membership and the still greater isolation of the Communist Party within British society.[28]

The German Communists' willingness to follow more unquestioningly the Comintern line – which meant, increasingly, Stalin's line – was especially disastrous for the party and its members. Whether, if the KPD had acted together with the social democrats, the rise to power of Hitler could have been prevented remains extremely uncertain. But by treating the social democrats, who were a still larger party than the Communists, as more dangerous enemies than the fascists, and by even taking comfort in the idea that the Nazi advance meant that the Weimar Republic was weakening, the German Communists were paving the way for their own destruction. The opening of the Soviet archives in the 1990s provides documentary evidence of the instructions being issued to the German party by the Comintern which most of the leaders of the KPD loyally accepted. The term 'social fascist' was used as a synonym for social democrat, with the former virtually replacing the latter in Comintern correspondence.[29] The Nazis won more votes than the Communists in the Reichstag elections of 1929 and twice as many in November 1932. In March 1933, after the Nazis had come to power, their electoral support (43.9 per cent) was substantially greater than that of the social democrats (18.3 per cent) and the Communists (12.3 per cent) put together.[30] The KPD leader, Ernst Thälmann, who had been backed by the Comintern to replace two more intellectual Communists, Ruth Fischer and Arkadi Maslow (who was of Russian parentage, but born in Germany), was himself almost replaced as party leader when he attempted to cover up embezzlement of party funds by his brother-in-law in 1928. With only one abstention, the Central Committee of the KPD voted to relieve him from his functions. The special significance of this episode was its illustration of where true power lay within the international Communist movement. The support of Stalin and the Comintern for Thälmann meant that he was reinstated and it was his KPD Central Committee opponents who began to be removed from the leadership.[31]

In March 1933, one German Communist Party activist broke ranks not only by warning that the policy of eschewing possible allies in the struggle against Hitler was leading to disaster but also by writing directly to Stalin. This KPD member, Karl Gröhl, using his party pseudonym, Karl Friedberg, recognized where real power lay in the international Communist movement. His letter to Stalin, which began 'Dear Comrade' and closed 'With Communist greetings', insisted that it was necessary for the German Communist Party to join forces with worker members of the Social Democratic Party and their organizations in a 'united front and combined struggle'. The Communist Party itself needed to create a parallel underground apparatus to continue the work of the activists who had been arrested. The national question – the Treaty of Versailles of 1919 (which had disadvantaged Germany) – should be treated as a second-order question. The top priority was the struggle for bread and work and against fascism. 'Today', Friedberg/Gröhl concluded his letter to Stalin, 'we are talking about the life or death of the party. If the party in these days is not able to open up a mass struggle, it will be smashed for many years. Not only the result of fascism, but also the undermining of faith in the party within the working class.'[32] Being correct ahead of the party line – with the Comintern taking a further two years before embracing the idea of a Popular Front – seldom did a Communist activist much good. Gröhl was wise that when he went into exile from Germany he spent only a short time in the Soviet Union. Otherwise he would have met the same fate as did many other German Communists who sought refuge in Moscow.[33]

Even after the Nazis had come to power in Germany in early 1933, a much more prominent Communist than Friedberg 'anticipated the resistance to fascism that the Communists squandered in the ultra-leftist atmosphere of the "Third Period" (1928–1935)'.[34] This was Georgi Dimitrov who succeeded in overcoming the bias of a courtroom in Leipzig, using it as a forum to attack fascism, thus turning the tables, rhetorically, on his accusers. Dimitrov won, thereby, admiration from party members throughout Europe, and this enabled him to receive also cautious approval from the Comintern. Dimitrov was born in 1882 into a Bulgarian Protestant family. His mother had wanted him to become a pastor, but he was expelled from Sunday school at the age of twelve for distributing anti-religious literature. A militant socialist before the Bolshevik revolution, he became a significant figure in the international Communist movement after it. Dimitrov was used by the Comintern as an emissary to various western European countries, but was arrested in Germany in 1933 and accused (falsely), with others, of setting fire to the Reichstag.[35] He denied the charges, defended 'Communist ideology, my ideals', and, during a trial which lasted from 21 September to 23 December 1933, portrayed himself as a patriotic Bulgarian, indignantly rejecting the Nazi charge that he came from a 'savage and barbarous country'. That description, he said, applied to Bulgarian fascism but not to the Bulgarian people. Dimitrov, along with fellow Bulgarian co-defendants, was acquitted for lack of evidence, though all of them were in danger of being executed if returned to Bulgaria. After a further two months in prison, they were released to the USSR and granted Soviet citizenship.[36] Dimitrov rose rapidly through the higher echelons of the Comintern to become its head, and unlike many of his Comintern colleagues, survived Stalin's Great Purge of 1937–38.

The German Communists he left behind were much less fortunate. By the end of 1933, between 60,000 and 100,000 had been interned by the Nazis. By 1945, more than half of those who were party members in 1932 – and party membership was then approximately 300,000 – had been in Nazi jails or concentration camps.[37] Thälmann was arrested in March 1933 and spent the rest of his life as a prisoner of the Nazi regime. During the Second World War he was transferred from jail to Buchenwald concentration camp and executed there in August 1944. In all, some 20,000 German Communists were killed by the Nazis. Many German Communists, including some of the more senior party members, managed to make their way to the Soviet Union. Approximately 60 per cent of them met their deaths in the Stalin terror. (At a time of Soviet–Nazi rapprochement, hundreds of them were even handed over to the Gestapo by the Soviet secret police.) More members of the Politburo of the German Communist Party were killed in the Soviet Union at Stalin's behest than in Germany on the orders of Hitler.[38]

POPULAR FRONT

Even the arrest of German Communists by the Nazis on such a massive scale did not jolt the Comintern into an immediate change of course. Belatedly, the leadership in Moscow was waking up to the threat which the rise of Hitler and Nazism represented for the Soviet Union, but this was still played down in 1934. It was in the summer of 1935 at the Seventh Congress of the Comintern – with Dimitrov making a major speech entitled 'The United Front Against Fascism and War' – that the policy of creating a Popular Front was fully enunciated. As ever, a changing perception of Soviet needs determined the policy of the Comintern. Thus began its fourth period, in which social democrats could be allies, as could even liberals and members of religious groups, provided they were ready to unite against fascism. This period, which lasted until the Nazi–Soviet Pact of 1939, was the time in the history of the Comintern when its international appeal was greatest to many idealists and staunch anti-fascists. The nature of Stalin's Soviet Union was poorly understood by them, but even if it had been better known, there was a case for an alliance with the Soviet Union to prevent Hitler's expansionist plans from being implemented. Western democracies were more than content to be in alliance with the Soviet Union during the Second World War when the Soviet army made a disproportionately great contribution to the victory in Europe. Though Stalin was no more to be trusted than was Hitler, and though he was responsible for the deaths of more citizens of his own country than Hitler in Germany, he was a much more cautious actor on the international stage. The threat of Soviet expansion by military means was less – certainly less immediate – than that from Nazi Germany.

The high point of the Popular Front era for the international

Communist movement was the Spanish Civil War, waged between 1936 and 1939. For the Soviet Union it presented both an opportunity and a dilemma, as the inauguration of the Popular Front 'coincided with the total polarization of Spanish society'.[39] The Comintern had welcomed the strengthening of the left in Spain and, in particular, the progress of the Spanish Communist Party. Much less welcome was the onset of civil war. The growing strength of Communists within the coalition of republicans, anarchists, socialists and Communists that emerged victorious in elections in 1936 was entirely positive from the standpoint of the Comintern and the Soviet Union. When, however, this victory was threatened by a military revolt, supported by conservative forces and the Catholic Church, leading to full-scale civil war, there was a tension between the need for the Comintern to be seen to be supporting the revolutionary left and the desire of the Soviet leadership to bring Western democracies, and Britain and France in particular, into a united front against the threat from Hitler's Germany. To the extent to which the Soviet Union was perceived as aiding and abetting a Communist takeover in Spain, this had little appeal for other West European governments and the Conservative-dominated 'National' government in Britain, in particular.

Both sides in the Spanish Civil War had internal differences in addition to their hatred of each other. These were especially pronounced on the republican side, where liberal republicans, a variety of socialists (including the anti-Stalinist party, POUM, which was substantially Leninist and 'half-Trotskyist')[40] and anarchists vied for supremacy with the Spanish Communist Party. The Soviet Union sent military support, both equipment and people. The latter were supposedly 'volunteers', but the nature of the Soviet system did not allow such matters to be left to chance. The Soviet Union sent not only airmen and tank specialists but also many intelligence officers, both from the NKVD and from military intelligence (the GRU). It did not do this without recompense – all the aid was charged for. Since the Soviet Union had taken possession of the greater part of the Spanish gold reserves, each piece of equipment as well as the salaries and expenses of the Soviet personnel in Spain was registered and billed, resulting in the Spanish republican government being told in mid-1938 that their gold supply in Moscow was now exhausted.[41]

Many Communists in a wide range of countries were genuine volunteers in the Spanish Civil War, joining the International Brigades, whose recruits included also non-Communist socialists, and whose total number was in the region of 50,000.[42] Later in the war they came under the command of the government of the Spanish republic and also became less international and increasingly composed of Spaniards. In the first year of the Brigades' existence, however, they 'constituted a semi-autonomous Comintern force' under the direction of Comintern advisers and Soviet military commanders.[43] The direct Soviet contribution included 800 pilots, of whom 17 per cent were killed in the conflict, and 584 advisers.[44] Since the Spanish Civil War also coincided with the period when the purges reached their height in the Soviet Union – 1937–38 – there were times when the NKVD was as intent on seeking out and killing Trotskyists, supposedly their allies in Spain, as in fighting their conservative and fascist enemies. The contribution of the Soviet Union to the republican cause in Spain was glorified in Soviet propaganda, but this did not mean that the citizens who fought there were all acclaimed when they arrived home. Many of the Soviet advisers and military men who served in Spain were shot in the Great Purge. The head of the NKVD in Spain, Alexander Orlov, when he was told in July 1938 to report to Paris, from where he would be taken to a Soviet ship in Antwerp harbour, realized what fate would be awaiting him and succeeded in fleeing to the United States via Canada.[45] (Orlov's cousin, Zinovy Katsnelson, the deputy head of the NKVD in Ukraine, had already been arrested the previous year and subsequently executed.)[46]

The Spanish Civil War resulted in the deaths of about half a million people and ended in defeat for the republican, socialist and Communist forces and victory for the nationalists led by General Francisco Franco. The victorious side had also been a coalition, in which fascists played a prominent part, and they had more foreign military assistance than had the republicans. Hitler and especially Mussolini committed far more troops to this struggle than did Stalin. Approximately 16,000 Germans and 70,000 Italians served at one point or another in the Spanish Civil War.[47] The Soviet Union, with Comintern as a pliable instrument, had attempted to square the circle in Spain by seeking a 'democracy of a new type', meaning one in which Communists would gradually assume full control, while simultaneously pursuing an anti-fascist alliance with Western democracies. That project failed, since they did enough, militarily, to arouse concern that they were going to install a pro-Soviet government in Spain, while being unprepared to commit sufficient troops to secure actual victory, fearing that this might precipitate war with Germany.[48]

THE NAZI–SOVIET PACT

The fifth and final stage in the activity of the Comintern before Hitler's attack on the Soviet Union in June 1941 – and the Soviet Union's entry into the Second World War – was that which began with the 1939 Nazi–Soviet Pact. Partly as a result of his failure to secure an anti-German military alliance with Britain and France, Stalin decided to seek an understanding with Hitler. He did not rule out a future attack by Nazi Germany on the Soviet Union, but thought that there was much to be said for the major capitalist states destroying each other while, in the meantime, the Soviet Union gathered strength for a future conflict.[49] Taking the rest of the world, not least Communists and admirers of the Soviet Union, by surprise, the Soviet Foreign Minister Vyacheslav Molotov and his German counterpart Joachim von Ribbentrop signed the Nazi–Soviet Non-Aggression Pact in late August 1939. It contained secret clauses agreeing to the partition of Poland, and to Soviet repossession of Estonia, Latvia and Lithuania. Earlier, the two leading military powers among Europe's democratic states, Britain and France, had come to an agreement with Nazi Germany and Italy of a much more limited nature, but one which tarnished the anti-fascist credentials of the democracies. The Munich Pact of September 1938 ceded Sudetenland – the north-western territory of Czechoslovakia, with its large German population – to Hitler's Germany. By this agreement the British prime minister, Neville Chamberlain, believed that the negotiators had saved 'Czechoslovakia from destruction, and Europe from Armageddon'.[50] Stalin's pact with Hitler was much more far-reaching and, as distinct from Chamberlain's attitude to the Munich agreement, it was not intended by either Stalin or Hitler to be a substitute for eventual armed conflict.

The Popular Front period had seen the successful recruitment of Communists in the democracies. Many people on the radical wing of the political spectrum in Europe and, to a lesser extent, also in North America, worried by the rise of militaristic fascism, came to view the Communists as the most determined opponents of Hitler, Mussolini and Franco. The about-turn signalled by the Nazi–Soviet Pact came, accordingly, as a profound shock to tens of thousands of Communists in different continents. The Comintern policy up to the moment at which the Molotov–Ribbentrop pact was signed was to emphasize, on the one hand, the imperative need to defend the world's 'first socialist state' and, on the other, to combat fascism.[51]

On the first day of September 1939, Nazi Germany attacked Poland both by land and air, and in response, Britain and France two days later declared war on Germany. The Soviet Union, meantime, was given a relatively free hand by Germany to deal with its near neighbours. It incorporated what had been part of Poland into Ukraine and launched an attack on Finland. The Soviet–Finnish war of 1939–40, known as the Winter War, was far costlier than Stalin had bargained for. The Finns put up a ferocious resistance, and though some 24,000 of them were killed and 420,000 were made homeless, it is likely that as many as 200,000 Soviet troops lost their lives. Estimates of the war dead vary hugely. The figure given to the Soviet leadership at the time was 52,000 dead on the Soviet side.[52] The estimate of Finnish fatalities given to the same plenary session of the Central Committee of the Soviet Communist Party was 70,000. Finnish sources, however, had no incentive to underestimate their losses, and so the figure of 24,000 is likely to be much more accurate. Stalin, in contrast, had every incentive to make Finnish deaths higher than Soviet losses. Nikita Khrushchev, in his later years when he had turned decisively against Stalin, went to the opposite extreme and suggested, implausibly, that as many as a million Soviet troops died in the Winter War.[53] A peace was signed in March 1940, in which Finland had to cede territory, including Finnish Karelia, to the Soviet Union, but the remainder of Finland was able to stay independent.[54]

In the first three weeks after the Second World War began, western Communists had continued to attack fascism as the main enemy, but when on 24 September the Comintern declared that the war was not primarily anti-fascist but 'imperialist', most of the highly disciplined Communist parties swung into line, condemning the war as such and making no distinction between the guilt of the fascist countries and the democracies. The Italian Communist Party (PCI) was largely an honourable exception, being especially condemnatory after Mussolini brought Italy into the war in June 1940.[55] In that same month, the Soviet Union, as part of its secret agreement with Nazi Germany, seized the three Baltic states of Estonia, Latvia and Lithuania. These countries had been lost to the Russian Empire by the Treaty of Versailles in 1919, following the Paris Peace Conference in which Bolshevik Russia had not been allowed to take part. The Nazi–Soviet Pact had given Stalin the opportunity to restore this part of the old imperial borders. Opponents in the Baltic states, real or potential, of the 1940 Soviet takeover were dealt with ruthlessly. Tens of thousands were killed or deported to Siberia, the arm of the Soviet secret police falling especially heavily on the political and intellectual elites.

The National Communist Parties between the Wars

The relative strength of German Communism until it was comprehensively crushed by the Nazis has already been noted. Fascism in Italy and authoritarian regimes throughout most of Eastern Europe also drove the Communist parties underground. The strongest party in Europe became that in France. The success of recruitment in Western democracies depended both on economic depression in these countries and on Comintern policy, with the years of the Popular Front against fascism providing much more fertile ground for the parties than the sectarian 'Third Period'. During that time, the most influential of Italian Communist theorists (over the long run), Antonio Gramsci, was in prison. Arrested in Italy in November 1926, he remained a prisoner of the fascist regime until, with his physical health destroyed, he was allowed in August 1935 to move to a clinic in Rome, where he died in 1937.[56] But between 1929 and 1935 he was writing his *Prison Notebooks*,[57] which were to exercise a posthumous influence on international Marxism, including the 'Eurocommunist' movement of the 1970s. Although not incompatible with much of the thinking of Lenin, the ideas were sufficiently different from the Marxism-Leninism of Stalin's Russia that Gramsci would not have been able to express them had he been with his PCI colleague Togliatti at the Comintern headquarters in Moscow rather than in an Italian prison. It has been correctly observed that Gramsci's writing 'contained approaches, particularly to political culture, that were foreign to the classical Marxist and the Leninist traditions'.[58] These included the role of 'organic intellectuals', in Gramsci's terminology, people who could 'construct an intellectual-moral bloc which can make politically possible the intellectual progress of the mass and not only of small intellectual groups'.[59] Similarly distinctive within the spectrum of Marxist thought was his view that 'the hegemony of the bourgeoisie lay in its dominance of civil society rather than its control of the repressive force of state power'.[60]

Promising members of foreign Communist parties were sent to the Lenin School of the Comintern in Moscow for training, among them in 1929–30 a future Secretary-General of the French Communist Party of working-class origin, Waldeck Rochet. When some of these students were directed to a Soviet factory for additional experience, the discussion within the group no longer focused on the superiority of the Soviet to the capitalist system but on the disparity between the theory of socialist production they had imbibed at the Leninist school and the reality of factory life in the Soviet Union they had just witnessed. The one student who was not impressed by this intrusion of real life was Rochet. Rather like Groucho (as distinct from Karl) Marx – 'Who are you going to believe? Me, or your own eyes?' – Rochet simply refused to accept the factual information the students had brought back from the factory.[61]

The French Communists had more success than any other western European party after the German Communists fell victim to Hitler. As early as 1928 they attracted more than a million votes (just over 11 per cent of the total) in elections for the French parliament. This declined in 1932, but rose during the period of the Popular Front to 1,487,000 votes (15.3 per cent) in 1936.[62] In that year 72 out of 608 deputies elected to the National Assembly were from the PCF.[63] Between 1933 and 1937 the size of the PCF grew fivefold, with workers constituting the bulk of the new members.[64] The strong showing of the French Communists in the parliamentary elections of 1936, in this period of co-operation with other parties of the left, allowed a government to be formed in France in that year which was headed by the Socialist Léon Blum.

During these years the PCF had a capable leader. A prominent figure in the French Communist Party from the early 1930s, and its definitive leader (with Moscow's blessing) from 1934, Maurice Thorez was a wily and secretive politician of working-class background who spent a lot of time in his study. He worked briefly as a miner, but in 1923 (when he was only twenty-three) he became a full-time party functionary. His 'endless desire to learn', in the words of the historian of the PCF, Annie Kriegel, led him to acquire a knowledge of Latin, German and Russian.[65] Given the relationship between his party and the Soviet Union, it was the last of these languages which was of much the most practical use. The PCF, however, did not have to deal with Moscow on a day-to-day basis. The party, and Thorez personally, also received a great deal of guidance from the Comintern's permanent representative in France during the 1930s, Eugen Fried, who had been a founder member of the Communist Party of Czechoslovakia. A talented Communist intellectual, who also possessed organizational skills, Fried had in 1919 liaised between the short-lived Hungarian Soviet Republic and Slovak revolutionary groups. For much of the 1930s he lived in Paris under the pseudonym Clément and met with Thorez almost daily.[66]

Another moderately successful European Communist Party was that of Czechoslovakia. Although a state founded only in 1918, Czechoslovakia was alone among central European countries in remaining a democracy throughout the inter-war period. In the first election after the Communist Party and the Social Democrats had split – that of 1925 – the Communist Party polled 943,000 votes and secured 41 out of 300 seats in the legislature. By the end of the twenties the Communists' support had declined drastically, largely as a result of following the intransigent Moscow line, but a combination of the economic depression of the 1930s and the party's greater attractiveness in the era of the Popular Front saw it gain just under 850,000 votes in 1935 and over 10 per cent of all votes. While even at its most successful in the inter-war period the voting strength of the Czechoslovak Communist Party never exceeded 13 per cent, it was always one of the country's four strongest parties.[67] Its actual membership ranged from a high of 150,000 in 1925 to a low of 28,000 in 1930.[68]

COMMUNISM IN AMERICA AND BRITAIN

In contrast with the relative, though still fairly modest, success of the French and Czechoslovak parties (with the party's strength in the latter case much greater in the Czech lands of Bohemia and Moravia than in Slovakia), Communist parties made little or no electoral progress in the English-speaking world. In the United States, they spent the early years after the Bolshevik revolution in faction-fighting and splits. Two Communist parties were founded in 1919, the Communist Party of America, headed by Charles Ruthenberg, and the Communist Labor League, which numbered among its leaders John Reed, who witnessed the Bolshevik seizure of power in Moscow and wrote an enthusiastic and vivid account of it, *Ten Days that Shook the World* (1919). Lenin himself wrote a short introduction to the Russian edition, recommending it unreservedly 'to the workers of the world' and adding that he would like to see the book 'published in millions of copies and translated into all languages'. Reed took an active part in the Second Congress of the Comintern in 1920, but died later that year in Moscow. He is the only American whose ashes are buried beside the Kremlin wall with a plaque there honouring his memory.

The American Communists, in the second half of the 1920s, split along lines similar to those of the Soviet party, with followers of Bukharin and followers of Trotsky both being expelled from the party, which had a legal existence from 1923, having earlier been repressed by the government for several years. Even before enormous pressure to conform to Soviet ortho-doxy was exerted from Moscow, copying Russia was voluntarily carried to absurd extremes by some American Communists. Even though he belonged to the small minority of early members of the Communist Party in the United States who had actually been born in America, Israel Amter (who, in his writings, sometimes used the pseudonym John Ford) began a speech in New York with the immortal words: 'Workers and peasants of Brooklyn'![69] Among the leading American Bukharinites was Bertram D. Wolfe, who later became a prominent analyst of Communism and the author of a notable book on the Russian revolutionary movement, published in 1948, *Three Who Made a Revolution* (the three being Lenin, Trotsky and Stalin). Wolfe was one of the leading figures in the Communist Party of the USA who spent weeks in Moscow in 1929 trying to defend the autonomy of their party. They were, however, outmanoeuvred by Stalin, who took a close personal interest in even such an insignificantly small party, since it was situated in the world's foremost capitalist state.[70] This was in the Third Period when, in Wolfe's words, the Comintern was turned into 'the Stalintern'.[71] From 1930 until 1945 the undisputed leader of the party was Earl Browder, appointed at Stalin's behest. Browder contested the presidential elections of 1936 and 1940 as the Communist candidate. He was, however, imprisoned in the United States from 1940 until 1942 and at the end of the war fell foul of the Soviet leadership. At Moscow's instigation he was expelled from the

Communist Party in 1946. The American Communist Party faithfully followed the Comintern line, so that, especially during its Third Period, not only the CPUSA's hated Trotskyist rivals (who had formed the Communist League of America in 1929) but also Franklin D. Roosevelt and the New Deal Democrats were dismissed as 'social fascists'.

As was the case in other democracies, the period of the Popular Front saw a rise in support for the American Communist Party, although it was on a very small scale compared with France or Czechoslovakia during those years. Even at its highest point in the inter-war period – in 1939 – membership of the CPUSA did not rise above 75,000. It had, however, many more sympathizers. When the party was founded, the great majority of its members were first-generation immigrants from the Russian Empire and it was as late as 1936 before a majority of the party's members had been born in the United States.[72] The attraction of the party grew in response to the Great Depression and to the rise of fascism. It won support from some leading writers and film-makers, especially Hollywood screenwriters, although the films which made it to the screen seldom showed much sign of radicalism, still less Communism. Anti-Communism in the United States was always a very much stronger force, backed not only by those in charge of funding (a bigger issue for film-makers than for writers of books) but also by the full authority of the state.[73]

The British Communist Party in its earliest years was, like its American counterpart, torn by factionalism but by 1924 was a disciplined organization. Its policy in the first half of the 1920s was both to establish itself as an institution in its own right and to infiltrate the British Labour Party, an organization which already had strong working-class support. Although the Labour Party, at the time of its first period in office (as a minority government) in 1924, was more sympathetic to the Soviet state than were its Conservative opponents, it took care to curtail Communist influence within the party. Labour refused to allow individual membership of the Labour Party to Communists or to permit their endorsement as Labour candidates. The British Communist Party hesitated to characterize the Labour Party as 'proto-fascist', when that became the Comintern's Third Period line, but made the personnel changes demanded of it in 1929. They removed Andrew Rothstein, the son of a Russian revolutionary – who stayed on in Britain when his father was sent back to Russia in 1920 – from the top leadership group, although Rothstein remained a prominent member of the party for the rest of his life. Another leading member to be accused of deviation, in response to the Comintern's proddings, was John (J.R.) Campbell, a Scottish trade unionist who had fought, and been decorated, in the First World War, before becoming a founding member of the British Communist Party. He was removed from the inner leadership of the party but kept his Central Committee membership. When, in the next zig-zag of the Comintern, the focus shifted to fighting against fascism, Campbell regained his former prominence and became editor of the party newspaper, the *Daily Worker*.

While a few secret Communists were able at various times to acquire membership of the Labour Party, they remained an insignificant minority. Such influence as Communists wielded within Britain was mainly through the trade union movement. Since the Trade Union Congress did not infringe the autonomy of individual trade unions, Communists could – and in many cases did – come to the fore as activists and leaders in the inter-war period and especially in the early post-Second World War decades. The two leading figures in the British Communist Party for a generation were Harry Pollitt and Rajani Palme Dutt. The Stalinization of the party was completed in 1929 and thereafter the leadership did not suffer fluctuations and expulsions to the extent of many other Communist parties. Born into an English working-class family in 1890, Pollitt became in 1929, on the prompting of the Comintern, the CPGB's secretary-general. Palme Dutt had a still keener nose for the way the wind was blowing in Moscow, possibly aided in this by his Estonian wife, Salme Dutt (née Pekkala), who was rumoured to be a NKVD agent.[74] Born in 1896, the son of an Indian doctor and a Swedish mother, Dutt did not inspire the same affection among the party rank-and-file as Pollitt, but he was inexhaustible in producing a stream of literature which elaborated whatever was the current Kremlin line. Neither Pollitt nor Palme Dutt spoke out against the Moscow trials of old Bolsheviks between 1936 and 1938 but Pollitt, unlike Dutt, did object in the Politburo of the British party when the Stalin–Hitler pact was announced. As a result, he was removed from the party leadership and dispatched to a subordinate position in South Wales. After the Soviet Union entered the war and the party line changed, Pollitt was reinstated as party leader.

In the inter-war period the highest membership attained by the British Communist Party was in 1939, when it reached 17,756 – in 1930, during the 'Class against Class' era of the Comintern, it was as low as two and a half thousand.[75] Party membership was to become higher during the war and early post-war years. If the 1930s were the 'heyday of American Communism', that term is more applicable to the 1940s in Britain.[76] Nevertheless, if that was true of party membership in absolute numbers, the 1930s were the time when many idealists of a radical disposition were drawn to Communism, believing that the Soviet Union had overcome the problems of economic slump which were affecting Britain and the rest of the capitalist world. The attraction of the Communist Party also reflected deep concern about the rise of fascism. The aggressive activity of the British Union of Fascists, led by Oswald Mosley, was an important contributory factor in bringing numerous Jewish recruits, in particular, into the CPGB. The Communists were perceived to be the people who were doing most to stand up to Mosley and his followers, including physically resisting them on the streets.[77] During the period between the signing of the Nazi–Soviet Pact and the German attack on the Soviet Union, the British Communist Party, like its counterparts in other democracies, lost members and supporters. Many were disillusioned or outraged at this about-turn by the people whom they had regarded as the most dedicated anti-fascists.

THE ORIGINS OF CHINESE COMMUNISM

The most prominent Asian Communist at the time of the founding of the Comintern in 1919 was the Indian M.N. Roy. At the Second Congress of the Comintern his view that the most decisive advances of the movement would be made in Asia was greeted with scepticism. Roy, in turn, was pessimistic about the prospects for revolution in the advanced industrial countries.[78] When Lenin was writing on national and colonial issues, he consulted with Roy and valued his advice. For some years after Lenin's death, Roy continued to be a prominent member of the Comintern. However, in the period of the Stalinization of that organization, he was accused of being a 'right-wing deviationist' and expelled from it. Still a revolutionary, he returned in secret to India, which remained under imperial British rule, but was arrested in 1930 and spent the next six years in prison.

It was, however, in China, not India, that the foundations were laid for Communist success. A nationalist revolution in 1911 had overthrown the imperial dynasty. It was given further impetus by the First World War – in particular, when in a secret deal made in 1917, Britain and France agreed that German colonies in China would become Japanese possessions after the allies had won.[79] Chinese students in Paris prevented the Chinese delegates to the Versailles conference from physically taking part in the signing of what they saw as a humiliating treaty, while in Beijing on 4 May 1919 3,000 students demonstrated in Tiananmen Square against the Chinese government's docility.[80] Few of the students at this time were Communists but the Comintern had taken a keen interest in setting up a Communist Party in China and succeeded in establishing a socialist youth league and a monthly magazine. One of those influenced by these developments was Mao Zedong, who formed a Communist group in Hunan. Two other of the most important Chinese Communists of the twentieth century were among the young students who went to Paris in 1920 – Zhou Enlai and Deng Xiaoping. It was in France that they were attracted to Communist youth groups, after which they became active proselytizers for the cause among the Chinese in Europe.[81]

The Chinese Communist Party (CCP) was founded in 1921, but was incomparably weaker than Sun Yat-sen's Nationalist movement – the Kuomintang. Excluding overseas members, the CCP had only some 200 people within its ranks in 1922.[82] In that same year it was agreed that Communists should enter the Kuomintang as individuals, although the CCP would retain its separate and independent identity. The Communists became part of the May Fourth Movement, which sought national unification that involved defeating hundreds of local warlords. Disappointed by the Western powers, Sun Yat-sen gained support from the Soviet state. This made the alliance between Chinese Communists and the Nationalists viable in the short run, although the CCP leader Chen Duxiu expressed nervousness about it.[83] A Comintern emissary, Mikhail Borodin, played an important part in liaising not only with the Chinese Communists but with Sun Yat-sen. The three principles of the Kuomintang were declared to be anti-imperialist nationalism, democracy, and socialism, but Borodin succeeded in introducing into the movement the Leninist principle of 'democratic centralism', making majority decisions binding on all party members.[84]

The links between the Chinese nationalist and socialist movement, on the one hand, and the Soviet Union, on the other, were close in the mid-1920s, especially before the death of Sun Yat-sen in 1925. The Soviet leadership set about strengthening the Kuomintang military. One of Sun's allies, Chiang Kai-shek, was a member of a delegation which spent several months in Moscow studying military organization. On his return to China he was appointed commandant of a new military academy. Thanks to the influence of Borodin, the future Communist prime minister Zhou Enlai, recently returned to China from Paris, became director of the political department of the academy.[85] Tensions, however, arose between the Kuomintang and the CCP in 1926–27. The Soviet Union had been keen to maintain good relations with China, which it saw as an ally against British imperialism, and they encouraged the CCP to keep in with the Kuomintang for longer than was in their interests. Chiang Kai-shek turned against the Communists, and when anti-leftist regional leaders killed large groups of them, Chiang not only sympathized but ordered some of the killings himself. M.N. Roy and Mikhail Borodin returned to the Soviet Union, disillusioned with the prospects of the Communists in China.

Borodin had a chequered career. His real name was Mikhail Gruzenberg. In the early years of the twentieth century he was a member of the Jewish Bund in Russia and also an early convert to the Communist cause. Following the failure of the 1905 revolution in Russia, he spent most of the years between then and the Bolshevik revolution in the United States, becoming a school teacher in Chicago. By 1922 he was a Comintern secret agent in Britain – using the name George Brown – before being sent, with greater success, to China the following year. Sun Yat-sen named him 'special adviser' to the Kuomintang.[86] After his return to Moscow in 1927, Borodin's political work was of a more modest nature – on foreign-language Soviet propaganda publications. He was not among the Cominternists to be rounded up during the Great Terror of the late 1930s. However, he did eventually die in a Soviet labour camp – in 1951 – having been arrested in 1949 as part of Stalin's anti-semitic onslaught of that period.

The Nationalists, headed by Chiang Kai-shek, set up their government in Nanjing in 1928. Although Chiang had got the better of the Communists, and disappointed the hopes that Stalin had placed in him, those Communists who survived, Mao Zedong notable among them, retreated into the countryside and staked their hopes on the peasantry. Mao, in particular, developed the idea that a rural-based revolution was strategically preferable to the more orthodox Marxist and Leninist notion of city-based seizure of power.[87] Mao, the son of a relatively well-off farmer against whom he rebelled early in life, was by the mid-1930s the de facto leader of the Chinese Communists. Chiang Kai-shek's Nationalist government by the early 1930s regarded the Communists as one of the main threats to their central authority and pursued 'extermination campaigns' against the main base of the CCP in Jiangxi province. This led to the Communists' retreat to the north-western province of Shaanxi in the 'Long March' of 1934–35. Although some 80,000 men and 2,000 women embarked on the march, only 8,000 reached their destination.[88] The Long March itself, and the role of Mao in the inter-war years, has become the subject of much myth-making and huge controversy, but what is not in dispute is that a nucleus of Communists lived to fight another day and, in due course, to stage the first successful Communist Party-led revolution in Asia.[89]

6

What Do We Mean
by a Communist System?

For Communists themselves, 'Communism' had two different meanings. It referred *both* to an international movement dedicated to the overthrow of capitalist systems *and* to the new society which would exist only in the future when Marx's higher stage of socialism had been reached. Given that ruling Communist parties described their existing systems as 'socialist', it is reasonable to ask: what is our justification for calling them 'Communist'? Many former Communist politicians have objected to the use of that term because, they remind us, 'communism' was to be the ultimate stage of socialism which they never claimed to have reached.' Yet the members of these ruling parties described *themselves* as Communists, and Western scholars, categorising the *systems* as 'Communist', did not imagine for a moment that they were depicting what Marx or Lenin had in mind by the stage of 'communism' – that self-governing, stateless, co-operative society which has never existed anywhere. (Using a capital 'C' for real Communist systems, with their enormous and oppressive state power, and a lower-case 'c' for the imaginary, stateless 'communism' of the future helps to keep clear the distinction.)

Communist leaders and ideologists have claimed that the countries ruled by them were – or, in the case of the five remaining Communist states, are – democratic. Yet many Western observers who would not dream of accepting the democratic credentials of these regimes have been content to take at face value Communists' descriptions of their own system as quintessentially socialist. Communist states had (and, to the extent that they still exist, have) a distinctive political and economic organization, sharing important common features to be discussed later in the chapter. The main problem with calling them 'socialist' is that this term has embraced a far wider range of political parties, movements and governments than those which accepted Marxist-Leninist ideology.² Governments have been formed, following free elections, in countries as diverse as Great Britain, the Federal Republic of Germany, Spain, Sweden, the Netherlands, Norway, Australia and Israel by people who regarded themselves as socialists, even if they never went so far as to claim that they had created a socialist system. Indeed, in recent decades social democratic parties have moved away from the idea that a radically different socio-economic system bearing the name of socialism will ever be created.[3] Long characterized by the evolutionary nature of their aims, these parties have become increasingly content to pursue greater social justice within an essentially market economy in which public ownership has been very much the exception rather than the rule.

Moreover, even before the most recent evolution of social democratic parties, many socialist theorists saw the essence of socialism not in central-ized, statist ownership but in social or public ownership which could be in the form of co-operatives, guilds, or municipal control as well as of – or as an alternative to – nationalized industries. They saw these as inextricably linked with democratic institutions.[4] A British political theorist, Michael Lessnoff, writing during the heyday of Communism, defined socialism succinctly as 'democratic control of the economy'. On that basis, he had no difficulty in reaching the much more unorthodox conclusion that not only were capitalism and socialism conceptually compatible rather than irreconcilable opposites, but also that states such as the USA and Britain 'are undoubtedly more socialist than the USSR or the People's Republic of China'.[5] They were certainly more democratic, and if democratic control of the economy is to be the main criterion of socialism, Lessnoff's conclu-sion may be paradoxical, but it is not illogical. In political practice, contin-uing globalization of the economy has put stricter limits on democratic control over the economy in any one state. That is one major reason why socialists, in the non-Communist sense, have had to modify and adapt some of their former goals, although the global financial crisis of 2008 reinforced social democrats' longstanding belief that unfettered capitalism was neither the only nor the best non-Communist answer to the world's problems.

In contrast with the activities and aspirations of democratic socialist parties, Communist parties, in most states which came under Communist rule, were very ready to *impose* that form of government on the society. In at least half of all cases, this was a result of foreign support (usually, but not always, Soviet), backed by armed force, for the local Communist takeover. The parties certainly could not rely on coming to power through free elections. Communists throughout most of Europe were far less successful electorally in gaining working-class support than were socialist parties which accepted the values of pluralist democracy. Indeed, in the Western world in the twentieth century, socialism did *not* generally mean the body of doctrine and the political practices associated with Communist parties. Socialists and Communists could be temporary allies, but they were separ-ated by fundamental differences concerning the relationship between means and ends. Thus, for example, in its annual report of 1933 the highest body of the British Trade Union movement, the Trade Union Council, scoffed at the Communist claim that in capitalist states there was no freedom worth defending, observing: 'The State has not yet the authority to shoot citizens without trial. Nor do people disappear at the hands of a secret police; nor is criticism of the Government a crime . . . The institutions of free citizenship and the organizations of democracy are our strongest safeguards.'[6]

Although socialists of a social democratic type sometimes found themselves on the same side as the Communists – in opposing fascism, for instance, during the Comintern's Popular Front phase and during the Second World War – in general there was a struggle within trade unions and their political wings between Communists and non-Communist socialists. The firmness of Ernest Bevin, Britain's formidable first foreign secretary of the post-World War Two era, in opposing the policy of Stalin's Soviet Union owed much to his experience of dealing with Communists during the inter-war years in which he built up the Transport and General Workers' Union as the largest trade union in Western Europe. A man of great ability and self-confidence, Bevin would brook no lectures on 'the workers' from any Communist. He was born in a Somerset village in 1881, never knowing his father, and to a mother who died when he was eight. He had a poverty-stricken childhood and left school at the age of eleven.[7] By the time of his death he had become the most respected British foreign secretary of the first half of the twentieth century.

In Western Europe, not least in Britain, the labour movement provided a way for talented individuals of humble origins not only to develop their own talents but also to advance and defend the interests of the social class from which they came. While in Communist countries the scale of social mobility was undoubtedly greater, this was purchased at a terrible price. It is hardly surprising that, for their part, Communist leaders and theoreticians viewed the democratic socialist parties of Western Europe as their most dangerous ideological enemies.[8] It was very late in the Soviet era before reformist Communists in Russia and in Eastern Europe became part of a one-way convergence whereby a good many of them increasingly embraced a social democratic conception of socialism. This led a Hungarian writer to complain at the time of 'a traffic jam on the road to Damascus'.[9]

Communist systems vary greatly over time as well as significantly from one country to another. The early years of establishing a Communist order, including the securing of the Communist Party's monopoly of power and the nationalization of all industry, are quite different from the period in which the fire of revolutionary zeal has died away, a party leadership has come face-to-face with long-term problems of government and development, and a new generation has grown up under Communist rule. The differences between one Communist system and another had by the 1960s become sufficiently great that towards the end of that decade the American political scientist John H. Kautsky (the grandson of the leading Communist theorist Karl Kautsky, who at one time was known as 'the Pope of Marxism' but who, after attacking the Bolshevik conception of the 'dictatorship of the proletariat', was dubbed by Lenin and his followers the 'renegade Kautsky') wrote: 'Communism has come to mean quite different things in different minds, and quite different policies can hence be pursued in its name. As a descriptive, analytical category, "Communism" has thus become useless, that is, it is no longer meaningful to describe a particular individual, movement, organization, system, or ideology as "Communist".'[10]

Although an exaggeration, there was a significant element of truth in that statement, especially in relation to individuals. A point I made in the Introduction bears repetition. To be told that a person was a Communist, meaning a member of a Communist party, could convey surprisingly little about the person's basic beliefs and values. Even at the stage of a Communist seizure of power, there were revolutionaries who joined the party with a burning desire to construct a just and harmonious society and others whose primary goal was to wreak vengeance on their class enemies and who were more interested in destroying than building. Within an established Communist system, the differences became much wider. To make only the most obvious distinction, many people with little or no interest in Marxism-Leninism opted to join the Communist Party to advance their careers, while others took the official doctrine seriously. The former could be closet social democrats or liberals, even monarchists or fascists. Many evolved into conservatives, defenders of what had become the established order in which they had found a comfortable place. Reformers could rationalize their party membership differently – by telling themselves that only from within the party would it be possible to influence the course of change within their country. The extent to which that turned out to be true, or not true, in different Communist states will emerge in later chapters.

Not only was there a wide diversity of opinion among individual members of Communist parties. There were also substantial differences from one Communist country to another, persisting to the present day, as the cases of contemporary China and North Korea clearly illustrate. Yet there are certain common features which make it entirely meaningful to call a political system Communist. When these are specified, it becomes clear that the only Communist regime that has ever existed in Latin America is that of Cuba. The Chilean government headed by Salvador Allende from 1970 until it was overthrown in a military coup in 1973 was not, by any stretch of the imagination, Communist, although it included some members of the Communist Party in its ruling socialist coalition.[11] And no African state has ever been Communist. The term 'Communist' should be used precisely and parsimoniously. It should not be applied indiscriminately to any government which contains Marxists or to Third World dictators who have employed vaguely Marxist rhetoric. It is worth noting also that a system can stop being Communist even when its 'Communist' rulers have not actually been overthrown. Thus, as will be argued in a later chapter, the Soviet Union ceased to be a Communist system in the course of 1989, although its chief executive was the same person at the beginning of that year and its end, namely Mikhail Gorbachev, and though the Soviet state did not come to an end until December 1991. China, as a later chapter will attempt to show, is today a hybrid, possessing still some essential features of Communism but having discarded others.

It may seem paradoxical to specify what Communist systems have in common as a prelude to showing their diversity and how they change, but it is a necessary preliminary if we are adequately to comprehend the differences between one Communist country and another and the significance of political change over time in a variety of Communist states. Of course, 'Communism' was used in everyday discourse throughout most of the twentieth century, especially in the years of the Cold War. Without defining the term, many people had an adequate idea of what they meant by it, though what made Communist systems different from other totalitarian or authoritarian systems was seldom spelled out. In a largely misplaced effort, political scientists who studied the USSR spent a lot of time inventing a variety of labels for the Soviet Union and arguing about which was the most appropriate, often missing the more basic point that the term which most illuminatingly encapsulated the system was Communist. Indeed, the Soviet Union was the archetypal Communist system, and hugely influential, even though the Soviet state and society themselves changed significantly over time.

The defining characteristics of a Communist system are, as I see them, six. They can be grouped into three pairs, relating, first, to the political system; second, to the economic system; and, third, to ideology. The first two categories also, of course, have substantial ideological content, but in a more operational, not merely aspirational, sense.

The Political System

The *first* defining feature of a Communist system is *the monopoly of power of the Communist Party*. In Stalin's time this was known as 'the dictatorship of the proletariat', since it was taken as axiomatic that the party represented the interests, and the real will, of the proletariat (if they knew what was good for them). In the post-Stalin period, especially from the beginning of the 1960s, the more common official term was 'the *leading role* of the party'. There were other important institutions within a Communist state besides the ruling party, among them government ministries, the military, and the security police, but all the senior officials in the ministries were party members, as were all military and security police officers. Every ministry, as well as every military unit and branch of the political police, also had its primary party organization – in the earlier days known as the party cell. Moreover, every organization – whether ministry, military, police or judiciary – was supervised by an appropriately specialized department of the Central Committee of the party. Within Communist states there was only a partial differentiation of functions and no separation of powers. All institutions were overseen by the organs of the Communist party, which had a higher authority than any other body.

By the beginning of the 1980s variants of the concept of the 'leading role of the party' appeared in the constitutions of all consolidated Communist states, including Vietnam, where the whole country had been Communist only since 1976. Three examples illustrate the general point. The relevant passage (Article 6) of the 1977 Soviet constitution began: 'The leading and guiding force of Soviet society and the nucleus of its political system, of all state organizations and public organizations, is the Communist Party of the Soviet Union.' The last sentence of the preamble to the 1979 constitution of the Mongolian People's Republic read: 'In the M.P.R., the guiding and directing force of society and of the state is the Mongolian People's Revolutionary Party, which is guided in its activities by the all-conquering theory of Marxism-Leninism.' In the case of Vietnam, Article 4 of the 1980 constitution declared: 'The Communist Party of Vietnam, the vanguard and general staff of the Vietnamese working class, armed with Marxism-Leninism, is the only force leading the state and society, and the main factor determining all successes of the Vietnamese revolution.'

The monopoly of power of the Communist Party long preceded its mention in most of the constitutions. Indeed, this was what the 'dictatorship of the proletariat' meant in practice, since it was the *party* which dictated policy in the name of the proletariat. In Communist states the politics of power always trumped law. Courts and judges were not independent, and in periods before the constitutions mentioned the party's 'leading role', the ruling parties in Communist countries were in no way inhibited from dominating the other institutions of the state. It could even, therefore, be regarded as a sign of modest progress when from the 1970s the constitutions were brought somewhat closer to existing political reality.

The *second* defining feature of a Communist system was a concept which has already cropped up in this book, *democratic centralism* – a term adopted by Lenin and invoked throughout the entire Communist era. In theory it meant that there could be discussion of issues – the 'democratic' component – until a decision had been reached, but thereafter the decision of higher party organs was binding and had to be implemented in a strictly disciplined manner throughout the party and society. Communist ideologists liked to compare 'democratic centralism' (good) with 'bureaucratic centralism' (bad). The latter denoted party officials acting in a high-handed manner, *not* taking into account the views of party members, including party committees at various levels, even in the early stages of policy-making. In political reality, democratic centralism *was* bureaucratic centralism. It became the codename for a rigidly hierarchical, severely disciplined party in which rights of discussion and debate were rigorously circumscribed. Though in principle many different interpretations of 'democratic centralism' could be offered, in practice in Communist systems the slogan was appropriated, at times of intra-party struggle, by those who wished to maintain strictly hierarchical, disciplined relations within the ruling party, to restrict free debate, and to prevent horizontal, as distinct from vertical, links between party organizations. It became both the name for a defining feature of Communist systems and the euphemism for one of the pillars on which such systems rested.

A combination of the Communist Party's 'leading role' and its highly centralized character meant that a vast amount of power was concentrated in the highest party organs – the Central Committee with its powerful Secretariat and departments. Even more power lay with its inner body, the Politburo (Political Bureau) and in the hands of the individual who stood at the apex of the system, the General Secretary. The relationship between the individual top leader and the Politburo varied greatly over time and from one country to another. In other words, while oligarchical rule has been the norm in a majority of Communist countries at most times, the power of the top leader in a number of instances has been such that the system became essentially autocratic – a personal dictatorship rather than collective rule by an oligarchy. The elevation of the party leader over his colleagues reached extreme heights under Stalin during the second and third of his three decades in power in the Soviet Union, under Mao Zedong in China, and under Kim Il-Sung and then his son Kim Jong-Il in North Korea. The pronouncements of Stalin, from at least the mid-1930s until his death in 1953, were accorded a status which put them on a par with those of

Marx and Lenin. In China, 'Mao Zedong Thought', understood as the definitive adaptation of Marxism to Chinese conditions, was raised on a pedestal
higher than Leninism. Even after some modification of the 'cult of personality' of Mao soon after his death, the 1978 Constitution of the People's
Republic of China put Mao's thought on a level comparable to that of Marx
and Lenin. Article 2 of that constitution stated: 'The guiding ideology of
the People's Republic of China is Marxism-Leninism-Mao Zedong Thought.'
As for North Korea, Kim Il-sung has been modestly described by the ruling
Communist Party as 'superior to Christ in love, superior to Buddha in benev-
olence, superior to Confucius in virtue and superior to Mohammed in
justice'.[12]

The Economic System

The *third* defining feature of a consolidated Communist system is *non-capitalist ownership of the means of production*, and linked to this is the *fourth* – the
dominance of a *command economy, as distinct from a market economy*. Even in
established Communist systems some private economic activity continued,
whether on a legal or illegal basis – or, quite commonly, as a mixture of both.
In agriculture, in particular, exceptions in favour of private enterprise were
not uncommon, and in two of the systems (Yugoslavia and Poland) the preponderant part of agriculture was in private hands. However, non-agricultural
production within established Communist systems was state owned and
controlled. State or social ownership of the means of production was regarded
as one of the basic objectives of all ruling Communist parties.

This was combined with the *fourth* defining feature of a Communist
system – a command economy. Its essential features are well summarized
by Philip Hanson, a prominent specialist on the Soviet economy:

> The fundamental difference from a market economy was that decisions about
> what should be produced and in what quantities, and at what prices that
> output should be sold, were the result of a hierarchical, top-down process
> culminating in instructions 'from above' to all producers; they were not the
> result of decentralised decisions resulting from interactions between customers
> and suppliers. Producers were concerned above all to meet targets set by plan-
> ners. They had no particular reason to concern themselves with the wishes
> of the users of their products, nor with the activities of competitors. Indeed
> the concept of competition was absent: other producers in the same line of
> activity were simply not competitors but fellow-executors of the state plan.[13]

There were ministries for each major branch of industry, which were in turn supervised by the state planning committee and by departments of the Central Committee of the Communist Party. At the apex of the system was the Politburo, for the polity and economy were even more intertwined in Communist than in capitalist states.

While there was scope for disagreement among Communists on how the economy should be organized, the overtly ideological character of the system also imposed limits. If leaders were to go beyond these, they would be embarking on the risky path of systemic change. As the political economist Alec Nove put it: 'Ideological commitment limits choice. Most people, presented with a cheese and a ham sandwich, can choose either. An Orthodox rabbi can not. The Bolsheviks could not choose to revive the Stolypin reform, or long tolerate a mixed economy.'[14] Thus, all four features of a Communist system discussed so far – the leading role of the Communist Party, democratic centralism, state ownership of the means of production, and a command rather than market economy – have a strong ideological component. They were part of the belief system of the Bolsheviks and of their Communist successors who held that 'socialism', as they understood that concept, was not only a higher stage of development than capitalism, but also one which was inevitable. However, the process could be speeded up, and successfully directed, only if political power was firmly in the hands of the party. These defining features of Communism, while ideologically significant, were also of clear organizational importance. They were part of the operational code of Communist rule with an everyday relevance to the task of maintaining power. That was obviously true of the monopoly of power of a highly disciplined ruling party. The merging of political and economic power served the same purpose. The absence of private ownership and a market economy meant that the state had control over the career possibilities of all its citizens. To fall foul of the state authorities at times led to imprisonment or death. Even, however, in more relaxed periods of Communist rule, to dissent publicly from the state authorities meant that a person's career was threatened, for there was no one else you could turn to for employment.

The Ideological Sphere

Communism was an all-encompassing system of beliefs. It purported to offer a key to understanding social development. It had authorities whose word could not be questioned, and whose interpreters and guardians acted also as gatekeepers, deciding who 'belonged' and who did not. The last two defining features of a Communist system belong, even more than the previous four, to this ideological sphere. The *fifth* such feature of a Communist system I take to be the *declared aim of building communism* as the ultimate, legitimizing goal. Clearly, in terms of everyday politics, this was much less important than the 'leading role' of the party or democratic centralism. It was, though, a feature which differentiated Communist systems both from other totalitarian or authoritarian regimes and from countries governed by socialist parties of a social democratic type. It had an important place in the official ideology, even though it was not of immediate practical import. In the early years after a Communist party had come to power, the idea of the building of communism doubtless had some motivational and inspirational significance for at least a substantial number of party activists. As years went by, though, there were ever fewer believers in the notion of a harmonious society in which the state would have withered away. And yet a Communist leadership could not renounce this goal without abandoning one of the sources of their legitimacy (such as that was). As Nove put it, writing in early 1989 when dramatic change in the Soviet system was under way:

> The essential point is that the open debate is now concerned with the very essence, the fundamentals, of the Soviet system – this for the first time in living memory. What kind of society did they have, and where are they now? Where are they going? One has a feeling that no one quite knows. Does this matter? After all, where are *we* going? In the Soviet Union it does matter, since the legitimacy of party rule rests upon its role of leading the people towards a goal.[15]

If political activity knows, in the words of Michael Oakeshott, 'neither starting-place nor appointed destination',[16] a political party could not claim the right to rule on the grounds that it had discerned how to guide society to an ultimate goal. It was because, however, Marxist-Leninist ideologists claimed that there *was* an appointed destination – that of communism, the classless, self-administering society – that they could justify the permanent exercise of the leading role of the Communist party. It was that party which possessed the theoretical insight and the practical experience to guide less advanced citizens to this radiant future.

While successive leaders of ruling Communist parties sincerely believed in the 'leading role' of the party and in democratic centralism, since this directly served their interests, it is open to doubt whether any Soviet party leader after Nikita Khrushchev (who headed the CPSU from 1953 until his forcible removal in 1964) believed in the future communist society in anything like Marx's or Lenin's sense. The same scepticism is in order about East European Communist leaders. However, whatever their private reservations, none of these leaders could publicly renounce the destination, for they led a goal-directed party and society. The doyen of Australian specialists on Communist systems, T.H. Rigby, wrote some years ago:

> In communist societies the structural and ideological features of a country totally mobilised for war have been converted into a permanent, 'normal' condition. The 'war', however, in which they engaged, is the 'struggle for communism'. 'Our Goal is Communism!' proclaims the enormous banner in the machine-shop, and indeed it is in terms of this goal that the Politburo justifies its Five-Year Plan guidelines, that Gosplan spells these out into annual and quarterly plans for the industry concerned, and that the ministry running it translates into specific targets for the particular plant, and the latter's management sets the tasks of individual workshops and workers.[17]

The final goal was the justification for all the toil and hardship that might be encountered along the way. Once that goal was abandoned, Communist regimes were in danger of being judged – and found wanting – on the basis of their capacity to deliver more immediate results. Without the goal of communism, the 'leading role' of the party would become far harder to legitimize. The moment leaders were to come clean on the fact that their aspirations were for more mundane improvements and that communism was a mythical heaven-on-earth, Communist parties could no longer be perceived as the possessors of sacred truth, and political religion would give way to secularization.

That the last leader of the Communist Party of the Soviet Union, Mikhail Gorbachev, although devoted to what he called the 'socialist idea', had long been sceptical about the ultimate goal of communism was evident from the fact that he recalled with relish a joke from Khrushchev's time, albeit committing it to print only after the Soviet Union had ceased to exist:

> A certain lecturer, speaking about future communist society, concluded with the following remarks, 'The breaking day of communism is already visible, gleaming just over the horizon.' At this point an old peasant who had been sitting in the front row stood up and asked, 'Comrade Lecturer, what is a horizon?' The lecturer explained that it is a line where the earth and the sky seem to meet, having the unique characteristic that the more you move toward it, the more it moves away. The old peasant responded: 'Thank you, Comrade Lecturer. Now everything is quite clear.'[18]

The *sixth* defining feature of Communism was the *existence of, and sense of belonging to, an international Communist movement*. This did not necessarily mean that the party concerned was officially called the 'Communist Party'. Communist parties in many countries changed their names over time, whether in an attempt to broaden the base of their support or to suggest that they were offering something new. Thus, for example, the Hungarian party, throughout the period 1948–89, was known successively as the Hungarian Communist Party, the Hungarian Workers' Party, and the Hungarian Socialist Workers' Party.[19] What mattered was that Communists both within and outside Hungary recognized the party as Communist. Equally, their opponents had no difficulty in similarly identifying them. In this book I use not only the official title of such a party at any given time but also the generic term Communist party, for any ruling or non-ruling party accepted as a member of the international Communist movement.

The existence of that movement was of great ideological significance. It was the supposed internationalism of Communism which attracted many of its adherents. Stalin had, of course, recognized the reality of the Soviet Union's early isolation when he came up with the doctrine of 'socialism in one country', and even the Communist International – the Comintern – had served above all Soviet interests. Yet there was a dual-track policy in Moscow whereby the Comintern concerned themselves with the international Communist movement while the Ministry of Foreign Affairs dealt with the more immediately practical business of state-to-state relations. The Comintern was abolished in 1943, when the Soviet Union was in coalition with the Western democracies in the war against Hitler's Germany. Between 1947 and 1956 a body called the Cominform (the Communist Information Bureau) existed, but it had both a more limited membership and more limited functions than the Comintern. The real successor to the Comintern in terms of keeping an eye on non-ruling Communist parties and revolutionary movements was the International Department of the Central Committee of the Communist Party of the Soviet Union. The continuity was exemplified in the person of Boris Ponomarev, who from 1955 until 1985 headed the International Department, having in the 1930s served on the staff of Georgi Dimitrov in the Comintern. The International Department provided not only guidance and encouragement but also frequently monetary help for non-ruling Communist parties, including small ones which seemed unlikely ever to come to power.

For individual members of Communist parties the consciousness of belonging to a great international movement was of huge importance, the more so if their own party occupied only a small part of the political spectrum in their home country. Writing in 1969, Eric Hobsbawm, a distinguished

historian and longstanding member of the Communist Party, whose childhood was spent in Central Europe and his adult life in Britain, observed:

> Today, when the international communist movement has largely ceased to
> exist as such, it is hard to recapture the immense strength which its members
> drew from the consciousness of being soldiers in a single international army,
> operating, with whatever tactical multiformity and flexibility, a single grand
> strategy of world revolution. Hence the impossibility of any fundamental or
> long-term conflict between the interest of a national movement and the
> International, which was the *real* party, of which the national units were no
> more than disciplined sections.[20]

Raphael Samuel was born almost two decades later than Hobsbawm, the
son of a militant Communist mother. He himself joined the CPGB but,
when still a young man, became a leading figure in 'the first New Left' of
British intellectuals who broke with Communism, but not with Marxism.[21]
He too testifies to the significance of internationalism for true Communist
believers. At one with Hobsbawm in his emphasis on the supranational, his
imagery is, in contrast, far more religious than military:

> The Communism of my childhood was universalist. We no longer advocated
> World Revolution, but we believed that socialism was a cosmic process, and
> though allowing for the existence of national peculiarities (we only half
> believed in them), we thought of the transition from capitalism to socialism
> as being 'identical' in content everywhere. Communism, like medieval
> Christendom, was one and indivisible, an international fellowship of faith . . .
> 'one great vision' uniting us, in the words of a communist song.
> Internationalism was not an option but a necessity of our political being, a
> touchstone of honour and worth.[22]

Among members of the worldwide Communist movement, there were
many who were genuinely devoted to the ideal of internationalism, but
since they recognized the unique role of the Soviet Union as the country
which had successfully put their ideology in power, and which thus served
as a teacher and exemplar, they became vulnerable to being used as instruments of Soviet state policy and of shifting coalitions within the highest
power structures in Moscow. 'What convinced in Lenin,' Hobsbawm has
written, 'was not so much his socio-economic analysis . . . but his palpable
genius for organizing a revolutionary party and mastering the tactics and
strategy of making a revolution.'[23] For non-ruling parties the international
Communist movement was, accordingly, something to which they for long

voluntarily submitted, believing both in its collective wisdom and in the special authority which accrued to the party that had been led by Lenin.

To be recognized as part of the international Communist movement by the existing members distinguished Communist countries and parties from socialist governments and parties of a social democratic type. Given that the Soviet and other Communist states described themselves as 'socialist', being accepted as a member meant conforming to 'socialism' in their terms. For many Communist governments, this was unproblematical, since they owed their existence to Soviet support, but it involved accepting Soviet leadership (and at times crude domination) of the international Communist movement. For Communist parties which had made their own revolutions – as was the case, for example, with Albania, China and Yugoslavia – it was much more difficult to accommodate themselves to Soviet hegemony. Their relationship with the Soviet-dominated international Communist movement will be discussed in later chapters. Other countries, in which Communist rule had been installed under the aegis of the Soviet Union, in due course also found ways of asserting their independence. Some of them ceased to meet several of the six criteria of a Communist system even before the ruling party lost its monopoly of power. The variety of ways in which that happened is explored in Parts 4 and 5 of this book. Before that, however, we need to examine the spread of Communism from the Second World War until Stalin's death – the theme of Part 2.

PART TWO

COMMUNISM ASCENDANT

7

The Appeals of Communism

In most Western countries the Communist Party was *not* the major party of the left at any point in the seventy years separating the formation of the Comintern in 1919 from the fall of Communism in Europe in 1989. More commonly, Communists were but a tiny minority of the population. With their organization and discipline, they could, however, sometimes wield influence well in excess of their numerical strength, especially in the trade union movement. What kind of people became Communists differed significantly in countries where the Communists were the main alternative to conservative or liberal parties from those, more common in Europe, in which Communist membership and electoral support trailed far behind socialist parties of a social democratic type.

In France, Italy and, to a lesser extent, Finland, the Communist Party was, however, for much of that seventy-year period a serious political force. In the first post-Second World War elections these were the three democratic countries in which the Communists did best, except for Czechoslovakia where they emerged as the largest single party in free elections in 1946. In the Czech lands of Bohemia and Moravia the Communist Party got 40 per cent of the vote (well ahead of the socialists), although in Slovakia its support was significantly lower at 30 per cent. The appeals of Communism in Czechoslovakia owed much to disillusionment with the Western powers for colluding with Hitler – in the Munich Agreement of 1938 – to hand over part of Czech territory to Germany; to the Czechs' historically good relations with Russia; and to the role of Soviet troops as the principal liberators of their country from German occupation. The Czechs and Slovaks were not to know that this would be their last free election for more than four decades. For the majority of those who supported the Communist Party at the polls, that was not what they were voting for. The immediate post-war years were, however, a time of genuine enthusiasm for 'building socialism' in Czechoslovakia, although different people meant different things by that notion.

In the other countries where the Communist Party did relatively well in the first post-World War Two elections, and which, unlike Czechoslovakia, *remained* democracies, the Communists attracted, in broad terms, between a fifth and a quarter of the electorate (26 per cent in France, 23.5 per cent in Finland and 19 per cent in Italy).[1] It was many years before the socialist parties overtook the Communists in France and Italy as the main party of the left, though in Finland this was achieved as early as 1948.[2] The very fact that in Italy the Communists constituted over several decades the party which seemed to be the main spokesman for working-class interests meant that comparatively recent immigrants were not (as was the case in countries as diverse as the United States, Canada, Britain and South Africa) a major component of their membership. This was, on the contrary, made up almost entirely from the indigenous population.[3] That was true up to a point also of France, especially in comparison with the English-speaking countries. However, in the 1920s and 1930s there was a large influx of immigrants, especially Poles, Italians and Spaniards, many of whom became industrial workers, with some being drawn into the Communist movement.[4]

The Communist Party was, moreover, quite effective in appealing to regional groups who felt neglected by the political elite in both France and Italy. France, in particular, with its own Jacobin tradition, was a natural home for a revolutionary party. The PCF made the most of this, portraying the Bolshevik revolution as a continuation of the French Revolution of 1789 and noting Lenin's affinity to Robespierre.[5] Class, even more than regional, differences throughout the twentieth century were sharp, as was the predominance of elitist educational institutions which, in turn, were a gateway to political power and influence. Intellectuals who had gone to French universities – most notably the Sorbonne in Paris, rather than the exclusive *grandes écoles* – were also a social group from which the PCF recruited in large numbers. The attraction of Communist ideas thus, at least partly, cut across the class divide, with the goals of the Communist Party being seen in France and also in Italy as 'coinciding with the socialist-humanitarian aspirations which were deeply rooted in those countries before the advent of Communism'.[6]

More generally, we can say that the appeals of Communism worldwide included country-specific factors; international developments (whether the Great Depression of the early 1930s or the rise of fascism later in that decade); and the varying attraction of the Soviet Union at different times. The last point is of great importance. Depending on the period and on the eyes of the beholder, the Soviet Union could be perceived as a model to be admired and copied or, alternatively, as a dreadful warning. The policies of the Comintern, heavily influenced (to put it at its mildest) by Soviet

interests, also played a different role at various times. In both Europe and
North America there was a deep economic depression at the end of the
1920s and mass unemployment at that time and in the early 1930s. That
led some recruits directly to the Communist Party, but the worst years of
the economic slump in the West coincided with the Comintern's Third
Period of narrow sectarianism which reduced the attractiveness of this
apparent alternative to a crisis-riven capitalism. As a result, in most countries the Communist parties picked up more members in the later 1930s
than earlier in the decade, even though by then the Western economies
had begun to recover and although the years 1936–38 were ones of show
trials and massive purges in the Soviet Union. The change in Comintern
policy and in the international situation played crucial parts in the expansion of Communist ranks in the later 1930s. The period between 1935 and
1939 was, as noted already in Chapter 5, that of the Popular Front. The
threat of fascism, combined with the Comintern's call for solidarity in the
face of it, was much more conducive to winning new supporters than its
earlier policy of making no distinction between democratic socialists and
fascists. The fast-growing Soviet economy, with its Five-Year Plans and full
employment, was also a source of attraction. It seemed to many in the
West, dissatisfied with what they saw as avoidable hardship occasioned by
a capricious capitalism, that a system of central planning provided a more
rational way of running an economy than the booms and busts of the
inter-war market economy.

Since even in the inter-war years (not to speak of the Cold War era) party
membership was treated with great suspicion in Western democracies, there
was a much wider body of people who were highly sympathetic to the
Soviet Union and to the Communist Party than those who actually took
out a membership card. They became known as the 'fellow travellers'.
Although the leaderships of the democratic socialist parties generally
distanced themselves from Communism and, as noted in an earlier chapter,
the strongest of them, the British Labour Party, took pains to prevent
Communists joining their ranks as individual members, some non-
Communist socialist intellectuals turned out to be especially starry-eyed
admirers of the Soviet Union.

Writers and Communism

The American novelist Howard Fast, the product of a poverty-stricken childhood, was working in a Harlem branch of the New York Public Library
when in 1932 a female librarian gave him George Bernard Shaw's *The Intelligent*

Woman's Guide to Socialism and Capitalism[7] to read. Fast recalled that he read through this 'wonderful book' in one night and 'Shaw was my idol and teacher ever afterwards'.[8] British Communists who joined the CPGB before or during the Second World War frequently mention this same book, first published in 1928 and in an updated paperback edition in 1937, as the work which converted them to a belief in socialism – and Communism. The Irish playwright, who spent his adult life in England and was one of the most prominent of the early Fabians, wrote much more accessible prose than that of the classical Marxist theorists. While strongly sympathetic to the Soviet Union, and taking a benign view of both Lenin and Stalin, Shaw was, nevertheless, sceptical about the turning of Marxism into a political religion. Although he noted that he himself had been convinced of the superiority of socialism over capitalism by reading Marx's *Capital*, he wrote in 1927 (for publication in 1928):

> There is, however, a danger against which you should be on your guard. Socialism may be preached, not as a far-reaching economic reform, but as a new Church founded on a new revelation of the will of God made by a new prophet . . . They preach an inevitable, final, supreme category in the order of the universe in which all the contradictions of the earlier and lower categories will be reconciled . . . Their prophet is named neither Jesus nor Mahomet nor Luther nor Augustine . . . but Karl Marx . . . Two of their tenets contradict one another . . . One is that the evolution of Capitalism into Socialism is predestined, implying that we have nothing to do but sit down and wait for it to occur. This is their version of Salvation by Faith. The other is that it must be effected by a revolution establishing a dictatorship of the proletariat. This is their version of Salvation by Works.[9]

Arguing that Marx was a teacher from whom much could be learned, not someone to be worshipped as an 'infallible prophet', Shaw urged his readers not to vote for anyone who spoke contemptuously of Marx, but added: 'Do not, however, vote for a Marxist fanatic either, unless you can catch one young enough or acute enough to grow out of Marxism after a little experience, as Lenin did.'[10] While Lenin certainly adapted Marxism to Russian conditions, whether the pre-revolutionary society or the exigencies of government, the idea that he 'grew out of Marxism' is but one of Shaw's more dubious observations on the Soviet scene.

The poet Hugh McDiarmid who, in the course of a contentious life, managed to get himself expelled at different times from the Communist Party for being a Scottish nationalist and from the Scottish National Party as a Communist, had an even more exalted view of Lenin than did Shaw.

In his poem 'First Hymn to Lenin', he compares him to Christ and says that Lenin marked the greatest turning point in the history of humanity since the birth of Christianity.* He makes clear his awareness of the killings perpetrated by the punitive arm of the Bolshevik revolution, the Cheka, but takes a cosmic view of their activities as both necessary and insignificant. What matters is 'wha [whom] we kill' in order:

> To lessen that foulest murder that deprives
> Maist [most] men o' real lives.[11]

That poem by McDiarmid is dedicated to Prince D.S. Mirsky, who fought on the side of the Whites in the Russian civil war, emigrated to Britain in 1921, taught Russian literature at the University of London, and acquired a growing enthusiasm for what he saw as a 'National Bolshevism' developing in Russia. He joined the British Communist Party in 1931 and returned to his homeland in 1932. Five years later he was arrested by the secret police. He perished in a Soviet labour camp in 1939.

The most notorious example of Fabian socialists becoming infatuated with 'the Soviet experiment' is that of Sidney and Beatrice Webb. They wrote a vast book which purported to show in detail how the Soviet Union was governed. Called *Soviet Communism: A New Civilization?* when it was first published in 1935, it appeared in its second edition with the question mark removed. Writing in October 1937, the Webbs observe: 'What we have learnt of the developments during 1936–1937 has persuaded us to withdraw the interrogation mark.'[12] The Webbs wrote much other work worthy of respect (including, not least, the first of Beatrice's two autobiographical volumes, *My Apprenticeship*) – and they were the main founders in 1895 of a great educational institution, the London School of Economics and Political Science. In their October 1937 preface to the second edition of *Soviet Communism*, they self-deprecatingly ascribe their writing of an enormous book on the USSR 'to the recklessness of old age'. They add that their reputation 'will naturally stand or fall upon our entire output of the past half-century, to the load of which one more book makes no appreciable difference'.[13] However, it would have been

---

* This poem was first published under a different title, 'To Lenin', in an anthology of *New English Poems*, edited by Lascelles Abercrombie, in 1930. By the following year it had become 'First Hymn to Lenin' and the title of a collection of McDiarmid's own verse. In another poem in that same volume, 'The Seamless Garment', addressed to a mill worker in McDiarmid's native Langholm, he describes Lenin as 'The best weaver Earth ever saw'.

better for their posthumous reputations not to have published a book replete with statements such as 'During the present year (1937) strenuous efforts have been made, both in the trade union organization and in the Communist Party, to cut out the dead wood.'[14] The year 1937 was that in which the physical annihilation of Communists reached a grotesque height, as the Great Purge hit the ruling party itself with full force. The Webbs engaged in mild, and misleadingly qualified, criticism of 'the deliberate discouragement and even repression, not of criticism of the administration, which is, we think, more persistent and more actively encouraged than in any other country, but of independent thinking on fundamental social issues . . .' in the Soviet Union.[15] However, they happily concluded that 'the ancient axiom of "Love your neighbour as yourself"' is embodied in Soviet society and that 'in the USSR there is no distinction between the code professed on Sundays and that practised on week-days'.[16] All that in the worst years of Stalinist repression.

Quite apart from socialist writers such as George Orwell, who were never attracted to Communism – with Orwell's *Animal Farm* (1944) and *Nineteen Eighty-Four* (1949) providing two of the most effective indictments of Stalinism and totalitarianism – there were also writers who did feel the pull of Communism but who before the end of the 1930s had seen through the fundamental falsity of Stalin's Soviet Union. The most prominent among them was the French writer André Gide (like Shaw, a winner of the Nobel Prize for Literature). Gide, without joining the party, was attracted by Communist ideals and the kind of society he thought was being developed in the Soviet Union. In 1932 he wrote: 'My conversion is like a faith . . . In the deplorable state of distress of the modern world, the plan of the Soviet Union seems to me to point to salvation. Everything persuades me of this . . . And if my life were necessary to assure the success of the Soviet Union, I would gladly give it immediately.'[17]

On the invitation of the official writers' organization in the Soviet Union, Gide visited Russia in 1936. While many other foreign authors were flattered by the attention they received, with numerous banquets being given in their honour, Gide was repelled by being offered 'all the prerogatives and privileges which I abhorred in the old world', since he had not failed to observe the widespread poverty in the USSR.[18] He also discovered that the officially approved 'criticism and self-criticism' was a sham. Although he was on the kind of politically sanitized conducted tour which had deadened the intellectual faculties of many another foreign visitor during this period of 'high Stalinism', Gide, in contrast to them, wrote:

It is not the Party line which is discussed or criticized, but only the question whether a certain theory tallies or not with this sacred line. No state of mind is more dangerous than this, nor more likely to imperil real culture. Soviet citizens remain in the most complete ignorance of everything outside their own country and – what is worse – have been persuaded that everything abroad is vastly inferior to everything at home. On the other hand, although they are not interested in what prevails outside their country, they are very much interested in what foreigners think of them. What they are very anxious to know is whether they are sufficiently admired abroad . . . what they want from them is praise and not information.[19]

In contrast, Arthur Koestler, a central European Communist in the fullest geographical sense – born in Budapest to an Austrian mother and Hungarian father, educated in Vienna, but a member of the German Communist Party from 1931 – was able to rationalize the poverty he saw at first hand in the Soviet Union in 1932–33, including the ravages of famine in Ukraine. He remained in the Communist Party until 1938. What finally led to his resignation was his experience as a journalist with the republican side in the Spanish Civil War and, still more, the purges in the Soviet Union in 1936–38, in which his brother-in-law and two of his closest personal friends were arrested on absurd charges. Koestler's influential novel Darkness at Noon, published in 1940, sensitively portrays an old Bolshevik, Rubashov, arrested and shot at the age of forty – the same age as was Nikolai Bukharin, to whom Rubashov bears a resemblance, when he was shot in the Great Purge. Rubashov is persuaded that his 'last service to the Party' is to confess to the fabricated charges brought against him in order 'to avoid awakening sympathy and pity' among the population as a whole, since the arousal of such feelings would be dangerous for the party and the Communist cause.[20]

Social and Psychological Appeals

In the case of non-ruling Communist parties, it was not generally the poorest in the community who joined – not so much the unemployed or unskilled workers as skilled and semi-skilled workers. What was true of the British Communist Party membership applied also to many other European parties – the recruits were drawn largely from well-organized sections of the working class, notably engineers, miners, and builders. There was also generally a fair sprinkling of teachers, especially those who had themselves come from politically conscious working-class backgrounds.[21] The Scottish and Welsh coalfields provided some of the CPGB's leading members, and though the party's General Secretary over many years, Harry Pollitt, was a Lancashire boilermaker before becoming a full-time party official, the English membership of the party was never proportional to their overwhelming numerical predominance in the British population. After the lengthy period in which Pollitt and Palme Dutt were the principal duo within the CPGB, members of Jewish origin (discussed in a broader context in the next section), as well as Scots, held a large number of positions of leadership. The Welsh miners' leader, Arthur Horner, who, after heading the South Wales Miners' Federation, became Secretary-General of the National Union of Mineworkers, was also one of the most prominent Communists from the 1930s to the 1950s. For a leading party member he showed an unusual independence of mind and a willingness to defy party discipline – to the extent that he was accused as early as 1931, and on more than one subsequent occasion, of 'opportunistic deviations' and of 'Hornerism'. Irish immigrants to Britain, many of whom worked in the building industry, were quite strongly represented in the Communist Party, even though the Catholic Church in Britain, as elsewhere, was in the forefront of opposition to the Communists. A number of the Catholic converts to Communism were, indeed, rebelling against their upbringing.

While the Communist Party attracted people who were vehemently opposed to conventional religion, it is notable how many members of non-ruling Communist parties (as distinct from party members in Communist states) have compared their belief in the party to religious conviction. That applies to many who remained in the Communist Party as well as those who left it. The religious-like zeal of their commitment to the Communist cause was especially true in the smaller parties, whether these were clandestine organizations in authoritarian regimes or more open ones within democracies. It also, however, varied over time. It was more true of those who joined the Communist Party before, rather than after, 1956 when Nikita Khrushchev's speech to the Twentieth Party Congress of the CPSU, with its attack on Stalin, inadvertently exposed the myth of the party's infallibility.

It is important to recognize that many Western Communists joined the party dedicated to building a better society worldwide. If, however, they were to maintain their ideals while conforming to the twists and turns of policy – emanating in most of its essentials from Moscow – this required considerable intellectual contortions. Above all, it meant believing that those in higher authority knew better than they did what policies and tactics were required for Communism to prevail or holding the overriding belief that the long-term goal justified disciplined obedience and the suppression of doubts about any particular change of tack. At the time at which he joined the American Communist Party, Howard Fast felt that he had 'now become part of an edifice dedicated singularly and irrevocably to the ending of all war, injustice, hunger and human suffering – and to the brotherhood of man'.[22] Even after he had broken with Communism and had become a severe critic of it, Fast wrote: 'Intimately, I know only the Communist Party of the United States; yet of this tiny organization I can say, honestly and forthrightly and under oath if need be, that never in so small a group have I seen so many pure souls, so many gentle and good people, so many men and women of utter integrity.'[23] To the extent that this was true – and it does not sit well with turning a blind eye to, or condoning, mass terror in Stalin's Soviet Union – it was more applicable to rank-and-file members than to the party functionaries, who were in the forefront of defending the indefensible. The Communist Party leaders in Western democracies displayed no qualms about defending the arrests and executions in the Soviet Union during the 1930s. And Earl Browder, the American Communist Party leader, just six weeks before the signing of the Nazi Soviet Pact, denounced rumours of a German–Soviet rapprochement, saying there was as much chance of that happening 'as of Earl Browder being elected President of the Chamber of Commerce'.[24] He duly swung into line when the unthinkable occurred.

The life of the Communist Party member within a Western democracy also had something in common with that of members of a sectarian Church. Membership was extremely arduous and demanding. Such time as was left for social life was spent in the company of party comrades. People met their spouses in the party, and when this was not possible because of the under-representation of women, the male spouse was expected to recruit his wife to party membership, and usually did. A less common case was that of Betty Dowsett, who qualified as a doctor in 1943 and worked for the Medical Research Council before being dismissed, apparently on political grounds, in 1949. She became a bus conductor, married her driver, and before long succeeded in adding him to the ranks of the British Communist Party.[25]

For some who joined the Communist Party, a search for belief and a craving for certainty were important parts of their psychological make-up. One English Communist, Douglas Hyde, moved from being a young Methodist lay preacher, with an interest also in other religions, to becoming a Communist activist for twenty years, finishing up as news editor of the CPGB party newspaper, the *Daily Worker*, before resigning from the party in 1948 to become a proselytising member of the Catholic Church. Although Hyde's political memoir, *I Believed*, written in the late Stalin period, is also a reasoned attack on Communist Party strategy and tactics, it holds that a majority of those attracted to Communism in those years were 'subconsciously looking for a cause which will fill the void left by unbelief, or, as in my own case, an insecurely held belief which is failing to satisfy them intellectually and spiritually'.[26] Raphael Samuel, who, when he left the CPGB, was not tempted by any religious substitute but became one of the leading intellectual voices of the British New Left, has written: 'Joining the Party was experienced as a momentous event, equivalent in its intensity, as numerous memoirs testify, to taking a decision for Christ, and it is indicative of this that new recruits, according to a phrase in common currency, were those who had "seen the light". By the same token full-time organizers – translated rather than elected to their posts – were obeying a vocation or call.'[27]

Although joining the party was less often seen in quite such terms in a mass party such as that in Italy, a study of the PCI by Robert Putnam in the 1970s found that, as compared with other Italian political activists, whether of the left or right, Communists defined 'their satisfactions more often in terms of commitment to broad ideals and goals, less often in terms of opportunity for personal influence'.[28] Italian Communist deputies were found to be much more optimistic at that time than their political opponents, and inclined to describe their politics as 'life itself' or as 'not a career, but a mission'.[29] The generalizations of Raphael Samuel about Communism as like 'a church militant'[30] are, on the whole, more applicable to Communist parties which were out of the mainstream of their countries' political life than to those of, say, France, Italy or Finland, and they applied more to some generations of Communists – particularly those who joined at any time between the Bolshevik revolution and the death of Stalin – than to those who became party members as late as the 1970s. Nevertheless, there is a broad applicability to Communist parties internationally in what Samuel writes on the basis of his own intra-party experience:

> The ambitions of the Communist Party – and the self-perception of members – were unmistakably theocratic. Organizationally, we conceived ourselves to be a communion of the elect, covenanted to a sacred cause. Politically, we aspired to be teachers and guides. As a visible church, we traced an unbroken line of descent from the founding fathers, claiming scriptural precedent for our policies . . . Authority in the Party was theocratic too, an institutionalized form of charisma which operated at every level of Party life. Reports were handed down with all the majesty of encyclicals and studied as closely as if they were Bible texts.[31]

Part of the attraction of Communism for many – and it was an especial comfort for members of the smaller parties – was the emphasis in the doctrine on inevitability. If all history was a history of class struggles in which the penultimate stage – before the establishment of socialism and its higher phase, a classless communism – was the assured victory of the proletariat, led by its vanguard party, then it was possible to look to the future with optimism. As one former member of the British Communist Party put it: 'The emphasis on inevitability in the theory is a tremendous comfort. It counterbalances the discouragement of failure in one's own lifetime.'[32]

While this psychological dimension to the appeal of Communism was of significance quite generally, there were other, still more important factors at work in the countries where Communism was most successful. Asian Communism, as will become clearer in later chapters, owed much of its success in China, Vietnam, Laos and Korea – as well as its significant support, which fell short of taking power nationally, in India, Indonesia and the Philippines – to its identification with anti-colonialism and national liberation. While in the West European countries where the Communist Party was strongest, nationalism did not play anything like so large a role, there was in the French Communist Party a strong identification with a current to be found more broadly in French society – namely, resistance to the encroachment of American culture, not to mention suspicion of the American military presence in Western Europe following the Second World War. Of course, the emphasis of the PCF on the French revolutionary tradition and the attempts of Communist intellectuals to present themselves as 'the zealous guardians of French culture against the rising tide of American barbarity' ran up against the contradiction 'between a class-based and national conception of culture'.[33] No less of a contradiction was the French Communists' acceptance of the ideological and, to some extent, cultural hegemony of Moscow at the same time as they made a virtue of rejecting that of Washington, New York and Los Angeles. That is not to deny that French Communism had its own indigenous roots. Although the development of the Soviet system after 1917 exerted a strong appeal to French intellectuals, their identification with the PCF rested on 'the particular blend of Marxism, Leninism, and Jacobinism which was so unique to the political culture of the French left'.[34]

Up until the end of the 1970s, Communism appealed to a broad range of French intellectuals, but their influence within the party was kept within strict limits. The major constituency of the party consisted of workers, and not only did they predominate within the membership but most of the leading positions within the party were held by people who began as manual workers. For these officials of proletarian origin, social and economic conditions had been of prime importance at the time of their recruitment. France and Italy differed in this respect. A study of Communist mayors conducted in the 1970s in those two countries found that 40 per cent of the French mayors named economic and social (or occupational group) factors as their reasons for joining the Communist Party, whereas only 7 per cent of the Italian mayors stressed such motives. For the latter, resistance to fascism had been the key factor.[35] In the late Stalin period a comparison of the French, Italian, British and American Communist parties found that the PCI, as befitted the largest Communist Party in Western Europe, was the most integrated with the broader society and the least indoctrinated. It contained the largest contingent of people who had *not* been exposed to official Communist doctrine prior to joining the party and the largest proportion who received no doctrinal training once they were within it.[36] The PCI was the most 'normal' of West European Communist parties in its psychological relationship with its own society. It wielded power successfully in a number of localities. However, unlike the French Communist Party, it was not allowed entry into any national government coalition – not, at least, until after the party had been disbanded and had re-emerged in the 1990s in social democratic colours.

Communists of Jewish Origin

One significant aspect of party membership is the extent to which Communism attracted recruits from long-settled indigenous populations or from recent immigrants. Ethnicity as a factor was played down in Communist doctrine. What mattered was class origin and class solidarity. And in countries such as China, Korea and Vietnam, the party attracted the nationals of those countries rather than any particular minority. This was true, in the main, also for the largest European non-ruling parties. In both Italy and France the parties had a mass membership – apart from the periods when they were forced underground by the fascist regime in Italy and the wartime Vichy regime in France – and both the rank-and-file and the party officials overwhelmingly came from the indigenous population.[37]

In contrast with these two cases, and as distinct especially from Asian Communism, relatively recent immigrants were massively overrepresented in the Communist parties of many other countries. As a study by the Institute of Contemporary Jewry of the Hebrew University of Jerusalem noted, in much of Europe, the Americas, and South Africa, Jews in particular 'at various times and in various places were disproportionately represented in the Communist movement (be it in the total membership, the apparatus, or the leadership)'.[38] There is no one explanation for this, although part of the answer is to be found in the position occupied by Jews in Russia and Eastern Europe in the nineteenth and early twentieth centuries. That goes some way to explaining not only the high incidence of Jewish participation in the Russian revolutionary movement and in East European Communist parties but also the disproportionately large number of Jews in such

Communist parties as those of the United States, Britain and South Africa, since it was from the Russian Empire and from other parts of Eastern Europe that the Jewish immigrants came.

Communist and socialist parties drew their support predominantly from the cities and large towns, and in both their Russian and Eastern European places of origin and the countries to which they emigrated, Jews were an overwhelmingly urban community. Over centuries they had been banned from owning land throughout most of Eastern Europe and so their economic activity was concentrated in the urban commercial economy, whether as traders and entrepreneurs or as workers in manufacturing industry.[39] Clearly, Jews could not belong to parties which were defined by Christianity or be much attracted either to peasant parties or to parties representing the interests of the wealthier landowners. Nor could they readily become members of nationalist parties, especially since the latter more often than not were anti-semitic in both ideology and political practice. Thus, the internationalism of Communism drew many young radicals of Jewish origin into the Communist movement as well as, where they were available, into socialist parties of a social democratic type. The fact that people from a Jewish background came to occupy a disproportionately large and prominent place in Communist parties does not, of course, mean that they were anything other than a small minority within the Jewish population. Indeed, joining the Communist Party meant distancing themselves not only from Judaism but also from distinctive Jewish customs. Alec Nove notes the irrelevance of the origins of Jewish Communists – with the significant possible exception of a greater attachment to internationalism – when he observes of the Soviet Union in the 1920s:

> Few would deny that Jews played a disproportionate role in the first decade of the Soviet regime. But since the individuals concerned had broken with Jewish traditions, it is hard to discern what difference their origin made to their ideas. The excesses of War Communism, under the joint impact of ideology and war emergency, destroyed the livelihood of millions of Jewish craftsmen and traders. The many Jewish parties were *anti*-Bolshevik. However, there was internationalism. Thus, it may not be accidental that 'right' ideologues of 'socialism in one country' (Bukharin, Rykov, Tomsky) were Russian, while the 'lefts' who opposed them (Zinoviev, Kamenev, Trotsky, Radek) were Jews.[40]

In Poland, the Communist Party was banned for most of the inter-war period and so party membership statistics are not precise. Nevertheless, one careful study notes that the proportion of Jews within the pre-World War

Two Communist Party of Poland (KKP) 'was never lower than 22 per cent countrywide, reaching a peak of 35 per cent (in 1930)'.[41] In Poland, as in many other countries, Jews were partly reacting against anti-semitism and their own marginality in society. There was the more general factor that 'given a certain level of literacy, education, and exposure to the injustices of society, members of discriminated minorities are more likely than others to join radical movements for change'.[42] There was also much revolutionary romanticism, encapsulated in the remark of one Polish Communist of Jewish origin that 'We waited for the revolution as for the messiah' and of another that 'I believed in Stalin and in the party as my father believed in the messiah.'[43] Communism may have appealed 'to a certain Jewish sense of justice and redemption', but it has also been appositely observed that 'the involvement of individuals in this radical movement was in most cases an act of rebellion against the traditional world of their parents or against the concern with particularistic Jewish issues as expressed by movements such as Zionism . . .'[44]

Of all Western Communist parties, there was none in which Jews were so overrepresented as that of the United States. This was especially true just after the Russian Revolution and in the earliest years of the Comintern. It was a time and place when internationalism was carried to an extreme. At one New York mass meeting in 1917, Trotsky spoke in Russian and the other speakers in German, English, Finnish, Lettish, Yiddish and Lithuanian.[45] In the early years of the CPUSA, the great majority of members were foreign-born. When the party abandoned foreign language branches as its basic unit of organization in 1925, it lost half its membership (dropping from just over 14,000 to a little over 7,000) in one month. During the 1920s, the Yiddish equivalent of the American *Daily Worker* had a larger circulation in the United States than the *Worker* itself.[46] It was not until 1936 that 'the Party was able to claim that a majority of members were American-born'.[47] As late as the 1930s and 1940s, approximately half of the party members were of Jewish origin, many of them from Eastern Europe.[48]

Paradoxically, although Communist parties such as those of the United States and Great Britain were marginal to the mainstream of politics, the act of joining them was for immigrants partly a way of overcoming their marginality and seeking integration in the new country.[49] In the words of Raphael Samuel: 'For my mother's generation Communism, though not intended as such, was a way of being English, a bridge by which the children of the ghetto entered the national culture.'[50] Joe Jacobs, who was secretary of the Stepney branch of the CPGB in East London in the late 1930s, has described how, as a Jewish working-class youth, he got into conversation at street corners with older men who discussed at length the Russian

Revolution, adding: 'The names and places talked about were familiar to us because many of our parents had come from Russia and Poland.'[51] The conversations ranged also over local and national events in Britain, and soon Jacobs was being invited to meetings, classes and demonstrations, 'all of which I was only too pleased to attend'.[52] Before long, he had been recruited by these older Communists into the CPGB. As a historian of the relationship between Jews and Communism in Britain observes: 'Here we can detect the combination of Jewish cultural memory and the partial integration of the second generation into British society – common themes in Jewish Communist biographies.'[53]

The rise of fascism in the 1930s led radicals in many European countries and in North America into the Communist Party. Its threat was perceived especially strongly by Jews and, to the extent that the Communist Party appeared to be the most unrelentingly anti-fascist of political parties, this drew a substantial number of Jewish recruits to its ranks. Taken in conjunction with the apparent collapse of capitalism in the early 1930s, Communism seemed to some young Jewish intellectuals the obvious alternative. Indeed, Eric Hobsbawm, who was born in 1917 and whose family moved to Berlin in 1933, argues that there was practically no choice:

> What could young Jewish intellectuals have become under such circumstances? Not liberals of any kind, since the world of liberalism (which included social democracy) was precisely what had collapsed. . . . We became either communists or some equivalent form of revolutionary marxists, or if we chose our own version of blood-and-soil nationalism, Zionists. But even the great bulk of young intellectual Zionists saw themselves as some sort of revolutionary marxist nationalists. There was virtually no other choice. We did not make a commitment against bourgeois society and capitalism, since it patently seemed to be on its last legs. We simply chose *a* future rather than *no* future, which meant revolution.[54]

Hobsbawm adds that 'the great October revolution and Soviet Russia proved to us that such a new world was possible, perhaps that it was already functioning'.[55] Although he remained a member of the British Communist Party during decades after others had left, the ebbs and flows of Soviet policy challenged the faith of less dogged members. What Jason Heppell says of the Communist Party of Great Britain was true of Western Communist parties more generally: 'The CP . . . was dependent on the lottery of Soviet policy: with the Nazi–Soviet pact of 1939, it had a losing ticket, but with the German invasion in 1941, it became a winner.'[56] If Communists of Jewish origin played a disproportionately large role in the leadership and membership of Marxist-Leninist parties, they were also to become a disproportionately large component of the victims of Communist purges – an aspect of the relationship between Jews and Communism that will be discussed in later chapters.

Recruitment to Ruling Parties

As was noted as early as the Introduction to this book, joining a Communist party in a Communist state was a very different matter from joining a non-ruling party. It was still voluntary up to a point, but obligatory if an individual wished to pursue a career in particular professions. It was also an enormous asset for those ambitious for success, whatever their occupation. To belong to the ruling group in a Communist state, whether at the national or local level, party membership was obviously a prerequisite, since the party organs themselves wielded most power. At the top of the hierarchy these were constituted by the Central Committee and its departments and the two inner bodies, the Politburo and the Secretariat. At the city level it was the party's City Committee and its inner body, the party Bureau, which was the ultimate local authority. There was a similar structure in the regions of the country and the urban and rural districts. For officials within ministries and for army and security police officers, party membership went with the job. Since, however, in Communist states the party did not normally include more than 10 per cent of the adult population in employment within its ranks, this meant that the party 'saturation' was much greater in some professions than others. The more ideological a profession, the greater the incidence of party membership. Thus, in research institutes, social scientists and academic lawyers would, overwhelmingly, be members of the Communist Party, whereas membership was more optional for mathematicians and natural scientists. It was optional, too, for creative writers and others in the artistic professions. In any career, however, to belong to the party assisted advancement and it was essential for those who wished to move into the higher administration of their profession.

If an average of one in ten adults within the party was a desideratum, and yet in some professions the overwhelming majority of people belonged to the Communist Party, then clearly there had to be categories and occupations underrepresented within the party ranks. That was notably true of women, whose numbers within the ruling Communist parties were very far from reflecting the fact that they generally (as a result of two world wars) constituted more than half the population. Clerical and shop workers – and this point links up with the last, for they were mainly women – were greatly underrepresented. Peasants also did not have a party presence in proportion to their percentage of the population. So far as the criterion of education is concerned, people with only the most basic levels had a far lower incidence of party membership than those with higher education. The one category of the population where the one-in-ten average was also the norm was that of manual workers, certainly in the case of the Soviet Union.

The appeals of party membership within a Communist state were, naturally, different for different people. For anyone who wanted to be a boss, this was a necessary first step. For many people, however, it was a prerequisite of having the kind of interesting career to which they aspired, and by no means necessarily a political career – for example, an economist, historian, or head teacher in a school. If a person wished to travel abroad from a Communist country, the chances of doing so were very much better if he or she were a party member. For a minority there were also greater privileges – including the possibility to purchase goods from special shops. That applied to those who were members of what was, in effect, the inner party – the *nomenklatura*.

The *nomenklatura* consisted both of a list of posts which could be filled only with the permission of a party committee at one level or another – the Central Committee in the case of an editorship of a national newspaper, the city or town committee in the case of a school principal – and a list of people (kept by the party organs) deemed suitable for appointments to such responsible posts. In some accounts the *nomenklatura* has been treated as if it were a ruling class within Communist states. That was always an oversimplification, for the powers and privileges of a woman teacher who had risen to be head of a school, even though her post was on the *nomenklatura* of the local party committee, were incomparably less than those of occupants of positions that required the imprimatur of the Central Committee or Politburo. Neither the party membership as a whole nor even those who were on the *nomenklatura* of a party committee at a local level can sensibly be identified as members of a ruling class. If that term is to be used, and its usefulness in this context is debatable, it would apply, at most, to the full-time party functionaries and to those holding high state appointments which could be filled only with the approval of the central party organs.[57] They certainly constituted an elite, and among their privileges was access to the special shops. Given the shortages in the shops open to the general public in most Communist states at most times, that was quite a perk, even though the *nomenklatura* shops themselves had less on display than was to be found in a typical Western supermarket or large store.

For those eager for upward social mobility, joining the Communist Party could also be seen as a mark of recognition from the powers-that-be of their worth and political reliability. In the Soviet Union in the 1920s and even in the 1930s it could, less prosaically, be associated with an idealistic desire to build a just society. A combination of the speed of social change and the effectiveness and all-pervasiveness of Communist propaganda and education meant that in those decades there were many true believers in the construction of socialism and communism. During the Second World War, to join the Communist Party was linked in the Soviet Union with the patriotic struggle against the Nazi invaders of their country. In the early post-war years, pride in the part played by the Soviet army in the defeat of fascism and a patriotic desire to rebuild a shattered country could also be factors leading an individual to seek party membership. In a other words, not all who joined ruling parties were careerists. However, the fact that being in the Communist Party was a *sine qua non* for some careers and an undoubted aid to advancement in others was the single most important appeal of party membership in countries in which the Communists had a monopoly of power.

The distinction between membership of a ruling and non-ruling Communist Party is, then, fundamental. Members in both cases may have shared a sense of mission and of being a group apart – an advance guard of ideologically armed citizens of a future society – but in the case of party members in a capitalist society (whether possessing an authoritarian or democratic regime), they represented a counterculture rather than the official culture. And where they had mass support, as in Italy or France, they were a counter-elite rather than the established elite, whereas in Communist states party membership was a necessary passport to elite status, even if not all rank-and-file members could be said to belong to it. The more idealistic members – in non-Communist *and* Communist states – believed, especially before fresh light was shed on the realities of Communist rule following Stalin's death, that a 'new man' or 'new socialist person' would become the norm in the communist society of the future. In the meantime, they accepted the discipline, arduous work and social bonds which were necessary if they were to hasten the day when a world of harmony would replace the world of class conflict and capitalist exploitation. Within actually existing Communist states, as distinct from the communist utopia of the imagination, lip service to the creation of the 'new man' was all too easily combined with an acceptance of privilege and career advantages and conservative defence of a status quo which worked to the benefit of party members, especially those in the higher reaches of the *nomenklatura*.

8

Communism and the Second World War

For western and central Europeans, the Second World War began earlier than it did for Russians and Americans. German troops marched into Prague on 15 March 1939, but that was not yet the beginning of European war. The Czechs, having been deserted by their democratic allies (although France had been bound by treaty to come to their aid), offered no resistance. On 1 September 1939, Nazi Germany attacked Poland. The Poles did resist, and two days later Great Britain and France declared war on Germany. Earlier that year the British government had given the Poles advice similar to that which they had offered Czechoslovakia in 1938 – namely, that it would be in Poland's interest to reach a negotiated settlement with Hitler. They had also said, however, that they would fight if Poland were to be attacked, and this they did. Stalin's pact with Hitler, already discussed in Chapter 5, delayed the war between the Soviet Union and Germany, although on neither side was there a belief that peace between them would be long-lasting. It was Hitler who ended it with the German invasion of the Soviet Union in the midsummer of 1941. The United States became a combatant country when the Japanese attacked the USA at Pearl Harbor later that same year – on 7 December. President Roosevelt had, though, already given much-needed economic aid to Britain's war effort, with the Lend-Lease Act passed in 1940. This was extended to provide support for the Soviet Union once the USA had entered the war. Hitler declared war on the United States on 11 December 1941, and from 1942 the USA played a major part in the war in both Asia and Europe.

The Soviet Union, however, not only suffered the greatest losses, but also contributed most to the ultimate defeat of the Nazis. Stalin was taken completely by surprise when German troops crossed the Soviet border on 22 June 1941. He had received a number of warnings of impending attack, but chose to ignore them. There were Soviet spies in Berlin who picked up information about plans to invade the Soviet Union, and their agents were able to observe the movement of German troops and equipment towards the Soviet border. Stalin, however, assumed that this was no more than bluff

on Hitler's part (perhaps to confuse the British) and that Germany's immediate priority was to knock Britain out of the war. Soviet military intelligence
– the GRU – had a talented spy in Japan, Richard Sorge, whose intimate
relationship with the wife of the German ambassador to Tokyo was one of
his sources of valuable intelligence. Sorge warned the Soviet leadership of
the impending attack on the USSR but was branded by Stalin as a liar.
Warnings came also from Germans sympathetic to the Soviet Union as well
as from Winston Churchill, who could hardly have been less sympathetic.[1]
Churchill, however, did not want the USSR to suffer losses in a surprise
attack, since he knew how badly Britain needed such a formidable military
ally in the struggle against Hitler's Germany.[2] (Having been the main propo-
nent of armed intervention against the Bolsheviks in the Russian civil war,
Churchill in 1920 had described Communism as 'a pestilence more destruc-
tive of life than the Black Death or the Spotted Typhus'.[3] When, however,
Germany invaded the Soviet Union in 1941, the British prime minister
remarked that if Hitler invaded Hell, he would make at least a favourable
reference to the Devil in the House of Commons.)[4]

Even the German ambassador to Moscow told his Soviet counterpart,
Vladimir Dekanozov, in early June 1941 that Hitler had come to a firm
decision to invade the Soviet Union, adding that he was conveying this infor-
mation to him as he had been 'raised in the spirit of Bismarck, who was
always an opponent of war with Russia'.[5] This led Stalin to complain to the
Politburo that disinformation had now reached ambassadorial level. Since
Stalin had convinced himself that a German attack was *not* imminent, no
one close to him dared express a contrary view. The head of the NKVD,
Lavrenti Beria, was especially zealous in following in his master's footsteps.
On 21 June 1941 – one day before the Nazis invaded – he said that four
NKVD officers who had persisted in sending reports of an impending inva-
sion must be 'ground into labour camp dust'[6] and on the same day he wrote
to Stalin:

> I again insist on recalling and punishing our ambassador to Berlin, Dekanozov,
> who keeps bombarding me with 'reports' on Hitler's alleged preparations to
> attack the USSR. He has reported that this attack will start tomorrow . . . But
> I and my people, Iosif Vissarionovich, have firmly embedded in our memory
> your wise conclusion: Hitler is not going to attack us in 1941.[7]

Beria was surely aware that his head would potentially be on the block if
there were a catastrophic failure of prediction. This, no doubt, explains his
stress on the fidelity within the NKVD to *Stalin's view* that there would be
no German attack in 1941. That was a precaution lest things turned out

differently from what Stalin and Beria expected, even though there could be no guarantees of immunity from Stalin's wrath, with its appalling consequences for those at the receiving end. Dekanozov was himself a protégé of Beria and had been a brutal NKVD officer in Georgia. Far from being especially perspicacious about Hitler's intentions, even as he passed on warnings of war, he was much more inclined than other senior members of his own embassy staff to regard all talk of a German invasion of Russia as deliberate disinformation.[8] (Beria, unlike his purged predecessors as head of the NKVD, succeeded in outliving Stalin, though not by long. He was executed later in the year of Stalin's death at the instigation of Khrushchev and the ruling group within the Politburo.[9] And among those arrested along with Beria and similarly accused of the heinous – and at that time imaginary – crime of plotting 'to revive capitalism and to restore the rule of the bourgeoisie' was former NKVD officer and Soviet ambassador Dekanozov, who was also executed.)[10]

As a result of Soviet unpreparedness, in spite of all the warnings of impending attack – received substantially earlier, and from sources independent of one another – the Red Army suffered horrendous initial losses. Stalin greatly compounded his failures of interpretation of the intelligence he received by forbidding Soviet generals from implementing defensive measures against an invasion. He had no wish to provoke Hitler and, having persuaded himself that a German attack was not imminent, there seemed no need to do so. Although the Second World War was ultimately to strengthen both the Soviet system and the spread of Communism internationally, that was not the way things looked during the remainder of 1941. The Soviet army lost four and a half million men before the end of the year. Stalin's culpability was immense. He had killed off a large proportion of the senior officer corps in the purges of 1937–38, including Marshal Tukhachevsky, who in 1936 had told the recently established General Staff Academy that the enemy against whom the Soviet Union should be preparing to defend itself was Nazi Germany, whose favoured form of attack was a lightning strike – the Blitzkrieg.[11] Tukhachevsky, who had first found himself on the opposite side of an argument with Stalin as long ago as the Soviet–Polish war in 1920, was arrested and shot in June 1937.[12] Three of the Soviet Union's five marshals perished in 1937–38 and the two who were left, Voroshilov and Budenny, were far from the most impressive. Both were removed from important positions of command very early in the war after they had demonstrated their incompetence. And not only had Stalin refused to believe well-founded intelligence concerning the imminence of a German attack in 1941; he proceeded, in the earliest weeks of the war, to authorize the shooting of a number of senior officers for 'cowardice' when they failed to prevent the advance of the invading army.[13] Later the NKVD would arrest not only Soviet troops who had been captured by the Germans and remained in captivity until the end of the war but also those who had succeeded in escaping from their captors. Moreover, senior officers who brought bad news were liable to be arrested on Stalin's instructions.[14] In his Order No. 270, issued on 16 August 1941, Stalin decreed that those who surrendered to the Germans 'should be destroyed by all means available, from the air or from the ground, and their families deprived of all benefits', while deserters should be shot on the spot and their families arrested.[15]

Soviet losses were much greater than they need have been for those and other reasons. An indirect result of the war was that many more political prisoners in Soviet labour camps died in the years immediately after June 1941 than in the 1930s, since shortages and privation were now such that they were more than ever undernourished. The ruthlessness with which the Red Army senior officers (including, notably, Marshal Zhukov) deployed their own troops – with punishment battalions being sent to clear mine-fields by marching through them – also contributed to the scale of the death toll. All that notwithstanding, it should never be forgotten (though it often is) that the Soviet Union lost a larger number of people than any other combatant state during the Second World War, that the great bulk of these deaths were caused by the barbarity of the Nazi invasion, and that it was the forces of the Soviet Union, more than those of any other country, which defeated Nazi Germany in the ground war in Europe. The Red Army war dead numbered nine million, and almost eighteen million Soviet civilians were killed in the war. The total was five times higher than the number of German war dead.[16]

Nazi ideology regarded Russians (and Slavs more generally) – as well as Jews, who came still higher on their hate list – as subhuman, and this dehumanization of entire populations led to a brutality on the Eastern Front far in excess of that in the western war zones. Politically, the Nazis saw Communists as their most bitter enemies, and so Communist Party members and Jews (categories which the Nazis often conflated) were killed in cold blood. Slav villagers who had assisted partisan fighters – even inadvertently, when guerrilla fighters entered their village and helped themselves to whatever they could find – were killed and the village destroyed.[17] Not only in Russia, but in other Slav countries, among them Poland and Yugoslavia, German units would shoot a hundred civilians in retaliation for every German killed by partisans. Sometimes, as in Poland, they would take a hundred hostages in advance, publish their names on posters, and then execute them in public to discourage further resistance.[18] The extraordinarily high proportion of Soviet prisoners of war who died in captivity – some 3,300,000 out of the 5,700,000 who fell into German hands – was a consequence of two main factors. The first was the aforementioned Nazi ideology, which placed no value on these lives, and the second Hitler's concerns about the economic burden on the German population (which might have led to discontent on the home front) of keeping them prisoner. Many of the deaths occurred in the first months of the war before the Nazi leadership decided that bringing prisoners to Germany and making them do productive work would better suit their war aims. The death toll among those engaged in forced labour was somewhat lower than in the prison camps, but the ruthless manner in which the Soviet prisoners were exploited led to mass deaths among those workers also, especially in 1943.[19]

As Omer Bartov has written: 'On the Eastern Front, Nazi Germany exercised barbarism on an unprecedented scale; its declared intention was extermination and enslavement; the only way to prevent her from achieving this goal was to defeat her militarily, for whatever we may think of the [German] resistance, it proved itself incapable of toppling the regime.'[20] The official figure for Soviet war dead now given in Russia is approximately twenty-seven million.[21] Even the two western countries which played a great part in the war against Nazi Germany, the United States and Britain, suffered incomparably smaller losses – some 400,000 in the case of the USA and 350,000 in that of Britain, with the latter figure representing a substantially higher proportion of the population than the former.[22]

In their advance into the Soviet Union in 1941, the German army had reached the outskirts of Moscow by November. There, however, they were stopped by the Soviet forces defending the city, and a counteroffensive, led by a new military elite, Georgy Zhukov, Ivan Koniev and Konstantin Rokossovsky, began in December.[23] In the battle for Moscow, which lasted from September 1941 until April 1942, 926,000 Soviet soldiers were killed. In other words, Soviet losses in that one battle came to more than the combined casualties of Britain and the United States in the whole of World War Two.[24] The Germans had hoped to take Leningrad as well as Moscow in 1941, but in the event captured neither. However, they began a blockade of Leningrad which lasted almost 900 days, causing over a million civilian deaths. The siege was finally ended only in January 1944.

Approximately 90 per cent of the German army's fighting strength was tied down on the Eastern Front for as long as three years. The battles at Stalingrad in 1942 and Kursk in 1943 took a huge toll of German lives as well as, in still greater numbers, on the Soviet side. In one of the most celebrated of British victories over German forces, the battle at El Alamein in 1942, the German army under the command of Rommel lost 50,000 men, 1,700 guns and 500 tanks. At Stalingrad in the same year the Germans lost

800,000 men, 10,000 guns and 2,000 tanks.[25] The battle for the city of Stalingrad, waged in the winter of 1942 and the beginning of 1943, was of huge symbolic importance, since the old town of Tsaritsyn had in the Soviet period been renamed in honour of Stalin. (After Nikita Khrushchev exposed at least some of the crimes of Stalin, the city was renamed again – as Volgograd, which was safe enough, since the city was, and remains, situated on the banks of the River Volga.) In addition to the significance of the city bearing Stalin's name, its capture was seen by Hitler as opening the way to exploitation of the Soviet Union's oil resources. The horrendous battle which took place in and around Stalingrad became, in the words of Antony Beevor, 'a personal duel by mass proxy' between Hitler and Stalin which Stalin, at immense cost, won.[26] Although 50,000 Soviet citizens fought in the *German* army at Stalingrad,[27] the vast majority of the Soviet population – though driven to the limits, and often beyond, of human endurance – resisted the invaders. When the remnants of Hitler's Sixth Army finally surrendered at Stalingrad, this was a massive boost for the Communist movement worldwide. It greatly strengthened Stalin's hand in his negotiations with Roosevelt and Churchill.[28]

Conscious of the huge contribution the Red Army was making to the defeat of Nazi Germany, the Soviet Union's wartime allies turned a blind eye to atrocities committed by the Soviet side, although atrocities there were. One, which for long was mendaciously attributed to the Germans, was the slaughter of thousands of Polish officers in cold blood in Katyn forest, near Smolensk, in 1940.[29] This was the year before the Soviet Union entered the Second World War, but followed their acquisition of Polish territory as part of the partition of Poland agreed in the Molotov–Ribbentrop pact. The Russian archival evidence on the Katyn massacre is now available. A letter from the head of the NKVD, Beria, to Stalin of 5 March 1940 proposed the shooting of some 25,700 Polish prisoners, the majority of them officers, though Beria's letter distinguishes between a group of 14,736 officers and officials held in prisoner-of-war camps, and a further group of 18,632 people being held in prisons in western Ukraine and Belorussia, of whom 10,685 were Poles. This latter group, Beria claimed, was composed of former officers, former police spies, actual spies and diversionists, and former landowners, manufacturers and bureaucrats. Stalin personally approved the proposal that they all be shot, and his signature was followed by that of Politburo members Klement Voroshilov, Vyacheslav Molotov and Anastas Mikoyan.[30]

Between 1941 and 1944, during the Second World War, Stalin ordered the deportation of entire nationalities – including the Chechens, their neighbours the Ingush, the Volga Germans (who had been in Russia since the eighteenth century) and the Crimean Tatars – from their traditional home-lands to Kazakhstan or Siberia. They were regarded as harbouring disloyal or potentially disloyal elements and so entire nations were victimized. Transported in cattle trucks, many of them died on the journey eastwards.[31] When Soviet troops finally entered Germany in 1945 they took brutal revenge – on the civilian population as well as German combatants. It is estimated that more than 110,000 women were raped in Berlin, and there was massive looting.[32]

Little attention, however, was paid on the Allied side to any of this. The British Foreign Office, for example, while aware that the Katyn killings had been the work of the NKVD rather than the Germans, took care to keep the information out of the public domain. Their priority was the decisive role the Soviet Union was playing in the defeat of Nazi Germany. Some aspects of the Communist system, such as its exceptionally rapid build-up of industrial capacity in the 1930s and its ability to mobilize vast numbers of people to meet specific targets, contributed to their ultimate wartime success. Thus, for example, Soviet industry, especially military production, was moved from western Russia to beyond the Urals at remarkable speed. Other features of the system – including NKVD surveillance and harass-ment of army officers (even one as high as Rokossovsky, who was to become a marshal in the course of the war but on its eve had been a political pris-oner) – were wholly counterproductive.[33]

Nevertheless, Stalin was sufficiently astute to realize that in a desperate war for survival, Communist ideology was not enough. It had to be supple-mented by traditional beliefs and symbols if the population of Russia, in particular, were to be inspired to fight to the end in the face of immense sacrifice and suffering. Thus, persecution of religion largely ceased during the war years and the Orthodox Church was encouraged to add its patri-otic weight to the struggle. Stalin, deeply shaken by the German invasion of the Soviet Union, did not broadcast to the Soviet people until eleven days into the war. In that speech, however, he addressed them not only as 'Comrades' but also as 'Brothers and Sisters'. On the anniversary of the Bolshevik revolution, 7 November 1941, he took the risk of inspecting a parade on Red Square and, in a speech, invoked great names from Russia's martial past – among them, Alexander Nevsky, a thirteenth-century Novgorod prince who was later canonized by the Orthodox Church; Alexander Suvorov, an eighteenth-century general regarded in pre-revolu-tionary times as the greatest of all Russian soldiers; and Mikhail Kutuzov, the military leader who outfoxed Napoleon in the Patriotic War of 1812–13. It is not for nothing that the Second World War became known in Russia as the Great Patriotic War. There was a conscious echo here of 1812, but the mid-twentieth-century conflict was a greater, and still more terrible, war. Most Soviet soldiers were fighting for their homeland, not for Stalinism or Marxism-Leninism. Indeed, in spite of the permeation of the army by a special category of political officers (successors of the commissars whom Trotsky had inserted in the Red Army during the civil war to ensure the political loyalty of officers who had formerly served the tsar), Communist doctrine was subordinated to patriotic and anti-German propaganda. Given the barbarous actions of the invading army, the latter met a ready response.

The Nazis were victims of their own ideology. If they had treated decently peasants who had lost family members during the forced collectivization of agriculture and who were still not reconciled to the Stalinist version of Soviet rule, they might have picked up more support. In western Ukraine, had they made concessions to nationalist sentiments, they would have won even more collaboration than they did.[34] In fact, German forces occupied Ukraine for longer than any other part of the Soviet Union and left it devastated. More than two million citizens of Ukraine were sent to Germany as slave labour.[35] The cities were deprived of sufficient food to sustain the life of their inhabitants. In December 1941, German economic administrators decided to increase the supply of foodstuffs from Ukraine to Germany by eliminating 'superfluous eaters', by whom they meant 'Jews and the population of Ukrainian cities such as Kiev'.[36] The population of Kharkiv dropped from 850,000 in 1939 to 450,000 by December 1941, with between 70,000 and 80,000 residents of that Ukrainian city dying of famine during the German occupation. Two hundred and fifty Ukrainian villages and their inhabitants were totally annihilated in the Nazi response to resistance.[37]

The Second World War was a period when the stock of the Soviet Union was higher in Western democracies than at any time before or after. American president Franklin D. Roosevelt and British prime minister Winston Churchill, in their wartime correspondence, habitually referred to Stalin as 'Uncle Joe' – often, indeed, by the abbreviation 'U.J.'.[38] (They also, as was common within their and other Western countries, called the people over whom 'Uncle Joe' ruled 'Russians' and spoke of the country as Russia rather than the Soviet Union. That obscured the fact that in this multinational state, Russians, although the most numerous, were far from being the only nationality suffering and fighting in the war against Nazi Germany.) After the dismay caused by the Molotov–Ribbentrop pact of 1939, the new esteem for the role being played by the Soviet Union came as a relief to many Communists throughout the world. As Donald Sassoon has observed, the Second World War, after the German attack on the Soviet Union, turned out to be the 'finest hour' also of Western Communists. For the first – and, indeed, last – time: 'They could fight fascism and Nazism, be true internationalists, defend the USSR, be flawless patriots and all without inconsistency.'[39] In occupied Europe, Communists were particularly active participants in partisan resistance to fascism, whether in its German Nazi or Italian manifestations.

In Greece and Yugoslavia this took the form not only of resistance to German occupation but also of bitter civil wars. In the case of Greece, it was war between two wings of the resistance movement. If the Soviet Union had put its weight behind the Greek Communists, they might have come to power in 1944 after the Germans withdrew from Greece, but on this occasion an agreement made between Stalin and Churchill that the Soviet Union would not intervene in Greece was adhered to. It is likely that it was not so much his promise to Churchill as the priority Stalin gave to gaining control of east-central Europe which persuaded the Soviet leadership to stand aside and allow British troops to play an important role in defeating the Communist insurgency in Greece during the last year of the Second World War.[40] As usual, the interests of 'fraternal' Communist parties were subordinated to those of the Soviet Union as Stalin perceived them, and the Greek Communists were mistaken in thinking that their armed struggle 'would receive Moscow's blessing as part of a broad move to expand Soviet control into the Mediterranean'.[41]

In Yugoslavia, civil war consisted of both ideological and military struggle between Communists and anti-Communists and bitter conflict among the country's different nationalities, especially between Serbs and Croats. In Croatia, where a puppet fascist state was established under extreme Croat nationalists called the Ustaše, a policy close to genocide was pursued against the Serbian part of the population as well as against Serbs in Bosnia and Hercegovina. The Communist partisans in Yugoslavia were led by Josip Broz, who had become known since 1934 as Tito – the name he then assumed on his release from prison for Communist activity. One of the strengths of the Communists was that they transcended the ethnic divide. On the eve of World War Two they were, in the words of a historian of Communism and nationality in the Balkans, 'perhaps the only truly Yugoslav party'.[42] They recruited people on the basis not only of their willingness to risk their lives in the fight against the German occupiers of their country but also of their readiness to work for the creation of a post-war Communist state. Serbs and Montenegrins were disproportionately strongly represented in the ranks of Communist guerrilla fighters, but Tito was born in a Croatian village in 1892 to a Croat father and Slovene mother. Among the Serbs there was a fierce struggle between the Chetniks, the Serbian nationalist part of the guerrilla resistance to the Germans (who at times, however, collaborated with them), and Tito's Communists, with their large Serbian contingent.

Given that Tito did succeed in establishing a Communist state in

Yugoslavia when the war ended, the decision of Winston Churchill and his government in 1943 to transfer British logistical support from the Chetniks, led by Draža Mihailović, to Tito's partisans became controversial in the post-war years. As Dennison Rusinow observed: 'While Western military aid was of only marginal if welcome importance, Churchill's advocacy of the Partisans and the King's reluctant acquiescence gave the nascent regime a much needed international recognition and legitimacy.'[43] Nevertheless, the Communists, led by Tito, took power largely as a result of their own efforts. Unlike a majority of the post-war European Communist states, they had not been propelled into the offices of state by Stalin and the Soviet army. The Red Army did play a very important role by liberating Belgrade, but by far the greatest part of the fighting on Yugoslav soil had been conducted by the partisans, and, in contrast with most of east-central Europe, the Soviet forces departed once the immediate task had been accomplished. Thus, when the war ended, it was the Yugoslav partisans who were in charge. It was not accidental that the first great split in the Communist movement to affect ruling parties was that between the Soviet Union and Yugoslavia. Communist leaderships which had made their own revolutions were able to sustain a position independent of that of Moscow (China and Albania were later examples) in a way in which regimes that were essentially Soviet-created found far harder to achieve, even when some of them tried.

For Churchill, during the Second World War, the overriding issue was which resistance movement to the Nazis was holding down more German divisions and killing more German troops. Two military missions, the first led by Captain (subsequently Lieutenant-Colonel) Bill Deakin – who, in the later 1940s, became the first head of St Antony's College, Oxford – and the second by Brigadier Fitzroy Maclean, who was both then and later a Conservative MP, helped to convince Churchill that Tito's partisans were the people to back. Deakin was parachuted into Yugoslavia and pitched immediately into battle, fighting alongside Tito. Less than two weeks after he made contact with the partisans, he and Tito were wounded by the same bomb in an attack which killed many of the partisans and the only other British officer who had accompanied Deakin on this dangerous mission.

Milovan Djilas, a close ally of Tito during the war and a leading figure among Yugoslav Communists who was later to become Tito's most notable domestic political opponent, observed on the arrival of the British military mission on 29 May 1943: 'The mission was led by Captain F.W. Deakin, who was outstandingly intelligent despite his general reserve. We found out that he was a secretary of a sort to Churchill and this impressed us, as much for the consideration thus shown to us as for the lack of favouritism among the British top circles when it came to the dangers of war.'[44] In that context, it is worth noting that Churchill's son Randolph, a Conservative MP as well as an army officer at the time, later joined the British military mission to Yugoslavia. As Djilas recalled:

> We, of course, felt honored, though it did occur to us that Randolph might be the gray eminence of the mission. But he himself convinced us by his behaviour that he was a secondary figure, and that his renowned father had decided on this gesture out of his aristocratic sense of sacrifice and to lend his son stature. Randolph soon enchanted our commanders and commissars with his wit and unconventional manner, but he revealed through his drinking and lack of interest that he had inherited neither political imagination nor dynamism with his surname.[45]

Winston Churchill himself sent a number of letters to Tito, hand-delivered by members of the British military mission. He tried unavailingly to persuade Tito to take a more favourable view of Yugoslavia's young king in exile, and to retain the monarchy after the war, while enthusiastically backing the partisans' current military efforts. On 17 May 1944 he wrote: 'I congratulate you once more upon the number of enemy divisions which you are holding gripped on your various fronts.'[46] Just one week later, writing again to Tito, Churchill said: 'I wish I could come myself, but I am too old and heavy to jump out on a parachute.'[47]

The limited Soviet participation in the war in Yugoslavia did not prove decisive. In Albania the Communists came to power without any Soviet help at all. They did, however, get assistance from the Yugoslavs – both instruction on party organization and guidance on how to conduct guerrilla warfare. Initially, Tito and his colleagues were mentoring the Albanians as part of a division of labour agreed by the Comintern. On the day the Italians invaded Albania – 7 April 1939 – King Zog, who had been the authoritarian ruler of Albania for fifteen years, left the country immediately with his entourage, creating a political vacuum.[48] Mussolini's army was far less effective than Hitler's, and gradually the Communists, allying organization to willpower, became the major element in the resistance. There was no Albanian government in exile or any other political parties with whom they needed even the pretence of sharing power. In October 1944, the Anti-Fascist National Liberation Committee became the provisional government and subsequently, under the same leadership, the rulers of a monolithic Communist state.[49]

Elsewhere in Eastern Europe, the Soviet Army played a decisive role in establishing the conditions for Communist takeover. It was the Red Army which recaptured the Baltic states from the Nazis. They had been taken into the Soviet orbit by Nazi–Soviet agreement before Hitler's invasion of the Soviet Union, but were occupied by German forces during the conflict. The Red Army also liberated from Nazi domination Poland, Hungary, Bulgaria and Romania. They ended Nazi control over the greater part of Czechoslovakia, including the capital Prague, but departed after the war ended. There had been no widespread resistance or partisan movement in Czechoslovakia during the war, in which the Czech lands of Bohemia and Moravia were a German protectorate while the Slovaks had their own clerico-fascist state. The head of the Czech protectorate, Reinhard Heydrich, was killed in 1942 on the initiative of the democratic Czech government in exile in London. However, the revenge the Nazis took, with the villages of Lidice and Ležaky destroyed, all the men in the villages shot, and the women and children sent to concentration camps, was enough to ensure that little further resistance ensued. In Slovakia in 1944, Communists and social democrats co-operated in an abortive rising, one of whose leaders was Gustáv Husák, who was later to become a political prisoner in Communist Czechoslovakia, and later still, the party's leader and the country's president. In Czechoslovakia, the Communist Party had sufficiently widespread support that there was a real possibility of its gaining power without the need to rely on Soviet armed force. It became, indeed, an intermediate case between that of the Yugoslavs and Albanians, on the one side, and states such as Poland and Hungary, on the other. The latter pair could not have become Communist in the absence of Soviet power and presence, whereas no Soviet troops were present in Czechoslovakia when the Communists (as described in the next chapter) seized full power in 1948.

Meanwhile, the Second World War had an effect also on the fortunes of Communists in Asia, where it was linked to national liberation. Japanese expansionism became a catalyst for Communist advance in China. The Japanese had seized Manchuria in 1931 and established a client state there. This did not stop the Chinese Nationalist leader of the Kuomintang, Chiang Kai-shek, from focusing on the extermination of Communists in the rest of China. As noted, however, in Chapter 5, a nucleus of Communist Party members survived the Long March to the north-western province of Shaanxi in 1934–35. One reason why the Nationalists and the Communists were such bitter rivals was not that they were polar opposites but that they had significant things in common.[50] They were both believers in modernizing China and the Nationalists did not in reality have a monopoly of national appeal. That the Communists could respond to the desire for national liberation as well as to local peasant grievances was to serve them well.

Chiang Kai-shek was on the verge of another extermination campaign aimed at the Chinese Communist Party when the Japanese forces invaded in 1937 and attempted to take control of the whole of China.[51] The Communists then became, along with the Nationalists, one of the two wings of the resistance. The Nationalists bore the brunt of the fighting, the Communists being the junior partner.[52] The Communist forces developed effective guerrilla warfare but they gave priority to building up their strength for the post-war struggle with the Kuomintang.[53] By the time the Japanese were defeated – above all, by the United States – the Kuomintang had been worn down by eight years of warfare. Chiang Kai-shek's government was also blamed for much of the hardship, including food shortages, of the war years. Thus Chiang ended the war weaker than he had been at the beginning, whereas the Communists had been able to gather strength and consolidate. In areas they controlled during the war, the Chinese Communist Party were often able to win local support with reform policies, by distributing land to poor peasants, and by punishing unpopular local elites.[54] Thus, in China, too, though in different ways from Eastern Europe – where the advance of the Soviet army was generally the most decisive factor – war turned out to be the prelude to, and facilitator of, the Communist seizure of power.

9

The Communist Takeovers in
Europe – Indigenous Paths

The single most important reason for the establishment of Communist regimes in Eastern Europe following the Second World War was the success of the Soviet army in ending Nazi rule in the region. In a speech in August 1927, Mao Zedong, in words that were to become famous, told Communists that 'power comes out of the barrel of the gun'.[1] While not a maxim of universal validity, this one applied well enough to east-central Europe in the immediate post-war years. Yet it was not the whole story. Socialism, whether in its democratic form or in its Soviet-style variant as preached by Communist parties, had gained greatly in popularity. In Western Europe there was not only revulsion against Nazism and fascism but also a response to the failures of capitalism – especially the existence of mass unemployment – in the 1930s and a reaction against the inadequacies of the democratic governments of those years. Among their mistakes had been that of trusting the promises of Hitler. Stalin had made the same error, but in 1945 he was held in high esteem in the West because of the huge role played by the Red Army in winning the war.

In many parts of Europe, then, there was ideational change as well as the strategic change brought about by Soviet force of arms. Socialism was increasingly believed to be a more just and more rational way of organizing an economy than capitalism. Planning was seen as a panacea which would either replace the vicissitudes of the market or, at the very least, moderate the inequality to which market relations gave rise. Public ownership in one form or another was widely held to be more socially just than private owner-ship of large swathes of land and industry. In particular, there was quite broad support for taking into state ownership both natural monopolies and what Lenin called, in the first stage of Bolshevik rule, the 'commanding heights' of the economy. Many people who counted themselves as social-ists and shared these beliefs in 1945 were subsequently to modify or even abandon them, but the immediate post-war era, for all its hardship, was one of optimism about the prospects of socialism. A belief that 'capitalism could offer only unemployment and misery' was also combined with illusions about the advantages of the Soviet system.[2] Collectivization had destroyed the lives of millions of peasants. Stalin, in his own country, was responsible for the imprisonment and execution of political opponents, real and imagined, on an even larger scale than Hitler in Germany, but all this was, for the time being, overlooked. Soviet secrecy and censorship, combined with the suspension of critical faculties on the part of many Westerners who provided rosy accounts of Stalin's USSR, meant that such facts were not nearly as widely known as they should have been.

The failures of the inter-war period, the breakdown of many social barriers which the war had accelerated, and the belief that something better than the pre-war order must be constructed with the coming of peace profoundly influenced thinking in parts of Europe where Soviet power did not impinge. Where socialist parties of a democratic type were already strong, they became the beneficiaries in Western Europe of the egalitarian and anti-capitalist tide of opinion. In Britain and Scandinavia, the Labour and socialist parties had great electoral success while the Communists received negligible support. In Italy, France and Finland, Communist as well as democratic socialist parties attracted broad support. Eastern and central Europe had a different political inheritance. With the exception of Czechoslovakia, right-wing authoritarian regimes had been the norm in the 1930s and they were now thoroughly discredited. Socialist parties of a social democratic type, as well as the Communists, had generally been suppressed – not only under Nazi rule but throughout much of the inter-war era. After the Soviet Union was attacked, and thus resistance to the German invaders became a Communist internationalist duty as well as a matter of local patriotism, Communists were very active in partisan movements. They had an additional incentive to work underground against the fascist enemy, for if they simply waited and hoped for the best, their chances of survival in Nazi-dominated Europe were going to be slim. Their party membership made them prime candidates for shooting or dispatch to a concentration camp.

The Communist takeovers of Eastern European countries which were directly Soviet-orchestrated are discussed in the next chapter. There are, though, three cases where local Communists achieved power for themselves – Albania, Yugoslavia and Czechoslovakia, although the Czech and Slovak case differs significantly from the first two.

Albania and the Leadership of Enver Hoxha

As noted in Chapter 8, the success of the Communists in resistance movements in Albania and Yugoslavia was on a scale which enabled them to prevail without Soviet support in the first case and with relatively modest help from the Soviet Union in the second. The Albanian Communists in the war years were, though, closely overseen by their Yugoslav comrades. The coming to power of Communists in these two countries, while largely independent of the feats of the Soviet army, rested, nevertheless, on the coercive power which the party leaderships had already built up during the war. In the Albanian case, since representatives of the old regime had left the country, the Communists faced no real competition. In Yugoslavia, Tito had got the better of his domestic enemies, whether the Serbian nationalist Chetniks or the Croatian fascist Ustaše.

Yugoslav help to the Albanians was primarily organizational and ideological and the Albanian Communists in the war years were heavily influenced by the Yugoslavs, who looked forward to being the leading player in a new federation which would embrace Bulgaria as well. Stalin and the Comintern approved of the idea, always on the assumption that Tito in Yugoslavia and Communist leaders in Albania and Bulgaria would be unswervingly loyal to Moscow. In 1943 Tito wrote to the Albanian Communists telling them that they needed to appeal to young peasants and that they had to bring into their partisan groups 'as many as possible honest Albanian nationalists and patriots besides Communists'.[3] On the foundation of the Albanian Communist Party in 1941, Enver Hoxha was chosen as its leader, and he was to remain in charge until his death in 1985, making him the longest-lasting party leader in Eastern Europe. Given that the Albanian Communists came to power in 1944, his forty-one years at the helm of the Albanian state made him, moreover, the person who held power longer than any other non-hereditary ruler in the twentieth century.[4] Hoxha, the son of a landowner, attended a French lycée in Albania and pursued his higher education in France, where he was attracted to Communism and wrote articles for the French Communist Party newspaper, L'Humanité, under a pseudonym.[5]

Even during the war years Hoxha was less enthusiastic about subordinating to Yugoslavia the party he led than were some of his colleagues, notably party secretary Koçi Xoxe, who headed both the party's Orgburo (Organizational Bureau) and the secret police in the immediate post-war period. Hoxha came close to losing his party leadership, which for a time was largely nominal, since Xoxe was more in tune with both Tito and Stalin. In 1947, Xoxe approved a plan for a merger of Albania with Yugoslavia (which would also have involved Bulgaria), but the Soviet–Yugoslav split of 1948 – to be discussed in Chapter 12 – put paid to that. It also led to the execution of Xoxe in 1949 for the twin crimes of having supported union with Tito's Yugoslavia and having opposed Hoxha.[6]

The Albanian Communists' path to power had been smoothed by their earlier acceptance of Yugoslav advice. Members of the Communist Party (renamed the Albanian Party of Labour in 1948) constituted the leading eche-lons of a broad movement known as the National Liberation Front (or NLM). It attracted young people from well-to-do families as well as from the villages. As its military power increased during 1944, its ranks swelled. Albania – one of Europe's poorest countries, with a population at that time well under three million – scarcely registered in the mind of President Roosevelt. The British had an ambivalent attitude to the contending Albanian groups. Some of those who took part in military intelligence missions to occupied Albania took the same view of the Albanian Communist-dominated partisans as they did of those whom Tito led in Yugoslavia – what mattered was that they were the people bearing the brunt of fighting the Italian and German invaders of their country. But whereas the main British concern was the defeat of the Axis forces in Albania, Hoxha's highest priority was to attain political power, and he wanted to achieve victory over his domestic opponents (among them supporters of King Zog) in advance of liberating the country from foreign occupiers. This was strongly resented by some in the British Special Operations Executive (SOE) and the Foreign Office. Such was the confusion that at one point in July 1944 Churchill, referring to the internal struggle in Albania, sent a memorandum to Foreign Secretary Anthony Eden which read: 'Let me have a note on this, showing which side we are on.'[7]

The seizure of power by the Albanian Communist Party in the autumn of 1944 was facilitated by the lack of any clear Western policy. The Soviet Union was clearly in favour of the Communists coming to power in Albania, while the USA and Britain were relatively permissive and not particularly well informed. By the time the German-supported government in the capital, Tirana, was overthrown, the partisan forces numbered more than 50,000. The Albanian Communists' seizure of power is rivalled only by that of the Yugoslavs as the most indigenous of takeovers in Eastern Europe. Neither the Soviet army nor Tito's partisans set foot in Albania. It was not a revo-lution, in the sense of a popular uprising against the old order, which produced a Communist government. This was, rather, a seizure of power which was the direct result of the invasion of Albania by the Axis powers and of the dominance within the resistance movement which the Communists had achieved.[8]

Tito and the Yugoslav Partisans

In Yugoslavia, Tito's partisans had by 1945 prevailed in the bitter civil war which had accompanied their struggle against the Germans. Yugoslavia was among the countries which suffered most in the Second World War, losing

11 per cent of its pre-war population between 1941 and 1945. Having been dismembered by its invaders, it was essentially reborn in 1943 when the National Liberation Movement, as the partisans led by Tito were known, met in Bosnia and established a National Committee of Liberation of Yugoslavia. It was headed by Tito, who in addition was the General Secretary of the Communist Party of Yugoslavia and the supreme commander of the National Liberation Army. He was given the title of Marshal of Yugoslavia. The second session of the National Committee of Liberation determined that post-war Yugoslavia would be a federal state, in which the Serbs, Croats, Slovenes, Macedonians and Montenegrins would each have a republic of their own, while Bosnia and Hercegovina, a historical unit with an ethnically mixed population, would constitute the sixth republic.[9]

In 1944, a new Yugoslav government in exile was imposed on King Peter by Churchill. It was headed – for the first time since the creation of the Yugoslav state at the end of World War One – by a Croat, Ivan Šubašić. His period in office was short-lived, for he and his government were pressed by Stalin, Churchill and Roosevelt – the 'Big Three' allies during World War Two – to form a provisional government with Tito. In that government Tito became prime minister and minister of defence. Thus, very briefly, Tito was the Yugoslav king's first minister, but the earliest act of the Constituent Assembly, which was formed in Yugoslavia in 1945, was to abolish the monarchy and declare Yugoslavia a Federal People's Republic.[10] Tito had accepted three royalist representatives in his provisional government only under heavy pressure from his Western allies, and he later said that he regretted doing so.[11] Neither they nor anyone else, however, proved a serious obstacle to the Communists gaining exclusive possession of state power. Known collaborators with the occupying forces were, in many cases, killed; other opponents were intimidated or imprisoned. In the general election held on 27 November 1945, the voters were presented with a single list of candidates and so had a choice only of being for or against those nominated by the Communist Party. As Tito's biographer Phyllis Auty put it:

> Few wished to vote against the party which had won the war and had such evident power; fewer still dared to put their voting disc in the opposition polling box. Tito's movement obtained ninety-six per cent of the total votes cast ... Though everything possible had been done to persuade people to vote for the communists, and though it can be presumed that the percentage for it would have been less had opposition parties been allowed, there is no doubt that Tito and the Partisans had massive genuine support at this time, and that they would in any case have obtained a majority.[12]

The Communists in Yugoslavia achieved in 1945 the monopoly of power which took most East European parties several years to attain. The Yugoslav power structure followed closely that of the Soviet Union, which meant that key decisions were taken in a small Politburo, chaired by Tito, endorsed by the substantially larger Central Committee of the party, and rubber-stamped by the parliament, which was entirely obedient to the Communist Party.

Many of the Chetniks took the opportunity to flee from Yugoslavia during 1945, but their leader, Draža Mihailović, who could have done so, decided to remain in the country in the hope of leading a Serbian national rising that would overthrow the Communists. He was captured in 1946, put on trial in 1947 on the basis of the Chetniks' collaboration with the German occupying forces, and executed, along with other Chetniks, in July of that year. Of the 12,000 Yugoslav Communists on the eve of the war, only 3,000 had survived the next four years. However, some 300,000 men and women joined the party during and immediately after the war. One of the strengths of the Communists, in a country with deep-seated inter-ethnic tensions, was their ability to bring together different nationalities, and for several decades they had some success in sustaining an all-Yugoslav identity. That this was based on consent as well as coercion was in part a result of Stalin's excommunication of Tito and Yugoslavia from the international Communist movement, an action which strengthened patriotism on a Yugoslavia-wide basis. The 'Yugoslavism' of the Communist Party was reflected in the national composition of the top leadership. Tito himself bridged the ethnic divide. Not only was he (as noted in the previous chapter) by birth and paternity, a Croat and, on his mother's side, a Slovene, but he was much respected by the Serbian Communists. His closest comrades-in-arms, who made up the central core of the early post-war leadership, were Edvard Kardelj, a Slovene; the Serbs Moša Pijade (who was also of Jewish origin) and Aleksandar Ranković; and Milovan Djilas, a Montenegrin. A still broader, and more methodical, representation of Yugoslavia's different nationalities was to be found in the Central Committee of the party, the body to which the Politburo was nominally responsible but which, in fact, it dominated.[13] There were anomalies in the nationality policy, however, which were to become sources of acute tension in later years. As David Dyker observed: 'Serbs, Croats, Slovenes, Montenegrins, Hungarians, Macedonians (for the first time) and Albanians (under the pseudonym of Šiptari) were all given official recognition. An uneasy note was, however, struck by the relegation of the Ethnic Muslims to the limbo of 'undetermined Muslims', with the implication that the sooner they declare themselves Serbs or Croats the better.'[14] Decades later, the 'Ethnic Muslims' were to emerge as the new Bosniak nation.[15]

Czechoslovakia

The seizure of power by Communists in Czechoslovakia was a more gradual affair than in Albania or Yugoslavia. It was not so dependent on the position that Communists had secured in wartime and least of all on a partisan movement, for that scarcely existed in the Nazi-controlled Czech lands during World War Two, but it had deeper social roots as well as pre-war legitimacy. Czechoslovakia had been the most democratic, libertarian and tolerant country of any in central and eastern Europe between the two world wars. One aspect of this was the fact that the Communist Party enjoyed a legal existence and, as noted in Chapter 5, a respectable level of support. When Czechoslovakia was liberated from German occupation in May 1945, about 40,000 Communist Party members had survived the war. A conscious and successful effort speedily to build up the party membership meant that by the end of that year it stood at 826,527.[16] In Czechoslovakia, as in other countries of central and eastern Europe which were to become Communist, a broad popular front was created, known as the National Front. In the Czech and Slovak case, however, although the Communist Party was the largest single component of the National Front (having emerged as the most successful party in free elections in 1946), this was a genuine coalition until February 1948. Like the Communist Party itself, the National Front had some roots in pre-war Czechoslovakia, where the five main political parties habitually formed a coalition known as the Pětka (The Five), in which they discussed and determined government policy.[17] Another element of continuity was to be found in the continuation of the institution of the presidency. Except, temporarily, in East Germany – and, after the break with the Soviet Union, in Tito's Yugoslavia – only in Czechoslovakia did the post of president exist in Communist Europe. It had enjoyed immense prestige during the incumbency of its first holder, the founder of the Czechoslovak state, Tomáš Masaryk, and continued to be accorded great authority when his close ally, Edvard Beneš, succeeded him in 1935. Beneš spent most of the war years in London as head of the Czechoslovak government in exile and returned to Prague as president in 1945. His re-emergence as head of state seemed to confirm that there had been a return to democracy.

In Czechoslovakia there was no anti-Russian tradition. Indeed, the Russians had traditionally been seen as a friendly Slav big brother – in a genuinely fraternal, not Orwellian, sense. In the whole of eastern and central Europe outside the Soviet Union, probably only in Bulgaria were remotely similar feelings toward Russia to be found.[18] A positive attitude to Russia and the Soviet Union was further engendered by the fact that most of Czechoslovakia was liberated by the Red Army, while memories of the Munich Agreement of 1938 meant that Britain and France were still viewed with some suspicion. Whereas Poles had witnessed the Soviet Union actively conniving with Germany, in the Nazi–Soviet pact, to dismember Poland, the Czechs had fresh memories of the British and French attempt to appease Hitler by agreeing to the transfer of Sudetenland, the part of Czechoslovakia heavily populated by Germans, to the Third Reich. In each case, historic perceptions of Russia were reinforced – still more distrustful in the case of the Poles, more supportive on the part of Czechs (especially) and Slovaks. Moreover, the Communist Party of Czechoslovakia had especially vigorously opposed the 1938 Munich Agreement and had argued at that time for an alliance with the Soviet Union.

Since Soviet troops had left Czechoslovakia after the end of the war, the emerging regime was not one put in place by Soviet tanks and bayonets. There was very strong support for socialist parties in the 1946 elections, especially in the Czech lands of Bohemia and Moravia. The Communist Party, which at that time appeared to embrace political pluralism, gained over 40 per cent of the vote in the Czech lands, 38 per cent in the country as a whole. When the votes of the Social Democratic Party and the National Socialist Party – a democratic socialist party having nothing in common with the pre-war German National Socialists – are added to those of the Communists, it can be seen that almost 70 per cent of the Czech population freely voted for some form of socialism. During the period of political pluralism between 1945 and the beginning of 1948, a number of socialist measures were implemented, including the nationalization of banks, insurance companies and key industries.

Throughout the first two post-war decades, in particular, the Communist Party had a higher proportion of the population within its ranks than any other East European Communist Party. The norm of around 6 per cent of the total population and one in ten of the working population in the party – which was typical of the Soviet Union during much of the post-war period – was always exceeded in Czechoslovakia. The party found it easy to recruit members immediately after the war both because of the Czech perceptions of Russia and of the Munich Agreement, already noted, and because, as elsewhere, there were people who were very willing to join, for careerist reasons, what looked likely to be the winning side.

The moment at which Czechoslovakia moved from being a socialist-inclined pluralistic political system to construction of a Communist state came in February 1948, when the Communists seized full power. They were led by Klement Gottwald, the son of a Moravian peasant, who had become the general secretary of the Communist Party as early as 1929 and who was to remain Czechoslovakia's leading Communist until his death in 1953. Elected a deputy in the Czechoslovak parliament in 1929, he spent much time in the 1930s, as well as the whole of the war years, in Moscow, working in the Secretariat of the Comintern until the dissolution of that body in 1943. After the war Gottwald continued to be the most authoritative member of the leadership of the Communist Party. Next to him in authority in the early post-war years was Antonín Zápotocký, who had survived imprisonment in the German concentration camp of Sachsenhausen from 1940 to 1945. Although Gottwald always paid lip service to the superiority of the Soviet system, he was less committed to establishing a Soviet-type system in Czechoslovakia than was his counterpart, Walter Ulbricht, in East Germany.

THE MARSHALL PLAN

Alone among east-central European Communist leaders, Gottwald, in his capacity at that time as Prime Minister of Czechoslovakia, would have been willing to receive American economic aid. In June 1947, the US Secretary of State George Marshall had announced America's European Recovery Programme, which involved massive aid to Western Europe, partly to ensure that economic hardship in the aftermath of the war did not play into the hands of the Communists. Gottwald presided over a Cabinet meeting in July 1947 which accepted an invitation to the forthcoming Paris conference on the Marshall Plan.[19] Stalin immediately summoned Gottwald to Moscow, for he had committed the cardinal sin for a Communist Party leader of going against the known wishes of the Soviet Union without even consulting Moscow in advance of the decision. The Soviet leadership did not allow any country it could control to receive such aid, even though the denial of it helped to widen the gap in living standards between the West and the East (understood as political categories, for, geographically, Czechoslovakia was in central, not Eastern, Europe). The Czechs were not bound to follow Soviet wishes, for it is very unlikely that – with no Soviet troops stationed in Czechoslovakia by 1947 – Stalin would have dared to invade the country, given the extent to which the Truman administration in the United States was now alert to what the American president and his principal advisers perceived as a dangerous Communist expansionism.

Gottwald, however, was conditioned, in the final analysis, to follow the Soviet lead. He told the two non-Communist members of his Cabinet who had accompanied him to the Soviet Union, Foreign Minister Jan Masaryk (the son of the country's founding father and first president) and Minister of Justice Prokop Drtina, that he had 'never seen Stalin so furious'. After seeing Stalin alone, Gottwald told them: 'He reproached me bitterly for having accepted the invitation to participate in the Paris Conference. He does not understand how we could have done it. He says that we acted as if we were ready to turn our back on the Soviet Union.'[20] From that time onwards Gottwald was ultra-responsive to Soviet wishes. He reversed the decision on the Marshall Plan, rejecting any idea of Czechoslovak participation in it. With opinion polls showing that the Communist Party was much less popular than it had been at the time of the 1946 elections, a membership recruitment campaign was intensified.[21] In the second half of 1947, the party increased its aggressiveness, with Gottwald fearing both the loss of support at home, should free elections be held as planned in 1948, and the loss of support from Moscow, since his flirtation with the Marshall Plan had so outraged Stalin. Later, Czech and Slovak democrats were to recall a remark Gottwald addressed to representatives of the 'bourgeois' parties in the Czechoslovak parliament as long ago as 21 December 1929: 'You are saying that we are under Moscow's command and that we go there to learn. Yes, our highest revolutionary staff is in Moscow and we do go to Moscow to learn. And do you know what? We go to Moscow to learn from the Russian Bolsheviks how to break your necks, you patriots.'[22]

The Marshall Plan was part of an American policy whereby Communism was being challenged both militarily and economically. In March 1947, the American president had enunciated what became known as the Truman Doctrine. Paying special attention to Greece (which was in the throes of civil war) and Turkey (on which Stalin had made territorial claims), and alluding to the 'significant threats' posed by Communist parties in France and Italy, Truman said it would be 'the policy of the United States to support free peoples who are resisting attempted subjugation by armed minorities or by outside pressures'.[23]

THE COMINFORM

The Soviet Union established a successor organization to the Comintern a few months later. Called the Cominform, it was less powerful than its predecessor and did not embrace so many parties, but it did include all the ruling Communist parties in Europe, among them the Communist Party of Czechoslovakia, the majority party within the government coalition in that country. At the inaugural gathering of the Cominform in Poland in September 1947, a meeting dominated by the two senior Soviet representatives, Andrey Zhdanov and Georgy Malenkov, the delegates were told by Zhdanov: 'The world is divided into two camps: the anti-democratic imperialist camp on the one hand and the anti-imperialist, democratic camp on the other.'[24] The latter camp – which, in the Soviet terminology, was described equally as the 'democratic camp' and the 'socialist camp' – was engaged in a 'progressive unification', and it was made clear to the Czechoslovak delegates that they should be part of that process.

By late 1947, the Communist leadership in Czechoslovakia were determined to seize full power, and accordingly, they set about creating a crisis which would facilitate their takeover. They made demands and presented bills in parliament which were 'politically or economically impractical but had the demagogic impact of being socially attractive'.[25] When these were rejected either within the National Front or by parliament, there was dire talk of threats to the state 'from without and within' from the agents of the forces of reaction. They also stepped up pressure on the Slovak Democratic Party, which had gained 62 per cent of the vote in the elections of 1946 as against the Communists' 30 per cent in Slovakia, and were thus the strongest party there. Czechoslovakia was not at that time a federal state, and so the Slovaks were still essentially subordinated to Prague, where the Communist-controlled Ministry of the Interior made difficulties for the democratic forces in Slovakia. The leadership of the Czechoslovak Social Democratic Party was moving in a more anti-Communist direction. Thus, the Communists set about splitting both it and other democratic parties, partly by suborning, as Pavel Tigrid put it, 'any third-rate politician in the other parties who was ambitious and venal enough' with the promise of ministerial positions provided their name could be used at the right moment in support of a united list of candidates and on condition that in the meantime they also provide the Communist Party with inside information on what their own parties were planning to do.[26]

The Communists also had a fellow traveller as Minister of Defence in the shape of General Ludvík Svoboda, who years later was to emerge during the 'Prague Spring' as President of Czechoslovakia, for a short time acquiring a liberal reputation, helped somewhat by the fact that his surname was in Czech (as well as in Russian) the word for 'freedom'. He had actually wanted to formalize his relationship with the Communist Party in 1945 by becoming a member, but Gottwald told him that it was much more useful, when the Communists had to have parity within the government with non-Communists, to keep him in the ranks of the latter, while voting, nevertheless, with the former. When the push for full power in the hands of the Communist Party came in February 1948, Svoboda was able to announce that the army was 'on the side of the people', by which he meant the Communists.[27] Things came to a head with the Communists, on the one side, demanding a single list of National Front candidates in the forthcoming elections rather than competition among the various political parties, and the non-Communist parties, on the other, demanding a commission of inquiry into the manipulation of the police and security forces by the Ministry of the Interior (which was headed by the Communist Václav Nosek).

When the democratic politicians failed in this and other attempts to prevent the Communists gradually taking over all the coercive instruments of power, a majority of those who held ministerial rank offered their resignations to President Beneš. Already in failing health, Beneš unwisely accepted the resignations and did not demur when the Communists used their now clear majority within the Cabinet to implement all the measures, such as the single list of candidates for future elections, which they had been pushing for. They had been ready to use coercion if need be. The People's Militia of Communist workers, which had been created by them after the war, had between 15,000 and 18,000 active members, 6,650 in Prague alone.[28] The army and the police were in reserve, but they were not required to play a major role in the Communist seizure of power. With the windfall of the resignations of the non-Communist ministers, Gottwald and the Communist leadership were able to move rapidly and peacefully to the imposition of a Soviet-type system. Beneš himself stayed on as president for several months, thus giving the Communist takeover an aura of legitimacy. However, just days after Gottwald's coup, the Foreign Minister, Jan Masaryk, in what was probably suicide rather than murder, was found dead outside the ministry building, having fallen from a high window.[29] Beneš resigned in June, just three months before his own death. Gottwald succeeded him as president, with Zápotocký becoming prime minister. The Communist takeover in Czechoslovakia was frequently cited by its apologists over the next two decades as a textbook example of the 'parliamentary road to socialism'.

For many non-Communist socialists, it was a textbook example of political chicanery and skulduggery. Yet support for the Communists in early postwar Czechoslovakia came from idealistic young people as well as from cynical power-grabbers. It would be mistaken to imagine that the kind of system which was created in Czechoslovakia after 1948 corresponded with the wishes of a majority of Communist voters in 1946. As Vladimir Kusin observed:

To say that these voters and supporters of the 'Czechoslovak road to socialism' were privy to Gottwald's and Stalin's long-term plans is ridiculous. After all they voted in 1946 to make the Communist Party the strongest in the country but not to endorse its monopoly of power for all times to come. If such monopoly had been at issue in a democratic election, the result would certainly have been different. The Communist voters were victims just as much as the more provident, who saw the danger clearly.[30]

What occurred in February 1948 was not so much a struggle between capitalism and socialism as a clash between two concepts of socialism. Victory went to the Communist variant and took a form which overwhelmingly reflected the Soviet model as distinct from Czechoslovakia's pluralistic traditions. The system soon produced (as will be seen in Chapter 12) a wide range of Stalinist excesses, including the execution of Communists who had fallen out of favour and the persecution on a wider scale of their democratic opponents.

10

The Communist Takeovers in
Europe – Soviet Impositions

Of all European regions, the Balkans was the one in which the Communists had the best chance of coming to power as a result of their own efforts. It was not in Albania and Yugoslavia alone that they might have done so. They had real possibilities also in Greece, but this is where the broader international context has to be considered. Stalin accepted that Greece was outside his sphere of influence and so didn't lift a finger when Western intervention against the Greek Communists tilted the balance away from them. As early as October 1944, in a piece of traditional Great Power diplomacy, Churchill, on a ten-day visit to Moscow, discussed with Stalin spheres of influence in post-war Europe. Churchill proposed a division of responsibility that would be 90 per cent Soviet for Romania, and 90 per cent British in Greece. These suggestions were accepted by Stalin, and when Churchill proposed a fifty–fifty supervisory share of Yugoslavia and Hungary, Stalin, initially, on Churchill's account, accepted both. Stalin may, however, have had more confidence about the strength of Tito's Communists (and at that time no doubts about their loyalty) than the situation in Hungary, and had reason to expect that, whatever Churchill may have hoped, a staunchly pro-Soviet regime would be established in Yugoslavia. Accordingly, that notional division of influence over Yugoslavia was retained even after further discussion involving the British foreign secretary, Anthony Eden, and Stalin's foreign minister, Vyacheslav Molotov. In those talks, however, the percentage for Hungary was altered to 80–20 in the Soviet favour. The same balance of influence was established for Bulgaria. Churchill, in his memoirs, cites the figures he agreed with Stalin. The Soviet leadership apparently took the exercise seriously enough, given that Molotov haggled further on the percentages even after Stalin had placed a large tick on the paper Churchill passed to him before handing it back. Albania did not figure in these British–Soviet bilateral discussions.[1]

Churchill was, on reflection, somewhat embarrassed by his percentage proposals. In a letter addressed to Stalin, which he did not send (on the advice of Averell Harriman, President Roosevelt's personal envoy to Churchill and the British government from the beginning of 1941 until October 1943, when he became the American ambassador in Moscow), he wrote:

> These percentages which I have put down are no more than a method by which in our thoughts we can see how near we are together, and then decide upon the necessary steps to bring us into full agreement. As I said, they would be considered crude, and even callous, if they were exposed to the scrutiny of the Foreign Offices and diplomats all over the world. Therefore they could not be the basis of any public document, certainly not at the present time.[2]

What would happen to Poland and to Germany was even more contentious and could not be settled until the Yalta and Potsdam conferences of 1945, involving all the 'Big Three', with the opinion of President Roosevelt at Yalta counting for more than that of Churchill. By February 1945, when the Yalta conference was held, Britain was weakened and over-stretched by the war, and the economic and military predominance of the United States was increasingly evident. Moreover, Stalin, in particular, hosting this conference on Soviet home ground in the Crimea, had briefed himself much better than had Churchill.[3] By the time of the Potsdam conference in the second half of July and early August, Roosevelt had died and the new president, Harry Truman, headed the American delegation. Halfway through the conference Churchill and his foreign secretary, Eden, were replaced by the new British prime minister Clement Attlee and foreign secretary Ernest Bevin, since Labour had defeated the Conservatives by a landslide in the first post-war election. (That election, when it was still a future prospect, had already come up in conversation between Churchill and Stalin in Moscow in October 1944, when 'Stalin said that he had no doubt about the result: the Conservatives would win'.[4] After the election had taken place and Churchill was about to return from Potsdam to London to learn the result, Stalin showed his psephological limitations by predicting that the British prime minister would secure a parliamentary majority of eighty.[5] He was not alone, of course, in overestimating the extent to which people would vote for a war leader rather than on a different set of issues. Churchill himself had been confident of victory.)

At Potsdam it was agreed that Poland would shift to the west. The Soviet Union would retain those parts of Poland which it had seized as a result of the Nazi–Soviet Pact and which roughly corresponded to the 'Curzon Line', the border established at the Paris Peace Conference of December 1919 and named after Lord Curzon, the British foreign secretary at that time. Subsequently, as a consequence of the Russo-Polish War, the Polish border moved further eastwards and so remained throughout the Second Polish

Republic which existed from 1921 until 1939.[6] Relations between Poles and Ukrainians during World War Two were extremely tense and there were many civilians killed by both sides. The Poles did not want a substantial Ukrainian minority living within their territory and the Polish Communists as well as Polish nationalists appeared to share that view. During the war the Communists 'dropped language about the rights of minorities from their programmatic documents', thus jettisoning the traditions of the Polish left.[7] However, as Timothy Snyder has observed:

> . . . by the summer of 1944, Stalin's preferences mattered more than Polish traditions of any kind. The population exchanges were preceded by, and based on, a Soviet–Polish accord that no Polish nationalist (and few Polish Communists) found acceptable. A secret agreement of 27 July 1944 shifted the Soviet border to the west once again, as in 1939, thereby removing 85 per cent of Ukrainians from Poland, leaving only about 700,000. Most of Poland's prewar Ukrainian minority thus left Poland without physically moving at all.[8]

To compensate for the post-World War Two loss of the eastern part of its inter-war territory to the Soviet Union, Polish borders were moved significantly westwards. Discussing this issue with President Truman at Potsdam, Stalin said: 'Of course the proposal . . . to shift the frontier westward will create difficulties for Germany. I do not object to the claim that it will create difficulties for Germany. Our task is to create more difficulties for Germany . . .'[9]

The loss to the Soviet Union of territory which had previously been part of Poland was, however, a bitter pill to swallow for those Poles who were not Communists (the vast majority) and, accordingly, not programmed to accept the view that Stalin and Moscow knew best. Churchill in 1944 was torn between his respect for the heroic efforts of the Red Army and desire to be on good terms with Stalin, on the one hand, and his admiration for the bravery of Polish soldiers and airmen who fought with the Allied armies, on the other. In the later stages of the war, however, he gave precedence to Soviet interests over those of any émigré group. In mid-October 1944, he spoke harshly to the Polish government in exile in London, telling them that they had to accept that the Curzon line would be their eastern border and that they must co-operate on a fifty–fifty basis with the Soviet-backed Lublin Poles. When the leader of the government in exile in London, Stanisław Mikołajczyk, attempted to argue with him, Churchill responded: 'If you want to conquer Russia we shall leave you to do it. I feel as if I were in a lunatic asylum, I don't know whether the British Government will continue to recognize you.'[10] Exasperated with both Polish governments in waiting but knowing which he disapproved of the more, Churchill wrote to King George VI on 16 October 1944: 'The day before yesterday was "all Poles day". Our lot from London are, as Your Majesty knows, a decent but feeble lot of fools but the delegation from Lublin seem to be the greatest villains imaginable.'[11]

What had been East Prussia was divided between Poland and the Soviet Union, with the German city of Königsberg becoming part of Russia and renamed Kaliningrad in 1946 in honour of Mikhail Kalinin, who had been titular head of the Soviet state (while wielding little power) and had died that year. Poland was granted what had been German territory east of the rivers Oder and the western Neisse. Both there, and in other Slav countries with a German population within their borders, it was agreed at Potsdam that German inhabitants could be expelled to Germany (with its redefined borders).[12] Germany was not yet in 1945 split into two states, but a de facto division developed from the outset. The territory which had been occupied by the Red Army was under the tight control of the Soviet Union, and that within the American and British sphere was profoundly influenced by the occupying powers and took a quite different direction from the Soviet zone. Shortly after the Federal Republic of Germany (West Germany) became a separate state in 1949, the Soviet satellite of East Germany was granted statehood as the German Democratic Republic.

The spread of Communism throughout east and central Europe in the early post-war years must, then, be seen in the context of the military outcome of the Second World War, of the vast range of territory conquered by the Soviet army, and of Western respect for the Soviet contribution to the Allied victory and for the scale of their losses. Thus the leaders both of the United States and of Britain in the later war years, and at the Potsdam conference, accepted Stalin's argument that the USSR must be secure from the threat of attack from the West – and from Germany in particular. Diplomacy played a role. Stalin had 'a computer-like memory'.[13] He could argue effectively, although it was many years since any Soviet politician had dared contradict him, and he could persuade as well as coerce. Even Churchill – who more than Roosevelt or even Truman (in the earliest months of his presidency) was suspicious of Soviet intentions – allowed himself to be charmed by Stalin and to say in 1944 that if they could dine together once a week, they would solve the vexed problem of Poland. More than once during the Second World War Churchill remarked of Stalin: 'I like that man.'[14] Roosevelt was still more of an optimist than Churchill about Stalin and on the prospects for continuing good relations with the Soviet Union after the war.

When Truman succeeded Roosevelt as president, he had little experience of foreign policy, and in a letter in May 1945 to his predecessor's widow,

Eleanor, he said that the 'difficulties with Churchill are very nearly as exasperating as they are with the Russians'.[15] His initial assessment of Stalin was: 'He is honest – but smart as hell.'[16] The second part of the judgement was sounder than the first. As one of America's most distinguished observers of the Soviet Union, George Kennan, put it: 'Stalin's greatness as a dissimulator was an integral part of his greatness as a statesman.'[17] By the following year, Truman fully shared Churchill's suspicion of the Soviet Union's post-war ambitions. At the Potsdam conference, however, Churchill's electoral defeat had led the American president to reflect on Stalin's mortality. He confided to his diary at the end of July 1945 his worries that Stalin might disappear from the scene:

> If Stalin should suddenly cash in it would end the original Big Three. First Roosevelt by death, then Churchill by political failure and then Stalin. I am wondering what would happen to Russia and Central Europe if Joe suddenly passed out. If some demagogue on horseback gained control of the efficient Russian military machine he could play havoc with European peace for a while. I also wonder if there is a man with the necessary strength and following to step into Stalin's place and maintain peace and solidarity at home. It isn't customary for dictators to train leaders to follow them in power . . . Uncle Joe's pretty tough mentally and physically but there is an end to every man and we can't help but speculate.[18]

In a letter which he composed, but did not send, to Dean Acheson in March 1957, Truman noted that at the Potsdam conference 'a large number of agreements were reached in spite of the setup – only to be broken as soon as the unconscionable Russian Dictator returned to Moscow!' Truman was irked, though, by the fact that some press comment had made him out to be 'the little man in stature and intellect' at Potsdam, when, so far as size was concerned, Stalin was 'a good six inches shorter than I am and even Churchill was only three inches taller than Joe!' Of Stalin he regretfully added: 'And I liked the little son of a bitch.'[19]

Poland

Although Churchill himself had talked with Stalin in 1944 in terms of percentages and spheres of influence, he had not envisaged this as paving the way for the establishment of Soviet-type systems throughout Eastern Europe. He did, however – earlier than two successive American presidents – become concerned that this was precisely the path Stalin was pursuing. The plight of Poland particularly exercised Churchill, since, as he reminded Stalin, it was the invasion of Poland which had brought Britain into the war. The Warsaw Rising against the Germans of August 1944 had led to the destruction of the city and the deaths of almost 200,000 Poles, while a large contingent of the Soviet army were camped nearby on the eastern side of the River Vistula. To the extent that the Warsaw Rising had been co-ordinated, it was with the Polish government in exile in London and not with Moscow or the Soviet-created Polish Committee of National Liberation at Lublin. Yet the fact that the Soviet army did not intervene, when it seemed to the Poles in Warsaw that they were in a position to prevent the city's inhabitants from being slaughtered or dispossessed (for the Germans expelled the survivors, around 800,000 people), added one more source of bitterness to a long history of animosity in Polish–Russian relations.[20]

Nothing could have been more hollow than the Soviet claim that the Communist government established in post-war Poland reflected the wishes of the Poles. The small inter-war Polish Communist Party had been dissolved by the Comintern in 1938, accused of being infiltrated by Polish secret police and Trotskyists. Many of its leaders and members were in exile in the Soviet Union and most of them were either executed or sent to labour camps. A new party was created, under Soviet tutelage, during the war and given the name initially of the Polish Workers' Party. Later it became the Polish United Workers' Party – the PUWP. The two leading Polish Communists in the early post-war period, Bolesław Bierut and Władysław Gomułka, had spent much time in Moscow. Gomułka was of working-class background. He had left school at the age of fourteen, worked as a mechanic, and from an early age was an active trade unionist and socialist. He was expelled from the Polish Socialist Party in 1924 because of the extremity of his views, and two years later he joined the illegal Communist Party. Bierut, who was born in 1892, was thirteen years older than Gomułka and had been a founder member of the Polish Communist Party in 1918. He was the more Russified of the two, having divided his time in the 1920s between the Soviet Union and Poland, while undertaking secret missions for the Comintern.

Both Bierut and Gomułka were students for two years at the Comintern School in Moscow, and each spent a substantial part of the 1930s in Polish prisons. When the Nazis invaded Poland, both men succeeded in escaping to Moscow. Gomułka returned to Poland in 1942 and was active in the Communist resistance movement (which was very much smaller than that of the Polish non-Communists). Bierut took part in the founding of the Polish Committee of National Liberation at Lublin after that city had been taken by the Red Army from the Germans. By January 1945 the Soviet Union had recognized the Lublin committee as the provisional government of

Poland, with Bierut as the prime minister and Gomułka as deputy premier. The Polish Communists were comparatively few in number at the beginning of 1945 – the party had 30,000 members in January of that year. By the end of the year this had risen to 210,000, and by January 1947 it had reached over 500,000.[21] Given the identification of the Communist movement with the Soviet Union, and in view of the historically bad relations between Poland and Russia, for Polish Communists to win support within their own society was especially difficult. However, here, as elsewhere, there were people who were ready to join the winning side and to benefit from the enhanced career prospects that would accrue. Hence the rapid rise in party membership between January 1945 and January 1947.

The Soviet-imposed regimes in Eastern Europe were not at the outset regarded as 'socialist' by Moscow. The name given to them was 'people's democracies' – a piece of nonsense from a linguistic point of view, since democracy literally means rule by the people. Politically, however, it was intended to distinguish these regimes from what in Marxist-Leninist terms were the 'bourgeois democracies' of the West. The terminology also reflected the fact that these did not become fully fledged Communist systems (or, in Soviet terms, 'socialist') overnight. They moved, in almost every case, from, first, a partially genuine coalition in which Communists predominated; to, second, a pseudo-coalition in which the Communists had, in reality, a monopoly of real power; and, third, to a Communist system similar to that of the Soviet Union, even if in several east-central European cases the government included one or two members of puppet parties intended to provide the illusion (though virtually no one was deceived) of non-Communist participation.[22]

Poland was important to the Soviet Union strategically, and for that reason Stalin, in common with the Polish Communist leaders, was predisposed to take account of its specific features. Thus, the local Communists, with Soviet support, were among the most cautious in Eastern Europe in how they implemented their capture of power. The change in Poland's borders gave the Communists one notable card they could play – namely, that the guarantor of the territory they had taken from Germany was the Soviet Union. Indeed, the potential threat of a possibly resurgent Germany, and the importance, accordingly, of alliance with the Soviet Union, was a theme of which Poland's Communist leaders made much over the next several decades. The policies of the Nazis (especially the physical annihilation of Poland's substantial pre-war Jewish population), the change in the borders, and the expulsion of Germans from what was now Polish territory meant that the country was much more homogeneous than pre-war Poland. That fact was by no means necessarily to the Soviet advantage. Poland had become 98 per cent Polish and, thus, overwhelmingly Catholic. It was also both russophobic and predominantly peasant, the more so since its industrial base had been destroyed in the war.[23]

It is a myth that the fate of Poland was determined at the Yalta conference. What defined the limits of Poland's future for several decades was Soviet military strength, together with the determination of the Communist leadership in Moscow that Poland should be an obedient ally of the Soviet Union. Moreover, far from consigning Poland to Communist statehood, the Yalta agreement had stipulated that there should be 'free and unfettered elections as soon as possible'. Elections – which turned out to be far from free and unfettered – were not held until the beginning of 1947. Both the Soviet leadership and the Polish Communists had realized that some time was required to achieve the right result. The former leader of the London Poles, Stanisław Mikołajczyk, headed the Peasant Party, which had refused to join a coalition with the Communists. Thousands of its members were arrested, including 142 of its parliamentary candidates.[24] A combination of gerrymandering of electoral districts and plain vote-rigging contributed to an electoral outcome whereby the Communist bloc was accorded 80 per cent of the vote.

For some of the Communists' policies there was, however, quite broad support, including that of the Polish Socialist Party, which had joined the coalition. Thus, the nationalization of industry and banking was broadly accepted, the more especially since these had been in German hands during the war. Similarly, there was support across the political spectrum for land reform, whereby the large estates of a wealthy landowning class were broken up and land was redistributed to Polish peasants. With their increasing control of the mass media and effective propaganda, the Communists were able to ensure that they, rather than the Peasant Party, gained most of the credit for that popular measure. In Poland, unlike what was to happen in the vast majority of Communist states, agriculture was not collectivized. The Catholic Church was not attacked to the extent to which religious institutions were elsewhere in east-central Europe. Bierut, who became president, even took a religious oath, and Gomułka, as Communist party leader, defeated the most extreme pro-Soviet group within the party, people who would have liked Poland to become a constituent republic of the Soviet Union.[25]

In other words, Poland in the immediate post-war years had characteristics in common with other Communist takeovers, but there were also concessions to the specific features of Poland, partly as a result of Gomułka's sensitivity to them. What was typical of the time and region was the rapid growth of political censorship and the decision in the autumn of 1947 to arrest a major figure from the political opposition, in this case Mikołajczyk. However, the leader of the Peasant Party learned of this in time and was able, once again, to go into exile. Also typical was the gradual absorption of malleable political figures from other political parties and the exclusion from political life of those who were intransigent. In Poland the Socialist Party was absorbed by the Communists in 1948, and that was the point at which the Polish Workers' Party was renamed the Polish United Workers' Party. Less typical of the coming to power of Communists, in addition to the relative tolerance of the Church and the survival of private agriculture, was the fact that Gomułka dared to criticize looters from the Soviet army and publicly recognized the contribution of Western, as well as Soviet, forces to the defeat of Nazi Germany.[26]

Hungary

Many of the leading Hungarian Communists and founding members of the party, who had sought respite in the Soviet Union, were killed in Stalin's purges. They included at least sixteen former members of the Central Committee. Among them was Bela Kun, the leader of the 1919 short-lived Hungarian revolution. Shortly after Stalin had telephoned Kun in June 1937 telling him to deny allegations in the Western press that he had been arrested (an instruction which Kun promptly obeyed), he was *arrested*! His last words to his wife were: 'Don't worry. Some misunderstanding. I will be home in half an hour.'[27] After interrogation, torture and confession, he was executed on the last day of November 1939. Wartime Hungary was allied with Nazi Germany and the party suffered further severe losses as a result. Hundreds of Communists were arrested during those years, most of them dying in German concentration camps.[28]

At the time Soviet troops liberated Hungary from Nazi rule in 1944 there were fewer than 3,000 Hungarian Communists left. By the end of the Second World War that number had risen to 150,000, and by March 1947 it was 650,000. Initially, the National Independence Front, formed by the Communists, included leaders of the main non-fascist parties – the Social Democratic Party, the Smallholder Party and the National Peasant Party, in addition to the Hungarian Communist Party. Just as the Polish Socialist Party was merged with the Communists in 1948, so in Hungary the Social Democratic Party was absorbed by the Hungarian Communist Party in the same year.[29] In Hungary's first post-Second World War elections in November 1945, which were honestly conducted, the Smallholder Party had emerged victorious. Further elections took place in 1947, this time fraudulently. The Communists received less than 23 per cent of the vote (and that owed much to the stuffing of ballot boxes) but emerged as the largest single party. Moreover, this under-stated their growing dominance, for the Communist-led leftist bloc emerged with 45.3 per cent of the votes. A further major breakthrough for the Communist cause came with the establishment of unity with the Social Democratic Party. This brought membership of the Communist Party to well over a million, representing 12 per cent of the population.[30] Soviet troops had remained in Hungary and a great deal of pressure was exerted on the Social Democrats to co-operate. In their new guise, the now-ruling Communists were known as the Hungarian Workers' Party. In an election in May 1949, a still broader umbrella group dominated by the Communists, the unified list of candidates of the Popular Front, was credited with 95.6 per cent of votes cast. The Communists were now able to move quickly to establish their monopoly of power.[31]

Those Hungarian Communists who had been in Moscow in the 1930s and had avoided being purged by Stalin formed the bulk of the leadership of the party in the immediate post-war period. It was headed by Mátyás Rákosi, and his Moscow associates included Ernő Gerő and Imre Nagy. The leading figures in the 'native', as distinct from Muscovite, wing of the party – Communist activists who had stayed in Hungary during the war – were János Kádár and Lászlo Rajk. Rákosi applied his 'salami tactics' of slicing off political opponents one by one, pursuing a policy of divide and rule with rival parties, and gradually extending Communist control to all ministries. He secured from the outset the Ministry of the Interior, thus combining control over the police with the power which flowed from the party organization.[32] Elements of political pluralism survived in Hungary until 1948, but in that year the comprehensive Stalinization of the system got under way and continued until Stalin's death in 1953. Rajk was arrested in 1948, along with his 'Titoist friends', and following a show trial he was executed. Kádár was arrested in 1950, and although he was tortured, he survived and, following Stalin's death, was released in 1954, along with Hungarian veterans of the Spanish Civil War and alleged 'Rajkists'.[33] The one institution which retained some autonomy until late in 1948 was the Catholic Church, but a series of restrictions on its activities brought protests from the head of the Church in Hungary, Cardinal Mindszenty, and he (followed by many other religious activists) was arrested on Christmas Day 1948.[34]

Romania

During the war, the small Romanian Communist Party was divided geographically between those who were in prison in Romania – among them two future leaders of the country, Gheorghe Gheorghiu-Dej and Nicolae Ceauşescu – and those in exile in the Soviet Union, who included

Ana Pauker, the daughter of a rabbi, and a revolutionary since 1918. She spent much of the inter-war period working for the Comintern but the years between 1935 and 1940 in a Romanian prison. In post-war Romania, Pauker was foreign minister from 1947 until 1952, when she was expelled in quick succession from the Politburo, Central Committee, the Foreign Ministry and the Communist Party. Although placed under house arrest, she was less harshly treated than leading Communists who fell out of favour elsewhere in Eastern Europe.

Romania, under its right-wing authoritarian regime, had fought on the side of Nazi Germany in the Second World War. The government of General Ion Antonescu, which had been formed in 1940, made clear to the monarch, King Michael (who had recently succeeded his father, who had abdicated and left the country in haste), that he was to play a merely symbolic role and take no part in the making of state policy.[35] In August 1944 King Michael was able to turn the tables on Antonescu. By this time Soviet forces were advancing into Romanian territory; it seemed prudent either to stop fighting altogether or to change sides. Antonescu informed the king that he was going to seek an armistice but that he would first inform the Germans about this. The king, having quickly decided that the Antonescu government was in no position to safeguard the territorial integrity and political independence of Romania, went to an adjoining room and instructed his allies to arrest Antonescu. The new government, formed under a premier appointed by the king, General Sanatescu, had representatives from four political parties, and when Soviet forces entered the Romanian capital, Bucharest, on 31 August 1944, the two countries were, in principle, no longer enemies.[36] Hardly surprisingly, however, the Soviet authorities did not set aside all that happened prior to the 'king's coup' and treated Romania as a defeated enemy. Molotov was the implacable Soviet negotiator when an armistice was signed on 12 September. He insisted that the Soviet annexation of the formerly Romanian territory of Bessarabia and Northern Bukovina be ratified. Punitive economic demands were imposed on the Romanians, while the military clauses brought the Romanian army back into the war, fighting side by side with the Soviet army against Germany and her allies. The Romanians made a significant contribution to liberating parts of Hungary and Czechoslovakia, took 100,000 prisoners and lost in this part of the war almost 170,000 of their own men.[37] Although Gheorghiu-Dej was not a 'Muscovite', he succeeded in convincing Stalin that he would be a faithful follower of the Soviet line, and his election as general secretary of the party – and thus the de facto ruler of Romania – took place in 1945. In a later struggle for power with the 'Muscovites', which led to the 1952 arrest of Ana Pauker, Gheorghiu-Dej was again to receive Stalin's blessing.

Bulgaria

Bulgarian Communists had taken part in partisan activities on a modest
scale during the Second World War and they were able to gain influence in
a Popular Front movement formed in 1943. In September 1944 that movement, called the Fatherland Front, seized power. The Communists were in
a minority in the coalition which made up the Fatherland Front, and in the
government which was formed in September. However, true to form, they
seized the most crucial positions for a party intent on consolidating its hold
on power. Through the Ministry of the Interior they controlled the police
and through the Ministry of Justice they held sway over the courts. In
Bulgaria, as in other states making a transition to Communist rule, a parallel
police force known as the People's Militia was created, and it was entirely
Communist-dominated.

The political party which had the strongest support at the end of the
war was the Agrarians, but the Communists, successfully applying divide-
and-rule tactics, succeeded in splitting both the Agrarian party and the
Social Democrats. Georgi Dimitrov returned to Bulgaria to become the
leading figure in the Bulgarian Communist Party. While still in Moscow,
he was very active behind the scenes and orchestrated many of the moves
made by the Bulgarian Communists, having access both to them and to
Stalin.[38] He returned to Bulgaria to head the government in November
1945. He wished to include the two main leaders of democratic oppositional parties, Nikola Petkov of the Agrarians and Kosta Lulchev of the
Social Democrats, in the governing coalition. However, both of them
insisted on removing the Ministry of the Interior and Ministry of Justice
from Communist control. This the Communist party (known temporarily
as the Bulgarian Workers' Party, reverting to Bulgarian Communist Party
in 1948) refused to countenance, and so Petkov and Lulchev stayed in
opposition.[39] Petkov continued to mount vigorous attacks on the
Communists and noted that they were spending far more on the police
and prisons than had the right-wing government of Bulgaria during the
war. In June 1947 Petkov was arrested and given a travesty of a trial. It
ended with his being sentenced to death and hanged. This effectively put
an end to democratic opposition to Communist rule in Bulgaria, although
Lulchev defied warnings from Dimitrov and voted against the budget in
January 1948. In spite of his advanced age, he was arrested later that year
and sentenced to fifteen years in prison.[40] The 'Dimitrov Constitution',
which had been formulated in the Soviet Union, was adopted in December

1947 and Marxism-Leninism became within the space of a few months the official ideology. The means of production were nationalized, and the Communist Party had by 1948 achieved a monopoly of power, although they kept in existence as a puppet party that section of the Agrarians which had been willing to co-operate with them.[41]

East Germany

What became the separate East German state known as the German Democratic Republic (GDR) began as the Soviet zone of Germany. It was the part of the country which had been occupied by Soviet troops and thus fell under Soviet control. This meant that it was administered by German Communists chosen by the Soviet leadership to do their bidding. In West Germany the GDR was known until 1971 – when Willy Brandt was the Social Democratic chancellor as either the 'Soviet Occupied Zone' or 'Central Germany', with the German provinces to the east of the Oder–Neisse Line, which had been lost to the Soviet bloc (especially Poland), referred to as 'East Germany'.[42] There was never any likelihood of that lost 'East Germany' being restored to German rule, not least because it had been 'ethnically cleansed' of Germans. However, the actually existing East Germany, ruled from 1945 by German Communists in close communication with their Soviet mentors, developed in ways similar to Communist regimes elsewhere in east-central Europe.

Thus they began by constructing a broad base, in which many of those whom they appointed to political offices, such as mayors of important towns, were from the Social Democratic Party or were prominent local professional people of liberal views. However, these citizens, who often accepted their posts in good faith, were invariably shadowed by a reliable Communist (in the office, for example, of deputy mayor) who would ensure that nothing contrary to the longer-term interests of the Communists occurred. All four powers – the Soviet Union, the United States, Britain and France (the last-named a presence in Germany only because Churchill had pressed for this in meetings of the 'Big Three') – had their zones of influence in Germany. Stalin was conscious that what happened in the Soviet zone would be the subject of scrutiny and comparison, so he was ready to tolerate some minimal democracy in the initial stage of building new political structures in East Germany. The German Communist Party's manifesto of June 1945 was modest, advocating neither a socialist economy nor a one-party state. It even included a commitment to 'complete and unrestricted development of free commerce and private enterprise on the basis of private property', making it, on the face of things, much less committed to socialism than was the German Social Democratic Party.

When the proclamation of policy was announced from on high by Walter Ulbricht to a conference of German Communists, a majority of whom had belonged to the underground party during the war, one of them asked in what respect the policy differed 'from the programme of any party you care to name'. Ulbricht's answer, which was accompanied by a wink, was: 'You'll soon see, Comrade! Just wait a bit!'[43] The top leadership of the German Communists, most notably Ulbricht and Wilhelm Pieck, were in full accord with Stalin on both tactics and longer-term strategy. On neither side was there an initial desire to commit to separate statehood for the Soviet zone, the preference being to keep their options open. Ideally, they wished for a united Germany – or, at least, a united Berlin – under Communist control. Failing that, they wished to 'build socialism', Soviet-style, in East Germany and at the same time to ensure that the part of Germany under Western influence would remain neutral and disarmed. If Germany *were* to be split into two separate states, Stalin wanted the initiative for this to come from the Western powers, so that they would be blamed by Germans for dividing the nation.[44]

In charge of the gradual transition to a Communist regime was a group of German Communists who had survived both the purges and the war in the Soviet Union. A dominant figure from the outset was Ulbricht, who went on to lead the party until 1971. He was a cold and calculating personality of little imagination but possessed of a remarkable memory. His years in the Soviet Union had left him well fitted to behave in a highly authoritarian manner in Germany, which he combined with obsequiousness in his relations with Stalin. It had become second nature for Ulbricht to think like a Stalinist and to be ready to follow every twist and turn of Soviet policy.

The youngest person on the first planeload of German Communists flown from Moscow to Berlin in 1945 was Wolfgang Leonhard, a graduate of the Comintern School, who was a true-believing Communist at the age of twenty-three, even though his mother had been arrested by the NKVD in 1936 and was to spend the next twelve years in a Soviet labour camp and subsequent exile to a remote Siberian village. Only in 1948 was she allowed to join her son, following representations to Moscow by Wilhelm Pieck, a veteran German Communist who, remarkably, was a leading figure in the party from 1918 until his death in 1960. Leonhard himself has written a vivid account of his years in Russia and of his experiences in early post-war Germany when he precociously entered the ruling circles and became disillusioned with what he saw. The hierarchy of privilege which he had learned to take for granted in the Soviet Union looked different when he saw the reactions of Communists who had known only an underground existence. Along with idealistic German

Communists, including some who had been in Nazi concentration camps, he was increasingly revolted by Ulbricht's style of rule and by the German leadership's slavish adherence to the Soviet line. The last straw was their endorsement of the excommunication of Tito's Yugoslavia in 1948. In common with many Communists in central Europe, Leonhard and a number of his colleagues in East Germany had admired the fighting spirit of Tito's partisans and the fact that they were able to come to power through their own efforts rather than courtesy of the Soviet army.[45]

Some of the German Communists, including one who had spent the war years in the Soviet Union, Anton Ackermann, argued in 1945–46 for a 'German road to socialism' which would be distinct from the experience of the Soviet Union. This was tolerated by Ulbricht and by the Soviet leadership for a time, since their policy was initially a gradualist one. Under pressure from Marshal Zhukov, who was head of the Soviet Military Administration in Germany, the Communist Party merged with that part of the Social Democratic Party which was prepared for such a fusion. In April 1946 they became the Socialist Unity Party (SED in its German initials). Notwithstanding that merger, in elections later in 1946 the SED failed to secure a majority in any province of East Germany. In greater Berlin, where the presence of the other four powers permitted those social democrats who had remained independent (the SPD) to compete, the SPD gained 48.7 per cent of the vote as against a mere 19.8 per cent for the SED. Although the Communists had many organizational advantages, they were beaten into third place in the Berlin election by the Christian Democrats, who obtained 22.1 per cent of the vote. After that experience the Communists made sure that in future the electorate would be offered no choice. For Leonhard and those who thought like him within the SED it was clear that the German Communists' greatest disadvantage was that they were thought of as 'the Russian party', and experience of rape, looting, and the dismantling of German factories had made even apolitical German citizens deeply resentful of the Soviet army and Soviet control.[46]

Marshall Aid to the countries of Europe within the Western sphere of influence had, as noted in the previous chapter, been launched in 1947. In West Germany the need to administer such economic aid underlined the necessity of having state political institutions. That necessity was accentuated when in 1948 the Soviet Union and their German Communist allies made an attempt to gain control over the whole of the city of Berlin, taking advantage of the fact that the surrounding territory was in the Soviet zone, by making subsistence impossible in the American, British and French zones. They did this by closing the roads, railways and canals leading into the Western part of the city. The plan did not work because Western aircraft, especially American and British, airlifted supplies to the population of West Berlin, making some 277,000 flights between the imposition of the blockade and its lifting in May 1949.[47]

Marshall Aid and the Berlin blockade between them underlined the de facto existence of two Germanies, and this was formalized in 1949. In the summer of that year the Federal Republic of Germany was formed on the territory of West Germany, and national elections in August led to Konrad Adenauer becoming the first chancellor of this new state. The German Democratic Republic, as East Germany now termed itself, was founded in October 1949, with Wilhelm Pieck becoming its first (and last) president, Otto Grotewohl the prime minister, and Walter Ulbricht pulling most of the strings as the leader of the SED.[48] Even before this the party had been removing many of the recently recruited social democrats from its ranks. Between the late 1940s and the early 1950s around 5,000 social democrats were imprisoned, another 20,000 were dismissed from their jobs, and 100,000 fled to the West.[49] The intense pressure on social democrats was part and parcel of the more thorough establishment of Communist political structures and norms, which gathered pace with the establishment of a separate East German state. While the Communist party (under its new name, the SED) held supreme power, it began to develop a security apparatus. In 1949 a Main Directorate for the Defence of the People's Economy was established which reported to the German Central Administration of the Interior. In February 1950, fear of Western influence led the GDR leadership to take the Stalinization of their state a step further with the creation of a Ministry of State Security, an organization that was to be permitted to grow to an extraordinary extent and become known as the Stasi.[50]

The 'Iron Curtain' Dividing Europe

The countries of east-central Europe became more Stalinist and the division of Europe more rigid from 1948 until the death of Stalin. I have more to say in Chapter 12 about that phase of post-war Stalinism both in the Soviet Union and in its now consolidated satellite states. The division of Europe remained in place until 1989, but the terminology which Winston Churchill made ubiquitous with his speech in Fulton, Missouri, on 5 March 1946 – 'from Stettin in the Baltic to Trieste in the Adriatic an *iron curtain* has descended across the Continent . . .' – was in later years to obscure the extent to which ideas crossed national boundaries, with the dividing curtain, in many cases, acquiring the permeability of gauze rather than iron.

However, the metaphor of the iron curtain was apt enough in the context of 1946, and it was the timing of Churchill's use of the term – allied to the fact that he was a world-renowned war leader who was being accompanied on the visit to a small Midwestern college by no less a person than the incumbent President of the United States, Harry Truman – which gave his speech such resonance. The political systems of Eastern Europe were already being constructed along Soviet lines. The mass media and security police in those countries were, with increasing effectiveness, cutting their citizens off from a free flow of information and greatly restricting the populations' Western contacts. It was not the originality of the term, 'iron curtain' – for it was far from original – but its political context which accounts for most of its impact. Just two weeks before Churchill's speech, George Kennan had sent what was to become celebrated as the 'long telegram' from the American Embassy in Moscow to Washington. It gave a penetrating analysis of Soviet strengths, weaknesses, stratagems and subterfuges, together with sensible counsel on how the United States and the West as a whole should respond. While advocating 'cohesion, firmness and vigor' in dealing with the Soviet Union, Kennan was at the same time dismissive of 'hysterical anti-Sovietism', saying that it was necessary to study Stalin's Soviet Union 'with the same courage, detachment, objectivity, and the same determination not to be emotionally provoked or unseated by it, with which a doctor studies unruly and unreasonable individuals'. Warning against 'prestige-engaging show-downs', Kennan advocated a policy of containment of Soviet ambitions, observing: 'Soviet power, unlike that of Hitlerite Germany, is neither schematic nor adventuristic . . . It does not take unnecessary risks.' And though it was 'impervious to logic of reason' it was 'highly sensitive to logic of force'.[51]

Kennan's telegram was read by President Truman as well as by senior officials, and the Secretary of the Navy 'made it required reading for hundreds, if not thousands, of higher officers in the armed services'.[52] Kennan set out, vividly and without illusions, what he saw as Soviet thinking in the immediate post-war period, taking cognizance not only of official policy but of its informal projection – 'policy implemented through "front" organizations and stooges of all sorts'.[53] In his memoirs, Kennan notes that the sensational impact of his 'elaborate pedagogical effort' rested on its timing: 'Six months earlier this message would probably have been received in the Department of State with raised eyebrows and lips pursed in dis-approval. Six months later, it would probably have sounded redundant, a sort of preaching to the converted.'[54] Generalizing further about American politics (though the remark has still broader application) he said: 'All this goes to show that more important than the observable nature of external reality, when it comes to the determination of Washington's view of the world, is the subjective state of readiness on the part of Washington offi-cialdom to recognize this or that feature of it.'[55]

Whereas Kennan's telegram was circulated in the most influential Washington circles, it was not known at the time to the wider world. In contrast, Churchill's speech, warning of the Soviet Union's desire to gain the fruits of war (albeit without war) through 'the indefinite expansion of their power and doctrines', was widely reported and highly controversial. It was not so long ago that the Soviet Union had been a wartime ally of the United States and Britain, and one of decisive importance. Nevertheless, Truman in private – though not immediately in public – agreed with Churchill, as, essentially, did the dominant figure in British foreign policy at the time, Ernest Bevin, foreign secretary in the Labour government. As Roy Jenkins put it, 'Bevin's foreign policy was moving very much in the direction of Fulton, even if a little more slowly.'[56] It was the iron curtain imagery which stuck in the public mind, although the term was not Churchill's coinage – or, indeed, that of Goebbels, though he also (as Soviet propagandists did not fail to note) used it during the war.

Even as a metaphor the term had been used quite often. Its literal origins lay in the iron curtain which, for safety reasons, separated the stage from the audience before, and during the intervals of, theatre performances. Later the iron curtains were replaced by asbestos ones. As a metaphor, the term had been used by pacifists, especially by Vernon Lee, as early as 1914, objecting to the 'iron curtain' which, as a result of imperial rivalries, divided peoples.[57] It seems to have first been applied to the division between Bolshevik Russia and the West by Ethel Snowden, the wife of a future Labour chancellor of the exchequer, Philip Snowden, in 1920.[58] Churchill himself had used the phrase several times in correspondence with President Truman as well as in the House of Commons in 1945. But when in 1946 Churchill (who had the theatre safety curtain in mind) spoke of the iron curtain which had descended in Europe, the impact of the metaphor was much greater. Even Stalin felt obliged to respond and, unusually, used the device of an inter-view given to *Pravda* to reply to Churchill's warnings. For Soviet politicians and historians Churchill's Fulton speech was seen over the next four decades as the moment at which the Cold War began. Since the term 'Cold War' is also a metaphor – it signified greatly increased tension, ideological struggle, economic competition, and armaments build-up, but it was *not* a war – there can be no definitive answer to the question: when did the Cold War begin? However, the Soviet imposition of Communist regimes on the countries of east-central Europe, with no regard for the wishes of their peoples, was the cause of the division of Europe – and that was the single most important manifestation of what became known as the Cold War.

II

The Communists
Take Power in China

The Second World War, so important for Communist parties coming to power in Europe, was crucial also in China. It weakened Chiang Kai-shek immensely, for his Kuomintang had borne the brunt of the fighting against the Japanese. The Communists had played a relatively modest part in the resistance to the foreign occupiers of their country. A higher priority for them, and for Mao Zedong in particular, had been to prepare for the coming struggle with the Nationalists for control of the entire Chinese state. The Communists had strengthened their power base to such an extent that in 1937, when the war with Japan began, they controlled areas whose population totalled only four million people, and had then 100,000 troops under their command, whereas by 1945, when the war ended, that had grown to command of territories comprising over ninety-five million inhabitants, by which time there were 900,000 soldiers in the Chinese Red Army.[1]

At the Yalta meeting in Soviet Crimea in February 1945, Roosevelt and Churchill had readily agreed with Stalin that the USSR should enter the war against Japan.[2] Stalin, who had his eye on territorial gain, was eager to do so. In fact, the Soviet Union took possession of the Kurile Islands – known in Japan as the Northern Territories – and in the twenty-first century they remain a serious bone of contention between Russia and Japan. As the Pacific war entered its last stage, Soviet troops advanced into Manchuria.[3] The Chinese Communists linked up with the Soviet forces and were able to hold on to Manchuria, in spite of the efforts of Chiang Kai-shek to dislodge them. Between 1946 and 1949, the Communists gradually extended their territorial control to other parts of China, eventually taking the major cities of Beijing and Shanghai. Although the Kuomintang claimed the mantle of nationalism, they produced no solutions to the country's problems, whereas the Communists appeared to be reasserting national dignity and providing a vision of China's future.[4] Many young revolutionaries of Mao's generation had viewed Marxism-Leninism as a doctrine which pointed the way to ending China's economic and political backwardness and would put a stop to the humiliation at the hands of foreigners which their country had suffered throughout the nineteenth and first half of the twentieth centuries.[5] The Chinese Red Army's role in fighting the Japanese, even though very limited in comparison with that of the forces led by Chiang Kai-shek, was significant in northern China, and it succeeded in adding a patriotic and national hue to the Communists' class struggle. This was partly a result of their effective propaganda, which made the most of the several battles in which they did engage. Most of the operations under the control of the Chinese Communist Party (CCP) were local guerrilla raids to seize land not garrisoned by the Japanese or their Chinese auxiliaries.

The social order the CCP set out to destroy, and to replace with new social and political relations, was one vastly more entrenched than that which any European Communist parties had to contend with. Although there had been changes in landholding over time, it was a class structure that had existed in major respects for some 3,000 years.[6] But no matter how sharp a break with national tradition the Communists represented, there was an appeal to national solidarity and to patriotic aspiration in Mao Zedong's words, used on more than one occasion, and most notably around the time of the foundation of the Chinese People's Republic. The Chinese people, he said, had 'stood up'.[7]

Conventional Marxist views on social class were problematic in the Chinese context. Even before 1917 there had been some interest in them on the part of a small minority of Chinese intellectuals. It was, however, the Bolshevik revolution in that year which aroused interest in Leninism. After the incorporation of the Chinese Communist Party into the Comintern in 1922, both plentiful advice and material assistance were offered to the Chinese party by Comintern and Soviet advisers, but their orthodox Marxist-Leninist theoretical emphasis on the working class was inappropriate to Chinese conditions. In Russia also – though not to the same extent as in China – the peasantry had been by far the largest social stratum at the time of the revolution. Nevertheless, in Russia it was the city battleground that mattered most, especially St Petersburg, and workers played a significant role in the revolutionary struggle. In its doctrine, as well as in political practice, the Communist Party of the Soviet Union kept the peasantry firmly in a subordinate place. Even when Soviet leaders and ideologues stopped speaking about 'the dictatorship of the proletariat', they replaced that phrase by 'the leading role of the working class'. In China, in contrast, the Communists got nowhere until they substituted the peasantry for the proletariat, thereby standing orthodox Marxist-Leninist theory on its head.[8] Although there had been a gradual growth in the urban population of China during the first half of the twentieth century, at the time the CCP came to power in 1949 it stood at only some 57 million out of a total population at that time of around 550 million people.

The war of resistance to the Japanese took a tremendous toll on China. Chiang Kai-shek's troops struggled for eight years against a ferocious Japanese fighting force. The Communist army, deploying guerrilla tactics, suffered less severe losses than did the Nationalists. Having undertaken fewer major campaigns in the last years of the war, their troops were, as a result, much fresher than Chiang's.[9] Following the Japanese surrender on 15 August 1945, the two sides of the Chinese resistance set about establishing their authority in different parts of the country in readiness for a resumption of their civil wars, which had been interrupted by the Japanese invasion. Chiang's troops were able to operate in most of the area south of the River Yangtze, while the Communist stronghold was in the north. There they controlled much of the countryside, although the Kuomintang succeeded in occupying the cities.[10] An attempt to bring the Nationalists and Communists together in a coalition was brokered by the United States, and backed (at least for appearance's sake) by Stalin. After hostilities had been resumed in full measure between the Nationalists and the Communists, Mao was persuaded to take part in talks with Chiang Kai-shek. Fighting between the Kuomintang and the Communists continued, as in August 1945 Mao flew in an American plane to Chongquing for what turned out to be forty-five days of talks with Chiang. He was accompanied, at his own insistence, by the American ambassador, since his distrust of the Nationalists was such that he did not rule out an attempt to arrange an accident. In the light of Chiang's dependence on the United States for the supply of armaments, the company of a high-ranking American was a useful insurance policy for Mao. There was deep distrust between Chiang and Mao, and each had every intention of achieving total victory in the continuing civil war. However, Chiang, in particular, had to go through the motions of seeking a compromise agreement with his Communist rivals. This was partly a result of his reliance on American support.[11] It also reflected the fact that public opinion in China was strongly against the civil war and in favour of national reconstruction. The meeting ended on an ostensibly constructive note with an agreement to hold a political consultation conference and to recognize all political parties. However, almost immediately both sides resumed their struggle for territorial control, with the conflict intensifying in 1946.

The civil war lasted until 1949. In 1947 the Communist military forces were renamed the People's Liberation Army (PLA), and by 1948 they had gone beyond guerrilla fighting to fielding armies with large units, using artillery, mostly of Japanese origin, which had been handed over to them by their Soviet allies. Mao Zedong headed the Revolutionary Military Committee, although the commander-in-chief of the PLA was a more professional military man, Zhu De.[12] A combination of redistribution of land to win peasant support, ideological conviction, strong party discipline, impressive organizational capacity and military prowess brought the Communists to power. The Nationalists were so heavily dependent on conservative regional power-brokers and large landholders that it was impossible for them to compete with the Communists in the area of land reform. They were also much more internally divided and suffering from the loss of their leading military professionals. Over 100,000 officers were among the Kuomintang troops lost in the Sino-Japanese war.[13] Chiang Kai-shek also made some serious errors. After the defeat of the Japanese, demobilization of the Chinese army had proceeded apace, with no provision for the demobilized soldiers to earn a new livelihood. Moreover, the Chinese puppet forces who had fought as auxiliaries of the Japanese were also disbanded, and the CCP did not hesitate to recruit large numbers of these former soldiers who had been trained by the Japanese to a higher level of military skill than their own troops.

Neither the Soviet Union for the Communists nor the United States for the Kuomintang was an entirely wholehearted ally. Mao's troops undoubtedly benefited from the Soviet capture of Manchuria after they had entered the war. This enabled the Chinese Red Army to join up with their Soviet counterparts, after which the Soviet army departed to their side of the border. The Communist forces also benefited from a vast supply of captured Japanese arms which the Soviet Union handed over to them. However, Stalin was more cautious than Mao and seemed content for the Chinese Communists to control only the north of China, and to be in no hurry to attempt to wrest control of the south from Chiang Kai-shek. Stalin and Chiang had reached an understanding whereby China would recognize (Outer) Mongolia as an 'independent' state, though it was essentially a Soviet satellite, rather than lay any claim to a unified Mongolia. Yet in November 1948, a time when the Communists were gaining ground on the Nationalists in the civil war, Stalin urged Mao Zedong to consolidate their existing northern gains, leaving the south to Chiang Kai-shek's administration.[14] Mao disregarded the advice. In conversation with a group of Bulgarian and Yugoslav party leaders (which included Dimitrov from Bulgaria but not Tito from Yugoslavia) in Moscow in February 1948 – just before the Soviet–Yugoslav rupture – Stalin admitted that the Soviet leadership had been wrong and the Chinese Communists right in believing that they could take power in the whole country. He said: 'True. We, too, can make a mistake. Here, when the war with Japan ended, we invited the Chinese comrades to agree on a means of reaching a *modus vivendi* with Chiang Kai-shek. They agreed with us in word, but in deed they did it their own way when they got home: they mustered their forces and struck. It has been shown that they were right, and we were not.'[15]

On the other side of the political divide, the United States also urged restraint. While generally supportive of the Kuomintang, the Truman administration persuaded the Nationalists to seek an armistice in June 1946, just as they were on the point of capturing the Chinese city closest to the Russian border, Harbin. The Chinese Communist forces in the area, under the command of Lin Biao, were given a much-needed respite. In an effort to end the fighting, the United States even introduced an embargo on supplying arms to China, which harmed the Nationalists more than the Communists. Ultimately, however, the outcome of the civil war was determined by the differing ability of the leadership of the two Chinese armies to inspire their forces and to mobilize support within the society. In 1949, when the Communists finally established their ascendancy, neither the United States nor the Soviet Union played a decisive role in the outcome.

Although all these factors – not least Mao's skilful, and ruthless, leadership – played a big part in the Communists' successful capture of power in mainland China as a whole in 1949, there were also deeper-rooted conditions for their success. China, throughout the first half of the twentieth century, had been a country experiencing dire poverty. The Nationalists had failed to produce a programme for alleviating it. Moreover, corruption in their ranks, both at the local level and within Chiang Kai-shek's family circle, aroused widespread resentment. Immediately after the war there was hyperinflation. Whereas in 1937 one American dollar was the equivalent in value of 3.42 yuan (the unit of Chinese currency), by 1945 it had become 1,705 yuan to the dollar and in August 1948 the US dollar was worth a startling 8.6 million yuan. The Nationalist government brought in a new yuan that month, attempting to peg it at four to the American dollar. By mid-May 1949, one dollar purchased 22.3 million new yuan.[16] The Kuomintang could find no answer to this massive problem, which was tackled by the Communists in their earliest years in power.

While Soviet support for the Chinese Red Army was significant, China remained a very different case from the East European countries discussed in the previous chapter. Notwithstanding Stalin's help, the coming to power of the Chinese Communists was essentially an indigenous movement, comparable with that of Yugoslavia rather than the Communist takeovers in, say, Hungary or Poland. In Yugoslavia and China, Soviet troops played a supportive role in recapturing territory (in the former case from the Germans, in the latter from the Japanese), but in both countries the local Communists' ability to generate domestic support was more decisive. And while Soviet military aid was of great help to the CCP after the Second World War in the Pacific ended, it had also been given in substantial quantities to Chiang Kai-shek while his army was fighting the Japanese.

Mao Zedong and the Chinese Communist Leadership

The rise of the Chinese Communist Party and the rise of Mao Zedong are closely interlinked, however absurdly exaggerated Mao's achievements were to become during the cult of his personality, which he promoted when in power. He emerged from the Long March as the de facto leading figure in the party, although it was only during the Second World War that this was made official. Well before the war, he was recognized in the Soviet Union as the leader of China's Communists. The book by the American journalist Edgar Snow, *Red Star Over China*, highly sympathetic to Mao, was published in the USSR in Russian translation in 1938. In 1939 a glowing biography of Mao was published in Moscow, and in the same year a Soviet brochure was devoted to the two *vozhdi* of the Chinese people, the second *vozhd'* being Zhu De, the military head of the Chinese Red Army.[17]* Mao's leadership was institutionalized when he became Chairman of the Politburo and Secretariat of the Chinese Communist Party in 1943, and his topmost position was ratified at the Seventh Party Congress in 1945.[18]

Mao had an up-and-down relationship with Stalin long before he met him for the first time in 1949. He recognized the Soviet leader, however, as the ultimate authority within the international Communist movement. He was aware that Stalin's control over the Comintern and his prestige among Communists worldwide, including China, was such that he had it in his power to bestow on someone else the accolade of leader of the Chinese Communists. The person concerned would then be accorded that status not only by a sufficient number of Chinese party members but also by the Comintern, and thus the whole Communist movement internationally. In the light of this knowledge, Mao was especially wary of China's representative at the Comintern, Wang Ming, who, by virtue of that post, spent most of his time in Moscow until the Comintern was wound up in 1943. Wang really did aspire to the top post in China and so was viewed by Mao as a deadly rival. What is more, he also had a cautious supporter in Moscow in the head of the Comintern administration, Georgi Dimitrov, who had adopted as his child Wang's young daughter.[19] Stalin, though, was the ultimate arbiter of the leadership of non-ruling Communist parties and he took a less rosy view of Wang Ming than did Dimitrov. Wang at one stage

---

* *Vozhd'* (the singular of *vozhdi*) implies a more than ordinary leader. Although used more broadly than Führer (as its application to two contemporaneous Chinese Communists indicates), it is the nearest Russian equivalent to the German word.

seriously blotted his copybook with Stalin. When one of the Chinese warlords with links to the Communists captured Chiang Kai-shek in 1936, Stalin was furious that Wang Ming's response had been to propose a telegram suggesting that Chiang be killed – or so, at least, Stalin was informed.[20] Stalin saw Chiang as integral to his plans for a united front against the Japanese.

At midnight on 14 December 1936, Dimitrov received a telephone call from Stalin in which the Soviet leader asked: 'Who is this Wang Ming of yours? A provocateur? He wanted to file a telegram to have Chiang Kai-shek killed.'[21] For a Comintern official to be called a 'provocateur' by Stalin was normally a prelude to a death sentence, but Wang Ming, with Dimitrov's support, survived.[22] In discussion in the Comintern, Wang was frequently dismissive of Mao Zedong's qualities as a leader, but Stalin, for all his reservations about Mao, combined grudging respect for him with continuing suspicion of Wang Ming. A recent scholarly article in a Russian journal (based on a study of Comintern documents) is even entitled 'How Stalin helped Mao to become leader (vozhd')'.[23] Stalin appears to have come down firmly in favour of Mao in 1938. A delegation of the Chinese Communist Party to the Comintern was told by Dimitrov, echoing the preferences of Stalin: 'You must convey to all that they must support Mao Zedong as the vozhd' of the Communist Party of China. He is hardened in the practical struggle. There is no need for such people as Wang Ming to fight for the leadership.'[24] Stalin's wishes and his strong doubts about Wang Ming clearly prevailed over Dimitrov's personal friendship with Wang.

More generally, Stalin's policy, until the moment when the Communists succeeded in gaining power throughout the whole of China, was to urge caution on the Chinese party, for he had welcomed the part played by Chiang Kai-shek's army in the war against Japan and saw him as a counterweight to British imperialism. Chiang had the additional advantage, in Stalin's eyes, of uneasy relations with his American allies. During the war Stalin wanted the Chinese Communists to maintain their alliance with the Kuomintang and to concentrate more on fighting the Japanese. Both then and in the civil war which followed, Mao and the Chinese Communists pressed ahead regardless with their domestic political agenda of supplanting the Nationalists entirely. Victory came quicker than even they expected. Stalin, looking ahead to an eventual Chinese Communist victory, in April 1948 urged Mao to be cautious also in the early period of Communist rule. Having in mind the East European example – of genuine coalition giving way to pseudo-coalition, and, in due course, to Communist monopoly of power – Stalin emphasized the need for a broad-based government after eventual victory in the civil war. He wrote to Mao: 'It should be kept in mind that after the

victory of the people's liberation armies of China – at least, in a post-
victory period for which the duration is difficult to define now – the Chinese
government, in terms of its policy, will be a national revolutionary-
democratic government, rather than a Communist one.'[25] That, he continued,
would mean a necessary delay in nationalization and confiscation of properties from large, middle and small landowners. In the meantime the Chinese
Communists pressed on with the military struggle, and in February 1949
they took Beijing. In October of that year they gained control of the last
major city in the south, Guangzhou. Chiang Kai-shek appealed to the United
States for more aid, but to no avail. He had little option but to leave with
what remained of his government and army for the island of Taiwan.[26]

The Soviet Model and Communist China

Though prepared to acknowledge the pre-eminence of the Soviet Union as
the world's first 'socialist state', which he combined with prudent respect
for the authority of Stalin, Mao regarded himself, not without reason, as a
better judge of conditions on the ground in China. His disregard for Stalin's
advice from time to time did not at this stage cause any crisis in the relationship between Soviet and Chinese Communism because the outcomes
of Mao's policies were sufficiently positive from a Soviet point of view. The
war in the Pacific had ended with the defeat of Japan – albeit thanks more
to the Americans and to Chiang Kai-shek's army than to Mao's forces – and
in 1949 the Communist Party did come to power throughout China. Mao
moved somewhat faster than Stalin had recommended in 1948, but the extent
to which the system constructed by the CCP was a copy of what existed
in the USSR could not but be pleasing to the Soviet leader. Although some
China scholars would argue that even in the early stages of Communist
rule there were significant differences from, as well as similarities to, the
Soviet system, a Russian historian convincingly contends that what was
constructed in China was 'the Soviet model of political, social and economic
development' and goes on to describe what were, indeed, fundamental
features they had in common: 'the undivided power of the strictly centralized and hierarchical Communist Party, the unbounded cult of the party
leader, all-encompassing control over the political and intellectual life of citizens by the organs of public security, state seizure of private property, strictly
centralized planning, priority given to the development of heavy industry,
and huge resources devoted to national defence'.[27]
   Mao had irritated Stalin from time to time by his unorthodox doctrine
as well as by a number of his initiatives when Stalin was urging caution.

But while Mao, for his part, undoubtedly had reservations about Stalin, he had taken care, even in the 1930s, to present himself to emissaries from the Soviet Union as the devoted pupil of the *vozhd'* in the Kremlin. Thus, when a Soviet documentary film-maker, Roman Karmen, came to China in the spring of 1939 to make a film about him, Mao posed with a work by Stalin in his hands, studying it intently, and making sure that Stalin's picture was clearly displayed to the camera. Karmen was able to report to Moscow on the warmth with which Mao spoke of Stalin.[28] It was, however, as late as December 1949 when Mao met Stalin for the first time. The visit was timed for the celebration of Stalin's seventieth birthday, which had the effect of overshadowing Mao's arrival. The Chinese Communists had come to power just two and a half months earlier, and that event was welcomed in Moscow as evidence of the onward march of Communism – in a country, moreover, of great international significance. Yet if anyone were to judge by the Soviet press coverage, they would have been forced to conclude that of the two occurrences, the Communist Party's accession to power in the world's most populous state was a less momentous occasion for celebration than Stalin's reaching his three score years and ten.

Mao over the years had taken care to discredit potential rivals within the party or make them dependent on him. When the Communists came to power in China, there were, nevertheless, talented individuals of high prestige apart from Mao in the country's leadership. One such person was Liu Shaoqi. While Mao was the undisputed top leader, with his power base in the party, Liu, who in the civil war with the Nationalists had operated skilfully in the 'white areas' behind enemy lines, occupied second place. Third in the ranking order was the head of the government administration, Zhou Enlai, who combined that post with the office of foreign minister.[29] A party veteran of great ability, who had on occasion opposed Mao in the early 1930s, Zhou's instincts were to soften some of the more extreme of Mao's policies. Like Anastas Mikoyan, a similarly intelligent and flexible long-serving member of the Soviet Politburo under Stalin and Khrushchev, Zhou was content never to seek the top post. (In this respect he differed from Wang Ming.) Thus he was able to stay in the leadership of the party over four decades at the price of sharing responsibility for costly mistakes and bloody repression. Remaining committed to the Communist cause he had embraced in his youth, Zhou Enlai accepted the twists and turns of Mao's leadership just as Mikoyan accepted his subordination to Stalin. (In the Soviet Union, still more than in China, to do so or not to do so was a matter of life or death.) Commenting on Mao Zedong's 'glaring contradictions', a leading specialist on Chinese politics, Lowell Dittmer, has written that while Mao was 'absolutely determined to have his own way and crush all opposition, he was sneeringly contemptuous of those (like Zhou Enlai) who fawned on and flattered him'.[30]

Yet in spite of these unequal and uneasy relationships, during the years in which the Chinese Communists consolidated their state power – from October 1949 until the mid-1950s – the ruling elite remained stable. The great majority of Central Committee members elected at the Seventh Congress of the party in 1945 who were still alive in 1956 were re-elected at the Eighth Congress in that year.* Elite unity then contrasted with later turmoil, but the Leninist principle of democratic centralism within the party worked to its advantage as it consolidated power. In political practice this meant projecting a monolithic image to society, based upon the strict discipline and steeply hierarchical organization which prevailed within the Communist Party. There was also at that time genuine agreement in the CCP that Soviet experience provided the model of how to build socialism, although that 'model' itself had varied over time – from Lenin's New Economic Policy to Stalin's compulsory collectivization of agriculture and the introduction of five-year plans of economic development. The Chinese Communists, in the early years of rule, tended to look to the Soviet experience of the late 1920s when considering *economic* development but to the *political* institutions of the consolidated Soviet political system.[31]

Among the slogans disseminated by the Chinese Communist Party in the early 1950s was 'The Soviet Union of today is our tomorrow.'[32] Remarkably, as late as January 1956, Mao declared that the Chinese Communists had merely elaborated on Soviet achievements.[33] During this period of constructing a Communist system, as Frederick Teiwes observes, Soviet influences affected the policy of the Chinese Communist Party and Chinese society in a variety of complex ways. Teiwes continues: 'In some senses the process was beyond the control of Party leaders, but more fundamentally it reflected their conscious choice. And when those leaders – or a dominant group of them – saw the need to break away from the Soviet path after 1957, it was well within their capabilities to do so, even though many Soviet influences inevitably remained.'[34]

The sheer breadth and immense population of the Chinese state, and the size of its Communist Party, put it in a very different category from the Soviet-imposed regimes of east-central Europe when, just a few years after

---

* 'Elections' to the Central Committee or its inner body, the Politburo – in China, as in other Communist states – were not by the free choice of delegates to the Party Congress. They endorsed a list of names of people who had been chosen by the inner-party leadership, with Mao, in the Chinese case, having a disproportionately large say in the outcome.

Stalin's death, serious differences with the Soviet leadership began to emerge. During the CCP's first years in power, however, there was a large measure of accord between the two largest Communist parties in the world.

The Communist parties in Eastern Europe whose path to power had at least something in common with that of the CCP were those of Yugoslavia and Albania, for in both cases it was Communist armies which won an essentially military victory, in which national liberation from foreign occupation and social and political revolution went hand in hand. Another, and especially significant, common feature was that, in spite of the importance that armies played in all three victories, the supremacy of the Communist Party was preserved. Mao put the point clearly as early as 1938: 'Our principle is that the Party commands the gun, and the gun must never be allowed to command the Party.' When the CCP came to power this principle was strictly adhered to. The party first secretary in each region was, as elsewhere in the Communist world, the most authoritative figure within that territory, and in every Chinese region except one – the Central-South, where the post was given to Lin Biao, one of the most successful commanders in the Chinese Red Army – that office was held by a civilian political figure.[35] Like Communist parties in Eastern Europe, the CCP rapidly increased its membership during the period in which it was coming to power, expanding from some 2.8 million members in 1948 to about 5.8 million in 1950. The speed with which the party more than doubled in size meant that many of the new recruits lacked knowledge not only of Marxist-Leninist ideology but even basic literacy. They were, moreover, joining the winning side, which meant that those who had taken part in the long struggle against the Nationalists were unsure how genuine was the new recruits' commitment to the Communist cause.[36]

The Korean War and Internal Crackdown

Initially, many Kuomintang local officials were left in their posts, for the Communists did not have sufficient cadres to fill all of them. The new Communist government succeeded in bringing the rampant inflation under control, partly by taking over the banking system and thus gaining control over the issuing of credit, partly by controlling the supply of goods and paying people mainly in commodities, such as grain and oil. The inflation rate was quickly brought down to 15 per cent annually.[37] In its early days, Communist rule evoked enthusiasm in a large part of Chinese society. In the words of John King Fairbank:

Here was a dedicated government that really cleaned things up – not only the drains and streets but also the beggars, prostitutes, and petty criminals, all of whom were rounded up for reconditioning. Here was a new China one could be proud of, one that controlled inflation, abolished foreign privileges, stamped out opium smoking and corruption generally, and brought the citizenry into a multitude of sociable activities to repair public works, spread literacy, control disease, fraternize with the menial class, and study the New Democracy and Mao Zedong Thought. All these activities opened new doors for idealistic and ambitious youth.[38]

If much, though by no means all, of this was positive, the darker side of Communist rule did not take long to emerge. Maintaining strict control over political behaviour and over access to information, while introducing revolutionary change in social and political relationships, led logically to physical repression and party dictatorship. It is probable that the period of relative tolerance of non-Communist strata within the society was even briefer than it might otherwise have been because of China's entry into the Korean War. This was a sharply ideological struggle as well as a conflict which was costly in terms of soldiers' lives. Three million Chinese troops took part, and estimates of those killed vary between 400,000 and a million, with little credence accorded the official figure of 152,000 dead, given by the Chinese authorities at the time.[39] Among those killed in Korea – in an American bombing raid – was Mao Zedong's eldest son, who was working as a Russian translator for the Chinese commander in the Korean War, Peng Dehuai.[40] The Soviet Union did not overtly take part in the war, but it provided massive assistance to the otherwise poorly equipped Chinese and North Korean forces, sending clandestinely air crew, advisers, and large-scale deliveries of military technology.[41]

We now know, through perusal of documents from the Soviet archives, that the Korean leader, Kim Il-sung, persuaded Stalin that he could prevail quickly in a war to incorporate the south in a united Communist Korea, and that Stalin gave him the go-ahead to plan an attack. When initial successes by the North Koreans were reversed by American resistance, Stalin expressed the hope, and expectation, to Kim Il-sung that Chinese 'volunteers' would come to the North Koreans' rescue.[42] Mao, however, hesitated to commit Chinese forces to the conflict, citing, in a message to Stalin of 2 October 1950, the longing for peace in China after so many years of war. Mao also faced serious doubts in the Chinese Politburo about disturbing the reconstruction of their country and worries that they might be exposing China to direct attack by the United States (with the atomic bombs dropped on Japan in 1945 fresh in their minds).[43] In mentioning some of his difficulties to

Stalin, Mao may also have been strengthening his bargaining position vis-à-vis the Soviet Union with a view also to consolidating his ascendancy over his Politburo colleagues. He had to ensure that there would be sufficient covert military support from the Soviet Union to compensate for the technological backwardness of the Chinese armed forces. The Chinese Communist leadership, with Zhou Enlai and Lin Biao sent to Moscow for a meeting with Stalin, stressed the importance of Soviet air support if the Chinese were to take part in the war. In a letter he wrote on 4 October 1950, delivered to Mao a day later, Stalin pressed the Chinese to send troops to Korea – a minimum of five or six 'volunteer divisions'. He argued that China would not receive the international recognition it craved through 'passive temporizing and patience', and he was even ready to risk world war, involving the United States (though he did not believe that would be the outcome) for the sake of preventing defeat of the Communists in Korea. Stalin wrote:

> One can suppose, that the USA, despite its unreadiness for a big war, could still be drawn into a big war, which in turn would drag China into the war, and along with this draw into the war the USSR, which is bound with China by the Mutual Assistance Pact. Should we fear this? In my opinion, we should not, because together we will be stronger than the USA and England, while the other European capitalist states, without Germany which is unable to provide any assistance to the United States now, do not present a serious military force. [The passages in italics are Stalin's handwritten amendments to the typed draft of the letter.][44]

In the same letter, Stalin said he took Mao to be saying that the presence of bourgeois parties in the Chinese coalition meant that they would be able to exploit discontent in the country against the Communist Party and its leadership in the event of war. He said that he understood Mao's 'predicament', but reminded him that he had earlier declared his readiness to send troops to Korea. Stalin managed to imply that he thought Mao was showing signs of backtracking and displaying insufficient revolutionary solidarity. Indeed, Mao later was to say that Stalin suspected he was a second Tito and trusted him only after he had intervened in Korea.[45] Three days after Mao received Stalin's letter, and after what he said were three sleepless days and nights, he gave a secret order for Chinese 'volunteers' to cross the Korean border. Thus, Chinese participation in the Korean War began – with the aim, in Mao's words, of resisting 'the attacks of U.S. imperialism and its running dogs'.[46]

It may be that Mao's hesitation was partly because he did suspect that, in addition to the danger of a wider conflict, Chinese participation in the Korean War – with the diversion of funds and loss of life it would necessarily entail – would sharpen opposition to the new regime at home and engender greater domestic turmoil. However, he saw that there would also be opportunities to be exploited. External threat could help consolidate domestic control, and by taking the fight to the Americans, Mao would strengthen his prestige among Communists internally. He was certainly ready to make use of heightened tension as an excuse for cracking down on even potential opposition. The number of executions of their own citizens by the Chinese Communists increased sharply after the Korean War began. Estimates of the number of people executed in China between 1949 and 1953 vary greatly – between a low of 800,000 and a high of five million. The great majority of the executions were after Chinese troops entered Korea in October 1950. The number imprisoned or intimidated by the authorities was many times more.[47] Ideological pressures on incorrect thinking – 'thought reform' – also began in earnest in 1950. It has been persuasively argued that it was a combination of deliberately deployed terror and paternalism which enabled the Chinese Communist Party to succeed where the Nationalists in the 1930s and 1940s had failed with their strategies of mobilization and indoctrination.[48] The state would give material support to those who co-operated with the new rulers, while dealing ruthlessly with its opponents. Exhibitions devoted to the activities of counterrevolutionaries were set up, at which those who had been accused of such crimes would explain the nature of the counterrevolutionary threat, express penitence, and say how grateful they were to the authorities for pointing out the error of their ways.[49]

Merely to abstain from counterrevolutionary activity was soon to be far from enough. The trigger for attacks on intellectuals who were sitting on the fence and not wholeheartedly embracing the goals of the Communist Party was a film, *The Life of Wu Xun*, which was released in December 1950. It portrayed a nineteenth-century philanthropist who rose from being a poor beggar to becoming a wealthy landlord, after which he used his fortune not only to create schools for the poor but also to persuade the imperial government to join in that endeavour. The film was popular and had been well reviewed. However, from the spring of 1951 it was ferociously attacked on the initiative of the Film Steering Committee of the Ministry of Culture. A possible instigator of the criticism was Jiang Qing, a recently appointed member of that committee, who became Mao's fourth wife. Soon newspapers were devoting a quarter of their pages to denouncing *The Life of Wu Xun*. The fundamental political error of the film had been to suggest that progress could be achieved through idealistic reformism rather than revolutionary class struggle.[50]

A dichotomous way of thinking has been characteristic of orthodox Communist doctrine.[51] This means that, in essence, there are only two sides in the struggle – the forces of revolutionary progress and the forces of reaction. There can be no 'third way'. This the film-makers were told in no uncertain terms, and the message was quickly spread to intellectuals as a whole. Artists, writers, university academics and schoolteachers were among those who were forced to take part in mass meetings at which they had to discuss the works of Marx, Lenin and Mao, denounce their former thinking, engage in self-criticism and face the criticism of others. Whereas landlords and overt opponents of the revolution were imprisoned or executed, the purpose of the thought-control campaign was to retain the abilities of educated people but to completely reshape their thinking in conformity with the new ruling ideology. At the same time the Chinese educational system was restructured along Soviet lines, which meant giving high priority to practical subjects – engineering and the natural sciences – and dismantling liberal educational programmes which had produced highly educated generalists (albeit a small minority of the total population).[52]

A series of campaigns characterized the period between 1951 and 1953. In 1952 the 'Three-Anti' campaign was quickly followed by the 'Five-Anti' project. The focus of the 'three' was on corruption, waste and bureaucratism, and the 'five' referred to bribery, tax evasion, stealing state property, cheating on government contracts, and stealing governmental economic data.[53] The social targets of the campaigns were urban officials, especially those engaged in financial management, and capitalists. An earlier campaign in 1951 had led to the arrests of 'counterrevolutionaries' and 'spies'.[54] Alongside these campaigns, the leadership had set about constructing a Communist system in a relatively orthodox manner, giving priority to the nationalization of heavy industry, between 70 and 80 per cent of which was state-owned by the end of 1952 (with some 40 per cent of light industry in state ownership by then). In the meantime, the Communist Party had removed the party cards of about 10 per cent of the members who had joined in recent years, but had added new recruits, so that by the end of 1953 membership stood at 6.5 million.[55] What all this meant is that so long as Stalin was alive – he died in March 1953 – the Chinese Communist system, notwithstanding the party's distinctive path to power, was developing in recognizable and acceptable ways for the arbiters of ideological and organizational rectitude in the Kremlin. Mao, so far as the rest of the international Communist movement was concerned, had not yet become a 'Maoist'.

12

Post-War Stalinism and
the Break with Yugoslavia

The years between the end of the Second World War and the death of Josif Stalin in March 1953 saw dramatic change in the Communist world and in its relations with Western democracies. First of all, the number of Communist states increased from the pre-war two to twelve. Second, the first great split occurred within the international Communist movement which hitherto had been remarkable for its cohesion. Just one year after the creation in 1947 of the Cominform (the successor organization to the Comintern, which had been abolished in 1943), Yugoslavia was expelled from that body. Third, the co-operation which had existed between the democracies and the Communists during World War Two gave way to the division of Europe, Cold War, and high tension.

For the Soviet leadership, and most of the population, the dramatic rise in the number of Communist-ruled countries could be judged a cause for celebration. The average citizen was not aware of the extent to which a majority of these regimes had been far from voluntarily embraced by the workers in those countries. Within Russia and most of the other Soviet republics (the Baltic states of Estonia, Latvia and Lithuania being the most obvious exceptions) there was in the immediate aftermath of the war a sense also of relief and optimism – relief that a horrific conflict had come to an end and optimism about rebuilding their shattered motherland and a better life. Not only were the buildings in countless cities and villages in ruins, but there was scarcely a family that had not been bereaved in the war. For many, the premature loss of a close relative had occurred earlier – in the famine of the early 1930s or the purges later in that decade, but the wartime losses were far greater. In 1945 nevertheless, Stalin was more popular than ever throughout most of the Soviet Union – especially in Russia – although there were aspirations for something better than the Soviet Union's pre-war existence.

It would be wrong to think that a majority of Soviet citizens in the early post-war years rejected the system they had grown up in, however horrendous some of its manifestations had been. A famous study of former Soviet citizens, known as the Harvard Project, found, through systematic interviews conducted in 1950, that the younger generation, in particular, accepted many aspects of the system, although not, for example, the collective farms. Those interviewed were people living outside the Soviet Union who, if unrepresentative of the population as a whole, were likely to be untypical in their greater hostility to the system. These were former Soviet citizens who had either used the opportunity in war to leave the USSR or had been displaced by the war and chose not to return. Those among them, a member of whose own family had been arrested by the secret police, were, unsurprisingly, the most hostile to the Soviet system. There was, however, strong support among the early post-Second World war émigrés for state ownership and control of industry and for a welfare state. Support for institutionalized civil liberties and political pluralism was fairly weak even within this émigré group. The kind of freedom they wanted was quite basic: mainly the freedom to talk openly among their friends, to be able to move about freely, and not to have to live in fear of arbitrary action by the state authorities.[1]

Naturally Soviet citizens aspired also to greater material comfort. There were soldiers who had fought in the war and thus become aware of the higher standard of living of people in other countries, even when those lands had been devastated by the conflict. The Russian writer Viktor Astafiev observed the influence of the West on soldiers returning to the Soviet Union who had seen with their own eyes that the defeated enemy was living better than they did and that life 'under capitalism was healthier and richer'. Astafiev suggested that Stalin's campaign against 'cosmopolitanism' (discussed later in the chapter) was partly in order to destroy any admiration for the West that this might have instilled. The temptation for those who had fought beyond the Soviet borders to compare favourably what they had witnessed there with their own lot, when they returned to their native village and 'looked at the cockroaches and at their hungry children', had to be stamped out.[2] Catherine Merridale, who made a study of letters written by Red Army soldiers during the Second World War, found that in the summer of 1945 officers' letters 'asked for more freedom, more education, and a livelier cultural life'. None of them, however, 'demanded democracy, let alone Stalin's scalp'.[3] In the course of the war, Stalin – 'because he lived mainly in men's imaginations' – had seemed to the overwhelming majority of those who fought in the Soviet army to embody 'progress, unity, heroism, deliverance'.[4]

It was Stalin, people believed, who had led them to a great victory. The fact that no alternative standpoint – such as information about Stalin's culpability for the earlier losses – could be aired in the mass media, or published even in the smallest-circulation book, naturally reinforced rosy views of Stalin and of the invincibility of the Soviet system. The connection between faith in the *vozhd'* and trust in the system was not accidental. Stalin himself believed that the extravagant build-up of his 'image' (though that was not then a term in use – it was four decades later that it entered Russian political discourse) as a charismatic, almost superhuman, leader helped to solidify support for Communism and to bestow on it legitimacy.[5] After Nikita Khrushchev had denounced the cult of personality of Stalin at the Twentieth Congress of the Soviet Communist Party in 1956 (a momentous event to be discussed in the next chapter), he received a letter from an old Bolshevik, P. Chagin, which is now in the Russian state archives. Chagin mentioned that he had been a member of the party since July 1917, and recalled a supper in Leningrad in 1926 to which he had been invited by Sergey Kirov (who in that year became head of the Leningrad party organization). The principal guest at the meal was Stalin. In the course of the conversation, Kirov said that without Lenin it was difficult, but 'we still have the party, the Central Committee, and the Politburo, and they will lead the country along the Leninist path'. Stalin responded:

> Yes, it's all true – the party, the Central Committee, the Politburo. But keep in mind, our people understand little of all that. For centuries the people in Russia were under the tsar. The Russian people are tsarist. For many centuries the Russian people, and especially the Russian peasants, have been used to being led by just one person. And *now* there must be *one* [italics added].[6]

This was a persistent belief of Stalin. It was self-serving, since it was his power and prestige which was being augmented, but there is no reason to doubt that this remark also reflected his deep conviction. These were not sentiments Stalin could express in public, for they were too far removed from Marxist-Leninist ideology, but he uttered them on other occasions in private. In a conversation with a fellow Georgian in the mid-1930s, Stalin said that 'the people need a tsar, i.e., someone to revere and in whose name to live and labour'.[7] It was the embodiment of those beliefs in the Stalin cult that led a distinguished student of Soviet history and politics, Robert C. Tucker, to argue that in the last fifteen years of Stalin's life the Soviet Union had moved from being a regime of a Bolshevik type to one of a Führerist type.[8]

Communism, as was to become clear after the Second World War, took significantly different forms in different places at different times. However, the defining features of a Communist system, outlined in Chapter 6, remained in place in the Stalinist post-war years. Compared with the 1920s, the Soviet Union had become more autocratic than oligarchic, but the monopoly of power of the Communist Party and iron discipline within it remained keystones of the system. Throughout the Soviet period, the political police were on tap rather than on top. They were an instrument of control at the disposal of the top party leadership, though sometimes that meant just the top leader and at other times it meant the party leadership collectively. When it meant the top party leader alone – as was the case of the Soviet Union during Stalin's last two decades – this significantly modified the notion of party control over the political police. Although they were under the jurisdiction of the Communist Party leader, who could hire, fire, or kill the head of the security police, these forces could, nevertheless, be used against party members, including very senior ones. They were ultimately accountable to only one person, and that was Stalin, who remained the party chief.

The repressive organs of the Soviet state had a complex lineage. In the post-war Stalin years Beria (who headed the NKVD directly from 1938 until 1945) had partial supervisory responsibilities over the security forces in his capacity as a deputy chairman of the Council of Ministers, while within the party Secretariat Alexey Kuznetsov was their overseer. Neither man had comparable control over them to that of Stalin. Moreover, Kuznetsov was himself arrested and shot in 1949. A year earlier Stalin had reprimanded him and the head of the MGB, Viktor Abakumov, for having taken an important decision 'without the knowledge or consent of the Politburo'.[9] Stalin took care to ensure that the actual ministers in direct charge of the repressive organs, such as Abakumov, did not have close personal relations with either of their supervisors within the Council of Ministers or the Central Committee, whether Beria, Malenkov or Kuznetsov.[10] While Stalin could not devote equal attention to all spheres of policy, two areas over which he was exceptionally protective were the security organs and foreign policy. Abakumov, who headed the MGB from 1946 until 1951, had earlier been in charge of 'Smersh' (an acronym from the Russian words for 'Death to the Spies!'), the wartime counterintelligence organization. Abakumov was, however, arrested in 1951, while Stalin was still alive, and executed in 1954, a year after the leader's death. Immediately following Stalin's demise, Beria's power increased. The MGB was amalgamated with the MVD, and Beria became the head of this new organization, wielding potentially vast punitive powers. (At the same time he was promoted from the rank of deputy chairman to that of first deputy chairman of the Council of Ministers.)[11] After Beria had departed from the scene, the two police organizations were separated again – in 1954. The part with political police functions became the KGB. The 'K' stood for Committee – Komitet – a symbolic downgrading from Ministry.

Stalin from 1941 until his death was head of the official governmental machine as well as of the Communist Party. Until 1946 that post was known as the Chairmanship of Sovnarkom (the Council of People's Commissars). It was then renamed the Council of Ministers. 'Commissars' had revolutionary connotations, and Stalin explained the change by saying that there was no need for a term which reflected revolutionary rupture, since the war had shown that 'our social order is now secure'.[12] Ministries were important political institutions in the late Stalin years and senior ministers were well represented on the Politburo. Yet the Communist Party allowed not the slightest challenge to its own hegemony. No other party was allowed to exist and no other organization was allowed any autonomy, although there was a significant differentiation of functions, with the ministries having a real job of work to do. But the system was highly ideologized, and the various campaigns – which for the targets of criticism could, ultimately, have fatal consequences – were orchestrated by the Department of Propaganda and Agitation (known as Agitprop) of the party's Central Committee.[13] Throughout the Soviet Union, moreover, the supremacy of the Communist Party was reflected in the fact that in every territorial unit of the country the top official was the party first secretary of that area, whether it was a republic, such as Ukraine, where for most of the 1940s the first secretary was Nikita Khrushchev (he was briefly replaced by another senior Politburo member, Lazar Kaganovich); an industrial region, such as Dnepropetrovsk, where, from 1947 to 1950, Leonid Brezhnev was the party boss; or an urban or rural district. At the most local level of all, that of the collective farm, a façade of democracy allowed peasants to 'vote' on who the farm chairman would be, but they were presented with just one name, that of the person chosen by the district party organization.

Stalin and His Circle

At the top of the hierarchy stood Stalin, still fully in charge. This does not mean, of course, that he took every decision himself – a physical impossibility – but that he could intervene in any area and impose his views. Moreover, other members of the leadership team lived in fear of him. The fear and the ingrained habit of obedience were such that Stalin's supreme authority remained equally unquestioned when he departed, as he grew older, for increasingly long holidays in the south of the country. Later Soviet leaders, Nikita Khrushchev and Mikhail Gorbachev, had coups mounted against them while they were on vacation. When their hands were thus removed from the levers of power, there was an opportunity for disgruntled senior colleagues to strike. Stalin, who kept in close touch with the group of senior Politburo members left in temporary charge in Moscow, was in no such danger. He did not in the post-war years engage in bloodletting on the same scale as in the late 1930s, but what had happened in those years was firmly implanted in the minds of all around the Soviet leader. A number of them had put their signatures on the death sentences of old Bolsheviks and so had become Stalin's partners in crime.

Sergo Mikoyan, the son of one such leader, the longstanding Politburo member Anastas Mikoyan, has written of those like his father moving as if in 'a cage', constrained not only by Stalin but by their unquestioning belief in 'the interests of the Party', the crucial importance of party discipline, the interests of 'socialism', and the need to maintain 'Soviet power'. Mounting a partial (in both senses) defence of his father, and distinguishing him from NKVD 'butchers', Sergo Mikoyan also compares the behaviour of Stalin's circle with those who surrounded his successors, Khrushchev and Brezhnev. 'The latter', he says, 'served the dictators, who were not murderers. The former had to deal with a first-class murderer. Extenuating circumstances for the latter are evident – they did not serve a murderer. But "extenuating" circumstances can also be found for those who constantly felt the coldness of a gun barrel at the back of their heads.'[14] (Mikoyan is somewhat misleading in his reference to Khrushchev and Brezhnev in two respects – first, calling them 'dictators'. Under both, especially the latter, power at the top was more oligarchical than autocratic, even though the party leader wielded significantly greater power than anyone else. Second, neither of them, especially Khrushchev, was guiltless of the blood of fellow citizens.) Stalin had 'only' one member of the Politburo executed in the years between the end of the war and his own death, the victim being Nikolay Voznesensky, an economist and the chairman of the State Planning Committee (Gosplan). He was arrested in 1949 and put to death, aged forty-six, in 1950. Those who had been Stalin's allies for many years were somewhat safer from arrest than newer members of the higher party echelons, but they too were given stark reminders of their relative powerlessness vis-à-vis the top leader.[15] Thus, for example, Polina Zhemchuzhina, the wife of Vyacheslav Molotov, who had long been the right-hand man of Stalin in the Politburo, was arrested and imprisoned in early 1949, and released only after Stalin's death. A long-serving Politburo member, Mikhail Kalinin, who was of less political consequence than Molotov – even though he was the formal head of state, as Chairman of the Presidium of the Supreme Soviet – fared still less well in family terms. His wife was imprisoned in 1938, and Kalinin's pleas for her release were granted only in 1945, when he was already terminally ill. He died in 1946.

Stalin could be irrational, seeing conspiracies and dangers where they did not exist. His purges before the war also went much further than was necessary simply to secure his unrivalled power. Even from that cold-blooded perspective, they were, in the most literal sense, examples of overkill. In the post-war period, however, Stalin did not engage in repression on the scale of that between 1936 and 1938.[16] For much of the time he employed the 'rational political calculation' of the 'mafia boss'.[17] As T.H. Rigby put it:

> Stalin wanted to be obeyed, he wanted to be secure against conspiracy, and he believed that instilling fear was essential to winning and maintaining that obedience and security. Having achieved this by egregious display of his power to kill, he thenceforth avoided the obvious mistake of so abusing his power as to drive his entourage to collective desperation. The prudent despot or gangster boss will seek to ensure that those around him, those on whom he depends for information and for executing his will, are men whose unqualified subservience and sensitivity to his needs has been tested over many years, and whose strengths and weaknesses he knows inside out.[18]

Stalin's favour could be bestowed upon or removed from a Politburo member at will. He operated through a smaller group than the Politburo as a whole and the insiders varied over time. Even Molotov and Mikoyan, surviving old Bolsheviks and his longstanding allies, were severely reprimanded by Stalin in late 1945 and 1946. The nature of the relationship was such that, though Molotov brought himself to abstain in a Politburo vote in late December 1948 to expel his wife, Polina Zhemchuzhina, from the Communist Party, a few weeks later he wrote to Stalin to say that he realized he had been politically mistaken in not voting for her expulsion. In the meantime Stalin had circulated copies of the correspondence between them in late 1945, bringing to the attention of other members of the ruling group Molotov's earlier mistakes. One of those errors in 1945 had been to allow excerpts from a speech by Winston Churchill to be published in *Pravda*. Even though Churchill had been quoted warmly praising not only the Russian contribution to winning the war but also Stalin personally, the publication had been condemned at the time by Stalin as displaying dangerous servility to foreign politicians who were thereby masking their 'hostile intentions toward the USSR'.[19] 'Such praise' from that source, said Stalin, writing from his holiday home on the Black Sea, 'only grates on me'.[20]

The day after Molotov's retraction of his failure to vote against Zhemchuzhina – in January 1949 – she was arrested.[21] Although they remained personally devoted to one another, less than a month earlier they had divorced on Stalin's instructions. Zhemchuzhina was of Jewish origin, and when Stalin's policies took a strongly anti-semitic turn from 1948, she came under suspicious scrutiny. Whereas many people were arrested who had not broken the rigid rules of the Soviet game, still less committed any crime, Zhemchuzhina had done enough to incur Stalin's wrath. She greeted the first head of the Israeli diplomatic mission to Moscow, the future prime minister of Israel, Golda Meir, very warmly at a reception on the anniversary of the Bolshevik revolution – 7 November 1948. She spoke with her in Yiddish, and when Meir expressed surprise that she spoke it well, Zhemchuzhina replied: 'I am a daughter of the Jewish people.'[22] Her enthusiasm for the new state of Israel was visible, and was duly reported to Stalin.[23] Yet her loyalty to the Communist Party was transcendent. Moreover, the extent to which Stalin had become the personification of the party is indicated by Zhemchuzhina's response when Molotov told her Stalin's words, 'You need to divorce your wife!' Molotov recalled her saying: 'If that is what the party demands, then that is what we shall do.'[24] Equally revealing is the tone of Mikoyan's response after he had been severely rebuked by Stalin: 'I shall devote all my energy so that I may learn from you how to work correctly. I shall do all I can to draw the lessons from your stern criticism, so that it is turned to good use in my further work under your fatherly guidance.'[25]

A more recent recruit to the leadership team who had risen fast, Georgy Malenkov, who had been in day-to-day control of the party organization in the immediate post-war period, was replaced in that role in 1946 by Andrey Zhdanov, a secretary of the Central Committee and former head of the Leningrad party organization, who was in Leningrad throughout the wartime siege. Zhdanov became the agent of a crackdown on intellectual and cultural life in the early post-war years, but although this period between 1946 and his death at the age of fifty-two in 1948 became known as the *Zhdanovshchina* (the time of Zhdanov, with the *shchina* having a pejorative connotation in Russian), the policy was essentially Stalin's.[26]

No branch of intellectual life was exempt from the official philistinism. Russia's most distinguished living composers, Shostakovich and Prokofiev, were severely criticized for their 'formalism'. Among the writers who were scurrilously attacked were one of Russia's greatest poets of the twentieth century, Anna Akhmatova, and the popular prose writer, especially renowned for his humorous short stories, Mikhail Zoshchenko. Neither of them was imprisoned, but both were expelled from the Writers' Union and denied the right to publish. In this period, more than ever, there was a sustained attack on any literature which might be deemed to be 'un-Soviet', Western or bourgeois. Although Zhdanov was the principal spokesman for the policy which combined 'party-mindedness' with an increasingly nationalist conservatism, its initiator was Stalin. Intense pressure was placed on the most outstanding representatives of 'high culture', although an important exception to that generalization is that the Russian classics continued to be published. Long-dead great writers fared better than living ones. Some, such as Dostoevsky, because of their religiosity, were published only rarely, but it was still possible for readers in the Soviet Union to get their hands on the works of, for example, Pushkin, Tolstoy, Lermontov and other outstanding representatives of nineteenth-century Russian literature. These works provided access to different values and a different way of looking at the world from that purveyed by Marxist-Leninist-Stalinist orthodoxy. That had long-term political significance, especially since this was a time when cultural influence from the outside world was being rigorously excluded.

In addition to such high culture, the post-war Stalin years saw the creation of a middle-brow literature which catered for the tastes of the 'new class' or 'middle class' of Soviet officials and technocrats. Its appeal was to the broad readership represented by upwardly mobile Soviet citizens. In the words of Vera Dunham, who made an innovative study of this social stratum, which she dubbed the middle class, and its reading matter:

> Stalin's political leadership had nurtured certain allies in the past. It had relied in those earlier days on the workers. It had appealed, too, to the intelligentsia. But this time [in the post-war period] it looked for a new force, sturdy and pliable. And it was the middle class which offered itself as the best possible partner in the rebuilding of the country. The middle class had the great advantage of being 'our own people': totally stalinist, born out of Stalin's push for the industrialization, reeducation, and bureaucratization of the country, flesh of the flesh of Stalin's revolutions from above in the thirties, and ready to fill the vacuum created by Stalin's Great Purge and by the liquidation of the leninist generation of activists.[27]

This was part of a more conservative turn in Soviet politics, with the party leadership – perhaps only semi-consciously – looking for a new social base. Labour laws remained harsh and the peasantry continued to be treated badly. During the war, peasant plots, tended usually by women and children, had been expanded spontaneously. A decree of September 1946 put a stop to that, insisting that this family-cultivated land be returned to the collective or state farms. However small they were, the private plots throughout the Soviet period produced a disproportionately large share of the vegetables and fruit available for purchase by nearby townspeople, while helping, in most years, to keep the peasants themselves alive. Manual workers, too, in spite of the lip-service paid to them, continued to be subject to draconian labour laws. In the post-war Stalin years, moreover, there was much less emphasis than in the twenties and thirties on giving preference for places in higher education to children of worker or peasant background. When a nineteen-year-old student from a southern Russian village, and peasant family, called Mikhail Gorbachev was offered a place in 1950 at Moscow State University – one of the Soviet Union's most prestigious educational institutions – this was very much the exception rather than the rule. A larger proportion than in pre-war days of the entrants to leading universities now came from the new 'middle class' or from intelligentsia backgrounds.

Yugoslavia: From Stalinism to 'Titoism'

While the leadership of the USSR was preserving strict discipline and control at home, it was expanding Soviet power and influence abroad. The Communist takeovers in Eastern Europe have been discussed in Chapters 9 and 10. The notion, accepted at the time within the international Communist movement, of 'different roads to socialism' was often misunderstood by gullible sympathizers to imply tolerance of a variety of systems. In the world beyond Marxist-Leninist straitjackets, there could, indeed, be a variety of 'socialisms' and significant differences even from one Communist system to another, but that was not recognized by the Soviet leadership and not at all what in orthodox Communist doctrine was meant by 'different roads'. This was an endorsement of different ways of reaching the same destination. The paths might vary, but the road being traversed was to the one and only 'socialism', the type which prevailed within the Soviet Union.

Yugoslavia was especially quick to adopt many of the essential features of the Soviet system, since the wartime victory of the partisans had brought them to power without having to make such significant concessions to non-Communist parties as occurred elsewhere, albeit temporarily, in Eastern Europe. The Yugoslavs adopted the Soviet system of five-year plans and took a decision to move ahead with rapid industrialization as early as 1946. By the end of that year, over 80 per cent of Yugoslav industry and a number of banks had been nationalized. The leadership moved more cautiously in agriculture, with only a little over 6 per cent of the country's arable land in state or collective farms by 1948.[28] The break with the Soviet Union, which occurred in that year, was not a result of the Yugoslavs being in any sense soft-liners. Not only had they moved faster than most other East European leaderships in establishing a Communist system at home, they were also eager to help the Greek Communists come to power, although Stalin had already accepted, in his wartime talks with his Western allies, that Greece was outside the Soviet zone of control.

There had been a number of areas of irritation in Soviet–Yugoslav relations even before the break between the two countries occurred in 1948. When Tito learned after the war that, during it, Stalin had been discussing with Churchill how much influence the Soviet Union and Britain would have in post-war Yugoslavia, he was far from pleased. And although Stalin had earlier been attracted to the idea of a federation aimed at uniting Yugoslavia, Bulgaria and Albania, he did not take kindly to Tito's immediate post-war travels in the region and Yugoslav initiatives in seeking a Balkan federal state. Another area of friction was over the creation of Soviet–Yugoslav joint-stock companies. The Yugoslav negotiator, Vladimir Velebit, broke off negotiations with the Soviet Union because he regarded the conditions the Soviet side wished to impose as exploitative. The Yugoslav Communists, although deeply conditioned to admire the Soviet Union and Stalin, were not going to be pushed around. As Dennison Rusinow put it:

> The basic issue in the great quarrel of 1948 was very simple: whether Tito and his Politburo or Stalin would be the dictator of Yugoslavia. What stood in Stalin's way was Tito's and hence the Yugoslav regime's autonomous strength, based on the uniqueness in Eastern Europe of Yugoslavia's do-it-yourself and armed Communist revolution and its legacy: a large Party and People's Army recruited primarily on the basis of patriotic rather than socialist slogans, and the independent source of legitimacy as well as power which came from the Partisan myth of political founding.[29]

In 1947 the Yugoslavs had enthusiastically supported the formation of the Cominform. It was all the more pleasing that, on Stalin's suggestion, the headquarters of the body was to be in Belgrade. The Cominform embraced not only the East European Communist parties but also the two largest parties in Western Europe, those of France and Italy. Stalin's assumption was that through the Cominform, as in the past via the Comintern, other parties could be kept in line, and if need be, their leaderships would be replaced. Stalin was highly displeased by what he regarded as lack of consultation in advance concerning the foreign policy moves of Yugoslavia, in particular, and Bulgaria, although both the Bulgarians and the Yugoslavs rejected the idea that they had failed to keep the Soviet authorities informed. The leaderships of these parties were summoned to Moscow for a meeting with Stalin which took place on 10 February 1948. As the number one Bulgarian Communist, Dimitrov came in person. Tito, more cautiously, stayed at home and sent other senior colleagues, including Edvard Kardelj, to join Milovan Djilas, who had gone on ahead to Moscow. One of Stalin's concrete complaints was the fact that Yugoslavia had sent two army divisions into Albania, the Yugoslavs arguing that they were necessary in order to protect Albania from possible attack by Greek 'monarcho-fascists'. Dimitrov was criticized for having spoken about the creation of an East European federation, in which Greece would be included.[30]

When Stalin told the Yugoslavs that the Soviet Union had not been consulted about the entry of their army into Albania, Kardelj responded that this action had been taken with the consent of the Albanian government. Stalin shouted: 'This could lead to serious international complications. Albania is an independent state. What do you think? Justification or no justification, the fact remains that you did not consult us about sending two divisions into Albania.'[31] Kardelj said he could not think of a single foreign policy issue on which the Yugoslav government had not kept in touch with the Soviet leadership, to which Stalin replied: 'You don't consult us at all. That is not your mistake, but your policy – yes, your policy!' On the issue of support for the Greek Communists in their insurgency, Stalin was especially adamant. He asked Kardelj if he believed in the success of the Greek uprising, to which Kardelj replied that he did if foreign intervention did not grow and if serious political and military errors were not made. Stalin's response was scathing:

If, if! No, they have no prospect of success at all. What, do you think that Great Britain and the United States – the United States, the most powerful state in the world – will permit you to break their line of communication in the Mediterranean? Nonsense. And we have no navy. The uprising in Greece must be stopped, and as quickly as possible.[32]

Stalin was a cautious international actor. He had two reasons above all for upbraiding the Bulgarians and (especially) the Yugoslavs. One was his fear that they would inflame the international situation and antagonize the Western powers unduly at a time when the Soviet Union was still in the early stages of recovery from the devastation of the Second World War.[33] The other was his perennial concern to be in control of the entire international Communist movement and have every major policy of another party cleared in advance by the Soviet Union. That applied particularly to foreign policy and especially to parties that had taken over the reins of state power. At the February 1948 meeting Stalin spoke aggressively to Dimitrov, saying: 'You wanted to astound the world, as though you were still Secretary of the Comintern. You and the Yugoslavs do not let anyone know what you are doing, but we have to find out everything on the street. You face us with a *fait accompli*!'[34] Dimitrov humbly admitted to errors and added that through errors they were learning how to conduct foreign policy, to which Stalin's response was: 'Learning! You have been in politics fifty years – and now you are correcting errors. Your trouble is not errors, but that you are taking a line different from ours.' Milovan Djilas, who was a participant-observer in this meeting and who recorded these exchanges in literary form some years after he had written an official account of them, adds that he felt sorry for Dimitrov: 'The lion of the Leipzig Trials, who had defied Goering and fascism from the dock at the time of their greatest power, now looked dejected and dispirited.'[35]

While Dimitrov accommodated himself to Stalin's wishes, relations between the Yugoslav and Soviet leaderships deteriorated rapidly. In the course of March 1948, the Soviet side suspended negotiations on a renewal of the Soviet–Yugoslav trade agreement, and then withdrew Soviet military advisers and civilian specialists from Yugoslavia. An increasingly acrimonious correspondence between Tito and Stalin commenced with a letter from Tito sent on 20 March. Some of the accusations from the Soviet side were, in fact, true – that the Yugoslavs had not nationalized the land or collectivized agriculture, though they had pursued a 'left extremist' policy in other areas. They had also obstructed the recruitment of Soviet agents in Yugoslavia. But their most basic sin had been to refuse to take orders from the Soviet Union. The response was put delicately, but clearly, in one of the Yugoslav replies to Stalin: 'No matter how much each of us loves the land of socialism, the USSR, he can in no case love his own country less.'[36]

The exchange of letters between the Yugoslav and Soviet leaderships included an invitation to the CPSU to send a delegation to see how badly informed they were about developments in Yugoslavia. The Soviet rejoinder was to summon the Yugoslavs to attend a Cominform meeting, which on this occasion would be held in the Romanian capital, Bucharest. Each side declined the invitation of the other. Tito was particularly alert to the dangers of attending, and said to Djilas: 'If we have to be killed, we'll be killed on our own soil!'[37] There is some evidence that Stalin did attempt to have Tito assassinated. In 1948 the Yugoslav party leaders were accused by Moscow of having adopted an 'anti-Soviet stand . . . borrowed from the arsenal of counterrevolutionary Trotskyism'.[38] It is plausible to suppose that Stalin would wish to subject Tito to the same fate as Trotsky, especially in the period when Tito was isolated both from the Communist bloc and the rest of the world – before, that is, Yugoslavia began to improve its external relations with both the developing and developed world. And, indeed, a former aide to Khrushchev claimed that among the very few papers found in Stalin's desk after his death was a note from Tito written in 1950 which read: 'Stalin.

Stop sending assassins to murder me. We have already caught five, one with a bomb, another with a rifle ... If this doesn't stop, I will send one man to Moscow and there will be no need to send another.'[39] There is also a document found in the archives of the Soviet security organs (called the MGB at that time), which discusses various ways in which Tito could be assassinated. The proposal was addressed to Stalin personally, and though it does not carry his signature of authorization, it is likely that he approved it, for preliminary preparations had begun. The assassination project was terminated after Stalin's death.[40]

At the Bucharest meeting on 28 June 1948, Yugoslavia was expelled from the Cominform. The Yugoslav party leadership was accused of 'leftist', 'adventurist' and 'demagogic and impracticable' measures. 'Healthy elements' within the party, 'loyal to Marxism-Leninism', were urged either to force their leaders to mend their ways or to replace them.[41] Stalin had little doubt that he would prevail in a trial of strength with Tito, one way or another. Khrushchev recalls Stalin, characteristically, saying: '"I will shake my little finger – and there will be no more Tito. He will fall." ... But this did not happen to Tito. No matter how much or how little Stalin shook, not only his little finger but everything else that he could shake, Tito did not fall.'[42] There were, indeed, people within the ranks of the Yugoslav party who believed that Stalin and the Cominform could not be wrong, and therefore the fault lay with their own top political leadership. Tito's former army chief of staff was killed by Yugoslav border guards while trying to reach Romania. The assumption about his intentions was that he would either prepare an invasion of Yugoslavia or head a pro-Soviet government in exile.[43] Some senior Yugoslav 'Cominformists' were jailed. Their number eventually reached around 14,000.[44] Even after the Soviet–Yugoslav rupture came out into the open in June, there was widespread hope within the Yugoslav party that the breach with the Soviet Union could be healed. How little the desire to break with the USSR came from the Yugoslav side is illustrated by the words of Tito, in July 1948, as he closed the Fifth Congress of the Communist Party of Yugoslavia: 'Long live the Great Soviet Union with the genius Stalin at its head!'[45]

At that time the Yugoslav Communists did not have an ideological position which was in any way distinctive from that of the rest of the international Communist movement. Indeed, their first reaction to Soviet criticism was, voluntarily, to try to speed up their assimilation to the established model of a Communist system. In particular, they greatly accelerated the collectivization of agriculture. The number of collectivized farms increased almost tenfold between 1947 and 1950 – from 779 to 6,797. There was peasant resistance to this, and the possibilities of higher productivity in larger farms were not realized because of lack of appropriate farm machinery. Overall agricultural production fell to 73 per cent of pre-war levels. The situation was greatly exacerbated by severe drought in 1950 which led a Soviet diplomat to observe to a Western counterpart that 'God is on the side of the Cominform.'[46] Nevertheless, the growing tension with the Soviet Union and the rest of the Communist bloc brought about a patriotic surge of support within Yugoslavia for the new regime. Tito and the Communists had been losing popularity between 1945 and 1948 with a substantial part of the 94 per cent of the population who did not belong to the party. Now a majority of the people rallied behind them. In the words of Rusinow, the Yugoslav leadership could look for support to only two sources: 'on the one hand, a disciplined and loyal Party apparatus in unchallenged, monopolistic, and fear-inspiring control of the country; on the other hand, a populace ready to acknowledge the legitimacy of the regime and defend its existence with more effort and better results than sullen fear alone could ever invoke'.[47]

Before long, however, they were to get an additional source of support, perhaps unexpectedly given the fact that Yugoslavia was still, in most key respects, a Communist system. This came in the form of economic aid from the United States. Following the expulsion of Yugoslavia from the Cominform, the Truman administration took a decision to offer economic assistance which would help keep an independent Yugoslavia afloat. US Secretary of State Dean Acheson, in a communication with the American embassy in Belgrade in early 1949, said that it was in the 'obvious interest' of the United States that 'Titoism' should continue to exist as an 'erosive and disintegrating force' in the Soviet sphere.[48] In November 1950, President Truman sent a letter to Congress in support of a Yugoslav Emergency Relief Act, making no mention of Yugoslavia's Communist political and economic structure, but using a strategic argument: 'The continued independence of Yugoslavia is of great importance to the security of the United States. We can help preserve the independence of a nation which is defying the savage threats of the Soviet imperialists, and keeping Soviet power out of Europe's most strategic areas. This is clearly in our national interest.'[49] In other words, the White House's strategic calculation clearly outweighed American ideological hostility to Yugoslavia's Communist system.

Having initially tried to prove to the Soviet leadership and the Cominform that they could be as Stalinist as Stalin, the leadership of the Yugoslav party, in the face of the vituperation directed at them from the rest of the international Communist movement, started to question the credentials of that very Soviet model they had earlier uncritically admired. Since, however, they had copied it as faithfully as they could, they had to look with fresh eyes at what they had themselves constructed if they were to differentiate themselves both organizationally and ideologically from Soviet orthodoxy. The main direction of the reforms undertaken in Yugoslavia was towards decentralization. A new law in 1949 gave more power to local government. The most striking innovation, although it was more impressive in theory than practice, was the introduction of what was called self-management.

In principle, social ownership by the workers of their own factories was to replace bureaucratic state ownership and control. Tito introduced a new law to this effect in 1950, and much was made of it, although the state continued to possess most of the functions accorded to it by the Soviet-style command economy, and the factory manager remained an agent of state control. The move in the direction of 'workers' control' of the factories was, in part, an ideological counteroffensive against the Cominform, but it was also the beginning of a process by which work councils did gradually acquire greater powers. After their creation in June 1950, 'workers' self-management' took its place alongside the Partisan war as one of the two basic sources of legitimation of the regime.[50] Collectivization of agriculture was abandoned in the first half of the 1950s, although restrictions on the size of household farms meant that they still did not maximize economic efficiency. More generally, there was a gradual development of a distinctive 'Yugoslav model'.

Symbolizing the change, the name of the Communist Party was altered in November 1952 to the League of Communists. In the course of the 1950s the Communists gradually adjusted themselves to a less rigid application of the party line (for the League was still, in essence, the party), not deciding in advance in the party group how to vote on every item of the agenda in the public bodies to which they belonged.[51] The party also gradually accepted a reduced role in economic management. The Soviet planning system, with its compulsory targets, gave way to indicative planning and a gradual move to market prices, so that by the mid-1960s 'market socialism' became another distinctive feature of the Yugoslav model.[52] From its foundation, the Yugoslav Communist state had federal forms; however, both state and party institutions were initially highly centralized. But yet another distinguishing mark was to be the development of a real federation. By the later 1960s, much power had passed from the centre to the republics. Thus, a federalism of substance, rather than simply of form, became an additional feature of the Yugoslav model that distinguished it from what was to be found within the Soviet Union.

The Purges under Late Stalinism

Yugoslavia had become the first Communist state to attempt to reconstruct and revise the Soviet model, and so it is hardly surprising that, even in its earliest manifestations, these deviations were vehemently condemned by the Cominform. Before long, Stalin had instigated a search for 'Titoist agents' in the upper echelons of other Communist parties and the Eastern European governments.[53] So long as the Yugoslav system existed, and increasingly diverged from the Soviet model, it was seen by Stalin as a dangerous deviation to be eliminated. The greatest worry was that the idea of different models of 'socialism' might catch on. The American hopes expressed by Dean Acheson that Yugoslavia would turn out to be an 'erosive and disintegrating force' precisely encapsulated Soviet fears. The expulsion of Yugoslavia from the Cominform had been a manifestation, in part, of a hardening Soviet line. A Russian historian has argued that rather than being interpreted primarily as a split in the international Communist movement, it should be seen as a means by which the Soviet leadership was able to unify it by cracking down much harder on any independent tendencies in East European Communist parties, thus enabling Moscow more fully to achieve its strategic goals throughout the region.[54] Fighting Titoism and 'national deviations' now became a major theme of Soviet foreign policy. It was the justification employed for a wave of arrests and trials throughout Eastern Europe. Later the arrests acquired an anti-semitic hue and were connected with the too enthusiastic welcome, as it seemed to Stalin, which had been given by Soviet Jews to the creation of the state of Israel (even though the Soviet Union had supported its establishment). The arrests were followed by show trials in which false confessions were obtained from prisoners – often through beatings, in some cases by more subtle means. They were reminiscent of what had occurred in the Soviet Union in the 1930s – and not coincidentally. Soviet advisers from the MGB arrived in the East European countries to provide expert organizational advice.

Those arrested included very senior members of the party leadership in every European Communist state. In Albania, the Minister of the Interior, Koçi Xoxe, who really had been well disposed towards Tito, was arrested, and executed in 1949. A leading member of the Politburo of the Bulgarian Communist Party, Traicho Kostov, who was certainly no 'Titoist', was arrested in March 1949 and put on trial in December of that year. To the consternation of the authorities, he repudiated his confession in court. The public broadcast of the trial came to a sudden halt and 'the simultaneous translations provided for foreign journalists developed immediate technical difficulties'.[55] Kostov was executed promptly thereafter. Not every leading Communist who was a victim of this purge had been chosen specifically in Moscow, but many of them had been identified there. In the case of Kostov, for example, the Soviet archives show that Stalin himself linked him with Tito and urged the Bulgarians (with the help of their Soviet advisers) to investigate him.[56] In Hungary, László Rajk, who had been General Secretary of the Hungarian Communist Party, and at the time of his arrest was foreign minister, was hanged in 1949. In the course of numerous beatings, he refused to confess to the imaginary crimes of which he was accused – they included conspiring with Tito to have the Hungarian leadership assassinated – but in the end confessed at the trial.

Among those who took part in questioning Rajk was the person who succeeded him as Minister of the Interior, János Kádár, acting on the instructions of Mátyás Rákosi, the party leader. Although Kádár, who was later to lead the Hungarian party for many years, was sometimes said to have played a decisive role in getting Rajk to confess to imaginary crimes, more recent research suggests that was an exaggeration. Nevertheless, he helped to deprive Rajk of hope that he would get a fair hearing even from people in the leadership from whom he might have expected sympathy.[57] While all party leaders were under pressure to prove their total loyalty to Moscow, lest they be not only replaced but eliminated, the choice of local victims left a degree of discretion to the top leaders of each national party. Rákosi took the opportunity to get rid of potential rivals. Communists who had remained in their own countries, rather than having spent years in Moscow, were especially dangerous in the eyes both of the 'Muscovites' in these parties and of Stalin and the Soviet security organs. Kádár was one such 'national Communist', and in 1951, just eighteen months after he had been prevailed upon to witness the execution of Rajk, he was arrested.[58] Broken by interrogation, Kádár confessed, later retracted his confession, and then, under further duress, confessed again. He was sentenced to life imprisonment, but released from jail in July 1954, more than a year after Stalin's death. Having experienced imprisonment as a Communist in the 1930s under a right-wing authoritarian Hungarian regime, Kádár wrote to Rákosi at the time of his release: 'If I could choose my fate, I would always rather spend twelve years as a Communist in the jail of a capitalist country than spend twelve months in the jail of my own people's republic. Unfortunately, I had reason to compare them – the two are not the same, they defy comparison.'[59]

Rákosi shared Stalin's suspicions of Communists who had spent the war years underground in their own country and, in general, was zealous in trying to root out unreliable leading party members not only in Hungary but also elsewhere in Eastern Europe. In the trial of Rajk and other Hungarian Communists, Rákosi decided, however, that seven death sentences was excessive and wrote to Stalin that he thought three would be enough, though the first of the three he named was Rajk. Stalin replied that he had no objection to what Rákosi was proposing, but he agreed that Rajk must be put to death, 'for the people would understand no other verdict'.[60] Rákosi went on to play a vigorous part in 'internationalizing' the Rajk affair. He sent leaders of other Communist parties a list of 526 people whose names had emerged during the Rajk investigations. By far the largest group in that list was from Czechoslovakia – 353 citizens of that country.[61]

Rákosi's list included thirty-three Romanians, but even before he produced it, several leading Communists had been arrested in Romania in 1948. Among them there was at least one who *was* a nationalistic Communist, Lucreţiu Pătrăşcanu – he was executed in 1954. Later, when the arrests had taken an anti-semitic turn, the Foreign Minister Ana Pauker, who had represented Romania at the Cominform meeting which expelled Yugoslavia from the organization, was in 1952 herself arrested, although she received the relatively light punishment of several years under house arrest. In Poland there were no executions of Communists, even though in the person of Gomułka, the security forces had a strong candidate for a national deviationist. He lost his position as general secretary of the party and was indeed accused of right-wing nationalist deviations, and imprisoned for three years, but – against the odds, given the atmosphere in Communist Europe at the time – he survived.[62] He had led the underground Polish Communist resistance during World War Two, and though this had been on a much smaller scale than Tito's Partisans, he had established his position of authority independently of Moscow. He had also accepted the need for an accommodation with the Catholic Church in Poland and, on similar tactical grounds, not to undertake the collectivization of agriculture. The mildness of the Polish purge, which the Soviet leadership tolerated, may have owed much to the weakness of the party within Polish society, combined with the Poles' proven willingness to fight, even against overwhelming odds. It also reflected unwillingness on the part of some Polish leaders, including Bolesław Bierut, a former Comintern agent who had succeeded Gomułka as general secretary of the Polish party in 1948, to add further killings of Polish Communists to those already perpetrated at Stalin's behest in the Soviet Union prior to World War Two.[63]

While in a majority of Communist countries there were executions of suspect Communists at the end of the 1940s and in the early 1950s, they were not on the scale of the Soviet Great Purge of the 1930s. In the other sense of the term, 'purge', namely removal from the Communist Party – political as distinct from physical death – they were, however, massive. Even in East Germany, where no leading Communists were arrested, the party was reduced in size from two million members in 1948 to 1.2 million in 1951, with former members of the German Social Democratic Party the most affected.[64] In Eastern Europe as a whole, approximately one in every four members of a Communist party suffered some form of persecution in the years between 1948 and 1953.[65]

Although Czechoslovakia was the last of the European states to become Communist (in 1948), it was the one in which repression was most severe. This may have been a Stalinist tribute to the very strength of Czech democracy. No country in central Europe was more democratic between the wars than Czechoslovakia, and in the first three post-war years political pluralism had been preserved, even though the Communists had the largest and strongest political party. A party with a larger than normal share of the population within its ranks, and one having mass support, was also less easy to control from Moscow. The work of Russian researchers, once the archives became more open after the Soviet Union ceased to exist, has confirmed how central to Stalin's thinking in those post-war years was the insistence not only that all East European countries subordinate their foreign policy to that emanating from the Soviet Union but that they model their Communist parties on the Soviet party, expelling all members who showed any sign of thinking differently, especially any who could be tarred with the brush of Rajk or Tito.[66]

The political trials directed against Communists themselves in Czechoslovakia took two forms. There was the repression of 'national Communists', especially Slovaks, following the expulsion of Yugoslavia from the Cominform. It was not difficult to find Slovak Communists who could be suspected of national deviation. And there was the repression which reflected the intensified anti-semitism emanating from the Kremlin. The most notorious case of this throughout the whole of Eastern Europe was the Slánský trial of 1952. Rudolf Slánský was the General Secretary of the Communist Party of Czechoslovakia from 1945 until 1951, when he was demoted to the post of deputy prime minister. Unusually, the general secretaryship did not mean that he was the number one Communist. That person was Klement Gottwald, who by the time of Slánský's arrest was both chairman of the party and president of the country. Slánský, however, had been in second place and was a potential rival to Gottwald. He had been critical of the moderation of the party's policy between 1945 and 1948, hinting that power should have been seized immediately after the war, and that there had been no need to reach a compromise with bourgeois parties.[67] The choice of Slánský to be the Czech equivalent of the leading Hungarian Communist purge victim, Rajk, was, ultimately, that of Moscow rather than Prague. On his fiftieth birthday on 31 July 1951, Slánský was awarded the Order of Socialism in Czechoslovakia and lauded by Gottwald, although he was careful to remove from the draft eulogy some of the superlatives as well as the phrase stating that Slánský was among Gottwald's most faithful colleagues.[68] He was praised also by the third member of the leading triumvir-ate within the party, Antonín Zápotocký. Congratulations came from other Communist countries, but ominously, there was silence from Moscow, where, traditionally, a great fuss was made of birthdays of political figures in good standing.

Slánský was arrested in November 1951 and eventually brought to trial as one of fourteen leading Communists one year later. Gottwald had been somewhat reluctant to authorize his arrest, but in the end approved it. He was presented with testimony against Slánský which had been obtained from other leading Communists who had worked with him. This had, of course, been given under duress. Ultimately, however, it was the Soviet leader, not the President of Czechoslovakia, who had the decisive word, although if Gottwald had been a Tito, he could have refused to give way. According to testimony given to an investigation of the trials by a commis-sion of inquiry during the 'Prague Spring', Gottwald assented only under pressure from Anastas Mikoyan and Stalin. Mikoyan arrived in Prague on 11 November 1951 to convey Stalin's view that Slánský should be arrested right away. When Gottwald continued to hesitate, Mikoyan broke off his meeting with him and telephoned Stalin from the Soviet embassy. When he returned, he said that Stalin 'insisted on his view and reminded Gottwald of his grave responsibility'. The Czech commission in 1968, composed of leading members of the Communist Party (but operating in an atmosphere of growing freedom), observed: 'Although he had no facts, Gottwald ulti-mately drew the conclusion that Stalin, as usual, had reliable information and that his advice was sound. He sent back a message through Mikoyan agreeing to Slánský's arrest.'[69]

Eleven of the fourteen convicted in the Slánský trial were of Jewish origin, and this fact was emphasized. The Soviet advisers wanted to list the eleven as being of 'Jewish nationality', Jews being classified as a nationality within the Soviet Union. This, however, was one piece of advice which was not followed to the letter. The eleven were described as of 'Czech nationality, Jewish origin'.[70] Among the non-Jews who stood trial along with Slánský was the Slovak Vladimír Clementis, who had succeeded Jan Masaryk in 1948 as Foreign Minister of Czechoslovakia. Of the fourteen accused men, eleven (who included Slánský and Clementis), were sentenced to death in late November 1952 and were hanged one week later. The remaining three defend-ants were sentenced to life imprisonment.

A number of the accused had committed crimes for which they were not charged – in particular, being responsible for the arrest and, in some cases, execution of innocent non-Communists. However, the charges to which they confessed, following months of interrogation, were a Stalinist fantasy. Taken together, they were 'Trotskyist-zionist-titoist-bourgeois-nationalist traitors, spies and saboteurs, enemies of the Czechoslovak nation, of its people's democratic order, and of socialism'. The confessions were obtained by a variety of means, including, in some cases, violence, threats of torture of their wives and children, and actual torture of some of those who gave false evidence against them. Not only did these leading members of the Communist Party then confess to the imaginary crimes, but several of them requested the death sentence, so that others might be deterred from following their terrible example.[71] Other trials of Communists followed in Czechoslovakia, including, as late as 1954 (and thus, after the deaths not only of Stalin but also of Gottwald, who died immediately after attending Stalin's funeral in March 1953), that of prominent Slovak Communists accused of 'bourgeois nationalist' tendencies. Among them was Gustáv Husák, who had been a major figure in the Slovak 'national rising' of 1944. He was arrested in 1951, and at his trial three years later was sentenced to life imprisonment. Although released in 1960, he had thus spent nine years in prison. (In 1969, half a year after Soviet tanks had put an end to the 'Prague Spring', Husák, in another twist to his circuitous career, was to become Communist Party leader and, subsequently, President of Czechoslovakia.)

The purpose of these trials of leading party members was to reinforce iron discipline within the international Communist movement, and especially to ensure that conformity with the line emanating from Moscow prevailed in all the ruling parties. The form taken by the repression made clear that no one was safe from retribution, least of all any Communist with international links other than with the Soviet Union. In several of the countries, veterans of the Spanish Civil War were among those imprisoned. The trials were also meant to underline Stalin's view that Jews, who had been disproportionately well represented in almost all the parties, should be regarded as potentially unreliable holders of the highest party and state offices. This was intended also to strengthen support for the Communists by appealing to popular anti-semitism. That was more effective in some countries than others and varied even within the same state. In the Czech lands, as distinct from Slovakia, anti-semitism had not been a strong current. By pointing to the activities of 'saboteurs', the trials were also offering a reason why overoptimistic economic targets had not been met.

At the same time the trials were meant to strike further fear into the heart of the populations as a whole. They accompanied a militarization of the economies and a war psychosis in which the prospect of Cold War, which had existed from the earliest post-war years, turning to hot war had by the early 1950s become a more serious threat. Actual war was already being waged in Korea, and east-central Europeans were being psychologically prepared for armed conflict with the principal imperialist enemy, the United States. Tito's rejection of Soviet hegemony also played its part in bringing about the arrest of East European Communists. It had driven Stalin to more severe measures to ensure that the Yugoslav example would not be followed elsewhere. Soviet advisers with long NKVD/MGB experience helped throughout the region to prepare the trials and to write the scripts of the Communist victims of Communist terror. The defendants had to learn these scripts, and after their resistance was broken, they were rehearsed until they knew their lines by heart. When the judge in the Slánský trial missed one of the questions, Rudolf Slánský answered the omitted question as programmed.[72]

These were trials of people who had been raised to the pinnacle of power by the Communist takeovers in Eastern Europe. The court cases were given huge publicity, and their impact was especially dramatic. However, the number of non-Communists repressed in Eastern Europe between the Communists coming to power and the death of Stalin vastly exceeded that of the Communist victims. Quite apart from the tens of thousands who were arrested, several million people across Eastern Europe lost their jobs because of their class origin or non-Communist political activism. 'Bourgeois' professors, for example, were hounded out of the universities. As with the repressed Communists, people with non-Soviet international links were especially suspect. That category included, once again, Jews, but also transnational organizations such as the Boy Scouts, which were banned. Many thousands of people were deported from the capital cities of Eastern Europe.

The Churches were persecuted, to varying degrees, in all the Communist countries. Even though the Catholic Church was treated with more circumspection in Poland than elsewhere, that did not prevent the arrest of a number of priests in 1952 on spurious spying charges, and in February 1953 a bishop and three priests were given lengthy prison sentences for 'anti-state and anti-people activities'. Under pressure from the Communist authorities, the episcopate condemned the four men, but Cardinal Stefan Wyszyński refused to do so, and as a result was himself placed under arrest later in 1953.[73] In all other Communist countries the persecution of the Church was greater. In Albania an attempt was made to eliminate religious organizations entirely. Among those arrested throughout Communist Europe were peasants and farmers who had opposed collectivization. Many of the victims were made to do dangerous work, ranging from building canals to working in uranium mines. So far as the number of political prisoners is concerned, it is reckoned that in Romania, for example, in the early 1950s it amounted to 180,000 people; estimates of those imprisoned for political reasons between 1948 and 1954 in Czechoslovakia range from 150,000 to 200,000.[74]

From the 'Leningrad Affair' to the 'Doctors' Plot'

In the Soviet Union itself there were purges in the late 1940s and early 1950s, albeit on a much smaller scale than the 1930s. Within the Communist Party the most important repression was of the so-called Leningrad group. The most prominent Leningrad Communist, Zhdanov, who died a natural death in 1948, had been seen as a rival by the secret police chief Lavrenti Beria, and by Georgy Malenkov. In 1946 he had succeeded the latter as the secretary of the Central Committee overseeing the party organization. Zhdanov's death left exposed Aleksey Kuznetsov, who had been his deputy in the city and regional party organization throughout the Second World War. From 1946 until 1949 Kuznetsov was a secretary of the Central Committee of the party, in which role he had, as already noted, partial responsibility for the security organs. That made him a potential rival of Beria, the godfather within the government of the secret police. Like Stalin, Beria was from Georgia, and although that was no guarantee of support, Beria did have influence over the Soviet leader and he knew how to feed his chronic suspicion. Thus, Kuznetsov's party responsibilities provided neither the power nor the protection they would have afforded someone in that position throughout most of the Soviet period. Khrushchev, in his memoirs, suggested that it was Beria and Malenkov who poisoned Stalin's mind against Kuznetsov and against the other leading Leningrader in the party leadership, Nikolay Voznesensky. In his 1956 speech to the Party Congress, Khrushchev had blamed Beria and the MGB chairman, Viktor Abakumov, not mentioning Malenkov – for the good reason that Malenkov at the time was still in the party leadership. In that speech Khrushchev said:

> As is known, Voznesensky and Kuznetsov were talented and eminent leaders. Once they stood very close to Stalin. It is sufficient to mention that Stalin made Voznesensky first deputy to the chairman of the Council of Ministers and Kuznetsov was elected secretary of the Central Committee. The very fact that Stalin entrusted Kuznetsov with the supervision of the state security organs shows the trust he enjoyed.[75]

But, said Khrushchev, the 'elevation of Voznesensky and Kuznetsov alarmed Beria' and so he fabricated declarations and anonymous letters which led to them, and the others who were caught up in the 'Leningrad Affair', being branded as 'enemies of the people' and subsequently liquidated.[76] That it was Beria, in particular, and Malenkov who played an important part in turning

Stalin against the Leningraders is supported by the evidence of Dmitry Shepilov, who was very much an insider at the time. Shepilov was first deputy head of the Department of Propaganda and Agitation of the Central Committee from 1947 to 1948, working with Zhdanov. Following Zhdanov's death, he became head of that department. Beria and Malenkov conspired against Shepilov also, and he was dismissed from the Central Committee apparatus in July 1949, but spared the fate of the Leningrad group. In posthumously published memoirs, Shepilov wrote that there were times when Stalin seemed to favour Voznesensky above everyone else, and that was 'enough reason to set the blades of Beria's infernal machine against him'.[77]

Men like Voznesensky and Kuznetsov were younger high officials, loyal to Stalin, who had distinguished themselves during the war. Beria and Malenkov perceived them as threats to their power and prospects. Stalin, though Chairman of the Council of Ministers, did not like to conduct its formal meetings, and after Voznesensky had been appointed first deputy chairman, he was the person who presided over its Bureau. This was uncongenial to Malenkov, who had hopes of becoming Stalin's successor – and, for a very brief period, succeeded. Voznesensky had also antagonized Beria by refusing to sign off on a long list of people who should be shot, when it was sent to him by the political police chief. He told one of his aides, who recounted the story: 'I am not a judge and I don't know whether the people on the list need to be shot. And tell them never to send such lists to me again.'[78] If the list had come from Stalin, Voznesensky would have found it much harder to decline to append his signature, but for Beria his refusal was an affront that would not be forgotten.

Khrushchev claims that there would have been a 'Moscow Affair', with many people executed, as well as a 'Leningrad Affair', but for him. Soon after he was recalled from Ukraine to Moscow at the end of 1949 to be first secretary of the city, he rejected as the work of a provocateur a letter shown to him by Stalin, which stated that his predecessor in Moscow and many of the district secretaries and factory managers in the capital were conspiring against the Central Committee.[79] However, Khrushchev's contention is very dubious. Stalin set up a commission consisting of Malenkov, Beria, Kaganovich and Mikhail Suslov to investigate the charges against the Moscow Party first secretary, Georgy Popov. They found the letter (which Stalin showed to Khrushchev) to be a standard anonymous denunciation and the most serious charges in it invented, as were the names of the 'three engineers' who had supposedly written it.[80] Stalin had taken the opportunity, however, to demote Popov (to a ministerial position) and to bring Khrushchev from Ukraine to Moscow as a counterweight to Malenkov and Beria, since the removal of the Leningraders had left them potentially more powerful.[81]

No one, however, came to the defence of the Leningrad officials. Kuznetsov and Voznesensky were both arrested, tortured, and executed in 1950, along with many other leading figures from the Leningrad party organization.[82] One Leningrader who had a very narrow escape was Aleksey Kosygin, who went on to play a major role in Soviet politics in the 1960s and 1970s (when he was Chairman of the Council of Ministers for sixteen years). Of Kosygin in 1950 Khrushchev writes:

> ... his life was hanging by a thread. Men who had been arrested and condemned in Leningrad made ridiculous accusations against him in their testimonies. They wrote all kinds of rot about him. Kosygin was on shaky ground from the beginning because he was related by marriage to Kuznetsov. Even though he'd been very close to Stalin, Kosygin was suddenly released from all his posts and assigned to work in some ministry. The accusations against him cast such a dark shadow over him that I simply can't explain how he was saved from being eliminated along with the others. Kosygin, as they say, must have drawn a lucky lottery ticket, and this cup passed from him.[83]

The repression of Stalin's last years affected tens of thousands of people who were far removed from the party leadership. Often it was enough to be the son of 'an enemy of the people' – a child of one of those incarcerated for no good reason in the 1930s – for that person to be arrested and sent to a labour camp. The growing anti-semitism under late Stalinism, the effects of which in Eastern Europe have already been discussed, also had dire consequences for many Soviet citizens of Jewish origin. There was a campaign against what was called 'cosmopolitanism', directed against all foreign influences and linkages but in particular at those citizens deemed by Stalin to be archetypal 'cosmopolitans', namely the Jews. Marxist-Leninist ideology could not be twisted to such an extent as to embrace overt anti-semitism, and thus, when it was deployed as a weapon in the Soviet Union, it was in the guise of attacking cosmopolitanism or Zionism.

Soon after the German attack had brought the Soviet Union into the Second World War, one of the organizations officially sanctioned in Moscow was a Jewish Anti-Fascist Committee, on which prominent Soviet Jews were glad to serve. In November 1948 that body was abolished and accused of being a centre of anti-Soviet propaganda and, still worse, of providing 'anti-Soviet information to foreign intelligence services'.[84] The committee chairman, Solomon Mikhoels, an outstanding actor and director, was killed in 1948 at Stalin's behest, as were a number of other prominent Soviet Jews.[85] The Yiddish theatre in Moscow, which had been directed by Mikhoels, was shut down. Among those arrested was Mikhail Borodin, the Comintern's talented envoy to China, and close associate of Sun Yat-sen (whose early career has been observed in Chapter 5). The English-language Soviet publication of which he was editor at the time, *Moscow News*, was closed down in January 1949 (resuscitated only in 1956), and Borodin was arrested in March. He died in captivity two years later.[86]

The final manifestation of anti-semitism in Stalin's Soviet Union, and also of the increasing paranoia of Stalin, took the form of the 'doctors' plot'. A cardiogram specialist, Lydia Timashuk, who had been involved in the care of Zhdanov, wrote several letters after Zhdanov's death in August 1948 claiming that she had been forced to change the wording of her report on the latter's condition and implying that the doctors treating him had wilfully hastened his death.[87] Timashuk was used by the MGB – she paid two visits to their headquarters in 1952 – and by Stalin to launch a campaign against those whom Stalin, at the beginning of December 1952, called 'Jewish nationalists', who believed that 'their nation has been saved by the United States'. He added: 'Among the doctors there are many Jewish nationalists.'[88] Over the two previous months some of the most prominent doctors in the Soviet Union – who had treated the country's leaders, including Stalin – had been arrested. They were tortured to secure confessions, and on 13 January 1953, *Pravda* made public the arrest of a 'group of saboteur-doctors'. The same issue of the paper published an editorial – drafted by Shepilov (by this time restored to favour as chief editor of *Pravda*) and amended by Stalin personally – beneath the heading 'Base spies and killers masked as professor-doctors'.[89] Six of the nine were Jews. The reports linked them with international Jewish bourgeois organizations and with American intelligence. Opinion remains divided on whether the doctors were being prepared for a show trial, comparable to those of the 1930s and that of Slánský in Czechoslovakia. It is possible that Stalin had in mind one more Great Purge, which would have involved many more Jews, but would also have ranged more widely. However, no evidence of that has emerged from the archives, and in general, Stalin pursued a more cautious policy in the post-war years, preferring the closed trial – as in the case of the Anti-Fascist Committee members – to the theatrical show trial.[90] Following Stalin's death in March 1953, the doctors were all cleared of the absurd charges against them.

Science and the Arts

The post-war Stalin years were a dismal time for the Soviet arts, and for many but not all of the sciences. Mathematics and physics, for example, flourished. This was partly because they could not be understood by those at the top of the party hierarchy or in the political police, but it was also because conscious priority had been given to physics in particular. Stalin was desperate to achieve nuclear parity, or better, with the United States and wanted the first Soviet atomic bomb as early as possible. Nuclear physicists were, accordingly, given generous resources and privileged living conditions. The first Soviet atomic bomb was successfully tested on 29 August 1949 in the steppes of Kazakhstan. Beria, who was chairman of the commission responsible for work on the bomb, arrived at the test site, and his presence was a reminder to the scientists involved, starting with their leader, Igor Kurchatov, that their personal fates were bound up in the success of the project. As a mushroom cloud formed above the test site, Beria embraced Kurchatov and another leading physicist, Yuly Khariton, and kissed them on the forehead.[91] Given the times, Khariton was vulnerable on many counts if things had gone wrong for the project. He was Jewish and had spent two years in Britain, taking his doctorate in physics at Cambridge in 1928. His father had been arrested in 1940 in Latvia by the NKVD and his mother had moved to Palestine with her second husband. Like most of the scientists involved, Khariton felt relief not only on personal grounds but also because they had solved the problem they had been set. Moreover, whatever Stalin or Beria may have had in mind, the scientists saw the advent of Soviet nuclear weapons in terms of deterrence. Khariton said that the successful test made him happy, because 'in possessing such a weapon we had removed the possibility of its being used against the USSR with impunity'.[92]

Other areas of Soviet science suffered from the presence of charlatans and of the illusion of Stalin and some of his associates that they understood the essence of the subject. A scientist much favoured by Stalin, Trofim Lysenko, played an enormous role in destroying genetics as a scientific discipline in the Soviet Union. He gained Stalin's approval for his assertion that it was incompatible with Marxism-Leninism – approval also for various quack experiments designed to demonstrate the validity of an extreme environmentalism. In Shepilov's words, 'Lysenko and his circle dismissed all preceding advances in genetics . . . as idealist notions and bourgeois inventions.'[93] At the end of the 1940s, thousands of geneticists and also plant biologists were dismissed from their teaching or research positions. Before long, the quest for ideological orthodoxy spread to other sciences, including astronomy, chemistry and ethnography. The stress on eliminating 'cosmopolitan' influences was accompanied by generally fanciful claims concerning the discoveries and inventions of Russians in practically every sphere of scientific activity.[94]

In cinema, the theatre and literature, a fantasy world of plenty in the Soviet Union was portrayed. Many works were devoted to the glorification of Stalin. A compulsory optimism – especially faith in the ultimate victory of 'socialism', as defined by the Soviet leadership – and 'party-mindedness' (*partiynost'*) were demanded of all who worked in the creative arts. It may be that cinema-goers were relieved to see a film such as *The Cossacks of Kuban*, made in 1948, which showed the joyous life of peasants in southern Russia and tables laden with food. For some city-dwellers this was probably welcome escapist entertainment. When, however, a young Czech Communist, Zdeněk Mlynář, saw the film with his Moscow University friend Mikhail Gorbachev in the early 1950s, it was Gorbachev, a native of the part of Russia portrayed in the film, who told him how utterly removed from the reality of rural life it was. In literature, the 'varnishing of reality' in the last years of Stalin's life was taken to such lengths that these works were, in the main, rapidly and deservedly forgotten in the years that followed.[95]

Stalin's Death

Stalin suffered a severe stroke on 1 March 1953 and died on 5 March. It is unlikely that prompt and efficient medical attention could have saved him, but in the event, the best doctors in Moscow were in the cells of the Lubyanka (the political police headquarters) and there was a delay in getting Stalin any attention at all. The medical team who did attend him were alarmed by his condition. His colleagues in the party leadership badly needed to know whether there was any chance that he would recover. No one would dare take control even on an interim basis if there was a possibility of Stalin suddenly reviving. Thus, the former Kremlin doctors who had just undergone weeks of torture were, to their great surprise, approached and Stalin's symptoms described to them. Their judgement that his condition was 'grave' strengthened Beria and Malenkov in their desire to take charge. The imprisoned medical specialists' opinion confirmed the view of the doctors who had attended Stalin, and by 3 March the Bureau of the Presidium of the Central Committee were told that he had no chance of recovering. That very day they agreed that Malenkov should become Chairman of the Council of Ministers, while retaining his secretaryship of the Central Committee. This decision was endorsed by an emergency session of the Central Committee held the next day. It was opened by Malenkov, who told the members that Stalin was seriously ill. He was followed by Beria, who proposed that Malenkov should takeover Stalin's duties.[96] It was 6 March, the day after Stalin expired, before the Soviet mass media announced the death.

Stalin's body lay in state, and so many hundreds of thousands tried to see it that an unknown number of people were crushed or trampled to death in the crowds. According to Khrushchev, speaking to Polish Communists in March 1956, the death toll was 109.[97] Once someone being swept along in the dense crowd slipped on the ice, there was no hope of getting up.[98] The great majority of people in the Soviet Union regretted Stalin's passing. Even the eminent physicist and future dissident Andrey Sakharov 'mourned the great man's death'.[99] Among the numerous encomia published in *Pravda* were tributes from writers. Aleksandr Fadeev (the head of the Writers' Union, who killed himself in 1956 following Khrushchev's exposure of some of Stalin's crimes) described the dead leader as 'the greatest humanitarian the world has ever known'. Mikhail Sholokhov, author of *The Quiet Don*, wrote: 'Father, farewell! Farewell, our own and, to our last breath, beloved father! . . . You will always be with us, and with those who come after us.' From France, Louis Aragon declared that Stalin was the 'great teacher whose mind, knowledge, and example nurtured our party, the party of Maurice Thorez'. Thousands of France's sons, he said, 'died in the cause of liberty with the names of Stalin and France on their lips!' The editor of *Pravda*, Dmitry Shepilov, to whom these and thousands of other tributes were addressed, had mixed feelings at the time, but later wrote: 'For Stalin, in the final period of his life, the exposure of "terrorists", "poisoners", and "conspirators" became as vital as vodka to a hardened alcoholic.'[100] However, among Communists across the world (with the principal exception of those in Yugoslavia), the mourning was genuine. They had identified the party and the international movement so much with Stalin that some dared to wonder if things could ever be the same again.

PART THREE

SURVIVING WITHOUT STALIN

13

Khrushchev and the
Twentieth Party Congress

The immediate aftermath of Stalin's death saw intense rivalry among the most forceful members of the Politburo. This succession struggle also became a test of the power of different institutions. Lavrenti Beria was Commissar of Internal Affairs between 1938 and 1945, and from 1941 to 1953 he was a deputy head of government with some responsibility for the security organs. The most odious member of Stalin's top leadership team, he could hardly conceal his satisfaction when Stalin died, and he quickly set out to consolidate his position. The Ministry of Internal Affairs (MVD) and the Ministry of State Security (MGB) were amalgamated, with Beria in direct charge of both. However, the person who had ranked next to Stalin on the eve of his death was Georgy Malenkov, the de facto second secretary of the Communist Party supervising the party apparatus. He, too, showed a keen interest in becoming the new supreme leader and seemed well placed to do so, given that in addition to his high party position he was a deputy chairman of the Council of Ministers.

Another member of the Politburo who was seen as a potential successor to Stalin was Vyacheslav Molotov, a significant Politburo member since the 1920s. Although he had been out of favour with the *vozhd'* at the time of Stalin's death, his colleagues brought him (and also Mikoyan) back into their inner circle during the several days when Stalin was in a coma. Molotov appears to have agreed with most of Stalin's policies not only out of prudence but also on principle. Indeed, he helped to shape Stalin's foreign policy. He did not, however, actively seek the top political post following Stalin's death. Beria, Malenkov and Molotov were the three orators at Stalin's funeral, with Molotov the only one of them who appeared genuinely upset. To onlookers it appeared as if they would be the ruling triumvirate.[1]

Beria, though, may well have guessed that if he were not to be in full personal charge, he would be a target for reprisal, given his central role in all the post-war repressions. He was ready to use Malenkov as the nominal new leader, believing that he could outwit and replace him in due course. With his massive police powers, Beria bugged, as a matter of course, the

telephones and homes of the other leaders. Several hundred thousand security troops came under his command, as did the border guards and the
labour camps.[2] In addition to being in charge of the unified political police
and ordinary police, Beria became on 5 March 1953 a first deputy chairman
of the Council of Ministers. Malenkov was appointed chairman. Moreover,
in a surprise tactic, Beria presented himself as something of a reformer,
hinting at a softer line both at home and towards Eastern Europe. He
appeared to be ready even to accept a unified, neutral and non-Communist
Germany.[3] He also spoke in favour of the heads of all Soviet republics being
nationals of that republic, and of stronger support for the language of the
titular nationality of the republic. None of this meant that Beria was any
kind of closet liberal. Rather, he was a highly authoritarian politician with
an especially murderous past who was trying to broaden his appeal. As a
non-Russian himself, he may have believed, with his proposal to make concessions to the non-Russian republics, that he could draw support from these
other nationalities who, taken together, comprised roughly half of the Soviet
population.[4]

One thing which Beria, Malenkov and Molotov had in common was that
they all underestimated Nikita Khrushchev. Born into a poor peasant household in southern Russia, Khrushchev had at most four years of schooling.
(His own accounts of how long he was able to study at elementary school
varied between two and four years.) From an early age he worked on the
land, and then in a factory and mine, before becoming a revolutionary. He
was one of the socially and educationally deprived whom the Bolshevik
revolution set on a path of upward political mobility. To the end of his days,
Khrushchev rarely put pen to paper, but preferred to dictate – and invariably did so when he held high political office. He had no problem with
reading, but he did not wish to undermine his authority by displaying his
inability to spell. Lack of education and lack of intelligence are, however,
very different things. Khrushchev had plenty of native wit, a prodigious
memory, political shrewdness, and what many who worked with him called
'peasant cunning'. He was also a true believer in building a communist
society. (All leaders of the Communist Party of the Soviet Union – except,
in the second half of his period as party leader, Mikhail Gorbachev – were
concerned to sustain, and extend internationally, the Communist *system*. But
only Lenin and Khrushchev, the latter in his own peculiar fashion, believed
in Marx's 'withering-away of the state'. Even Stalin had to pay lip-service
to the building of 'communism', but hardly believed in a future stateless
society, although he accepted many other tenets of Marxism and Leninism.)
These varied characteristics of Khrushchev emerge in his memoirs – dictated
at his dacha several years after he had been removed from political office.

By that time every room in his home was bugged, and the Communist Party leadership were extremely anxious to prevent his memoirs being published. His son, however, was able to arrange for a set of tapes to survive the close attentions of the KGB and make their way abroad. The memoirs were published around the world, although not in the Soviet Union until late in the Gorbachev era.[5]

Having dinner with Stalin was always an ordeal, Khrushchev notes in those memoirs, for he plied the members of his inner circle with an excess of alcohol and then watched and listened closely for signs of the slightest disloyalty or political error. He did not hesitate to humiliate them or to show who was boss. On one occasion, Khrushchev, who readily admitted in his retirement to being one of the world's worst dancers, was told by Stalin to perform the gopak, a Ukrainian folk dance which involves the dancer getting down on his haunches and kicking his legs out. 'Which frankly wasn't very easy for me', the rotund Khrushchev recalled with some understatement. 'But', he says, 'I did it and I tried to keep a pleasant expression on my face. As I later told Anastas Ivanovich Mikoyan, "When Stalin says dance, a wise man dances."'[6] Khrushchev could cope with such ordeals and even turn compulsory socializing with Stalin (whom he portrays as lonely as well as vindictive) to his own advantage. As he also recalled:

If there was anything worse than having dinner with Stalin, it was having to go on a vacation with him. To have dinner with him or to go on vacation with him was, of course, a great honor. But it was also a terrible physical strain . . . The friendliest relations always had to be demonstrated outwardly. You had to make this sacrifice. But putting up with the ordeal had its rewards and advantages, too. Conversations were always going on which you could use profitably and from which you could draw useful conclusions for your own purposes.[7]

On his way to the top of the Soviet political hierarchy Khrushchev, too, had authorized numerous arrests – which in many cases meant executions – in the course of zealously demonstrating his Stalinist credentials in Ukraine. His attitude to Stalin combined elements of admiration, revulsion and guilt. He was impressed by Stalin's abilities, but ultimately revolted by his methods, especially the annihilation of fellow Communists. His feelings of guilt derived from the active part he had played in the repression, especially in Ukraine, while demonstrating utter loyalty to Stalin and surviving physically and politically himself. Khrushchev was a naturally spontaneous, indeed impulsive, person, but he was able to keep his emotions in check when this was necessary for political advancement. Once he had became the most powerful politician in the Soviet Union, the spontaneity and impulsiveness were given fuller scope – for better, and for worse.

Communist regimes have often been described as party-states, and the description makes sense, so closely intertwined were party institutions and governmental structures. Yet official Communist doctrine was generally misleading or ambiguous about this. On the one hand, the party was accorded a monopoly of political power – supposedly exercising it from the 1920s to the end of the 1950s, as the 'dictatorship of the proletariat' or, later, playing what was more modestly described as the 'leading role' within the system. On the other hand, it was also in official theory a public (or social) organization rather than an organ of state power. In fact, for most of the time, paradoxical though it may seem, it was both. The *ordinary party member* did not wield state power, but belonged to what was the most authoritative 'public organization' within the country. At the same time real state power was wielded by the *party officials* at every level of society – from the district party committee right up to the Politburo. At the top of the political system, the Politburo and Secretariat of the Central Committee were the most powerful collective bodies of all, and the individual who had his hands on the most levers of power was the de facto Communist Party leader. Usually, this person had the title of general or first secretary of the Central Committee, although the top party leader was not called that in every Communist state at all times. Indeed, even when Stalin became general secretary of the party in 1922, Lenin was still universally recognized as the party leader, although he was in day-to-day charge of the government rather than the party organization and his job title was Chairman of Sovnarkom.

The intertwining of party and state was even more conspicuous in the Soviet Union during Stalin's last dozen years – to the extent that it could appear that some state institutions were more powerful than the Communist Party. Stalin had during the war given himself the title of Generalissimo, and he was head of the armed forces. From 1941, as noted in the previous chapter, he had been Chairman of Sovnarkom – Chairman of the Council of Ministers after that name was adopted instead of 'Commissars' in 1946. He remained party leader, but he projected himself much more as the embodiment of the Soviet state than as the head of the party. Although the Communist Party bureaucracy continued to function, with departments of the Central Committee supervising every sphere of activity, including ideology, propaganda and culture, other party institutions had become virtually moribund. The most striking example was the party congress, which, according to the party rules, was the highest policy-making body and was supposed to be convened every three years. (In the post-Stalin era the rules were changed, so that it was due to be held every four years – later at five-yearly intervals.)

There was, however, a gap of more than thirteen years between the Eighteenth Congress, held in March 1939, and the Nineteenth, summoned in October 1952. This illustrated the fact that while Stalin needed the party bureaucracy at least as much as he required the ministries and the political police, he was able to treat even the Communist Party with some disdain. Khrushchev observes that when Stalin suggested to members of the Politburo that a party congress be held in 1952, he didn't need to use any persuasion, since they all thought it 'incredible' that there had been such a long gap between congresses.[8] While ready to greet the proposal as a splendid idea, not one of them had dared refer to the party rules or point out some years earlier that a party congress was overdue.

At that Nineteenth Congress Stalin changed the name of the Politburo to the Presidium of the Central Committee and substantially increased its size. At the same time he created a secret inner body called the Bureau of the Presidium. Thus, people who were falling out of Stalin's favour – among them Molotov and Mikoyan – had their names published as being still members of the Presidium, but they were not included in the inner circle. On the evening of 5 March 1953, the day Stalin died, an unprecedented joint meeting of the Central Committee of the party, the Council of Ministers and the Presidium of the Supreme Soviet of the USSR jointly authorized the abolition of the Bureau of the Presidium of the Central Committee and reduced threefold the size of the Presidium, so that it became, in fact, simply the old Politburo under a new name.[9] A Politburo minus Stalin, but including a number of very senior Soviet politicians, was, of course, a quite different political institution from the group of men at Stalin's beck and call who lived in awe and fear of him.

The coming together of party and state bodies on 5 March was soon followed by a greater differentiation between the ministerial and party hierarchies. Malenkov, as already noted, became Chairman of the Council of Ministers, and for just over a week he also remained a secretary of the party Central Committee. He was very soon, however, forced to choose between these functions. On 13 March 1953, he decided in favour of heading the government, giving up his seat on the Central Committee Secretariat. He believed that the chairmanship of the Council of Ministers was the highest office in the land.[10] There were precedents, going back to Lenin, for the head of the government to chair meetings of the Politburo, and Malenkov assumed that this position of authority would fall to him, as it did for some time. Moreover, the post of general secretary had been formally abolished by Stalin at the Nineteenth Party Congress in 1952, so that in principle even Stalin was then just one among several secretaries, though the reality was utterly different. This meant, though, that in March 1953 there was not a position of individual pre-eminence in the Communist Party in the way in which there was a slot for just one person at the top of the ministerial hierarchy.

From 1950 a Bureau of the Council of Ministers, consisting of its leading members (but not Stalin, who, as age took its toll, cut back on his commitments), had met weekly to consider major economic issues. Thus, the early prominence of the Council of Ministers following Stalin's death was in many ways a continuation of a trend which became apparent in the last years of Stalinism. In the immediate post-Stalin period, the highest executive committee of the Council of Ministers was called its Presidium, and that institution, thus named, continued until almost the end of the Soviet era. As we have seen, the inner body of the Central Committee of the Communist Party was called *its* Presidium (though after the fall of Khrushchev in 1964, the old title of Politburo was brought back in 1966). Between 13 March and the beginning of July 1953, the Presidium of the Council of Ministers met more than three times as often as the Presidium of the Central Committee of the Communist Party.[11] This was an indication that key decisions in that brief period were more often taken in the former body than the latter. In an important sense, however, it did not mean that the monopoly of power of the Communist Party had been usurped, for the leading politicians in the governmental Presidium were party members of long standing who had seats also in the Presidium of the Central Committee.

Nikita Khrushchev was both First Secretary of the Moscow party organization and a secretary of the Central Committee at the time of Stalin's death. He immediately gave up his Moscow post in order to focus on his work in the Secretariat of the Central Committee. What Khrushchev had realized, much better than Malenkov, was that the party organization was the key political resource which an aspiring political leader had to control. It had been Stalin's means of rising to his position of pre-eminence, after which, however, he became a dictator over the party as well as over every other institution. Khrushchev set himself the task of revitalizing the party as well as advancing the careers of people he had worked with and whom he regarded as loyal to him. By September 1953 he was strong enough to acquire the title of First Secretary of the Central Committee – the old general secretaryship under a different name. (The title of the party leader reverted to general secretary in 1966.) Although Khrushchev was gradually strengthening his position within the leadership, he did not initially push too far too fast. As late as March 1954, Malenkov was chairing meetings not only of the Presidium of the Council of Ministers but also the Presidium of the Central Committee.[12] In the course of the year, that changed. Khrushchev began to preside at those meetings, and his name now appeared before that of Malenkov when the leadership team was listed in Soviet newspapers. Malenkov's spell as number one in the Soviet leadership lasted for little more than a year, and during that time he was far from being a dominant leader.

The Arrest of Beria

Khrushchev had already asserted his authority by taking the lead in having Beria arrested. He had carefully sounded out the senior members of the Central Committee presidium one by one about removing Beria. 'What, just remove him?' was Molotov's response. 'After a question like that,' said Khrushchev, 'everything was clear, and we talked candidly.'[13] Khrushchev was apprehensive about approaching Malenkov, for he had always seemed close to Beria, but eventually he risked it and found that Malenkov, too, was ready to come on board. It was essential to take Beria by complete surprise, for otherwise he could call on the security forces to strike at those who were moving against him. As part of the process of ensuring that Beria got no forewarning, and that his suspicions were not aroused, Khrushchev and his allies had to use the army rather than the police to arrest him. Beria was to get his comeuppance at a meeting of the Presidium of the Council of Ministers on 26 June 1953. The previous evening, after a meeting of the Presidium of the Central Committee, Khrushchev, Beria and Malenkov shared the same car on their journey home. After Malenkov had been dropped off, Khrushchev accompanied Beria to his front door and, as he later recounted, 'complimented him shamelessly', talking about how Beria had 'managed to raise such large and valid questions after Stalin's death'. After an apparently jovial conversation, Khrushchev recalled: 'I gave him a long and warm handshake. All the time I was thinking, "All right, you bastard, I'm shaking your hand for the last time . . . Tomorrow, just in case, I will have a gun in my pocket. Who the hell knows what may happen."'[14]

The next day, after the last member of the Presidium entered the large Kremlin room in which the meeting was held, armed soldiers took up their positions outside. Malenkov was in the chair and announced that, in addition to the items on the agenda, there was 'a proposal to discuss the issue of Comrade Beria'. In the words of Dmitry Shepilov, editor of *Pravda* at that time: 'The carefully prepared sequence took its course. Lavrentii Beria was told bluntly and angrily everything that he needed to be told: first and foremost, that he was trying to make himself dictator, that he placed the state security services over and above the party and the government, and that he hatched and implemented his own plans.'[15] The operation had been a difficult one, for the people who looked after the security of other Presidium members were all answerable to Beria, there were two divisions of the security police in Moscow, the Kremlin guards were under Beria's command, and even the head of Moscow's Military District, General Pavel Artemev, was a former NKVD officer. The plotters against Beria arranged, however, for Artemev to be out of Moscow on manoeuvres, and they called in their most senior military allies.[16] Khrushchev had telephoned a wartime friend, General Kirill Moskalenko, the chief of Moscow air defences, who was asked to come with some trusted men to the Kremlin for a discussion on air defence. Malenkov and Nikolay Bulganin went one better and recruited Marshal Zhukov. After Khrushchev, Malenkov and others had spoken against Beria – Khrushchev adding to Beria's real crimes some imaginary ones, such as the claim that at one time he had worked for British intelligence – Malenkov pressed a button and the military men in the next room entered, with guns drawn. Zhukov shouted at a dumbfounded Beria that he was under arrest.[17]

The same day many of Beria's closest allies in the state security services were rounded up. They were kept in army prisons until December, when they were brought to court – in Beria's case in a secret trial, lest he attempt to incriminate any of those who had overthrown him. Although Beria was guilty of countless crimes, the trial itself was in the Stalinist tradition.[18] Beria was shot on the same day that the guilty verdict was reached. The contents of his safes provided ample evidence that he had eavesdropped on his leadership colleagues. They also contained the names and addresses of numerous women, among them well-known actresses, and teenage girls he had raped.[19] At a meeting of the Central Committee of the party in July 1953, Beria was condemned as 'an enemy of the Communist Party and the Soviet people'.[20] At that stage, the portrayal suggested that he and his henchmen were entirely responsible for all the worst crimes of Stalinism. Beria was accused of trying to usurp power by attempting to elevate the security police above the party and government. Khrushchev presided over the Central Committee plenary session, which lasted from 2 until 7 July, and in one of his numerous interventions he summed up Beria's personal qualities by saying: 'Cunning, effrontery and insolence – these are the basic qualities of Beria.'[21] Fittingly, Khrushchev's were the sharpest attacks on Beria at the plenum, since he had been the person bold enough to make the first move against the hated secret police chief.[22] One of Khrushchev's most severe critics, Shepilov, interprets his actions primarily in terms of his 'inordinate ambition' to be the country's leader and his need, accordingly, to dispose of the other person who most aspired to supreme power.[23] While this may well have been part of

Khrushchev's motivation, there is no reason to doubt his genuine revulsion at Beria's methods or his desire to ensure that the Communist Party subordinated the security forces to its will, not the other way round.[24]

The fact that the Central Committee had been summoned in July 1953 had significance beyond the personal fate of Beria and other political policemen. This was the beginning of the revitalization of the Communist Party, a task to which Khrushchev devoted himself energetically. The Central Committee had met only three times during the last twelve years of Stalin's life.[25] Under Khrushchev it began to meet at least twice a year. According to the party rules, it had a higher authority than its inner body, the Politburo/Presidium. In reality, the Central Committee normally supported whatever was proposed to it by the inner circle of the top leadership. However, at a time when Khrushchev was surrounded by people in the Presidium of the Central Committee who in some cases were his rivals and in no case his personal protégé, it made sense for him to upgrade the actual, as distinct from purely theoretical, authority of the Central Committee. As First Secretary of the Central Committee, he was able to place many of his own supporters within it. Membership of the Central Committee depended on the person's full-time job. Thus, all first secretaries of the union republics of the Soviet Union belonged to it, as did the first secretaries of a majority of the regions, including the most important industrial and agricultural areas. Most ministers also had Central Committee membership, but it was not only Malenkov, as Chairman of the Council of Ministers, but several other senior members of the Presidium who had a say in their appointment, and so no one in the official government acquired such extensive patronage vis-à-vis the Central Committee as did the party first secretary. Khrushchev set about installing as party bosses in the regions people who had worked with him in the past, while an ally who had been his subordinate in Ukraine, Leonid Brezhnev, became first secretary of Kazakhstan, the second largest of the republics territorially and the third largest in population after Russia and Ukraine. In Ukraine a Khrushchev client, Alexey Kirichenko, was returned to the first secretaryship. At least 35 per cent of the posts carrying Central Committee membership were in the direct gift of Khrushchev.[26]

Immediately after Stalin's death, Khrushchev was number five in the Soviet hierarchy. Following the arrest of Beria, he was by July 1953 third in the ranking order, after Malenkov and Molotov. One year later he was number one. Even then, this was still very much a collective leadership with real discussion and disagreement in the Presidium. However, in 1955 Khrushchev was able to increase his power by having Malenkov removed as Chairman of the Council of Ministers and the more pliable Bulganin appointed in his place. By the time of the first post-Stalin party congress, the Twentieth Congress, in February 1956, Khrushchev was quite clearly the dominant personality and the most authoritative political figure in the Soviet leadership. That congress, discussed in a later section of this chapter, represented the great breakthrough towards overt de-Stalinization, but between the arrest of Beria and the congress, significant changes were already taking place.

The Thaw

Stalin's death led to almost immediate policy innovation in several areas. In foreign policy the change was partial at best, but an important development, and a sign that the new leadership might be less intransigent than Stalin, came in June 1953 when the Korean War was ended as a result of Soviet pressure on China to reach agreement on an armistice. In the same month, however, Soviet tanks were used to put down strikes and demonstrations in East Germany.[27] At the time of Stalin's death, the Soviet foreign minister was Andrey Vyshinsky, who had been the chief prosecutor in the political trials of the 1930s. He had overcompensated for having been a Menshevik (it was as late as 1920 that he joined the Bolsheviks) through consistent ruthlessness as a prosecuting lawyer (as early as the Shakhty trial in 1928) and as Chief Procurator of the USSR between 1935 and 1939. He strongly favoured the use of ferocious methods for procuring confessions. After moving into the field of foreign policy, Vyshinsky spent nine years as a deputy minister and was Minister of Foreign Affairs from 1949 to 1953.

It was only a slight improvement, however, when he was replaced as foreign minister in the latter year by Molotov, returning to his old post. Intransigent in his view of the capitalist West, Molotov was no less implacably opposed to any deviation on the part of Communists, such as had occurred in Yugoslavia. When others in the post-Stalin leadership decided it was time they tried to improve relations with Tito, Molotov's response, at a meeting of the party Presidium on 19 May 1955, was to say: 'In 1948 Yugoslavia moved from a position of people's democracy to one of bourgeois nationalism. Yugoslavia is trying to weaken our camp.'[28] At another meeting of the Presidium four days later, he said there were only two kinds of state, proletarian and bourgeois, and asked his colleagues rhetorically: 'What kind of state is Yugoslavia?'[29] For Molotov, the Yugoslavs were evidently in the 'bourgeois' camp. At a plenary session of the Central Committee two months later, there was open disagreement between Khrushchev and Molotov, with the former blaming Molotov and Stalin jointly for the break with Yugoslavia.[30]

It was Molotov who first became known to Western diplomats and foreign ministers as 'Mr Nyet', although the sobriquet was later inherited by Andrey Gromyko.

The years immediately after Stalin's death acquired a name from a famous novella written by Ilya Ehrenburg called *The Thaw*, which was published in 1954. Although far from a great work of art, it conveyed the miserable state of Soviet culture under Stalin and was suggestive of a new optimism following his demise. All this was done without as much as an explicit mention of Stalin's death. Ehrenburg was adept at keeping his writing within the realm of the publishable at any given moment in the Soviet Union, but sometimes, as on this occasion, he pushed the limits a little wider. He was attacked both for the contents of his story and for the title – one editor suggested calling it *A New Stage* – but the author, who had accommodated himself to what was required of a writer in Stalin's Russia, refused to alter *The Thaw*, symbolizing, as it did, the perceptible change of political climate in the Soviet Union. One of Ehrenburg's friends 'wondered if he had written an entire story solely to inject the title into the country's vocabulary'.[31] Ludmilla Alexeyeva, a longstanding campaigner for human rights in the post-Stalin Soviet Union, in a book which she called *The Thaw Generation*, noted that 'a thaw is tenuous', for a frost could return at any moment. She adds: 'Its symbolism notwithstanding, *The Thaw* was a book I read, then forgot all about. I had no inkling that it would give the name to an era.'[32]

In the absence of open politics, literature became a battleground between writers with different values and of different political dispositions. This had been true of nineteenth-century Russia, and notwithstanding the harsher Soviet censorship and ideological pressures, it was an important feature of Soviet life from the time of Stalin's death until the late 1980s, by which time real political contestation had largely superseded its literary surrogate. Already in 1953 an important essay entitled 'On Sincerity in Literature' by Vladimir Pomerantsev had openly accused the Soviet literary establishment of 'varnishing reality'. Not only was Pomorantsev attacked for putting sincerity ahead of party-mindedness, but the editor of the journal *Novy mir* (*New World*) which had published the article, Alexander Tvardovsky, was dismissed. He was later to return as editor in 1958, and *Novy mir* was to become the best, and most anti-Stalinist, literary journal throughout the 1960s.

The early post-Stalin thaw included the release of many thousands of political prisoners. Initially, they were mainly old Communists who had fallen foul of Stalin's machinery of repression.[33] There was a distinction between those who were simply released from prison or labour camp before the end of their sentences and those who were formally rehabilitated, with all the charges against them declared to have been false. Prior to the Twentieth Party Congress in 1956, the overwhelming majority of those who had their punishments reduced, or were freed entirely, were in the former category. The Presidium of the Central Committee of the party set up a central commission to look into the cases of those who had been repressed on political grounds. In the period between then and March 1956 they considered 337,183 victims, and in 153,502 cases they cut the sentences or freed the prisoners immediately.[34] In mentioning in his speech to the Twentieth Congress only the 7,679 people who had been fully rehabilitated (many of them posthumously) since 1954, Khrushchev was understating the measures of de-Stalinization which had already occurred.[35] Following the Twentieth Congress, ninety-seven regional commissions were set up to investigate trials that had taken place in different parts of the country. Reappraisals of political crimes then proceeded more quickly. As a result, between March and October 1956, over 81,000 people who for political reasons had been condemned to slave labour in the Gulag were released, though only 3,271 of them were fully rehabilitated by a court.[36] *

The Soviet leadership themselves, even as they sanctioned releases from the camps, were afraid in the earliest post-Stalin years of things getting out of hand. Khrushchev, in his forced retirement, spoke openly about this:

> We in the leadership were consciously in favor of the thaw, myself included, but without naming Ehrenburg by name, we felt we had to criticize his position. We were scared – really scared. We were afraid the thaw might unleash a flood, which we wouldn't be able to control and which could drown us . . . We wanted to guide the progress of the thaw so that it would stimulate only those creative forces which would contribute to the strengthening of socialism.[37]

As a pensioner Khrushchev was more tolerant of cultural diversity than he generally was when in power, observing: 'What a bore it would be if everybody wrote in exactly the same way, if everybody used the same arguments', adding in his characteristic style, 'If there's too much monotonous cud-chewing in literature, it will make a reader vomit.'[38]

---

* The word Gulag entered the English language as a result of Alexander Solzhenitsyn's book, *The Gulag Archipelago*. Completed in 1968, this account of life and death in the labour camps was published abroad in 1973 and first published in Russia in 1989. Before Solzhenitsyn made it internationally recognizable, the term was already in use in the Soviet Union as an acronym of three Russian words, *Glavnoe upravlenie lagerey*, meaning the Main Administration of the Camps, a branch of the political police.

In the years between 1953 and 1956, Khrushchev was concerned both with ensuring that the Communist system – in his terms, 'Soviet power' and 'socialism' – was sustained, as well as with advancing and consolidating his own power within that system. He succeeded in asserting the clear supremacy of the party bureaucracy over that of the political police and over the Council of Ministers. In the former case, all the senior members of the Communist Party had a common interest in ensuring that no one should ever again be given as much leeway as Beria had acquired. At a meeting of the Presidium of the Central Committee in February 1954, a new delineation of powers between the MVD and a Committee of State Security (KGB) was agreed and formalized in a decree of the Presidium of the Supreme Soviet the following month.[39] The political police functions went to the KGB, and Khrushchev helped to ensure that they would be loyal to him personally by putting at their head Ivan Serov, who had been the NKVD chief in Ukraine when Khrushchev was first secretary there. Serov's own record was little better than that of a number of NKVD colleagues who, along with Beria, were shot in 1953.[40] There was some opposition to him at the Presidium of the Central Committee session of 8 February 1954 at which he was appointed as KGB chairman. A majority, however, voted for Serov, although he was warned by several presidium members that he must be more party-minded and be aware that the KGB was in essence a branch of the party. Malenkov, who chaired the meeting at which the governmental structures were reorganized, said: 'We are talking about a major reconstruction (*perestroika*).'[41]

During the first two years after Stalin's death, Malenkov took a more reformist position than did Khrushchev on domestic policy and a softer line on international issues. He supported boosting light industry and doing something for the long-suffering Soviet consumer. This was used against him by Khrushchev, who at that time was championing heavy industry, a policy which appealed to the Soviet military and military industry. (Later, once he had got the better of Malenkov, Khrushchev was to embrace a number of the policies his defeated rival had favoured, including higher investment than hitherto in consumer-goods industry.) In early 1955, Khrushchev widened the attack to undermine Malenkov's authority more comprehensively. The Chairman of the Council of Ministers was accused of being a weak economic administrator, of being indecisive, and – more damagingly – of having been too close to Beria. He was held to have been morally responsible for the 'Leningrad affair', which had led to the deaths of Voznesensky and Kuznetsov, among others, and for many more gross miscarriages of justice. Malenkov was demoted to the much lower governmental post of Minister of Electricity Power Stations. He was given one of the deputy chairmanships of the Council of Ministers and was allowed to retain his seat in the Presidium of the Central Committee.[42] This was partly because Khrushchev believed that Malenkov's support on foreign policy would come in useful against the much harder line taken by Molotov.[43]

Malenkov was replaced as Chairman of the Council of Ministers by Nikolay Bulganin, an appointment for which there was wide support within the Presidium of the Central Committee. The odd one out was Molotov, who, somewhat surprisingly, proposed that Khrushchev himself become head of the government as well as the Communist Party.[44] It was another several months, however, before Khrushchev and Molotov were to clash over Yugoslavia. Meantime, the fact that in the first two years after Stalin's death Khrushchev had taken a harder line than Malenkov on many issues commended him to Molotov. The clear supremacy of the party over the Council of Ministers was evident from the fact that these decisions were taken in the Presidium of the Central Committee and only later ratified in the Council of Ministers and by the rubber-stamp legislature, the Supreme Soviet. Having succeeded in getting the Presidium to support him against Malenkov, Khrushchev was now ready for the biggest challenge of his political career thus far – the Twentieth Congress of the Communist Party of the Soviet Union.

The Twentieth Congress

The decision to broach the culpability of Stalin was a far from straightforward one for the Soviet leadership. Within the party Presidium there was a sharp division between those who wished to keep criticism of the former leader to a minimum and those, with Khrushchev in the vanguard, who were looking for a more radical de-Stalinization.[45] Anastas Mikoyan was very much on Khrushchev's side on this issue. In the fullest version of his memoirs, published posthumously, Mikoyan gives a many-sided portrayal of Khrushchev, elaborating on both his strengths and his weaknesses. When Khrushchev had taken hold of an idea, he said, he moved forward 'like a tank'. While the efficacy of that depended on whether he was moving in the right direction, it was an excellent quality for a leader in the struggle for de-Stalinization.[46] Molotov, in contrast, had even wished to see in the official Central Committee report to the congress recognition that 'Stalin was the great continuer of Lenin's work'.[47] He and Kaganovich were the most concerned about the consequences of any debunking of Stalin. Along with Voroshilov, they were against the very idea of the 'Secret Speech'.[48]

However, the Presidium had set up a commission in 1955 to look at the reasons for 'the mass repression of members and candidate members of the Central Committee elected at the 17th Party Congress'. It was chaired by

Petr Pospelov, who was both a historian and, from 1953, a secretary of the Central Committee. According to Shepilov, 'you couldn't find a more zealous Stalinist' than Pospelov, and for Mikoyan also, Pospelov was undoubtedly 'pro-Stalinist'.[49] Yet the evidence uncovered by Pospelov and the fellow members of his commission pointed overwhelmingly to Stalin's guilt and to the innocence of the victims – at least of the crimes of which they were accused. It was their report which provided the factual basis for much of Khrushchev's Secret Speech. Shepilov also contributed material to the speech, but the final version was Khrushchev's own.[50] Mikoyan claims to have been the first person to propose that such a speech be delivered at the Twentieth Congress, but his idea was that it should be given by Pospelov, as chairman of the investigating commission. Khrushchev responded that this was wrong. It would look as if the first secretary was avoiding responsibility for addressing such an important issue. Mikoyan readily accepted that Khrushchev was right and that the significance of the speech would be much greater if it were given by the party leader.[51] At a Presidium meeting on 13 February 1956, the decision was taken to have a report on 'the cult of personality' presented by Khrushchev at a closed final session of the Twentieth Congress.[52]

Even though Khrushchev had been acutely worried about the thaw becoming a flood, he risked just such an outcome with the revelations contained in his Secret Speech. The congress began on 14 February 1956, and in the main official report, in open session, delivered by Khrushchev there were coded references to Stalin, such as the Central Committee having 'resolutely condemned the cult of the individual as alien to the spirit of Marxism-Leninism'.[53] There were many unexciting speeches, differentiated from the past by the paucity of references to Stalin, although praise for Stalin from the French Communist guest speaker, Maurice Thorez, produced a standing ovation.[54] Mikoyan, in contrast, had provided a brief foretaste of what was to come from Khrushchev in a speech on 16 February in which he spoke of people who had wrongly been declared to be 'enemies of the people', and said that 'for roughly 20 years we did not really have collective leadership'.[55] Mikoyan's younger brother, Artem (co-designer of the MiG fighter aircraft, one of the two famous engineers after whom the planes were named), who was also at the congress, came up to him some time afterwards and said that many delegates were cursing him for criticizing Stalin. Why had he taken that initiative when Khrushchev had said nothing similar? Mikoyan told him to wait, for he would hear much more dreadful things about Stalin in the speech which Khrushchev would deliver in closed session.[56] The other delegates, however, had no idea of what was in store for them. They were all set to return home on 25 February when they were called back for the unreported session. It was Khrushchev's four-hour peroration then which became known as the Secret Speech. It did not remain secret for long, since it was distributed to foreign Communist leaders as well as to Communist officials in the Russian regions.

The Poles were the least careful in safeguarding its confidentiality. They authorized the printing of three thousand copies for reading in party cells, but the printers showed considerable initiative and ran off another fifteen thousand.[57] By early April a copy had reached the CIA. It was not long before it was published in the West – for the first time in the United States by the *New York Times* and in Britain by *The Observer*. Khrushchev, in the view of his son, was not unhappy that the speech became known in the wider world. A copy was even leaked as early as March to a British journalist, John Rettie, who was working for the Reuters news agency in Moscow. Certainly Khrushchev was by no means averse to gaining the credit due to him for mounting the first sustained attack on Stalin by a leading Soviet politician. Domestically, moreover, other members of the party's Presidium were still more closely associated with, and more likely to be damaged by, the crimes and errors of Stalin which he divulged. The official text, published in the West by June 1956 and in the Soviet Union not until 1989,[58] did not include all of Khrushchev's colourful asides, but it was a far sharper and more vivid onslaught on Stalin than a majority of the Presidium wished.

The individual cases Khrushchev mentioned in his speech were but a tiny fragment of the number which could have been adduced, but their impact was immense. Thus, for example, he cited the case of Robert Eikhe, who had been a Bolshevik since 1905 and who, at the time of his arrest in 1938, was a candidate member of the Politburo and the Commissar for Agriculture. Eikhe managed to send two declarations to Stalin in which he stated that his confessions were entirely false and were extracted from him under extreme duress. He wrote: 'Not being able to suffer the tortures to which I was submitted by [NKVD interrogators] Ushakov and Nikolayev – and especially by the first one – who utilized the knowledge that my broken ribs have not properly mended and have caused me great pain, I have been forced to accuse myself and others.'[59] Eikhe, as Khrushchev informed the delegates to the Twentieth Congress, retracted everything that was in his confession when he was finally brought to court in 1940. His faith in the Communist Party undimmed, he said: 'The most important thing for me is to tell the court, the party and Stalin that I am not guilty. I have never been guilty of any conspiracy. I will die believing in the truth of party policy as I have believed in it during my whole life.' As in all such show trials, the verdict had been predetermined. Two days later Eikhe was shot.[60] The only thing untypical about this was that he had been sufficiently unbowed, and enough of a Bolshevik true believer, despite everything that had happened to him, to retract his confession in court. As already noted in Chapter 4, it was in his Twentieth Congress Secret Speech that Khrushchev informed the party delegates that close to three-quarters of the Central Committee who had been put in place at the Seventeenth Party Congress in 1934 were arrested and shot before the end of that decade, and that well over half of the delegates to that earlier congress had also been arrested.

Khrushchev was also able to show how sedulously Stalin engaged in self-glorification while maintaining a front of modesty. In the 1948 edition of the hagiographical *Short Biography* of Stalin published in the Soviet Union, which, as Khrushchev noted, turned its subject into 'an infallible sage', Stalin made a number of emendations to the manuscript by hand. After enhancing still further his achievements, he himself inserted: 'Although he performed his task as leader of the party and the people with consummate skill and enjoyed the unreserved support of the entire Soviet people, Stalin never allowed his work to be marred by the slightest hint of vanity, conceit or self-adulation.'[61]

How dangerous the report was for international Communism, especially for the regimes which had been established by Soviet force of arms in Eastern Europe, was soon to become clear. (The international repercussions of the speech are among the issues discussed in Chapter 15.) Khrushchev's revelations came close to sweeping Communists from power in more than one country and, in their aftermath, threatened his own position. By exposing some of the crimes of Stalin, albeit very partially – with an almost exclusive emphasis on the arrests of party members on trumped-up charges, rather than on Stalin's policies which caused immense suffering to many more *non*-Communists – Khrushchev pricked the bubble of infallibility with which the Communist Party had surrounded itself. That the highest echelons of the party could get things so badly wrong, that the Great Leader, admired by Communists throughout the world, could have been personally responsible for the deaths of so many of their comrades came as a profound shock to Communists and their sympathisers worldwide. In many ways, the breakthrough to a higher level of honesty in Khrushchev's speech, however incomplete its disclosure of facts and however simplistic its analysis, was the beginning of the end of international Communism, but that end was a long time in coming.*

---

* Although party congresses were, after the 1920s, carefully choreographed events, the period leading up to them was important for the top leadership. Once the dates of a congress had been announced, the leaders had an incentive to examine past policy and to contemplate something new. That applied overwhelmingly to the Twentieth Congress which, in its international repercussions, was the most momentous of all.

14

Zig-zags on the Road to 'communism'

After decades of adulation of the man who had led the Soviet Union for a generation, Communists worldwide had to come to terms with the fact that Stalin was, to put it bluntly, a mass murderer. Some refused to believe it, and held that Khrushchev's Secret Speech must be a forgery – perhaps an invention of the CIA. In 1961, however, Khrushchev went on to attack Stalin in open session of the Twenty-Second Congress, thus putting an end to any doubts about the authenticity of his 1956 speech. What he did *not* do at either of those de-Stalinizing congresses was to call into question the political system which had allowed Stalin and the secret police to get away with their atrocities.

Much of what Khrushchev said in his speeches on those two major occasions was known in essence in the West to those who had taken the trouble to inform themselves. Among the sources of information were Russian and East European émigrés, former Communists and anti-Stalinist Marxists, including Trotsky and some of his followers, as well as people who had been close to Bukharin. Others were democratic socialists, among whom the most insightful and influential was George Orwell,[1] or academic authors such as Harvard's Merle Fainsod.[2] But there were many Communists and fellow travellers who regarded *all* such sources as tainted and untrustworthy. It was the more dispiriting for them when they heard some of the most shocking charges, with new details added, from the mouth of the leader of the Communist Party of the Soviet Union. There was an exodus of members from Western Communist Parties, and in the Soviet Union itself questions were asked at meetings which went well beyond the bounds within which the party leadership had hoped to confine discussion. In Stalin's native Georgia there was a large demonstration protesting against Khrushchev's speech and in favour of their most famous son.[3] The most serious repercussions of the Twentieth Congress for the Soviet leadership were, however, in Eastern Europe.

The 'Anti-Party Group' Crisis

The East European events of 1956 – in particular, profound unrest in Poland, leading to a change of policy and of leadership, and the Hungarian revolution in the same year – are discussed in the next chapter. Not surprisingly, the problems in Eastern Europe contributed to a backlash against Khrushchev from a number of those in the Soviet leadership whom he had alienated. Those who continued to revere Stalin believed that Khrushchev had gratuitously undermined the credibility, unity and strength of the international Communist movement. They were joined by others who strongly disliked Khrushchev's style of leadership, which had become increasingly assertive and dismissive of criticism. This culminated in what became known as the 'Anti-Party Group' crisis of 1957. Khrushchev found himself outnumbered and outvoted on the Presidium of the Central Committee by people who did not really form an organized group but were united by their desire to replace him.

In order to meet without Khrushchev in the first instance, those who wished to depose him as first secretary called a meeting on 18 June 1957 of the Presidium of the Council of Ministers, of which Khrushchev was not a member, so that they could confer among themselves. Bulganin then contacted Khrushchev and summoned him to join them. Khrushchev reluctantly agreed. The gathering was turned into a meeting of the Presidium of the Central Committee, but Khrushchev was not allowed to chair it. Malenkov, who was the first to speak, insisted that Bulganin preside.[4] There was a majority among the full (or voting) members of the Presidium who, each for his own reasons, had had enough of Khrushchev and decided to remove him. Some were unreconstructed Stalinists, notably Molotov, Kaganovich and Voroshilov; others were people who were no less implicated in Stalin's crimes, such as Malenkov, but who in recent years had embraced a more reformist position. Bulganin, the Chairman of the Council of Ministers, whom Khrushchev had regarded as a supporter or, at the very least, someone he could control, also became a member of the anti-Khrushchev coalition.[5] Among the members of the Presidium of the Central Committee, the line-up was seven–four against Khrushchev. The other two full members who opposed him, though less actively, were the industrial minister Mikhail Pervukhin, and the economic planner Maksim Saburov. Especially distressing for Khrushchev was the participation in the attacks on him of the relatively anti-Stalinist Dmitry Shepilov, whose career Khrushchev had advanced. Shepilov had replaced Molotov as Minister of Foreign Affairs in 1956 and he was a candidate member of the Presidium. In the Presidium meeting, called with the aim of ousting Khrushchev, Shepilov criticized him sharply for purporting to be an expert on everything in spite of his lack of education. Khrushchev never forgave him. The four votes in support of Khrushchev continuing as party first secretary were made up of Khrushchev himself, Mikoyan, Mikhail Suslov (who was a secretary of the Central Committee as well as full Presidium member) and Alexey Kirichenko, the first secretary of the Communist Party in Ukraine and an ally of Khrushchev, known to him since 1938. Kirichenko missed the first part of the meeting because, unaware of the move against his patron, he was addressing a meeting in Kiev that day.

Even some of those round the table who did not join the attempt to remove Khrushchev from the party leadership, whether they were full members of the Politburo, like Mikoyan and Suslov, or a candidate member such as Marshal Zhukov, who was by now Minister of Defence, had their reservations about Khrushchev. For a variety of reasons, however, they preferred him to the alternatives. Not everyone had given sufficient thought to what those might be. In 1991, when he was aged eighty-six, Shepilov was interviewed by his grandson, who asked him whether, in speaking up against Khrushchev, he had realized that the removal of Khrushchev 'could mean a return to Stalinism'. His reply was revealing:

> Never. I never gave any thought to it. That is unpardonable. I deserve a lashing for it. I never asked myself: Whom will we get instead of Nikita? It was either naiveté on my part or plain stupidity . . . to go into all the gross violations of the principle of collective leadership, all the nonsensical schemes that were leading us to disaster, but not to ask myself who would be there to take Nikita's place.[6]

The Anti-Party Group could not deal with Khrushchev in the way in which they had joined forces with him to arrest Beria. Through Serov, Khrushchev controlled the security police, and Marshal Zhukov was in charge of the army. Zhukov had many criticisms of Khrushchev but felt still more strongly about the way in which the army had been decapitated in the late 1930s – a time when several leading members of the opposition to Khrushchev shared responsibility with Stalin for the mass arrests of Red Army officers. Not being in control of the forces of coercion, the Anti-Party Group had to prevail politically. They had assumed that their majority among voting members of the Presidium would be enough.

Although clearly outvoted by the full members of the Presidium, Khrushchev had on his side a majority of those who attended these meetings with the right to speak but not to vote. These were the candidate members of the Presidium and secretaries of the Central Committee. They included younger people who had worked with Khrushchev in the past, such as Brezhnev, whose careers he had advanced. Brezhnev's own attempt to defend Khrushchev at this marathon meeting ended somewhat ignominiously. Kaganovich, whom Khrushchev later described as the 'knife-sharpener' of the group, aggressively berated the younger colleagues who had the audacity to contradict the majority of the voting members. In the face of this verbal onslaught, Brezhnev fainted and had to be carried out of the room by the guards.[7]

As these members of the outer ring of the top leadership team lacked Presidium voting rights, it looked as if the old guard aligned against Khrushchev would prevail. Among the most senior members of the Presidium, only Mikoyan was firmly on Khrushchev's side. But Mikoyan played an important part in convincing Mikhail Suslov to support Khrushchev, even though he privately took a dim view of Suslov, regarding him as a 'real reactionary'.[8] Suslov's support for Khrushchev in 1957 was prudential rather than principled. 'I convinced him', recalled Mikoyan, 'that in spite of everything Khrushchev would emerge as the winner.'[9] Playing for time, Khrushchev succeeded in dragging the meeting on into a second and third day. In the meantime, word of the attempt to remove him from the party leadership got round to members of the Central Committee. At this point the rules which the majority of the Presidium had used against Khrushchev, insisting that only full members could vote, worked against the Anti-Party Group. In principle, the Presidium was the body which took decisions in between plenary sessions of the Central Committee, with the latter institution possessing ultimately the higher authority. That was not the way things normally happened in practice, but Khrushchev made the rule work.

His political manoeuvring since Stalin's death also worked to his advantage. His support for heavy industry and cultivation of the military had ensured on this occasion Marshal Zhukov's crucial support, even though Zhukov had already complained to Shepilov of Khrushchev's disregard of collective leadership.[10] Military aircraft were used to bring some Central Committee members from the more distant parts of the Soviet Union to Moscow. By 21 June, more than a third of the Central Committee members were in the capital, and on that day eighty of them signed a letter demanding that a plenum be held immediately. They refused to accept Bulganin's assurance that such a session would be convened within two weeks, and, in the face of the Central Committee members' insistence, Khrushchev's opponents had to give way. The plenum opened the following day.[11] This was the key turning point in the struggle, for Khrushchev had more supporters within the Central Committee than had his opponents put together. While the latter were Communist Party members of extremely long standing, there was one point at which the 'Anti-Party' label connected with reality. Khrushchev's strongest support came from people in the party apparatus, many of them his protégés, and they were heavily represented within the ranks of the Central Committee. His leading opponents were, overwhelmingly, people working in the governmental, rather than party, machine at the time of the showdown. The adage of bureaucratic politics that where you stand depends on where you sit was an additional factor here. Khrushchev had alienated large swathes of the ministerial network by earlier in 1957 abolishing many of the central ministries and transferring their functions to regional economic councils, the *sovnarkhozy*. By doing so, he had hoped to find a cure for the sin of 'departmentalism', whereby Soviet economic ministries would hoard material and personnel and put their institutional interests above the common good. Unfortunately for Khrushchev, the same kind of bureaucratic behaviour re-emerged in the regions, with 'localism' taking the place of departmentalism.

Suslov, as a senior secretary of the Central Committee, opened the attack on a group who had, he said, been trying to take over the party. Marshal Zhukov, the formidable second speaker, upped the ante by referring to the role Molotov, Kaganovich and Malenkov had played in the repressions of the 1930s. Other speakers added details of their bloody past, including the fact that on one day alone – 12 November 1938 – Stalin and Molotov had approved the execution of 3,167 people.[12] When the phrase 'Anti-Party Group' was introduced into the discussion, the dreaded party sin of factionalism appeared to count for no less than the mass murders of the 1930s in the eyes of Central Committee members. In the face of prolonged attacks, the fragile unity of the group was exposed, and before long the hard core of Molotov, Kaganovich and Malenkov had been left isolated. Even they were united by not much more than their dislike of Khrushchev and their intimate linkage to many of the crimes of Stalin.

The plenum ended in complete victory for Khrushchev. Molotov, Kaganovich and Malenkov were removed from the Presidium and expelled from the Central Committee. Other members of the opposition to Khrushchev were able to retain their positions for the time being, for to expel them all would have made clear to the world that Khrushchev had been in a minority within the Presidium. The candidate member, Shepilov, was, however, also removed from the Central Committee. He became known for the rest of his life by a phrase Khrushchev used which implied that he had opportunistically attached himself at the last moment to the Anti-Party Group. Referring to the group, Khrushchev (and, subsequently, his supporters) invariably added 'and Shepilov who joined them', giving him, it was later joked, the longest name in the Russian language.[13] Shepilov remained an implacable critic of Khrushchev, although he acknowledged his positive role in freeing political prisoners, attacking Stalin and trying to repair relations with Yugoslavia.[14]

Khrushchev's opponents were people of disparate views and intentions, rather than a cohesive band of brothers. Their victory, however, given that the most determined among them were Molotov and Kaganovich, would almost certainly have resulted in a rehabilitation of Stalin and increased repression. The 'group' would not have stayed together for long, as there was no love lost among them. Even Molotov and Kaganovich, in spite of their shared admiration for Stalin and dislike of Malenkov, could not stand each other.[15] The defeat of the Anti-Party Group provided some illumination on the changing role of Soviet institutions since the death of Stalin. It was clear that a real struggle had gone on within the party Presidium. It was now evident, furthermore, that the Central Committee could, when the Presidium was seriously split, play a decisive part in the political outcome. In particular, the Anti-Party Group crisis underlined the significance of the relationship between the first secretary and the Central Committee. This was named the 'circular flow of power' by the American historian Robert V. Daniels.[16] The phrase encapsulated the important political point that the first secretary (or general secretary, as in Stalin's and Brezhnev's cases) had a disproportionately large say in appointments to key posts, especially party secretaryships at the all-union, republican and regional levels, and that those people, by virtue of the offices they held, would become members of the Central Committee. There they could be expected to support the patron who had appointed them, thus completing the circle.

The 'circular flow of power' explanation of a first/general secretary's security of tenure raises, however, the question of how a Communist Party leader could ever lose power, other than by dying. That, indeed, was the most common way in which the party chief in the Soviet Union demitted office. The East European cases can be left aside for the moment, for those were penetrated political systems in which leadership changes were heavily influenced by, and sometimes determined from, Moscow – not only, therefore, by the relationships within the Central Committee of each country. But in the Soviet case indigenous politics prevailed – and so usually did the general secretary. Of the six Soviet leaders who held that office, four of them died in post, and only one of the quartet, Yury Andropov, was under the age of seventy at the time. There are those who have suggested that Beria poisoned Stalin, but there is no evidence for that, and it seems safe to say that no leader of the Communist Party of the Soviet Union died other than a natural death. In contrast, between 1926, when Felix Dzerzhinsky, the first head of the Soviet political police, died of a heart attack, and Beria's arrest and execution in 1953, the only political police chief to die *other* than an *un*natural death was Semyon Ignatiev, who headed the MGB between 1951 and Stalin's death in 1953. (Ignatiev lived until 1983.)

Of the Communist Party leaders, Khrushchev alone was successfully ousted from that post by his colleagues. The case of Gorbachev's loss of office had some similarities, but more differences. It does not really belong to this discussion because by 1991 so much else that was fundamental had changed. Nevertheless, Khrushchev's removal from office in 1964 – and, to a lesser extent, Gorbachev's loss of power twenty-seven years later – illustrates two points. The first is that even if a leader appoints people to prestigious positions of responsibility, if he then pursues policies which go against their interests, they are liable to turn against him. This, as we shall see, applies strongly to Khrushchev's policies after the Anti-Party Group crisis and, especially, to his actions between 1962 and 1964. The second point is that, since the party leader also invariably became the country's chief executive, and over time was increasingly involved in foreign policy and international diplomacy, appointments within the party apparatus were largely devolved to the de facto second secretary of the party, who was in charge of personnel. Between 1960 and 1963 that office was held by the neo-Stalinist Frol Kozlov. (There was at least an echo of this, in terms of appointments lower down the party organization, between 1985 and 1988, when the radically reformist general secretary, Gorbachev, had as his second secretary the relatively conservative Communist Yegor Ligachev.)

Marshal Zhukov, as we have seen, was among those who attacked Stalin and the Anti-Party Group at the June 1957 plenum of the Central Committee. He also, however, hinted at Khrushchev's role during the Stalinist repression. In general, Zhukov's increasing assertiveness had worried Khrushchev, who saw him as a potential rival, notwithstanding the invaluable support he had rendered in the arrest of Beria (which had led Khrushchev to bring Zhukov into the political leadership) and in the defeat of the Anti-Party Group. In the closed system of Soviet politics, when a member of the leadership team was about to be removed, he was usually sent on a mission far from Moscow or was already on holiday. The person concerned was thus caught unawares (most business trips or vacations did not, after all, end in dismissal) and prevented from mobilizing the support of his most influential friends in high places. In Zhukov's case, he was dispatched on a lengthy visit to Albania and Yugoslavia on 4 October 1957. Khrushchev was then able to spend the next two weeks making sure that he would have a majority of the presidium behind him in his move to oust Zhukov from political office. In this he succeeded, for when the Presidium met to discuss the minister of defence on 17 October, one speaker after another criticized Zhukov severely.[17] One of Khrushchev's new recruits to the Presidium, the veteran Finnish Communist (but Soviet citizen) Otto Kuusinen, who had been a leading figure in the Comintern, was among those who stressed the importance of party control over the military and the unacceptability of Zhukov's resistance to this. According to Kuusinen, the linkage between the party and the army had been weakened and the army was becoming the monopoly of one person.[18]

Zhukov had travelled by ship to the Balkans, but having heard about the moves against him in Moscow, he hastened back by plane. At a Presidium meeting on 26 October, he complained about that body discussing his behaviour in his absence and asked for a commission to be set up to investigate his conduct.[19] Voroshilov, still in the Presidium since his own 'Anti-Party' activities had not yet been made public, called Zhukov a person with little interest in the party (*malopartiynyy chelovek*). Having been utterly outshone by Zhukov during the Second World War, he no doubt relished turning the tables politically. The accusations of Voroshilov and others were, however, overdrawn. While Zhukov did not show the usual deference, according to Soviet norms, of a candidate member of the Presidium towards full members (including the first secretary), his speech to party activists in the Ministry of Defence at the time of the Anti-Party Group crisis a few months earlier had been quite orthodox in party terms. It stressed the importance of the Communist Party, which was 'leading the Soviet people to communism', and pledged fidelity to the course set by the Twentieth Party Congress.[20] It laid great stress on the role of Malenkov, Molotov and Kaganovich in the repression of the 1930s. The only note in this unpublished speech which might have raised Khrushchev's eyebrows, if he read the transcript, was a reference to the Anti-Party Group plotters having taken advantage in their factional activities of 'some shortcomings in the work of the Presidium and Secretariat of the Central Committee'.[21] Be that as it may, the 26 October meeting of the Presidium of the Central Committee ended with Zhukov accepting that he had lost the confidence of his colleagues and that he could not therefore continue as minister of defence. It was agreed that he would be succeeded by Marshal Rodion Malinovsky, a Ukrainian with strong links to Khrushchev.[22] At a subsequent meeting of the Central Committee which ratified the dismissal of Zhukov, no fewer than four Soviet marshals joined in the attack on their former comrade-in-arms, whom they clearly resented. Rokossovsky complained about his rudeness, Moskalenko denounced his 'limitless arrogance', Malinovsky referred to his 'self-glorification', and Marshal Bagramyan added that 'self-aggrandizement is in his blood'.[23] As Khrushchev's biographer William Taubman observed: 'With friends and colleagues like these, Zhukov needed no enemies.'[24]

The Limits of de-Stalinization

In the short term Khrushchev was enormously strengthened by his victory over Molotov, Kaganovich, Malenkov and the rest of the Anti-Party Group, as well as by his removal of the potential threat which Marshal Zhukov's strength of will and popular standing represented. Over the next two years Khrushchev brought an increasing number of people who had worked with him in the past, especially in Ukraine, into the Presidium of the Central Committee (in addition to the Secretariat, where they were already well represented). In demoting his rivals he even displayed his sense of humour. Molotov, who had been the foreign minister, representing the Soviet Union in many major international negotiations, was dispatched to Ulan Bator, where he spent the years between the June 1957 plenum of the Central Committee and 1960 as Soviet Ambassador to Mongolia. Malenkov, who had been in charge of the entire Soviet economy before being demoted to minister for electrical power stations, was sent to manage a hydro-electric power station in eastern Kazakhstan. Kaganovich was shunted off to the Urals as manager of a cement works in Sverdlovsk. While Khrushchev's defeated rivals could feel hard done by, their fate was a dramatic improvement over that of oppositionists under Stalin. The execution of Beria turned out to be the end of the era in which the price of intra-party opposition was a bullet in the head – and, if anyone deserved such a fate, it would have been hard to find a better candidate than Beria.

Bulganin kept his post as Chairman of the Council of Ministers until 1958 (it was only in that year that his membership of the Anti-Party Group was revealed to the Soviet public and the wider world), when Khrushchev took this office in addition to his party first secretaryship. Heading the government as well as the party enhanced Khrushchev's powers still further, but by broadening his responsibilities, it pointed up his evident culpability when things went wrong. It also led to growing ill-feeling in the highest echelons of the party about the apparent abandonment of collective leadership and Khrushchev's desire to concentrate immense power in his own hands. In retirement, Khrushchev came close to admitting that adding on the chairmanship of the Council of Ministers to his party first secretaryship had been a mistake, conceding that it 'represented a certain weakness on my part'. However, he was content to leave the final judgement on its wisdom to 'the court of history'.[25]

Having taken on this new role, Khrushchev proceeded to work from his office in the Council of Ministers more than from his office in the party Central Committee building. Along with the extra duties he had taken on, this meant that the second secretary of the Central Committee had all the more leeway in dealing with the party organization. When, at the end of the 1950s, that office was held by Khrushchev's ally Kirichenko, this did not represent any danger to the party leader, but the Ukrainian Kirichenko had enemies within the top leadership team, and Kozlov succeeded in turning Khrushchev against him. In 1960, Kirichenko was demoted and Kozlov, who aspired to be Khrushchev's successor as party leader (with, for a time, Khrushchev's apparent blessing),[26] became the second secretary in charge of the party bureaucracy. Kozlov thus played an important role in supervising the selection of delegates to the Twenty-Second Party Congress in 1961 as well as in choosing the membership of the Central Committee formally elected on that occasion.

Khrushchev himself at times wavered in his anti-Stalinism, partly as a result of pressure from more conservative colleagues, but more because of his own worries about a loosening of party control. He remained an ideologically convinced Communist who actually, as his own daughter remarked, agreed with Stalin on many matters.[27] At a diplomatic reception on the eve of 1957 – thus, after the Twentieth Congress but before the struggle with his opponents came to a head the following summer – Khrushchev announced that he and his colleagues were 'Stalinists in the consistency with which they fought for communism and Stalinists in their uncompromising fight against the class enemy, as was Stalin, who devoted his whole life to the victory of the working class and socialism'.[28] The Yugoslav ambassador, who reported these and other pro-Stalin remarks made by Khrushchev at the time, saw them as 'a passing tactical move', aimed especially at pleasing the Chinese Communists.[29] But Khrushchev, in the enforced leisure of his retirement, recognized the profound imprint that Stalin had left on him. Reflecting on his refusal of permission to Petr Kapitsa, a distinguished physicist and later Nobel Prize winner, to go abroad in the mid-1950s, Khrushchev observed that 'possibly Stalin was still belching inside me'.[30] *

Even in his memoirs, by which time his views were, on the whole, more moderate than when he was in office, Khrushchev declared:

> The struggle will end only when Marxism-Leninism triumphs everywhere and when the class enemy vanishes from the face of the earth. Both history and the future are on the side of the proletariat's ultimate victory . . . We Communists must hasten this process by any means at our disposal, *excluding war* . . . There's a battle going on in the world to decide who will prevail over whom: will the working class prevail, or the bourgeoisie? . . . Every right-thinking person can see clearly that the basic questions of ideology can be resolved only when one doctrine defeats the other . . . To speak of ideological

---

* Kapitsa, a Russian by birth, worked in Britain – as a physicist at Cambridge University – from 1921 until 1934. When he visited the Soviet Union in the latter year, Stalin refused to let him leave again. A new institute was created for him and he went on to play a major role in Russian science, often showing great courage, as when he refused to work on the atom bomb project under Beria's direction.

compromise would be to betray our Party's first principles – and to betray the heritage left to us by Marx, Engels, and Lenin.[31]

De-Stalinization in Literature

Khrushchev pursued an inconsistent cultural policy. The Twentieth Party Congress had encouraged talented writers to believe that work which could not previously be published was now within the realms of the possible. Some of it did make its way into print. A short story by Alexander Yashin called 'The Levers' pointed to the dichotomy between the way people spoke in everyday discourse and the wooden language they would adopt when the situation required a switch to official clichés. The story is set in a collective farm with a group of people making clear how dilapidated the place was and how badly things had gone under the direction of the district party secretary. Then they are called to order and it transpires that they are the members of the primary party organization of the collective farm. As soon as the party meeting begins, they speak in the kind of official language they have just been mocking. The disjunction between state and society, between conformism and spontaneity, was not just a phenomenon existing among very different sets of people. It was also often to be found in the heads of the same people.[32]

A more famous literary work – Vladimir Dudintsev's novel *Not by Bread Alone* – portrayed an inventor's struggle against the protection accorded an inferior designer by Soviet bureaucratic authority. Such aspersions on the social order brought a storm of criticism from Soviet literary functionaries no less than from party ideologists. Both sets of conservative officials were adept at manipulating Khrushchev to join the attack on innovative work in literature and art. A notorious example was when Boris Pasternak, one of the most important twentieth-century Russian poets, was awarded the Nobel Prize for Literature in 1958 for his novel *Doctor Zhivago*. It had been published abroad, although Pasternak had offered it to *Novy mir* and hoped it would be published in Moscow. (The novel eventually appeared in Russia – in *Novy mir* – in the very different political climate of 1988.) Pasternak was crudely and scathingly insulted by Soviet officials, especially by the head of the Komsomol (Young Communist League) and later KGB chief Vladimir Semichastny, with Khrushchev's full support. He was put under great psychological pressure and was compelled to refuse to accept the award of the Nobel Prize. Pasternak's death in 1960 was almost certainly hastened by the campaign of abuse against him. Khrushchev, when dictating his memoirs, admitted that he had not read Pasternak's novel during his years in power, and in retrospect he regretted the harsh treatment to which the author had been subjected.[33]

While he *was* in power, Khrushchev, however, showed some sympathy for another poet, Alexander Tvardovsky, who returned to the chief editorship of *Novy mir* in 1958 where he struggled to defend literature against dogma.[34] Young poets who attracted mass audiences to readings of their work, Yevgeny Yevtushenko and Andrey Voznesensky, also managed to combine wide popularity with cautiously nonconformist views, and were met with a degree of official tolerance, although they too could attract the wrath of party conservatives and the cultural bureaucracy. Yevtushenko combined a spirited anti-Stalinism with what seemed – in the Khrushchev era, at least – to be a rosy view of Lenin.[35] If what could be published under Khrushchev was far removed from some of the root-and-branch criticism of the Soviet system and Soviet society that was to appear in print in the second half of the 1980s, it was, nevertheless, a refreshing contrast with the cultural desert of late Stalinism. In Soviet intellectual life following the Twentieth Party Congress there was a division not only between Stalinists and anti-Stalinists but also strong echoes of a much older divide – between Westernisers and Russophiles (or Slavophiles, as they were known in the nineteenth century). The latter included both Russian nationalists who were sympathetic to Communist rule – applauding the extent to which this had made Russia, in its Soviet form, into one of the world's two greatest powers and nationalists with religious sympathies who were fundamentally (though not overtly in their Soviet published work) opposed to the Communist system. The most important writer in the last-named category was Alexander Solzhenitsyn, about whom more will be said later, for in 1962 he was able to break the literary silence on the Soviet labour camps, following Khrushchev's renewed attack on Stalin at the Twenty-Second Party Congress the previous year.

Socialism Built – 'communism' Coming Soon

That congress also saw the approval of an ideologically innovative new party programme. While non-Stalinist in spirit, the document was a remarkable combination of self-delusion, wishful thinking, and utopianism. Khrushchev himself was not much interested in abstract ideas, but having defeated his most dogmatic opponents, he was eager to be associated with movement to a new stage in the development of Soviet society. The programme endorsed by the Twenty-Second Congress on 31 October 1961 declared that the Soviet Union had become a 'state of the whole people' and that the Communist Party was now a 'party of the entire people'. It was no longer a dictatorship of the proletariat. This, in a way, was good news for the intelligentsia and, indeed, the peasantry who, doctrinally (and for much of the time in practice), had been treated as less praiseworthy citizens than industrial workers. It should also have been good news for bureaucrats, although they (with the exception of those who were arbitrarily caught up in Stalin's purges in the 1930s) had flourished perfectly well during the 'dictatorship of the proletariat'. What the state was called did not directly affect people's lives, although different terminology often reflected different political tendencies. Behind the scenes party intellectuals had agonized over the phraseology of the party programme, with the most conservative guardians of Marxism-Leninism very reluctant to accept the idea of the all-people's state. Indeed, in that respect they were the more orthodox followers of Marx, who had held that for as long as there was a state, there had to be a ruling class.

The 1961 programme was also, however, the last authoritative document produced by the Communist Party of the Soviet Union to take entirely seriously the building of a communist society – as distinct from a Communist system, which the programme, of course, called socialism, declaring that socialism had now been built in the Soviet Union. Its final words were: 'The Party solemnly declares: the present generation of Soviet people shall live in communism.'[36] The Programme stated that '*a communist society will in the main be built in the U.S.S.R.*' by 1980, and that the construction of communism would be 'fully completed in the subsequent period'.[37] In the meantime, the role of the party would become greater rather than diminish. As the programme put it: 'The period of full-scale communist construction is characterised by a further *enhancement of the role and importance of the Communist Party* as the leading and guiding force of Soviet society.'[38] The authors of the programme, running no risk of understatement, further declared:

> The achievement of communism in the U.S.S.R. will be the greatest victory mankind has ever won throughout its long history. Every new step made towards the bright peaks of communism inspires the working masses in all countries, renders immense moral support to the struggle for the liberation of all peoples from social and national oppression, and brings closer the triumph of Marxism-Leninism on a world-wide scale.[39]

If such rhetoric was to be something of an embarrassment to Khrushchev's successors, still more embarrassing were the concrete predictions of economic achievements also made in the programme, for the latter were what Soviet citizens remembered. Thus, the programme declared that by 1970 there would be no housing shortage in the Soviet Union, that they would have surpassed the United States in production per head of population, and that by 1980 the real income per head would have increased by more than 250 per cent.[40]

At this same party congress which approved the new programme, Khrushchev returned to the attack on the Anti-Party Group and on Stalin in sessions which were reported. He implied that Stalin was responsible for the murder of Kirov, which the Soviet leader had then used as an excuse to launch the intra-party repression of the 1930s. Some other speakers attacked Stalinism more strongly, and younger delegates could be even more outspoken about the role of Molotov, Kaganovich and Voroshilov than Khrushchev himself, since his own hands were far from clean. Molotov and Kaganovich were expelled from the Communist Party. The congress also passed a resolution approving the removal of Stalin's body from the mausoleum in Red Square where it had lain alongside that of Lenin. By the very next morning Lenin lay there alone.[41]

Achievements and Failures

The years in which Nikita Khrushchev headed the Communist Party of the Soviet Union were packed with policy initiatives, many of which backfired on Khrushchev. They were also, though, a period of social change and intellectual ferment. Some of the developments were willed by Khrushchev, while other changes were more of an unintended consequence of de-Stalinization. One change – Khrushchev's massive house-building programme – had elements of both at the same time. Khrushchev had a genuine concern for the average Soviet citizen's living conditions and placed a high priority on improving the quality of housing. The apartment blocks were drab and not particularly well built, but they transformed the lives of millions of people for the better.[42] During Khrushchev's years at the helm, the annual rate of housing construction, from prefabricated materials, almost doubled, and tens of millions of people moved into homes of their own.[43] Most of them were rented from the local authorities – the soviets – but there was also a growth of co-operative apartment blocks which were co-owned by the various occupants. Previously, whole families in the cities had lived in one room in communal apartments – in the worst cases more than one family to a room, with their territory separated by a curtain – during the years of rapid urbanization and industrialization under Stalin. Even if the new apartments consisted of only one or two rooms plus kitchen and bathroom, they greatly enhanced the quality of everyday urban life.

A Russian dissident and literary scholar, Leonid Pinsky, in a conversation I had with him in Moscow in early 1976, picked out Khrushchev's housing programme as the most important social and political change of the post-Stalin years up to that time. Its significance, he observed, lay in the fact that millions of people acquired the possibility to shut their own front door. The unintended consequence of the policy of constructing self-contained apartments was that it provided privacy and thus liberated conversation. People who were known political dissenters had their homes bugged. One of the 'privileges' of being in the top leadership team was that those high officials, too, were wise to assume that their apartments and dachas contained listening devices. But most citizens were spared such intrusion. The economy would have ground to a halt if half the population had been employed listening to the conversations of the other half. The KGB had to rely on selected informers to report the existence of dangerous opinions. The task of the latter was very much easier in communal apartments. Once people had their own home, with a door they could close to the outside world, they began to talk uninhibitedly with members of their family and with trusted friends. Paradoxical though it may appear, some of the freest and broadest-ranging conversations in the world took place round the kitchen tables in the apartments of the intelligentsia in Moscow and Leningrad during the Khrushchev and Brezhnev years of oppressive Communist rule in Russia.

Many of the conversations were not, of course, overtly political, but among those which were, the nature of the departure from current Soviet orthodoxy varied radically. Some intellectuals criticized the system on the basis of an idealized view of Lenin. Others did so drawing on the writings of pre-revolutionary Russian liberals or on the basis of Western liberal ideas and practices. Others were impressed by democratic socialism. A minority within the Russian intelligentsia knew something about Scandinavian social democracy, which had achieved a far higher standard of welfare for the average citizen at infinitely less social cost than Soviet Communism. There were also some in the Khrushchev years, and many more in the Brezhnev era, whose critique of the system was grounded in Russian nationalism. Between the mid-1950s (after the Twentieth Congress) and the mid-1980s, it was possible only obliquely to advance these ideas in works which had passed through the hands of the Soviet censorship. Nevertheless, the public glasnost (openness or transparency) which was embraced during Gorbachev's perestroika could not have taken off as quickly as it did had it not been preceded by the private glasnost developing over the three previous decades.[44]

The educational expansion which had been one of the positive features of Soviet rule already under Stalin continued in the 1950s and 1960s. What was most distinctive about Khrushchev's approach was an attempt to improve the chances of workers and rural youth entering higher educational institutions and to emphasize the importance of vocational training. He spoke out against the disproportionately large number of children from privileged families who were entering universities. He also noted a tendency to look down on manual work. This he regarded as a personal and ideological affront. Khrushchev's way of trying to resolve these problems was to attempt to make it a condition of entry to higher education that a student should have completed two years of work experience. There was much resistance to this, with scientists and mathematicians being the first to point out that people in their fields tended to produce their most innovative work at an early age. To delay their university entrance was, accordingly, a mistake. In a policy area such as education, Khrushchev could set the tone but he found himself obliged to accept practical objections from within the relevant ministries and the policy community of specialists. Between April and December 1958 – from the time he made some of his most radical proposals until the promulgation of the law on education – the policy innovations were watered down. The new law raised the period of compulsory education from seven years to eight and it recommended that in admissions to higher education, preference be given to students with work experience. However, it neither specified how long the period of work had to be nor made it mandatory.[45]

If Khrushchev showed more genuine interest in improving the everyday lives of the average Soviet citizen than did many of his colleagues in the leadership, who had long insulated themselves from the travails of lesser mortals, there was one category of people whom he treated with especial disdain – namely, religious believers. In his desire to push ahead on the road to communism, Khrushchev was convinced that all religious belief was a hopeless relic of the past which needed to be swept aside as soon as possible. Between 1959 and 1964, about three-quarters of all Christian churches in the Soviet Union were closed down in defiance of the wishes of the believers. In comparison, the years between the Second World War and 1958 were a period of *relative* tolerance of religion in the Soviet Union.[46] A leading specialist on religion in Communist countries, Michael Bourdeaux, went so far as to describe Khrushchev as 'one of the greatest persecutors of the church that Christian history has known'.[47]

Khrushchev's policy in this area bore especially harshly on the peasantry, whose village churches in many cases were closed. In other ways, too, he made life more difficult for those who worked in the countryside. Campaigns to catch up with the United States in meat production within the space of two or three years led to the excessive slaughter of cattle at the behest of party secretaries desperate to meet their targets, with a corresponding shortage of livestock in subsequent years. Khrushchev had a special interest in agriculture, but his frequent reorganizations and new ideas did more harm than good. His policies were not helped by the fact that, like Stalin, he had confidence in the quack agronomist Trofim Lysenko. This led him to support some entirely useless agricultural techniques. Khrushchev's agricultural policy was notable, above all, for his encouragement of the growing of maize in the Soviet Union and for his extension of agriculture to hitherto uncultivated land, especially in northern Kazakhstan and southern parts of Siberia – the 'Virgin Lands' campaign. Both had mixed results. Maize was grown not only in soil suited to it but also in places where it was inappropriate. Khrushchev himself was popularly deemed to have a maize-mania. The Virgin Lands project was also, at best, a temporary and mixed success. It was on such a massive scale that between 1953 and 1956 the *increase* in the area of land culti-vated was equivalent to the total cultivated land of Canada.[48] Exploitation of the Virgin Lands led to increases in the tonnage of grain produced in the country, but the short-term successes were vitiated by the political campaigning nature of the enterprise, with an emphasis on the speedy achievement of ever higher yields leading to lack of crop rotation and, in turn, to soil erosion.[49] Nineteen sixty-three was a particularly bad year in the Soviet Union for both livestock and the harvest, and the leadership were forced to import grain from abroad. It was remarked in Russia at the time that Khrushchev was the first person to sow in the Virgin Lands and to reap in Canada.

Measured purely in quantitative terms, discounting the poor quality of many Soviet goods, economic growth was impressive in the 1950s. The economy grew more slowly thereafter. There was a long-term decline in the rate of growth from the 1950s to the 1980s. However, the nature of the command economy was such that massive investment of material and human capital could be devoted to certain areas of production, and in these the Soviet Union was able to achieve world standards. This was true of much of Soviet military industry, an area in which Khrushchev emphasized nuclear weapons and rocket production rather than conventional forces, thereby (in the years after he had defeated the Anti-Party Group) causing discontent in large sections of the military. Above all, the Soviet Union under Khrushchev took a lead in space research and exploration. In August 1957 the first successful test of an intercontinental ballistic missile was carried out, and in October of the same year that rocket was used to launch the world's first man-made satellite in space.[50] It was a tremendous boost for the Soviet Union, and an achievement in which the average citizen as well as the Soviet leaders took pride, when a Soviet spacecraft – the sputnik – became the world's first satellite in space. The excitement was, if anything, still greater when a Russian, Yury Gagarin, became the first man in space in 1961. A year earlier he had been encouraged to join the Communist Party and he was subsequently given the honorific role of a deputy to the Supreme Soviet. (Gagarin was killed in an aircraft accident in 1968.) The principal genius behind the Soviet Union taking an early lead in the space race was Sergey Korolev. His career trajectory illustrated the severe risks and disadvantages of life as a Soviet scientist as well as the opportunities. Korolev was already working on rockets from the beginning of the 1930s, but he was arrested later in that decade and not released until the summer of 1944. During some of that time he endured severe conditions in a labour camp at Kolyma, but for part of his sentence he was allowed, under guard, to work in a special prison (of the kind described by Solzhenitsyn in his novel *The First Circle*) in which scientists and engineers could do research in their area of expertise for the benefit of the Soviet state. The secrecy with which the Soviet authorities surrounded his later work was such that Korolev's name was publicly revealed only when he died in 1966. Until then he was known as 'the Chief Designer'.[51]

The success of Soviet space research, and also Khrushchev's boastfulness about the country's military rocketry, led the outside world to overestimate Soviet progress. Alongside Soviet economic aid to some developing countries, including Egypt and India, the conquest of space helped boost the prestige of the Soviet Union in the Third World. (That was assisted still more by the Soviet Union's anti-colonial stance in world politics, with its admirers in Africa and Asia overlooking the nature of the relationship between the USSR and the states subordinated to it in Eastern Europe.) However, Khrushchev's exaggeration of Soviet missile capacity turned out to be counterproductive in the 'First World'. In particular, it led to American perceptions of a 'missile gap' in favour of the Soviet Union and so to massive investment in US military production. Similarly, the shock of the first sputnik and Gagarin's flight in space produced an American response so successful that the first men to set foot on the moon – in 1969 – were Americans. (The space programmes of both the Soviet Union and the United States, it is worth adding, benefited from their acquisition of talented German rocket scientists and engineers at the end of the Second World War.) Nevertheless, in the years between 1953 and 1964, the Soviet Union became a still more formidable military power than it had been hitherto, far stronger than any country apart from the United States. It was not, though, until the early 1970s that it reached a rough military parity with the USA.

In foreign policy the record of the Khrushchev years was a very mixed one. Some of the major events – among them, Soviet reaction to unrest in Eastern Europe and the Sino-Soviet split – are discussed in other chapters. Nevertheless, this was an area where Khrushchev's impetuousness at times made the world a much more dangerous place. In 1960 he took the decision to wreck a Paris summit meeting with President Eisenhower, President de Gaulle of France and British prime minister Harold Macmillan by demanding a public apology from Eisenhower for the intelligence-gathering flights made by American aircraft over Soviet territory. The evidence for these flights was in Soviet hands, for one such U-2 flight had been downed, and the pilot, Gary Powers, who had bailed out, was in Soviet custody. This being so, Eisenhower owned up to prior knowledge of the spy flights but, in such circumstances, could scarcely apologize for them. For Khrushchev this meant that 'Eisenhower had, so to speak, offered us his back end, and we obliged him by kicking it as hard as we could.'[52] Since, however, Khrushchev had actually wanted to achieve better relations with the United States, this style of diplomacy was, to say the least, unhelpful.[53]

Although Khrushchev was firmly convinced that nuclear war would be a disaster for all humankind, and profoundly disagreed with Mao Zedong's more insouciant view of the prospects, he brought the world closer to nuclear catastrophe than it had ever been by placing missiles, with nuclear warheads, in Cuba in 1962. Fidel Castro had initially been reluctant to accept the missiles, but he regarded it as a humiliation when, on the insistence of the Kennedy Administration that the missiles be withdrawn, they were removed. In the Soviet Union also, both in political and military circles, there were many who had thought the original idea foolhardy but also perceived the return of the rockets to Soviet soil as a diplomatic victory for the United States. In fact, the backstairs diplomacy during the crisis produced results which were not at all bad from a Soviet standpoint. President Kennedy gave an assurance that there would be no US attack on Cuba and, on condition that the promise was not made public, agreed to withdraw American missiles from Turkey. Yet the venture did Khrushchev much more harm than good in the circles of those who mattered at home. His impulsiveness had risked war with the one country which was militarily stronger than the Soviet Union – and whatever the concrete results of the showdown, the perception was that Khrushchev had blinked before Kennedy.[54] The extreme dangers which the Cuban missile crisis had highlighted contributed to the current of opinion internationally, and in scientific circles in the Soviet Union itself, in favour of banning nuclear tests in the atmosphere. Igor Kurchatov, the leading Soviet atomic scientist, was among those who lobbied Khrushchev to agree to such a ban, which had gained the support of the Western nuclear powers. A limited nuclear test-ban treaty was duly signed in Moscow in 1963.[55]

Contradictions of the Khrushchev Era

When conservative party bureaucrats, notably the ideologist Leonid Ilichev, joined with the leading officials of the Artists' Union to take Khrushchev to an exhibition of abstract art, they knew exactly what they were doing. They accurately predicted that there would be an explosion of rage from Khrushchev and that this would be conducive to stepping up the pressure on writers and artists who deviated from Soviet orthodoxy. This was late in the same month, November 1962, in which Solzhenitsyn had published his *One Day in the Life of Ivan Denisovich* in *Novy mir*. This ground-breaking short story, which in an understated way illuminated life in the Soviet labour camps, had been published with the personal support of Khrushchev. That came after Khrushchev's aide, Vladimir Lebedev, on the urging of Tvardovsky, who was enthusiastically in favour of publishing the work, had read the story to Khrushchev when the latter was in a receptive mood.[56] Thus, in the very same month, Khrushchev's support had been successfully enlisted on opposite sides of the battle on the artistic and literary front. (Soviet officials were fond of such military metaphors.) An already grumpy Khrushchev, who thought he had better things to do than attend an exhibition of recent and contemporary art, was duly outraged by the sculpture and abstract paintings he encountered in the Manezh hall, just a few hundred yards from the Kremlin.

The approved form of art was 'socialist realism'. This meant representational art which was realistic only up to a point. It had to be imbued with optimism and to present an idealized view of workers and peasants. The key word was 'socialist', in the sense of whatever was currently meant by that term at the top of the Soviet hierarchy. (Irreverent Soviet citizens asked: 'What is the difference between impressionist, expressionist and socialist realist art?' The answer: 'Impressionists paint what they see, expressionists paint what they feel, and socialist realists paint what they hear.' To listen to the guidance of party and state officials and the guardians of orthodoxy in the state-sponsored artistic unions was the path to a comfortable existence for the artist.) The outstanding sculptor Ernst Neizvestny was one of those targeted at the Manezh exhibition for the full range of crude Khrushchevian invective. He was also bold enough to answer back and even to tell Khrushchev that the people around him were exploiting his ignorance of art. That produced another explosion. The ploy of the conservative bureaucrats worked in the way they had intended it should. A backlash got under way not only against innovative artists but also against writers such as Solzhenitsyn who were raising dangerous questions about the Soviet past.[57]

Subsequently, a group of writers and artists were invited to a meeting with Khrushchev in the Central Committee. Yevtushenko, with a mixture of daring and orthodoxy, raised the issue of anti-semitism. This annoyed Khrushchev, who said it was not a problem in the Soviet Union. Yevtushenko insisted that it was and that it was to be found among people who occupied official posts. Addressing it would 'lead us to even greater success in all areas of Communist construction'.[58] Neizvestny was among those called to this Central Committee meeting, and again he got a dressing-down from

Khrushchev. The name 'Neizvestny' means 'unknown' in Russian, and Khrushchev told the sculptor that he was well named because he would remain unknown. Later in the 1960s, when dictating his memoirs, Khrushchev recalled this episode and said, 'it was rude of me to say it . . . If I met Neizvestny now, I'd apologize for what I said during our discussion at the Central Committee.'[59] Seven years after he was ousted from the Soviet leadership, Khrushchev died – in September 1971. Remarkably, the person his family asked to sculpt a memorial to him, to stand above his grave in Moscow's Novodevichy cemetery, was none other than Neizvestny. He agreed. The very striking monument has intersecting white marble and black granite (in equal proportions) and on one of them rests a bronze head of Khrushchev. For most observers it symbolizes the good and the bad which Khrushchev did in his life, the two sides of a remarkable personality who lived through turbulent times.

The Khrushchev era was one of profound contradictions. Much that was important in these years occurred regardless of Khrushchev's intentions, no matter how hard he tried to keep his finger on every pulse. However, the pull in two different directions also reflected contrasting sides of Khrushchev's own personality. He was a Stalinist who did more than anyone to shake the foundations of Stalinism, a hard and ruthless politician who yet retained some human warmth, a poorly educated worker with a remarkable capacity for learning, and a true believer in the goal of a humane world communism who did not hesitate to use tanks to put down popular resistance to Communist rule in Hungary in 1956 or to support, although this time with misgivings, the shooting of striking workers in the Soviet city of Novocherkassk in 1962.[60] (The strikes and demonstrations were a product of deteriorating working conditions in local factories as well as more general discontent at price rises. Even the KGB report from Novocherkassk noted that new work norms in one of the factories had earlier in the year led to a decline in the wages of some categories of workers of up to 30 per cent.)[61]

The Fall of Khrushchev

Between 1962 and 1964 Khrushchev was at his most imperious. In general, he liked to shake up institutions and he gave full vent to this desire in his final years in power. This style of leadership, and the upset his reorganizations caused, adversely affected the interests of a majority of Central Committee members, the very constituency which had come to his rescue in 1957. It sealed Khrushchev's fate when his colleagues in the Presidium of the Central Committee finally moved against him. They had no difficulty in getting the Central Committee as a whole on their side. How much Khrushchev's institutional changes of the early 1960s were disliked by the Soviet establishment was shown when within a year of his departure almost all of them were reversed. That applied also to earlier changes, such as Khrushchev's uniting of the party leadership and the chairmanship of the Council of Ministers and his creation of the regional economic councils. The first two posts were separated in October 1964 and most of the central ministries that had made way for the *sovnarkhozy* were soon reinstated.

In November 1962 Khrushchev had created a new body called the Committee of Party-State Control, which had the avowed aim of checking up not only on state organs but on Communist Party officials as well. This could be perceived as yet another centralization of power in his hands, although the chairman of that body was the ambitious Alexander Shelepin, who was already a secretary of the Central Committee and had previously been Chairman of the KGB. The greatest blow to regional party first secretaries, who had earlier formed Khrushchev's main power base, was dealt to them in the same month, when Khrushchev divided the regional party organizations into organs for industry and organs for agriculture. This meant that whereas previously the regional party first secretary was responsible for everything that went on in his area – in effect, a powerful regional governor – now he (and it was invariably a man) was in charge of either industry or agriculture, but not both. The other sector became the responsibility of a different secretary. But the Central Committee in 1964 was the same Central Committee that had been selected at the Twenty-Second Party Congress in 1961, thus consisting of people whose powers and functions had in the meantime been curtailed. To this diminution of their authority was added uncertainty about their future. One of the changes introduced at the Twenty-Second Congress was the imposition of a compulsory percentage turnover of membership of party committees at all levels at every 'election'. This even applied to the top party leadership. There was to be a turnover of at least a quarter of the members of the Central Committee and of its Presidium at every congress of the Communist Party. At lower levels of the party organization the percentage turnover was to be still higher. All of those changes were reversed very soon after Khrushchev was removed from power.

Naturally, his opponents chose to strike when he was on vacation. He was accompanied on this occasion by Mikoyan. Khrushchev had provided plenty of opportunities for his enemies to conspire against him. He had become an inveterate traveller, and in the course of 1963 had spent 170 days away from Moscow and in the first nine and a half months of 1964 150 days away, either in some other part of the Soviet Union or abroad.[62] On the evening of 12 October 1964, when he was holidaying at Pitsunda, on the Black Sea coast of

Georgia, Khrushchev received a telephone call from Leonid Brezhnev.[63] The latter had succeeded Kozlov, who was incapacitated by a stroke in 1963 (dying in 1965), as second secretary of the party. Brezhnev told him he must return to Moscow at once to attend a Central Committee meeting. When Khrushchev asked him what the issues were, he was told they would be 'agriculture and some others'.[64] Khrushchev guessed what was coming. His son, Sergei, had been told by a friendly KGB officer of an impending move to oust his father, and he had passed the warning on to both Khrushchev and Mikoyan. They had given it some thought, but decided that there was little danger. Since, however, it was normally Khrushchev who decided when there was going to be a Central Committee plenum, it was not difficult for him to work out that Brezhnev's call meant the warning had, after all, been well founded.

Khrushchev attended a meeting of the Presidium of the Central Committee the following day. It had been well prepared. Every member criticized him. He was accused of errors in both agricultural and foreign policy, of adventurism in the Cuban missile case, of being unpredictable, erratic, overbearing and conceited. Among the lesser charges, he was blamed for having awarded the title of Hero of the Soviet Union to President Nasser of Egypt. Khrushchev telephoned Mikoyan that evening – on a phone which was, of course, bugged – and said that he would not put up a fight but would go quietly. The Presidium reconvened the following day, on 14 October, and the criticism continued. Only Mikoyan suggested that Khrushchev be allowed to keep one of his two posts, that of Chairman of the Council of Ministers. But when Brezhnev called for a vote on ousting him from both his positions, even Mikoyan did not vote against or abstain. Later the same day the Central Committee met and ratified the decision. Only Suslov spoke, reading the indictment, while Khrushchev sat silently. Since Khrushchev was quite popular in parts of the outside world, the leadership who had united against him produced the formula that they had accepted his request to retire 'in connection with his advanced age and deterioration of his health'.[65] Khrushchev was in fact aged seventy, and Brezhnev and others had paid sycophantic but utterly insincere tributes to him on his seventieth birthday earlier the same year. He was also in reasonably robust health. But in 1964, unlike 1957, he knew he was beaten. The people he had trusted, but often treated extremely roughly, had turned against him. Khrushchev, though, noted how much had changed. He remarked later: 'Perhaps the most important thing I did was just this – that they were able to get rid of me simply by voting; Stalin would have had them all arrested.'[66]

15

Revisionism and Revolution in Eastern Europe

So long as Stalin was alive, he had been the ultimate arbiter on relations between the Soviet Union and Eastern Europe. He also had a large say on the speed of the changes introduced from above in the East European countries. The main exception to that rule was, of course, Yugoslavia where the strong domestic position of Tito's Communists had enabled them to defy the Soviet leadership. The Albanian Communist Party had also come to power without significant help from the Soviet army, but during Stalin's lifetime that did not lead to clashes between Tirana and Moscow. In the time and places with which this chapter is concerned – Eastern Europe in the post-Stalin years up to the mid-1960s – that harmony was to disappear. The Albanian break with Moscow was linked to the much more important Sino-Soviet dispute which got under way in the late 1950s and became an open split in the 1960s. That momentous rupture is, however, discussed in Chapter 17, which focuses on political and ideological change in China.

In countries where local Communists' hold on power was much less secure than in Yugoslavia or Albania (not to speak of China), open defiance by them of the Soviet Union was not an option. Weakness, however, could also be turned to advantage by a determined East European Communist politician seeking to acquire or retain a position of supreme power. If he could portray himself as the one person who was either tough enough or, alternatively, popular enough to be able to keep his country in line, this counted for much with the ultimate overseers in Moscow. The very fragility of the relationship between local Communists and their own society could become a bargaining chip vis-à-vis the Soviet Union in the hands of a shrewd operator. Thus, Walter Ulbricht survived a period of diminishing trust from Moscow by demonstrating that he could maintain the Communists' grip on power in East Germany. In Poland, Władysław Gomułka fell into a somewhat different category. While no Communist in Poland came close to gaining widespread popularity, Gomułka for a time was by a large margin the least unpopular of the country's Communist politicians. He was seen by Poles in the 1950s as a patriot; they overlooked then the fact that he was

also a Leninist. In September 1948 he had been replaced as general secretary of the party by Bolesław Bierut. He was arrested in July 1951, though
never brought to trial. Released from prison in 1954, Gomułka was not re-
admitted to the Communist party until August 1956. Two months later he
had become the leader of Poland's Communists as First Secretary of the
Polish United Workers' Party (PUWP).

To have been imprisoned in the Stalin period was a point in Gomułka's
favour with the Polish population and even with many rank-and-file party
members. After much hesitation, the Soviet leadership went along with the
sudden return to power of such a popular Communist. It turned out to be
a worthwhile gamble. Although Gomułka was never a mere puppet, he
became a sufficiently reliable leader from Moscow's standpoint. In Poland,
as throughout most of Eastern Europe, local Communists could not have
remained in power for long without the ultimate backing – by force, if need
be – of the Soviet Union. However, they had some leeway to manoeuvre
between Moscow and their own populations. Direct rule of the countries
of Eastern Europe by Russians was out of the question, not least in a country
such as Poland where there was a long tradition of Russo-Polish hostility.
It was also unthinkable on ideological grounds. There had to be at least a
minority within the society – preferably, of course, a majority of the working
class – who had discerned the 'laws of history' and were ready to build
'socialism' of a Communist type.

German and Czech Worker Resistance

The earliest popular resistance, after Communist regimes had already been
established, came – though this is often overlooked – in Czechoslovakia. It
was soon followed by more serious unrest in East Germany, with the latter
case presenting the post-Stalin Soviet leadership with a major dilemma.
Stalin's death had introduced a new uncertainty into the Soviet–East
European relationship, and that was particularly so in the German
Democratic Republic (GDR), which had formally come into existence in
October 1949 under the leadership of Ulbricht. The post-Stalin collective
leadership that emerged in Moscow was far from united on foreign policy,
especially in the few months in which Beria played an important role within
it. At the plenary session of the Central Committee in July 1953, at which
the members of the party's Presidium explained to the broader leadership
the reasons for Beria's removal from office, he was accused of having been
ready to give up East Germany. Nikolay Bulganin observed that, in discussion in the Presidium, the central argument was over the direction in which

Germany should be led – 'the path of strengthening the German Democratic Republic or the path of its liquidation and the transmutation of Germany into bourgeois Germany'. Beria, he said, had chosen the second option, which, however, other members of the Presidium had rejected.[1]

Beria, however, had not been alone in considering the possibility of a united Germany that would not be a threat to the Soviet Union but which would, in Soviet terms, be a 'bourgeois democratic' rather than 'socialist' state. Malenkov was at various times accused not only by Bulganin but also by Khrushchev and his allies of having been unsound on the German question. Even if Beria and Malenkov took the lead, though, in considering a bold change in policy towards Germany, new evidence suggests that, for a short time, a majority of the leadership had been prepared to go along with the idea of a united Germany. Beria, as head of the secret police, was better informed about the growing tensions within East German society than other members of the party Presidium, whereas Malenkov was simply sceptical about the feasibility of sustaining a divided Germany indefinitely. They were influential initially, but the mood in the whole Soviet leadership hardened after the arrest of Beria and, more especially, after the uprising that occurred in Germany on 17 June. Malenkov's position also changed in the light of that event.

Among Malenkov's papers which have come to light in recent years is one drafted in late May or early June 1953 in which he said it was 'profoundly mistaken' to believe that Germany could remain divided over the long term. He stated that its unification would be possible only on the basis of its becoming a 'bourgeois-democratic republic'.[2] However, when Malenkov gave a report to the Central Committee plenary session on 2 July, convened to discredit Beria, the tone was very different and was one of support for the existing East German state.[3] Khrushchev and his allies had an interest in damning Beria and, later, Malenkov on policy grounds and not only for their role in repression, since the latter sphere was one in which their own pasts were open to question. The views attributed exclusively to Beria and Malenkov were, however, more generally, if briefly, held. Malenkov's earlier paper, taking a soft line on the German question, was prepared for a meeting with the East German leadership on 2 June 1953, in which Ulbricht and his colleagues were criticized for the harshness of the policy they had been pursuing. Since the document was designed for an inter-party meeting, it required the assent of the Soviet party Presidium. Thus, prior to the popular uprising in East Germany in mid-June 1953, the top Soviet leadership as a whole had endorsed such judgements in Malenkov's paper as 'Germany's unity and its transformation into a democratic and peaceful state' being 'the most important prerequisite' and 'one of the essential guarantees' for maintaining peace in Europe and beyond.[4]

What emerges from the archival evidence is a contradiction between two different notions of a future Germany, both of them desirable from the standpoint of the Soviet Union. The problem for the Soviet leaders was that they were mutually incompatible. On the one hand, there was the Soviet desire to build a strong Communist system in East Germany. On the other, there was the idea that a united Germany, which would remain disarmed and non-aligned, would best serve Soviet security interests. Between Stalin's death and the East German uprising a few months later, discussion around these issues took place in the Soviet leadership, but after the latter event, the emphasis was very much on 'building socialism' in East Germany.[5] This was accompanied by a desire to ensure that West Germany (the Federal Republic) would not become part of a military alliance directed against the Soviet Union. Since the goals, however, could not be reconciled, pursuit of the first of them led to the Federal Republic of Germany becoming in 1955 a member of NATO.

Events in Germany itself in 1953 played a decisive role in reinforcing the preference for strengthening the GDR as a Communist state. Stalin's death had raised hopes in the minds of the German population of some relaxation on the part of their hard-line regime. The idea, however, of a 'new course', leading to greater reconciliation with the population, emanated from Moscow, not from Ulbricht. Quite independently of any policy preferences of Beria and Malenkov, members of the Soviet Control Commission in East Germany reported to Malenkov in May 1953 that the German Communists were underestimating 'the political significance of the populace's departure from the GDR to West Germany'. The document found in Malenkov's papers, prepared for the meeting with Ulbricht on 2 June, contained the stark statement: 'The analysis of the internal political and economic situation in the GDR, the facts of the mass flight of the population of East Germany to West Germany (about 500 thousand have already fled!) shows conclusively that we are really heading at full steam – not towards socialism, however, but towards an internal disaster. We are obliged to soberly face the truth and to recognize that without the presence of Soviet troops the existing regime in the GDR is unstable.'[6] Part of the problem, according to the Soviet Control Commission in Germany, was the harshness with which 'basically correct' decisions were being implemented. They noted numerous cases of 'incorrect arrests' and of 'unlawful and groundless searches in apartments and offices'. They recommended freeing many people who had been convicted for Nazi crimes, saying that an amnesty should enable between 15,000 and 17,000 people to be released from prison.[7]

Ulbricht was highly sceptical of the softer line, and in fact, work norms were made tougher in the GDR. More work, in other words, was demanded for the same pay. In response to popular discontent, the GDR leadership adopted on 11 June 1953 their own version of a 'new course', with some economic concessions, but they did not rescind the higher work norms. Building workers in East Berlin went on strike on 17 June and they were soon joined by workers in many other localities. Within a matter of hours, over half a million people were involved in the strikes and demonstrations, and the demands quickly escalated from complaints about work norms to a call for free elections. Soviet tanks, however, moved in. Dozens of the demonstrators were killed, many were arrested and there were subsequent executions. By 19 June the uprising was over.[8] The response was characteristic of Communist leaderships when faced by serious working-class opposition – economic concessions, but a hard line, including the use of whatever force was necessary, to preserve the existing power structure. In East Germany there was subsequently a greater effort than hitherto to make basic foodstuffs, housing and utilities available at affordable prices through the use of subsidies.[9] A distinctive feature of the Communist regime in the GDR in the 1950s was the possibility for people to vote with their feet – to move to the Federal Republic of Germany (FRG) by going from East to West Berlin. That option was eventually cut off with the building of the Berlin Wall in 1961. However, the GDR leadership always had another difficulty peculiar to their state: its nationals could compare their standard of living with that of their fellow Germans in the FRG. This did not, following the June 1953 unrest, lead to political relaxation, but it did stimulate an attempt at economic amelioration, including now a retreat from the higher work norms.

Two weeks prior to the uprising in Berlin, workers had taken to the streets in the western Bohemian town of Plzeň – better known as Pilsen, not least for its beer, outside the Czech Republic. Although they were much less of a headache for the new Soviet leadership, since they were on a smaller scale and the Communist Party in Czechoslovakia was in a much stronger position than its East German counterpart, the fact that it was workers opposing the Communist authorities at the beginning of June 1953 alarmed the Communist rulers in Prague. Those who took part in this rebellion were not armed, but some of the young workers acquired knuckledusters. Among the seventy or so people who were quite seriously injured, a majority were secret policemen or members of the local workers' militia. Some of the latter, as well as army units stationed locally, refused orders to fire on the demonstrators, and the revolt was crushed only when special police units from the Ministry of the Interior and a contingent of the workers' militia from Prague were sent to the scene.

The cause of the unrest had been a currency reform which wiped out people's savings. Very quickly, however, the slogans became anti-Communist, pro-Beneš (although he had been dead already for five years), and pro-American (Pilsen was in a part of the Czech lands which had been liberated at the end of the Second World War not by the Soviet army but by the Americans). No one was killed, but particularly unpopular local Communists were beaten up, and busts of Stalin and Gottwald were thrown out of windows of official buildings which the demonstrators had stormed. Although prison sentences were imposed on many of the participants, the punishment was not so draconian as to draw undue attention to the events, which were a significant embarrassment to the Communist Party. This was, after all, a working-class revolt in a state in which the workers had supposedly become the ruling class. The secretariat of the party's Central Committee in Prague came up with the convenient formula that the rebels 'were not workers but bourgeois elements dressed up in overalls'.[10]

The 'new course' in East European policy immediately following Stalin's death was associated with Beria, in particular, and with Malenkov. The fact that it appeared to have contributed to serious trouble in East Germany led to a more cautious Soviet approach and made Beria and, later Malenkov, convenient political scapegoats for the policy failures. (Both of them, especially Beria, were guilty many times over of conspiracy to murder innocent Soviet citizens, so the attempt to ameliorate conditions in east-central Europe might, more reasonably, have been regarded as mitigating factors, however inadequate, to be counted against their long list of real and atrocious offences.) The fundamental problem for the Soviet leadership was the gap between their demands and aspirations and those of a majority of the people in East Europe living under Communist rule. The way in which they tried to square the circle was, in some of the more difficult cases – notably Poland and Hungary – to place a wager on leaders who had a degree of popularity in their own societies and to count on them being sufficiently loyal followers of whatever line was emanating from Moscow. In East Germany, however, after some dithering in 1953, they opted for short- and medium-term stability by supporting successive leaders who were not even the most acceptable Communists in the eyes of their fellow citizens – Walter Ulbricht and his successor, Erich Honecker. In the long run it was to become clear that such a regime could collapse as quickly as one in which a softer line had been pursued.

Change in Poland and Hungary

Communist rule brought about changes in the societies of Eastern Europe that had longer-term unintended consequences as well as short-term

1. Karl Marx in 1880.

2. Friedrich Engels in 1870.

3. Vladimir Lenin in 1920.

4. Josif Stalin in 1942.

5. Leon Trotsky.

6. Georgi Dimitrov in 1933 when he was awaiting trial accused of setting fire to the German Reichstag.

7. Leaders of the Yugoslav Resistance during the Second World War: (*from left to right*) Aleksandar Ranković, Josip Broz Tito, and Milovan Djilas.

8. German tanks advancing through a burning village following the invasion of the Soviet Union in 1941.

9. Soviet leaders in celebratory mood in August 1945, Stalin leading the way. Behind Stalin is Nikita Khrushchev (*left*) and (*in white suit*) Georgy Malenkov. Vyacheslav Molotov is on the right of the picture.

10. Hungarian resistance fighters on a captured Soviet tank: Budapest, 1 November 1956.

11. János Kádár addressing the Hungarian legislature on 12 May 1957, his first speech there since the crushing of the 1956 Hungarian revolution.

12. East German leader Walter Ulbricht checking his watch on 8 August 1956. His successor, Erich Honecker, would be told by Gorbachev that history punishes those who come late.

13. (*From left to right*) Fidel Castro, Che Guevara and Anastas Mikoyan during the veteran Soviet politician's February 1960 visit to Cuba.

14. Fidel Castro in conversation with Nikita Khrushchev on 20 September 1960 in the United Nations building, New York.

15. Visitors to the Moscow Exhibition of National Economic Achievements – above them a poster showing the first man in space, Yury Gagarin, with Soviet leader Khrushchev.

16. (*From left to right*) Zhou Enlai, Mao Zedong and Lin Biao at a Tiananmen Square parade on 3 October 1967. This was during the Cultural Revolution and Zhou and Lin are dutifully waving the Little Red Book of sayings of Chairman Mao.

17. Mao Zedong (*left*) with Deng Xiaoping. Later Deng was to reverse many of the policies which Mao had espoused.

18. The burning of banned books in China during the Cultural Revolution.

19. The leader of the Prague Spring, Alexander Dubček, in July 1968.

20. 26 August 1968: Soviet troops occupying Czechoslovakia are confronted in Prague by angry young Czechs.

21. American military aircraft bombing North Vietnam: 31 January 1966.

22. A German student protester against the American involvement in the Vietnam war holds up a Ho Chi Minh placard: Berlin 1968.

23. The most vicious of Communist leaders from the Cambodian Khmer Rouge in 1975: (*from left to right*) Pol Pot, Noun Chea, Leng Sary and Son Sen.

intended outcomes. Especially important were the growth of urbanization and, still more, of education. Thus, even one of the most trenchant, and erudite, of Polish philosophical critics of Communism (and, more generally, of Marxism), Leszek Kołakowski, wrote: 'In the Stalinist years the state was quite generous in subsidizing culture, so that a good deal of rubbish was produced but also much work of permanent value. The general standard of education and access to universities soon rose considerably as compared with before the war.'[11] Kołakowski is also probably correct in suggesting that the Soviet-imposed orthodoxy did less damage in Poland than elsewhere in Eastern Europe because of the deep-rooted Polish distrust of everything emanating from Russia. Partly as a result, 'cultural Stalinism in Poland was comparatively short-lived', purges in institutions of higher education were less drastic than elsewhere in Eastern Europe, and fewer books were removed from library access.[12]

The extension of education – and, in particular, the rapid widening of opportunities to enter higher educational institutions – was not, though, a specifically Polish feature. It was a more general achievement of Communism. It was one, however, which did much more to undermine than to sustain Communist systems. That became especially clear in the long term – with the Soviet Union the most important case – but even in the short run students could, in some instances, make life very difficult for Communist leaders. In Hungary, as the author of a lively history of the Hungarian revolution of 1956 has observed: 'To the Communists' credit they had made big strides in education, raising literacy standards in the countryside and massively increasing the number of places at colleges and universities for children of peasants and workers.'[13] Yet the same students, whose heads had been stuffed full of Marxist-Leninist ideology as well as more useful knowledge in the course of their university studies, were in the vanguard of resistance to Communist misrule as early as 1956.[14]

The years between the death of Stalin and Khrushchev's Secret Speech were a time of reassessment for a number of those who had earlier enthusiastically embarked on what they perceived as 'building socialism' in Eastern Europe. While the tempo of change was to increase in 1956, there were important developments earlier than that in Poland and Hungary. A plenary session of the Central Committee of the Polish Communist party (PUWP) in January 1955 went further in criticism of Stalinism than any party other than the Yugoslavs had gone up to that point. Unofficial critics were still more outspoken, and in the course of the year the boundaries of permissible debate were extended. The Poles and Hungarians, with their large Western diasporas, were – next to the East Germans – the peoples least cut off from information about Western democracies. Like others in east-central

Europe, they also listened to broadcasts by fellow nationals emanating from Western Europe. In the Polish case an important role was played at this time by a lieutenant-colonel in the Communist security police, Józef Światło, who defected from Poland in December 1953 and, in broadcasts from Radio Free Europe in Munich which he began the following year, provided accurate information on, for example, the barbaric methods used to convict innocent people.[15]

In both Poland and Hungary the mid-1950s were, briefly, a period of classical 'revisionism' inasmuch as, following the death of Stalin, members of the party who had been enthusiastic about building socialism, but were disillusioned with what had been constructed thus far, began to voice criticism of the way Communist doctrine was being interpreted. Since anti-Communism had been dealt with ruthlessly, and non-party members had no opportunity to contribute to political discourse, members of Communist parties – arguing with each other on the basis of different understandings of Marxism and Leninism – became the main dissenting voices. Later, most East European Communist intellectuals were to move beyond revisionism, no longer believing that Marxism-Leninism, even when stripped of its Stalinist excrescences, remained the best way of understanding the world. In the mid-1950s, however, they were still convinced that there was something worth reviving or revising. A generation later a majority of them saw Communism as a body of doctrine which was fundamentally flawed and a set of institutions fit only for dismantling.

Those party members in the 1950s who were beginning to have doubts were more readily influenced by people who were arguing from within Marxism than by overt anti-Communists. Thus, for example, the renowned Hungarian economist János Kornai has said that in the period between 1953 and 1955 he was much influenced by Isaac Deutscher's biography of Stalin and by the writings of the Yugoslav Edvard Kardelj, who argued that the Stalinist model of economic management led to bureaucratic centralism.[16] As Kornai put it: 'I was still half or three-quarters a Communist at the time. The works that affect a person most strongly in the state of mind I was then in are not ones diametrically opposed to the views held hitherto by the doubter – that is, not attacking the Communist Party from without.'[17] Some of the most innovative economic thinking, while remaining within the bounds of revisionism, emanated from Poland, with Oskar Lange and Włodzimierz Brus among the most prominent theorists. Their arguments for a form of 'market socialism' were also to influence Communist reformers elsewhere at a time when the ideas of orthodox Western economists were still taboo.[18] Transnational influences within east-central Europe took many different forms. Thus, unrest and open defiance of the authorities in

Poland in 1956 was a stimulus to protest in Hungary which eventually took a more dramatic turn. There were also, however, the less politically overt, but in the long run important, influences of party intellectuals in one Communist country on their counterparts in another.

In Hungary, revisionist thinking had been given a boost by Moscow's insistence in mid-June 1953 that Mátyás Rákosi give up the prime ministership. He was allowed to remain party leader, but a much more reformist Communist, Imre Nagy, became prime minister. Nagy pursued a 'new course' with an enthusiasm and measure of popularity which increased the hostility to him of Rákosi and the Communist old guard, although Nagy, too, was a 'Muscovite'. He had spent a lot of time in the Soviet Union in the 1930s and the war years. The declining power of Malenkov within the Soviet leadership over the next two years made it easier for Rákosi to strike back at Nagy. In 1955, the same year in which Malenkov lost his chairmanship of the Council of Ministers, Nagy was dismissed as prime minister in Hungary. Indeed, Malenkov, conscious of his weakening position, himself criticized Nagy at a Kremlin meeting in January of that year at which the Hungarian prime minister was given an extremely uncomfortable time by the whole Soviet leadership. Malenkov accused Nagy of economic incompetence and, worse, of 'bourgeois nationalism'.[19] Once it was clear that Nagy no longer had highly placed supporters in Moscow, Rákosi, who had never been reconciled to his own de facto demotion, was free to strike, and he lost little time in doing so. Nagy was accused, at a Central Committee in March, of 'rightist deviation', removed from the headship of the government and from the Politburo a month later, and expelled from the Communist Party by the end of 1955.

There were, then, revisionist stirrings in Eastern Europe before 1956, as well as workers' revolts such as that in Czechoslovakia in 1953. The uprising in East Germany in the same year involved a great many workers, but it brought together different social groups. Declassified Stasi records show that intellectuals, especially students, were arrested in disproportionately large numbers in relation to their percentage of the population. In 1956, however, protest involved workers and intellectuals together, opposing the authorities over a longer period, thereby turning a problem into a crisis for the Soviet leadership. And the impetus to events with a revolutionary dimension in Communist Europe came – as it was to come also in the late 1980s – from Moscow. The leadership of the Communist Party of the Soviet Union played a decisive role not only in the development of Communist rule in Eastern Europe but also, as will be shown in Part 5 of this book, in its demise. Khrushchev's attack on Stalin at the Twentieth Congress of the CPSU in February 1956 made life vastly more difficult for East European

Communist leaders who had prided themselves on following closely in Stalin's footsteps. Thus, the First Secretary of the Hungarian Communist Party, Mátyás Rákosi, rejoiced in the title of 'Stalin's best pupil' (or, slightly more modestly, 'Comrade Stalin's best Hungarian disciple'),[20] a slogan which accompanied his unprepossessing features on placards and posters.[21] (Rákosi's nickname, quite widely used behind his back in Hungary, was 'Arsehead'.)[22]

For more idealistic members of Communist parties, for whom life under Communism had been far removed from what they had envisaged, Khrushchev's speech was both a spur to self-questioning and an impetus to reform within their own societies. The leaderships of the East European countries had been put in an awkward position not only by the Twentieth Congress of the CPSU but by Khrushchev's reconciliation with Tito. Along with Bulganin, Khrushchev came to Belgrade in May 1955 and apologized for Soviet mistakes in the relationship with Yugoslavia. He got off to a bad start by placing all the blame for ostracizing Yugoslavia on Beria rather than Stalin, a position the Yugoslavs greeted with frank incredulity. However, the visit ended with the Soviet visitors accepting Tito's basic conditions for a joint communiqué stating that 'different forms of Socialist development are solely the concern of the individual countries'. Tito was insistent that the negotiations were between independent states, not between ruling Communist parties. For the same reason he was adamant that Bulganin, as Chairman of the Council of Ministers of the USSR, not Khrushchev as party leader, must sign the communiqué.[23] A number of notable East European Communists, especially from the ranks of those who had remained in their own countries rather than spending years in the Soviet Union, had been either imprisoned or executed as alleged Titoists at the end of the 1940s and the beginning of the 1950s. Thus the revelation that Tito was, once again, a comrade rather than a renegade was a severe embarrassment for Eastern Europe's unreconstructed Stalinists. The corollary was that reconciliation with Yugoslavia gave encouragement to reform-minded, or 'revisionist', Communists in other parts of East Europe.

Poland in 1956

The repercussions of these developments, and especially of Khrushchev's Secret Speech, were felt, to a greater or lesser degree, in every Communist state, but in none more so than Poland and Hungary. The Polish Communist leader Bierut died just a fortnight after Khrushchev's bombshell at the Twentieth Congress – probably of a heart attack, although there were suggestions of suicide.[24] He was succeeded as general secretary by Edward

Ochab, who at one time had been close to Gomułka and who was to attempt to steer a middle course between the 'national Communists', on the one hand, and the hard-liners, on the other. The liberalization from above was accompanied by radicalization from below. The weekly *Po Prostu* (Quite Simply) was an especially important forum not only for the expression of critical views but as the initiator of discussion clubs for young intellectuals throughout the country.[25] Khrushchev's secret speech led to a wave of debate and questioning within the Polish Communist party, as well as to the release of tens of thousands of prisoners in 1956, of whom some 9,000 had been jailed for political reasons.[26] The first serious manifestation of working-class protest came in late June 1956, when factory workers in Poznań demonstrated to demand higher wages. A peaceful demonstration turned into a full-scale uprising, involving more than half the population of Poznań. Communist party offices were set on fire. Following two days of clashes between the demonstrators (with factory workers in the vanguard) and the Polish army and security forces, at least seventy-four people were dead and hundreds wounded.[27] The Soviet as well as the Polish leadership were seriously worried by the growing unrest.

Four months later, what became known as the 'Polish October' saw a groundswell of support for the return of Gomułka. Public opinion, given the crisis within the ruling party, had a huge impact. At the beginning of October, Gomułka returned to the Politburo, and by 19 October he was once again First Secretary of the Polish Communist party. The Soviet leadership were concerned both by the fact that Gomułka had been swept to power independently of them and by the evidence that anti-Soviet sentiment had played a significant part in swelling his support. Soviet troops, already in Poland, were brought closer to Warsaw to put pressure on the new Polish leadership. Yet Gomułka was able to get his way on a number of issues on which he was at odds with Khrushchev and the Soviet leadership. Thus, the Russified Pole Konstantin Rokossowski (in the Polish spelling of his name) had been minister of defence since 1949, and Gomułka insisted on his removal.[28] As Marshal Rokossovsky, he had been one of the heroes of the Red Army in the Second World War, although (as noted in Chapter 8) he had been in a Soviet prison on the eve of the German attack on the Soviet Union. Khrushchev, who had a high regard for Rokossovsky, only reluctantly acceded to Gomułka's demand. However, a combination of massive popular pressure in Poland and a growing, and potentially more severe, crisis in Hungary led Khrushchev to seek a more general compromise solution to the Polish impasse.

In a number of Polish cities on 22 October there were pro-Gomułka rallies, involving in each case as many as 100,000 people. Two days later, around half a million people demonstrated in Warsaw. Khrushchev noted at a meeting of the Presidium of the Soviet Communist Party held on 24 October that there was no shortage of reasons for embarking on armed conflict in Poland. He prudently added, however, that 'finding a way to end such a conflict later on would be very hard'.[29] One important reassurance Gomułka offered the Soviet leaders was that Poland would remain a loyal member of the international Communist movement and, most specifically, of the Warsaw Pact. In retrospect, the somewhat reluctant Soviet endorsement of the Poles' choice of Gomułka bought them a lot of time. In the long run it produced more disillusionment in Poland than in the Soviet Union. Reflecting years later on the decisions made in those days, Khrushchev was able to say of Gomułka: 'Here was a man who had come to power on the crest of an anti-Soviet wave, yet who could now speak forcefully about the need to preserve Poland's friendly relations with Soviet Russia and the Soviet Communist Party. Perhaps I didn't appreciate this fact right at that moment, but I came to appreciate it afterwards.'[30] Radical Polish critics of the system came to the same conclusion as Khrushchev. Unlike him, of course, instead of rejoicing in Gomułka's trajectory, they deplored it. Thus the philosopher Kołakowski wrote:

> The Russian leaders, at first highly mistrustful, decided in the end – quite rightly, as it turned out – that although Gomułka had taken over without Kremlin sanction he would not prove too disobedient, and that invasion would be a greater risk. The 'Polish October', as it was called, far from ushering in a period of social and cultural renewal or 'liberalization', stood for the gradual extinction of all such attempts. In 1956 Poland was, relatively speaking, a country of free speech and free criticism, not because the government had planned it so but because they had lost control of the situation. The October events started a process of reversal, and the margin of freedom which still remained grew less year by year.[31]

Hungary in 1956

Whereas in Poland the turmoil stopped short of either revolution or armed conflict, events in Hungary took a different course. Hungary also had a relatively popular Communist who had been banished from the leadership and likewise expelled from the Communist Party in the person of Imre Nagy, who had been appreciated as a reformer during his prime ministership of 1953–55. In other respects, Nagy's past fitted much less well with the idea of a 'national Communist', especially when compared with the record of

Gomułka as a resistance leader of Poland's home Communists during World War Two. Nagy, in contrast, not only spent many years in the Soviet Union but he was also, while there, an active informer for the NKVD, denouncing to the authorities a number of other Hungarian exiles. When he volunteered in 1941 to join the Red Army, he was placed in a special NKVD unit.[32] When all allowances are made for the fact that Nagy's own life was in danger in the Soviet Union, not least because of his known preference for the relatively gradualist approach favoured by Bukharin (who perished in the Great Purge), this was an unpropitious background for someone who showed great courage in the last two years of his life and who was to become a hero to anti-Communist Hungarians.[33]

Under Soviet pressure, Rákosi was obliged to give up the leadership of the Hungarian party in July 1956. The person who conveyed the message was the Kremlin's leading troubleshooter, Anastas Mikoyan, on a mission to Budapest. Mikoyan had a friendly meeting during that visit with János Kádár who, as noted in Chapter 12, had been released from prison in the summer of 1954. Kádár may have been coming under scrutiny as a possible future leader of the Hungarian Communist party. In fact, however, Rákosi's immediate successor, Ernő Gerő, was a Communist in the same mould as himself – a Stalinist who had spent years in Moscow. He was also of Jewish origin, though the Soviet leadership believed that the disproportionately strong representation of Jews at the top of the Hungarian hierarchy made it harder for the Communists to win more widespread support from the society. Nevertheless, at a meeting of the Central Committee of the Hungarian party, Mikoyan, as Moscow's envoy, eventually spoke in favour of Gerő, who was duly appointed. (Later, Khrushchev acknowledged that this was an error, saying at a meeting of the Presidium of the Soviet Communist Party on 3 November 1956, at which Kádár was present: 'Mikoyan and I made a mistake when we proposed Gerő instead of Kádár. We were taken in by Gerő.')[34] Mikoyan, however, surprised the July meeting in Budapest by speaking also in favour of reinstating Imre Nagy's party membership.[35] In a report to the Presidium of the Soviet Communist Party, Mikoyan said that it had been a mistake all along to expel Nagy from the party, 'even though he deserved it with his behaviour'. Had he remained, however, he would been bound by party discipline. Although Mikoyan was not ruling out the possibility that Nagy might play some future part in the Hungarian leadership, in his half-hour speech to the Central Committee of the Hungarian party, he observed that Nagy must distance himself from the 'anti-party group' which surrounded him.[36]

Mikoyan was the most flexible member of the Soviet top leadership team and the only one who consistently opposed Soviet military intervention in

Hungary. He was also readier than Rákosi to accept relatively free discussion among Hungarian intellectuals. The equivalent of the discussion clubs fostered by *Po Prostu* in Poland consisted in Hungary of the writers and journalists who had attached themselves to the 'Petőfi Circle', named after the national poet who helped inspire the Hungarian revolution of 1848 against their Austrian overlords. That organization had been created by the Communist party's youth movement as a way of allowing intellectuals to let off steam. It began as a body seeking incremental change, but the tone of its proceedings became increasingly radical.[37] Most of the speakers were thinking in terms of a reformed Communism, and one of their calls (in advance of the same suggestion coming from Mikoyan) was for the readmission of Nagy to the party. They were reformers, not revolutionaries, in the spring and summer of 1956, but by the autumn many of them were moving rapidly in a revolutionary direction. The developing freedom of speech owed much to the influence of the de-Stalinization Khrushchev had accelerated with his Twentieth Party Congress speech.

In Hungary, as in Poland, October was the month in which political tensions came to a head. The reburial of László Rajk gave huge impetus to the movement for change. Rajk, as Minister of the Interior, had been no liberal, but his arrest and execution had turned him into a martyr and the leading Hungarian victim of Stalinist oppression. With Tito once again accepted as a comrade within the international Communist movement, those such as Rajk who had been condemned for their supposed Titoist sympathies had to be rehabilitated. At the reburial, Rajk's widow, Júlia, holding close their seven-year-old son, stood next to Imre Nagy, who assured those around him that 'soon it will be Stalinism that will finally be buried'.[38] For 100,000 Hungarians who lined the streets of Budapest, that was the minimum they hoped for. The reburial of Rajk had been officially approved by the Hungarian authorities, in contrast to the demonstration by some 500 students shouting anti-Communist slogans which followed it. That was broken up by the police. Gerő, who had been out of the country at the time, later acknowledged to the Soviet ambassador, Yury Andropov, that Rajk's reburial had 'dealt a massive blow to the Party leadership', even though their 'authority was not all that high to begin with'.[39] One day later, Nagy was readmitted to the party. A more prominent personality than Kádár, he seemed to represent the best hope for stabilization on the basis of reform.

Events took another course. Five thousand students gathered at the Budapest Technological University on 22 October and produced what amounted to a revolutionary manifesto. It consisted of sixteen points. The very first on the list was the demand that all Soviet troops leave Hungarian soil immediately. The demands included a call not for a multi-party system but rather for election of Communist party (Hungarian Workers' Party, as it was called at that time) officials by secret ballot of all party members. The third point read: 'A new Government must be constituted under the direction of Comrade Imre Nagy; all the criminal leaders of the Stalin–Rákosi era must be immediately relieved of their duties.' The authors of the manifesto declared their solidarity 'with the workers and students of Warsaw and Poland in their movement towards national independence' and called for 'complete recognition of freedom of opinion and expression' and 'of freedom of the press and radio'.[40] The next day the students demanded that their sixteen-point manifesto be broadcast on Hungarian radio. The director of the Budapest radio station tried to trick them into thinking this was being done. A woman announcer, in what purported to be the broadcast, read through the list of points, which were heard by the students listening through loudspeakers outside the radio building. In the meantime, however, people at home were hearing music from their radios. The subterfuge backfired, for when those in the crowd realized this had been an attempt to fool them, they laid siege to the building.[41]

On that same day, 23 October, the gigantic statue of Stalin in central Budapest was toppled, to the cheers of tens of thousands of Hungarians. By midnight on the 23rd, Nagy had been appointed prime minister. Gerő agreed to this reluctantly, on the instructions of Khrushchev. Nagy was told that he should sign a formal invitation to the Soviet leadership to send troops to restore order in Hungary. This he refused to do, although he did sign a declaration of martial law which authorized Hungarian forces to impose curfews and to resort, if need be, to summary executions.[42] There were many Soviet troops and tanks already in Hungary, and in the early hours of 24 October, 6,000 soldiers and 700 tanks entered Budapest. In the fighting which broke out, the Hungarian forces were divided. A Hungarian army colonel, Pál Maléter, whose charismatic presence owed something to his immense height, joined the rebels. Before long Nagy's position evolved from that of Communist reformer with ties to Moscow to leader of the Hungarian resistance to foreign domination. On 3 November, with fighting taking place between Hungarian insurgents and Soviet troops, who by now were being massively reinforced, Maléter was appointed Minister of Defence in a freshly formed coalition government which included members of the refounded Social Democratic Party and the Smallholders' Party. The Stalinists were all excluded. The government included János Kádár, who had been appointed First Secretary of the Communist party, in succession to the discredited Gerő, on 25 October. It was yet another indication, though, of how much had changed that prime minister Nagy, not party chief Kádár, was regarded even by the Central Committee of the party as the leader of Hungary during those days of revolutionary turmoil.[43]

Mikoyan and Suslov attended the meeting of the Hungarian Politburo which chose Kádár. They sent a four-page telegram to the leadership in Moscow late that night on the day's happenings – including the violent clashes involving Soviet tanks and Hungarian insurgents – and, though acknowledging that the situation in Budapest had become 'more complicated', they seemed content with the removal of Gerő and the promotion to the party leadership of Kádár. However, Mikoyan and Suslov had argued against those in the Hungarian leadership who had called for the withdrawal of Soviet troops, and they believed that their objections had been endorsed by Nagy, Kádár and the Hungarian Politburo as a whole. As an anguished postscript to their message to Moscow, they added that they had just received (late at night) a translation of what Nagy had said in a radio broadcast that evening: in contradiction 'to what was decided in the Politburo', Nagy had declared that the Hungarian government would take the initiative in holding discussions with the Soviet Union on the withdrawal of Soviet armed forces from Hungary.[44]

Mikoyan and Suslov approved the creation of a coalition government, even though this meant a definite retreat from previous Soviet positions. On 30 October, the Presidium of the Central Committee of the CPSU in Moscow had also opted for a peaceful resolution of the crisis. However, events in Hungary continued to spiral out of their control. This included the lynchings of particularly hated Communists, mainly secret policemen, on the streets of Budapest – spontaneous actions by a minority within the Hungarian resistance which were deplored by Nagy. News of their comrades hanging from trees and lampposts not only helped to produce a change of mind in Moscow but also engendered a change of mood among Communist leaders in countries to which the Soviet leadership could not dictate. Tito and Mao eventually endorsed the use of massive force to crush the uprising.[45] Both the Yugoslavs and the Chinese had been in favour of the Polish and Hungarian Communists being allowed to resolve their own difficulties. They had supported the appointment of Gomułka and of a Hungarian counterpart. Tito, for example, had urged the replacement of Gerő by Kádár, and his opinion almost certainly influenced the Soviet leadership at that time. The Yugoslavs also believed that a much earlier retreat from Stalinist policies, combined with the removal of leaders of the type of Rákosi and Gerő, could have prevented matters reaching the point of crisis. Yet the Yugoslav and also the Chinese leaders remained Communists orthodox enough to be unwilling to see 'counterrevolution' prevail in any country which had already, in their terms, become socialist.

The Soviet leadership as late as 30 October took a decision that they *would* be willing to withdraw their troops from Hungary 'provided that the Nagy government succeeded in (1) consolidating the situation while maintaining the socialist system and (2) preserving membership in the Soviet bloc'.[46] The Soviet leadership were united in insisting that a Communist system must be preserved in Hungary, but quite deeply divided in the last days of October 1956 on the tactical means to that end. There was some criticism in the Soviet Presidium, when Hungary was debated on 26 and 28 October, of Mikoyan and Suslov for making too many concessions. Molotov, Voroshilov and Bulganin were among those taking a hard line. Perhaps surprisingly, Marshal Zhukov was the first to press for more 'political flexibility'.[47] Events in Hungary on 30 October, the very day on which the Soviet leadership had agreed upon a conditional withdrawal of Soviet troops, led them the following day to reverse that decision. It was on 31 October that the decision was taken to use overwhelming military force to put an end to the 'counterrevolutionary' turmoil. As already noted, the Nagy government had been reorganized on a multi-party basis on 30 October, but on the same day unrest had increased, and among those killed in an act of mob violence was the first secretary of the Budapest city committee, Imre Mező (who was actually a Nagy supporter).[48] This last development, as well as the lynchings that day of Hungarian secret policemen, had a profound effect on Communist leaderships throughout the region. These latest events intensified their already acute concern, especially in Romania and Czechoslovakia, where the Hungarian minorities in Transylvania (part of Romania) and Slovakia had been in contact with their fellow nationals in Hungary.[49] The Soviet leadership now feared that the Hungarian infection could travel across Eastern Europe and the entire bloc might be affected.

Having changed their position on intervention, Khrushchev and Malenkov braved atrocious flying conditions to visit Tito in his island home of Brioni on 2 November to inform him that the Soviet Union was going to deploy massive force in Hungary. Among the reasons they gave were the lynchings of Communists there; Nagy's declaration after fighting had begun in Budapest that Hungary was withdrawing from the Warsaw Pact and was declaring neutrality; and the argument that if Hungary were lost to the 'socialist camp', this would be a massive gift to hard-line Stalinists in the Soviet Union.[50] (Nagy had first spoken in public on 31 October of Hungary leaving the Warsaw Pact, but of doing so after patient discussions with the Soviet Union.)[51] Khrushchev also referred in his talks with Tito to the advantage of crushing the Hungarian uprising at a time when the British and French, in collusion with Israel, had embarked on an attack on Egypt in response to President Nasser's nationalization of the Suez Canal. In the words of the Yugoslav ambassador to Moscow, who was at the Brioni meeting:

> Khrushchev said that British and French aggressive pressure on Egypt provided a favourable moment for a further intervention by Soviet troops. It would help the Russians. There would be confusion and uproar in the West and the United Nations, but it would be less at a time when Britain, France, and Israel were waging a war against Egypt. 'They are bogged down there, and we are stuck in Hungary', Khrushchev said.[52]

Thus, by the end of October 1956 the Soviet leadership had decided firmly on the use of overwhelming military force to ensure that Hungary remained Communist and a member of the Warsaw Pact. Even without the Anglo-French intervention in Egypt, they would have reached that decision. However, the foolhardy Suez escapade meant that there was a far from exclusive international focus on the crushing of the Hungarian insurgents. Israel had sent its forces into Egypt on 29 October, and the following day the British and French governments sent an ultimatum to Egypt and Israel, demanding that they cease their hostilities and ensure freedom of naviga-tion in the Suez Canal. The two Western governments had, however, acted dishonestly, colluding in advance with Israel and then, in the words of a retired senior British diplomat, claiming 'the right to intervene to stop what we had conspired to start'.[53] The Suez adventure, doomed to ignominious failure from the outset, was opposed by the Eisenhower administration in the United States, and it vied with the Soviet suppression of the Hungarian revolution for the attention both of the USA and of the United Nations.[54] Indeed, between 1 and 3 November 1956, President Eisenhower's attention was focused on the Middle East crisis, for he knew that the United States could play a more decisive role there than in Hungary.[55]

Kádár, during his brief period as a member of Nagy's coalition govern-ment, in a broadcast in Budapest on 1 November referred to 'our glorious revolution'. On that same day he voted in favour of declaring Hungary's neutrality, having already supported the re-establishment of a multi-party system.[56] He had come to be seen, however, by a part of the leadership in Moscow as the best hope for achieving some kind of reconciliation with the Hungarian population after the 'counterrevolutionary' uprising had been suppressed. It was an important consideration also that he had already been chosen in Hungary to be leader of the country's Communist party. Notwithstanding Kádár's support thus far for the policies of the Nagy govern-ment, there was hope in Moscow that he could be turned round. And indeed, on the evening of the same day on which he voted for neutrality, Kádár prepared to change sides. Along with a harder-line colleague, Ferenc Münnich, who was the favourite not only of Molotov and the more Stalinist members of the Soviet Presidium to become Hungary's leader, but initially also of Khrushchev, Kádár allowed himself to be taken to a Soviet air base and flown to Moscow. Once there, he did not renounce all his previous views. He told a meeting of Soviet leaders (not including Khrushchev, who was touring Eastern Europe, gathering the political support of other Communist leaders for the impending surge of Soviet forces to put an end to Hungarian resistance) that continued Soviet support for the wrong people in the Hungarian leadership – in particular, Rákosi and Gerő – had been 'the source of many mistakes'. Rákosi simply had to say: 'this is the opinion of the Soviet comrades' and everyone in the Hungarian leadership would fall silent.[57] Soviet Ambassador Yury Andropov has sometimes been given credit for spotting early on that Kádár could be the salvation of the Communist cause. But though the two men were to establish a strong political and personal relationship, which lasted to the end of Andropov's life, Andropov supported hard-liners in Budapest in 1956. In late April of that year, Andropov had called for greater Soviet support for Rákosi to prevent any more 'major concessions to rightist and demagogic elements'.[58] He had met Kádár only once before their fateful encounter on the evening of 1 November at a Soviet air base to the south of Budapest, when he told him that the Soviet leadership wished to speak to him in Moscow.[59]

As the Hungarian situation, in Soviet eyes, went from bad to worse in the second half of 1956, opinion within the Presidium of the CPSU became more volatile. Mikoyan, though, was alone in continuing to believe, after all his colleagues in the Soviet party leadership had given up any such hope, that a government led by Nagy could avoid the need for invasion. Even after the Soviet party Presidium had taken the decision to use massive force to put an end to the uprising in Hungary, Mikoyan, on his return to Moscow at the beginning of November, still expressed opposition to a military solution, urging that more time be granted to elaborate a political compromise. Khrushchev, however, told him that the decision had been taken and there would be no going back on it.[60] Mikoyan briefly contemplated resignation, but in fact remained in the Soviet top leadership team for another decade. Suslov, who had been in Budapest with him, fully agreed with the decision to invade.

Mikoyan observed the norms of collective responsibility and party unity in public, but the contemporary minutes of CPSU Presidium meetings, which became available only after the end of Communism in the Soviet Union and Eastern Europe, substantiate the fact that he consistently sought alternatives to the bloodshed which ensued.[61] Even in 1956 this required political courage, albeit not the suicidal courage which would have attended opposition to Stalin on such an issue. Mikoyan attended Politburo meetings (the Presidium of the Central Committee being the Politburo under another name) over a period of forty years, from the time he became a candidate member in 1926 to his retirement from high politics in 1966. He had known personally every Soviet leader from Lenin to Brezhnev (who succeeded Khrushchev as party chief in 1964). His legendary status as the ultimate survivor was captured by a Soviet joke from the later Khrushchev years. The Presidium members emerged from a meeting, so the story went, into a torrential rainstorm. The only person with an umbrella was Mikoyan. He handed it to Khrushchev, saying: 'You take it. I can dodge between the raindrops.'

The transcripts of the meetings which Kádár and Münnich had with the Soviet leadership on 2 and 3 November throw a somewhat different light on Kádár's actions during those early November days from what was for long assumed. He did not travel to Moscow aware that he would be chosen as Hungarian leader or knowing that a new influx of Soviet troops was imminent. In fact, he spoke in Moscow of the inadvisability of an invasion and openly admitted that he was among those who had voted within the government for Hungary's neutrality. He also told members of the Soviet party Presidium that the intelligentsia in Hungary supported Nagy. Kádár favoured renaming the Hungarian party (in fact it was changed from the Hungarian Workers' Party to the Hungarian Socialist Workers' Party) and said it was important that a successor to Nagy not be a marionette. Moreover, Stalinists such as Rákosi and Gerő should not be included in the Hungarian government.[62] Thus, though Kádár was to be regarded, following his return to Budapest, as a quisling, even at the outset he was not, as he put it, a marionette.

Nevertheless, Kádár did return to Hungary as Moscow's man, though there were serious doubts within the Soviet leadership about the wisdom of their choice. Kádár's own rationalization of the betrayal of his Hungarian colleagues was that he favoured reform but not a return to capitalism or 'bourgeois democracy', and, in face of the opposite danger from his standpoint, he wished to prevent the return to the Hungarian leadership of the Rákosi group. Because the Hungarian uprising had destroyed the authority of the Communist party, Kádár was installed as head of the Soviet-engineered government (with the emphasis initially on the government, rather than the party). Once a majority of the Soviet leadership were persuaded that he stood the best chance of making a reimposition of Communist rule palatable to Hungarians, Kádár was given some leeway over the composition of the new government. Rákosi had apparently been led to believe by his allies in the Soviet Union that he and other Hungarian Stalinist refugees would play a leading role in the Soviet-imposed (for a second time) Hungarian regime, but Khrushchev and the dominant group in the Presidium of the CPSU Central Committee had no intention of allowing that.[63] The new ruling group of Hungary was announced as a 'Revolutionary Worker-Peasant Government'. Kádár's power was far from supreme, for it was his deputy, Münnich, who was to be in control of the armed forces and the security police.[64] Münnich, furthermore, had long-standing links with Soviet military intelligence.[65]

Molotov was distinctly unhappy about the choice of Kádár. He voiced his fears at a Presidium meeting on 4 November, after Kádár and Münnich had returned to Budapest, saying that they had brought to power someone who would take Hungary down a Yugoslav road. He observed also that Kádár's reference to the 'Rákosi clique' was dangerous. Even Shepilov, who was not an ally of Molotov, expressed his concern about this precedent, remarking: 'Tomorrow it will be the "Ulbricht clique".'[66] There were still doubts about Kádár in the Soviet leadership throughout the following year. These were shared by Khrushchev, who noted that he 'made a number of trips to Hungary in 1957',[67] and at that time:

My own hopes rested with Münnich. I thought I could deal with him better than with Kadar. Munnich was a cunning and battered old wolf who had been through the Hungarian revolution with Bela Kun. He'd lived in the Soviet Union for a long time, and I thought he was better prepared than anyone else to handle the problems which were still facing Hungary.[68]

The Hungarian revolution was brutally suppressed by Soviet troops with Kádár's acquiescence. The process took only four days. Although many people had been killed earlier in the clashes with Soviet tanks, most of the 2,500 Hungarian deaths occurred between 4 and 7 November 1956. Almost 20,000 were sufficiently seriously wounded to be hospitalized. On the Soviet side, over 700 were killed or 'disappeared' and 1,450 were wounded. Over the next few years more than 100,000 people were arrested on 'counterrevolutionary' charges and almost 26,000 imprisoned. At least 300 people, and possibly as many as 600, were executed.[69] Following the Soviet invasion, some 211,000 people fled from Hungary to the West, of whom around 45,000 in due course returned.[70] Among those executed were Nagy and the colonel who became minister of defence in Nagy's short-lived government, Pál Maléter. Nagy had taken refuge in the Yugoslav embassy, a reflection of the ambivalence of the Yugoslavs concerning the Soviet onslaught. On the one hand, Tito did not wish to see capitalism

restored in Hungary. On the other, he did not want to see Soviet hegemony reinforced in Eastern Europe.

When Nagy, having been assured he would be unharmed, left the embassy
on 23 November, he was arrested and taken to Romania. The Yugoslavs
protested and argued that he should either live in freedom in Hungary or
be allowed to emigrate to Yugoslavia. That was acceptable neither to Kádár
nor Khrushchev. The Romanian Communist leader, Gheorghiu-Dej, was the
earliest to indicate that Nagy's lease on life would be a short one. He was
firmly in favour of handing back Nagy to 'the Hungarian comrades' as soon
as they had consolidated power, adding that he was sure that Nagy would
'be hanged for his crime – not by the neck, but by the tongue'.[71] The only
point of any validity made by the ghoulish Dej was that Tito had a more
indulgent attitude towards Nagy than towards the dissident views of his
former close comrade-in-arms, Milovan Djilas, who by that time had been
imprisoned in Yugoslavia. Nagy was kept under house arrest in Romania
until 1958, when he was tried in Budapest, sentenced to death, and hanged
(by the neck) on 16 June. Maléter and the writer Miklós Gimes were hanged
that same day. It was widely assumed that the death sentences were carried
out on Soviet insistence, but this was not so. Kádár himself supported these
extreme measures. He resented the fact that Nagy had not resigned his
prime ministership after the Soviet invasion, thus making his own task of
convincing Hungarians that he was their legitimate head of government all
the harder. He apparently believed that as long as Nagy was alive, he would
be a dangerous rival, given that he had come to symbolize Hungarian patriotism and the desire for independence. In his trial, Nagy refused to ask for
clemency, not acknowledging the competence of the court. When he was
addressed as the 'former' prime minister, he insisted that he was 'still' the
head of the legitimate government. In his last statement to the court, Nagy
said: 'If my life is needed to prove that not all Communists are enemies of
the people, I gladly make the sacrifice. I know that there will one day be
another Nagy trial, which will rehabilitate me. I also know I will have a
reburial. I only fear that the funeral oration will be delivered by those who
betrayed me.'[72] The last recorded words of Maléter were: 'Long live independent and socialist Hungary.'[73]

The Lessons and Legacy of 1956

The Hungarian revolution was anti-Soviet but not anti-socialist. It became
a national – indeed, nationalist – movement, but its leaders were members
of the Communist party. There was, however, widespread opposition to the

kind of Soviet-style Communist system which had been constructed under the leadership of Rákosi. Out of a Hungarian population of some ten million people, approximately 15,000 took up arms against the Soviet forces. Hundreds of thousands, though, had taken part in peaceful demonstrations, such as the reburial of Rajk. When the Soviet invasion came, the overwhelming majority of the Hungarian population supported those who, heavily outarmed and outnumbered, were resisting them.[74] Contrary to Soviet propaganda at the time, no Western 'imperialists' were in Hungary fomenting revolution – 'counterrevolution' in Soviet parlance. Indeed, the rhetoric of the Eisenhower administration (especially of Secretary of State John Foster Dulles) was shown to be just that. Talk of 'rollback of Communism' and 'freeing the Captive Nations' was evidently geared more to domestic American politics than to the real world of international relations.[75] Neither the United States nor, still less, any other Western power was going to go to war to end the de facto division of Europe which they had accepted at the end of World War Two.

The one partial exception to the lack of Western intervention in support of the Hungarian uprising was Radio Free Europe (RFE). Its broadcasts to the populations of Communist East Europe (which were usually jammed but not wholly successfully) varied from one country to another. Some of the Hungarian exiles who addressed their compatriots from the Radio Free Europe station in Munich were more inflammatory than, for example, their Polish counterparts.[76] This meant, though, that in October and November 1956, the Hungarian RFE broadcasts were more of a hindrance than a help to those in Hungary who were attempting to carve out greater independence while taking account of the bounds of possibility at that time in that place. The broadcasts made little or no distinction between Rákosi and Nagy, some of them calling for the overthrow of the latter at a time when it was almost certainly in the interest of Hungarians to rally behind him. The radio analysts also misjudged the balance of forces within Hungarian society. Whereas students, workers and intellectuals (including, not least, Communist intellectuals) were in the forefront of the resistance, the RFE broadcasters placed their hopes on the Catholic Church and the peasantry.[77] However, while there was fierce fighting on the streets of Budapest, life went on more or less normally in the countryside, and the Church was not the force it had been in the past or that it remained in Poland. The Hungarian Cardinal József Mindszenty had been condemned to life imprisonment in a show trial in January 1949. He was released from prison during the revolutionary turmoil of October 1956 and broadcast a stirring speech on 3 November, in which, however, he did not distinguish the government of Nagy from that of its Communist predecessors. Although his supposed incitement of 'counterrevolutionaries' was later blamed for provoking the Soviet invasion, it played no part in Kremlin thinking. The decision to intervene with overwhelming force had already been taken three days earlier.[78]*

The broadcasts of Radio Free Europe helped to foster the illusion among some of those who had taken up small arms against Soviet tanks that the might of the United States stood behind their insurgency, leading them to believe that they would receive American military assistance (even though RFE did not explicitly say this). One result of the crushing of the Hungarian revolution was to make foreign broadcasters, and Radio Free Europe (which was paid for by the American taxpayer) specifically, more careful about raising unwarranted hopes. Over many subsequent years that radio station and others – including, not least, the BBC – were to play important roles as purveyors of accurate information concerning events in Eastern Europe and developments in the outside world. After 1956, however, Radio Free Europe endeavoured not to encourage unrealistic expectations and avoided anything remotely resembling a call to arms.

One of the lessons which reformers in Eastern Europe drew from the Soviet crushing of the Hungarian revolution was the importance of pledging loyalty to the Warsaw Pact. Thus, Czech reformist Communists in 1968 believed that the big mistake of Nagy and his colleagues had been to declare neutrality and the intention, accordingly, of withdrawing from the military alliance with the Soviet Union. Reasonable though the supposition was that this had been the last straw for the Soviet leadership in 1956, the stated intention of remaining within the Warsaw Pact was not, as it turned out, enough to save Czechoslovakia from its own Soviet military intervention twelve years later. The 'Prague Spring' will be discussed in Chapter 19, but a more general point is that all such Soviet crackdowns – whether in Hungary 1956 or Czechoslovakia 1968 – had the immediate effect of strengthening hard-line forces throughout Communist Europe, including Russia.

In October 1956 the neo-Stalinist or, at best, conservative Communist leaders of East Germany, Bulgaria, Czechoslovakia, Romania and Albania (Walter Ulbricht, Todor Zhivkov, Antonín Novotný, Gheorghe Gheorghiu-Dej and Enver Hoxha) all supported, in private as well as in public, the Soviet intervention in Hungary. In Poland, Gomułka was privately opposed to the Soviet invasion (in contrast with the attitude he took to Czechoslovakia

---

* Later, Mindszenty took up residence in the US embassy in Budapest and stayed for fifteen years – to the embarrassment not only of the Hungarian authorities but, in due course, also of the United States and even the Vatican, who, in response to the evolution of Hungarian politics and society, wished to improve their relations with Hungary.[79]

in 1968), but he did not voice any public criticism of the Soviet actions in Budapest. Although there were great historical and cultural differences among all of these countries, systemic similarities generally prevailed. That is to say, the essential features of the Communist system remained firmly in place, and the way these internal structures operated had much in common from one country to another. That changed in 1968 with the culmination of the reform movement within the Communist Party of Czechoslovakia, but reverted back after the 'Prague Spring' was forcibly ended. In terms of its immediate goals, the Soviet military intervention in Hungary was a success. Soviet hegemony within the bloc was maintained and a surface stability was secured. That situation lasted in Eastern Europe, albeit with several serious interruptions, for more than a generation. Invading a 'social-ist' ally had, however, costs as well as benefits for the Kremlin. Coming on top of Khrushchev's revelations at the Twentieth Party Congress, the inva-sion of Hungary looked to many outside observers like a return to Stalinism and led to a massive loss of membership by Western Communist parties. The Scottish nationalist poet Hugh McDiarmid was very much the idiosyn-cratic exception to the rule in choosing the Soviet crushing of the Hungarian uprising as his moment to rejoin the Communist Party of Great Britain. This was especially ironic since Hungary, as well as Poland, had just shown what a potent threat to Communism a strong sense of national identity could be.

In Hungary itself the renamed ruling party had to be rebuilt almost from scratch and more than 8,000 officers were forced to leave the Hungarian armed forces at the end of 1956 and in 1957.[80] The Soviet Union lost support not only in Western Europe and North America, where in most countries that support was not high to begin with, but also in Asia. Later, Soviet rela-tions with Third World countries improved, but at the time some of their erstwhile friends regarded the invasion of Hungary as at least as much an act of imperialist aggression as the Anglo-French attack on Egypt.[81] Within Eastern Europe resistance developed from the end of the 1950s onwards in both Albania and Romania to Soviet aims of greater integration under Russian leadership. However, there was no trace of revisionism in either country. They were to become (Romania later than Albania) the two most oppressive Communist states in Eastern Europe. Proceeding with their pecu-liar forms of nationalist Communism, the Albanians formed an alliance with China, while the Romanian Communists maintained a somewhat uneasy alliance with the Soviet Union.

The Bulgarians and (until 1968) the Czechs were the most obedient members of the Soviet bloc. The development hardest to predict from the vantage point of October–November 1956 was the subsequent political course of Poland and Hungary. Gomułka was a strong personality, anti-Stalinist inasmuch as he had been a victim of Stalinism, but far from a liberal. He was a firm believer in the dominant role of the Communist party and in a centrally planned economic system. Before the end of the 1950s, the hopes that had been placed in him by many Poles in 1956 had largely vanished.[82] The radical reform they expected had not materialized, nor did it emerge in the 1960s, although, partly as a result of the authority of the Catholic Church, the Communists were far less dominant within Polish society than they were in most of the countries of Eastern Europe.

In Hungary, the last years of the 1950s were a time of severe repression. The immediate aftermath of the suppression of the 1956 revolution was just as bad as most Hungarians feared it would be. Few leaders, at the beginning of their period of office, could have been more despised by a majority of their fellow countrymen than János Kádár. But whereas Gomułka returned to office on the crest of high expectations, and disappointed them, Kádár began, as head of a Soviet-imposed government, with dismally low expectations and confounded them many times over. Until 1958 he was both prime minister and party first secretary, but he ceded the premiership to Münnich in January of that year.[83] In the meantime, the normal order of precedence in a Communist system had been restored. It became clear in the course of 1957 that the party leadership was the top job. From the early 1960s onwards, a cautious relaxation got under way in Hungary. By the mid-1960s, serious economic reform was being discussed, and an actual economic reform – the New Economic Mechanism (NEM) – was implemented from 1968. Living standards improved substantially, and there was a gradual liberalization of cultural life. Kádár wielded great power, but showed no interest in the trappings of power. He lived modestly, and there was no hint of a personality cult. Yet it is remarkable that shortly after his death on 6 July 1989, three-quarters of Hungarians polled in a survey agreed with the statement that 'with his passing Hungarian political life has lost one of its greatest figures'.[84] In late 1999, in a vote for the greatest Hungarians of the millennium, Kádár occupied third place. He was the only one of the three to have lived in the twentieth century, and so by implication was the greatest Hungarian of his epoch.[85] There is no necessity to agree with such assessments, but how such a turnaround in perceptions occurred – how such a gloomy and guilt-ridden man came to be admired as a consummate politician – is a topic to which I return in Chapter 26.

16

Cuba: A Caribbean Communist State

Cuba is an unusual Communist state. It is the only case of Communism prevailing either in the Americas or in the Caribbean. It is the only Hispanic Communist state, and also the only 'Third World' country outside Asia to have constructed and sustained a Communist system. Although it belongs to the sizeable category of Communist countries which had an indigenous revolution, it differs from all the other members of that group in that the seizure of power in Cuba was *not* by the Communist party. Indeed that party, called at the time the Popular Socialist Party (PSP), was dismissive of the guerrilla-war tactics adopted by Fidel Castro and his fellow revolutionaries – until they were on the eve of coming to power.¹ And although Cuba was to evolve into a Communist state over several years, the gradualism was not, as in Eastern Europe, primarily a tactical manoeuvre promoted by political caution. Rather, it reflected the evolution in the thinking of the foremost leader of the revolution. Faced by the new challenges of managing, as distinct from seizing, state power, Fidel Castro turned to the only available long-term example of non-capitalist, post-revolutionary governance, that offered by the Soviet Union and other Communist states.

Cuba was also unusual among Communist countries in having had a formally democratic system for most of the time from its independence (at the end of the nineteenth century) until the success of the Castro-led revolution. Among Communist states, the same could be said only of Czechoslovakia, although the quality of democracy was far higher and infinitely less corrupt in the Czech case than in Cuba. Throughout this period the substance of democracy was largely lacking in Cuba, and often even the forms were violated. Thus, the last ruler of Cuba before Castro, Fulgencio Batista, seized power in March 1952 just before presidential elections were due to be held. He had close links with business interests in the United States, especially from the seedy American underworld. A notable example was Meyer Lansky, who lost a sum estimated at more than one hundred million American dollars when his hotels, clubs, casinos and brothels in Cuba were confiscated by the Cuban state following the Castro-led revolution.² Indeed, such was the level of corruption of successive Cuban governments, with rulers in cahoots with American gangsters, that resentment of the United States was widespread in Cuban society long before the country became Communist. Although the USA had helped to liberate Cuba from Spanish rule at the end of the nineteenth century, it was perceived to have replaced Spain as the colonial power. Anti-Americanism was stronger in Cuba than anywhere else in Latin America. At the same time American material possessions attracted envy, and some intellectuals admired the political institutions of the United States. However, the level of attachment to the island's own deeply flawed democratic legacy was meagre and Batista's dictatorship was held in still lower esteem.

Successive Cuban leaders invoked the memory of the hero of their country's struggle for independence from colonial rule, José Martí, but none succeeded in doing so as convincingly as did Fidel Castro. Although no Marxist, Martí left a literary legacy of support for a socially just democracy as well as for an independent Cuba. He regarded domination by the United States no more favourably than he did Spanish colonial rule. An eclectic nationalist and internationalist, Martí was the inspiration behind the Cuban liberation struggle in the late nineteenth century. Moreover, he placed the resistance to foreign domination into a broader Latin American and, indeed, international context as 'a struggle of the oppressed for liberty and equality'.[3] His death in 1895 meant that he did not live to see post-colonial Cuba. He became, however, a potent political symbol and one whose ideals could be contrasted with the grubby reality of twentieth-century Cuban politics. So universally admired was Martí among Cubans that not only did Fidel Castro continue to cite him – even after his conversion to Communism, Castro quoted him with greater fervour than he did Marx and Lenin – but Castro's arch-enemies, the Cuban exiles in Miami, named their US-funded broadcasting station aimed at Cuba 'Radio Martí'.

Castro's Background and Rise to Power

Fidel Castro came from quite a wealthy landowning family, the third child of a relationship between his father and the cook-housekeeper, whom Castro's father later married.[4] He was much closer to his devoutly Catholic mother than to his strong-willed and irreligious father. The latter was a first-generation Cuban who arrived, moneyless, from Galicia in Spain and made good, gradually extending his landholding. Although Fidel Castro was to suffer some adverse discrimination because of his rural origins, birth out of wedlock, and late baptism, he went on to distinguish himself both academically and on the sports field in a leading Jesuit college before entering the law faculty of Havana University.[5] In his early teens Castro wrote a naïve letter to President Franklin D. Roosevelt (preserved in the National Archives of the United States), congratulating him on his election victory in 1940 and suggesting that the president might like to send him ten dollars, 'because I have not seen a ten dollars bill American and I would like to have one of them'.[6] He received a letter of thanks from the State Department but, hardly surprisingly, no ten-dollar bill. Castro remarked in his interview-based memoirs: 'And there are people who've told me that if Roosevelt had only sent me $10 I wouldn't have given the United States so many headaches.'[7] Nine years later, Castro turned down $5,000, which the New York Giants offered him as a signing-on fee, after American talent scouts had noticed his outstanding promise at baseball. Castro was a leading member of the Havana University baseball team, in spite of the fact that by then he had become politically very active.[8]

When Batista, a presidential candidate with little chance of winning, staged his military coup in March 1952, he declared it was a revolution, inaugurating a new legal order. In fact, Meyer Lansky became his 'official adviser for casino reform', and soon both men were accumulating millions of dollars.[9] One year later, Castro made his first attempt to bring down the Batista regime. By then he had read some Marx and Lenin, but though he was already thinking in terms of social revolution with a redistribution of the estates of the wealthy, he was far from being an orthodox Communist in 1953. He led a group of radical opponents of the Batista regime in an attempt to take over the Moncada Fortress in Santiago de Cuba. Castro's group numbered some 120 men and two women, whereas estimates of the number of troops in the barracks vary between 700 and 1,500.[10] They mounted their attack at 5.15 in the morning and had counted on an element of surprise and the fact that most of the troops would be asleep. They planned to seize all the weapons stored in the fortress, win over many of the soldiers, and then take over a radio station to announce their victory. A chance patrol at the crucial moment deprived them of the advantage of surprise, and Castro and his comrades were defeated. Those who were not killed in the attack – and a majority were not – were taken prisoner and the remainder, including Castro, hunted down. Most of the group were killed in cold blood after capture, often following gruesome torture and mutilation.[11] The failed attempt to take the Moncada barracks took place on Sunday, 26 July, and in the official historiography of Communist Cuba this date in 1953 has been portrayed as the beginning of the revolutionary process which was to succeed in overthrowing the Batista regime less than six years later.

Through good fortune – partly due to the decency of one of the officers guarding him – Fidel Castro was spared the fate of many of his followers. Nevertheless, in a trial which was not open to the public, he was sentenced on 16 October 1953 to twenty-six years of imprisonment. Castro was allowed to conduct his own defence. The sentence had been predetermined and so his speech to the court, lasting four or five hours, had no bearing on the immediate outcome of the trial. Castro, however, concluded with words which were to become famous: 'Condemn me. It does not matter. History will absolve me.'[12] He was confident that, regardless of the court's verdict, the revolution would be successful in much less than a quarter of a century. In his memoirs, Castro projects back to this period the strong influence of Marxism on him. There is scarcely any evidence of it, however, in his speech to the court, which was an eloquent defence of liberty, and a justification of the right of rebellion against tyrannical rulers. Castro cited numerous authorities in support of such a right, including Thomas Aquinas, John Milton, John Locke, Jean-Jacques Rousseau and Tom Paine. He also denounced Batista in no uncertain terms. Towards the close of his peroration, he said: 'It is understandable that honest men should be dead or in prison in a Republic where the President is a criminal and a thief.'[13]

In fact, Castro served just a year and seven months in prison, being released in May 1955 after Archbishop Pérez Serantes succeeded in persuading the authorities to free him and other surviving members of his group as part of a wider amnesty. The archbishop argued that they no longer posed any threat.[14] Castro himself, however, was in considerable danger of being assassinated by agents of Batista, especially after he founded his own political organization, the 26th of July Movement. Less than two months after his release from jail, therefore, he left Cuba for Mexico, where he joined his younger brother, Raúl. It was Raúl who introduced him to an Argentinian doctor who was already a Marxist revolutionary, Ernesto Guevara, much better known by his slang name, 'Che'. Fidel was aged twenty-nine at the time, Che Guevara twenty-seven. Guevara, writing in his diary about their first meeting, said of Castro: 'He is a young, intelligent guy, very sure of himself and extraordinarily audacious. We hit it off well.' Fidel observed years later that at that time Che's 'revolutionary development was more advanced than mine, ideologically speaking'.[15] In Mexico, Castro was also jailed for a time, and in November 1956 was told that he had three days in which to leave the country. With a group of fellow revolutionaries, he acquired an ancient boat, the *Granma* – a name which was later to become the incongruous title of the main Cuban Communist party newspaper – and set sail for Cuba. The craft was overloaded with weapons and came close to sinking in a storm in the Gulf of Mexico. The former leisure boat was meant to accommodate twenty-five people, not the eighty-two guer-rilla fighters who shared it with rifles, sub-machine guns, pistols and boxes of ammunition. The journey took a week, two days longer than intended, but eventually ran aground in Cuba, more than a mile short of the beach which was its intended destination.[16] This was just one of countless occa-sions when Castro survived against the odds.

The group of revolutionaries took to the hills of Sierra Maestra and fought a guerrilla war against the Batista regime over the next two years. The vagueness of Castro's ideology at this time, partly real and partly tactical, helped to attract tacit support from much of Cuba's middle class and parts of the upper class.[17] Castro was seen by them as the leader of what was essentially a democratic movement. The revolutionaries led by Castro relied on the Cuban rural workforce rather than on urban workers as their main source of support. However, the former were quite different from the rural peasantry elsewhere in Latin America. Many of them were employed by the sugar mills and earned adequate wages during the harvest season and very little outside it. They were described at the time as 'semi-proletarianized labourers'. These rural workers, who were organized in large groups, were among the most active of Castro's supporters. By early 1958, after many skirmishes, the revolutionaries controlled almost 2,000 square miles of territory in eastern Cuba, even though the core group of rebels comprised only some 300 armed men. By confiscating livestock from large landowners in the areas they dominated, and distributing them to peasants with little or no property, they were able to consolidate their social base.[18] However, it is part of the mythology of the revolution to describe those who fought the government in the late 1950s as a 'peasant army', for the nucleus of Castro's force consisted of young, middle-class revolutionaries.[19]

In July 1958, meeting in the Venezuelan capital of Caracas, eight Cuban opposition parties and anti-Batista groups issued a 'Manifesto of the Civil-Revolutionary Opposition Front', in which they declared that Fidel Castro was their leader. Castro's men had established a radio station in the terri-tory they controlled and were thus able to broadcast this manifesto. Conspicuous by its absence as a signatory to the declaration was the Communist PSP. However, immediately afterwards, realizing that he and his party might be missing a historic opportunity, the PSP leader Carlos Rafael Rodríguez made his way to the Sierra Maestra to pay his respects to Fidel Castro. Although Castro was later to part company with many other Communists, Rodríguez not only became a member of his future govern-ment but remained an important colleague until his death in 1997.[20] The understanding he reached with Rodríguez brought Castro ideologically and politically closer to his brother Raúl and also to Che Guevara.[21]

Castro in Power

In the last months of 1958, by which time Fidel and Raúl Castro now led a fighting force of around 3,000 people, the revolutionaries captured more and more territory, rarely meeting much resistance. The army was demoralized and no longer putting up a serious fight. The rebels captured Santiago and met no armed opposition as they made their way towards Havana. Batista, realizing that his days in power were numbered, transferred command of the armed forces to General Eulogio Cantillo, and on 1 January 1959 left by plane with his relatives and some of his friends for the Dominican Republic. Two more planes full of Batista's people followed within hours. Batista took with him almost the whole of Cuba's gold and dollar reserves.[22] General Cantillo had come to an agreement with Castro in late December not to oppose the 26th of July Movement, but tried to double-cross him by installing himself as Batista's successor. He had no basis of support, however, and by 3 January 1959 the game was up for the old regime. (Cantillo was arrested and spent some years in prison.)[23] Castro made good use of the relatively new medium of television (there were already some 400,000 television sets in Cuba, which had a population at that time of just under seven million.) He also made a triumphal tour of the island in an open jeep. After he entered Havana on 8 January, his speech from the balcony of the presidential palace, which lasted several hours, was greeted with vast enthusiasm. He appeared, according to the British ambassador to Cuba, to be 'a mixture of José Martí, Robin Hood, Garibaldi and Jesus Christ'.[24]

Although Castro had reached a modus vivendi with the PSP leader Rodríguez, he was still not a Communist when he came to power in January 1959. It was not until December 1961 that he declared himself to be a Marxist-Leninist. His acceptance of all the main features of a Communist system was a gradual process. Nevertheless, even in 1953, some of the people Castro gathered around him had been strongly influenced by Communist ideas, among them his younger brother, Raúl, who had been a member of the Young Communists. Che Guevara was also ideologically closer to Communism in the 1950s than was Castro, although Che's combination of revolutionary idealism and attraction to guerrilla warfare did not commend itself to Communist officials in Moscow. Fidel, as he himself has noted, was more of a utopian socialist than a Leninist. His primary political hero was José Martí. In the 1950s he was certainly more Martí-an than Marxian.[25] In an interview late in his career as Cuban leader, Castro himself emphasized

Martí as a continuing inspiration, saying: 'I was first a Martían and then a Martían, Marxist and Leninist.'[26]

It is not altogether surprising that neither Castro nor a majority of those who fought a guerrilla war against the dictatorship of Fulgencio Batista were initially admirers of Cuba's Communists. The Communists had rejected armed struggle. They had instead gone so far as to accept, opportunistically, several positions in Batista's government. And when Castro, with a small band of radical followers, took to the hills of Cuba in 1956 to begin the attempt forcibly to remove the corrupt authoritarian regime of Batista, the Cuban Communists dismissed him as a 'putschist' and referred to his movement as 'bourgeois' and 'romantic'.[27] The latter adjective was appropriate enough. Castro was a romantic revolutionary by temperament – his comrade-in-arms, Che Guevara, even more so – but he was also a much more inspirational leader than any of Cuba's official Communists. As we have seen, the Communist leader, Carlos Rafael Rodríguez, allied himself with Castro only when it was clear that the revolutionaries were in the ascendant and the Batista regime doomed. Notwithstanding this overture, the movement which triumphed was not a Communist one. Yet the success of the revolution led by Castro found him quite suddenly holding the reins of power 'without a real party, a real army or a real program'.[28] It was soon evident that all three were necessary and that the organizational experience of the Communists would come in useful.

In some respects Cuba followed the East European pattern of broad coalition which gave way before long to Communist rule. The first president of post-revolutionary Cuba was a judge, Manuel Urrutia, and most of the members of the first government were, like him, from the 'bourgeois-liberal' camp.[29] However, Castro, even when not holding supreme office, was recognized as the *caudillo*, the supreme leader and embodiment of the nation – an ascription familiar in Latin America and one which Castro claimed to despise, even though he benefited from such traditional personalization of power combined with what was, in other respects, a radical break with the past. For a month and a half following the flight of Batista, Castro held no government office but was commander-in-chief of the armed forces. In the fifteen-person cabinet there were only four members of the 26th of July Movement and no one from the Communist PSP.[30] Changes in the composition of this body came quite quickly, however. In mid-February 1959, the first post-revolutionary prime minister, Miró Cardona, resigned, dissatisfied with his lack of power, and Castro took over the prime ministership.

On a visit to the United States in April 1959, Castro was adamant that the revolution in Cuba had not been a Communist one and, moreover, that 'doors are open to private investments that contribute to the industrial development of Cuba'.[31] Behind the scenes in Cuba, though, there was a struggle going on for the direction the post-revolutionary regime would take. Raúl Castro and Che Guevara were the most prominent members of the Marxist and pro-Soviet camp. The revolution had been both national and social, but the negative attitude to it of both the American government and, not surprisingly, US business may have speeded up Castro's turn to the Communists. One month after his visit to the United States, Castro established a National Agrarian Reform Institute (INRA) which he himself chaired. It became for a time the main executive body in the country, marginalizing the official 'bourgeois-liberal' cabinet. It took over the land reform which was radically redistributing property. Castro was consistent in his implementation of this measure. The land of his own family was expropriated, with only the living quarters left for his mother to reside in until her death in 1963.[32]

In July 1959 Urrutia was replaced as president after he had complained about the growing influence of the Communist PSP, and in October it was the turn of army officers to object to Communist infiltration, among them Huber Matos, who had been a comrade of Castro in the struggle in the Sierra Maestra. He received a severe prison sentence – twenty years – for 'betraying the revolution'. This was a sign of the hardening of the new regime. Raúl Castro had even been in favour of shooting Matos, but Fidel vetoed this.[33] Opposition to the revolution and to the new leadership increasingly was equated with treason. By the middle of 1960, critical newspapers, radio and television stations had been taken over or closed down.[34] Although Cuba was becoming more like a Soviet-type system, the Cuban leaders' fear of enemies had a basis in reality. An anti-Castro guerrilla force operated in the mountains of central Cuba and there were many acts of sabotage, a majority of them apparently organized by Cuban exiles in association with the CIA.[35]

In 1961, Castro's 26th of July Movement was merged with the Communist PSP and became known as the Integrated Revolutionary Organization (ORI). Castro, however, kept a wary eye on Cuba's old Communists as they rapidly showed signs of taking over the coalition in a way reminiscent not only of East European experience but of his own recent tactics, whereby he replaced the liberal members of the briefly functioning broad coalition. In Cuba it was Castro, as he was to make clear time and again, who was calling the shots. The Communist who had taken charge of the ORI bureaucratic machine, Anibal Escalante, was dismissed from his post in March 1962 and exiled from Cuba. All six provincial secretaries of the ORI came from the pre-existing Cuban Communist party (PSP) and Castro removed four of them, keeping only the two on whose loyalty he could count. In 1965 the

ORI changed its name to the Cuban Communist Party (PCC), with Fidel Castro as general secretary, as well as prime minister. (It was not until 1976 that he became the official head of state as well, an office he continued to combine with the prime ministership, the party leadership, and the office of commander-in-chief of the armed forces.)[36] Cuba was officially recognized as 'socialist' (i.e. Communist) by the Soviet Union and other members of the international Communist movement in 1963, at the end of Castro's first visit to Russia in that year. It did not belong to the international Communist economic organization, Comecon, or the military alliance, the Warsaw Pact. Cuba did, though, benefit from its trade with the Soviet Union and from an ample supply of Soviet arms.

THE CUBAN MISSILE CRISIS

This recognition of Castro's Cuba as part of the international Communist movement followed the traumatic events of 1962 – the Cuban missile crisis – which had put a severe strain on the Cuban–Soviet relationship. This episode, which brought Cuba into the very centre of the world's attention, has been touched on already in Chapter 14, mainly in the context of Soviet politics and the damage it did to Nikita Khrushchev. When Khrushchev came up with the idea of installing nuclear missiles in Cuba, Castro was initially reluctant to accept them, since he was opposed to Cuba being seen as a Soviet base.[37] Indeed, Khrushchev himself had only the previous year publicly ridiculed the idea that Cuba could be used by the Soviet Union as a base for attacking the United States. By the early summer of 1962, however, he favoured placing nuclear missiles in Cuba with a view not only to deterring an American attack on Cuba but also for the potential they provided as offensive weapons against the USA. Although the Presidium of the Central Committee eventually approved Khrushchev's proposal on 24 May, there was some prior opposition to it, led by Anastas Mikoyan. In his view the policy was highly dangerous and the Americans, he said, would not accept it. From start to finish of the Cuban missile crisis Mikoyan was a voice of common sense within the Soviet leadership as well as the Kremlin's chief intermediary with Fidel Castro.[38] That latter task required all his diplomatic skills, for Castro's doubts about the wisdom of installing nuclear missiles in Cuba were as nothing compared to his anger when the sites were dismantled and the missiles withdrawn in bilateral negotiations between the Soviet Union and the Kennedy administration in which he was entirely bypassed.

In both Washington and Moscow those who favoured a diplomatic solution to the impasse prevailed. Of crucial importance was President John F. Kennedy's decision to reject advice to bomb without warning the missile sites which were being erected or to sink Soviet ships which were still conveying missiles to Cuba. Instead, he imposed a naval blockade around the island, preventing any more missiles being delivered and providing a breathing space for negotiations as well as more time for the Soviet Union to dismantle the sites under construction and to remove the missiles that were already there. As part of the deal for ending the highly dangerous stand-off, the United States pledged not to mount another attack on Cuba. Kennedy had earlier inherited from the Eisenhower administration a plan to back an attempt by Cuban exiles to recapture the island from Castro and the revolutionaries. Castro had forewarning of this adventure, and the force which landed at the Bay of Pigs in Cuba in 1961 was comprehensively routed. The Cubans captured more than a thousand of the invaders and later returned them to the United States in return for medical supplies and agricultural equipment.[39] In contrast, in the Caribbean missile crisis the following year, the Cubans had no opportunity to negotiate with the United States. Castro could make his case to Khrushchev, but all the key decisions were taken in Moscow and Washington. In addition to a promise not to invade Cuba, Kennedy, as a further concession to Khrushchev, agreed to remove American missiles from Turkey, provided that decision was not publicized by the Soviet Union. This sweetener, as it happens, was not strictly necessary. Khrushchev had already dictated his speech essentially accepting the American demands before he learned of Kennedy's concession over Turkey.[40] Since the price of having the American rockets removed from Turkey some months later was that the Soviet side had to keep quiet about it, Khrushchev did not benefit politically from the agreement. The Chinese as well as the Cubans thought that Moscow had backed down unnecessarily. The Soviet leaders had, though, been rational enough to pull back from the brink of catastrophe to which the world had been brought as a result of Khrushchev's impetuosity. As Mikoyan later observed, they had been 'on the verge of a Third World War'.[41]

Castro was outraged that he was not a party to the negotiations between the Soviet Union and the United States, even though he was exchanging letters with Khrushchev throughout the crisis. He maintained that the weapons should not have been withdrawn, even if this did lead to nuclear war. Indeed, if the United States attacked, using conventional weapons, he argued that the Soviet Union should be ready to use nuclear weapons, saying in a letter of 31 October to Khrushchev:

> It is my position that once the aggression has occurred, the aggressors must not be given the privilege to decide when nuclear arms will be used. The destructive power of these weapons is so great, and the means of transporting

them so swift, that the aggressor can count on a considerable initial advantage in his favour . . . I did not suggest to you, Comrade Khrushchev, that the USSR attack in the midst of the crisis . . . but rather that after the imperialist attack, the USSR act without hesitation and never commit the error of allowing the enemy to strike you first with nuclear weapons.[42]

Fortunately, the Soviet leadership had more experience of the politics of co-existence in a nuclear age than the still young Cuban revolutionary. Lessons were learned both by the United States and by the Soviet Union from the Cuban missile crisis and neither side brought the world so close to nuclear calamity during the remaining years of the Cold War as Khrushchev had done. Against the better judgement of some of his colleagues, Khrushchev had gambled that putting missiles in Cuba would be 'a quick fix not only to protect Castro's revolution but to redress the strategic imbalance' between the two superpowers, while enabling him to curtail Soviet defence expenditure.[43] After this dangerous episode, Khrushchev himself seemed more convinced that nuclear war would be 'sheer madness' and he was also readier to countenance the Nuclear Test Ban Treaty which was signed in 1963.[44]

Castro insisted, though, that if he had been involved in the negotiations, he would have extracted more concessions from the United States. He had a number of demands which he believed were realizable in October 1962 at a time when Soviet nuclear weapons were already in Cuba. They included an ending of 'the acts of aggression and terrorism against us'; a lifting of the American economic blockade; and the return of the land which became the location of America's Guantánamo naval base. In his memoirs Castro insists that these aims were eminently realizable because 'nobody was willing to march into a world war on account of a blockade, a few terrorist attacks and a naval base that was illegal and on land occupied against the will of the Cuban people'.[45]

Constructing Communism in Cuba

Indigenously established, as distinct from Soviet-imposed, Communist regimes face a particular problem of attempting to reconcile utopian aspirations with actual economic development and reliable political control. Where Communist rule was imposed by Soviet tanks, party leaders' ambitions rarely extended beyond achieving economic growth, political hegemony and a quiescent society. Cuba, however, was in a different category. At the time he came to power, Fidel Castro had never in his life met a Soviet citizen – his brother

Raúl had met one. As Castro put it, comparing – in the twenty-first century
– Cuban experience with that of Eastern Europe: 'Socialism didn't arrive
here through cloning, or through artificial insemination.'[46] The 1960s, in particular, were a time when Castro and his associates took seriously the idea of
creating a 'new man' or 'new socialist person' and the building of a 'moral
economy' rather than one based on material incentives. It was symptomatic
of such ambitions that the person appointed Director of the National Bank
– the Banco Nacional de Cuba – was none other than Che Guevara. There
was a Cuban joke at the time that Castro said: 'We need an economist' –
but this was misheard as 'We need a Communist', and so they brought in
Che.[47] Castro himself, though, stressed Guevara's 'talent, discipline, abilities
and integrity' as the reasons for the appointment. These qualities were needed
because the resources were extremely limited after 'the reserves had been
stolen by Batista'.[48]

Che Guevara had a series of jobs between then and his death eight
years later. He was also a major influence on Castro's thinking and hence
on official Cuban ideology. With the United States doing its best to keep
Cuba economically isolated, Guevara, who became minister for industry
(which was nationalized), and Castro emphasized the citizen's moral duty
to society rather than personal accumulation of material goods. From one
point of view, this was just as well, since the latter became increasingly
scarce. An ambitious programme of healthcare was introduced, and in
due course it achieved impressive results. The same was true of the Castro
government's literacy drive. However, Cuba's gross national product fell
between 1961 and 1963 and serious economic problems persisted. The Soviet
Union helped by agreeing in 1964 to buy most of the Cuban sugar crop
over the next five years at a better price than the world market rate.[49] Che
Guevara admitted in that same year that an earlier decision to reduce the
area of land devoted to sugar cane had led to 'a general decline in agricultural production' and had been a big mistake. It had been based on 'a
fetishistic idea' connecting 'sugar with our dependence on imperialism and
with the misery in rural areas'.[50]

The following year Guevara, tiring of mundane administration, set off
in the further pursuit of international revolution. His travels took him to
the Congo, Brazil and Bolivia, and it was in the last-named Latin American
country that he met his death. In the 1960s Castro, too, fully supported the
armed struggle in Latin America. In 1967 he distanced himself from a number
of Communist parties – including, ultimately, even that of the Soviet Union,
but also from parties nearer home, such as the cautious Venezuelan
Communists – when he declared:

Our position regarding Communist parties is based strictly on revolutionary principles . . . Those parties which call themselves Communist or Marxist and believe themselves to have a monopoly of revolutionary feeling, but who are really monopolizers of reformism, we will not treat as revolutionary parties. If in any nation those who call themselves Communists do not know how to fulfil their duty, we will support those who – even though they do not call themselves Communists – behave like real Communists in the struggle . . . What defines a Communist is his action against oligarchies, action against imperialism and, on this continent, action in the armed revolutionary movement.[51]

Castro made that resounding statement in March 1967. In July of the same year, President Lyndon Johnson complained to Alexey Kosygin, who was Chairman of the Council of Ministers of the Soviet Union at that time, about Guevara conducting revolutionary activity in Bolivia. This came as news to Kosygin, since the Cubans had not troubled to inform the Soviet leadership of Che's whereabouts. Kosygin, employing the sanction of potential withdrawal of Soviet aid, told Castro to stop supporting guerrilla movements in Latin America. Castro refused to take orders from the Soviet Union, arguing that their relations had to be based on mutual respect and independence. But the Soviet leaders were able to take advantage of Cuba's economic dependence upon the USSR, both as a market and as a supplier, and failed to provide the Cubans with an adequate amount of oil in the course of that year. Whether or not there was a direct connection with Moscow's economic squeeze, Castro in 1968 gave his support to the Soviet invasion of Czechoslovakia.[52] That his endorsement of the military intervention, which stopped the Czech radical reforms in their tracks, was not just a matter of temporary expediency is, however, suggested by the fact that Castro was still of the same mind years after the Soviet Union itself had ceased to exist. He observed that Czechoslovakia had been 'headed towards a counterrevolutionary situation, towards capitalism and the arms of imperialism' and that the Cuban leadership were, and remained, opposed to 'all the liberal reforms that were taking place there and in other places in the Socialist camp'.[53]

Che Guevara's role in revolutionary activity ended in 1967 in Bolivia when he was aged thirty-nine. He was wounded, captured, interrogated and then – on the orders of Bolivian president Barrientos – killed in cold blood and buried underneath an airport runway. How Che came to be captured gave rise to varied speculation, including the possibility that he had been betrayed by Bolivian Communists, the KGB, or the Stasi agent Tamara Bunke (known as 'Tania'), who had attached herself to him after serving as his interpreter in East Berlin in 1960.[54] For the most orthodox of Communists, Guevara had been too much of a follower of his own revolutionary conscience rather than official Soviet doctrine for them to be comfortable with him. He was also suspected, wrongly, of being in danger of taking the Chinese side in the Sino-Soviet dispute, which had acquired great intensity by the mid-1960s. Che's status in Cuba remained high, however. After his death he was made into even more of a national hero by Castro. His remains were excavated in 1997 – thirty years after his violent end – and returned to Cuba, where he was given a state funeral. Although Castro sometimes differed from Che on policy and tactics, he did not waver in his admiration for him or display any jealousy of his legendary status as a revolutionary. In learning from Soviet organizational experience (as well as occasionally challenging it), the Cuban revolutionaries created youth associations on the Soviet pattern. These included establishing a Soviet-style movement in which all young schoolchildren were enrolled, called (as in the USSR) the Pioneers. Teachers would shout out to these children of primary-school age: 'Pioneers for communism!' and they had to reply in unison: 'We will be like Che!' How widespread such aspiration was among the children is very doubtful. Probably the ballet dancer Carlos Acosta, growing up in an impoverished part of Havana, was not alone in having his own version: 'We will be like Pelé!' The great Brazilian footballer was more of a role model for children aspiring to a different life than the Argentinian revolutionary physician who had been ready to kill or die for his ideals anywhere in Latin America.[55]

In the 1970s there was something of a retreat from the utopian urge to create a 'new socialist person' and more emphasis on consolidating 'socialist' – meaning Communist – institutions. The Communist Party as an organization became increasingly central to the Cuban political and economic system. Raúl Castro observed that 'the institutionalization of our revolution began only in 1970 and was accelerated from 1972 onward'. Fidel in 1973 said that the party was now carrying out a more decisive role than individuals: 'Men die, but the party is immortal.'[56] New emphasis was placed on the fact that the Communist Party was the ultimate political authority, but the government was reorganized and attention paid to differentiating its functions from those of the party. The Communist Party's supremacy was enshrined in the 1976 Cuban constitution, in which it was stated that 'the highest leading force of the society and state' was the PCC. The strengthening of the institutions of a Communist system somewhat constrained the powers of Fidel Castro.[57] Since, however, he added the presidency of the Cuban state to his other offices following the adoption of the new constitution, there was no doubt about who had the most individual power. Moreover, Castro retained the authority which came from having been Cuba's 'Lenin', with the big advantage over Lenin that he not only remained alive but also retained his leadership for almost half a century after the revolution.

During the 1970s, while never becoming a mere client of the Soviet Union, Fidel Castro generally paid tribute to Soviet experience, from which Cuba borrowed institutional arrangements quite voluntarily. Even in the 1960s, on a visit to Moscow, he had described *Pravda* as 'the best newspaper in the world'.[58] While the remark was obviously intended to please his Soviet hosts, it doubtless owed something to the fact that Castro did not read Russian. In the course of the 1970s, Cuba increasingly adopted Soviet methods of planning and management. These measures helped improve the efficiency of the Cuban economy, which indicated just how much chaos the more utopian policies of the 1960s had created.[59] Neither in Cuba nor anywhere else, however, could Soviet-type planning provide a long term solution to economic problems. It was one way in which to organize a non-market economy and to do much to end its underdevelopment, but though it could mobilize resources very effectively in a few sectors, it invariably led to uneven development and to inadequate provision of consumer goods.

Achievements and Failures of Cuban Communism

Perhaps the greatest, and most surprising, achievement of Communism in Cuba is that it outlived the collapse of Communist regimes in Eastern Europe and the disintegration of the Soviet Union – Cuba's most powerful ally and by far its most significant economic partner. Fifty years after Castro's successful overthrow of the Batista regime – in January 2009 – Cuba had a population of just under eleven and a half million people. It is an island only ninety miles away from the United States. Yet Cuba has withstood for half a century the unremitting hostility and economic sanctions of the world's most powerful country. Fidel Castro, during his time in office, overlapped with no fewer than ten presidents of the USA. The failure of Communism elsewhere in Latin America underlines the uniqueness of the Cuban case. Communists were sometimes given ministerial office as part of a coalition in other Latin American countries, just as they had been in Batista's Cuba. They were part of Salvador Allende's socialist coalition in Chile from 1970 to 1973, but although Allende was a Marxist, Chile's political system during his presidency remained pluralist and certainly not Communist.[60]

The survival of the Cuban regime is due to a variety of factors. A point which applies generally to Communist rule is that these systems – however economically inefficient in many respects and however lacking in democratic accountability – are very effective at maintaining political control by a party elite over an entire society. These controls are all the more effective if the political elite are self-confident (rather than cynical or plagued by doubts) and have faith in the superiority of their system over capitalism and 'bourgeois democracy'. That has certainly been true of the top Cuban leadership, pre-eminently so in the case of the brothers Fidel and Raúl Castro. A willingness to employ an apparatus of coercive force in defence of the regime has been important in Cuba as elsewhere in the Communist world, but executions and arrests have been on a far smaller scale than they were in the Soviet Union or China. One reason why levels of coercion have been lower in Cuba than in a majority of Communist states is that successive waves of emigration from the island have been permitted. Thus, several hundred thousand of the most disaffected citizens have been able to move either to the United States or to other parts of Latin America.

Communist systems which have survived over the long term have never relied on either coercion or charismatic leadership alone. In a majority of cases they have had a base of mass support. Where this support was inadequate on its own to sustain the regimes, as in east-central Europe, the real prospect of Soviet intervention served to uphold the regimes. Cuba was in a very different category from Poland, Hungary or East Germany. Despite economic and ideological support from the Soviet Union, Cuba's rulers knew very well that they could not expect the Soviet military to save them from being unseated by popular unrest or even from attack by the United States. Hence, as well as attempting to build and sustain broad popular support, the Cuban leadership has built up a large army and had a fifth of the population bearing arms. They have been ready to resort to guerrilla warfare, if need be, thus raising the costs of hostile foreign intervention. Castro remained confident that the guns would not be turned against the political elite. The fact that Cuba had an indigenous revolution against a corrupt and unpopular dictatorship gave it a form of legitimacy from the outset. That the top leaders who made that revolution survived so long helped to consolidate that legitimacy through familiarity.

Cuba, especially during the 1970s and 1980s, played a role on the international stage disproportionate to its economic resources and became a significant power in the Third World, especially in Africa. The intervention of Cuban troops in African civil wars, on the side of those who were deemed to be the anti-imperialists, was independent of the Soviet Union inasmuch as the decision to intervene was taken in Havana rather than Moscow, but dependent, nevertheless, on the Soviet Union's supply of armaments. A substantial proportion of the Cuban population is black, and as this was true of the troops they sent to the Congo, Guinea, Ethiopia, Mozambique, Benin and Angola, it made their military contribution the more acceptable to local populations. Cuba supplied doctors as well as soldiers, which added to their reputation in the parts of Africa in which they served. The number of troops committed to Angola, in particular, was remarkably high for a country of Cuba's size. It reached a peak of 52,000 in 1988.[61] What was highly unusual, if not unique, was that a small Third World country was actively influencing the outcome of a military conflict thousands of miles from its own geographic region.

Castro has been described as a 'compulsive revolutionary', and the interventions in Africa were governed more by idealism than pragmatism, though there was a prudential consideration that it was politically safer to send troops to Africa in situations of anarchy than to other parts of Latin America where there were not only legal governments but where also the United States would take serious umbrage over further Communist incursion in its 'backyard'.[62] A scholar who compared American intelligence assessments of Cuban activity in Africa with the interpretations of American policy-makers finds that the former were generally correct and the latter usually wrong. The CIA and the Bureau of Intelligence and Research of the State Department (INR) recognized that Castro was acting in Africa on his own initiative, whereas the leading American politicians, among them Henry Kissinger, believed that he must be acting under pressure from Moscow to repay the Soviet Union for its economic support and supply of weapons. As Kissinger later admitted: 'Evidence now available suggests that the opposite was the case.'[63] The Cuban troops acquitted themselves well in the African conflicts, stopping a well-armed white South African army in its tracks in Angola. Nelson Mandela visited Havana in July 1991 and heaped praise on his hosts, saying: 'What other country can point to a record of greater selflessness than Cuba . . . displayed in its relations to Africa?'[64]

For the Soviet Union, the Cuban interventions in Africa were a very mixed blessing – at times a positive embarrassment. The long-serving Soviet ambassador to the United States, who later became the Secretary of the Central Committee of the Communist Party overseeing international policy, Anatoly Dobrynin, has observed that 'the myth of Cuba as a Soviet proxy was especially damaging for us in America, where the Cuban crisis of 1962 had fixed the idea firmly'.[65] But Castro, Dobrynin remarked, 'liked to make things difficult for the Americans', and Dobrynin was sent to Havana in 1986 to try to restrain him in order to improve Soviet–American relations. He received a fairly dusty response: 'Castro made it plain to me that what was happening in Angola was a Cuban show. "It is my command", he said. He wanted to be a player on the world scene, and that was one way he could do it.'[66]

There have also been real domestic achievements of post-revolutionary Cuba which have helped to sustain support from a sufficiently broad spectrum of the population. These have been, above all, in the realm of health and education. There was a substantial improvement in public health in Cuba throughout the 1960s and 1970s. Life expectancy in Cuba had risen to over seventy by the end of the 1970s and became as high as seventy-seven early in the twenty-first century. By the beginning of the 1980s Cuba's infant mortality rate was less than twenty per thousand live births, half the death rate of a decade earlier.[67] In the early years of the twenty-first century, even though the Cuban economy had suffered a severe setback with the collapse of the Soviet Union, its health service continued to perform impressively, given its economic base. Harvard public health specialists suggested that the 'paradox of Cuba's health care system' was that the country had so few resources that prevention became 'the only affordable means of keeping its population healthy'.[68] However, by conscious choice Cuba has placed a disproportionate share of its limited resources into public health provision and has the highest proportion in the world of physicians per 100,000 of the population (591 as compared with 256 in the United States and 198 in Mexico). Its infant mortality rate and average life expectancy are very much on a par with the USA, in spite of the vastly greater wealth of the United States.[69]

Education in Cuba has also been an area of substantial development. Cuba, even before the revolution, had one of the highest literacy rates in Latin America – at 75 per cent – but there were huge inequalities in both education and health between the towns and the countryside. The eradication of illiteracy became a top priority for Castro's government and was to become almost wholly successful in that regard.[70] Cultural life, however, was stultified, and many of Cuba's best writers emigrated. As in other Communist states, there was a qualitative difference in higher education between the intellectual freedom accorded to scientists and technologists and that accorded scholars in the humanities or social sciences. Scientific and technical education prospered, since the best efforts of scientists and engineers were of direct and obvious benefit to the state. In contrast, heterodox ideas in the humanities and the social sciences posed a threat to the ideological hegemony of the ruling party. Medical education became a particular speciality, and a generous supply of doctors was a significant component of Cuba's foreign aid to other Third World countries.[71]

The spread of free health and educational services to those previously deprived of such resources is an important element of support for Cuba's post-revolutionary social and political order. In Cuba, however, just as elsewhere in the Communist world (not to speak of non-Communist countries),

it was discovered that even an egalitarian educational policy could not eliminate the educational advantages of children born into families where the
parents had themselves benefited from a higher education. This continuing
disparity of life chances troubled Castro, just as it had disturbed Khrushchev
in the Soviet Union. Another persistent problem of post-revolutionary Cuba
has been the link between class and colour. Although the Cuban regime has
consciously opposed racism, and although Castro personally was a dedicated
opponent of racial discrimination, black Cubans are over-represented among
manual workers in the island and under-represented not only in higher education but also in the higher echelons of the Communist Party.

While the brothers Fidel and Raúl Castro would not recognize it as such,
Cuba's biggest failure is the absence of political pluralism and intellectual
freedom. While the abuse of human rights has been less than in some other
Communist states – and less than that at times in some right-wing Latin
American regimes – it has been substantial and accompanied by political
repression. A political police force, on the model of the Soviet KGB, was
created in the earliest post-revolutionary years, and its activities were supple-
mented by neighbourhood groups called Committees for Defence of the
Revolution. These social organizations kept a vigilant eye on potential 'counterrevolutionaries' and became, in effect, a network of government
informers.[72] They reflected Castro's hard-line view that 'To be a traitor to
the revolution is to be a traitor to the country.'[73] This has been a feature of
Communist systems. In the prototype of all such systems, the USSR, the
notion of 'anti-Sovietism' was conflated with hatred of the motherland, a
point to which I return in Chapter 28.

The relative economic failure in Cuba is a feature of a system which has
greatly reduced inequality but at the expense of shared low living standards
for the majority of the population. Some of the problems which Fidel Castro
has himself criticized in the Cuban economy are features intrinsic to a
Communist economic system. Thus, at the beginning of 1985 Castro
inveighed against what he called a 'sectorial spirit' which was dominating
organizations and to be found 'in all the ministries'.[74] In the Soviet Union
this was called 'departmentalism'. In a non-market system a ministry responsible for a particular sector of the economy hoards as many resources as it
can lay its hands on and, unless led by a revolutionary as pure as Che
Guevara, gives priority to its own bureaucratic interests over any notion of
the common good. Bureaucratic rivalry occurs, of course, also in democracies, but in a system in which political power and economic power are
both concentrated in state agencies, with the concomitant absence of
countervailing market forces, departmentalism becomes the main arena of
political struggle. As noted in an earlier chapter, Khrushchev attempted to

deal with the problem by abolishing most of the central ministries and creating in their stead regional economic councils, only to discover that departmentalism was rapidly replaced by 'localism'. The pattern of bureaucratic behaviour which he deplored at the centre was promptly replicated in the localities.

If the achievements in health and education have helped to sustain support for the existing system in Cuba, an unwitting ally of Castro's regime has been the United States. The more contact people in relatively closed societies have with people in open societies, the harder it is for the former regimes to retain their authoritarian control. By imposing a trade embargo on Cuba and by making it difficult for citizens of the USA to visit the island, the American government has not only helped the Cuban leadership by sustaining the external threat, thus reinforcing Cuban patriotism, but has reduced the opportunities for interaction in which each side might have learned something from the other. It would have been likely, however, to be more corrosive of a system imposing controls on free enquiry than of one in which liberal, conservative, and, indeed, Communist ideas were readily accessible, although the Communist Party of the United States was already past its far from impressive peak before Fidel Castro came to power.

17

China: From the 'Hundred Flowers' to 'Cultural Revolution'

The coming to power of the Chinese Communists has been discussed in Chapter II. That account ended in 1953, the year of Stalin's death. This chapter covers a no less tumultuous period – from 1953 to the demise of Mao Zedong in 1976. It was a period of huge significance both for China and in its implications for the rest of the Communist world. Just as momentous as the years of civil war and revolution in China were the four major events on which I focus in this chapter: the 'Hundred Flowers' campaign and the repression which followed it; the 'Great Leap Forward', which ended in disaster; the Sino-Soviet split, which was a turning point in the history of the international Communist movement; and the 'Great Proletarian Cultural Revolution' of Mao's last decade as Chinese ruler – a movement which caused immense suffering and had important unintended consequences.

Until the mid-1950s, the policy of the Chinese Communists in power drew very heavily on Soviet experience. A five-year plan running from 1953 to 1957 aimed to double industrial production and to raise agricultural output by a quarter.[1] Soviet aid, though not great in financial terms, was significant in providing expertise. Russian engineers and technologists undoubtedly played a constructive part in helping to develop China's industrial infrastructure during the 1950s. Industrial policy yielded better results than the attempt to collectivize agriculture – even though the Chinese tried to avoid the excesses of Stalin's compulsory collectivization of the late 1920s and early 1930s in the Soviet Union. Agricultural Producers' Co-operatives were set up which embraced everyone in small villages. They were expected to expand gradually – from a few tens of households to several hundred in each co-operative. Growth of agricultural output was much slower, however, than predicted and argument broke out in the Communist Party between those who favoured a more gradualist approach (including the retention of private plots and some free markets) and the harder-liners, led by Mao, who favoured more rapid socialization.[2] Yet by 1956, in the Chinese economy as a whole, the basic transfer of the means of production from private hands into state or collective property had been accomplished.[3]

As in other Communist countries, substantial progress was made in education. At the highest levels there were losses – especially, and crucially, of
intellectual freedom in the humanities and social sciences (although Mao
thought there had been *too little* ideological indoctrination) – but the spread
of basic education was on a huge scale. The number of children attending
primary school rose from 24 million in 1949 to 64 million in 1957.[4] In the
same period the numbers in higher education doubled. There remained,
however, vast differences between town and country, with few good schools
outside the cities, as well as great disparities between men and women.
Even in the primary schools, boys outnumbered girls by two to one.[5] There
were substantial improvements in public health during the Communists'
first decade in power. This brought problems in addition to benefits. The
death rate declined much more sharply than the birth rate and an annual
population increase of 2 per cent put a further strain on scarce resources.[6]

Soviet experience and the most recent developments in the Soviet Union
continued to influence Chinese politics. Thus, at the Eighth Congress of
the Chinese Communist Party in September 1956, Mao's role was less emphasized than at the previous congress in 1945. Mao Zedong Thought was
removed (for the time being) from the party statutes and there was a strong
emphasis on collective leadership. These changes were at least partly a consequence of the dethroning of Stalin at the Twentieth Congress of the Soviet
Communist Party and the more general attack there on 'the cult of personality'.[7] The inner core of the Chinese party leadership was retained at the
Eighth Congress, although a significant promotion to it was of Deng
Xiaoping, later to become one of the most important figures in twentieth-
century Chinese history. Talking to the Soviet leader Nikita Khrushchev in
1957, Mao pointed to Deng and said: 'See that little man there? He's highly
intelligent and has a great future ahead of him.'[8] The remark seems particularly apposite in retrospect, but since Deng's future involved reversing much
that had been said and done by Mao Zedong, it was hardly what Mao had
in mind. The Eighth Congress appeared to mark a new stability in political
life, with various bureaucratic interests, notably economic ministries and
provincial party organizations, making their claims heard.[9] It turned out,
however, to represent no more than a lull before a series of storms.

The Hundred Flowers

For a brief period it looked as if the congress was, unexpectedly, going to
be followed by a developing pluralism. It appeared to many in China and
abroad that Mao Zedong had inaugurated a new phase of post-revolutionary

development when he encouraged people to take a more critical look at what had been achieved thus far. What became known as the Hundred Flowers movement in 1956–57 derived from Mao's remark, 'Let a hundred flowers bloom, let a hundred schools of thought contend.'[10] Although inaugurated in 1956, the campaign was stepped up in the first half of 1957. Mao encouraged criticism of what had been accomplished since 1949, although he had in mind the pinpointing of specific shortcomings rather than root-and-branch critiques. In general, he took a positive view of conflict, holding that party members should criticize not only themselves but each other. He drew the line, though, at criticism of himself or of the Communist system. But some of the criticisms aired were of fundamentals. They included questioning even the Chinese Communist Party's right to rule without any checks on its power or accountability for its decisions. By the time Mao issued an instruction to high-ranking party officials in May 1957 that they should allow the criticism to continue, his motives were suspect. By then, if not earlier, he was attempting to lure his enemies and those who were opposed to the system into the open. That would enable him, like Lenin in 1921, 'to put the lid on opposition' or, in Mao's own words (as he continued to favour horticultural metaphors), to dig out 'the poisonous weeds'.[11]

The Soviet leadership had been alarmed by the Chinese talk of allowing a hundred flowers to bloom, since it added to the pressure for freer expression in the Soviet Union and Eastern Europe. In retrospect, at least, Khrushchev believed that 'Let a hundred flowers bloom' was nothing but a provocation: 'Mao pretended to be opening wide the floodgates of democracy and free expression. He wanted to goad people into expressing their innermost thoughts, both in speech and in print, so that he could destroy those whose thinking he considered harmful.'[12] The partial liberalization which had, however briefly, allowed an airing of heterodox ideas, meant, nevertheless, that Mao's position had been temporarily weakened. The campaign damaged his authority and revealed sharp differences of opinion within the ruling party. Mao's response was to mount an 'anti-rightist campaign' and to re-emphasize the importance of class struggle.[13]

Not only intellectuals of 'bourgeois' background but also students who had received their higher education in the Communist period had been among those who expressed their discontent, some of them questioning the party's competence. All this pointed to a growing alienation from the system of many of the most educated segments of society.[14] The attack on the 'rightists' which followed hit the intellectuals hard. Over half a million of them were tarred with the 'rightist' brush and put under great psychological pressure, leading to a number of suicides. Many of the intellectuals were consigned to manual labour. It was one of the ironies of Communist systems – the same thing was to happen in Czechoslovakia after the crushing of the Prague Spring and at various times in other Communist states – that, although manual workers constituted the official ruling class, a standard punishment for intellectuals who had been guilty of unorthodox writings or of politically suspect activities was to remove them from the ranks of professions requiring a higher education and to turn them into workers. Paradoxically, then, they were 'demoted' into the 'ruling class'.

The Chinese leaders were sensitive to what was going on elsewhere in the Communist world. They had taken some account of Khrushchev's Secret Speech to the Twentieth Congress of the CPSU in 1956, although Mao had serious reservations about its wisdom and was furious at having been given no forewarning of such a dramatic change of line. They were also greatly concerned about the political role being played by intellectuals in Poland and Hungary in the same year. The lesson Mao and his closest allies took from the Hundred Flowers movement was that Chinese intellectuals, too, had turned out to be ideologically unreliable. The party leadership remained aware that they needed the expertise of higher professionals. Accordingly, they stressed that the anti-rightist campaign, which followed the failure – from their standpoint – of the Hundred Flowers initiative, was not targeted at the majority of the Chinese intelligentsia. However, the attack on those who had been sufficiently bold, or naïve, to take at face value the idea of open contention of different schools of thought was to dampen, rather than stimulate, the already waning enthusiasm of many intellectuals for the party's goals.

The Great Leap Forward

Visiting Moscow in October 1957, Mao was complimentary about Soviet achievements, especially in the light of the USSR's recent feat of being the first country in the world to put a spacecraft in orbit. In the East–West conflict, he declared, the East wind was prevailing over the West wind.[15] However, just one year later, Mao and those close to him were moving away from the Soviet model of development which they had followed, in its essentials, hitherto. The idea of a Great Leap Forward, which they espoused, was a programme of mass mobilization in which the enthusiasm and willpower of the mass of the people were to be fully harnessed. Mao aimed to bring managers, technicians and workers closer together, rejecting the more technocratic and hierarchical approach of Soviet advisers. The Soviet engineers and technologists were largely sidelined, as were the bureaucratic agencies of the Chinese central government. So that the countryside could become more self-sufficient in all respects, every locality was encouraged to establish small-scale technology to complement the large-scale industry already constructed. This Mao called 'walking on two legs'. It meant, among other things, the creation of backyard furnaces which were a waste of labour and economically useless. The Great Leap Forward heralded a redistribution of power. It handed the initiative from central officials and managers to political generalists in the provinces whose task it was to inspire the workers ideologically.[16]

Mao, while jealously guarding his personal power, also took ideas seriously, and he was eager to advance the communization of Chinese society. In particular, this meant converting the Agricultural Producers' Co-operatives into much larger 'people's communes'. Many more women were brought into the workforce when these massive farms were created, with men often working far away from their native village. The utopianism of the Great Leap Forward may have been initially inspiring, but its results were disastrous. Disdain for material obstacles and for professional expertise alike led to chaos in the countryside and, in turn, to a devastating famine. False reporting of increased grain output contrasted with the harsh reality of a drastic drop in production. Rural transport was disrupted and farm equipment neglected. Matters were made worse by floods and droughts in 1959 and 1960. The best estimate of the number who died as a result of the economic turmoil created by the Great Leap between 1958 and 1961 – the 'excess deaths', in statistical terms, in that period – is in the order of thirty million people. That means that one person in twenty in the Chinese countryside was a fatal victim of this largely man-made disaster.[17]

In Tibet, which had been incorporated in the Chinese People's Republic (PRC) in 1950, the threat of the kind of change involved in the Great Leap was enough to create serious unrest in 1959. Tibetans are one of fifty-five officially recognized different ethnic groups within the PRC, although the Han Chinese are numerically overwhelmingly dominant in China as a whole, making up more than 90 per cent of the population. However, with their distinctive language, culture and religion, Tibetans were already at loggerheads with the Han Chinese who had migrated to their region. The revolt in 1959 was put down forcibly by Chinese troops, and the Tibetans' spiritual leader, the Dalai Lama, took refuge in India. While the Chinese authorities were able to maintain their control over Tibet in the years that followed, the issue of religious and political autonomy for the indigenous population of Tibet remains a contentious international issue to the present day.[18]

As it became increasingly clear to some in the Chinese leadership at the end of the 1950s and the beginning of the 1960s that the Great Leap Forward had been a monumental mistake – a giant step backwards, in fact – it brought into public view tensions which, in some cases, had been there below the surface for years. Prominent among those who criticized Mao for the fiasco of the Great Leap Forward was Peng Dehuai, who had distinguished himself as a general in charge of Chinese forces in the Korean War. Peng favoured close relations with the Soviet Union and, as minister of defence, wished to model China's armed forces on the Soviet army. Mao suspected Peng, without any real evidence, of co-ordinating his attacks on him with criticism that was soon to emanate from Moscow. Peng was promptly dismissed from his post, but Mao's somewhat weakened position was reflected in the fact that he gave up his office as head of state in 1959, although he retained the more powerful post of chairman of the Chinese Communist Party.

Deng Xiaoping had become general secretary of the party and, as such, wielded great authority within its secretariat, but so long as Mao was alive, the general secretaryship, unusually for a Communist Party, was not the most powerful post. The chairmanship of the party, since Mao held it, was the top job. At the time when Mao spoke highly of Deng Xiaoping to Khrushchev in 1957, Deng was still the chairman's strong supporter, but that changed in the course of the Great Leap Forward. He became less deferential to Mao, who later – during the Cultural Revolution – complained that Deng 'had not listened to him since 1959'.[19] Mao's successor as head of state, Liu Shaoqi, announced in 1961 that, notwithstanding the serious flooding which had occurred in a number of Chinese provinces, 70 per cent of the various famines which had afflicted the country were due to human errors rather than being natural disasters.[20] This was not presented by Liu as an indictment of Mao but, especially in retrospect, could be seen as a veiled criticism of him. It was Liu and Deng together who developed the policies from 1961 until the middle of the 1960s which put the Chinese economy back on a somewhat more rational course. Expertise was again given its due and steps were taken to strengthen the party apparatus as a disciplined body.[21]

The Sino-Soviet Split

The Sino-Soviet split had its origins in 1956 – with Khrushchev's speech to the Twentieth Congress, which troubled the Chinese, since they had given uncritical public support hitherto to Stalin.[22] That was also the year in which, with his Hundred Flowers initiative, Mao began to promote policies which were strikingly divergent from, and potentially embarrassing for, the Communist rulers of the Soviet Union and Eastern Europe. By 1957, a number of differences were emerging. The outcome of the Anti-Party Group crisis in Moscow was a case in point. Mao disagreed with Khrushchev's removal from the Soviet leadership of such old Bolsheviks as Molotov, even though Mao himself was a decade later to treat his own old comrades with still less respect.[23]

In the wake of the crisis within the Soviet leadership in 1957, following the much more tumultuous events in Poland and Hungary the previous year, the Soviet Communist Party set about trying to restore and reinforce the unity of the international Communist movement. A conference of Communist Party leaders was convened in Moscow in November 1957 at which an effort was made to bring together all the major parties. This meant, in particular, securing the attendance of both Mao and Tito. Mao turned up, but Tito did not. The Yugoslav leader had objected to a draft declaration which referred to the 'socialist camp' – a term he did not like, since it might call into question Yugoslavia's freedom of action. He also objected to the phrase, the 'struggle against dogmatism and revisionism'. The term 'dogmatism' referred to hard-line Stalinist policies and was to be increasingly applied to China. 'Revisionism' had long been the term of abuse in the international Communist movement for deviation in the opposite direction – concessions to the market or to political tolerance. Ever since the expulsion of Yugoslavia from the Cominform, 'revisionist' had been one of the epithets applied by other Communists to the Yugoslavs.

By 1961–62, Yugoslavia was no longer the outcast from the international Communist movement it had been in the last years of Stalin's life, but the term 'revisionist' was repeatedly applied to them in those years by the Chinese leadership. *Yugoslavia*, however, had by then become a codename for the Soviet Union. This was in the period shortly before the Chinese Communists began publicly attacking Khrushchev and the *Soviet* leadership as 'revisionists'. And just as the Chinese initially directed their open polemics at Belgrade rather than Moscow, the Soviet Union publicly criticized the 'dogmatism' of the 'Albanians' (standing in for the Chinese) who, under Enver Hoxha's leadership, had transferred their allegiance in 1960 from Moscow to Beijing. There was a reluctance in the Soviet Union, in particular, to reveal to all and sundry that the world's two most important Communist states were at loggerheads. Serious analysts of the Communist world had little difficulty, however, in discerning the depth of disagreement between China and the Soviet Union. In the course of 1962 that fact became still more abundantly clear, although some obtuse Western politicians, especially in the United States, chose to believe for years to come that the Sino-Soviet dispute was an elaborate ruse to deceive the 'free world'.

Differences between China and the Soviet Union had been emerging gradually, but Mao shocked many of his listeners when, in a speech during his November 1957 visit to Moscow, he contemplated with equanimity the prospect of nuclear war. Perhaps 700 million people would be killed (about a third of the world's population at the time), or possibly as many as half of all people on earth, but they would soon be replaced, Mao said, and the gains would be enormous. Imperialism would have been crushed and the whole world would have 'become socialist'.[24] Even Khrushchev at his most impetuous (as in the early stages of the Cuban missile crisis) never thought, still less said, anything remotely as irresponsible. The reaction of the Czech and Polish Communists was one of horror. Mao could say that he was prepared to lose half the population of China in a nuclear war – which, in the late 1950s, would have meant the deaths of 300 million Chinese – but, as the Czech Communist leader Antonín Novotný said to Khrushchev, Czechoslovakia would lose 'every last soul' in such a war.[25]

When Khrushchev visited China in 1958, he found Mao highly resistant to the idea of allowing Soviet submarines to use Chinese ports or of a radio station being located on Chinese territory for communication with the Soviet fleet. Mao offended Khrushchev by comparing his desire to make such use of Chinese territory to the activities of Britain and Japan in the past. He did not yet use the word 'imperialist', but the implication was clear. He also went out of his way to humiliate Khrushchev in other ways. Mao was a notable swimmer. At the age of seventy-two, in 1966, he joined 5,000 participants in an annual swim in the River Yangtze and, aided by a strong current, covered a distance of ten miles.[26] Khrushchev, in contrast, was not much better a swimmer than he was a dancer. If Stalin had embarrassed him by instructing him to dance the gopak, Mao's method of oneupmanship was to conduct political discussions in a swimming pool. As Mao swam around effortlessly, expounding views which were immediately translated, Khrushchev was left to splutter his answers in between mouthfuls of water. 'Of course', he remarked in his memoirs, 'I couldn't compete with Mao in the pool – as everyone knows, he's since set a world record for both speed and distance.'[27]

Signs of rapprochement between the Soviet Union and the United States were anathema to Mao, who disapproved of Khrushchev's visit to the USA in September 1959. Three months previously, Moscow had reneged on an earlier promise to supply China with the atomic bomb (which before long they were to develop by themselves). The Chinese leadership assumed that the backtracking had occurred to please the Americans, although, in fact, there were Soviet worries that the United States might retaliate by supplying nuclear weapons to West Germany.[28] (There was no factual foundation for that supposition, but memories of the Second World War remained sufficiently fresh in 1959 for the Germans still to be seen as the Soviet Union's major potential enemy in Europe. It was with the election to the chancellorship of West Germany a decade later of Willy Brandt – and his government's policy of constructive engagement with the Soviet Union and the countries of Eastern Europe – that perceptions of Germany in Russia and East Europe underwent a major shift.)

By the time Khrushchev made his third and last visit to China in October 1959, the tensions between the two countries – as well as the testiness between the two top leaders – had become much more pronounced. Border skirmishes between China and India had been an embarrassment to the Soviet Union. Although diplomatic mediation was not his strongest suit, Khrushchev counselled restraint. The USSR enjoyed good relations with Nehru's India and yet remained, officially at least, the fraternal Communist ally of China. Khrushchev did not endear himself to his hosts by fulfilling a promise he had made to President Eisenhower whereby he brought up the subject of five Americans who were being held in captivity in China. Both Mao and Zhou Enlai treated these and other remarks of Khrushchev's as if he were a spokesman for the USA. When Mao complained about the United States having sent its fleet close to the Chinese coast, Khrushchev responded frankly: 'One should keep in mind that we also are not without sin. It was we who drew the Americans to South Korea' – a reference to Stalin's responsibility for starting the Korean War.[29] It was Khrushchev's turn to be belligerent, however, when the conversation turned to Tibet. Mao said that they had intended to 'delay the transformation of Tibet by four years', to which Khrushchev responded: 'And that was your mistake.' Mao was also forced to defend China's failure to stop the Dalai Lama from leaving Tibet. Khrushchev made it clear that he regarded this as political incompetence, saying: 'As to the escape of the Dalai Lama from Tibet, if we had been in your place, we would not have let him escape. It would be better if he was in a coffin. And now he is in India, and perhaps will go to the USA. Is this to the advantage of the socialist countries?' Mao replied that the border with India was very long and the Dalai Lama could cross it at any point.[30]

By July 1960, Chinese Communist leaders, in their internal communications, were referring to a struggle between 'Marxism and opportunism' in the international Communist movement, in which, of course, they were the Marxists and Khrushchev was the number one 'opportunist' and also a 'schemer'.[31] The dispute moved beyond words when that same month the Soviet Union informed Beijing that they were withdrawing immediately the 1,400 or so specialists who had been working in China. In a confidential letter, the Soviet side gave their reasons for this sudden action. They included the allegation that criticisms had been made in China of the specialists' work, disregard of the specialists' advice (although it was Chinese rejection of Soviet political, rather than technical, counsel that weighed more heavily), and, especially, Chinese Communist Party propaganda against the CPSU.[32] Nevertheless, whatever their disillusionment with Khrushchev and the Soviet leadership, the Chinese recognized the practical help which the Soviet engineers and technologists had provided. At a farewell dinner, held in mid-August 1960, in honour of the departing Soviet specialists, Zhou Enlai thanked them for the contribution they had made to the construction of 'socialism' in China.[33] As part, however, of the worsening of relations between the two major Communist powers, in that same year Soviet–Chinese trade virtually ended, adding to the difficulties of the Chinese economy in the throes of its Great Leap Forward.

The Chinese tried to propagate their ideological position and their view of the dispute with the Soviet Union inside Russia, handing out documents in Moscow research institutes giving the Chinese side of the story. The Soviet leadership retaliated by expelling three Chinese diplomats and two other Chinese citizens. They returned to Beijing in early July 1963 to a heroes' welcome, attended by Zhou Enlai.[34] This was the month in which the dispute became a public one. *Pravda* published on 14 July, as an open letter, the response of the Central Committee of the CPSU to proposals the Chinese had made a month earlier.[35] By this time the Chinese were openly attacking Soviet 'revisionism', and the years 1963–64 marked a watershed in the international Communist movement. The two largest Communist parties in the world engaged in open polemics against each other and had clearly moved into an antagonistic relationship. The idea of Communism as an ideology which united revolutionaries and 'anti-imperialists' throughout the world suffered a blow from which it could never fully recover. The Soviet leadership, accustomed as it was to the idea that the Communist Party of the Soviet Union played a leading, if not dominant, role within the international Communist movement, sought to maintain unity, but not at the price of ideological surrender to the position of the Chinese. Mao, however, was content to keep the polemics going, partly because he feared 'revisionism' at home as well as within the broader movement. By putting himself at the head of the assault on Soviet apostasy, he was strengthening his position for an attack on domestic backsliders. Some of the Chinese leaders, such as Deng Xiaoping and Liu Shaoqi, who had assiduously argued with their Soviet counterparts in support of Mao's line, were to find that similar accusations of 'revisionism' – and, indeed, stronger terms, such as 'capitalist roaders' – would be levelled against them in the Cultural Revolution.[36]

When Khrushchev was toppled by his colleagues in October 1964, Mao briefly hoped this meant that the Soviet leadership had accepted *his* critique of Khrushchev's policies. Equally briefly, the Soviet leaders imagined that the removal of the less than tactful Khrushchev would make it easier for them to resolve their differences with the Chinese Communist Party. However, the dispute was much more than personal. There were profound political and ideological issues at stake. Zhou Enlai led a delegation to the celebration of the anniversary of the Bolshevik revolution on 7 November 1964, just three weeks after the removal of Khrushchev. Leonid Brezhnev, in his official speech on this occasion, called for a new international meeting of the fraternal Communist parties. This remark was greeted by stormy applause in which, however, Zhou Enlai conspicuously failed to join. At a reception later the same day the Soviet minister of defence, Marshal Rodion Malinovsky, told a military member of the Chinese delegation that they should follow the Soviet example and get rid of Mao, just as they had rid themselves of Khrushchev.[37] Malinovsky was fairly drunk at the time, but Brezhnev's attempt to persuade the outraged Chinese that this was not official policy – merely a result of Malinovsky's over-imbibing – met with the response from Zhou that, on the contrary, the alcohol had simply enabled Malinovsky to say what he believed.[38] Given that Malinovsky's remark would have been reported to Mao, Zhou himself would have been in dire trouble in Beijing had he reacted in any way other than vehemently denouncing it.

Incidents on the Soviet–Chinese border added to the tensions between the two sides. Later – in 1969 – they were to result in scores of deaths in the border regions of both countries and raise fears of a full-scale war between the two Communist giants. However, the territorial disputes, while real, were not fundamental to the break between the Soviet Union and China. Central to it were ideological differences. The Chinese at that time were more committed to world revolution and the Soviet Union had become tolerably content with the European and broader international status quo, so long as they occupied one of the two most important places in the world hierarchy, along with the United States. The Soviet Union was in favour of 'peaceful co-existence', which meant that it did, indeed, wish to avoid war, though it was resolutely opposed to ideological co-existence. (The Soviet authorities, like Communist rulers elsewhere, tried hard to avoid the dissemination of non-Communist ideas in their own country, while doing their best to promote their own ideology worldwide.) In contrast to the Soviet stress on peaceful co-existence, Mao appeared ready to consider war as a way of advancing Communism, although he was more cautious in practice in the international arena than his rhetoric might suggest.[39]

There was also disagreement between the two leaderships in their attitude to Stalin. This became less pronounced after October 1964, for Khrushchev's successors soon decided that criticism of Stalin and Stalinism was potentially destabilizing, and put a stop to it at home. Although, however, there were those within the Soviet political elite who wished to rehabilitate Stalin, this did not happen, and between the fall of Khrushchev in 1964 and the death of Mao in 1976, Stalin was lauded much more in Beijing than in Moscow. Moreover, in a number of his actions – not least in his (pyrrhic) victory over party officialdom which was at the heart of the Cultural Revolution – Mao seemed to be following in Stalin's footsteps. Certainly, in China's 'Great Proletarian Cultural Revolution', there were echoes of Stalin's purges of the late 1930s in which so many party members of long standing perished. There were disagreements between the leaderships of the two Communist states on the way the economy should be run, with Mao despising the highly bureaucratized nature of the Soviet state and concerned to combat such tendencies in his own country. In addition to the real ideo-logical differences must be added Mao's personal ambition to be the leading theorist in the Communist world and his aspiration to make a transition to communism, in the utopian sense of the term, ahead of the Soviet Union. After the fall of Khrushchev, Soviet leaders paid no more than occasional lip-service to the very notion of this supposedly final stage of development of society, so Mao had that field to himself.

The Cultural Revolution

With the collapse of the Great Leap Forward, Chinese government in the first half of the 1960s had become more orderly and increasingly institu-tionalized. Although Mao Zedong sat at the top of the political hierarchy, a number of institutions wielded real power and authority. They included the Politburo of the Central Committee of the CCP; the Central Committee Secretariat, led by Deng Xiaoping; regional and city party organizations, especially that of Beijing, headed by Peng Zhen; the State Council, which comprised the ministerial network, at whose head stood Zhou Enlai; and the official headship of state, a post occupied by Liu Shaoqi, who, more importantly, had a strong base in the party machine. He was number two in the Politburo after Mao and had been identified as Mao's successor. In the early 1950s the slogan 'The Soviet Union's today is our tomorrow' had been seen as a cheerful forecast of speedy economic progress and a cause for optimism. By the 1960s, Mao, with his increasingly dyspeptic view of Soviet developments, saw it as an awful warning.[40] If China was not to slip into a pattern of bureaucratism and revisionism, the system must undergo another fundamental shake-up.

Hence, Mao was susceptible to the urgings of those who felt they had been held back by the old guard who were now running the country's major institutions. He was influenced, not least, by the faction led by his wife, Jiang Qing, who had an especially keen eye for any departures from revolutionary correctness on the cultural front. The Cultural Revolution, in the fullest sense of the term, lasted from the spring of 1966 until the spring of 1969. Since, however, it was never formally declared to be at an end so long as Mao lived, in milder form it lingered on until his death in 1976. Along with Chen Boda, the Communist Party intellectual (though a man of poor peasant origin) closest to Mao, Jiang Qing led what became known as the Cultural Revolution Small Group. Initially, it lacked a serious power base in the party, but with Mao's crucial support it became one of three organizations with whom he principally interacted during the Cultural Revolution, the others being the People's Liberation Army (PLA), headed by the minister of defence, Lin Biao, and the State Council, led by Zhou Enlai.[41] Peng Zhen and Liu Shaoqi, paying in part for previous unwillingness to take Jiang Qing seriously as a political actor, were among the earlier victims of the Cultural Revolution. Zhou Enlai survived by taking positions that were 'just radical enough to avoid destruction while he worked to minimize the chaos'.[42]

Lin Biao, although he ultimately became a casualty of the Cultural Revolution, was a key ally of Mao throughout the greater part of it. In spite of some similarities with Stalin's Great Purge, Mao came much closer to overthrowing the party than did Stalin, who remained aware that he needed it. Another notable difference was in the role played by the Soviet and Chinese armies. In the late 1930s, the Soviet army was decimated by Stalin and his henchmen and very far from playing a serious role in domestic politics. In contrast, the PLA, as both the party organizations and the ministerial network came under attack, became the main institutional bulwark on which Mao Zedong could rely between 1966 and 1969. Mao was also enthusiastically supported by young people, the Red Guards, who had been introduced as a new force in Chinese politics, but the PLA, as befitted an army, were much more disciplined. Unbound by rules, and disdainful of hierarchy, the Red Guards ultimately scared even the CCP chairman. Although Mao was psychologically ready to initiate conflict within the party and society, and to re-establish the dominance of his own views, it was Jiang Qing who, with his approval, struck the first blow. She argued that a play by a historian, Wu Han, *Hai Rui Dismissed from Office*, which had been performed in Beijing in 1961, had been a covert attack on Mao's policies. Wu Han, in addition to his academic background, happened to be deputy mayor of Beijing. He thus enjoyed the protection of the party first secretary in the capital, Peng Zhen. Accordingly, Jiang Qing could find no author in Beijing who would write a polemical article against Wu Han – a good indication of the power wielded by the city party boss. Undaunted, she went off to Shanghai, and the party first secretary there, aware that Mao had approved his wife's enterprise, assigned two propagandists to the task of unmasking Wu Han. They duly described the play as 'a reactionary intervention in the great class struggle between the bourgeoisie and the proletariat'.[43]

The publication of the denunciation of Wu Han (the text of the article having been edited by Mao personally) launched the Cultural Revolution. From this time on it became ever more meaningful to speak of Maoism and of Maoists, for it was the chairman who defined what was authentic revolutionary doctrine, distinguishing it from what had been accepted hitherto. He used his authority, and the manufacture of a cult of his personality which reached new heights, to replace one senior member of the Chinese political and cultural establishment after another. Wu Han and Peng Zhen were among the first to be ousted. Lin Biao, whose PLA had given crucial support to Mao, was among the last. In 1971 he was accused of conspiring with his son, a PLA officer, to assassinate Mao. With his wife and that son, Lin Biao made a midnight dash to an airport, where they commandeered an aircraft. They attempted to fly to the Soviet Union, but the plane crashed in Mongolia, in all likelihood having run out of fuel.[44] Earlier in the Cultural Revolution Lin Biao had taken Liu Shaoqi's place as heir apparent to Mao, but that was always a dangerous position to be in. Lin was still being denounced at orchestrated meetings in China several years after his death. Liu Shaoqi himself had been the most senior target of the first and most manic stage of the Cultural Revolution between 1966 and 1969. Removed from office in 1967, he died under house arrest in 1969. He had been formally denounced as a 'traitor, renegade, and scab'. His wife, Wang Guangmei, was imprisoned for twelve years. After Mao's death Liu was posthumously rehabilitated, with all the allegations against him dismissed as baseless.

Far fewer people died during the 'Great Proletarian Cultural Revolution' than during the Great Leap Forward. That was partly because the Cultural Revolution affected mostly the urban population, whereas a majority of people – some 620 million in the late 1960s – still lived in the countryside.[45] Yet it is estimated that a minimum of half a million people, out of some 137 million living in the towns in 1967, died as a direct result of the Cultural Revolution.[46] The political purge of officials was, in percentage terms, even higher than that conducted by Stalin between 1936 and 1938, although a lower proportion in China were executed or imprisoned. Between 60 and 70 per cent of officials in the central organs of the Communist Party were removed from office. Of thirteen members of the Central Committee Secretariat in 1966, only four were still there by 1969, and only fifty-four out of 167 members of the Central Committee retained their positions. Half of the ministers in the State Council lost their posts. Many of these ousted officials from the central and regional party and government organs were sent to 'cadre schools' in the countryside, where they had to undergo ideological re-education interspersed with hard physical labour. Some, however, suffered worse treatment, being beaten to death or tortured. Wu Han, the author whose disgrace Jiang Qing organized, was among those who attempted suicide.[47] Deng Xiaoping was denounced as a 'capitalist roader' (a description that was a gross exaggeration at the time, but might be thought to have contained a grain of truth when he wielded supreme power a decade and a half later) and dismissed from all his posts. He was sent to work as a fitter in a factory, a job for which he was not without qualifications, albeit somewhat dated, since during his studies in France forty years earlier he had worked part-time in that capacity in a Renault factory. Deng's elder son was crippled for life when he jumped out of an upstairs dormitory window of Beijing University in an attempt to escape from his Red Guard tormentors.[48]

It was, in fact, the schools and universities which suffered the worst effects of the Cultural Revolution. Millions of teachers were pilloried, and universities were shut down for several years from 1966 so that the students could participate as Red Guards in the revolutionary process. Most of the young people who took part began as true believers in the 'purification' of the revolution that was going on and with implicit faith in the wisdom of Mao Zedong. The distillation of Mao's thoughts in the ubiquitous Little Red Book became compulsory reading – and not just for students. (I well recall, from the academic year I spent at Moscow State University in 1967–68, seeing diplomats from the Chinese embassy walking in single file, in Mao-style uniforms, each of them reading, as he walked, the Little Red Book.) Turmoil in the Chinese educational system continued in the first half of the 1970s, and many former Red Guards who were relocated to the countryside, with their education interrupted for up to a decade, had ample time to repent of their youthful revolutionary zeal.

UNINTENDED CONSEQUENCES IN CHINA

There was a partial re-evaluation of the Cultural Revolution even while Mao Zedong was still alive. Mao by 1975 was using the formula that it had been 70 per cent a success and 30 per cent a failure.[49] Once he had pronounced, it took a bold person to disagree. Deng Xiaoping, who had been brought back into the leadership as a vice-premier, found himself under attack, however, for his understandable reluctance to agree that the Cultural

Revolution had, all things considered, been a success story. He had to engage in self-criticism, but what he said fell far short of satisfying Mao. Deng was once again demoted after he attributed his errors to 'a profound inability to understand what the Cultural Revolution was all about'.[50]

As well as insisting that the Cultural Revolution had been successful, Mao in 1975 criticized factionalism within the Communist Party, including the faction most fanatically engaged in this revolution, of which his wife, Jiang Qing, was a member. Mao described it within inner party circles as the 'Gang of Four' – a phrase which after his death was to become far more famous than he intended. (Jiang's relationship to Mao was not as close as her status as his spouse would suggest. Among the duties of the head of Mao's security, General Wang Dongxing, was maintaining a constant supply of young women whose sexual services the 'Great Helmsman' enjoyed. They were euphemistically known as the 'Cultural Work Troupe'.)[51] The other members of the Gang of Four, apart from Jiang Qing, were Wang Hongwen, a radical labour leader in the early years of the Cultural Revolution who in the early 1970s was considered a possible successor to Mao; Yao Wenyan, the Shanghai literary critic who was the major author of the attack (at Jiang Qing's behest) on the play, Hai Rui Dismissed from Office; and Zhang Chunquiao, a senior propagandist in Shanghai who by the mid-1970s was chairman of the Shanghai Revolutionary Committee and a vice-premier of the State Council.

The Cultural Revolution was a personal disaster for millions of Chinese people. The more educated they were, the more likely they were to be among its victims. It was also in almost all respects an anti-Cultural Revolution, inasmuch as it involved the wanton destruction by Red Guards (often acting on their own initiative) of cultural artefacts, whether books, paintings, the contents of museums, graveyards or historical sites.[52] The Red Guards had, though, been encouraged already in 1966 to attack the 'Four Olds'. Old thought, old culture, old customs and old habits had to be eliminated.[53] One of the things, it seems, which motivated Mao in the launch of the Cultural Revolution was the desire to secure his legacy. He wanted to be followed, and revered, by radicals, not by 'revisionists'.[54] However, the disaster of the Cultural Revolution, following fast on the even greater disaster of the Great Leap Forward, helped to ensure the triumph of what he would have regarded as extreme revisionism.

The Cultural Revolution did, indeed, have unintended consequences that were ultimately beneficial for China, however tragic it was that such a heavy price had to be paid for a resurgence of common sense. One major reason why radical economic reform was almost impossibly difficult to introduce in the Soviet Union was the strength of vested interests – in the first place, the bureaucracies of the economic ministries and the regional party organizations. In *China*, the Cultural Revolution totally disrupted those structures and they never fully recovered their former coherence and domination. Thus, bureaucratic resistance to market reform was much weaker than it otherwise would have been when economic innovation got seriously under way after Mao Zedong's death. Moreover, the campaign against 'revisionism' had led to such irrational extremes that the zealots of the Cultural Revolution soon found themselves on the defensive when their mentor and protector, Mao, was no longer there. The Gang of Four were arrested on 6 October 1976, less than a month after Mao's death, and were kept in prison for four years before being brought to trial in 1980. As a group, they were accused of causing almost 35,000 deaths. Two of them – Mao's widow, Jiang Qing, and Zhang – were given death sentences which were later commuted.[55] The publicity given to their crimes helped still further to discredit the extremism of the Cultural Revolution and to aid the full rehabilitation of officials, including those of reformist disposition, who had been persecuted in those years. The party leadership could not afford to discredit Mao comprehensively, for he was their Lenin as well as their Stalin. Thus, too much of the legitimacy of Communist rule would have been lost had they done so. Nevertheless, a Central Committee 'Resolution on Party History', without going so far as to turn the Gang of Four into a Gang of Five, did not evade Mao's ultimate responsibility for the disastrous decade from the mid-1960s to the mid-1970s. It noted: 'The "cultural revolution", which lasted from May 1966 to October 1976, was responsible for the most severe setback and the heaviest losses suffered by the Party, the state and the people since the founding of the People's Republic. It was initiated and led by Comrade Mao Zedong.'[56]

The hold of Communist ideology could never be the same again in China. Neither Marxism-Leninism nor Mao Zedong Thought, although lip-service continued to be paid to both, dominated people's minds in the way in which they had before and, to an extreme extent, during the earlier stages of the Cultural Revolution. Utopianism was out, pragmatism was in. Indeed, almost everything Mao had intended to destroy for ever, and which constituted his primary motivation for launching and persisting with the Cultural Revolution, was given a new lease of life in the reaction against the turmoil and arbitrariness of 'Mao's Last Revolution'.[57] The old officials who returned to their posts, after suffering to varying degrees at the hands of revolutionary zealots of their own generation and, still more, from the youthful fanaticism of the Red Guards, were united in their determination never again to put up with such extremism and insubordination. (Recent experience of what young people could do when they were apparently given their heads did nothing, however, to incline the returning cadres toward political democracy.) While many Chinese continued to believe that Mao, in the course of his long career as a revolutionary and ruler, had done more good than harm, he was no longer deified. Both Mao and Mao Zedong Thought had been secularized.

UNINTENDED INTERNATIONAL CONSEQUENCES

Even during the lifetime of Mao Zedong there was a retreat from some of the violent disorder engendered by the Cultural Revolution. Mao had to call on the services of the PLA to curb the wilder excesses of the Red Guards. But it was in foreign policy that he reversed course most spectacularly. Having chastised and ridiculed the Soviet leadership for being soft in its attitude to the arch-imperialist power, the United States, Mao began in 1970–71 to send signals to Washington that a less antagonistic relationship would be welcome. It was in 1969 that China had come closer to war with the Soviet Union than ever before, and to be on equally bad terms with both superpowers seemed inadvisable. The Cultural Revolution had exacerbated the Sino-Soviet conflict. It had united most of the Soviet establishment – whether reformers or conservative Communists – against China, for it reminded them of the Great Terror of the 1930s. Indeed, one unintended consequence of events in China for Soviet politics was that, at a time when the Brezhnev leadership had put a stop to criticism of Stalin, a number of anti-Stalinist – indeed, thoroughly 'revisionist' – Soviet authors wrote books and articles which were ostensibly about Mao and China but which their more discerning readers realized were about Stalin and the Soviet Union. Just as 'Yugoslavia' for a time served, in Chinese polemics, for the Soviet Union, and 'Albania', in the Soviet responses, stood in for China, so Mao became a surrogate for Stalin and writings about him became a way of pressing the case for moderation, reform, and a rule of law in the USSR.[58]

Conscious of their international isolation at the beginning of the 1970s, the Chinese leadership began to show a new interest in being accorded a seat at the United Nations. For most of the outside world, it had long been regarded as an absurdity that they were not already there. The stumbling block had been the United States – hence the tentative Chinese overtures to the Nixon administration, to which President Richard Nixon and his secretary of state Henry Kissinger responded. Although American recognition of China was little more than a belated recognition of the obvious, and while Nixon's meeting with Mao Zedong in 1972 was less consequential than Nixon and Kissinger made out, the fact that a Republican president – and one who, during the McCarthyite period, had been an enthusiastic red-baiter – took the plunge, changed the contours of international diplomacy.[59]

From that time on, the United States could attempt to play the 'China card' against the Soviet Union, although this turned out to be of no significance whatsoever at the time when relations between the USA and the Soviet Union improved most dramatically – during the second half of the 1980s. Historically, the Sino-Soviet split was a far more important occurrence than the development of a Sino-American working relationship. The latter was overdue and it made sense. It often, however, involved hypocrisy on both sides, with the Soviet Union, during the presidencies of several of Nixon's successors, much more castigated for its human rights record than China. That was in spite of the fact that China's record of repression and intolerance – especially in Mao's lifetime – was very much worse than even Brezhnev's USSR.

18

Communism in Asia and Africa

It is striking that of the five states in the world today which count as Communist (though the degree to which they embody the main attributes of a Communist system varies), four are in Asia. Apart from China, they are Vietnam, North Korea and Laos.* Moreover, in 2008 a Maoist party came to power in Nepal, although it would be, to say the least, premature to count Nepal as a Communist state. Two other countries which did have Communist systems, and no longer have them, are in Asia: Cambodia (known as Kampuchea during the Communist period) and Mongolia, a much longer-lasting Communist regime. Another Asian country which, for a time, came close to establishing a Communist system was Afghanistan, although it was not held to be a 'socialist country' by the Soviet Union and other members of the international Communist movement.

This chapter is mainly concerned with the evolution of Asian Communist states up to the mid-1980s. Less attention will be devoted to Communism in Africa, for no African country has ever had a fully fledged Communist system. None was recognized as such by the Soviet Union and the international Communist movement, although some were considered to be states 'of socialist orientation', as distinct from being 'socialist' (i.e. Communist) countries.

In Asia and Africa, unlike Europe, the advance of Communism has been linked not only with class struggle but, at least as crucially, with the movement for national liberation and with anti-colonialism. Communist parties, in the countries in which they came to power in Asia, have been able to tap into patriotic and anti-imperialist sentiments as well as to the desire of the poor to reduce inequality and take revenge on those perceived to be their

---

* China, as the world's most populous country and now a major economic power, is examined separately in three chapters of this volume. It is also an especially important subject of the question asked in Chapter 30, 'What's left of Communism?' The present chapter, therefore, excludes China from the discussion except where it has a bearing on one of the other countries considered here.

class oppressors. Communist rule, however, put new forms of exploitation in place and, especially in Cambodia and North Korea, imposed infinitely more suffering on the great majority of the population than the regimes they displaced. Communist governments which have come to power indigenously, rather than by courtesy of Soviet bayonets, have been difficult to dislodge, and Asia has provided examples of these. However, though making your own revolution was a good way to start for Communists wishing to have a long lease on government, it was not the only way. As the case of North Korea has demonstrated, ruthless exercise of totalitarian state power can sustain a Communist regime, even though initially Soviet support may have been more important than a negligible domestic power base.

The first Asian country to become Communist, as noted in Chapter 5, was Mongolia. It is still sometimes known as Outer Mongolia, inner Mongolia being part of China. If Mongolia had not been under the protection and ultimate political control of the Soviet Union, it would hardly have survived as a sovereign state during its lengthy period of Communist rule. China had long regarded the whole of Mongolia as being part of its domain and it was not until 1946 that the Nationalist government in China recognized the Mongolian People's Republic as an independent state. Its satellite status in relation to the Soviet Union made it the odd one out among the Asian Communist countries. The other Communist states in Asia sooner or later stopped following so closely Moscow's lead. It was in keeping with Mongolia's dependence on its Soviet neighbour that it ceased to be a Communist state at the same time as the Soviet Union itself was wound up.

The Communist party in Mongolia was known from 1924 until the end of Communist rule as the Mongolian People's Revolutionary Party – MAKN in its Mongolian acronym. In the inter-war period, collectivization of agriculture had been resisted by a reluctant and, in large part, nomadic population. However, the party leader and the country's ruler from the 1920s until his death in 1952, Horloogiyn Choybalsan, ruthlessly followed the Soviet example, earning himself the sobriquet of the 'Stalin of Mongolia'. Although the Mongolian economy remained predominantly agricultural, it adopted a series of five-year plans of economic development after the Second World War. In 1949 the leadership proclaimed that Mongolia was now a 'socialist' state – as distinct from merely building, or aspiring to, socialism. Internationally, Mongolia's leaders had good relations with the Chinese Communists after the latter came to power in 1949, but their Soviet satellite status was confirmed when the Sino-Soviet dispute made equally harmonious relations with the Chinese People's Republic and the USSR impossible. Mongolia continued, in all essentials, to support the Soviet Union, its main trading partner, from whom it also received substantial economic aid.

North Korea

The emergence of North Korea as a Communist state after 1945 owed much to the occupation of that part of Korea by the Soviet army as the Japanese were driven out. While Communists generally came to power without widespread support from their own populations, the takeovers count as indigenous if power is seized without decisively important outside help. Even on those grounds, North Korea's path to Communist rule was hardly indigenous. Not only were the country's Communist groups small and lacking in popular support, but Soviet troops provided crucial backing for the North Korean Communists in the years in which the latter acquired power. Nevertheless, in the establishment, and especially consolidation, of North Korea's Communist regime there was a strong nationalist component. The Soviet military left Korea in 1948, making it more imperative for the new regime to develop its system of control and means of mobilizing domestic support.

Korea had been annexed as a colony by Japan in 1910 and remained so throughout the Second World War, becoming a battleground only at the end of the war. There were various Korean resistance groups against Japanese occupation, and the future Korean dictator, Kim Il-sung, was but one of many who had at various times been involved in guerrilla activity against the Japanese. He did enough, however, to make a favourable impression on some senior Soviet officers, and he was brought to Russia for further military and political training.[1] Kim, on his return to his homeland, became, with Soviet support, the leader of the North Korean Communists and, in due course, of the new state. He made use of the tradition of national liberation, and an exaggerated version of his own role in it, as one of the main sources of his legitimacy.

The partition of Korea at the 38th Parallel was agreed between the Soviet Union and the United States in 1945, leaving North Korea occupying approximately 55 per cent of the Korean peninsula. Koreans were one of the minority nationalities in the Soviet Union, and several hundred of them, especially from the Soviet republics of Kazakhstan and Uzbekistan, were brought over to join forces with the group led by Kim.[2] The early stages of the Communist takeover of North Korea had much in common with what happened in Eastern Europe. The military and the administrative apparatus were brought under the control of the Communists. Other political parties were merged with the Communist party, the membership of which reached 600,000 by December 1946. This was already close to 10 per cent of the adult population, although almost all the members had been recruited since the end of the war.[3] They were led by Kim, who from December 1945 headed the North Korean branch of the Korean Communist party. As chairman of what was called the Interim People's Committee, he held also the highest administrative position in the North. It was not until September 1948 that a North Korean state was formed. It was named the Democratic People's Republic of Korea, and it followed the declaration two months earlier of the statehood of South Korea, called simply the Republic of Korea. That country was led by the conservative nationalist, Rhee Syngman, who at the time enjoyed the support of the United States administration and the American occupying forces. Both Rhee and Kim Il-sung, who agreed on nothing else, shared a belief that before long Korea could be united, and each aspired to be the leader of that state. South Korea for the next several decades was at best a flawed and corrupt democracy and, for much of the time, a conservative authoritarian state. However, a serious and successful democratization process got under way in the 1980s. North Korea, in contrast, became – even by the standards of Communist states – one of the harshest and grimmest of totalitarian regimes.

A peculiarity not only of the takeover of North Korea but also of Kim Il-sung's assumption of power in the North Korean revolutionary party is that to most of Korea's prominent Communists, who were in the South, Kim was a virtual unknown. Envisaging a reunification of Korea in which they would resume their place in the leadership of the Communist movement, these senior party members made no attempt to block Kim's leadership of what in December 1945 was no more than the North Korean branch of the party.[4] By the time two separate states were formed in 1948, it was too late to stop Kim Il-sung. The Korean War began in 1950, when Stalin finally acquiesced with Kim's desire to mount an attack on the South, something he had been urging on Stalin since March 1949.[5] Mao Zedong also gave his agreement, and Chinese forces, as noted in Chapter 11, played a prominent part in the conflict. The war ended in July 1953, a few months after Stalin's death. Korea, though, remains a part of the world where the Cold War continues to the present day, with one nation divided into two hostile states.

More than three million Koreans managed to move from the North to the South in the course of the war. After it ended, Kim set about strengthening the patriotic support for his state by injecting a strong element of strident nationalism into the official ideology. Another distinctive feature of North Korea was that Stalinism long survived the death of Stalin. Indeed, the glorification of Kim Il-sung exceeded even that accorded the Soviet leader, especially since the personification of power led him to groom his son, Kim Jong-il, to succeed him. The younger Kim became a Politburo member in the early 1970s and was officially designated as the future successor in 1980. He duly succeeded as North Korean leader when Kim Il-sung died in 1994, although it was 1997 before he assumed all of the offices that had been held by his father. The elder Kim had been universally referred to in the North Korean mass media as the 'Great Leader'. His son became the 'Dear Leader'. Surrounded by a court, and with personal access to every luxury the West can offer, Kim Jong-il has presided over extreme measures to eliminate any possibility of foreign influence on the population as a whole. The major responsibility of one party department is to send officials into people's homes to check that the dials of their radios are tuned to fixed frequencies, thus ensuring that they are on no account able to receive foreign broadcasts.[6] Ruthless use of coercion by both father and son, with elimination of even potential opponents, and systematic social controls combined with constant propaganda, have kept in place a regime which, on most measures, has been a grotesque failure.[7] By 1978 the GDP of South Korea was almost four times that of the North. Yet the poverty of the people did not deter either the Great Leader or the Dear Leader from spending disproportionately vast sums on the military as well as on grandiose construction projects.[8] And there is no automatic link between economic failure and collapse of a Communist regime if all the resources of an oppressive state are brought to bear to keep its rulers in office.

In comparison with the rest of the population, those who are key to keeping Kim Jong-il in power – senior army generals and leading party and police officials among them – have been well rewarded. Even the most stringent autocrat has to win the support, either through ideological persuasion or an appeal to their interests, of the groups necessary to sustain him and the regime. That is as true of Communist rulers, including those who have taken personification of power to extremes such as the Kims, father and son, as of despots of an earlier age. In the early sixteenth century, Niccolò Machiavelli, in *The Prince*, noted the importance of what subjects thought about even an autocratic ruler. 'The prince', he argued, 'is highly esteemed who conveys this impression of himself, and he who is highly esteemed is not easily conspired against.'[9] A little over 200 years later, David Hume reflected on the necessity for tyrannical rulers to influence the opinions people hold, since coercion alone is not enough to guarantee their security. Hume observed that 'the bodily force' even of a tyrant as an individual could 'reach but a small way'. If, therefore, he was obeyed, this depended in part on his influence on the opinions of other people, including what *they* presumed to be the opinions of yet others.[10] One can be certain that neither Kim Il-sung nor Kim Jong-il ever read Hume, and it is improbable that they read Machiavelli. However, the cult of personality in North Korea, and in other Communist states (though rarely taken to such extremes as by the Kims), had a logic similar to that elaborated by Machiavelli and Hume. The works of Marx, Engels and Lenin contained no words of support for the glorification of leaders, but the classics of Marxism-Leninism were not widely read in the peasant societies of Asia in which Communists seized power. A quicker way to secure compliance, and a necessary supplement to physical coercion, was to instil adulation of the Great Leader.

Vietnam and Laos

For many Asian Communists, hostility to colonialism and hostility to capitalism went together, for the kind of capitalist system they first encountered was one which seemed to radical intellectuals to involve extreme exploitation of the local population by foreign business. The euphemism for this used by staunch supporters of the British Empire was that 'trade follows the flag'. The reality was that companies from the colonial rulers' mother country were granted privileges not accorded to nationals of other countries or to the indigenous population. In this context, therefore – even though, intellectually, nationalism and Marxism are poles apart – a significant minority of young intellectuals in Asian countries in the first half of the twentieth century linked in their own minds national liberation with the replacement of capitalism by a socialist or Communist system. This was true of a number of Vietnamese radicals, among them the person who has the strongest claim to be regarded as the father of the Vietnamese revolution and of the Communist state in Vietnam, Ho Chi Minh. When he read Lenin's 'Theses on the National and Colonial Questions' in French translation in the newspaper L'Humanité, in July 1920, the young Ho was overjoyed. Lenin seemed to be providing a key to understanding the plight of Indochina, where Western capitalist countries found both markets and raw materials to sustain a system which exploited the peoples of the region. It is significant that it was Lenin's writings on colonialism specifically which set Ho Chi Minh (who at that time went under the name of Nguyen Ai Quoc) 'on a course that transformed him from a simple patriot with socialist leanings into a Marxist revolutionary'.[11] Of this work of Lenin, Ho Chi Minh later wrote: 'What emotion, enthusiasm, clear-sightedness, and confidence it instilled in me!'[12]

The 'confidence' of which Ho spoke was important. When the odds seemed to an individual discontented with imperial rule to be stacked on the side of the colonial powers, the writings of Marx and Lenin provided not only an explanation of their woes but also the conviction that it was only a matter of time before they prevailed over their foreign exploiters. We have seen in earlier chapters how the consolation offered by belief in the inevitability of the downfall of capitalism and the triumph of 'socialism' (as that concept was understood by the Communist Party) gave heart to party members in advanced Western countries, in which they often seemed marginal to the political life of their nation. For Third World revolutionaries, the firm belief that history was on their side was even more inspiring. Although, contrary to the predictions of Marx, it turned out that Communism had a broader appeal in peasant societies than in the most advanced industrialized countries of the world, this worked to the advantage of Communists in Asia. Why there should have been more indigenous revolutions, leading to Communist rule, in predominantly peasant than in industrialized societies is an interesting question. The idea of factories belonging to the people as a whole had a romantic appeal for a minority, but the actual experience of nationalization was more prosaic. However, land redistribution within what were highly unequal peasant societies turned out to be an altogether more effective instrument for mobilizing support for Communist parties. In the first stage of the revolutionary struggle, and in the earliest implementation of Communist rule, the emphasis was invariably on redistributing land from wealthy landlords and the richest peasants to the majority who hungered after more land. It was, as a rule, only significantly later that collectivized or state farms were introduced. These evoked much more hostile sentiments in the countryside. By that time, however, a Communist power structure had been established and resistance to the policies of the ruling party had become difficult and dangerous.

Ho Chi Minh, in common with the Indian Communist M.N. Roy (with whom, though, he had difficult relations), maintained as early as the 1920s that 'communism could acclimatize itself more easily in Asia than in Europe'.[13] Ho, like so many of the early leaders of revolutionary movements, was of middle-class origin. His father was a civil servant of scholarly disposition, and Ho himself acquired a good education, including knowledge of several languages. Early radicalism, however, caused him to be expelled from more than one school as a troublemaker and he embarked on many different careers – including a sailor, a photographer's technician in Paris, and an assistant chef in London. He adopted numerous pseudonyms – Ho Chi Minh was just one of dozens, but the name by which he was to become known to the world. After spending several years in the early 1920s in Paris, where he joined the French Communist Party, he went to Moscow in 1923 to work for the Comintern. He was on good terms with Borodin, who, as noted in earlier chapters, became the chief representative of the Comintern in China. Ho joined Borodin there later in 1923 and remained in China for two and a half years, getting to know some of the leading members of the Chinese Communist Party, among them Zhou Enlai.

In the remaining years of the inter-war period Ho moved between Moscow and Asia. He was the main organizer of the founding conference of the Indochinese Communist Party in 1930 in Hong Kong, but the following year was arrested there by the British police. By 1934, however, he was back in Moscow, from where in 1938 he set out on the hazardous journey to the Yanan province of northern China, where those who had survived the Long March were encamped. Throughout these years Ho was in close touch with the major underground Communist movements in Asia. He was arrested in China in 1942 but released by the Nationalist Chinese authorities in September of the following year, although with limits on his freedom of movement. Long years as a professional revolutionary, changing his residence and his name at frequent intervals and disappearing from the view of police forces in different countries who thought they had him in their sights, had prepared him well for the new opportunities which were to arise at the end of the Second World War.

The French rulers of Vietnam had dealt rigorously with sporadic strikes and demonstrations organized by the Communists in the inter-war period, but with the Japanese surrender in August 1945 there was a power vacuum into which Ho Chi Minh and the Communists moved rapidly. They formed a National Liberation Committee, with Ho as chairman, and issued an 'appeal to the people', demanding independence. Signing the appeal, Ho used for the last time his pseudonym, Nguyen Ai Quoc (which means Nguyen the Patriot).[14] By September 1945 the committee had been transformed into a provisional government, chaired by Ho Chi Minh. It was, characteristically, a Communist-dominated coalition. When Ho addressed a vast crowd in Hanoi on 2 September, he calculatedly quoted from both the American Declaration of Independence and the French Revolution's Declaration of the Rights of Man. His emphasis on national liberation and democracy was aimed partly at engaging the sympathy of the United States. He hoped that anti-colonialist sentiments in Washington would lead them to support Vietnamese demands for independence from French rule. Whereas, however, President Roosevelt had spoken up for the liberation of Asians and Africans from colonial rule, his successor, Harry Truman, was more concerned with rising tensions between Washington and Moscow. He was receptive to the argument of the Division of European Affairs in the State Department that American opposition to French control of Indochina would complicate relations with Paris.[15]

Talks in France between representatives of the provisional Vietnamese government and the French government broke down without any agreement to grant Vietnam independence. Ho Chi Minh made numerous compromises in the endeavour to get a promise of independence, and his prestige at home was lowered by the failure of that mission. Having not succeeded in securing liberation from French colonial rule by peaceful means, Ho and the Vietnamese Communists turned to force. What became known as the First Indochina War (the American war in Vietnam was the Second) began on 19 December 1946 when, under the direction of Ho Chi Minh, Vietnamese units launched attacks on French installations throughout Hanoi, including the municipal power station. By late evening the French had regained control over central Hanoi, but Ho escaped capture. The Communist Party Politburo could no longer safely remain in Hanoi, so they took to the hills and embarked on guerrilla warfare.[16] In the course of the war, which was to last until 1954, Ho changed his living quarters regularly. A prisoner of war reported in 1952 that Ho, then aged sixty-two, was moving from one place to another every three to five days and that he could still walk thirty miles a day with a pack on his back.[17]

As well as using guerrilla tactics against the French, the Communists were fomenting class war in the countryside. Kangaroo courts were set up in which landlords were condemned, deprived of their property, and often executed on the spot. Since, however, their property was redistributed among the neediest peasants, there were more winners than losers from this ruthless process. In early 1950, first China and then the Soviet Union recognized Ho's Democratic Republic of Vietnam (DRV) as the sole legal government of the country. In fact, the Communists controlled much of the North of Vietnam and were able to pass legislation which could be implemented in that territory. In late 1953 they passed a law enforcing rent reductions and 'extending the confiscation of landholdings to the entire landlord class'.[18] The Communists' dominance in the North was eventually conceded by the French and recognized internationally. At a conference in Geneva in 1954, agreement was reached on the partition of Vietnam. Both the Soviet and Chinese foreign ministers, Molotov and Zhou Enlai, favoured this compromise. The head of the DRV delegation, Pham Van Dong, only reluctantly agreed. Zhou helped to persuade him that this was a necessary, and temporary, price to pay for French withdrawal and that the French prime minister, Pierre Mendès-France, needed a face-saving formula. Moreover, the Eisenhower administration in the United States had watched the negotiations with concern and had resolved not to accept any agreement which did not retain at least part of the future Vietnam under non-Communist rule. Zhou's assurance to Pham Van Dong that it would be a simple matter to take over the whole of Vietnam once the French had departed turned out to be overoptimistic. The Vietnamese Communists, though, remained determined to achieve the goal of national unity under their leadership and saw partition as but a short-term setback.[19]

By the mid-1950s the United States had emerged as the main backer of the non-Communist South Vietnamese government, whose headquarters were in Saigon, while in the North the Chinese had become increasingly influential. Following the Chinese example meant an intensification of class war in the countryside, with several thousand people executed and many more severely harassed. The tilt of the Vietnamese Communists in the direc-tion of China was reinforced by some of the actions of Moscow. There was no enthusiasm in Hanoi for the emphasis at the Twentieth Party Congress of the CPSU on 'peaceful co-existence', since it was feared this might lead to Soviet disapproval of the resumption of revolutionary war to unite Vietnam. Even more worrying was a Soviet proposal, made without consulting Hanoi, that both the South (the Republic of Vietnam) and the North (the Democratic Republic of Vietnam) be admitted to membership of the United Nations.[20] With the reinstatement of the DRV in 1954, about a million people fled to the South. Since those who left included many of the better-off and most anti-Communist Vietnamese, this exodus – as well as the intimidation of landowners – greatly reduced the possibility of serious resistance to the Communists within the territory they administered.[21]

Moreover, when they took their struggle to the South, the Communists were able to attract substantial peasant support, as they had done in the North. A Vietnamese-speaking American, Jeffrey Race, who served with the United States army in Vietnam as a specialist adviser, came to the conclu-sion that the Communists had a better-thought-out strategy than the govern-ment in Saigon which American troops had been sent to support. Revolutionary war was for the Communists part of a broader social process. They had some success in presenting as their ultimate goal a more just society. In the meantime, their redistribution of land in areas they controlled brought immediate benefits to many. The Communist guerrillas were also able to instil fear in those who supported the Saigon government. Race concluded, nevertheless, that in the first half of the 1960s the South Vietnamese government 'terrorized far more than did the revolutionary movement' – by, for example, artillery and ground attacks on 'communist villages'. Their methods led to a strengthening, rather than weakening, of the revolutionary movement.[22]

The United States was drawn into the conflict in Vietnam partly because of what it did *not* do in Laos. Vietnam is today a country of over eighty million people – a population over ten times greater than that of the economically backward, land-locked and mountainous Laos. It would be reasonable to conclude that it was of greater consequence both to Western countries and to the Communist world which way Vietnam went. Nevertheless, when President Eisenhower handed over power to John F. Kennedy in 1960, he spent more time talking to him about Laos than about either Cuba or Vietnam.[23] Already during the Eisenhower presidency the United States was dropping supplies to anti-Communist forces in Laos, but for more than one reason it avoided direct military involvement there. The difficult terrain would have made it a 'logistical nightmare', but no less important was the assessment in Washington that the Lao people would not put up much of a fight to resist a Communist takeover. Sweeping generalizations and ethnic stereotypes portrayed the Lao people as 'drowsy', 'diffident', 'docile' and 'dreamy'.[24] The CIA director Allen Dulles informed the National Security Council that there were 'few people of any courage' in Laos and that the population had 'a long tradition of not liking bloodshed'. An American journalist, Oden Meeker, put a much more positive spin on the same stereotype, saying that the Lao were 'gentle' and 'utterly charming'.[25] For Henry Kissinger, reflecting on his years as US secretary of state, the people of Laos were distinguished by 'the grace of their life-style rather than martial qualities'.[26] The Washington consensus was, indeed, that the Lao people were 'incorrigible pacifists' and far from ideal allies with whom to make a stand against the march of Communism.[27] The economist John Kenneth Galbraith, at a time when he was US ambassador to India, wrote from New Delhi to Kennedy, sarcastically declaring: 'As a military ally, the entire Laos nation is clearly inferior to a battalion of conscientious objectors from World War I.'[28]

The United States backed a compromise solution on Laos in 1962, abandoning their support for the most anti-Communist forces and settling for a neutralist government headed by the nationalist Prince Souvanna Phouma. The Communist insurgents in Laos, the Pathet Lao, with the support of the North Vietnamese, were gradually able to take over the country territorially and to establish Communist rule by the mid-1970s. Souvanna, in a speech at a dinner on the outskirts of the Laotian capital, Vientiane, in honour of Henry Kissinger in 1973, pointed out that as a result of war and loss of territory, the population of the country, which at one time had been seventeen million, was down to three million. In Souvanna's eyes, too, the Lao people were 'pacific by tradition and by religion'. All they asked for was peace and sovereignty.[29] The British prime minister, Harold Macmillan, and French President Charles de Gaulle had been among those who in the early 1960s pressed for a neutral Laos under the leadership of Souvanna. However, in the coalition government which was formed, the Communists exercised increasing influence. That finally gave way to outright Communist rule in 1975. The Vietnamese influence was very evident, for this followed fast upon the victory of the Viet Cong and the unification of the whole of Vietnam under Communist rule. Although the regime in Laos turned out to be milder than other Communist systems in Asia – with few executions in comparison with Vietnam, not to speak of Cambodia – almost 10 per cent of the people fled from the country. This was a higher proportion of the population than that constituted by the 'boat people' who left by sea from Vietnam. The size of the exodus from Laos is partly to be explained by the relative ease of crossing the Mekong river into Thailand.[30]

How important giving up on Laos was for the United States embroilment in Vietnam has been shown by recent scholarship. At the time of the Eisenhower–Kennedy handover, Kennedy's secretary of defense, Robert McNamara, had been left with the impression that 'if Laos were lost, all of Southeast Asia would fall' to Communism. Eisenhower's warnings, he said, 'heavily influenced our subsequent approach to Southeast Asia'. Kennedy, though, decided that Laos was not the place to make a stand – and possibly suffer a humiliation comparable to the recent Cuban Bay of Pigs fiasco. He sought to reassure anxious members of his administration in 1961 by saying: 'If we have to fight for Southeast Asia, we'll fight in South Vietnam.'[31] The American president had decided that a neutral Laos, with an uncertain future, was as good a result as he could obtain in that country. However, as Seth Jacobs has observed, this meant that 'Kennedy's Laos policy came with a hidden trip wire. He did not believe he could retreat any further in Southeast Asia. If the Viet Cong pressed their advantage against the US-sponsored Saigon regime, America would have to fight. By cutting his losses in Laos, Kennedy narrowed the range of options for himself and future presidents attempting to cope with Vietnam.'[32]

. The Vietnam War divided the allies of the United States and, ultimately, opinion in America itself. West European governments did not question the desirability of non-Communist government in Vietnam, but harboured doubts as to whether this could be achieved by military means, and also about how significant the Vietnamese system of government was for Western safety.[33] The officials in Washington with special responsibility for defence and security were much more eager to escalate American involvement in Vietnam than were either Presidents Kennedy or Johnson. National Security Adviser McGeorge Bundy and Secretary of Defense McNamara implicitly warned Johnson that he could not count on their support unless he did something to avert a humiliating American defeat in Vietnam.[34] Ultimately, Johnson heeded the advice of those who urged escalation of the bombing of Vietnam, although he had been given a very different, and more prescient, warning by his vice-president, Hubert Humphrey, in a document written in

February 1965. In a memorandum which long remained secret, the vice-president wrote that it was time for the administration to cut its losses, for disengagement in that year would be better than the alternative of deeper embroilment. Humphrey predicted that 'political opposition will steadily mount. It will underwrite all the negativism and disillusionment which we already have about foreign involvement generally – with direct spill-over effects politically for all the Democratic internationalist programs to which we are committed – AID, UN, disarmament, and activist world policies generally.'[35] Nevertheless, the United States was driven both by fears of growing Chinese influence throughout South-East Asia and by the 'domino theory' which had first been voiced by President Eisenhower at the time the French were forced out of Indochina in 1954.[36]

From 1966, with the Cultural Revolution under way in China, there were arguments within the Vietnamese Communist party as well as within the administration in Washington. Even Ho Chi Minh, who lost some of his influence from 1963 (and died in 1969), began to be criticized by a number of party members. He was blamed both for 'allowing' the French back into Vietnam in 1945 and for accepting the partition of the country in 1954.[37] The divisions among Vietnamese Communists in significant part reflected the Sino-Soviet dispute, with some party members supporting the Chinese line and others leaning towards Moscow. The fact that the Soviet Union over-took China by the end of 1968 as the main supplier of aid, including military equipment, made it the more important for the Vietnamese Communists to maintain good relations with the Soviet leadership. One of the assets of the aged Ho Chi Minh in the later 1960s was that he was able to command respect in both Beijing and Moscow.[38] By the early 1970s, however, the relative attraction of the Soviet Union for Vietnamese Communists was enhanced by worrying signs of rapprochement between China and the United States.[39]

When improved US relations with China were followed by an improvement also in American relations with the USSR, the Hanoi government had to curb their intransigence. They were urged by the Soviet leadership not to launch another offensive but to concentrate on diplomacy.[40] By 1972, as both the major Communist powers favoured a peace settlement in Vietnam which would not, at least initially, lead to a unification of Vietnam under the Communists, there were Hanoi politicians who perceived this as Soviet and Chinese kowtowing to America. Both the USSR and China did put pressure on Hanoi to reach a negotiated settlement, but neither the North nor the South Vietnamese governments had any faith in the peace agreement reached in Paris in January 1973 or the will to make it a lasting settlement.[41] Nor, even after making temporary concessions, did Communist Vietnam ever become a mere satellite of the Soviet Union or of China.

Although the Vietnamese Communists emerged in 1975 as the winners in their struggle, and the United States and its Vietnamese allies as the losers, that victory was obtained at a very high cost. There were some 700,000 Vietnamese casualties, and 45 per cent of the country's towns were destroyed. David Elliott, who arrived in Saigon with the US army in 1963 as an intelligence officer, and in the post-war period went on to become a major scholar on Vietnam, has noted that successive administrations in Washington 'thought that the Vietnamese were irrelevant to the big picture'. Having been complicit in the removal of the ally they initially entered the conflict to help, Ngo Dinh Diem, the Johnson administration in 1965 'thought so little of its nominal ally, the government of the Republic of South Vietnam, that it did not even bother to inform its own ally that America would escalate the war and send in combat troops'.[42] Moreover, Elliott has argued persuasively, Vietnamese society was divided not only between revolutionaries and their opponents but 'between the entire "political class" on both sides of this divide' and 'the risk averse, whose constant refrain was "do whatever you like, I'll still be a simple citizen"'.[43]

The Hanoi government was even more repressive than that in Saigon. Nevertheless, the South Vietnamese rulers lost credibility with a substantial section of their own population by having to rely on foreign troops, with their massive firepower, to assist them in a civil war. In the end it became clear that the anti-Communist forces in Vietnam could not win *with* United States active military support and could not win *without* it.[44] Reflecting on more than forty years of involvement with Vietnam, starting with his time as an American soldier there, David Elliott observed. '. . . self-deception is the surest road to disaster . . . the main reason I concluded that the U.S. presence was damaging to Americans as well as to the people we were trying to help was that for America, the Vietnam War was never about Vietnam, but always about some larger abstraction of concern to the United States – containing China, dominos, credibility'.[45]

Cambodia

The idea that Asian countries would fall like a stack of dominoes into the hands of Marxist-Leninists if Communism were to prevail in Vietnam turned out to be wholly fanciful, and a vast amount of blood was shed on the basis of that false premise. Most of Asia remained resolutely non-Communist. One country which did, however, for a time turn Communist, and for part of that period was run by a regime of exceptional viciousness, was Cambodia. Between 1976 and 1979, under Khmer Rouge rule, Cambodia slaughtered a higher proportion of its own citizens than any other Communist – or fascist – state in the twentieth century. During the period in which the country was run by the Khmer Rouge, under the leadership of Pol Pot, the idea of class war was taken to perverse extremes; the purges of the Communist party itself exceeded the worst excesses of Stalin and Mao Zedong; and an attempt was made to leap into communism even faster than in China's Great Leap Forward. In both cases the result was famine, but in Cambodia it was accompanied by far more killings for a vast range of offences than in China. Even sexual relations outside marriage and the consumption of alcohol were punishable by death.[46]

Cambodia had been part of French Indochina, but gained its independence in 1953. For over fifty years a key figure in the politics of the country was Prince Norodom Sihanouk. When not yet twenty he became King of Cambodia, having been placed on the throne by the French governor-general. Although he was a nationalist who aspired to independence, he bided his time, and when the French departed in 1953 he became prime minister. From 1960 until 1970 he governed as president. An authoritarian but not especially repressive ruler, Sihanouk managed to keep his country neutral between the United States and the Soviet Union, a task which became increasingly difficult as the Vietnam War unfolded. He was ousted by members of his own government in a coup in 1970 which had the backing, although not the active involvement, of the CIA. Sihanouk was made welcome in China and spent the first half of the 1970s there, during which time he established a National United Front of Cambodia. Meanwhile, in Cambodia there was civil war going on which lasted until 1975. The main antagonists were the government, which had become more pro-Western following the ousting of Prince Sihanouk, and the Communists. In 1973 the Cambodian Communists (Khmer Rouge) – who had, presumably, not read George Orwell – renamed their party 'Big Brother'. Between 1970 and 1973 they were joined in their struggle by Vietnamese forces. The stated goal of both Hanoi and the Khmer Rouge was the return to power of Sihanouk, who had allied himself with the Communists in angry outrage at his removal from office. Accordingly, the government troops, led by General – subsequently Marshal – Lon Nol, found themselves in the odd position of fighting 'royalist Communists'. Both the Vietnamese and the Khmer Rouge were, at that time, paying lip-service to Sihanouk, while being careful not to accord him any decision-making power.[47]

Before Congress cut off funds for this in 1973, the Nixon administration authorized the massive bombing of Cambodia to slow down the progress of the Khmer Rouge. Although this did interrupt supply routes, as well as killing many people, the main political effect of dropping over 540,000 tons of explosives in the Cambodian countryside was to win recruits for the Communists and to foster extreme hostility to the United States. It also caused an inflow of refugees from the rural areas to the cities.[48] In 1973 the North Vietnamese drastically cut back their support for the Khmer Rouge because the latter had refused to join the Paris peace talks which led to an end of the Vietnam War and which could have extended to negotiations over Cambodia. Thus, when the Kampuchean Communist party, in the shape of the Khmer Rouge, came to power, it was essentially an indigenous takeover. Though what was to occur later was often described as 'genocide', insofar as that term normally means the attempt to eliminate the people of a particular nation or ethnic group, it was a misnomer. Most of the violent deaths were of Cambodians killed by the Cambodian fanatics who had seized power, although it is true that the Vietnamese were killed in proportionately even larger numbers.[49] The Khmer Rouge killed Vietnamese wherever they came across them in Cambodia in a way which was close to what later would be termed 'ethnic cleansing'.[50] In their brutality during the civil war the Khmer Rouge had provided many foretastes of what was to come. When, for instance, they captured the former royal capital, Oudong, in 1974, they massacred tens of thousands of the inhabitants.[51]

The Communists took governmental power in April 1975 when the capital, Phnom Penh, fell to them. Sihanouk became the nominal head of state, but from 1976 he was put under house arrest. Hundreds of thousands of people were expelled from the cities, for which the Khmer Rouge seemed to have developed a special hatred.[52] This anti-urbanism was an odd interpretation of Marxism-Leninism. However, although Pol Pot had become a Marxist in the early 1950s, Marx and Lenin were little quoted during the Khmer Rouge reign of terror. Even Mao, to whom the Pol Pot branch of the Communist movement was closest, was not much cited. In many ways what occurred in Cambodia – called Democratic Kampuchea in those years – was a caricature of Communism. It had enough affinity with the Maoism of the Great Leap Forward to be not a totally new phenomenon, but it was worse by several degrees. There is no agreement on the exact numbers who died at the hands of the Khmer Rouge – mostly by assassination, although also of hunger – but a figure of about two million is widely regarded as likely. In the space of five years in the mid- and late 1970s, it is probable that one in five of the population perished prematurely as a result of Khmer Rouge barbarism. As of 1979, 42 per cent of Cambodia's children had lost at least one parent. In 1989, 38 per cent of adult women in Cambodia were widows, as compared with the 10 per cent of men who were widowers, for though many women were also executed, men were killed in much larger numbers.[53]

Like Mao, Pol Pot was attracted to the idea of starting the rebuilding of society with a 'blank slate'. He rewrote even the most recent history of his country, decreeing that Cambodia's revolutionary struggle began with the founding of the Kampuchean Communist Party in 1960. He himself became a member of its Central Committee then, and from 1963 was a secretary of that body. Rather than working in a bureaucracy, this meant operating from secret hideouts in the jungle and countryside. The Khmer Rouge version of history conveniently airbrushed out of the narrative the founding of the Indochinese Communist Party by Ho Chi Minh in 1951. The Cambodian Communists formed part of that organization, but its headquarters were in Vietnam.[54] Thus, it did not make a suitable founding myth for the society the Khmer Rouge wished to create. The extremism of the Khmer Rouge in the second half of the 1970s was out of kilter with what was happening in the rest of the Communist world at the time. The rule by systematic terror got under way around the time of the death of Mao and at the end, therefore, of even the later and somewhat milder variant of China's Cultural Revolution. From the point of view of the Khmer Rouge fanatics, 'revisionism' had become rampant – from the Soviet Union to Vietnam. Now it was rearing its head even within China. If there was any logic to the apparent madness of the Pol Pot regime's attempt to remodel Cambodian society through terror, it is perhaps that drawn out by the French scholar Jean-Louis Margolin:

China's Great Leap Forward had failed; so had the Cultural Revolution. The reason, in the Khmer Rouge's view, must be that the Chinese had stopped at half-measures; they had failed to sweep away every counterrevolutionary obstacle: the corrupt and uncontrollable towns, intellectuals who were proud of their knowledge and presumed to think for themselves, money and all financial transactions, the last traces of capitalism, and 'traitors who had infiltrated the heart of the Party'.[55]

In his style of rule, quite apart from the scale of the executions, Pol Pot was very different from Mao, not to speak of Kim Il-sung and Kim Jong-il. Rather than promoting a personality cult, he kept in the shadows, while making sure that any possible threat to his power was eliminated. His real name was Saloth Sar and he had a relatively privileged upbringing, partly spent within the circle of the monarchy. It included study in Paris from 1949 until 1953. He had, however, in common with other Communist leaders who became tyrants – among them Stalin, Mao and the North Korean Kims – a belief in his own genius. In reality, no one deserved more to be brought to justice for crimes against humanity – not even Stalin, Mao and Kim Il-sung.

Like them, however, Pol Pot died a natural death, in his case one month short of his seventieth birthday in 1998. Fortunately, he had by then been out of power for many years.*

The overthrow of the Khmer Rouge government was very largely the work of the Vietnamese. After almost two years of border clashes, Vietnamese forces invaded Cambodia/Kampuchea at the end of December 1978.[56] Their intention was to dislodge the Khmer Rouge – not, of course, to put an end to Communist rule. Most of the Cambodian population welcomed them as liberators, and in the course of that year a more 'normal' Communist government than Pol Pot's was established, under Vietnamese supervision. For the next decade – until the Vietnamese troops withdrew in 1989 – Cambodia had a more orthodox Communist system, with far less arbitrary violence. The system was still highly authoritarian, but it was unquestionably a vast improvement on the regime it replaced. As Margolin observes, 'given the increasing murderousness of the Khmer Rouge . . . the Vietnamese incursion saved an incalculable number of lives'.[57]

The Vietnamese military intervention, although undertaken of their own volition, was supported by the Soviet Union and opposed by a strange coalition which included China, the United States and most of the countries of Western Europe. Even the Carter administration, which ceased to overlook manifest abuses of human rights by some of the more dubious of America's allies in the Cold War struggle against the Soviet Union, opposed the Vietnamese intervention in Cambodia, seeing Hanoi purely as a proxy for Moscow. In a summit meeting in Vienna with Leonid Brezhnev in June 1979, President Carter, after complaining about the presence of Cuban troops in Africa, was critical of the fact that the 'Soviet Union has also encouraged and supported the Vietnamese in their invasion of Kampuchea'.[58] In response, as Carter notes, Brezhnev 'claimed that in Kampuchea the citizens were thankful to the Vietnamese for overthrowing the abhorrent regime of Pol Pot' and that it was understandable that the Soviet Union should support the intervention.[59] On this occasion Brezhnev happened to be right. The Communist government with which the Vietnamese replaced the regime of Pol Pot was manifestly a lesser evil than its predecessor.

However, when the Chinese decided to teach the Vietnamese a lesson

---

* Pol Pot spent some time in both Bangkok and Beijing after being removed from power. Mostly, however, he lived in encampments in forests of Thailand and northern Cambodia which were protected by Thai and Cambodian supporters. At the time of his death in 1998, he was living in a Khmer Rouge-controlled part of Cambodia close to the border with Thailand. He had been placed under house arrest by his former Khmer Rouge comrades-in-arms, but escaped international justice.

and, after informing the American president in advance of their intentions, launched a limited military action against Vietnam, this was met with understanding by the Carter administration.[60] The Chinese incursion caused the Vietnamese subsequently to place more troops on their border with China and fewer in Cambodia. Although Carter's National Security Adviser, Zbigniew Brzezinski, in his memoirs, refers to the 'Cambodian regime that the Vietnamese displaced' as that of 'the murderous Pol Pot', he evinced no doubts about the policy of opposing Vietnam's intervention against the Khmer Rouge. The fact that Vietnam was allied with the Soviet Union, and that China (with whom the US was now developing good relations) regarded Pol Pot as an ally, overrode humanitarian considerations.[61] Military invasion frequently makes a bad situation worse, but that was not the case with Vietnam's intervention in Cambodia. As the former Under-Secretary-General of the UN in charge of Peacekeeping, Marrack Goulding, wrote at the beginning of the twenty-first century: 'by today's humanitarian standards, [Vietnam's action] can be justified as something that had to be done, like Tanzania's military intervention in Uganda in 1979 to topple the monster Idi Amin'. At the time, however, the Western powers, having recognized the Pol Pot regime as the legitimate government of Cambodia/Kampuchea, denied recognition to the government installed by the Vietnamese which itself lasted for more than another decade before Cambodia ceased to be a Communist state.[62]

The Vietnamese withdrew all their troops from Cambodia in 1989, partly in response to promptings from the Soviet Union, by that time led by Mikhail Gorbachev. The withdrawal was a consequence also of the improved relationship between the Soviet Union and China, and that in turn helped to ease the tensions between China and Vietnam. Cambodia was the last country in the twentieth century to become Communist, although well before the century's end it had ceased to be a Communist state. The takeover, as we have seen, occurred as late as 1975, and the system lasted – as a different type of Communist regime from 1979 – until 1991. The Khmer Rouge, after being ousted from power, became once again an underground organization, but at the beginning of the 1990s the United Nations was able to oversee a peace process which led to elections in 1993 and a non-Communist Cambodia.

Afghanistan

The only country which might conceivably be regarded as Communist and which came to Communism later than Cambodia was Afghanistan. However, it was never considered socialist by the Soviet Union, and what Moscow meant by 'socialist' is very close to what, as I have already argued (especially in Chapter 6), it is less imprecise to call Communism. The Soviet involvement in Afghanistan was not, as was widely believed in Western capitals at the time, the beginning of a major new attempt at expansion, but part of a policy aimed at ensuring that Afghanistan would not acquire a regime hostile to the USSR. The seizure of power by Communists in Afghanistan came as a surprise to the Soviet leadership, who subsequently had the greatest difficulty in controlling the personal rivalries and bloodletting among their supposed close allies. Having failed to get their way by diplomatic means, the Soviet leaders made matters worse for themselves by invading their southern neighbour. The large-scale Soviet military incursion into Afghanistan failed, in the first instance, because of the strength and persistence of domestic Afghan opposition. It backfired also, in significant part, because of the assistance given to the coalition of oppositional forces by the United States, Saudi Arabia and Afghanistan's neighbour, Pakistan, employing all means short of overtly joining in the fighting. American support for Islamist guerrilla fighters – Osama Bin Laden among them – against the Soviet occupying forces was also, however, far from a success story in the long term. Indeed, the war in Afghanistan, with its aftermath of Taliban rule followed by further war, turned out to be one with *no* winners.

The Soviet leadership were quite relaxed about having a non-Communist and neutral Afghanistan, even when it was under monarchical rule from 1919 until 1973. (I happened to be in central Moscow at a moment in the late 1960s when the King of Afghanistan, Zahir Shah, was passing by in the course of a state visit. A rather bored rent-a-crowd of Muscovite spectators duly waved their government issue of welcoming Afghan flags.) When the king was deposed while he was out of the country in July 1973 by his prime minister (and cousin), General Mohammad Daoud, the Soviet Union had no hand in this conversion of Afghanistan into a republic. The new government continued to have unproblematic relations with its Soviet neighbour, although from 1976, on the advice of the Shah of Iran (whose own regime was overthrown just a few years later), Daoud began to take a tough line against potential opponents. These he identified as Communists and radical Islamists, and in 1977 he cracked down on the more extreme elements in both groups.[63]

The Afghan Communist party – the People's Democratic Party of Afghanistan (PDPA) – had been formed as recently as 1965 and was composed of two factions. The more radical of them, which became known as the Khalq (meaning 'the masses'), was headed by Nur Mohammad Taraki, whose closest colleague was Hafizullah Amin. The other group, called the Parcham (meaning 'flag'), was led by Babrak Karmal, an intellectual Marxist of aristocratic background. The Parchamis had been relatively supportive of Daoud, who had made a start on land reform.[64] The Soviet ambassador in the Afghan capital of Kabul, Alexander Puzanov, informed Moscow that the Parcham and the Khalq were almost like two different parties and that there was a great deal of animosity between them.[65] It was Karmal's faction which those in Moscow with responsibility for Afghanistan, whether within the CPSU Central Committee, the Ministry of Foreign Affairs or the KGB, favoured. Their policy during the period of Daoud's rule was a cautious one. They urged the Communists to achieve an accommodation with the Daoud government, so that their influence might be felt but without causing any violent rupture. It came as a complete surprise to Puzanov, and to his superiors in Moscow, when in April 1978 Daoud was assassinated in a coup successfully carried out by the Communist Khalq faction of Taraki and Amin. The Soviet ambassador reported, with some disapproval, that Taraki and Amin were prone to take ultra-leftist initiatives, although, on the brighter side, he noted that the new government would be 'more sympathetic toward the USSR'.[66] Indeed, in emphasizing the Khalq domination of the new regime, Amin stressed that not only would they be closer to the Soviet Union than the Daoud government, but that they would also be more faithful than the Parcham faction of the PDPA. In the event of disagreement between the leaders of the Khalq and 'Soviet comrades', Amin claimed, 'the Khalquis will say without a moment's hesitation that the Soviet comrades are right'. In contrast, he added, 'the Parchamis will say that *their* leaders are right'.[67]

In fact, relations soon soured both between Amin and Moscow and between Amin and his nominal superior, Taraki. The latter had become president and Amin prime minister. They began by excluding from power virtually the whole of the Parcham group, many of whom were imprisoned or killed. Karmal became Afghanistan's ambassador to Prague, a form of dignified exile. The Soviet Union, forced to deal with the Khalq faction because it held the reins of power in Kabul, supplied economic assistance and arms to the new government. However, the Afghan leaders, and, in particular, Taraki – who was Communist party first secretary as well as president – wanted more direct military assistance from the Soviet Union. They became conscious during their first year in power of the growing opposition to their regime. Taraki had an important meeting in Moscow on 20 March 1979 with the Chairman of the Soviet Council of Ministers Aleksey Kosygin, Foreign Minister Andrey Gromyko, Defence Minster Dmitry Ustinov and Central Committee International Department head Boris Ponomarev. Kosygin presided and made very plain his view that the

Afghan Communists should be able, through their own efforts, to defend their regime. More than once in the course of the meeting he held up to Taraki the example of the Vietnamese, who had seen off both the Americans and the Chinese.[68] Kosygin was firmly against direct involvement of Soviet troops in the fighting in Afghanistan, although ready to agree to the supply of arms and technical assistance. He went so far as to say to Taraki: 'Our common enemies are just waiting for the moment when Soviet troops appear in Afghanistan.'[69] While the reaction in Western capitals was not, in fact, one of joy when Soviet troops did move in later that same year, before long the evidence that the Soviet Union was getting bogged down in a morass analogous to the American experience in Vietnam evoked, especially in Washington, the reaction Kosygin predicted.

Taraki was reluctant to take Kosygin's 'no' for an answer, and since Kosygin was the senior Politburo member *most* opposed to direct Soviet military involvement in Afghanistan, he may have had hopes of persuading others. Taraki told Kosygin, Gromyko, Ustinov and Ponomarev that they badly needed helicopters and it would be even better if they came with pilots. Kosygin's response was to say that they could send specialists who would be able to service the helicopters, but 'of course' *not* fighting personnel, as he had already informed him.[70] Towards the end of the meeting Taraki tried Kosygin's patience further by asking if the Afghans could not be sent pilots and tank-drivers 'from other socialist countries'. Kosygin replied that he could not understand why this question about pilots and tank personnel kept being raised. It was quite unexpected and a very sharp political issue, and he doubted if the response of the 'socialist countries' would be any different.[71] Kosygin ended the meeting by questioning what he euphemistically called the 'personnel policy' of the Kabul regime, having in mind the number of people they had dismissed from office or thrown into prison. These included senior military officers and politicians. Kosygin said he didn't wish to interfere in the internal affairs of Afghanistan, but he could offer some advice on the basis of Soviet experience. Under Stalin, he told Taraki, many Soviet officers were imprisoned, but when war came Stalin released them and sent them to the front. Kosygin continued: 'These people showed themselves to be real heroes. Many of them rose to the highest positions of military command.'[72]

If Taraki seemed obtuse, it was not long before the Soviet leadership came to the conclusion that Amin was dangerous. The latter's promises of total loyalty to the Soviet Union were not matched by his actions. Some Soviet leaders, and in particular the KGB chief, Yury Andropov, began to fear that Amin would 'do a Sadat' on Moscow.[73] This was a reference to the change of direction taken by Egypt, which, during the presidency of Gamal

Abdel Nasser, had leaned towards the Soviet Union, whereas his successor, Anwar Sadat, moved closer to the United States. The Soviet leadership continued to be alarmed at the scale of arrests being carried out on Amin's orders and the extent to which he was alienating more and more groups instead of building a broader coalition. KGB officers in Kabul in the late summer of 1979 made clear to Taraki that good relations with the Soviet Union required the arrest of Amin. That was taken a step further when Amin was invited to Taraki's residence on 14 September for a meeting attended also by Soviet representatives. Taraki's presidential guards opened fire in an attempt to kill Amin. Two of the prime minister's assistants died, but Amin escaped. He had enough military units loyal to him to remove Taraki from power and to have him arrested. Amin appointed himself head of the Communist party. Taraki was executed in prison on 9 October, with Amin turning a deaf ear to Soviet pleas for clemency.[74]

The rule of Amin, who had become a Marxist while a student in the United States, was by this time much more problematical for the Soviet leadership than the docile Afghan monarchy had been. The Afghan leader's aggressive policies were creating enemies, including militant Islamic ones, inspired by the Iranian revolution which had taken place earlier in the same year. The deteriorating situation inside Afghanistan led to the fateful Soviet decision to intervene militarily and to replace Amin with the Communist who would have been their original first choice as leader, Babrak Karmal. The prime movers in urging military action were the Minister of Defence Dmitry Ustinov and KGB Chairman Andropov, but Foreign Minister Andrey Gromyko also gave his approval and the head of the International Department of the Central Committee, Boris Ponomarev, acquiesced. By 1979 the General Secretary of the Soviet Communist Party, Leonid Brezhnev, was in poor health and he was brought into the decision-making process only at a late stage. His agreement was, nevertheless, still crucial. Brezhnev, a cautious political actor, was persuaded that the conflict would be short-lived. He went along with the advice of his senior colleagues, and the decision to invade was accordingly presented to the CPSU Politburo as a fait accompli. Kosygin had remained strongly against sending a large Soviet fighting force to Afghanistan, but he was not present at the Politburo meeting which rubber-stamped the decision, and so the usual unanimity was maintained.[75]

The Soviet invasion meant that a second Afghan Communist president was executed within the space of three months in late 1979 – and again by fellow Communists. Taraki had perished in October and Amin was killed in December. The Soviet army moved in large numbers into Afghanistan in late December, along with more than 700 members of KGB special forces.

It was the KGB troops who attacked Amin's residence, overcame the resistance of his guards, and killed the Afghan leader, along with a number of his relatives and aides. The following day Karmal announced that he was now prime minister and also general secretary of the PDPA.[76] In a five-page document laconically headed 'On the events in Afghanistan 27–28 December 1979', Andropov, Gromyko, Ustinov and Ponomarev reported to the Soviet leadership on the change of government in Kabul they had successfully brought about. Amin, they said, had 'deceived the party and the people'. In the period since September alone, more than 600 members of the Communist party and military personnel had been eliminated without trial. What was going on was nothing less than 'the liquidation of the party'.[77] What was now occurring was the formation of a new government and revolutionary council, whose composition would include 'representatives of the former groups "Parcham" and "Khalk", representatives of the military and non-party people'.[78]

Karmal was described by Andropov and his colleagues in that report as 'one of the best prepared leaders of the PDPA from a theoretical point of view', as someone who was sincerely sympathetic to the Soviet Union, and as a man who possessed 'high authority among the party masses and in the country'.[79] Nevertheless, initially Karmal was a good deal less ecumenical in his appointments policy than his Soviet mentors wished him to be. Most of the other leading members of the government came from his party group and had been in exile along with him. He followed the example of his dead rivals by arresting many Communists who had been in the wrong faction. Having been put in power by Soviet arms, he was, however, more dependent on Moscow than Taraki and Amin. Although Karmal's predecessors had subsequently needed Soviet economic aid and weapons, they had at least seized power in April 1978 of their own accord. On Soviet insistence, Karmal had to release most of the Communists he had arrested and, for the sake of party unity, bring a number of them into the new government.[80]

The Afghan regime, though led by people who regarded themselves as Communists, had certainly not succeeded in creating a Communist system prior to the Soviet invasion, and it was, if anything, even less successful in doing so after it. Normally a Communist party, after coming to power, was able to increase party membership massively. In Afghanistan, as a leading specialist on the conflict has observed: 'it would have taken a miracle to resurrect Afghan Communism' because the latest round of factional infighting had destroyed 'most party members' belief in the building of a Communist Party as a viable project'.[81] The regime's survival depended heavily on the Soviet military. In the first half of the 1980s, around 100,000 Soviet troops at any one time were caught in a stalemate in Afghanistan.

At least 25,000 of them were killed and over a million Afghans perished in the conflict.[82] The Mujahedin opposition to the Soviet-supported leadership, based both on ethnic and religious identity, time and again retook territory which had been captured by Soviet troops. The supply of increasingly sophisticated weapons from the United States enhanced the firepower of the Afghan resistance to the Soviet occupying forces and raised the political costs of the operation for the Soviet leadership. The war was becoming more unpopular in the USSR, especially among parents of sons approaching military age. However, public opinion, while not totally negligible as a political factor in the post-Stalin Soviet Union, came low in the order of considerations of the pre-perestroika Politburo. Therefore, although some of the growing discontent with the war in Soviet society could be likened to the trend of opinion in the United States during the Vietnam War, public opinion did not have the same impact on high politics. Neither under Brezhnev nor under his short-lived successors Andropov and Konstantin Chernenko did the Politburo contemplate changing course. The decision to withdraw Soviet forces from Afghanistan was taken by Mikhail Gorbachev very early in his general secretaryship in 1985 but not made public at that time. It will be discussed briefly in Chapter 24 in the context of the links between domestic reform and the 'new thinking' on foreign policy which characterized the Soviet perestroika.

Alongside the fratricide, the Afghan Communists had some achievements to their credit. Even the divided Taraki–Amin leadership in 1978–79 tackled the problems of widespread illiteracy and of the gross gender inequality in educational opportunities. At that time only 5 per cent of girls attended school, as compared with 30 per cent of boys. The Communist government granted women equal legal rights and tried to ban forced marriage. They also attempted to introduce land redistribution.[83] The changes in education and the measures affecting the rights of women were popular in the towns but resisted in the countryside. They led to clashes with fundamentalist clergy and the beginning of fierce resistance to the secularization intrinsic to Communist rule. It was the strength of that backlash, as well as the internecine conflict within the ranks of the PDPA, which brought about the Soviet Union's ill-fated intervention.

Non-ruling Communist Parties in Asia

Elsewhere in Asia there have been Communist parties which have attracted more support than the PDPA in Afghanistan, but – with the exception of Nepal in the twenty-first century – they have not come close to success at national level. Nevertheless, in two of Asia's most important democracies, the Communists have performed better in elections than their counterparts in the Americas or in most of Western Europe. The Communist Party in India, while never coming close to power nationally, has governed in two of the regions of this federal state – the second most populous country in the world. At various times the Communists have been in control in Kerala and, from the mid-1970s and up to the present, they have enjoyed over-whelming majority support in West Bengal. The party which had such success, usually in coalition with other leftist parties, emerged from a split in the old CPI in 1964 between pro-Soviet members and Maoists. The former took the name Communist Party of India (Marxist) – or CPI(M) – and it is they who have had these significant regional successes. Their electoral support has come from the peasantry. As elsewhere in Asia, land redistrib-ution has been part of the Communists' appeal.

Just as Communist parties in Western Europe generally lost out to socialist parties of a social democratic type, so in India, the CPI – and subsequently the CPI(M) – was unable to compete nationally with the party which had led the struggle for independence and which had a generally leftist political orientation. In the 1930s Mahatma Gandhi's civil disobedience campaign against the British won overwhelming support for his Indian National Congress, and the party which emerged from this movement, the Indian Congress Party, consistently eclipsed the Communists at national level. There has been, though, wide regional variation. Of particular significance is the fact that in a democracy such as India, Communist rule locally has not been accompanied by the massive disadvantages of a Communist monopoly of power. In West Bengal, along with land redistribution, came security of tenure for the peasantry – not forced collectivization, which would be impossible in a genuine democracy. Increased spending on health and education, espe-cially in Kerala, also enhanced Communist standing. Of the two most funda-mental political attributes of a Communist system – *democratic centralism* and the 'leading role' (*monopoly of power*) of the party – only the first has been applicable in India, and practised by the Communist Party and its subsidiary organizations in the regions where it has governed. The CPI(M) has, indeed, generally maintained the strictly hierarchical organization and rigorous disci-pline characteristic of democratic centralism. In the Indian political system, this was not, and could not have been, accompanied by either a monopoly of power or a monopoly over the sources of information. Where the CPI has gained power locally, it has been in competitive elections, and even the local media – and, naturally, the national media – have been far from uncrit-ical of their performance. Thus, there is a qualitative difference between Communist government locally, or even regionally, and a Communist *system*.

The other Communist party which has performed respectably in elections in Asia is the Communist Party of Japan (JCP). As early as 1949, after it became a legal party in the post-war period, it secured just under 10 per cent of the vote and thirty-five seats in the House of Representatives, the lower and more powerful parliamentary chamber. That support dropped to much less than 5 per cent throughout most of the 1950s and 1960s – the coldest years of the Cold War. However, between 1972 and 1980 the party's vote exceeded 10 per cent in three successive elections to the House of Representatives. This was a period in which the JCP had distanced itself from Soviet policy. In outlook it had become close to the 'Eurocommunist' parties (discussed in Chapter 23). Together they examined ways of making a *democratic* transition from capitalism to socialism.[84] Compared with the Asian Communist parties which came to power, the Japanese Communists were not only more like their European counterparts (by the late 1960s, at least) but also more in line with what Marx would have expected. They were operating in an advanced industrial society and their greatest strength has been in the towns. Unlike the Asian Communist parties which took power, the JCP has had little appeal or success in agricultural areas. (Its support in the early twenty-first century is much diminished. The JCP won only nine seats in the elections to the lower house in 2005.)[85] In other flourishing democracies in Asia, such as Australia and New Zealand, the Communist parties have been a negligible electoral force, although in Australia for a time Communists held leading positions in a number of trade unions. Their hard work and organizational skills made them effective challengers to weak or corrupt non-Communist union leaders in the 1930s and in the earlier post-war years.

The largest Communist party in the world outside Communist-ruled countries was in Indonesia. It had been gaining in influence in the first half of the 1960s under the rule of President Ahmed Sukarno, a leading figure in the non-aligned group of nations, alongside Tito, Nasser and the Indian prime minister Jawaharlal Nehru. Sukarno was, however, more indulgent to the Communist Party than Nehru and much more so than Nasser. Although Nasser had good relations with the Soviet Union, he took a tough line against Egypt's own Communists. Sukarno, however, not only leaned more towards the Soviet Union than the West in his 'non-alignment', but was protective of the Indonesian Communist Party (PKI). Rhetorically, his policy came close to that of the Communists when on Indonesian Independence Day in August 1965 he said that Indonesia was only 'at the national-democratic stage' of development, but the time would come when it would 'build socialism'. Land in the ownership of landlords would be 'redistributed among the people'.[86] Earlier that year, Sukarno endorsed the claim of the PKI that they had three million party members. He added that the youth organization had another three million and that there were an additional twenty million Communist sympathisers.[87] Since the total Indonesian population was around 105 million at the time, this suggested that at least a quarter of adults were either affiliated to or supported the Communists.

The main stumbling block to further advance on the part of the PKI was the Indonesian army. Sukarno wielded extensive power within a system which he called 'guided democracy'. It rested, however, on an uneasy coalition – or rather 'peaceful co-existence', which was not to last – between the Communists and the armed forces. The military elite controlled not only a large fighting force but also the country's economic spoils. Either personally or through their family ties, they reaped the profits from the country's state industries. Accordingly, their nationalism, anti-Communism and economic self-interest were in perfect harmony.[88] To overcome the obstacle which the higher ranks of the military presented, the Communists urged Sukarno to introduce a system of political commissars in the armed forces and also to form a force of volunteers.[89] The latter would have been the equivalent of the 'workers' militias' the Communists created during the power seizures in Eastern Europe. Sukarno hesitated, and while he did so, Communist sympathisers in the armed forces in September 1965 abducted and killed six of the most senior army generals. The army, with General Hadji Suharto leading the way, retaliated ruthlessly, and they were supported by millions of previously suppressed Muslims. There was a massacre of Communists and those deemed to be sympathetic to them. According to Amnesty International, half a million people were killed. Other estimates put the figure at a million.[90] One of the world's largest Communist parties virtually ceased to exist. Sukarno was not deposed at once, but his position was greatly weakened. By 1967 he was replaced by General Suharto as national leader. In the following year Suharto became president. For the next thirty years he ruled Indonesia as a corrupt and nepotistic dictatorship, ameliorated only by the achievement of substantial economic growth.

South Africa

The most serious Communist Party on the African continent has been that of South Africa (the CPSA). Like the party in Japan, it recruited its members primarily in the urban areas. Unlike the Japanese party, it was illegal for the greater part of the second half of the twentieth century. In contradistinction from Japan, the South African Communist Party also had the 'advantage', as well as the disadvantage, of being opposed to a racist and manifestly unjust regime. The positive side of that for the party was that it was able to attract recruits who saw in the Communist Party the most viable radical alternative to the apartheid regime. The party remained small, but it attracted talented people who were to have an influence within the main opposition movement, the African National Congress (ANC), out of all proportion to their numbers. The party's strength as an organization lay also in the fact that it brought together people of different ethnic and social backgrounds in a common struggle. The Communist Party contained members not only of the black African majority, but also Indians, 'coloureds' of mixed heritage, and whites. The last category included a disproportionately large number of Jews.[91] The most prominent, and highly respected, party member of Jewish origin was Joe Slovo. Like many of the Jewish Communists, he was of East European background, in Slovo's case Lithuanian. Whereas for the African National Congress the basic task was to replace white minority rule by majority rule, the Communists saw this as being only part of a more fundamental class struggle.

Members of the Communist Party of South Africa had, since 1950, acquired plenty of experience of working underground. When there was a warrant for the arrest of Nelson Mandela at the beginning of the 1960s, CPSA members helped him to move from town to town, holding clandestine meetings over many months. This was done so effectively that some of the mass media took to calling Mandela the Black Pimpernel, a reference to the fictional character, the Scarlet Pimpernel, who evaded arrest during the French Revolution.[92] Communists were able to work within the ANC, for they were equally dedicated to ending apartheid, and their experience of operating in secret, together with their organizational skills, were valuable for the broader movement. It was partly thanks to South Africa's white Communists – though also, of course, to strong support from social democrats and liberals (as well as Communists) abroad – that the ANC were not tempted to think of all whites as the enemy.

In spite of that, in the late 1960s, the 1970s and the 1980s the International Department of the Communist Party of the Soviet Union was more comfortable with the ANC than with the CPSA. With Nelson Mandela in prison by then, Oliver Tambo led the ANC which had its headquarters in exile in Zambia. Through the Soviet embassy, there was close Soviet contact with Tambo and with other leading figures in the ANC.[93] In the 1970s the Africa specialists within the International Department of the CPSU suspected Joe Slovo of having Eurocommunist sympathies. They also saw as a disadvantage, rather than an advantage, the fact that some whites were prominent within the party leadership (as well as, to a lesser extent, within the ANC).[94]

The view from Moscow was that the successful overthrow of the apartheid regime depended on Africans very clearly playing the leading role in the movement for change. The strong Communist influence within the African National Congress did not necessarily make for greater radicalism within the ANC. While committed to ending apartheid as early as possible, the Communist members were often quite cautious political actors. When Nelson Mandela in June 1961 decided that the time had come to move from a policy of non-violence to armed struggle against the South African regime, there was a mixed reaction from the Communists. He had difficulty persuading Moses Kotane, a secretary of the Communist Party and a member of the ANC executive, of the need for this. He told Kotane that his 'opposition was like the Communist Party in Cuba under Batista. The party had insisted that the appropriate conditions had not yet arrived . . . Castro did not wait, he acted – and he triumphed.'[95] Nevertheless, Communists became integral members of the organization Spear of the Nation, which Mandela chaired and which set out to commit acts of sabotage to discourage foreign investment in the apartheid regime. Mandela, Joe Slovo and Walter Sisulu, the leading figures in Spear of the Nation, argued that the South African state was illegitimate and rested on violence and that they had exhausted purely non-violent attempts to overthrow it.[96]

The nature of the regime in South Africa made it possible to attract into the Communist Party people who would have been highly unlikely to join the party in a democracy. If that was an advantage for the CPSA, it does not alter the fact that being a Communist in South Africa also had some serious disadvantages. They included the threat of imprisonment or assassination. The Suppression of Communism Act in 1950 made the party illegal, and went much further. As Nelson Mandela wrote:

> The act outlawed the Communist Party of South Africa and made it a crime, punishable by a maximum of ten years' imprisonment, to be a member of the party or to further the aims of communism. But the bill was drafted in such a broad way that it outlawed all but the mildest protest against the state, deeming it a crime to advocate any doctrine that promoted 'political, industrial, social or economic change within the Union by the promotion of disturbance or disorder'.[97]

In his speech to the South African court in 1964 at the trial which saw Mandela sentenced to life imprisonment – he served twenty-seven years of that sentence, for more than eighteen of them on Robben Island – he had the opportunity to define his relationship to the Communist Party. Mandela told the court that he was not a Communist and had always regarded himself as an African patriot. Furthermore, whereas the Communist Party sought to emphasize class differences, the ANC sought harmony. He disagreed with the Communists' dismissal of parliamentary institutions. He told the court that he regarded the British parliament as 'the most democratic institution in the world' and that he admired the separation of powers and the independence of the judiciary which were prominent features of the political system of the United States.[98] He explained to a court which was very unreceptive to such an explanation why, nevertheless, he and other African politicians co-operated with and had friendly relations with Communists:

> Theoretical differences amongst those fighting against oppression are a luxury we cannot afford at this stage. What is more, for many decades communists were the only political group in South Africa who were prepared to treat Africans as human beings and their equals; who were prepared to eat with us; talk with us, live with and work with us. Because of this, there are many Africans who, today, tend to equate freedom with communism.[99]

Communists were a significant element in the ANC coalition which ultimately came to power in South Africa under Mandela's leadership. Their presence as an integral part of the African National Congress had made it easier for successive South African white minority governments to play the anti-Communist card against the African majority. It had also made a number of Western governments hesitate to support the ANC both because of their tacit acquiescence in armed struggle and because, in the context of the Cold War, they feared that they might thereby be embracing a future Communist South Africa. The National Party government in South Africa increasingly fell back on emphasizing the Communist threat as governments and public opinion elsewhere became unwilling to accept a racist justification of minority rule.[100]

Although it is moving beyond the period with which this chapter is mainly concerned, the changed international context by the end of the 1980s is crucial to an understanding of change in South Africa itself. What happened in the Soviet Union and Eastern Europe in the late 1980s had a profound effect on both the ANC and the more pragmatic members of the South African government. The Soviet leadership by this time was not interested in supporting armed struggle anywhere in Africa, and this had its effect on ANC thinking. Equally, the pluralization of the Soviet political system, the vastly improved East–West relations, and the peaceful transition of the countries of Eastern Europe away from Communism made invocation of the 'Communist threat' an anachronism. On 2 February 1990, the South African president, F.W. de Klerk, announced to the South African parliament the lifting of the bans on the ANC and the Communist Party and the freeing of political prisoners. By the time South Africa had its first democratic elections in 1994, which brought the ANC into government, the world had moved on still further. There was no longer a Soviet Union or a single Communist regime in Europe. Thus, the issue of whether South Africa might become Communist was also confined to the past. In the ANC government which was formed in the 1990s, Communists of long standing – including Joe Slovo, as well as Mandela's deputy and eventual successor as President of South Africa, Thabo Mbeki – played an important role. However, neither the system nor the policies the government pursued were remotely Communist. Whereas one of the ANC's staunch foreign allies, Fidel Castro, continued to swim against the tide of events elsewhere in the Communist world, especially in Europe, South Africa's most prominent Communists had swum with them.

The comparative strength, albeit for most of the time as an underground movement, of the Communist Party in South Africa was very much a product of the racist social order. In a country as industrialized as South Africa, a social democratic party on the European model might have been expected to develop and flourish. However, the reactionary and repressive nature of the South African regime made such moderate leftist opposition impossible. People who might have belonged to a democratic socialist party elsewhere joined the Communist Party and exerted real influence within the ANC. Although the South African Communists went through many of the intellectual contortions required of Communists who were basically loyal to the political line emanating from Moscow, their primary focus was on the problems of South Africa. While Communists elsewhere in the world had usually done far more to extinguish than promote democracy, in South Africa they played a significant part in the acquisition of democratic rights by the majority of the population. Along the way, some of them paid a heavy price for that endeavour.*

* A party activist, Ruth First, who was married to Joe Slovo (the latter for many years General Secretary of the South African Communist Party and, late in his life, a member of Nelson Mandela's government), was killed in exile in Mozambique in August 1982 by a letter bomb sent by agents of the South African regime. Slovo's comparatively young successor as General Secretary of the CPSA, Chris Hani, who might have played an important role in a post-apartheid South Africa, was assassinated by a Polish immigrant member of an extreme white supremacist organization in 1993. This was a deliberate attempt to provoke mob violence by those who aimed at all costs to disrupt the process of negotiation and reconciliation which was leading to majority rule. Mandela played a crucial part in ensuring that calm prevailed. See Mandela, *The Long Walk to Freedom*, pp. 728–30.

States of 'Socialist Orientation' in Africa

For a variety of reasons, including the way the African continent was originally carved up by the imperial powers, with little regard for ethnic boundaries and cultural communities, to say that pluralist democracy did not flourish in Africa during the twentieth century would be a gross understatement. In the first half of the century most of the continent was under colonial rule. But after decades of independence (varying between one and four), in 1989 only three out of fifty African states had sustained competitive elections among different parties over a lengthy period: Senegal, Botswana and Gambia. The great majority of countries were either one-party states or military dictatorships.[101] The regimes whose leaders had aspirations to build a Soviet-style 'socialism' – most notably Mozambique, Angola and Ethiopia – but who did not succeed in creating a Communist system, turned out to be both oppressive and inefficient. They were hardly more so, however, than a number of other clearly non-Marxist African dictatorships whose leaders were embraced in European capitals and in Washington as stalwarts of the 'free world'. The fighting of the Cold War by proxy in Africa, especially in the 1970s and the first half of the 1980s, added greatly to the sufferings of the people who lived in the countries concerned. Yet it achieved neither the ideological aims of the Soviet Union nor those of the United States if the goal of the former was taken to be the establishment of Communist systems and the goal of the latter the creation of democracies. In fact, for each of the 'superpowers', loyalty to *their* side in the Cold War counted, in the final analysis, for more than ideology or the form of government. Thus, the Soviet Union had good relations with Nasser's Egypt and the far more repressive regime of Saddam Hussein in Iraq, although in both countries Communists were either imprisoned or, in the case of Iraq, more often executed.

Nevertheless, when leaders in a few African countries appeared to have been seriously influenced by Marxism-Leninism, some of the aged members of the Soviet leadership in Moscow of the 1970s and early 1980s took encouragement from this. Not only had the Soviet Union attracted allies, but even the ideas were apparently winning some support. 'You see', said the Soviet leader, Leonid Brezhnev, speaking within a narrow party circle, 'even in the jungles they want to live in Lenin's way!'[102] Within the Soviet establishment there was, however, debate about what significance should be attached to countries such as Mozambique, Angola and Ethiopia apparently being eager to follow the Soviet ideological example. At no time were these countries counted as 'socialist' even by the Soviet leadership, within which the

International Department of the Central Committee had primary responsibility for maintaining links with them. The term that was invented for these countries – and for South Yemen, in the Middle East, which for a time received a large quantity of Soviet aid on the strength of purporting to be Marxist-Leninist – was that of 'states of socialist orientation'.

But within Soviet think-tanks there were sceptics who thought that even the term 'socialist orientation' was going too far. While most officials were ready to welcome support for the Soviet Union wherever it might arise, there were specialists who argued that some of the Third World countries in which leaders were talking about 'building socialism' were wildly premature in such aspirations. No good, they believed, would come of it; these countries should be applying themselves to building capitalism as a necessary prelude to socialism. While not directly attacking the party leadership, such nonconformists within the Soviet establishment were arguing against taking at face value self-proclaimed Marxist-Leninists and 'builders of socialism' in backward Third World countries. The basis of their critique was that Marx was right! The countries in question, whose very statehood was in several cases under threat, were not ready to 'build socialism'.[103]

No Communist system was ever established in Africa, but it is undoubtedly true that a number of African leaders were influenced by Marxism and some also by Leninism. Even a number of entirely non-Marxist African leaders, running authoritarian regimes, picked up some tips from Soviet methods of maintaining political control. There had been earlier attempts to create what was called 'African socialism' – by, for example, Kwame Nkrumah in Ghana and Julius Nyerere in Tanzania – but though they took on board just enough ideas from the Communist world to suffer from some of the defects of Soviet-type systems, they did not aspire to recreate such systems on the African continent. In Mozambique, Angola and Ethiopia, in contrast, leaders laid claim to such an aspiration, and received Soviet aid on the strength of it. In Mozambique the guerrilla movement Frelimo, led by Samora Machel, which had fought for independence from Portugal, in the 1970s espoused Marxist-Leninist ideas, nationalized plantations and businesses, and sought to introduce central economic planning. They also denounced religion and the traditional authority of chiefs. The result was a disastrous civil war. Three years after Machel's death in an air crash, with Soviet support drying up, Frelimo in 1989 renounced its Marxist-Leninist ideology.[104]

In the civil war in Angola, the Soviet Union and, still more enthusiastically, Cuba backed the Popular Movement for the Liberation of Angola (MPLA). Aghostino Neto, the MPLA leader, was impressed by the amount of economic aid and military equipment the Soviet Union was willing to provide – to the extent that the MPLA became the second most important Soviet ally in the region after the ANC.[105] The performance of Cuban troops was to be more impressive still. The United States, from the mid-1970s, stepped up its funding for the MPLA's main opponents, the National Front for the Liberation of Angola (FNLA) and also for a third group, UNITA, which had a following in the largest tribe in Angola. Both of these anti-MPLA and, by extension, anti-Soviet movements were supported with aid also from the Chinese.[106] The South African apartheid government joined in the struggle (on the same side as the USA and China), and it was an important boost for the morale of the ANC in South Africa when Cuban soldiers, mainly of African descent, helped the MPLA defeat the better-armed South African forces.[107] The MPLA emerged as the dominant grouping, and in late 1975 Cuban troops stopped several thousand South African regular soldiers in their tracks. The Organization of African Unity gave their official recognition to Neto's government in 1976, and a year later the MPLA declared themselves to be a Marxist-Leninist party. They needed the presence of Cuban troops and Soviet aid, however, to maintain even the semblance of power through a period of further turmoil which lasted until peace accords for south-western Africa were signed at the United Nations in 1988 by South Africa, Angola and Cuba.

The United States, which was also a party to the discussions, had reluctantly to agree to the participation of Cuba because the South African government by this time wanted a settlement. The Cubans had repulsed another major South African military offensive into Angola in 1987. There were as many as 55,000 Cuban soldiers at a time in Angola, and over a period of fifteen years some 300,000 Cuban combatants served there, in addition to almost 50,000 Cuban civilians, including doctors.[108] As Fidel Castro was to claim, this was a unique case of a Third World country, on its own initiative, playing a decisive role in another country outside its own geographic region.[109] By 1988, however, the Soviet Union was no longer willing to underwrite economically either Cuban revolutionary zeal in Africa or the cost of civil war in African countries. Gorbachev had replaced the veteran head of the International Department of the CPSU, Boris Ponomarev, in 1986 with Anatoly Dobrynin, who had for a quarter of a century been Soviet ambassador to Washington. Well aware of how Soviet intervention in Africa had complicated the task of improving relations with the United States, Dobrynin, while critical of some aspects of Gorbachev's 'New Thinking' on foreign policy, was fully supportive of his new Third World policy.

Soon after the overthrow and murder of the Emperor Haile Selassie, in the Ethiopian revolution of 1974, the leader who came to the fore was an army officer who proclaimed himself to be a Marxist-Leninist, Mengistu Haile Mariam. He first achieved prominence at the time of the revolution when he demonstrated his ruthlessness by ordering the execution of around sixty senior officials from Haile Selassie's regime. He also showed no compunction about killing intellectuals who had supported the revolution and members of rival factions. When Ethiopia came under attack by Somalia, Mengistu was saved from defeat by Soviet military hardware and the efforts of some 17,000 Cuban troops. The egalitarianism of the Cuban revolution was, however, being put to strange use, for Mengistu by 1978 was presiding from the same ornate chair in which Haile Selassie had sat and had come to be regarded even by former revolutionary allies as the 'new Emperor'.[110] Not only did the Communist party not play the leading role in Ethiopia. There was no attempt even to found such a party until ten years after the revolution – in 1984. And by that time Mengistu had killed most of the Marxists in the country. In the same year Ethiopia suffered a calamitous famine for which Mengistu's policies were at least as responsible as the drought. Requisitioning grain to feed his army, who were fighting rebels, favouring inefficient state farms over peasant farming, and employing scorched-earth tactics against rebel fighters contributed massively to the catastrophe.[111] From the late 1970s there were serious reservations even within the ranks of Soviet officialdom about continued involvement with regimes such as Ethiopia's, but a Politburo majority continued to support this element of Cold War struggle until the second half of the 1980s. Then, with Gorbachev the most decisive voice on foreign policy, the aid dried up. When Mengistu made a desperate appeal for more military assistance, he was given very little. Having been briefed on Mengistu's human rights record, Gorbachev rapidly developed a distaste for him. Africa did not bulk large in Gorbachev's foreign policy, but, to the extent it did, he advocated, whether in Afghanistan, Ethiopia or South Africa, a policy of national reconciliation.[112]

19

The 'Prague Spring'

The 'Prague Spring' of 1968 was in some respects a delayed reaction to Khrushchev's Secret Speech to the Twentieth Congress of the CPSU in 1956 and to his further attacks on Stalin at the Twenty-Second Congress in 1961. In other ways, it was a precursor of the Soviet perestroika. It had an importance greater than is generally realized today – even by most citizens of the Czech Republic. Its significance has several different strands. One is that what became known as the Prague Spring was the culmination of a reform movement inside the Communist Party of Czechoslovakia which got under way five or six years earlier. To a greater extent than in Poland and Hungary in 1956, this was a major reformist current within the Communist Party itself. It demonstrated that intra-party developments could produce change sufficiently fundamental as to lead to military intervention by other Communist states, led by the Soviet Union. This, for some observers, raised the question: what would happen should reform gather momentum within the CPSU itself, for who would intervene to put a stop to a 'Moscow Spring'? The answer, of course, was that no other country would or could do to the Soviet Union what the Soviet leadership did to Hungary in 1956 and was to do again – in Czechoslovakia in August 1968. This was, however, a question rarely posed. The conventional assumption in the West – and, indeed, overwhelmingly in the USSR itself – was that a 'Moscow Spring', analogous to the Prague Spring, was too fanciful a notion to be entertained even as a hypothetical possibility.[1]

The relevance of Czechoslovakia in the 1960s for the Soviet Union in the 1980s lay in the fact that there were people of serious reformist disposition in both parties and that a change of top leader – from a conservative Communist to an open-minded moderate in the case of Czechoslovakia in 1968, and from a Communist bureaucrat to an energetic reformer in the case of the Soviet Union in 1985, changed the balance of forces within these ruling parties. So great was the institutional power placed in the hands of a Communist Party leader that the emergence of a general secretary with an *open mind* also *opened doors*, including ones which had been firmly closed for decades. An early effect of the reform movement within Czech and

Slovak Communism (with more emphasis on democratization in the Czech lands of Bohemia and Moravia and more emphasis on greater national autonomy in Slovakia), together with its crushing by Soviet military intervention, was to stimulate some of the most important West European Communist parties to embrace a more reformist programme and to cease to follow slavishly Soviet ideological guidance. That movement, which I discuss in a section of Chapter 23, was known as 'Eurocommunism'. Within the Soviet Union and Eastern Europe, the immediate effect was the opposite. The fact that the Soviet Union, with the participation of the armies of its East European Warsaw Pact partners, put a stop to the Prague Spring set back the progress of reform throughout the entire bloc. The limits of the possible had been defined and it was now clear that the Communist Party in Czechoslovakia had transgressed them. Thus, in the Soviet Union and elsewhere in Eastern Europe, reformers in the 1970s and the first half of the 1980s had to be very careful if they were not to be tarred with the Czech 'revisionist' or even 'counterrevolutionary' brush.

Stimuli to Reform

If we divide states into those in which Communists came to power through their own efforts and those who were essentially put into government by external forces – most commonly those of the Soviet Union – Czechoslovakia is a slightly ambiguous case. There were no Soviet troops in the country when the Communists seized full power in 1948. Stalin took a proprietorial interest in Czechoslovakia, but, as was suggested in Chapter 9, it is unlikely that he would have invaded the country in the late 1940s had Czech politicians, including Czech Communists, resisted the political and psychological pressure from Moscow to create a Soviet-type system. The USSR, in the immediate aftermath of the devastation it suffered during World War Two, was far weaker, militarily and economically, than the United States. A good deal, in this hypothetical case, would have depended also on the resolution of the Western powers. Many Czechs, ever since the Munich Agreement of 1938, had concluded that the West had very limited interest in what kind of regime would be foisted on them.[2] The evidence gathered by the Czech security police in the immediate post-war years – with the Ministry of the Interior under firm Communist control from 1945 – was that the United States, Britain and France would do nothing to prevent the Communists bypassing the ballot-box in order to gain full power.[3]

At any rate, Gottwald and the Czech Communist leadership did succeed in staging their successful coup. Thereafter, members of the Czechoslovak party continued to believe that they had made their own peaceful revolution. Soviet guidance had always been important, however, and in the Twentieth and Twenty-Second Congresses of the CPSU it took a different form. Stimulated into more independent thought by Khrushchev's revelations at these congresses of 1956 and 1961, party intellectuals in Czechoslovakia began to blame their past and present leaderships for having voluntarily adopted the Stalinist Soviet model. They believed that there had been a choice in the second half of the 1940s and that they had a choice once again in the second half of the 1960s. When, in early 1965, I made the first of five study-visits to Czechoslovakia when it was under Communist rule, many party intellectuals were already going out of their way to emphasize how different their country, with its more democratic traditions, was from the Soviet Union. Copying Soviet institutions had, therefore, been a bad mistake.

There were veteran Communists who were to be found in the ranks of the radical reformers in 1968, among them three who were elevated to the Politburo or Secretariat of the Central Committee, František Kriegel, Josef Smrkovský and Václav Slavík (of whom the boldest was Kriegel). However, the political generation of those who came of age just after the Second World War played an especially active part in promoting change. As one of them put it, with just a little poetic licence: 'We were all twenty in 1948, so we were all forty in 1968.'⁴ It was not those who had in 1948 jumped on the Communist bandwagon for career reasons, sometimes moving rapidly from another political party to the Communists, but the people who had sincerely believed that they were about to build a new world who were in the vanguard of the Prague Spring. They were not only the most disillusioned with what had been constructed but also the most determined to do something to change matters. With more self-criticism than was strictly merited, the young woman Communist of 1948, cited above, said to me in Prague in 1969: 'We helped to get the country into this mess. The least we could do was help get it out again.'⁵ Many of those who in their youth in the early post-war years had voluntarily and enthusiastically embraced Communism believed that they were masters of their own destiny. This enabled them to embrace bolder political reform in 1968 than their counterparts in the Communist parties of Poland and Hungary. In August of that same year they were to discover the limitations on their sovereignty which Poles and Hungarians already knew and which Czech non-Communists had long assumed. Perceptions in politics are, however, crucially important, and the fact that Czech Communist intellectuals *believed* that radical political change was possible *made* it possible – for eight months.

If it was Khrushchev's boldness which shook the more reflective members of the Communist Party of Czechoslovakia into reassessing the post-war years, many of them drew conclusions in the 1960s that were not to be drawn in the Soviet Union until the 1980s. Czech reformist party intellectuals were dissatisfied with the explanation that the state-sponsored terror associated with Stalinism could be attributed simply, or even mainly, to the moral deficiencies of one man, Josif Stalin. By the mid-1960s they were raising questions about the political system which had allowed Stalin to get away with murder (in the most literal sense). Questions also began to be raised, even more widely, about the economic system. Pavel Eisler, a Czech economist who did not live to see the Prague Spring, observed in 1965: 'The greatest stimulus to change is failure.'[6] He had in mind specifically the economic failure which Czechoslovakia had recently been experiencing. In 1963 the country had a negative growth rate of 2.2 per cent. To the qualitative deficiencies of Czech and Slovak industry, which the party had learned to live with, was now added failure even in quantitative terms.

An important outcome was that economists were given a greater freedom of debate among themselves. Once this concession had been granted, it became easier for other specialists – including sociologists, historians and academic lawyers – to extend the limits of the possible within their own disciplines. The main arguments among the economists centred on the extent to which market forces could be introduced into a reformed economic mechanism. A large team headed by the Director of the Institute of Economics, Ota Šik, was formed at the beginning of 1964. Even their compromise conclusions were too radical to be welcome to the party leadership and to the first secretary, Antonín Novotný, in particular. But since economic failure had become a fact of life, a modest reform of the economic system was accepted in principle in 1965. It increased material incentives and aimed to introduce a three-tier price system, divided into different categories. Thus, there would be a number of fixed prices determined centrally; prices which were allowed to float between upper and lower limits; and free prices to be determined entirely by market forces.

Šik was a political as well as economic reformer. Alone among the speakers at the Thirteenth Congress of the Communist Party of Czechoslovakia in the summer of 1966, he had called for greater democratization of the society and for more intra-party democracy, arguing that economic reform would not work unless it were accompanied by political reform.[7] Although the speech was not fully reported in the mass media at the time, it gave encouragement to reformers. The widespread discontent which already existed within the party ranks was fertile soil for the ideas it expressed. The issue of whether economic reform would work only if it went together with political reform was one which was long debated in Communist countries. After the crushing of the Prague Spring, a realistic answer seemed to be: serious economic reform would be allowed to proceed only if it were *not* accompanied by political reform. In Hungary, in January 1968, the very month of the launching of the Prague Spring and the year of its crushing, an economic reform was introduced which raised living standards and was allowed to continue and develop throughout the 1970s and 1980s, albeit with some temporary setbacks. Crucially important for its resilience was the fact that it was not being accompanied by any fundamental reform of political institutions. More recently, the case of China, where economic success has been much more conspicuous, is cited by those who argue the case for economic reform *without* reform of the political system.

The crux of the matter can be boiled down to two points. The first is that reformers in Czechoslovakia and, twenty years later, in the Soviet Union *believed* that economic reform required political reform if it were to be successfully implemented. If the party and ministerial bureaucracies retained their existing powers, moves towards marketizing reform would be frustrated. The second, and more fundamental, point is that, in the absence of foreign intervention or domestic counterreformation, the end result would not be Communist reformation, but the evolution of the system to something different in kind. 'Reform Communism', as in Czechoslovakia in 1968 or the Soviet Union two decades later, was in unstable equilibrium. This was not, it should be added, the perception of Czech or Soviet Communist reformers at the time they embarked on political change. There can, though, be little doubt but that the reforms of the Prague Spring would have developed into a recognizably non-Communist political system, characterized by political pluralism, in the absence of armed intervention. But the reformers would, given the broad public support for a form of socialism at that time, have attempted to make a democratic socialism work. Dubček's slogan, 'Socialism with a human face', had real resonance in the Czechoslovakia of 1968. In contrast, by the time Czechoslovakia (and, after the division of the country into two states, the Czech Republic) did gain independence just over twenty years later, there was widespread disillusionment with any notion of socialism.

While failure (to recall Eisler) can, indeed, be an important stimulus to change, there is nothing automatic about one leading to the other. First of all, failure has to be perceived and acknowledged as failure. Second, even if a party leadership in a highly authoritarian state recognizes that failure has occurred, they can decide that the risks of the proposed remedies outweigh the dangers of muddling through. If the social consequences of the failure are so great that people take to the streets in massive numbers, throwing into question the continuing existence of the regime, the party leadership is forced to do something – either to make concessions or to use force to repress the discontent. No such unrest occurred in Czechoslovakia in the mid-1960s, any more than it did in the Soviet Union in the mid-1980s. (When people *did* take to the streets in vast numbers in the USSR at the end of the 1980s, it was as a result of the introduction of political pluralism, not a precursor to it.)

An orthodox Communist leadership, using all the levers of power at its disposal – from control over everyone's career prospects to the ability to arrest and determine the prison sentence of anyone brave enough to offer opposition – can live with economic failure (as well as other types of failure) for many years. In their quite different ways, Cuba and North Korea are countries which are still doing so. To make concessions to market forces, still more to tolerate the introduction of elements of political pluralism, are policies leading to an erosion of the party's political hegemony and control. Communist party leaderships, by virtue of the systems within which they operate, are not obliged to give priority either to economic efficiency or to the preferences of a broader public. Had that not been the case, a majority of the states in Eastern Europe would have ceased to be Communist decades before they did. In Czechoslovakia, although Novotný reluctantly acquiesced in the introduction of an economic reform (which was never fully implemented), he was not prepared to take risks with the 'leading role of the party', which had become, more precisely, the monopoly of power of the party bureaucracy.

Novotný, a Communist of working-class origin who joined the party in 1921 at the age of seventeen, survived the war years in the Nazi concentration camp, Mauthausen. He truly believed that a Communist system was preferable to capitalist democracy. He was also skilled in the arts of bureaucratic politics and an unscrupulous operator. He showed especial zeal in seeking out enemies within the party in the lead-up to the trial and execution of the general secretary Rudolf Slánský in 1951–52.[8] In 1953 Novotný himself became first secretary of the party. Zdeněk Mlynář, who was one of the most important of the Prague Spring reformers, gives a telling example of Novotný's moral standards. Having played his part in hounding to their deaths the leading Communists who perished in the Slánský trial, Novotný and his wife then bought the china tea service and the bedclothes of one of those who was hanged, Vladimír Clementis, since the property of the victims was being sold off cheaply to high-ranking officials. When, only a few years earlier, they had visited Clementis (at that time foreign minister) and his family socially, Novotný's wife, Božena Novotná, had expressed her admiration for the tea service.[9] Mlynář adds: 'The thought that the first secretary of the ruling party and the head of state slept between sheets belonging to a man whom he had helped send to the gallows is something quite incredible in twentieth-century Europe.'[10]

Ideas for political reform were already in the mid-1960s being aired in small-circulation journals and books, but with Novotný as party leader (and president), there was little chance of implementing them in practice. Even the reformist economists, it should be noted, were not in the 1960s arguing against state or other forms of public ownership, but wished to move in the direction of a socialist market economy. This already existed in Yugoslavia, and that country was a significant influence on a number of Czech and Slovak party intellectuals who were attracted not only to Yugoslav economic reform but also to the extent to which interest groups had been accommodated within the one-party system, and to the state's federal structure. Polish economists and sociologists also influenced their Czech counterparts, but nothing was more important for giving an impetus to the reformist tendency in Czechoslovak Communism than Khrushchev's open attack on Stalin at the Twenty-Second Congress of the CPSU in 1961. The last five years of Novotný's regime were a time of development of ideas which could then be expressed only very cautiously but which were given much fuller expression in 1968, a year which began with the removal of Novotný from the party leadership and his replacement by the Slovak Alexander Dubček.

The prime movers in the changes were from the party intelligentsia, by which is meant simply Communist Party members with a higher education who were employed in the professions or in the party and governmental bureaucracy. In Czechoslovakia, as elsewhere in Communist Europe, some sections of this stratum were more significant than others. Social scientists, writers, academic lawyers and some of the best-educated members of the party and government apparatus were much more important politically than natural scientists and engineers. Those in the party intelligentsia who *did* exert political influence can be divided into two broad categories – the *insiders* and the *outsiders*. There is a distinction, that is to say, between the influence wielded within party committees and party commissions and the influence on a wider audience exercised, for instance, by writers. The two categories were not completely compartmentalized, for some of those who worked for change within party organs also attempted to propagate their views in the mass media insofar as this was possible in the years leading up to 1968.

The broad division of labour between those whose main efforts were concentrated on intra-party change and those who were opinion-makers in a wider social context was not planned, but the roles played by the two categories of intellectuals were mutually reinforcing. So far was it from being part of a carefully worked-out strategy that both before 1968 and during it, people in the two groups frequently failed to appreciate what was being done by those who had adopted a different approach. Reformers who worked cautiously for change within the party machine were often suspected of being timid time-servers, while the insiders, especially in 1968 itself, had little respect for the political judgement of some of the writers and philosophers. Yet their roles in promoting change were complementary, albeit unplanned. The party intellectual insiders played a vital part in creating – in the years between 1963 and 1967 in particular – a greater receptiveness to new ideas within the party apparatus and in initiating some modest changes in party organization. The outsiders, for their part, attempted to rouse public opinion, which had been notable for its quietism, to demand more vigorous, radical action. A 'new wave' in the Czech cinema in the 1960s, which produced some brilliant and politically unorthodox films, was an especially important part of the activities of the cultural intelligentsia.[11] On the reformist Communists whom I have termed outsiders, Mlynář wrote:

> . . . the general political orientation of this group of reform Communists was more democratic and radical than that of groups inside the power structure itself. The contrast between *Literární noviny* [the Writers' Union weekly newspaper] and the party press in the 1960s is a good example of this. And it often led to conflicts between this more radical group and the political authorities, with the reform Communists inside the power structure caught in the middle. But such differences between the reform Communists were more a matter of style than substance.[12]

Insider-reformers from the party intelligentsia in Czechoslovakia in the years between 1963 and 1968 operated in ways familiar to their counterparts in other Communist states. They engaged in self-censorship and would sometimes write several articles which repeated current party orthodoxy in order to be able to publish the next article, which broke new ground. They became experts at knowing the limits of the possible and when an attempt to expand them might have a chance of success. The self-censorship, Mlynář admitted, extended to what they thought as well as to what they said. If some ideas were clearly unacceptable to those in power, they would set them aside for future resuscitation when the time was ripe.[13] Mlynář even engaged in criticism of 'revisionism', which was a high priority at the time for the Communist Party's ideologists. He did this 'for the most part insincerely', not least in his criticisms of 'certain Yugoslav conceptions which, in fact, I believed to be somewhat relevant for our own political transformation in Czechoslovakia'.[14] Through compromises of that kind, Mlynář (who wrote his doctoral thesis on Machiavelli) was able to publish articles in the main party newspaper, *Rudé právo*, was invited to join influential working groups which drafted party documents, and became, from 1964, the secretary of the law commission which had been set up by the Central Committee as an advisory body to them. It was one of several such commissions created in the five years preceding the Prague Spring which brought together members of the apparatus and scholars and helped prepare the ground for reform.

The outsider members of the party intelligentsia included some very prominent writers. Their most important criticism of the status quo, prior to the Prague Spring, came at the Fourth Congress of the Czechoslovak Writers' Union, held in Prague in late June 1967. Seventy-five per cent of members of the Writers' Union were also members of the Communist Party, but these were people whose influence was not exerted in smoke-filled rooms or the corridors of power but through their publications and, on this occasion, their speeches. What was said at the Congress was initially conveyed by word of mouth and by foreign radio broadcasts. The proceedings of the Writers' Congress were not published in Prague until 1968. However, they caused great embarrassment to the party leadership, who were especially worried about having blotted their copybook in the year of the fiftieth anniversary of the Bolshevik Revolution, which was to be celebrated in Moscow in November. The first speaker at the congress was the novelist Milan Kundera, who set the tone. He contrasted the flourishing of Czech culture over the previous four years with the twenty-six years which had preceded them, thus implicitly lumping together most of the Communist era with the years during the Second World War when the Czech lands of Bohemia and Moravia were a Nazi protectorate. He quoted Voltaire's famous 'I do not agree with what you are saying, but I will fight to the death for your right to say it', and added that 'the truth can only be reached by a dialogue of free opinions enjoying equal rights'. He poured scorn on a deputy in the legislature who had recently called for the banning of 'two serious and intelligent Czech films', and added: 'He inveighed brutally against both films, while positively boasting that he understood neither of them. The contradiction in such an attitude is only on the surface. The two works had chiefly offended by transcending the human horizons of their judges, so that they were felt as an insult.'[15]

Among many striking speeches at the congress, none more pertinently addressed the issue of democracy, and its absence in Czechoslovakia, than that by Ludvík Vaculík, himself a member of the Communist Party of working-class origin. In the course of it he said:

It seems that power has its own inviolable laws of development and behaviour, regardless of who exercises it. Power is a peculiar human phenomenon, due to the fact that even in the jungle someone in the tribe has to give the orders, and even in the most high-minded community someone has to sum up the discussion and draft the priorities ... Thousands of years of experience persuaded men to try to lay down rules of procedure. Hence the system of formal democracy with its feedbacks and control switches and limiting values ... the rules in themselves are neither capitalist nor socialist; they do not decide what should be done, but how to reach a decision on what to do.

They are a human invention which makes the job of ruling considerably harder. They favour the ruled, but when a government falls they also save its ministers from being shot. The maintenance of such a formal system of democracy does not bring strong government, but it brings the conviction that the next government may be better. So the government can fall, but the citizen is renewed.[16]

A letter which Alexander Solzhenitsyn had sent to the Fourth Congress of the Soviet Writers' Union, where it had been suppressed, in which Solzhenitsyn criticized both the Union and the Soviet censorship, was read out, in Czech translation, at the Czechoslovak Writers' Congress by Pavel Kohout. It was at this point that the Politburo member in charge of ideology, Jiří Hendrych, stormed angrily out of the hall.[17] The Solzhenitsyn letter, and the publicity given to it, was, however, praised by Václav Havel, addressing a Writers' Union Congress, for the first (and last) time. In a later speech, responding to the insubordination shown by the writers, Hendrych expressed particular outrage at 'efforts to disparage the revolutionary achievements of our people and the communist party, as well as efforts to negate and vilify 20 years of our socialist achievements and place them virtually on a par with the period of darkness and the Nazi occupation'. He also showed particular sensitivity to the reading out of the Solzhenitsyn letter, saying that this 'irresponsible move' had 'seriously damaged our fraternal ties'.[18]

THE SLOVAK QUESTION

When Dubček was chosen by the Slovak Central Committee to be their first secretary in 1963, he was not Novotný's favoured candidate for the post.[19] The latter's discontent was reflected in a long delay between the choice of Dubček by his Slovak colleagues and the announcement of his election in the press. Nevertheless, Dubček automatically became the principal spokesman for the grievances felt by the Slovak branch of the Communist Party of Czechoslovakia. Slovaks, dissatisfied with their role in the political system, were part of the coalition which turned against Novotný. Dubček played a significant role in triggering a crisis within the leadership of the Czechoslovak Party when in a speech at a plenary session of the Central Committee in October 1967 he sided with Novotný's opponents. He did not mention simply Slovak discontents but called, more generally, for different methods of political leadership. The party should not replace state organs and it 'should not direct society, but lead it'.[20] Novotný responded with a personal attack on Dubček and complained that he had yielded too much to 'narrow national interests'.[21]

The political system of Czechoslovakia up until 1968 remained highly centralized, and what Czech reformers called 'bureaucratic centralism' could be interpreted by Slovaks as a violation of their national rights or even as Czech chauvinism. In the person of the tactless Novotný, it was often both. Many Slovaks felt that they were, in the words of the Slovak writer Laco Novomeský, 'a tolerated race of vice-chairmen and deputy-ministers, a second-class minority generously accorded a one-third quota in everything'.[22] When Dubček clashed with Novotný at the October 1967 Central Committee plenum, this was an indication of a crisis within the leadership, for a Communist system could not long tolerate a second centre within the party. It meant that the Slovak question became a catalyst for the change of leadership, and even though it was not the top issue on the agenda of Czech reformers, it raised the standing of Dubček in their eyes.

The Reforms of the Prague Spring

In further Central Committee sessions in December 1967 and January 1968 the Central Committee was again divided. They were given a greater than normal decision-making power because the Presidium of the Central Committee was split down the middle – five–five – for and against Novotný remaining as party leader. Leonid Brezhnev, concerned about the divisions within a Communist Party which had given the Soviet Union little trouble hitherto, came to Prague and attended a meeting of the Presidium on 9 December 1967. He tried to support Novotný without, however, attempting to impose either him or any particular alternative candidate for the first secretaryship on the Czechoslovak party. He was confident enough that any alternative to Novotný, including Dubček, who had lived for years in the Soviet Union, would be a reliable partner. Dubček's father, a working-class founding member of the Communist Party of Czechoslovakia, had emigrated to the Soviet Union in the mid-1920s when Alexander Dubček was only three. In 1938 they returned to Czechoslovakia, where, during the Second World War, Alexander joined the underground resistance. He was wounded during the Slovak National Rising of 1944. His brother Julius was killed. The future Czechoslovak leader returned to the Soviet Union in the Khrushchev era, spending the years 1955–58 at the Higher Party School in Moscow when he was in his mid-thirties and evidently regarded as someone with future prospects.[23] The Soviet part of his background was doubtless sufficiently reassuring for the Moscow leadership. Brezhnev's meeting with the fluent-Russian-speaking Dubček in December 1967 passed off cordially. Before leaving Prague, and speaking privately, he told senior Czech and Slovak party members apropos of the party leadership: 'It's your business' – words which were to have a hollow ring less than a year later.[24] In fact, Brezhnev, as he later made clear in a message to the Hungarian leader János Kádár, would have preferred Novotný to remain in office. However, by acknowledging that it was ultimately a matter for the leadership of the Czechoslovak party to sort out, he weakened both Novotný's position and that of his strongest supporters within the Central Committee apparatus, including not only half the Presidium but the hard-line department head, Miroslav Mamula, who was the overseer of the armed forces and the security organs.[25]

The Central Committee plenum which launched the Prague Spring was held from 3 to 5 January 1968. It ended with Novotný's removal as first secretary and the election of Dubček in his place. For the time being, Novotný was allowed to retain his state function as President of Czechoslovakia, but following increased pressure on him, he resigned from that post on 22 March. Later in March, on the recommendation of another Central Committee plenum, Ludvík Svoboda was chosen to be Novotný's successor as president. He was a former army general who had fought alongside the Red Army during World War Two, commanding Czech military units, and who, as minister of defence, had played a part in helping the Communists to seize power in Czechoslovakia in 1948. He had, however, fallen from grace when, under Soviet pressure, the Czech security forces intensified their search for hidden enemies. He was arrested at the beginning of the 1950s and, although soon released, allowed to work only as a bookkeeper on a collective farm. He was rapidly rehabilitated when Nikita Khrushchev, as Soviet leader, visited Czechoslovakia in the mid-1950s and asked to see his old wartime comrade, Svoboda, who had been 'an outstanding military commander' on the First Ukrainian Front. When in 1968 Svoboda was brought out of retirement to become President of Czechoslovakia, he was already aged seventy-two.[26] The name *svoboda* means 'freedom' in both Czech and Russian. This helped the new president for a time (including the days immediately after the Soviet invasion of August 1968) to become one of the symbols of the Prague Spring. Svoboda went along with most of the reforms of 1968, but was very susceptible to Soviet pressure and lost the widespread respect he had acquired during the Prague Spring by remaining until 1975 as a figurehead president in post-invasion Czechoslovakia.

Following the January 1968 plenum, the political atmosphere in Czechoslovakia changed dramatically. The mass media, some sections more than others, became ever bolder as censorship virtually withered away.[27] As early as the beginning of February, the new chairman of the Czechoslovak Writers' Union, Eduard Goldstücker, related on television the true story of Novotný's downfall, exposing the way in which this had been covered up.[28]

In March, the issue of the political trials of the 1940s and early 1950s was reopened, as was the question of whether Jan Masaryk had committed suicide in 1948 or been murdered. In April, Evžen Löbl, one of only three of those accused in the Slánský trial who suffered long imprisonment rather than execution, published a book in 30,000 copies in Slovakia, parts of which were promptly republished in Czech weeklies, in which he exposed how the confessions were extracted and how these show trials were stage-managed.[29] Very early in the year there were calls for a return of Tomáš Masaryk to the place of honour in the history of his country which he enjoyed before the Communists came to power. One Czech writer put the point especially provocatively with a none too veiled reference to the fact that Peter the Great and even Ivan the Terrible were presented in Soviet historiography as great leaders and 'progressive for their time'. Writing in an educational newspaper, and complaining that truthfulness had been eliminated from the school curriculum in Czechoslovakia, Jan Procházka wrote:

> To the more intelligent boys and girls, it was hard to understand that, in the history of other nations, it was possible and permitted to pay homage even to tsars and tyrants, while in our own country, there was no place in history for a man who was the founder of our democracy, who was neither a usurper nor the murderer of his own children but an educated, democratic and highly moral man.[30]

The wide range of opinion and the reformist tendencies within the Communist Party which had struggled for recognition before 1968 were expressed as never before during that year. From the highest party organs to the lowest, there was real debate, and pressure from below played a significant part in influencing higher party appointments. Draft party rules, published shortly before the Soviet invasion of Czechoslovakia, were designed to ratify officially the new reality whereby, for instance, individual party members not only had the right to their own opinion but the right to attempt to convert others to their point of view. That was a considerable inroad into the doctrine of democratic centralism. Another was the development of horizontal links between party organizations. Thus, in 1968 links were established between the party organization in the university district of Prague and the organization in the industrial district of Prague 9. In a further glaring contravention of party norms – in this case of the *nomenklatura* system of appointment – the party organization in Prague 1 went so far as to advertise in the city's evening newspaper for a secretary responsible for ideology. This last sin was drawn to the attention of Brezhnev, who declared that it showed the Communist Party of Czechoslovakia was becoming social democratic. The Prague city party organization played an exceptionally important role in 1968. In the post-invasion period it was to be described by the conservative Communists, who had regained control thanks to the Soviet invasion, as having been a 'second centre' within the party. The charge was not without foundation, for the Prague organization set the pace in advocating radical reform. They shared a building with the Central Committee, and through the connecting doors there was regular contact between reformists within the Central Committee apparatus and the Prague City Committee.[31]

For conservative Communist leaders in Eastern Europe, the most alarming document to be produced during the Prague Spring was the Action Programme of the Communist Party of Czechoslovakia, which was published on 5 April. This was not because it was the most radical publication of 1968, for it was far from that, but because it marked a break with the past and with current Communist orthodoxy by the party leadership itself. The main author of the section on the political system was Mlynář. The programme itself was a compromise document and fell far short of advocating fully fledged political pluralism. It still envisaged a 'leading role' for the Communist Party, but argued that this should not be understood as a monopolistic concentration of power in party organs. It criticized the 'unthinking adoption' in the 1950s of 'ideas, habits and political concepts which conflicted with our circumstances and traditions', leading to the gradual development of a 'bureaucratic system'. The internal life of the country had been plagued by sectarianism, the suppression of liberty, legal violations, dogmatism and misuse of power! The Action Programme did not advocate a separation of powers but called for a 'system of mutual control'. It demanded an independent judiciary and called for clearer governmental and legislative control over the Ministry of the Interior.[32]

A much more radical document which became the subject of Soviet polemics against the developments in Czechoslovakia was the *Two Thousand Words*, a manifesto issued by a group of scholars and writers, including both party and non-party members, whose author was the writer Ludvík Vaculík. It was published in June 1968 – at a sensitive time when Warsaw Pact military manoeuvres were taking place in Czechoslovakia – in the Writers' Union newspaper (now called *Literární listy*), which by this time had a circulation as high as 300,000.[33] Unlike the Action Programme, it did not pull its punches. It gave credit to the Communist Party for starting the 'regenerative process of democratization', but qualified that praise by saying that there was nowhere else the process could have begun, for only the Communists were in a position to take action. 'No thanks, therefore', the document continued, 'is due to the Communist Party, although it should

probably be acknowledged that it is honestly trying to use this last opportunity to save its own and the nation's honour.'[34] One of the major points
made by Vaculík was that no institutional change had yet taken place in the
political system.[35] The liberalization and partial democratization thus
depended very much on the goodwill of the Communist Party leadership.
The document called on citizens themselves to set up watchdog committees to look at questions which no official organ would examine, and to
demand the resignation of people who had misused their power or acted
dishonestly. The means of doing so might include strikes and 'picketing
their houses', although no illegal methods should be employed, 'since these
might be used against Alexander Dubček'.[36]

The development of civil society, in the sense of the emergence of independent social organizations and pressure groups, quite rapidly followed the
changes which had been inaugurated by the January plenum of the party
Central Committee. Indeed, the creation of interest groups was endorsed
by the Presidium of the Central Committee on 21 March, although in the
changed atmosphere it is unlikely that those who formed the groups would
have been content to await such official approval.[37] Among the more important organizations politically was the Club 231 of former political prisoners
(its name deriving from the fact that they had been charged under Article
231 of the criminal code). It was concerned to secure rehabilitation of those
who had been unjustly condemned and to promote human rights more
generally. At much the same time – in early April – a Slovak Organization
for the Defence of Human Rights was established in Bratislava. And an
organization which became known as KAN (*Klub angažovaných nestraníků* –
Club of Non-Party Activists) was formed. The declared aim of KAN was
to share in the construction of a 'new political system' which would be one
of 'democratic socialism'.[38] Another very important development was the
spread, and publication, of professionally conducted opinion polls, even on
sensitive political issues. The reformists within the party leadership, in
rejecting a high level of coercion, welcomed the survey research, for they
had committed themselves to taking serious account of public opinion.
Dubček, though more a facilitator of reform than a radical reformer, acquired
the reputation of being a good listener. In turn, he became genuinely popular
across a broad spectrum of the population.

Although the time was too short for real institutional change to take
place, there were many important personnel changes in the leadership
between January and August 1968. The highest party organs, however,
remained divided. Along with an influx of reformers, hard-liners, as well as
people with special links to their Soviet counterparts, remained in post.
Apart from the three older Communists already mentioned who joined the

leadership – Kriegel, who had served in the Spanish Civil War as a physician attached to the International Brigade; Smrkovsky, who had been a leader of an uprising in Prague in 1945 against the Nazi-imposed regime, but was one of the Communists imprisoned in the 1950s; and Slavík, who had turned from Stalinist editor of the party newspaper, *Rudé právo*, in the early postwar years into serious reformer – they included Jiří Hájek, a former concentration camp prisoner who became foreign minister, and Josef Pavel, a former regimental commander in the Spanish Civil War and a political prisoner in Czechoslovakia in the 1950s. Pavel became minister of the interior and began to convert the ministry from a secret police machine into the more limited guardian of national security required in any state. From the political generation of those who had been students in 1948, Zdeněk Mlynář moved from being an academic with party insider credentials to becoming a member of the Central Committee Secretariat at the age of thirty-seven.[39] In addition to his work on the Central Committee law commission, Mlynář had headed an academic team examining the way the political system should be reformed. Communist reformers Jiří Pelikán and Zdeněk Hejzlar (the latter a political prisoner in the 1950s) became the directors of television and radio respectively.

Rehabilitation of those falsely imprisoned (or posthumous rehabilitation of those executed) was a major issue in 1968. A commission under the chairmanship of Jan Piller re-examined the major trials, especially the Slánský show trial, and completed a report in 1968. It was not, however, published before the Soviet invasion and had no chance of seeing the light of day in Czechoslovakia after it. Piller himself informed the party leadership in the summer of 1968 that the report (which was subsequently published abroad) 'contained such alarming facts' that its publication might damage the party and some of its leaders.[40] Several members of the Presidium saw it as a threat to themselves. Even in 1968 the main focus of the reformers in the party leadership had been on Communist rather than non-Communist victims. The latter, however, now had people who were both willing and able to speak up for them. A group of non-Communist writers was formed, with Václav Havel elected to be their principal spokesman. Among their pronouncements, they called for the automatic quashing of the verdicts in all political trials held after February 1948, with the onus put on the state authorities to prosecute anew, should there be any legal grounds for this.[41]

The process of re-examining the trials of Communists had begun five years earlier. The Barnabitky Commission of 1963 (named after the monastery in which its members met) exonerated, among others, Gustáv Husák, the Communist who had been a leader of the Slovak National Rising of 1944, and who had been imprisoned as a 'Slovak bourgeois nationalist'.

Although the formal membership of the commission included some of the most conservative figures in the party leadership, the detailed investigative and archival work was carried out by scholarly experts – historians, lawyers and economists. Novotný subsequently treated them as a dangerous group. While they came from different backgrounds, they did, indeed, develop close ties in the course of several months of work together. Several of them lost their jobs as a result of their show of independence. For example, Milan Hůbl was ousted from the pro-rectorship of the Party High School, although in 1968 he made a comeback, becoming rector of the very institution from which he had been dismissed in 1964. His main offence had been to write more frankly than was customary about the nationality question in Czechoslovakia and to espouse the cause of the so-called Slovak 'bourgeois nationalists' and, in particular, that of Husák. In 1968, when he headed the Party High School, Hůbl reinforced the reformist current that was already to be found among some of its staff. It briefly became a kind of school of political science, having been, as one party intellectual put it, 'secularized'. Husák, who succeeded Dubček as Communist Party first secretary in April 1969, in a spectacular case of ingratitude rewarded Hůbl, who had fought to clear Husák's name, by endorsing his removal once again from the Party High School and subsequently overseeing his expulsion from the Communist Party. Hůbl, who refused to recant the critical views he had developed, was sentenced in 1971 to six and a half years in prison.[42]

It was sometimes said of Husák that the only thing he thought was wrong with the unreformed system in Czechoslovakia was that he, Husák, had been imprisoned. There was an element of truth in that, but as early as 12 January 1968 he published an article in the Slovak Writers' Union weekly, Kultúrny život, calling for democratization. He was much attracted to power, and to gain political promotion he was prepared to adopt the line that seemed most conducive to it both before and after the Soviet invasion.[43] One reform which he pursued sincerely was to turn Czechoslovakia into a federation in which Slovaks would enjoy equal rights with Czechs. It was virtually the only reform of 1968 to survive the transition of leadership from Dubček to his fellow Slovak. What remained was a less radical variant of federalism, inasmuch as the Communist Party, as distinct from the government and legislature, was not federalized, as had been planned before the Soviet invasion. Nevertheless, the federation of state institutions enhanced the position of Slovaks within the political system. They now had their own ministries in Bratislava as well as holding many offices in Prague during the years in which Husák headed the party and, subsequently, as president, the state.

East European and Soviet Alarm

From very early in 1968, other Communist leaders in Eastern Europe – especially Gomułka in Poland and Ulbricht in East Germany – were alarmed by developments in Czechoslovakia. It was clear to them that the growing freedom of expression, intra-party debate and developing civil society could prove highly infectious. It was, indeed, not long before demonstrating Polish students shouted, 'We want a Polish Dubček!' The first sustained pressure put on the Czechoslovak leadership came at a meeting with five member states of the Warsaw Pact at Dresden on 23 March 1968. The Romanian leadership, keen to emphasize national autonomy, remained apart and did not attend these and other meetings convened to cajole the Czechs and Slovaks into reversing their reformist course. 'The Five', as they became known, consisted of the Soviet Union, East Germany, Poland, Hungary and Bulgaria. With the transcript of the Dresden meeting now available, the intensity of the pressure put on Dubček is very evident. Gomułka, already in March 1968, raised the spectre of counterrevolution in Czechoslovakia and reminded the Czech and Slovak leaders of the experience of Poland and Hungary. The trouble had started in both of those countries with the writers. He went on: 'We have to come . . . to decisions which unequivocally state that the counterrevolution will not succeed in Czechoslovakia, that the leadership of the Czechoslovak party and Czechoslovakia's working class will not permit that, that Czechoslovakia's allies, that is, those who are gathered here, will not permit it.'[44]

All the leaders present, but especially those from central Europe, were concerned with the spread of the Czech political infection. Kádár explicitly made the point that 'there is a direct connection between important events which happen in any socialist country, and the domestic situation in other socialist countries', and added that the process observable in Czechoslovakia was 'extremely similar to the prologue of the Hungarian counterrevolution at a time when it had not yet become a counterrevolution'.[45] Ulbricht said that Western influence had been observable in Czechoslovakia already for six or seven years and that no systematic ideological battle against it had been fought for ten years, and 'Now all this boils over. We see it in black and white.'[46] Alexey Kosygin, from the Soviet delegation, took an even harder line than Brezhnev. 'It is currently a fact', he said, that in Czechoslovakia 'the organs which convey the thoughts of the leadership and our thoughts to each worker, farmer, student, and intellectual, are in the hands of the enemy. These are the TV, radio and even the newspapers.'[47] Brezhnev complained about denunciations of the Communist Party – and the use of phrases such as 'decayed society' and 'outdated order' – even in *Rudé právo*: 'And this in the central organ of the party!'[48] The Czech leaders at Dresden listened respectfully to the criticism, but the prime minister, Oldřich Černík, gave the most spirited defence of what was happening in Czechoslovakia. He said it was 'overwhelmingly progressive and pro-socialist in character' and that thousands of meetings were being held in overcrowded halls, with millions of people enthusiastically participating in these gatherings. Previously, they had 'a situation in which halls have been empty, passivity was evident and increasing'.[49] What Černík did not realize was that to his Soviet and East European colleagues, empty halls were infinitely preferable to an active and newly emboldened citizenry, excited about politics and eager to join in.

There was nonstop pressure from the Soviet Union, as well as from the other Communist countries, whose leaders had taken part in the Dresden meeting, throughout the eight months of the Prague Spring. It was clearly better from their point of view that the Czechoslovak leaders should incur the odium of instituting the crackdown than that they should bear the political (and economic) costs of military invasion. While the Soviet leaders could be reasonably confident that the United States, embroiled in Vietnam, would not react too strongly to Soviet military intervention in Czechoslovakia, there might be a political price to pay in Europe, where the Prague Spring was being extensively reported by the mass media and followed with great enthusiasm. In May 1968, Marshal Grechko, the Soviet minister of defence, led a military delegation to Czechoslovakia, and in the same month Alexey Kosygin arrived, ostensibly to 'take the waters' at the famous Czech spa, Karlový Vary (Carlsbad). Kosygin's serious misgivings about what was going on in Czechoslovakia were doubtless reinforced by some of his personal experiences on this visit, as well as by his meetings with different members of the Czechoslovak leadership, when, in the words of Mlynář, his Czech hosts were unable to protect 'the second most powerful man in the empire . . . from prying journalists'.[50]

In early May a summit meeting between the Czechoslovak and Soviet leaders was held, at Soviet behest, in Moscow. The leading members of the Soviet Politburo expressed their outrage at what was happening in Czechoslovakia and their astonishment that stronger action was not being taken to put a stop to it. Brezhnev was incensed by the talk 'about some sort of "new model of socialism" that has not existed until now'.[51] When Dubček was asked what he was going to do about the kind of thing being published in the press, he responded that the only way was to work individually with editors and to win them over, as he had done in Bratislava. He went on: 'I'll have to work personally with these people and speak to them. In Prague, I don't have such a strong position in these circles, and past roots are stronger there than in Slovakia.'[52] Thus, even in circumstances where he had to try to assuage the concerns of the Soviet leadership, Dubček evinced some of the characteristics noted by people who knew him well, starting with the fact that he was 'clearly not authoritarian by nature'.[53] Dubček had reconciled in his own mind Leninism and a humane socialism, however oddly such a belief sits with a more hard-headed look at Lenin's words and deeds. At a time, Mlynář observes, when 'cynicism and formal faith had been dominant for years', Czechs and Slovaks responded to someone with 'a sincere, human, humanitarian faith', doing so almost regardless of the content of that faith. Dubček, for his part, incorrectly assumed that the fact that he was greeted with genuine warmth wherever he went in Czechoslovakia reflected agreement with his political ideas.[54]

Dubček was a very unusual first secretary of a ruling Communist party, not simply because he really believed in 'the ideals of communism', but even more because he did *not* believe in imposing them on society. He had, indeed, a genuine mistrust of the role of force. While he thought of himself as a follower of Lenin, in his democratic temperament and 'Masarykian rejection of dictatorial violence', he was closer in character to the first president of the Czechoslovak Republic, Tomáš Masaryk, than to the founder of the Soviet state.[55] These characteristics were not what Brezhnev wanted to see in the leader of a fraternal ruling party. He had begun by liking Dubček, and he continued to place some confidence in his Czechoslovak counterpart after others in the Soviet leadership had given up on him. However, Brezhnev regarded Dubček as indecisive, and he ended the Moscow meeting of May 1968 with what could be regarded as a veiled warning: 'Now, while we're still discussing all these matters with you, we hear you and we believe you. But if it becomes necessary, we can begin to speak in such a way that everyone can hear, and then the working class will hear the voice of its friends. But it is better for you to do this now yourselves.'[56]

A few days after the Czechoslovak leaders had left for Prague, 'the Five' met in Moscow. Brezhnev reported to Ulbricht, Gomułka, Kádár and the Bulgarian leader, Todor Zhivkov, on those early May talks and on the situation in Czechoslovakia since they had met at Dresden. The most vehemently concerned of the participants were Ulbricht and Gomułka, for whom the developing freedom of speech and organization in Czechoslovak society could clearly have a dangerous impact in their own countries. Kádár, too, was exercised by the spectre of 'counterrevolution', but adopted a tone more in sorrow than in anger, saying of Dubček and his colleagues: 'They are honest, albeit naïve, people, and we must work with them.'[57] All of the leaders agreed that they could not publish the Action Programme in their own countries, but in their public propaganda against the Prague Spring they were not yet directly attacking the leadership of the Czechoslovak

Communist Party and its official documents, but focusing on 'anti-socialist elements' and 'counterrevolutionaries'.[58] 'The CPSU', Brezhnev said at the May 1968 meeting of the Five, 'believes it is necessary to save scientific socialism in Czechoslovakia and to defend and maintain the communist party in power ... As for criticism of the Action Program, that can come in the second stage. For now, it is essential to discover and consolidate the forces that can undertake the struggle against counterrevolution.'[59]

The Soviet Union cultivated a group of politicians in Czechoslovakia who shared their views. Some were essentially Soviet agents, but two who were simply close to the Soviet embassy and to the view from Moscow, Vasil Bilak and Alois Indra, were people in whom the Soviet leadership began to place their hopes. Given Dubček's popularity in Czechoslovakia, as public opinion polls demonstrated, an optimal solution remained that of Dubček doing the Soviet job for them as, in a different context, Gottwald had done in 1948. A new peak in the crisis of relations among the ruling European Communist parties came in July, when Dubček and the presidium of the Czechoslovak party refused to meet the Five at a meeting to be held in Warsaw. (Not only Romania, but, still more, Yugoslavia remained aloof from these machinations. The Yugoslavs, unlike the Romanians, were not, of course, members of the Warsaw Pact. They were much more actively sympathetic to the growing independence of the Communist Party of Czechoslovakia. They believed that the party's leadership in 1968 enjoyed the support of the greater part of the membership and of the population, as Tito had informed Brezhnev personally when he visited the Soviet Union at the end of April.)[60]

The Five went ahead with their meeting in Warsaw to discuss what for them was 'the crisis' in Czechoslovakia without the participation of any Czechs or Slovaks. This led to a sharp letter of protest, signed by Dubček and Černík, sent to Brezhnev on 14 July, although the Soviet leader received it only after the meeting of the Five had concluded.[61] Gomułka, chairing the opening session since the meeting was being held on his home ground, said that their purpose was 'to exchange views and reach a common position on a matter of the utmost importance for each of our countries and for the whole socialist commonwealth'. Brezhnev intervened to say that there should be only one item on the agenda: 'On the situation in Czechoslovakia.'[62]

Gomułka, presenting the Polish Communist assessment, said that the Communist Party of Czechoslovakia 'is abandoning the precepts of Marxism-Leninism and is being transformed into a social democratic party', while 'the country is being peacefully transformed from a socialist state into a bourgeois republic'.[63] Kádár, however, perhaps because he was only too well aware of the logical conclusion of an analysis such as Gomułka's, took a less apocalyptic view. He did not agree that the Czechoslovak party was being transformed into a social democratic party, although there were dangerous tendencies within it. Neither Dubček nor Černík, he said, understood 'the full gravity of the situation'; they appear to be in 'a stupor'. The situation in Czechoslovakia was, though, steadily deteriorating – already much worse than when the Five had met in Dresden and Moscow.[64]

Ulbricht, nevertheless, launched an attack on Kádár for the relative mildness of his assessment of the situation in Czechoslovakia, saying that he was amazed that he spoke of 'revisionist forces' when he should have been talking about 'counterrevolutionary forces'. He went on:

> The Czechs' plans for counterrevolution are obvious. There can be no further doubt about this matter. The counterrevolutionaries want to prepare the party congress in such a way that they can crush and eliminate the Marxist-Leninists . . .
>
> I don't know, Comrade Kádár, why you can't grasp all this. Don't you realize that the next blow from imperialism will take place in Hungary? We can already detect that imperialist centers are concentrating their work now on the Hungarian intelligentsia.[65]

The Bulgarian leader, Todor Zhivkov, also criticized Kádár for continuing to vest some hopes in Dubček and Černík. Perhaps following some informal prompting from members of the Soviet delegation, given the weightiness of the issue, Zhivkov was the first person at this meeting to speak explicitly of military intervention (although Gomułka had already done so, in discussion with members of the Soviet Politburo, at the beginning of July),[66] saying:

> There is only one appropriate way out – through resolute assistance to Czechoslovakia from our parties and the countries of the Warsaw Pact. We cannot currently rely on the internal forces in Czechoslovakia. There are no forces there that could carry out the types of tasks we wrote about in our letter. Only by relying on the armed forces of the Warsaw Pact can we change the situation.[67]

The Soviet political and military leadership had been making contingency plans for months for a possible military intervention in Czechoslovakia, but the leadership had still not taken a definite decision in July to use force. At the beginning of that month a two-day Politburo meeting found Brezhnev and Kosygin still favouring intense pressure on Dubček – to remove the people in high office whom the Soviet leadership most objected to, and to crack down on the mass media – whereas several others already favoured the use of force. They included KGB chairman Yury Andropov and the

Central Committee secretary (later to be minister of defence) who super-vised the military and military industry, Dmitry Ustinov.[68] At a meeting at the end of July at Čierna nad Tisou in eastern Slovakia, just over the border from the Soviet Union, a tense confrontation took place between almost the entire CPSU Politburo on one side and the whole of the Czechoslovak Communist Party Presidium on the other. The latter had the disadvantage of being far less united than the Soviet Politburo. Some of their number actually agreed with the severe criticism of the Czechoslovak authorities meted out by Brezhnev, Kosygin, the First Secretary of the Ukrainian Communist Party, Petro Shelest, and others.[69] Dubček was not unduly cowed and, in fact, registered two strong complaints. The Warsaw meeting of the Five and the publication of their letter condemning what was happening in Czechoslovakia had, he insisted, been counterproductive, for it had been 'perceived by us, the communists, and by our whole society as a means of generating external pressure on our party'.[70] He also complained about the continuing presence in Czechoslovakia of two Soviet army regiments several weeks after the end of Warsaw Pact military exercises.[71] The meeting ended with the briefest of communiqués, but with an agreement to meet in the Slovak capital, Bratislava, on 3 August, when they would be joined by the Polish, East German, Bulgarian and Hungarian leaders.

The month of August, in the lead-up to the Soviet invasion, was one of extreme pressure on the Czechoslovak leadership, and on Dubček in partic-ular. The absence of any real information as to what went on at Čierna led to several thousand young people demonstrating in Prague, demanding to know the truth. They were not helped by the disunited leadership sending out quite different signals about what had been agreed. President Svoboda described the meeting as having symbolized Soviet–Czechoslovak friend-ship. Josef Smrkovský met the demonstrating students and assured them that no agreements on limiting press freedom had been agreed. Dubček spoke on radio and television and, in attempting to placate both his own people and the Five, did not succeed in reassuring either, in particular the Soviet and East European Communist leaders. For the latter he mentioned that Czechoslovakia would 'remain faithful to our friends and to proletarian internationalism' ('proletarian internationalism' having long become the accepted phraseology in the international Communist movement for following the Soviet line). For Czechs and Slovaks he promised 'to stand firmly on the post-January policy'.[72]

The meeting in Bratislava in early August produced what was in many ways a compromise document, which became known as the Bratislava Declaration. Being themselves internally divided, the Czechoslovak leadership team accepted much of the terminology demanded by the Soviet and East

European leaders, including such phrases as 'unswerving loyalty to Marxism-Leninism' and the need to educate 'the masses' in the 'spirit of proletarian internationalism', as well as accepting that further progress was possible 'only through strict and consistent adherence to the laws of building a socialist society and above all through a consolidation of the leading role of the working class and its vanguard, the communist party'. The Czechoslovak side was able, though, to insert the qualification that 'each fraternal party decides all questions of further socialist development in a creative way, taking into account specific national features and conditions'. Nevertheless, the document included a passage which was later used to justify the military intervention by the Five – that the task of 'supporting, consolidating and defending' the gains of socialism was 'the common international duty of all the socialist countries'.[73]

At the very time when the 'fraternal parties' were hammering out their declaration, the Soviet leadership were slipped a letter they had been soliciting in order to justify an invasion. It was a request from the hard-line members of the Czechoslovak leadership addressed to Brezhnev and calling for intervention to combat what the letter-writers called 'an anti-communist and anti-Soviet psychosis'. They wrote: '. . . we are appealing to you, Soviet communists, the leading representatives of the Communist Party of the Soviet Union, with a request for you to lend support and assistance with all the means at your disposal. Only with your assistance can the Czechoslovak Socialist Republic be extricated from the imminent danger of counterrevolution.'[74] When things did not go in the short run after the invasion as the Soviet and Eastern European leaders had planned, the authors of this document decided to remain anonymous. The letter was kept in the archive of the Soviet Politburo. Brezhnev's loyal associate, Konstantin Chernenko, the head of the General Department of the Central Committee of the CPSU, wrote: 'Not to be opened without my express permission.' The signatories to the letter, even its very existence, remained a mystery until 1992, when a copy was given to the Czechoslovak government. The five members of the 1968 party leadership who signed the letter were Alois Indra, Drahomír Kolder, Antonín Kapek, Oldřich Švestka and Vasil Bilak. By the time it came to light, only Bilak was still alive.[75]

The Invasion and Aftermath

The final decision to launch an invasion was taken in the Soviet Politburo, which met over three days between 15 and 17 August. Brezhnev had telephoned Dubček on 13 August and in a call which lasted almost one and a half hours accused him of deceit. Even at that stage he did not warn Dubček openly that the alternative to compliance with Soviet demands was imminent invasion. Until this actually took place, Dubček had refused to believe that the Soviet Union would take such a step against a country in which, after all, the Communist Party was still in office, albeit not – from a Soviet standpoint – in control. Moreover, the Czechoslovak leadership had never at any point proposed leaving the Warsaw Pact, which some of them believed had been the tipping point, bringing about Soviet invasion of Hungary twelve years earlier. The fact, indeed, that Czechoslovakia had a tradition of good relations with Russia, along with the friendship a number of the Czech and Slovak leaders enjoyed with their counterparts in the Soviet Union, meant that hardly any of them believed that an invasion was at all likely. It is arguable that they did not take the prospect seriously enough, but if they had done so, there could hardly have been a Prague Spring. Given the composition and views of the Soviet leadership at that time, fortified by the agitation of Gomułka and Ulbricht, it seems certain that the only way the Czechoslovak Communist leadership could have avoided a military intervention was by *not* giving the country eight months of substantial freedom (which were followed by seven months of partial freedom).

Dubček was pressed on many specifics by the Soviet leadership, not least to remove leaders of whom they disapproved, with František Kriegel top of that list. Responding in his long conversation with Brezhnev on 13 August to the latter's telephone tirade, Dubček told the Soviet leader that personnel changes were issues for a plenary session of the Central Committee, not something he personally could decree. He also refused to agree with Brezhnev that the Fourteenth Party Congress, which the reformers in the Czechoslovak party leadership wished to bring forward and hold in the coming weeks, should be postponed. The imminence of that congress merely confirmed the Soviet view that there was no time to lose in launching their invasion. The political atmosphere in Czechoslovakia was such that the Fourteenth Congress would have consolidated the position of the radical reformers and seen the removal of the hard-line pro-Soviet members of the Presidium and secretariat – the 'healthy forces', as they were known to the Soviet leaders and propagandists.[76]

The armed forces of the Soviet Union, with East German, Polish, Hungarian and Bulgarian contingents as well, crossed the borders of Czechoslovakia late on the night of 20 August. The Czechoslovak Presidium was in session, and a plan had been worked out between the Soviet Union and their collaborators in the Czechoslovak leadership. A majority in the Presidium were to denounce the 'rightists' who had allowed a counterrevolutionary situation to develop, and would seek the assistance of their Soviet and East European comrades. That was just the first of the interventionists' plans to go awry. Dubček had refused to accommodate their preferences on the order of business on the Presidium agenda. Those who had hoped to procure a majority vote against him had not yet had a chance to raise their concerns when the news broke that the armies of the Five had entered Czechoslovakia. Some round the Presidium table had been well aware that the invasion was about to take place, but it came a little earlier than they had expected.

An anonymous telephone caller to a Czech journalist in Budapest at 5 p.m. on 20 August had told him in an agitated voice that the occupation of his country would begin at midnight.[77] The message was passed on to the Czechoslovak ambassador to Hungary and subsequently to Černík as prime minister. (Midnight was also the time those in the Czechoslovak leadership who had colluded with the Soviet leadership expected the military intervention to commence.) Černík took the warning seriously enough to have the situation checked on the ground. He left the Presidium meeting to take a telephone call, and when he returned at 11.40 p.m. he announced. 'The armies of the five parties have crossed the borders of our republic and are occupying us.'[78] Two Presidium members, whom the collaborators had counted on to join them in a vote of no-confidence in Dubček but for whom the invasion was unexpected, were sufficiently aghast that they defected from the hard-line camp. Almost half a million troops had occupied Czechoslovakia, the great majority of them Soviet, but with thousands also from each of the other four collaborating East European Communist states.

The Soviet leaders knew whom they trusted in the Czechoslovak leadership and knew whom they could not abide, but there was also a group in between. They were prepared to wait and see who was willing to collaborate with them after Soviet troops were in control before making their personnel preferences clear. They had given up on Dubček. At a minimum, they had no intention of allowing him to play the leading role in a post-invasion regime. This was signalled not only in private – as when Brezhnev, in a meeting of the Five on 18 December, told the other leaders that at the Czechoslovak Presidium 'our friends' would 'wage an open struggle with the rightist forces, including Dubček'[79] – but also in their public pronouncements, with Pravda immediately after the invasion describing Dubček as the leader of a 'minority group' within the Presidium who had adopted a 'frankly right-wing opportunist position'.[80]

The Presidium members for whom the invasion had been totally unexpected were in shock when they heard Černík's news. Mlynář compared it to the way he felt when he had been in a car crash years before. He also had 'the clear feeling that this was the ultimate debacle of my life as a Communist'.[81] His facility as a writer, however, which had involved him in frequently drafting Prague Spring documents, led to his being the main author of a resolution which was approved by the Presidium members by seven votes to four. It included the sentence: 'The Presidium of the Central Committee of the CPC considers this act not only contrary to all the fundamental principles governing relationships between socialist states, but also as a denial of the basic norms of international law.'[82] In spite of the invading armies' occupation of all the major television and radio buildings, those who worked in those places found ways of broadcasting the Presidium's condemnation of the invasion the next morning. Meantime, the reformist members of the Czechoslovak leadership soon had guns to their heads after Soviet troops entered Dubček's office in the Central Committee building, where they had remained after the Presidium meeting ended in the early hours of 21 August. The two leading collaborators, Bilak and Indra, had made their way to the Soviet embassy.

Even without the broadcasting of the Presidium resolution, which confirmed that the occupation had been against the will of the country's top leadership, people would have taken to the streets. Eight months of reform and debate had revitalized the society. In the days following the invasion there was massive unarmed resistance by the Czech and Slovak populations. In Prague, in particular, young soldiers from the occupying forces in Soviet tanks were taken aback to be compared to fascists and to realize just how unpopular their 'fraternal assistance' was with the overwhelming majority of the population of Czechoslovakia. Street signs were changed to confuse the invading forces, and on 22 August technicians diverted the jamming of Radio Free Europe broadcasts and jammed instead broadcasts coming from East Germany aimed at giving the occupiers' view of the situation in Czechoslovakia. On 21 August Soviet troops killed fifteen unarmed Czech demonstrators in the vicinity of the main Prague radio building, and there were other deaths. The Czechs and Slovaks, however, offered only unarmed resistance, and the scale of it was such that the invading forces were soon more bewildered than belligerent. Many of them had arrived in Czechoslovakia without even knowing where they were going. Some thought they were being sent to West Germany.[83]

The fact that a majority of the Czechoslovak Presidium, including the top leaders, had rejected the 'fraternal aid' they had been offered by the Warsaw Pact forces, together with the overwhelming opposition of the civilian population of Czechoslovakia, forced the Soviet leadership to think again about replacing Dubček. He, along with other senior reformist members of the Presidium, had been flown to Moscow under duress for what were later termed 'negotiations', although the fact that they took place in the Kremlin, at a time when Soviet forces were occupying Czechoslovakia, made them somewhat one-sided. Unknown to the Czechoslovak leaders being held in the Soviet Union, a clandestine party congress, called at the time the Fourteenth Congress, had been hurriedly convened in a Prague factory in the industrial district of Vysočany. It met on 22 August, and remarkably, 1,290 of the delegates who had been chosen to take part in the scheduled Fourteenth Congress managed to make their way there – more than two-thirds of the elected delegates. They had to get past the patrols of the occupying troops and keep the location of the congress secret from them.[84] The congress fully supported the reforms of the Prague Spring, condemned unreservedly the invasion, and elected still more reformers to leading positions in the party. Zdeněk Mlynář, who had been among the party leaders held at gunpoint on the morning of 21 August, was not one of those involuntarily transported to Moscow. He was, however, now sent to Moscow on the instructions of the Vysočany congress to convey their decisions to those leaders who were in Soviet custody. From Mlynář they learned not only of the decisions of the congress but also of the remarkable passive resistance of the population as a whole.

Two others who joined the 'negotiations' in Moscow, President Svoboda and Gustáv Husák – who had emerged as Bilak's successor as first secretary in Slovakia – played very different roles from that of Mlynář. Svoboda was more accommodating of the Soviet leadership than of Dubček and the reformist wing of the Czechoslovak leadership. Husák refused to recognize the validity of the Vysočany congress because Slovak delegates had been unable to get there. He did, however, say that this would have to be done delicately because it had so much support among Czechs. He also informed the Soviet leaders that Bilak was now regarded at home as a traitor.[85] The 'Moscow Agreement' was signed on 26 August, and notwithstanding the intimidatory atmosphere in which the discussions had been held, the Czechoslovak side were able to remove any references to counterrevolution. The document did not condemn the whole process of reform, but it did include such familiar Soviet points as 'strengthening the socialist system on the basis of Marxism-Leninism'.[86] There were very diverse views among the Czechs and Slovaks who had arrived at different times in the Kremlin – they included a number of Brezhnev's 'favourite sons', such as Indra and Bilak – but the only person on the Czechoslovak side who refused to sign the agreement was Kriegel. There were disagreements on the Soviet and East European side as well. Ulbricht, Gomułka and Zhivkov were horrified by the idea of keeping Dubček in the leadership, most of all by allowing him to continue as first secretary. They wanted the formation of a 'revolutionary' government in Czechoslovakia, as did Andropov and Ustinov from the Soviet leadership.[87] Ulbricht asked: 'If Dubček and Černík are going to be in the government, then why did we send the troops?' Kosygin, although he referred to Dubček as the 'Number One Scoundrel', said he failed to see the people who could lead a revolutionary government.[88]

Brezhnev and Kosygin were the most influential of those who were making a tactical retreat from what had been the Soviet position on the eve of the invasion. They had decided by 23 August that the main office-holders in Czechoslovakia could not be replaced for the time being if Czechoslovakia was to be governable by Czechs and Slovaks. That meant that not only Svoboda, to whom the Soviet leaders were quite well disposed, but also Dubček, Černík and Smrkovský would temporarily keep their posts. Brezhnev told Svoboda that they were not raising the question of removing Dubček or the other two leaders who had also become symbolic figures of the Prague Spring.[89] Dubček stood up well to interrogation by Brezhnev, but took very little part in the negotiations on the text of the Moscow Agreement, for the strain of the past week had made him ill. The Czechoslovak side, however, conceded an important point which was not in the published agreement – namely, the removal from significant posts of some of the radical reformers to whom the Soviet side most strongly objected.

In the short term, things did not proceed in Czechoslovakia as the Soviet leadership and their East European governmental allies had hoped. A top-secret document compiled by the KGB was signed off by Andropov on 13 October 1968 and two days later approved by the CPSU leadership for dispatch to Ulbricht and Gomułka, who had asked for more information on what was happening in Czechoslovakia.[90] The report was a mixture of truth about the defiance of leading members of the party and public in Czechoslovakia (with concrete examples), and untruths. In some respects the KGB were not so well informed as they thought, putting together in a 'second centre' people who were not particularly close to one another. The report also, after placing Mlynář in that 'second centre', put in brackets after his name 'Müller'.[91] This was intended to convey that Mlynář was a Jew who had changed his name. In fact, he was not of Jewish descent on either side of his family and possessed the same surname all his life. The anti-semitic card was, however, to be played relentlessly in the Soviet mass media. Not content with listing Czech Communists who were indeed of Jewish origin as dangerous enemies – among them Kriegel, Šik, Pelikán and Goldstücker – Jewish 'original names' were invented for other prominent figures in Czechoslovakia, to damn them the more effectively. This had more resonance in Soviet Russia than in Czechoslovakia. It doubtless also went down well with one of the recipients of the KGB document, Gomułka, since his campaign against intellectual reformers in Poland in 1968 had a strongly anti-semitic flavour.

In many ways the compromise agreement which saw almost the same Czechoslovak leadership return to Prague had been a defeat for the Soviet leadership. Alexander Dubček, helped by the enormous and demonstrative support he was enjoying at home in Czechoslovakia, returned still holding the office of First Secretary of the Central Committee. Quite inadvertently, though, the Soviet Politburo had hit on a solution which worked very well, from their narrow point of view, for two decades. The deal struck in Moscow meant that during a period almost as long as the Prague Spring itself, Czechoslovakia's 'normalization would have a human face'.[92] However, the step-by-step retreat by the leaders in whom the people of Czechoslovakia had reposed great trust meant that by the time Dubček was replaced by Husák as party first secretary in April 1969, there was scarcely a murmur from the population, whereas millions would have taken to the streets if anyone other than he had been appointed to that office at the end of August of the previous year. One by one, those who favoured radical reform were demoted or dismissed. The people of Czechoslovakia had been politically and morally disarmed by the time hard-liners came to power and governed the country much more intolerantly. Many interesting – from a Soviet point of view politically objectionable – publications continued to appear in Czechoslovakia between September 1968 and April 1969, but in the changed circumstances brought about by military occupation, the relentless pressure on the country's leadership to concede positions they had earlier refused to give up took its toll.

After moving from the first secretaryship in Slovakia to becoming the political leader of the Czechoslovak state, Husák became a model Soviet-style 'normalizer'. He failed to meet even the modest desires of those who hoped he would turn into a Kádár and support economic reform and perhaps cultural liberalization. In the longer run, however, the years in which Czechoslovakia became a 'normal' Communist state brought no credit, or positive legacy, either to the leading Czech and Slovak normalizers or to those in the Soviet Union who had placed them in power. Indeed, as will be seen in later chapters, the Prague Spring and its crushing came to have a significance in Western Europe in the 1970s and for the Soviet Union in the second half of the 1980s quite different from anything that was in the mind of Leonid Brezhnev and his colleagues.

20

'The Era of Stagnation':
The Soviet Union under Brezhnev

'The Era of Stagnation' was the name given in the last years of the Soviet Union to the period between 1964 and 1982 when Leonid Brezhnev was the leader of the Soviet Communist Party and the most powerful politician within the Soviet state. It was in many ways a fitting description, for this was a period of a declining rate of economic growth, no political reform worthy of the name, and a conservative Communist regime led by the cautious Brezhnev. The term, though, can also be misleading, for Soviet society changed during these years in ways that were not and could not be wholly controlled from above. Moreover, in spite of the censorship and ideological pressures for conformity, there were struggles between different political and intellectual tendencies going on below the surface of politics.

Some Russian writers make a distinction between the early Brezhnev and the later Brezhnev. There certainly were contrasting features. In his early years as leader, Brezhnev was anxious to show how different he was from Khrushchev and did not try to hog the limelight.[1] In the 1970s, however, a mini-cult of his personality was created, and this continued into his declining years. In that last period, Brezhnev's physical and intellectual capacities had been severely reduced by illness and his speech was slurred. But the differences in policy between early Brezhnev and late Brezhnev were far from notable. The early Brezhnev approved the invasion of Czechoslovakia and the later Brezhnev approved the invasion of Afghanistan. The word 'approved' is used deliberately, for he was not, as we have seen, the person who was pushing hardest for the use of force in either case. Indeed, he was aware that he probably could not have survived as Soviet leader in 1968 had he *not* gone along with the idea of military intervention. As he told one of the reformist leaders of the Czechoslovak Communist Party, Bohumil Šimon (who had been allowed to remain in the party Presidium for the time being), in Moscow later that year: 'if I had not voted for Soviet armed assistance to Czechoslovakia you would not be sitting here today, but quite possibly I wouldn't either'.[2] We now know from the archival evidence that there were significant voices in the Soviet leadership calling for the immediate overthrow of the Prague Spring reformers and the installation of a 'revolutionary government' in Czechoslovakia in August 1968. Brezhnev, as we saw in the previous chapter, was one of those who judged it necessary to reach a temporary compromise with the reformist Prague political leadership, which had been shown to enjoy overwhelming domestic support. Thus, Brezhnev's remark rings true so far as Šimon's reprieve was concerned. More significantly, Brezhnev was doubtless right in thinking that his own survival as Soviet leader would have been in serious question had he opposed military intervention in Czechoslovakia. Failure to prevent a central European Communist state from acquiring political autonomy, thus setting a dangerous example for the rest of east-central Europe, was not an option he dared contemplate.[3]

In foreign policy, while having no desire to yield an inch of territory which came under Soviet control, Brezhnev favoured some easing of tensions in East–West relations. These were to be, as far as possible, on Soviet terms. That meant using every means available to try to prevent Western ideas from gaining a foothold in the Soviet Union. Nevertheless, Brezhnev's policy of détente enabled him to establish a measure of rapport with Willy Brandt when Brandt as West German chancellor introduced his *Ostpolitik*. Brandt's initiatives led to the signing of the Moscow and Warsaw Treaties in 1970, which recognized the state borders that had existed de facto since the end of World War Two.[4] His chancellorship was of decisive importance in reducing the fear of Germany which had persisted in the Soviet Union and in Poland. Memories of the war were still fresh, and they were constantly exploited by Brezhnev and by the Soviet mass media. The victory of the Soviet army and the sufferings of the civilian population during the Second World War were used as a particularly effective rallying cry, one which evoked a much more deeply felt response than references to Marx or Lenin. In that context, respect for Brandt's anti-Nazi record and his foreign policy initiatives had a more than temporary significance. Without the change of perceptions of Germany the *Ostpolitik* helped bring about, later Soviet acquiescence in the unification of the country would have been unimaginable. Détente extended to Soviet relations with the United States as well as with West Germany. Brezhnev signed arms control and trade agreements with American presidents Nixon and Ford, and shortly before détente collapsed, a treaty on strategic arms limitations (SALT II) with President Carter in 1979. Earlier the Soviet Union signed the Helsinki Final Act of 1975, following the Conference on Security and Co-operation in Europe. This was believed by many at the time to be a triumph of Soviet diplomacy, but it turned out to have more disadvantages than advantages for those in the USSR (including Brezhnev) who wished to keep the ideological hatches battened down. (The Helsinki agreement is discussed in Chapter 23.)

Domestically, as noted in Chapter 14, virtually all of Khrushchev's administrative reforms were reversed within the first two years after his removal from office. Still more important was the change of policy with regard to Josif Stalin. The Brezhnev-led Politburo soon decided that it was much too dangerous to allow a continuation of criticism of Stalin. Brezhnev was a practitioner of what seemed to him a kind of Soviet 'golden mean'. He abjured 'revisionism', on the one hand, and 'dogmatism', on the other. He was neither Stalinist nor anti-Stalinist, but projected himself, rather, as the voice of authentic Leninism. The retreat from criticism of Stalin and Stalinism in the Brezhnev era was a step backwards, but Brezhnev's caution prevented it from becoming a still greater leap into the past. Immediately after the fall of Khrushchev there was substantial support both from Brezhnev's personal entourage and within the top party leadership for a disavowal of the Twentieth and Twenty-Second Party Congresses (which were seen as part of Khrushchev's folly) and for the rehabilitation of Stalin. A battle was waged behind the scenes over every party document and the text of every Brezhnev speech.[5] Among the most influential Stalinists in Brezhnev's entourage was Sergey Trapeznikov, who had enjoyed his patronage ever since he worked for him in Moldova, where Brezhnev had been first secretary at the beginning of the 1950s. (It was there that Brezhnev also picked up the ever-loyal Konstantin Chernenko – his successor but one as general secretary. Chernenko was a conservative Communist, but less ideological than Trapeznikov. He became essentially Brezhnev's chief clerk.)

Having failed to secure the rehabilitation of Stalin at the Twenty-Third Congress, those who were angling for this tried again when they worked on the speech Brezhnev was to deliver in November 1966 in Stalin's native Georgia. Trapeznikov and a number of Stalinist Georgians were among the authors of a text which, in the words of Georgi Arbatov, an adviser to the Soviet leadership, was 'an utterly unabashed effort to glorify Stalin and proclaim him, once again, the Great Leader'.[6] Brezhnev had some doubts about the text and consulted more widely. Arbatov, backed by his chief at that time, Yury Andropov, who was head of the department of the Central Committee responsible for relations with other Communist states, was among those who put the arguments against the draft speech when Brezhnev asked for comments. Rather than focus on political morality, Arbatov chose arguments based on expediency likely to have more sway with Brezhnev. He pointed out, first, that a rehabilitation would complicate relations with East European Communist states (not least the positions of two leaders who had been victims of Stalin – Kádár in Hungary and Gomułka in Poland); second, that another about-turn on the Stalin issue would make life difficult for Western Communist parties; and third, he picked out the most strongly worded anti-Stalin passages from the speeches of existing members of the Soviet top leadership team at the Twenty-Second Congress in 1961 when they were still trying to please Nikita Khrushchev. Finally, he pointed out that Brezhnev had taken part in all the party congresses since the nineteenth. Might this not raise questions about his role?

Whatever Brezhnev's personal inclinations, these arguments sufficed, and Arbatov and others drafted a boring speech which the Soviet leader duly read out in Georgia. It had the sole merit of avoiding any glorification of Stalin.[7] Not only opposition from anti-Stalinists within the CPSU, but objections also from foreign Communist leaders and protests from prominent Soviet intellectuals played a part in ensuring that the rehabilitation of Stalin did not occur.[8] The issue was not just of historical interest. A victory for the Stalinists, while ostensibly about the role Stalin himself had played, would have meant a severe crackdown on any contemporary deviation from the strictest orthodoxy – still more than actually occurred in the Brezhnev era. As it was, the struggle between Stalinists and anti-Stalinists ended in a stalemate in which, however, even the euphemistic phrase, much used in Khrushchev's time, 'the period of the cult of personality' (which referred to the years from 1934 to 1953) was banished from use.[9] On the whole there was silence about Stalin, but it became significantly easier to publish a positive than a negative reference to him.

The Brezhnev years turned out to be, in many ways, the golden age of the Soviet bureaucrat. Under Stalin they progressed rapidly up the career ladder, but they lived with uncertainty. Especially in the late 1930s, senior officials did not know at the start of each day whether they would end it in their own bed or in prison. If Stalin had threatened their very lives, Khrushchev threatened their careers. His frequent administrative reorganizations meant that there was still little security of tenure for officials in the party and governmental apparatus. Brezhnev, in contrast, made a virtue out of 'respect for cadres' and maintaining bureaucratic stability. For Soviet officials, this was welcome after what had gone before and was in particularly satisfying contrast with what they could see happening in China during Mao's Cultural Revolution.

In Brezhnev's Soviet Union, politicians could grow old in the same job, whether as Politburo members, party secretaries, or ministers. The average age of the Politburo immediately after Khrushchev's removal was sixty. By 1975 it had risen to sixty-five, and on the eve of Brezhnev's death in 1982 it was seventy. There was no tradition in Soviet politics of honourable retirement, and the best way to ensure a good send-off in the Soviet mass media was to die in office. Provided officials were politically loyal and ideologically orthodox, life for them was more predictable than it had ever been before. For inefficiency they might be moved from one post to another, but usually to a job of comparable standing – on the same level of the *nomenklatura* as the post from which they had been transferred. For young officials the promotion blockage, which had not existed in Stalin's or Khrushchev's time, was frustrating, but there was nothing they could do about it. With seniority went power – notably, membership of the Central Committee of the CPSU, to which the first secretaries of the republican parties belonged, as did most of the regional first secretaries and a majority of the ministers.

The Top Leadership

Like Khrushchev before him, Brezhnev promoted people who had been his subordinates in the past, but he only very gradually secured a Politburo in which he had a majority of close allies. His most influential colleagues, especially in the 1960s, were Alexey Kosygin, who had made his career in the ministerial network and was Chairman of the Council of Ministers for sixteen of Brezhnev's eighteen years as party leader, and Mikhail Suslov, a senior secretary (a member both of the Politburo and the Secretariat of the Central Committee) throughout almost the whole of the Brezhnev era. His influence ended only with his death in office in 1980 at the age of seventy-nine. Brezhnev was fortunate that Suslov, who had people beholden to him in many parts of the apparatus, was satisfied with the substance of the great power he wielded within the Central Committee secretariat and did not aspire to the party leadership.

Another whose position was independent of Brezhnev was Nikolay Podgorny, a client of Khrushchev who (like Brezhnev) turned against his former patron. The long-serving Anastas Mikoyan was briefly Chairman of the Presidium of the Supreme Soviet in 1964–65, but Brezhnev and his colleagues, not forgetting that Mikoyan had been the only member of the leadership team to mount a partial defence of Khrushchev at the time of the latter's removal, invented a new rule (quickly forgotten, after it had been applied to Mikoyan) that no one should remain in the Politburo beyond the age of seventy. Podgorny took Mikoyan's place as Chairman of the Presidium of the Supreme Soviet, combining that with his Politburo membership. He held both offices until Brezhnev felt strong enough unceremoniously to remove him in 1977. By then Brezhnev decided he had waited long enough to add the dignity of becoming formal head of state to his party leadership. Yet another senior member of the Politburo throughout the Brezhnev era who did not owe his position to Brezhnev was Andrey Kirilenko. Like the general secretary, he was indebted to Khrushchev for his initial invitation to the top table. Kirilenko was a senior secretary from 1966 until Brezhnev's death in 1982. By that time, aged seventy-six, his mental condition had deteriorated to the point where he could scarcely remember the names of the other members of the Politburo. He was unable without help to write a short letter of resignation when begged to do so by Andropov.[10]

Kosygin, as already noted, had an importance initially which was at least comparable to Suslov's. And like Suslov he did not aspire to be general secretary. He was content to head the governmental rather than the party machine, although less happy at the way Brezhnev's gradual accretion of power reduced his own authority in the 1970s as compared with the mid-1960s. Kosygin was so prominent in the earlier post-Khrushchev years that as late as 1970 Henry Kissinger mistakenly thought that he was 'the dominant figure in foreign policy in the Politburo' and that summit talks with the recently elected President Nixon would mean meeting with Kosygin.[11] In fact, Brezhnev was busy demonstrating once again that the leader of the Communist Party would emerge as number one in Soviet politics and that discussions at the highest level must involve him. Kosygin continued, however, to be in charge of detailed economic administration in his role as Chairman of the Council of Ministers.

He introduced an economic reform of modest proportions in 1965. It aimed to increase material incentives and to reward factories and their managers for sales rather than simply for gross output. But in the absence of market prices, even the sales success indicator was of dubious value as a measure of economic efficiency. The Soviet economy, in fact, enjoyed stronger growth in the second half of the 1960s than it ever did thereafter, but the link between that and the 'Kosygin reforms' is tenuous. Kosygin, although an able administrator, was too much a product of the Soviet ministerial system, as it evolved under Stalin, to become a radical economic reformer. However, even his modest proposals for change became linked in arguments behind the scenes with the developments in Czechoslovakia. It seems likely that the harshness of Kosygin's criticism of Czech and Slovak reformers owed something to his realization that they had made his own attempt to achieve greater rationality within the Soviet economic system harder to realize. The fact that economic reform in Czechoslovakia had in 1968 been accompanied by dangerous political reform helped to discredit the very word 'reform' in the Soviet Union. Those, especially within the Communist Party apparatus, who viewed any attempt to make the economy more self-regulating as a threat to their political and administrative powers were happy to assist in the task of elevating Brezhnev to a position of significantly higher authority than Kosygin. In practical terms, a more important economic development than the Kosygin reforms was the removal of some of the restrictions, which had been imposed by Khrushchev after 1958, on peasant plots. The size of this subsidiary agriculture was still curtailed, but it was treated more benevolently under Brezhnev (who, like Khrushchev before him, made agriculture one of his special responsibilities). Peasants were allowed to keep more livestock on their personal plots than hitherto.[12]

If Brezhnev kept a wary eye on Kosygin, he turned a more baleful gaze on one member of the top leadership team who was a real potential rival, Alexander Shelepin. There is every reason to suppose that Shelepin, who was not alone in regarding Brezhnev as a temporary leader, aspired to the top job. Known as 'Iron Shurik', he had accumulated some important allies on his way to membership of the Politburo. He had been head of the Komsomol (the Communist youth organization), then head of the KGB, and from 1961 a secretary of the Central Committee. When in 1966 he became a full member of the Politburo, he was one of the handful of senior secretaries – those with a foothold in both the Politburo and the secretariat – who, as a result, carried special authority. Brezhnev handled Shelepin with care. In May 1967 he removed Vladimir Semichastny, an important ally of Shelepin, from the chairmanship of the KGB, replacing him with Yury Andropov. In September of the same year he eased Shelepin out of the secretariat, making him head of the Soviet trade unions. This was a dead-end job, given that the main function of Soviet-style unions was to keep workers docile and obedient rather than have them become an autonomous force defending workers' interests. Yet such was Brezhnev's caution that there was a gap of almost eight years between his moving Shelepin out of the secretariat and dropping him from the Politburo. That was engineered in 1975 while Shelepin was on a visit to Britain. As we have seen, it was common practice in the post-Stalin Soviet Union for politicians to be dismissed when they were far from Moscow and thus unable to mobilize support from potential allies. (In Stalin's time it didn't matter where they were. They could just as easily be arrested in their apartments in central Moscow.)

Although Brezhnev demonstrated what Stalin and Khrushchev had shown before him, that the general secretaryship of the Central Committee was the most powerful office in the Soviet Union, the period of almost twenty years in which he occupied the Kremlin was one of oligarchical rather than autocratic rule. Even the absurd personality cult which developed in the second half of the 1970s (albeit far below the scale of Stalin's) did not turn Brezhnev into a dictator. In Soviet society it was counterproductive, since it was seen as too much of a coincidence that Brezhnev was found to have been a major war hero, and thus the recipient of the highest award for military valour, the Order of Victory, in 1978 when he was at the height of his political dominance. Still more risible was the award to him one year later of the Lenin Prize for Literature for his ghosted memoirs. Pleasing as these and many other awards were for Brezhnev, who was not lacking in vanity, they were primarily a way of setting him on a higher pedestal than other members of the Politburo and thus bolstering the position of his closest associates within the political hierarchy.

Nevertheless, Brezhnev was a far less domineering leader than Khrushchev had been. Under Khrushchev, almost every major institutional interest had been adversely affected by his zeal for change and reorganization. Brezhnev, in contrast, was solicitous of the interests of the military (whom Khrushchev had tried to cut down to size), of the KGB (whose past was no longer to be associated with the crimes of Stalinism), and even of the ministerial network (who had the same chairman, Alexey Kosygin, from 1964 until his resignation two months before his death in 1980). Above all, he dealt benevolently with the party organization. Loyalty was rewarded with political longevity, and those who had worked successfully with Brezhnev in the past received generous promotion.

Diversity behind the Monolithic Façade

While there were some differences of outlook in the top leadership team – for example, between Andropov (who became a full member of the Politburo in 1973) and Suslov, to whom I'll return later in the chapter – they were all committed to the maintenance of the pillars of the Communist system both in the USSR and in Eastern Europe. Even overt dissent in the broader society seldom called into question such major features as the monopoly of power of the Communist Party. More often, the argument was that the Soviet Union should abide by its own constitution and allow the freedom of speech it seemed to provide. (As noted in a previous chapter, even the constitution contained important qualifications on the various democratic rights it ostensibly bestowed.) What became known as the dissident movement – though its size was scarcely large enough to be regarded as a movement – emerged in the Soviet Union in the earliest post-Khrushchev years. That was partly in response to the elimination of criticism of Stalinism and the arrest of two writers, Andrey Sinyavsky and Yuly Daniel, in 1965, followed by their trial and imprisonment in 1966, for publication of 'anti-Soviet' works abroad.

Two major novels submitted for publication by Alexander Solzhenitsyn in the mid-1960s, *The First Circle* and *Cancer Ward*, were refused publication, even though the editor of *Novy mir*, Alexander Tvardovsky, was eager to see them in print. The KGB had confiscated Solzhenitsyn's literary archive, which included much more overtly anti-Communist works, and he was by this time regarded with deep suspicion.[13] It was in the Brezhnev era that Solzhenitsyn

and the nuclear physicist Andrei Sakharov emerged as the two leading dissidents in the Soviet Union. The fact that the one was a major writer and the
other a great scientist meant that more attention was paid, both within the
Russian intelligentsia and in the outside world, to them than to other dissidents, some of whom were no less brave. Solzhenitsyn and Sakharov were
very different in outlook, although not in respect of their moral courage.
Solzhenitsyn had become an Orthodox Christian and Russian nationalist –
though at the moderate end of the nationalist spectrum – whereas Sakharov
had evolved from having in his youth absorbed 'Communist ideology without
questioning it'[14] into a liberal in the West European sense of that term.[15]

The 1960s saw the development of the phenomenon of *samizdat* – literally,
self-publishing – whereby writings were typed, with numerous and ever-
fainter carbon copies, and distributed by hand. Even when photocopying
machines began to be introduced in Soviet institutes and other work places,
they were kept under strict lock and key. Dissidents, therefore, had to make
copies of documents – and even long novels, such as those of Solzhenitsyn
– in a very labour-intensive way. A related phenomenon was *tamizdat* –
meaning publication 'there' (i.e. the West) – whereby works which emanated
from but could not be published in the Soviet Union were printed in Russian.
Some of them found their way back into the USSR. To be caught reading
such a book, still worse to be distributing it, was a seriously punishable
offence, and so the impact of *tamizdat* was not great. The typescripts of
samizdat, especially when they consisted of politically unorthodox but high-
quality creative literature (which the Russian intelligentsia craved), were,
however, seen by a significant proportion of intellectuals. They were mainly
people outside the political elite, but there were reform-minded officials
who read *samizdat* literature from time to time.

A stream of Soviet dissent which had some covert support even within
the Soviet establishment was that associated with the historian Roy Medvedev.
His first, and major, work was a lengthy and seriously researched manuscript
on Stalin and Stalinism called (in English) *Let History Judge*.[16] Medvedev represented a strand of opinion which was anti-Stalinist but took an idealized view
of Lenin. Before the archives were open, he was able, as a result of his meetings with and collection of materials from old Bolsheviks, to throw detailed
light on the crimes of Stalin. He also wrote about contemporary Soviet politics and was given information by people friendly to his point of view within
the party apparatus.[17] Medvedev's relationship to the system was vastly less
hostile than that of Solzhenitsyn or even compared with the position to
which Sakharov evolved, but he had overstepped the bounds of the permissible. As early as 1968, Andropov, by this time chairman of the KGB, was
calling the attention of heads of Central Committee departments to the

book on Stalinism which Medvedev was writing. Three of these department chiefs, including Trapeznikov, jointly signed a document saying that the Moscow city party organization should raise the question of Medvedev's continued party membership. Although Medvedev was treated more leniently than some dissidents, the KGB and Andropov personally came to regard him as dangerous. Medvedev had made no secret of his work on this book. In the Soviet archives there is a copy of a letter he wrote to Mikhail Suslov, enclosing the chapter headings of his work on Stalinism when it was still in progress, requesting a half-hour meeting with him. In fact, his reward for completion of the book was expulsion from the Communist Party in 1969.[18]

The dissidents who became known in the West were mainly those who were concerned with issues of human rights and civil liberties. While they caused concern to the party leadership and the KGB, by the later Brezhnev years their numbers had been reduced from small to infinitesimal. The overtly dissenting groups and movements 'made little or no headway among the mass of ordinary people in the Russian heartland', as the leading specialist on their activity noted. In the last three years of the Brezhnev era and the period of less than three years when Andropov and Chernenko were, successively, the Soviet leaders (i.e. from early 1979 until 1985), there was an especially severe and effective crackdown on the dissidents.[19]

The most dangerous segment of the dissident movement from the point of view of the Soviet authorities was that associated with nationalism, especially when national and religious identity coincided. The three Baltic states, which had been forcibly incorporated in the Soviet Union in 1940, remained the most disaffected of the union republics which made up the USSR. Most Estonians, Latvians and Lithuanians did not openly protest at their lack of political and cultural autonomy, for the price of doing so was too high. Nevertheless, it was clear that if they were given the freedom to argue for a high level of autonomy within a real federation, or outright independence, they would do so. As it was, in their literary journals, and in the foreign works they translated, they were able to get away (especially in Estonia) with material of a kind deemed politically impossible when presented to Moscow publishers. Moreover, samizdat was more widespread in Lithuania, in relation to population size, than in any other Soviet republic.[20]

Jews were a special case in Soviet nationality policy. Citizens of Jewish origin were counted as a nationality in the Soviet Union, but they were dispersed throughout the country. In the course of the 1970s, Soviet Jews emigrated in large numbers. To succeed in doing so involved a struggle with the authorities, and some were refused permission to leave. Emigration was, nevertheless, on a scale which had not occurred since the 1920s, and this was one of the areas in which Soviet policy under Brezhnev did change significantly. Although in the late Brezhnev years the number of Jewish emigrants declined, even in 1980 as many as 21,471 left for Israel or, via Israel, for the United States. By the end of that year, the number who had left the USSR over the past decade was close to a quarter of a million (with approximately 1.8 million of the Soviet Jewish population remaining).[21] Tens of thousands of Soviet Germans were also allowed to emigrate to Germany in the 1970s. Permitting people from these two communities to emigrate was deemed by the Soviet leadership to be a lesser evil than keeping against their will so many disaffected citizens, the more especially since they had strong support from abroad. This took the form of high-profile campaigning and lobbying in the United States, in particular, for the Jewish would-be emigrants, and quiet diplomacy from West Germany on behalf of the German Soviet citizens.

The emigration, even though grudgingly granted by the Soviet author-ities, was a change of policy in a more liberal direction. It did not, however, contribute to the longer-term liberalization of the Soviet Union. That is because the Soviet Jews, a particularly well-educated group, included a large number of people who were strongly in favour of reform of the system, among them, naturally, many of the emigrants. Even after the large-scale emigration, Jews remained the most overrepresented 'nationality' within the Communist Party of the Soviet Union, although the very fact that so many wished to leave the country did not make life easier for the even larger numbers of Soviet citizens of Jewish origin who wished to stay where they were. Ever since Stalin's anti-semitic purge at the end of the 1940s and begin-ning of the 1950s, Jews (with rare exceptions such as Kaganovich until 1957) had been kept out of the highest ranks of the party and the KGB, but there continued to be a significant number of academic specialists of Jewish origin in senior positions in major Soviet think-tanks.

The national dissent potentially the most corrosive of the Soviet system was *Russian* nationalism, given that Russians made up a little over half of the total population of the USSR and the Russian republic constituted three quarters of its territory. The union could survive large-scale Jewish emigra-tion and *a* union could continue even without the Baltic states (though that was scarcely an imaginable occurrence during the Brezhnev years). If, however, Russians were to give up paying even lip-service to Marxism-Leninism, the foundations of the Soviet state would be fatally undermined. In fact, the Brezhnev era saw the rapid growth of Russian nationalism, though it was a movement which had many different strands. There were Russian nationalists who saw the Soviet Union as a greater Russia and fully identi-fied with the Soviet state, glorying in its superpower status. There were others who saw the USSR as much too *internationalist*, and pointed to the fact that the other fourteen union republics had their own capital and their own republican institutions, such as academies of sciences, whereas Russia simply had the Soviet capital, Moscow, and Russians had largely to make do with being the preponderant nationality within a number of all-union institutions. For some, such as Solzhenitsyn, national feeling was closely connected to respect for the Orthodox Church and abhorrence at the way Christianity had been persecuted during the Communist era. Among the authors who might in varying degrees be described as nationalists, there was a school of 'village prose' writers who tended to idealize the Russian peasant and to deplore the way the Communists had destroyed traditional patterns of rural life. A complementary strand of writing – which one did not need to be a nationalist to support – involved a concern with ecological issues. This was a permitted form of dissent and included campaigning for the protection, for example, of Lake Baikal (the world's largest freshwater lake), although raising ecological concerns went against the Communist regime's relentless emphasis on economic growth and material progress.[22]

Russian nationalists who remained within the Communist Party were opposed to internationalism and to Western influences, and often were strongly anti-semitic, seeing Jews as archetypal internationalists with strong foreign links. In terms of broad movements of opinion within the CPSU, there was a fundamental division between those, on the one side, who constituted 'the Russian party' and those, on the other, who wanted greater integration with the rest of the world, many of whom could be accurately described as Westernizers. Although both Mikhail Suslov and Yury Andropov were orthodox enough Communists, Suslov was seen as the protector of the Russian nationalists and Andropov, strange though it may seem, was held to be the patron of the internationalists. Andropov himself never even visited a non-Communist Western country, but he was generally well disposed towards the international institutes, such as the Institute of the United States and Canada (founded early in the Brezhnev era) and IMEMO (the Institute of World Economy and International Relations, which had existed for much longer), in neither of which was there any shortage of Westernizers. Andropov was also a hate figure for many Russian nationalists.*

---

* A book published in Moscow in 2005 by a former Soviet specialist in anti-Western 'counter-propaganda', entitled 'The Russian Party Inside the CPSU', argues that this 'Russian party', with whom the author wholly identifies, was represented at virtually all levels of the Communist Party, and that their arch-enemy was Andropov. The book is permeated by anti-semitism. Andropov is referred to throughout as 'Andropov-Fainshstein' (an allusion to his mother's name and Andropov's half-Jewish origins) or, sometimes, the 'Jew-Chekist Andropov'. See Aleksandr Baygushev, *Russkaya partiya vnutri KPSS* (Algoritm-Kniga, Moscow, 2005), esp. p. 200.

Andropov was a complex character, and one side of his personality – the fact that he had intellectual interests and liked to be surrounded by intelligent people – is illustrated by the subsequent careers of party intellectuals who worked closely with him in the Central Committee before he became chairman of the KGB. Several of them turned into important reformers during perestroika, the most senior of their number being Shakhnazarov. Andropov also supported Kádár in the 1970s, after the Hungarian leader had embarked on economic reform which went beyond anything to be found elsewhere in the Soviet bloc at that time. Yet he had taken one of the hardest lines on Czechoslovakia in 1968, and in general there were strict limits to his reformism. He was, however, certainly no nationalist. Suslov, in contrast, was the senior member of the party leadership who did most to ensure that Russian nationalist deviation was the form of dissent treated most gently throughout the 1970s. Many books and articles which were more Russian nationalist than Leninist were passed by the censor. Towards the end of the Brezhnev era three journals (and they were far from alone) on whose editorial boards Russian nationalists predominated – *Molodaya gvardiya* (Young Guard), *Moskva* (Moscow) and *Nash sovremmenik* (Our Contemporary) – had a combined circulation of more than one and a half million copies.[23] This utterly dwarfed the circulation of *samizdat*, whose products also, however, included some of Russian nationalist orientation.

CULTURAL DEVIATION

In many ways pressure from below changed official policy, while not yet affecting the fundamental characteristics of a Communist system. Even though the 'leading role' of the party was maintained in the political system of the Brezhnev era, the party was more often than not following, rather than leading, within the realm of popular culture. Youth culture had become increasingly international. Cultural overseers fought prolonged battles against jeans and rock music, and lost both. Party propagandists might rage against 'decadent' Western influences, but to very little effect. Having failed to stop young citizens of the Soviet Union from buying jeans from Western tourists, the Soviet state began to manufacture its own. It was soon discovered, though, that only Western labels had the required cachet. Because the genuine article was not easy to come by and the price was high, a flourishing underground market emerged in fake Western jeans.[24] The dominance in popular music of Western groups, from the Beatles onwards, was scarcely less great throughout the Soviet Union and Eastern Europe than Western sartorial influence. This was not particularly linked with political nonconformity, other than in its defiance of the conservative cultural norms of officialdom.

More politically potent than Western rock music in the Soviet Union was an essentially indigenous form of musical protest which was part of neither official culture nor the dissident movement, but occupied a halfway house. Its three most famous representatives, known as the 'guitar poets', were Vladimir Vysotsky, Alexander Galich and Bulat Okudzhava, who sang nonconformist songs of their own composition.[25] Only a few of the recordings of the songs of Vysotsky, an outstanding actor at the Taganka Theatre as well as a poet, were approved for distribution in his lifetime. Along with the other guitar poets, his prolific output was circulated through *magnitizdat*, the tape-recorded equivalent of *samizdat* literature. When Vysotsky died in his early forties in 1980, the huge attendance at his funeral was a rare (for the Brezhnev era) public demonstration of the extent of critical thinking within the society. Galich, the least tolerated by the Soviet cultural authorities (who took, however, a dim view of all three of them), was also an actor, but one whose writing came to take precedence over acting. He was expelled from the Union of Writers in 1971 and from the Soviet Union itself in 1974. Okudzhava, whose Georgian mother and Armenian father were both arrested in 1937, was gentler in his satire than the other two, and his work was diffused with nostalgia for older values (and buildings). He was the only member of the trio still alive during perestroika, during which he was a strong supporter of liberalization and democratization. The work of all three poet-singers became widely and officially available from quite early in the Gorbachev era. Galich, who died in 1977, was fully rehabilitated in 1988. The audience for the taped songs of the guitar poets was not only, or perhaps even mainly, students, but a generation of the intelligentsia who had come of age in the Khrushchev era and whose anti-Stalinism was allowed no official outlet in the two decades that followed his removal from office.

INTRA-SYSTEMIC DISSENT

A number of people who became overt dissidents, and were punished for it by the party-state authorities, began by trying to bend, rather than break, the rules of the system. That was clearly true of Medvedev, but even Solzhenitsyn made minor cuts in some of his earliest published works in order to have them appear in *Novy mir*. Solzhenitsyn also became a member of the Writers' Union, from which, however, he was expelled in 1969. The following year, to the embarrassment of the Soviet authorities, he was awarded the Nobel Prize for Literature. It was only after it became clear that Solzhenitsyn's work would no longer be published in Russia that he revealed to the world the full extent of his anti-Communism. He had completed in secret his devastating account of the fate of political prisoners, *The Gulag*

Archipelago, in 1968, but did not authorize its publication abroad at that time. When it was first published in the West in 1973, the Politburo decided that Solzhenitsyn was too dangerous to remain in the country and too renowned to be imprisoned again (as he had been in Stalin's time). He was arrested in February 1974, deported from the USSR, and deprived of his citizenship.

Still more clearly, Andrei Sakharov tried to influence developments in the Soviet Union as an insider. As a distinguished physicist, and one who had made an important contribution to research on nuclear weapons, he did not hesitate to offer advice and to advocate changes of policy to Soviet leaders, urging Khrushchev, for example, to stop the testing of nuclear weapons in the atmosphere. A *samizdat* essay he wrote in 1968, on 'Progress, Peaceful Coexistence and Intellectual Freedom', was intended to influence governments, including his own, as well as public opinion. There was no chance, however, of it being published in Brezhnev's Soviet Union, and when it appeared in print in the West, Sakharov was banned from work involving state secrets and deprived of many privileges. He became an increasingly radical critic of Soviet policy throughout the 1970s, and at the beginning of 1980 he was sent into internal exile – banished to the city of Gorky (which has now been restored to its old name of Nizhny Novgorod). It was not until January 1987 that Sakharov was able to return to live and work in Moscow, following a telephone call from Gorbachev in December 1986 inviting him to do so. (In 1989 Sakharov was elected a member of the reformed Soviet legislature. He died suddenly in December of that year.)

During the Brezhnev era, however, thousands of people did succeed in surviving as reformers working within the boundaries of the system, pushing them wider when they could. If they went too far, they could find themselves turned from 'intra-systemic' to 'extra-systemic' reformers – in other words, overt dissidents. Yet over the long run, those gradualists who worked to change the system from within played the more important role in transforming the policy and character of the Soviet state. Their victories during the Brezhnev years were modest ones, but the fact that they had remained within the parameters of the system was crucially important when a reform-minded general secretary came to power in 1985. The system was such that a general secretary had to appoint to important positions people who already had some seniority within the party. If he wished to find people with fresh ideas, some of them (who could bring in others) needed to have experience already of the corridors of power of the Central Committee building. Three such people who played important roles during the perestroika period were Alexander Yakovlev, Anatoly Chernyaev and Georgy Shakhnazarov. All three of them had fought in the Second World War but defied the generalization which loosely associated Soviet war veterans with Stalinism. Resolute anti-Stalinists, they had all held senior positions in the Central Committee apparatus. In the Brezhnev era, Yakovlev had been an acting head of the Department of Propaganda, Chernyaev was a deputy head of the International Department, and Shakhnazarov a deputy head of the Socialist Countries Department.

Although their own views evolved and were not the same in the early 1970s as they became in the late 1980s, even in that earlier period they were relative liberals – or in at least one case, a closet social democrat – within the party apparatus.[26] Chernyaev and Shakhnazarov were still deputy heads of their respective departments in 1985, but Yakovlev had been sent into dignified exile as Soviet ambassador to Canada in 1973. His main offence had been to publish a newspaper article in late 1972 that attacked all forms of nationalism and chauvinism, including Russian nationalism. This provoked anger in conservative Communist and Russian nationalist circles. Yakovlev remained in Canada until 1983, when Mikhail Gorbachev, by that time an influential senior secretary of the Central Committee during Yury Andropov's brief period as Soviet leader, visited Canada and found a polit ical soulmate. At Gorbachev's request, Andropov agreed to Yakovlev being brought back to Moscow as director of the major foreign affairs think-tank, IMEMO. From there, Gorbachev, on becoming leader, brought Yakovlev back into the Central Committee.

The minority of reformists by inclination who held on to posts within the Central Committee apparatus during the Brezhnev era were to play a particularly important part in Soviet political life when Gorbachev came to power. The International Department (ID) of the Central Committee was widely regarded in the West as a citadel of Communist orthodoxy, and it was, indeed, the department which had inherited the role of the Comintern, keeping a supervisory eye on non-ruling Communist parties throughout the world. Yet it was from this department that Gorbachev was to draw many of the 'new thinkers' of the perestroika era into his foreign policy team. Part of the reason was that it recruited into its ranks as full-time consult-ants highly educated people with a knowledge of one or more foreign languages and expertise on the outside world. They were influenced by their travel and by their reading in ways unintended by the party leadership, who nevertheless relied on them for a better understanding of that outside world with which they had to deal.

A second department of the Central Committee with international respon-sibilities, the Socialist Countries Department, likewise contained people with linguistic and other expertise. Its main focus was on the countries of Eastern Europe, and albeit to a lesser extent than the ID, it too was a source of fresh thinking. In these departments, as elsewhere in the Central Committee appa-ratus, those who were profoundly dissatisfied with the way things were going in the Soviet Union during the Brezhnev era had to keep such ideas largely under wraps in their official capacities, although they would speak freely among close friends. Anatoly Chernyaev, an exceptionally influential 'new thinker' of the Gorbachev era, aptly draws on Orwell for the title of one of the Brezhnev-era chapters in his memoirs, calling it 'In the regime of double-think (the International Department of the Central Committee)'.[27]

Reformers, and people who were profoundly dissatisfied with the Soviet status quo, were to be found in much greater numbers in the research institutes than in departments of the Central Committee. They were especially numerous in those which involved travel and study visits abroad. Apart from the Institute of the USA and Canada, whose director, Georgi Arbatov, had at one time been head of Andropov's group of consultants in the Central Committee Socialist Countries Department, and IMEMO, whose director for almost the whole of the Brezhnev era was the pro-détente Nikolay Inozemtsev,[28] special note should be made of the Institute of Economics of the World Socialist System, headed by Oleg Bogomolov.[29] A higher proportion of radical reformers, it is arguable, emerged from Bogomolov's institute during perestroika than from any other. Even in Brezhnev's time, there was no bolder institute in giving advice which was not what the party leadership wanted to hear. On 20 January 1980, that institute sent a memorandum to the Central Committee of the CPSU in which they wrote of the 'hopelessness and harmfulness' of the Soviet military intervention in Afghanistan.[30]

Institutions which were set up for one purpose could gradually come to serve another, the second purpose being almost the opposite of the original intention of the founders. Thus, for example, Arbatov's USA institute was established to provide the party leadership with better knowledge of the United States and to help the Soviet Union effectively counter American propaganda. Many of its researchers, however, became not only sophisticated analysts of American politics but also rather pro-American – not in an unpatriotic way, but finding much to admire and which could be copied, with advantage, nearer home. Specialists in Bogomolov's Institute of Economics of the World Socialist System, part of whose task was to ensure that East European countries received Soviet guidance and kept to a straight-and-narrow Marxist-Leninist path, became enthusiastic about some developments in east-central Europe which were less than congenial for the Soviet party leadership. That applied not only to Hungarian economic reform but, for a few members of the institute, even to the rise of Solidarity in Poland.

An especially interesting example of this emerging dual character of institutions in Communist states – what a Chinese scholar analyzing Chinese developments called 'institutional amphibiousness'[31] – was to be found in the Department of Scientific Communism of the institute responsible for collecting information in the social sciences, INION. This department was staffed by people who were expected to read, in foreign languages, the most sensitive materials published abroad, including critical writings about the Soviet Union. INION had a series of quite liberal directors, of whom the first was the Sinologist Lev Delyusin, who had earlier been a member of Andropov's team of consultants in the Socialist Countries department of the Central Committee (as had been two other important institute directors – not only Arbatov, but also Bogomolov). Intellectuals who were highly critical of Soviet reality found INION's Department of Scientific Communism a very attractive place to work and happily congregated there. They were able to read in the office interesting materials which they would have been very hard pressed to find in *samizdat*.

One person who was employed in this supposed Marxist-Leninist redoubt was Ludmilla Alexeyeva, a leading Soviet dissident who in her spare time typed and distributed underground literature.[32] In the period when she worked under the roof of Scientific Communism, she was – as all who worked there had to be – a member of the Communist Party. Other people of critical views who worked in that office, as well as in other social science or international institutes, remained 'within-system reformers' or 'intra-structural dissenters'. The idea, quite widespread in the West during the Brezhnev years, that Soviet citizens could be divided into dissidents, on the one hand, and conformists, on the other, with members of the Communist Party constituting the ultra-orthodox members of society, was highly misleading. The membership of the CPSU included Stalinists, idealistic Communists (who put their faith in the late Lenin or the purged Bukharin), nationalists, social democrats and liberals, among others. The system was such, however, that only a change at the top could allow these 'hundred flowers' to bloom.

Successes and Failures

From the point of view of Communist rulers, the Brezhnev era was in many ways successful. This was the period when the USSR achieved a rough parity with the United States – by the early 1970s – as a military power, although the basis of its 'superpower' status depended very heavily on the disproportionately large resources it devoted to military expenditure. Although no economic superpower, the Soviet Union contained some of the world's richest mineral deposits. It was, however, a sign of the weakness of the economy that Soviet exports depended so heavily on the sale of natural resources, especially oil and gas. Yet what was termed the 'oil crisis' in Western Europe – the sharp rise in price of 1973 – turned out to be an energy bonanza for the Soviet Union. The Brezhnev leadership's ability to keep various elites content owed much to the sale at advantageous prices of its natural resources. Keeping them satisfied was, however, harder at the end of the Brezhnev era than earlier. The rate of economic growth was in long-term decline and in Brezhnev's last years had virtually ground to a halt.

To reduce the chances of outbursts of popular, as distinct from elite, discontent, Soviet party leaders were far from relying on the threat of coercion alone. Basic foodstuffs were subsidized and many commodities were in short supply. The shortage economy meant a lot of time was wasted searching for scarce products, but price increases caused resentment. Queuing was regarded as fairer than price hikes, which hit the low-paid hardest. The Brezhnev leadership displayed great caution in dealing with the problem, even as the cost of subsidizing bread and meat prices soared. By the later Brezhnev years, subsidies to farm products were, by international standards, on an exceptionally large scale. A quarter of all Soviet investment went into its highly inefficient agricultural sector.[33] In the long run, subsidies were at an unsustainable level and a radical reduction in their level would have been easier under the highly authoritarian (or, according to how the term is defined, totalitarian)* regime of the 1970s than in the liberalized system of the second half of the 1980s when marketizing policies could be openly advocated but whose adoption and implementation was too long delayed.[34]

---

* A vast amount of ink has been spilled on arguments between those who hold that all Communist systems were totalitarian at all times and others who argue that in certain Communist states at certain times the term 'totalitarian' is more misleading than helpful. Among those who take the second view, there is further scope for disagreement about precisely when and where 'totalitarian' might be an overstatement. Sometimes the arguments are based on failures of observation but quite often simply on definitional differences. If a 'pure' totalitarian system has not existed anywhere – other than in the pages of George Orwell's *Nineteen Eighty-Four* – it becomes absurd to object to the very concept of totalitarianism, or its application to high Stalinism, on the grounds that even a Stalin (who had the power, inter alia, to condemn to death his 'colleagues' in the political leadership) did not personally control *everything*. There are certainly Communist regimes that have come sufficiently close to the totalitarian ideal type to be appropriately called totalitarian. Brezhnev's Soviet Union does not seem to me to be quite in that category. It was a highly authoritarian Communist system, but classifying it as totalitarian is liable to obscure rather than illuminate important developments within the society. For a discussion of the concepts and their application, see Archie Brown, 'The Study of Totalitarianism and Authoritarianism', in Jack Hayward, Brian Barry and Archie Brown (eds.), *The British Study of Politics in the Twentieth Century* (Oxford University Press for the British Academy, Oxford, 1999), pp. 345–94, esp. pp. 354–60.

The Brezhnev era was a time when tens of millions of Soviet citizens could live a peaceful and more predictable life than hitherto. It was also a period of comparatively stable prices. Most people did not live in fear of the KGB. Whereas in Stalin's time it was easy to be caught up in the maelstrom of state terror through anonymous denunciation or sheer bad luck, in the Brezhnev era KGB interrogation normally came about only when people had significantly breached the rules of the Soviet game. Even then, for offences such as passing along *samizdat* (an activity which the vast majority of the population did not engage in), the KGB normally let miscreants off with a warning in the first instance. In many opinion surveys in post-Soviet Russia, more respondents named the Brezhnev era than any other when asked what was the best time to live in Russia during the twentieth century.[35] By the 1970s, there were more highly educated people in the Soviet Union than ever before. In the middle of that decade there were four and a half million students in higher education institutions. Educational advance was one of the successes of the Soviet system. It was also, however, a double-edged sword so far as the longer-term viability of the system was concerned.

Highly educated people were more likely to listen to foreign broadcasts and tended not to take at face value the upbeat accounts of Soviet life to be found in the domestic mass media. They became increasingly unhappy about the restrictions placed on their reading matter and about the curbs on travelling abroad, especially when they compared their situation with equivalent professionals in Western countries. For many decades Soviet people had tended to make comparisons with the past and take satisfaction from an enhanced standard of living over time. Once they made comparisons across space rather than time, a great deal depended on their reference group – that is to say, with whom they compared themselves. In the Baltic republics, citizens made the comparison with their near neighbours in Scandinavia and had every cause for dissatisfaction. In countries such as Sweden, Norway and Finland, far higher levels of economic well-being were combined with political freedom. For people in Soviet Central Asia, the comparison was very different. They could contrast their relative tranquillity very favourably with China during the Cultural Revolution, and their economic and educational levels were much superior to those in neighbouring Afghanistan. Russians, especially those in the professions who were already enjoying an educated middle-class lifestyle – reading widely, going to the theatre and cinema – were ever more conscious of the freedoms enjoyed by West Europeans and North Americans that were denied to them. Increasingly, it was with these advanced Western countries that they made comparisons.

There were ample grounds for dissatisfaction with the Soviet status quo. The Brezhnev era was one of growing social problems and disturbing long-term trends. In the first category came the growth of alcoholism and drunkenness and its consequences for health. Alcohol abuse was one of the major reasons why the life expectancy of men in the Soviet Union declined from sixty-six in 1964 to sixty-two in the early 1980s. It was unusual to have such a decline over a period of less than two decades in an industrialized developed country.* There was also a long-term demographic problem. Whereas the population was growing quite quickly in Soviet Central Asia, in the European part of the USSR it was stagnating or even declining. Some Soviet analysts worried about thinly populated Siberia, where so many of Russia's mineral resources were located, and the billion Chinese over the border.

The Soviet Union's foreign relations during the Brezhnev era are largely dealt with in other chapters. They hardly represented a success story. The Soviet Union in 1982 had bad relations with the United States, with China, and with Western Europe. The leaders had good relations with their East European counterparts, but the warm sentiments of the latter were not shared by the populations of those countries. In particular, the crushing of the Prague Spring had not been forgotten in Czechoslovakia, and the recent imposition of martial law in Poland, although undertaken by Poland's own Communist leadership, had done nothing to ease the animosity of Poles towards the Soviet Union. Soviet troops were also bogged down in a war in Afghanistan in which the most they could achieve was a costly stalemate. Whatever nostalgia may have been felt in post-Soviet Russia, especially in the first decade after the end of Communism, for the Brezhnev years, that era was a time of great hypocrisy. If public criticism and overt social conflict were rare during this period, that was largely because of the strictness of the censorship, the sophisticated system of rewards for conformist political behaviour, and the hierarchy of sanctions for deviation from that norm.

* The life expectancy of Russian men became still lower in the early post-Soviet era – 57.6 in 1994, rising to just under 60 by 1999 – a time when the life expectancy of women in Russia was 72.

PART FOUR

PLURALIZING PRESSURES

21

The Challenge from Poland: John Paul II, Lech Wałesa, and the Rise of Solidarity

At the beginning of the 1970s, it was often argued that pressure from intellectuals was not a significant threat to a Communist regime. It was only a revolt by workers that could really alter anything substantial. That was plain wrong. The dramatic changes under way in Czechoslovakia in 1968 were intelligentsia-led (by the party intellectuals, in the first instance) and it took half a million foreign troops to put a stop to the process. The generalization that only worker protest really mattered gained plausibility, however, from a comparison of what happened in Poland in 1968 and in the same country in 1970. Moreover, it is beyond doubt that worker unrest did, indeed, pose special problems for a Communist system. These were, after all, states in which the working class allegedly played the 'leading role', even if they no longer constituted a 'dictatorship of the proletariat'. In either case, the workers had supposedly 'delegated' the implementation of that role essentially to the Communist party.

Polish workers, more than those in any other European Communist state, challenged that orthodoxy. They had done so in 1956, and were to do so again at the beginning, middle and end of the 1970s. In the early 1970s it looked as if, in Poland at least, manual workers were the people who possessed real political muscle. In 1968 the Polish intelligentsia and the regime had been at odds, and workers had remained on the sidelines, showing no desire to get involved. The intellectuals lost that battle with the authorities. Some prominent academics left the country for good. Others were either sufficiently isolated or intimidated that they kept a low profile over the next several years. In December 1970, in contrast, a workers' revolt panicked and divided the Communist leadership, brought down Gomułka, and produced some changes in economic policy.

During 1968, intellectuals in Poland, stirred by the developments in Czechoslovakia, had became increasingly outspoken. Students in particular demonstrated in large numbers in March. In the same month some of Poland's most distinguished scholars were dismissed from their professorial posts at the University of Warsaw. They included the philosopher Leszek

Kołakowski, the economist Włodzimierz Brus, and the sociologists Zygmunt Bauman and Maria Hirszowicz. By the end of March, the rector of the university had announced the temporary dissolution of the faculties of economics, philosophy, sociology and psychology, thus denying 1,616 students the right to continue their studies. For good measure, students in the third year of mathematics and physics found their course had also been disbanded.[1]

The Polish leadership's way of combating the intellectual ferment had a strong element of anti-semitism. Many of those targeted by the regime were of Jewish origin. Although Gomułka launched this campaign, it derived its strength from a party faction known as the 'Partisans' (or 'the Patriots'), headed by the minister of the interior, General Mieczysław Moczar. Manoeuvring between them was the party boss of the Silesian industrial region of Katowice, Edward Gierek, although he was identified with a party grouping known as the 'Pragmatists'. The thrust of the campaign was to remove 'Zionists' (meaning Jews) from high political and academic posts and to oust 'revisionists' and liberals more generally. In fact, only a comparatively small number of people of Jewish origin were left in Poland. Ninety per cent of Poland's Jews had been killed during the Second World War. Subsequently, survivors who wished to leave the country, as many did, were allowed to emigrate. Those who remained were people who felt much more Polish than Jewish. They tended also to be lifelong Communists. The campaign against them was part of a struggle for power at the top of the party, aimed at undermining and replacing Gomułka. Had it not been for the 'crisis' (in the eyes of Europe's Communist leaders) in Czechoslovakia, and Gomułka's close liaison with the Soviet leadership throughout 1968, it is likely that the Polish party leader would have been ousted in that same year.[2]

The workers' demonstrations that did trigger leadership change took place in December 1970. Following a decade in which there had been very little increase in the real incomes of workers, price increases were announced just a fortnight before Christmas, thus adding insult to injury in this over-whelmingly Catholic country. Workers demonstrated in the capital, Warsaw, and several factories there were occupied. The largest-scale workers' protests, however, were in the Baltic ports of Gdańsk and Szczecin. Gomułka ordered the army and police to use force, and sixteen workers were shot dead in front of the Lenin Shipyard in Gdańsk.[3] This intensified the outrage already felt in the shipyards. Gomułka, who had come to power on a wave of popular support, left office unmourned by all. On 20 December 1970 he was replaced as party leader by Gierek.[4] While this clash between workers and the state authorities was going on, the Polish intelligentsia had stood aside.

But quite apart from the evidence from Czechoslovakia, the idea that workers as a social group were necessarily the most important instigators of radical reform was not really borne out. At the end of 1970 and over the next few years, Polish workers were, to an extent, bought off by short-term improvements in their material conditions that were not accompanied by fundamental political change. Gierek initially won their support. He visited shipyards and factories and appeared to be a good listener – even the future leader of Solidarity, Lech Wałesa, was impressed at the time.[5] That support was consolidated and lasted for several years as the revamped Communist leadership significantly raised Polish living standards. They did so thanks to reckless borrowing abroad, but in the first half of the 1970s it appeared to many Poles that Gierek's strategy was working. Sociological survey research – which had made progress in Poland earlier than in any other East European Communist state – showed that in 1975, three out of four Poles believed their material conditions had improved in recent years.[6] However, by counting on improved economic well-being to accord his leadership legitimacy, Gierek had embarked on a dangerous course. Since the boom had been financed by foreign credits, with Poland ultimately defaulting on many of the loans it had received, the marked improvement in living standards could not last. Economic problems that were tolerated when there was little hope of things getting better were not greeted with equanimity when they came during a period of rising expectations.

Gierek displayed an ability to manoeuvre politically which stood him in good stead for some years. Upon succeeding Gomułka as party first secretary, he lost little time in removing from the leadership the ambitious Moczar, who had played the national card so vigorously in 1968. Gierek himself, however, responded to national sentiments as well as to economic grievances. Under his leadership, the government launched the reconstruction of the Warsaw Royal Castle, which had been destroyed during World War Two and only partially restored subsequently. Overtures were also made to the Catholic Church, whose significance in Poland was closely linked with Poles' strong sense of nationhood. These included permission to build churches in newly developed housing areas, as well as the symbolic gesture of Gierek's well-publicized meeting with Pope Paul VI in the Vatican in 1977.

None of that could for long disguise the fact that the economic upturn was illusory. What has been termed Poland's 'premature consumerism' was bound to be relatively short-lived, for it was not in the least underpinned by the fundamentals of the Polish economy.[7] Gierek was buying time as well as meat from Western Europe. The December 1970 price increases had been completely reversed in response to worker unrest. This meant that food prices in 1976 were very much the same as they had been a decade earlier, although incomes had increased substantially in the first half of the 1970s.[8] And a third of the revenue from Polish exports was spent paying the interest on the foreign loans the government had received – loans which had been used to finance an import-led boom. Poland, having been an exporter of food in the 1950s, was a major importer in the 1970s. Afraid to introduce higher food prices gradually and earlier, the Gierek leadership got the worst of all possible worlds when, quite suddenly, they increased them by an average of 60 per cent (with meat going up by 69 per cent) in June 1976.[9]

The reaction was one which was already becoming a tradition in Poland under Communist rule. There were strikes and sit-ins across the country, with the Baltic shipyards again in the vanguard of resistance to the authorities. In Radom, a town to the south of Warsaw, workers reverted to a form of drastic action which had last been taken at Poznań in 1956, setting fire to the local Communist party headquarters. In a more novel development, several thousand workers from a tractor factory near Warsaw made their way to the transcontinental railway line and stopped the Paris–Moscow express, thus adding to the international impact of the protests. The government retreated much more quickly than they had done in 1970. Within twenty-four hours of the price hikes being made public, they were rescinded. Repressive measures, though, were applied to the workers who had forced this embarrassment on the authorities. These included beatings, arrests and the dismissal from their place of employment of several thousand workers.[10]

The next few years were to demonstrate that the problems for Communist rulers were liable to be especially severe if workers and intellectuals *co-operated*, rather than taking it in turns to be a thorn in the flesh of the authorities (as had happened, in an entirely unplanned way, hitherto). Already in December 1975 a large group of intellectuals had protested about the planned changes to the Polish constitution which were to enshrine in the country's fundamental law the 'leading role' of the party and Poland's membership of the Communist bloc. This followed a period of passivity after 1968 of that social group. However, the fact that civic protest had already been revived meant that there were intellectuals ready to rally to the defence of the workers who had been ill-treated following the June 1976 protests.[11] In September of that year, an organization was set up which was to become one of the most important examples of a developing civil society in Poland – the Workers' Defence Committee, known by the acronym KOR.[12] Those who formed it included writers, historians, lawyers, scientists, actors and a priest. Among the most active members of KOR were Jacek Kuroń, who had already by this time twice been expelled from the Communist party (PUWP) and had served almost six years in prison for his oppositional activities, and Adam Michnik, among whose many contributions was the encouragement of greater dialogue between the Polish left and the Catholic Church.[13] KOR developed into a serious opposition movement, fostering links with workers and producing a large number of uncensored publications whose circulation far exceeded those of Soviet *samizdat*.

The publications produced by KOR and by other oppositional groupings that sprang up were quite widely read in workplaces. Ironically, Lenin's idea that a newspaper (*Iskra*, in his case) could be important in raising the consciousness of workers was demonstrated in Poland, though it was used against the Communist authorities. Of the various unofficial publications, the most important was *Robotnik* (The Worker), produced as a collaborative effort by workers and intellectuals. It was concerned with workplace issues but also provided a broader critique of the Communist system. The Polish state still had a lot of coercive power at its disposal – as it was to demonstrate in December 1981 – and it caused some surprise in the outside world that the authorities did not crack down harder on the growth of independent political movements and unofficial publications between 1976 and the birth of Solidarity in 1980. KOR activists were harassed by the security police and some of them were dismissed from their jobs, but they were not imprisoned.[14]

A number of reasons for the relative restraint may be adduced. Within the political elite there were hard-liners who were urging stronger action, but Gierek knew that if he gave in to their demands he would be weakening his own position. That had rested on an element of dialogue with the society, rather than on coercion alone. At least as significantly, there was the problem of Western reaction. This was partly but not simply a matter of Poland having been a party to the Helsinki accords of 1975 (discussed in Chapter 23), by which it was pledged to observe human rights. That did not prevent other European Communist states, including the Soviet Union, from taking more resolute action against the purveyors of *samizdat*. The Polish leadership were, however, aware that a sharp response, involving further financial pressure, could be expected from the Carter administration in Washington to any internal crackdown. Carter's National Security Adviser was Zbigniew Brzezinski, who took a close interest in Eastern Europe as a whole and the land of his birth in particular. Poland had become more dependent on Western reaction than other East European Communist states because of its indebtedness to Western financial institutions.

Moreover, in the second half of the 1970s, the economy was in dire straits. With prices still on hold, shortages were increasing and inflation was rising rapidly. The imprisonment of well-known people would have had an adverse effect on the Polish government's standing in the West at a time when it could ill afford the economic repercussions.[15] Within Poland, the Catholic Church – a stronger institution enjoying independence from the state than was to be found elsewhere in Communist Europe – had since 1968 increasingly spoken up in defence of civil rights. (Earlier, more inward-looking, their emphasis had been especially on what they saw as the Church's historic rights.) In September 1976 the Polish primate, Cardinal Stefan Wyszyński, said that it was 'painful that workers should have to struggle for their rights against a workers' government'.[16] And he doubtless, in his own mind, put inverted commas round the last two words. Given the increasingly active role the Church was playing, and the proven readiness of Polish workers to take to the streets, the party leadership had reason to be concerned that a crackdown on the growing unofficial movements might provoke even more widespread domestic resistance than had greeted the price increases.

The Election of a Polish Pope

To add to the Gierek leadership's troubles, a dramatic election in Rome transformed the psychological atmosphere in Poland to the disadvantage of the Communist authorities. On 16 October 1978, Politburo member Stanisław Kania telephoned Gierek to give him the bad news that the Archbishop of Kraków (and former professor at the Catholic University of Lublin), Karol Wojtyła, had been elected pope. 'Holy Mother of God!' was the response of the first secretary of Poland's Communist party.[17] For a Pole to become the first non-Italian pope in four and a half centuries was a matter of enormous national pride and widespread rejoicing. Not, however, within the Central Committee of the Polish United Workers' Party. Although the party leadership had to put a brave public face on this remarkable outcome of the Vatican conclave, it was a blow from which they were ill equipped to recover.

The overwhelmingly non-Communist and Catholic majority of the population of Poland, including the opposition activists, were given a strong sense that God was on their side. This was magnified by the nine-day triumphal visit that Pope John Paul II (as he had become) paid to his native country in June 1979. Millions turned out to hear him speak at open-air services – almost two million in Kraków alone. As Timothy Garton Ash observed: 'For nine days the state virtually ceased to exist, except as a censor doctoring the television coverage. Everyone saw that Poland is not a communist country – just a communist state.'[18] The Pope's reception in Poland was viewed with some alarm not only by the Polish Communist party leadership but also in the Soviet Union. Its positive impact was felt most strongly in the Baltic republics of the USSR, especially Lithuania. Many Lithuanians travelled close enough to the Polish border to be able to watch the Pope's triumphal return to his homeland on Polish television.[19] While that did not give a complete picture of the extent of his rapturous reception, it was much fuller than anything available in the Soviet mass media.

The campaign against revisionism as well as 'Zionism' in Poland in 1968 and the crushing of the Prague Spring had, between them, reduced faith in reform coming from within the Communist party. What hope remained of that was further reduced when promises made by Gierek were not kept. These included the pledge to allow the building of a monument to the workers who were killed on the Baltic coast in December 1970 and the promise to make the official trade unions more responsive to workers' interests and demands. A coalition of social groups and institutions – workers, intellectuals, and the Catholic Church, who had never before come together in a common cause in a Communist state, even in Poland – co-operated increasingly effectively. Their efforts, initially, were focused not so much on changing the system as on bypassing it. They set up alternative organizations which, they hoped, would attract increasing support and turn their official Communist counterparts into empty shells.[20]

One key element of this was the idea of creating free trade unions. In sharp contrast with the official trade unions, they would be entirely independent of the state. They began to be set up in the late 1970s. The most important of these precursors of what was to become a mass movement in 1980-81 was the 'Founding Committee of Free Trade Unions on the Coast', established on May Day 1978 in the Baltic port of Gdańsk.[21] Lech Wałesa, an electrician who had been a strike leader in Gdańsk in 1970 and was dismissed from the shipyard for his part in the protests of 1976, was one of its earliest members. Four years after that, sharp price rises once again provided the trigger for mass resistance to the Communist authorities. On 1 July 1980, the Polish government increased prices of consumer goods and deregulated a number of meat prices. They rose between 60 and 90 per cent. This followed several years of growing inequalities of income and increasing popular resentment of the privileges of the Communist party and government elite. All that added to the sense of injustice which the price rises provoked, even though from a strictly economic standpoint a reduction in the enormous subsidies was overdue.[22]

A series of strikes began in July and were settled locally with the award of wage increases. Yet the strikes spread. A key moment came on 14 August, when the workers in the Lenin Shipyard in Gdańsk downed tools. They demanded not only a substantial wage increase but the reinstatement of two fellow workers who had been dismissed for political reasons, Lech Wałesa and Anna Walentynowicz. They also – once again – called for the erection of a monument to those who had been killed during the December 1970 strikes. The resistance almost collapsed when a majority of older workers on the strike committee decided on 16 August to settle for a wage increase amounting to 75 per cent of what they had demanded. The condition was that the workers must leave the shipyard by six o'clock that evening. A majority did go home, in spite of the efforts of Wałesa, who had emerged as the strike leader, to dissuade them. A determined minority, however, remained and the strike committee no longer included members who would be readily appeased by purely material concessions.

Other factories in the region, moreover, had come out on strike, most notably in Szczecin, and the last thing they wanted was capitulation by the largest shipyard, that in Gdańsk. An Inter-Factory Strike Committee (MKS) of thirteen people was formed, with Wałesa as leader. Over the weekend they worked out demands which they presented in a communiqué on 18 August. They were, in the first instance, political.[23] Top of the list was an insistence on free trade unions, independent of the ruling party and of employers. The document cited Convention 87 of the International Labour Organization (ILO), to which the Polish government had signed up. Other demands included the release of all political prisoners and respect for freedom of speech and print, with no repression of independent publications. The influence of worker–intellectual co-operation and of articles which had appeared in *Robotnik* was evident. Specific material and local grievances were also raised in the document, but these came only after the political demands. Radical though the political issues voiced were, they did not, following debate in the MKS, include demands for the complete abolition of censorship or for free elections. The workers on the committee remained well enough aware of Poland's position within the Soviet bloc not to wish to test to the limits the tolerance of the Soviet leadership.[24]

The first number of a strike bulletin, *Solidarność* (Solidarity), was issued in the Lenin Shipyard on 22 August. That same day and the next, the Polish government, in the persons of two deputy prime ministers who had travelled to Szczecin and Gdańsk, began negotiations with the MKS. On 24 August the Communist party leadership responded to what was clearly a major crisis – unrest having spread to many industrial regions, with 253 factories on strike – in a manner which had become as traditional to them as had political protest strikes by Polish workers. They made personnel changes. The prime minister Edward Babiuch was dismissed, as were a deputy prime minister and the head of the official trade unions. The same day Józef Pińkowski was appointed prime minister.[25] He promptly promised to implement the agreements that had been reached between the government representatives and the striking workers on the Baltic coast. Already on 17 August the Pope had sent a message to Cardinal Wyszyński in which he made clear his support for the striking workers. The Polish primate's response, however, was much more restrained. He was afraid that developments would get out of hand and that violent repression would be authorized by the party-state authorities.[26]

Solidarity as Mass Movement

Before the end of August, more than 700,000 workers were on strike, and the Polish party leadership at a Central Committee meeting on 30 August accepted in principle the demand for free trade unions. On 5 September it was Gierek's turn to pay the price for leading the Communist party and the country into crisis. He was removed as first secretary of the PUWP and replaced – with Soviet approval – by Stanisław Kania, who had been the Central Committee secretary supervising the security organs.[27] On 17 September, over thirty inter-factory strike committees from all over the country met in Gdańsk. There the historic decision was taken to establish the independent trade union with the name of *Solidarność*. The growth of the movement was startling. By October 1980, Solidarity could claim three million members. By December it was over eight million. The sheer numbers presented the Polish party-state leadership with a problem on an entirely new scale. The tacit support of the Catholic Church, even though its leadership favoured caution, was also important for Solidarity. Such was the wave of enthusiasm for the new movement, led by the thirty-seven-year-old electrician from Gdańsk, Wałesa, that even a third of the members of the Polish United Workers' Party decided to be united with the workers in an entirely new way and joined Solidarity.[28] This was, to say the least, a flagrant breach of democratic centralism.

For a period of at least sixteen months – until December 1981 – there was something close to dual power in Poland. This was reminiscent of the stand-off in Russia of 1917 between the soviets, dominated by the Bolsheviks, and the Provisional Government. But the roles were reversed. The challenge in Poland was to a Communist state and it was coming from anti-Communist workers. Moreover, the participation of the working class in what became known as the Polish Revolution of 1980–81 was vastly greater even in absolute numbers, and certainly as a proportion of the population, than the part played by workers in bringing the Bolsheviks to power. The developments in Poland in 1980–81 presented an ideological challenge, as well as a threat to the power of the party, and one which was felt acutely in Moscow. For all the talk of the 'leading role of the working class', whose absence in Czechoslovakia in 1968 the Kremlin could deplore, it was hard even for the most cynical propagandist to argue that workers were being bypassed in the politics of Poland. The argument became, rather, that they were being misled by counterrevolutionaries.

As early as 25 August 1980, the Politburo of the Communist Party of the Soviet Union set up a commission to examine the situation in Poland. How seriously the CPSU leadership regarded the Polish events was shown by the seniority of the people who made up this body. The commission was chaired by Mikhail Suslov, the second secretary of the party, and included KGB chairman Yury Andropov, Minister of Defence Dmitry Ustinov and Foreign Minister Andrey Gromyko, as well as the head of the General Department of the Central Committee and Brezhnev's closest associate, Konstantin Chernenko.[29] By 28 August, they were not only considering the possibility of military intervention in Poland but also proposing concrete measures. Troops and tank divisions were to be moved from their present locations in different parts of the Soviet Union to be in full combat readiness by the evening of the following day. Subsequently, 'up to 100,000 reservists and 15,000 vehicles' would be required. Later the Soviet leadership came round to the view that they should *not* send troops into Poland, and that it was essential that the Polish authorities themselves use whatever degree of force was required to restore the hegemony of the Communist party. There is no doubt, however, that at an early stage of the Polish crisis, a group of the most senior members of the Soviet Politburo had put the invasion option firmly on the table.[30]

The Soviet leadership were acutely concerned not only about what was happening in Poland itself but about its possible effect in other Communist countries. A secret report in late October for the Secretariat of the CPSU Central Committee noted that even in the Soviet Union, 'work stoppages and other negative incidents' had 'substantially increased' since August.[31] These were, however, isolated incidents and the Soviet authorities did not experience difficulties remotely comparable to that of the Polish party in dealing with them. In fact, in no other Communist country was a serious independent union, with a mass following, created. Since other European Communist states were being asked to help Poland economically – and thus prop up the party leadership – there was even some popular resentment in those countries of the work stoppages in Poland.[32]

The Soviet leadership were already in the autumn of 1980 discussing the likely need for martial law in Poland. In the Polish Politburo, Kania mooted it as a last resort and said it was something they had to prepare for, should the need arise. Yet while this was going on, Solidarity's political position was being strengthened. On 10 November 1980, the Polish Supreme Court registered it as a legally independent organization and confirmed that it did not need to include an acceptance of the leading role of the PUWP in its charter. As a result of this major concession, Solidarity withdrew its latest strike threat.[33] In late November, Erich Honecker, who had succeeded Ulbricht as the Communist leader of East Germany, made clear his determination to play the same role in relation to Poland as Ulbricht had played regarding Czechoslovakia twelve years earlier. In a letter to Brezhnev dated 26 November 1980, Honecker called for a meeting of the leaders of the European Communist states to consider what action they should take collectively against this latest threat of counterrevolution. Every delay, he said, was 'equivalent to death – the death of socialist Poland'. He said that 'Comrades Husák and Zhivkov have also expressed the desire that we urgently meet to discuss this issue' in the belief that 'collective advice and possible assistance from Comrade Kania's allies can only help'.[34]

Brezhnev acceded to the request, and when the leaders met in Moscow on 5 December, not only those mentioned by Honecker were present, but also Kania himself, the Hungarian party leader János Kádár, and the Romanian leader Nicolae Ceauşescu. Honecker was especially alarmist, saying that 'the survival of socialism in Poland is in acute danger' and that the Polish Supreme Court decision had 'resulted in a rapid escalation of counterrevolutionary activities and a massive deterioration of the situation'.[35] Ceauşescu chided Kania for having shown insufficient determination in combating 'anti-socialist, counterrevolutionary elements', and added: 'We also do not understand how it was possible for so-called independent free unions to be established.' They were, however, now a reality which had to be taken into consideration. He emphasized non-intervention, saying that 'the Polish comrades' must secure 'the socialist construction of Poland on their own and in their own ways'.[36] Brezhnev was cautious enough to say that a confrontation with the Polish Church 'would only worsen the situation' and that an attempt should be made to influence 'moderate circles within the Catholic Church in our direction'. Nevertheless, he added: 'A terrible danger hovers over socialism in Poland. The enemy has managed to open a rift between the party and a major segment of the workers.' He paraphrased an interview given by Lech Wałesa as saying: 'I brought Gierek to power and I deposed him, and I can also bring the new leadership down, if I want to.' Brezhnev did not advocate intervention by other Warsaw Pact countries in Poland, warning rather of Western 'interference in internal Polish affairs'. Stressing, however, the Soviet commitment to Poland remaining a Communist state, he added: 'We have made it clear to them that neither Poland's communists nor the friends and allies of Poland would allow them to tear Poland out of the socialist community. It has been and will be an inseparable member of the political, economic and military system of socialism.'[37]

Less than two weeks later, on the tenth anniversary of the December 1970 strike, the memorial which workers on the Baltic coast had long demanded, in honour of those who were killed, was finally dedicated in front of the Lenin Shipyard in Gdańsk. Notwithstanding the pressure from Moscow calling for no more concessions to Solidarity, the event was attended by government and PUWP officials. Warnings from the Soviet Union and from leaders of other Warsaw Pact countries continued unremittingly for the next year, but during that time Solidarity continued to defy the efforts of the Polish party leadership to curtail its progress by all means short of the declaration of martial law. At its height, Solidarity had a membership of ten million in a country whose total population was under forty million. (This, nevertheless, made Poland by a large margin the most populous country in Eastern Europe.) The counter pressures to those of the Soviet Union – from Washington – continued uninterrupted in spite of a change of government. The Carter presidency – with its stress on human rights and its Polish-American National Security Adviser, Brzezinski – was succeeded in January 1981 by the Reagan administration, which, across the board, took a harder anti-Communist line than its predecessor.

After the experience of Hungary in 1956 and Czechoslovakia in 1968, there could be no illusions that the United States – still less any other Western country – would intervene militarily on behalf of the Poles, should there be a Soviet invasion. The 'Brezhnev doctrine', enunciated in 1968, which held that other 'socialist' states had the right and duty to defend socialism in any part of the 'Socialist Commonwealth' where it might be threatened, was, however, still operative. Neither the Polish leadership nor the population as a whole could assume that there would not be a Soviet military intervention in the last resort. As we have seen, preparatory measures for an invasion had been put in place as early as August 1980. For the Soviet leaders, however, Poland was a special case. The size of the country, the fact that a vast oppositional organization was already mobilized, the tense relations with the Reagan administration, the consideration that the Soviet Union was engaged in a 'peace offensive' in Western Europe, and the fact that Soviet troops were already having a hard time in Afghanistan were among the major reasons why the Commission on Poland of the Soviet Politburo turned almost as strongly *against* Soviet invasion as they were *for* the imposition of martial law by the Polish authorities themselves.[38] There remained, nevertheless, certain circumstances in which a Soviet military intervention *might* have taken place. When the Polish Ministry of Internal

24. Communist leaders meeting at Sochi on the Black Sea coast, June 1973: (*from left to right*) Tudor Zhivkov, Nicolae Ceauçescu, Edward Gierek, János Kádár, Gustáv Husák, Leonid Brezhnev, Erich Honecker, Mongolian leader Yumjaagiyn Tsedenbal and Andrey Gromyko.

25. In the foreground Italy's Eurocommunist leader Enrico Berlinguer, to his left the leader of the French Communist Party Georges Marchais.

26. Soviet missiles trundle past the Kremlin during the Bolshevik Revolution anniversary parade of 1969.

27. American President Richard Nixon and Soviet leader Leonid Brezhnev exchange copies of the Strategic Arms Limitation Treaty, May 1972. The two balding men between them are (*foreground*) Nikolay Podgorny, the chairman of the Supreme Soviet, and behind him Boris Ponomarev, head of the International Department of the Central Committee. To Brezhnev's right is the bespectacled Mikhail Suslov.

28. Alexander Solzhenitsyn, mobbed by journalists in Zurich 1974, following his deportation from the Soviet Union.

29. Andrey Sakharov, not long before his death in 1989.

30. Yury Andropov – the official portrait after he became general secretary of the CPSU in November 1982.

31. Pope John Paul II was greeted by vast and enthusiastic crowds on his return to Poland in 1979.

32. Uneasy partners in the politics of transition: Communist President Wojciech Jaruzelski (*left*) and Solidarity leader Lech Wałesa in Warsaw, 1989.

33. Dancing on the Wall: Berlin citizens from both sides of the divided Germany celebrate the opening of the borders at the Brandenburg Gate on the night of 9–10 November 1989.

34. Václav Havel, the leading figure in Czechoslovakia's 'Velvet Revolution' (soon to become the country's first post-Communist president), acknowledges the cheers of a vast crowd in Prague's Wenceslas Square, 10 December 1989.

35. Mikhail Gorbachev with his two most influential aides and policy advisers,
Georgy Shakhnazarov (*centre*) and Anatoly Chernyaev (*right*).

36. Heads together – ideas far apart: Yegor Ligachev (*left*) and Alexander Yakovlev at the
Nineteenth Conference of the Soviet Communist Party in 1988.

37. In his first term as American president Ronald Reagan did not meet with any Soviet top leader. In his second term he had a summit meeting every year with Mikhail Gorbachev. They were marked by increasing bonhomie.

38. During the short-lived coup by Communist hard-liners in August 1991 (with Gorbachev and his family under house arrest on the Crimean coast) the eyes of the world were on Russia's president Boris Yeltsin. He denounced the attempted coup from the top of an army tank outside the Moscow White House, home at that time to the Russian parliament.

39. A North Korean poster on a hospital wall in Hwanghae province presents a characteristically idealized picture of the 'Great Leader' Kim Il-sung (*right*) and his son, the 'Dear Leader' Kim Jong-il (*left*).

40. The interior of a bookshop in Chengdu (in China's Sichuan province) photographed in July 2004. A poster on the wall portrays the three European founding fathers of Communism, Marx, Engels and Lenin, and the three Chinese leaders deemed to have made the greatest contribution to the development of Communist China: (*from left to right*) Mao Zedong, Zhou Enlai and Deng Xiaoping.

Affairs and the general staff of the Polish army deliberated on preparations for martial law in March 1981, one scenario they considered was that workers might occupy their factories in a general strike and that there might be 'attacks on party and administration buildings'. Should that be the case, 'assistance from the Warsaw Pact is not ruled out'. Those conclusions were endorsed by their Soviet counterparts.[39]

In February 1981 General Wojciech Jaruzelski, who had been minister of defence since 1968, became prime minister. At the same time, Mieczysław Rakowski, the editor of the journal *Polityka*, and a reformer within limits, became a deputy prime minister. The appointment of Jaruzelski was reassuring for the Soviet leadership, for he had trained in a Soviet officers' school during the Second World War (having earlier, at the age of sixteen, been one of the Poles deported to the Soviet Union for forced labour). He took part in the Soviet-sponsored Polish First Army's liberation of his native country from Nazi occupation. A fluent Russian-speaker, he was initially trusted by the Soviet leadership.[40] With his dark glasses and ramrod stiff back (the former the result of an eye ailment and the latter from constantly wearing a brace on account of a serious back injury), he was a somewhat enigmatic figure. On the other side of the coin from his Soviet connections, he was from a Polish gentry family, with a tradition of army service, and had attended a prominent Jesuit school. He had a deserved reputation for fighting corruption in the army and for being free of any greed or corruption himself. Most Poles – like the Soviet leadership – initially welcomed his appointment.[41]

At different times, however, Jaruzelski was to disappoint both the Soviet Politburo and the Polish citizenry as he tried to walk a tightrope between their conflicting demands. From early in his prime ministership he was preparing for the eventuality of martial law. Indeed, he and Kania in March 1981 presented plans for its imposition to the Soviet leadership. Nevertheless, this was to be a last resort. Jaruzelski's strong preference was to reach a modus vivendi with Solidarity. Jaruzelski and Lech Wałesa had several meetings in the course of 1981. While the Soviet leadership, for their part, did not wish to assume the military burden and economic costs of invading Poland, they took pains to remind Poles of what had happened in Czechoslovakia in 1968. Warsaw Pact manoeuvres began in Poland on 17 March 1981 and, as had occurred in Czechoslovakia, were extended beyond the date at which they were due to end. At a meeting of the Soviet Politburo on 2 April, Brezhnev reported on his latest telephone conversation with Kania, who was still First Secretary of the Polish Communist party. Kania had complained that at a recent Central Committee plenum he had been criticized by hard-liners. Brezhnev told his Politburo colleagues: 'I immediately said to him,

"They acted correctly. They should not just have critized you but taken a cudgel to you. Then perhaps you would understand." These were literally my words.'[42]

Deadlock continued, however, for many more months. There was debate within Solidarity on whether their revolution should continue to be self-limiting.[43] The desire, ultimately, among the overwhelming majority of their members was that they should come to power, replacing the Communist regime. However, they had to keep in mind what post-war history had suggested was a real possibility, namely the Soviet army crossing the border into Poland. Thus, they stopped short of demanding fully fledged political democracy, but insisted on maintaining their freedom as a mass movement. Solidarity held a national congress at Gdańsk in September 1981, while nearby Soviet naval manoeuvres took place in the Gulf of Gdańsk.[44] In some of the documents they approved, Solidarity delegates threw caution to the winds. One such was a 'Message to the Working People of Eastern Europe', which stated: 'We support those among you who have decided on the difficult road of struggle for free trade unions. We believe that it will not be long before your and our representatives can meet to exchange our trades union experiences.'[45] At a meeting of the Soviet Politburo less than a week later, Brezhnev was the first to refer to that appeal to East European workers adopted by the Solidarity congress. He said: 'It is a dangerous and provocative document. It does not contain many words but they all strike at one point. Its authors want to stir up sedition in the socialist countries and rouse up groups of various kinds of apostates.'[46]

Martial Law

Transcripts of meetings of the Soviet and East European leaders, especially those of the Soviet Politburo, show a growing impatience with Kania, in particular, but also with Jaruzelski, who in their view were vacillating in the face of the growing boldness of Solidarity. One response came when Kania, who had been much criticized by Polish as well as Soviet hard-liners, was dismissed as first secretary of the party by the Central Committee of the PUWP in mid-October 1981. He was replaced by Jaruzelski, who continued to be prime minister, minister of defence and chairman of the National Defence Committee. Before that month was out, Brezhnev and Andropov were complaining in the Soviet Politburo that Jaruzelski had done nothing 'constructive' or new. Making it clear that there were those in the Polish leadership who would welcome 'military aid from the fraternal countries', Andropov, however, said to Brezhnev: 'we must firmly stick to your line – not to introduce our troops into Poland'. Even more significantly, the minister of defence, Dmitry Ustinov, was firmly against military intervention. With some understatement he said: 'They, the Poles, are not ready to receive our troops.'[47]

Martial law in Poland was finally imposed in the early hours of the morning of 13 December 1981. At 3 a.m., Wałesa was awoken and taken into custody, and several thousand Solidarity activists were arrested the same day. Some of the leaders of Solidarity who escaped arrest helped to organize strikes which took place in more than 250 factories and in other institutions, including universities. Nine workers, resisting martial law at a Silesian coal mine, were shot. The official death toll as a result of the imposition of martial law reached seventeen. The whole operation was conducted by the Polish army and Ministry of the Interior troops, although the Russian commander-in-chief of the Warsaw Pact forces, Marshal Viktor Kulikov, was in Poland during the days of the crackdown. Some 80,000 Polish soldiers, 1,600 tanks and 1,800 armoured vehicles took part in the operation, which was conducted so effectively that, as a mass movement, Solidarity did not emerge again until the late 1980s, when fundamental change was already under way in Moscow.

Yet three days before Jaruzelski introduced martial law, the Soviet Politburo were quite uncertain whether he would do it. Andropov said that even though the Polish Politburo had made a unanimous decision on the introduction of martial law, Jaruzelski appeared to be still vacillating. There was some discussion about Jaruzelski's claim that Marshal Kulikov had spoken about involving Warsaw Pact forces. Andropov said: 'If Comrade Kulikov actually spoke about the introduction of troops then I consider that he did so incorrectly. We cannot risk that.' Andropov, remarkably, went significantly further and said that 'even if Poland comes under the authority of Solidarity', there should be no military intervention. Strengthening the Soviet Union, and avoiding 'economic and political sanctions' by 'the capitalist countries', was more important. Suslov, who had chaired the Politburo's Commission on Poland for the past sixteen months, spoke equally adamantly against Soviet military intervention, saying: 'If troops are introduced, that will mean a catastrophe. I think that we all share a unanimous opinion here that there can be no discussion of any introduction of troops.'[48] The Soviet leadership had shied away from action which a little over a year earlier they had come close to taking. Ultimately, therefore, the decision to introduce martial law was one which the Polish Communist party leadership took themselves. They had, of course, been under colossal pressure from the Soviet Union and from other East European Communist leaders to do this. Although martial law was described by the new Polish primate, Cardinal

Glemp (who had succeeded Cardinal Wyszyński in the summer of 1981, following the latter's death), as a 'lesser evil',[49] the unspoken greater evil of Soviet occupation had ceased to be an imminent danger. Glemp, of course, was not to know that.

Martial law was suspended on 31 December 1982 and officially terminated on 21 July 1983. Those who had been imprisoned on the night of its imposition, including Wałesa, were at various times released. To the embarrassment of the PUWP leadership, Wałesa in 1983 was awarded the Nobel Peace Prize. A gradual relaxation in Polish society recommenced. Pope John Paul II was, for example, allowed to make a pilgrimage to Poland in June 1983 and was able to insist, in the face of official resistance, on meeting with Lech Wałesa He did so again in 1987.[50] Cardinal Glemp, in contrast with the Pope, was publicly critical of Solidarity. The Church itself was divided between those who were prepared to strike a bargain with the state – political acquiescence in return for the building of new churches – and those who wished to keep alive the spirit of Solidarity. Prominent among the latter was the Warsaw priest Father Jerzy Popiełuszko, who was, as a consequence, murdered by state security officers in 1984. This, however, had been done without the knowledge of Jaruzelski, and the four security policemen who had committed the outrage were tried and imprisoned in 1985. The fact that the trial was held in public, and widely reported on national television, was part of a significant process of liberalization which Jaruzelski had initiated.[51] Nevertheless, until well into the perestroika period in the Soviet Union, Solidarity was no longer a mass movement, but had to live a subdued, underground existence, holding meetings in church halls. It was not until August 1988, with a wave of strikes taking place, that the Polish government offered to open talks with Wałesa on the legalization of Solidarity if he would get the strikers back to work![52].

That remarkable turnaround in Solidarity's fortunes was a result, partly, of Poland's grim economic circumstances. It depended even more, however, on the fundamental change which was by then under way in Moscow. For a period of a year and a half in 1980–81, Solidarity had transformed social and political life in Poland and alarmed Communist rulers throughout Europe. Yet even in Poland, the forces of coercion at the disposal of the state authorities had turned out to be enough to crush Solidarity as a mass movement once the leadership of the country had decided that this was a 'lesser evil'. For them, unlike the Catholic Church, the greater evil was Poland ceasing to be in any sense a Communist state. And for all they knew, that might lead to the additional evil of a Soviet invasion. By 1989, Solidarity was once again at the centre of Polish national life. For Poland itself, the significance of Solidarity can hardly be overstated. There was, however, no causal link between the political achievements of Solidarity at the beginning of the 1980s and the fall of Communism in Eastern Europe at the end of that decade. The example of Solidarity, which began as an independent trade union and then became a mass political movement, was not followed in any other country in the world.

22

Reform in China: Deng Xiaoping and After

The death of Mao was quickly followed, as noted in Chapter 17, by the arrest of the Gang of Four and by a significant change of course. The person who exercised greatest influence by far on the new direction of Chinese policy was the 'little man' with 'a great future ahead of him' (as Mao had predicted in 1957), Deng Xiaoping.[1] Deng had a number of advantages. They included the prestige which accrued to a veteran of the Long March and of the Sino-Japanese War. A member of the Chinese Communist Party since 1924, Deng was also, a quarter of a century later, one of the founding fathers of the People's Republic of China. Most importantly, his long experience in senior posts, combined with his political acumen, had enabled him to build up a network of supporters within the party-state structures. It did not take him long to become the dominant personality within the post-Mao leadership. Thereupon his pragmatism did more to undermine Maoism than Soviet and Western criticism of that ideology combined. Deng did not achieve this through a frontal attack on Mao, for, as he observed, 'discrediting Comrade Mao Zedong . . . would mean discrediting our Party and state'.[2] A resolution adopted two and a half years after Mao's death, on which Deng was the predominant influence, cautiously maintained that Mao's 'merits are primary and his errors secondary'. It noted that he had made 'gross mistakes' in his later years, but described Mao Zedong Thought as 'Marxism-Leninism applied and developed in China'. Deng and the Communist Party continued to uphold that doctrine, viewing it, in the words of John Gittings, as 'a synthesis of Mao's own ideas and the Party's collective wisdom'.[3] The whole history of the Chinese Communist state was inextricably connected with the name and activities of Mao. Thus, to debunk Mao so soon after his demise would have been a much riskier step for the Chinese leadership than was Khrushchev's attack on Stalin, though even that required considerable boldness.

However, from shortly after Mao's death in 1976, and especially between 1978 and the early 1990s, Deng was not only the most important of Mao's successors but also the person who did most to dismantle his legacy. Maoism rapidly ceased to be the ideological orthodoxy and became an endangered, minority creed. Deng reappeared in the State Council in 1977 and was re-admitted to the party's Central Committee. Unusually for a politician in a Communist system, he was able to effect decisive change within the party organization even though he was not the general secretary. While holding various offices which, in principle, were less powerful than that post, he was, nevertheless, able to restore the party Central Committee's Organization Department (which had been one of the casualties of the Cultural Revolution) and put it under the control of a longstanding ally, Hu Yaobang. Radical Maoists were ousted and Deng supporters were brought back within the fold.[4] Mao Zedong's immediate successor as party leader was the person Mao himself had chosen, Hua Guofeng. He led a group who became known by their critics as the 'Whatever'. Hua declared: 'We will resolutely uphold whatever policy decisions Chairman Mao made, and unswervingly follow whatever instructions Chairman Mao gave.'[5] The 'Two Whatevers' were mocked by Deng and his supporters, who found a useful quotation from Mao Zedong from a time when Mao had been stressing that policy should be based on reality rather than dogma: 'Seek Truth from Facts'.[6] Deng said that the Two Whatevers took Mao's statements out of context and ignored the fact that even Mao recognized that some of his ideas had been wrong. In December 1978, Deng posited against Hua's fundamentalist appropria-tion of the words of Mao a very different approach when he said:

> The more Party members and other people there are who use their heads and think things through, the more our cause will benefit . . . We hope every Party committee and every Party branch will encourage and support people both inside and outside the Party to dare to think, explore new paths, and put forward new ideas, and that they will urge the masses to emancipate their minds and use their heads.[7]

More interested in the substance of power than its trappings, Deng did not attempt to promote a cult of his personality, but more often than not he had the last word on major policy. Under the shifting coalition of leaders of different views which he formed, the goal of evolutionary economic progress took the place of mass mobilization and of great political campaigns. There were to be no more disasters like the Great Leap Forward or the Cultural Revolution. Social stability was prized above revolutionary consciousness. Building and maintaining a strong state took the place of Mao's encouragement of violent attack on state structures in the name of ideological purity. A famous remark of Deng Xiaoping in 1962, at the end of the disastrous period of the Great Leap Forward, was revived for a second time. It had first been revisited during the Cultural Revolution as a stick with which to beat Deng. A prominent woman Red Guard, Nie Yuanzi (with high-level political backing), proclaimed in November 1966 that four years earlier Deng Xiaoping had attempted to unleash a 'capitalist windstorm' with his call for peasants to be given back individual plots of land. She illustrated the apostasy by citing his remark, 'It doesn't matter if a cat is black or white; if it can catch mice, it's a good cat.'[8] As a popular way of encapsulating Deng Xiaoping's open-minded approach to economic reform, this saying was 'rehabilitated' in the 1970s and 1980s when Deng's fortunes were once again ascendant.[9]

There were parts of Marxism-Leninism in which Deng was a firm believer. That included, above all, the monopoly of power of the Communist Party. A leading Chinese reformer observed in 1988 that 'Deng is for free discussion, but only to the point where it would not threaten the leading role of the party.'[10] He added that Deng favoured 'very radical economic reform but, again, while preserving the leading role of the party'.[11] Deng Xiaoping had already demonstrated the limits of his tolerance at the end of the 1970s and he was to do so, more brutally, in 1989. What became known as the Democracy Wall, on which people were free to pin posters airing grievances and opinions, was given tacit encouragement by Deng in 1978, for the targets of attack were not only the Gang of Four but people close to the new party leader Hua Guofeng, whom Deng was in the process of discrediting. (In the meantime, Hua had been trying to promote a cult of his own personality, and had even grown his hair longer in an attempt to look more like Mao.) Once the wall-posters began to include criticism of Deng and of the system, tolerance evaporated for this new manifestation of 'a hundred schools of thought contending'. The Democracy Wall was moved from a main Beijing thoroughfare to a specially erected prefabricated building in a small park far from the city centre. Spontaneous criticism was further curtailed by the requirement that poster-displayers formally register their names. The following year the right to put up independent posters was removed from the constitution and the Democracy Wall ceased to exist.[12]

In the sixty years since the foundation of the People's Republic of China as a Communist state, the first thirty were a time of turmoil and conflict, much of it inspired by Mao. The second thirty, in contrast, can be seen as a period of *relative* tranquillity. Yet although the Communist Party has retained its control over the state and society, it has done so partly by a process of adaptation.[13] And though like all ruling Communist parties it has preserved a united front in its dealings with other countries and, for the most part, a façade of unity at home, behind that façade there has been great diversity of view. Moreover, underlying the apparent stability of the society, there has been social dislocation, extreme tensions and much (though little reported) unrest. During this time the Chinese Communist leadership have reasserted Leninist political organization while abandoning in fact, if not entirely in theory, any semblance of Marxist political economy. The remainder of the chapter will look at economic and social change in China after Mao, and the political challenge this has posed to the party-state authorities. It will also pay attention to the debate which has gone on behind the scenes and the way in which further political, as well as economic, change may be brought about in China.

Economic and Social Change

In China, as elsewhere in the Communist world at a time of change, the party intelligentsia began to play a more important role. As a category, that broad grouping included both people within the party-state structures and party members in research institutes and higher educational institutions. Academics, especially from the newly established Chinese Academy of Social Sciences, played an important role in policy innovation, criticizing what passed for economic theory under Mao and arguing for the creation of a socialist market economy. They paid attention to the views of East European economic reformers, including those who had been driven out of their homelands, such as the Polish economist Włodzimierz Brus, and reconnected with the discipline of economics in the West. The bolder Chinese economists were already arguing at the end of the 1970s for individual as well as collective ownership and urging movement towards market prices.[14]

An important pragmatic reformer brought into the leadership with (as in the case of Hu Yaobang) Deng Xiaoping's support was Zhao Ziyang, the son of a landlord but from his teens a member of the Communist Party and a fighter against Japanese occupation. By September 1980 Zhao had replaced Mao's designated successor, Hua Guofeng, in one of the posts he held, that of prime minister.[15] This post was in China, as in other Communist states, of great importance in relation to the management of the economy, but less powerful politically than the party leadership. In June 1981 Mao's nominee Hua lost his other two posts. Hu Yaobang became the leader of the Communist Party and Deng Xiaoping took over the chair of the Military Affairs Committee. Thus Deng had direct supervision of the armed forces, but he was also the senior figure in the system as a whole, with one or other of Hu and Zhao apparently being groomed to be his eventual successor.

The first and most immediately fruitful of the economic reforms, introduced under the aegis of Deng and Zhao, was the removal of shackles from the peasantry. Collectivization was essentially reversed in the early 1980s. When land was now parcelled out among the peasants, it was still perfectly well remembered which family had traditionally cultivated which area, and more often than not they recovered it. Peasant households became the basic farming unit.[16] The farmers had to agree to sell a certain quantity of grain to the state, but could earn more by exceeding that quota. They were also now free to develop sidelines, including, for example, pig-rearing and also non-agricultural activities.[17] It was possible to effect a dramatic improvement in agricultural productivity in China simply by freeing peasant farmers to use their initiative.

China had three great advantages over the Soviet Union in this respect. It had a large and able-bodied workforce which contrasted with the labour shortage and the ageing, predominantly female population in the vast expanses of the Soviet countryside. Second, whereas under Soviet conditions much depended on the availability of expensive capital equipment, which the peasantry were in no position to buy for themselves (even if there had been a market providing it), in China labour-intensive (as distinct from capital-intensive) production could, given adequate freedom and incentives, produce quick results. Third – and the most important point, though connected with the last one – China had not had collectivized agriculture for anything like so long as had the Soviet Union. Some time before he became General Secretary of the Communist Party of the Soviet Union, Mikhail Gorbachev, on a visit to Hungary, expressed enthusiasm for the successful agricultural reform he encountered there (which had much in common, notwithstanding the vast difference in population size, with that of China). Gorbachev was at the time the secretary of the Central Committee of the CPSU responsible for agriculture. His Hungarian counterpart asked why, if he liked the Hungarian reform so much, a similar policy was not being pursued in the Soviet Union. Gorbachev replied: 'Unfortunately, in the course of the last fifty years the Russian peasant has had all the independence knocked out of him.'[18] This had not yet happened in China.

In the economy as a whole there was a new emphasis on monetary rewards, including bonuses, and also on the production of consumer goods, for material incentives would have little effect if there was virtually nothing (as in Mao's time) to buy. The new leadership took full advantage of the Chinese diaspora's experience of the capitalist world. In 1980, four special zones of economic development were designated in China's coastal areas. Two of them were directly opposite Taiwan, one bordered Hong Kong and the other bordered Macao. The aim was to make use of the business experience of the Chinese who worked in market economies and to open the door to investment, tourism, trade and technology transfers.[19] Later, Japanese,

American, European and multinational companies were encouraged to participate in the expansion of the rapidly globalizing Chinese economy. A period of fast economic growth began, although the concessions to market forces brought new problems, including inflation and increasing unemployment. There was no longer the guaranteed 'iron rice bowl', a product of job security and subsidized food prices. In attempting to deal with the demographic threat to increased prosperity, the new leadership introduced a severe birth-control policy, restricting each family to one child. It was not entirely enforceable, especially in the countryside, but was rigorous enough to cause resentment, especially among the peasantry.[20]

The problems were more than sufficient to enable Chinese Communists who were not reconciled to the reforms to attack markets and what they saw as Western intellectual influences (which via some of the social scientists undoubtedly existed) and the undermining of Marxism-Leninism. Yet the internal battle in the 1980s was being won by the economic reformers, thanks to the changing balance of political forces. As in other Communist states, the Politburo was the powerful inner body of the party Central Committee. In China, however, there has been *an inner body within the Politburo* – its Standing Committee, consisting generally of between five and nine people, as compared with the twenty or more Politburo members.[21]At the Twelfth Congress of the CPC in 1982, the supporters of Hua Guofeng were removed not only from the Standing Committee but from the Politburo, whereas both Zhao Ziyang and Hu Yaobang, already members of the latter, were promoted to the inner sanctum of the Standing Committee. This was a significant victory for the reformers.

The social changes resulting from economic reform in some respects turned the clock back as well as providing new opportunities. The demise of the commune in the countryside and the return of the family as the basic production unit also reinforced the old patriarchalism. During the first thirty years of the People's Republic, progress towards reducing gender inequality had been made. Some of that was now reversed. When a woman left home to live with her husband, the family which had lost her labour demanded a 'bride price'. Children were more frequently taken out of school to work on the land, and female infanticide – a result of the one-child family policy and parents' desire to have the permanent economic support of a son – became distressingly frequent. Moreover, the dismantled communes had also provided some basic services – the 'barefoot doctors' and clinics, for example – which now disappeared. They were replaced by better but more distant hospitals, which were no longer free.[22] Rural schools also, in many cases, deteriorated during the 1980s, since within the more market-orientated economic system it was difficult to recruit teachers to work in the countryside. The picture in higher education, however, was much more positive. It began to recover from the ravages of the Cultural Revolution and research became more professional.

Political Struggle

The revival of higher education, however, made its own contribution to the problems of the party-state authorities. In 1986, Hu Yaobang, who was still general secretary – and Deng Xiaoping himself – permitted discussion of political reform, partly to rebuff criticism from more orthodox Communists of the economic changes. The response in the universities was more than they had bargained for. A leading Chinese astrophysicist, Fang Lizhi, speaking to an audience at Shanghai University, said that people possess rights that are not dependent on the will of a government. His call for more fundamental political change was followed later in the year by student demonstrations in almost twenty Chinese cities. The preference of Hu, as party leader, was to take a conciliatory line, but the student unrest gave his more conservative colleagues the opportunity they had been waiting for. Deng went along with their demand that Hu should be removed from the general secretaryship. As his replacement was Zhao Ziyang, this was only a partial victory for the hard-liners.[23] However, the much more conservative Li Peng became Zhao's successor as prime minister and set about curtailing the radicalism of the economic reform. Li, a former engineer who had studied in the Soviet Union, had already joined the five-man Standing Committee of the Politburo.

There was a real struggle between Zhao and Li Peng both over economic policy and on how protests should be handled. Meanwhile, problems in society were accumulating. Fluctuating grain prices worried the peasant farmers, while inflation and the risk of unemployment were causing dissatisfaction among urban workers. Critical intellectuals (including many students) were concerned about the lack of political reform and, linked to that, the demotion of Hu Yaobang. Official corruption had also become increasingly visible, adding to the anger.[24] The demonstrations in 1989 which led, ultimately, to the events that became known as the Tiananmen Square massacre, although most of the killings did not take place in that square, began with the death of the popular Hu Yaobang. He died unexpectedly on 15 April. It was rumoured that his heart attack had occurred during a Politburo meeting at which he was engaged in a fierce argument with party conservatives. Thousands of students took to the streets and began an encampment in Beijing's Tiananmen Square. The embarrassment this caused the party-state authorities was increased by the imminent arrival in Beijing of Mikhail Gorbachev. The following month he was to become the first Soviet leader since Khrushchev to visit China. Sino-Soviet relations had been improving after Gorbachev became General Secretary of the Central Committee of the CPSU in 1985, and the Soviet political reforms, which became more radical in 1988–89, were being followed with keen interest by Chinese intellectuals.[25] They constituted yet another stimulus to the demand for political reform in China. Gorbachev's impending visit made it more difficult for even those in the Chinese leadership who wished to crack down ruthlessly on the demonstrators in central Beijing to do so. Gorbachev's hosts took care to keep him away from Tiananmen Square, which was still full of protesters during his two days in Beijing.

On 16 May Gorbachev met with the eighty-two-year-old Deng Xiaoping, who told him that they could now officially declare that Soviet–Chinese state relations had become normal. Deng added that as Gorbachev would be meeting later in the day with the General Secretary of the CCP, Zhao Ziyang, this meant that the relations between their Communist parties had also been normalized.[26] When Gorbachev did meet Zhao, he was pleasantly surprised by his openness. Zhao raised as a perhaps rhetorical, but funda-mental, question for them both: 'Can a one party system ensure the devel-opment of democracy, and will it be possible in this system to have effective control over negative phenomena and to fight the corruption which is to be found in party and government institutions?'[27] He told Gorbachev that 'in China the political reforms in the Soviet Union are being followed with great interest', especially among the intelligentsia, who are 'demanding that China study and emulate your experience'.[28] It was clear that Zhao himself was seriously interested in political reform. Events were soon to show, however, that in the view of the person who mattered most, Deng Xiaoping, Zhao Ziyang was on the verge of taking a step too far. Zhao, indeed, favoured dialogue with the protesting students, many of whom had embarked on a hunger strike on 13 May.

One day after Gorbachev's meeting with both Deng and Zhao, Deng convened a meeting of the Standing Committee of the Politburo in his house. Deng himself was not a member of the committee, but though he raged at Zhao for informing Gorbachev that major decisions were referred to him, his calling the top leadership to his home graphically illustrated the truth of what the Soviet leader had been told. Deng's primary concern was to put a stop to what he saw as growing anarchy. To make matters worse, the protests were being reported in the Chinese media, which were getting out of control. The Standing Committee met again on 18 May and by four votes to one, Zhao being the only opponent, supported the imposition of martial law. Zhao's own earlier soundings had indicated that he was far from alone in being against resort to force of arms to stop the protests, but (as he noted in an interview he gave in 1995) it was Deng's views which mattered. Deng Xiaoping, he said, 'might have imposed military control even if all five had disapproved'.[29]

In the early hours of 19 May 1989, Zhao visited the students in Tiananmen Square in what was to be his last public appearance. Since the media had not yet been brought to heel, the meeting was televised. Zhao was accompanied by his protégé Wen Jiabao, who fourteen years later (in 2003) was to become prime minister. Zhao apologized to the students for coming so late, and said 'Your criticism of us is justified.' He appealed to the young people to give up their hunger strike before it was too late.[30] It was, however, already too late for Zhao, who ceased to be general secretary later that same day. He remained formally a member of the Politburo for a short time longer, but thereafter he was effectively under house arrest until his death in 2005.[31] The wish of the Chinese leadership to avoid embarrassing their Soviet visitor, with relations between the two Communist giants on the verge of being put on a constructive footing, was evident in the timing of the crackdown. Gorbachev left Beijing for Shanghai on 18 May. The de facto removal of his friendly interlocutor, Zhao, from the Chinese party leadership took place the following day. Without the Gorbachev visit, it would probably have happened earlier. On 20 May the Chinese leadership formally declared martial law.

In a speech which was televised nationwide late on 19 May, the prime minister Li Peng had said: 'To fulfil our responsibilities to our sacred motherland and to the entire people, we must take firm, decisive measures to put a swift end to the turmoil, protect the leadership of the Party, and protect the socialist system.'[32] The stand-off, however, continued for two more weeks, although by midday on the 20th there were an estimated quarter of a million troops in and around Beijing. The most unpleasant surprise for the authorities was that large crowds of Beijing residents came out on to the streets, remonstrated with the soldiers, and even erected road-blocks. On 21 May, an estimated million people demonstrated in the capital against the imposition of martial law. On the same day a similar number took part in a protest demonstration in Hong Kong (still at that time under British rule – it returned to China's jurisdiction in 1997).[33] In late May, students at the Central Academy of Fine Arts began work on a statue, thirty feet tall, to be called 'The Goddess of Democracy', which bore some resemblance to the Statue of Liberty. It was made of white Styrofoam and plaster and was taken in sections to Tiananmen Square, where it was unveiled on 30 May. It faced the portrait of Mao Zedong which had hitherto been the dominant image on the square.[34]

Perhaps this was the last straw for the party leadership. The mass media were now firmly back under their control and the statue was denounced on television as 'an insult to our national dignity'.[35] Even more worrying for Deng and his colleagues, however, was the emergence of an autonomous workers' movement which proclaimed its solidarity with the students, 'bringing', Richard Baum has observed, 'ever closer to reality Deng's recurrent Polish nightmare'.[36] It was later in 1989 that Communist regimes in Eastern Europe were toppled. If this had occurred in the first half of 1989, the Chinese leadership would have felt even more concern. However, as things were, thousands of officials from party and governmental organizations had taken part in the May demonstration against martial law.[37] So the situation was serious enough. The party leadership's patience was exhausted, and on the night of 3–4 June, tanks and armoured personnel carriers moved in. Most of the killings took place in the surrounding streets. Some of the troops fired above the crowds, others directly into them. Estimates of the total number of deaths caused by the military crackdown vary between several hundred and several thousand. Thousands more were arrested. A majority of the dead and wounded were Beijing residents, not students.[38] Tanks flattened the Goddess of Democracy on 4 June.

Political Conflict and Reform after Tiananmen

The initial reaction to Tiananmen was repression. Following several thousand arrests in June and July 1989, there were many trials. As many as thirty-five workers (but no students) are believed to have been executed. Active dissidents were given lengthy prison sentences. International fame could provide some limited protection. Thus, the astrophysicist Fang Lizhi and his wife Li Shuxian were charged with conspiracy to subvert the Communist Party and the socialist system. Although they were advocates of democratization, they had, in fact, little to do with the demonstrations. On 6 June 1989 they took refuge in the American embassy in Beijing. It was not until June of the following year that they were given permission to leave China for the United States.[39] There was a resumption of jamming of overseas broadcasts, such as those of the BBC and Voice of America. Newspapers warned of the dangers of Western campaigns of 'peaceful evolution' designed to subvert the ideas of the Chinese people.[40]

Although Deng had presided over the crackdown in early June 1989, he remained an economic reformer and an advocate of China taking its place in the global economy. He did not accept the idea that 'freedom is indivisible'. On the contrary, he contrived to divide it, according quite a high degree

of economic freedom to individuals and enterprises, while curtailing political freedom and dividing intellectual freedom by subject. The natural
sciences had more freedom than the social sciences, while strict censorship
remained in the theatre, cinema and the arts. But Deng and his family had
suffered too much during Mao's later years for him to have any interest in
a return to Maoism. In the short run, political constraints became tighter,
but the aftermath of Tiananmen did not produce the comprehensively hard-
line reaction that more conservative Chinese Communists had hoped for.
Yet what happened somewhat undermined Deng's own authority. Those
who, at least partially, sympathized with the student protests and the idea
of democratic reform were, naturally, distressed by the events of 4 June,
and more critical of Deng than hitherto. By now, however, they were but
thinly represented in the highest echelons of the party. The more numerous
senior officials, who had been concerned that the party was gradually losing
control, saw both the protests and the fierce crackdown as a logical consequence of the 'liberal' policies pursued by Deng and of his mistaken support
(up until the May–June 1989 political crisis) for Zhao Ziyang.

Deng still, however, retained sufficient authority to have a decisive influence on the choice of Zhao's successor. He ensured that the clock was not
turned back too far by going beyond the ranks of the Politburo's Standing
Committee and selecting the new general secretary from the broader
Politburo membership. The person agreed on was the first secretary of the
Shanghai party organization, Jiang Zemin. Jiang had closed down the
reformist Shanghai weekly newspaper, *World Economic Herald*, in May 1989,
a decision which Zhao had criticized but which Deng approved. The *Herald*
had published the speeches and writings of a number of political reformers,
among them Su Shaozhi.[41] Jiang had, however, managed the Shanghai
spillover protests from the 4 June events without bloodshed. Although not
exactly a reformer, he was also no fundamentalist Marxist-Leninist or Maoist.
He occupied the middle ground within the Politburo and was a cautious
operator. Before long he had accumulated the array of formal institutional
powers which had been possessed by Mao Zedong – and, very briefly, by
Mao's chosen successor, Hua Guofeng. But in spite of being General
Secretary of the Communist Party, President of the People's Republic of
China, and chair of the Military Affairs Commission, Jiang had to play second
fiddle to Deng Xiaoping until Deng's health began to fail in the mid-1990s.
Moreover, other colleagues also wielded considerable power, not least the
hard-line premier, Li Peng.[42]

Thus, the coalition at the top of the Chinese Communist Party hierarchy
had changed in a more conservative direction following the death of Hu
Yaobang and the removal of Zhao Ziyang. At a meeting of the Central

Committee of the party on 23–24 June 1989, the dismissal of three of Zhao's associates from the inner party leadership was approved. Zhao, who attended the session, was subjected to a number of severe attacks. The prime minister Li Peng said that after Zhao became general secretary, bourgeois liberalization had 'spread rampantly'.[43] The fact that later that year Communist systems collapsed in Eastern Europe further strengthened the conservative forces within the CCP, as did the disintegration of the Soviet Union at the end of 1991. Liberalization and 'peaceful evolution', major aims of Western policy for countries under Communist rule, now seemed to many senior figures within the CCP to represent a mortal threat to their system. Whereas Deng continued to take the view that economic development would promote social and political stability, others, such as Wang Renzhi, the head of the Propaganda Department of the Central Committee, called for ideological struggle against 'bourgeois liberalization' and a renewal of 'socialist construction'.[44]

Overt dissent was dealt with severely. The most renowned Chinese dissident, Wei Jingsheng, had already spent thirteen years in prison for his contributions to the Democracy Wall when he was released in 1993. He lost no time in resuming his campaign for democracy. He was arrested again in 1994 and the following year sentenced to fourteen more years in prison. A reporter was sentenced to six years in prison for revealing that the National People's Congress was a rubber-stamp assembly (as were, she might have added, all the 'parliaments' in Communist systems) and that while Deng Xiaoping was alive, it would be wrong to say that General Secretary Jiang Zemin held supreme power. She was accused of stealing state secrets, although these points were about as secret as the revelation that China has a Great Wall. She had also offended by publishing the information in Hong Kong, which was still under British colonial rule.[45] International pressure and China's diplomatic interests could sometimes have an effect on the fate of dissidents. Wei Jingsheng's 1993 release was on the eve of a bid from China to host the Olympic Games. He was finally let go – and instantly deported to the United States – in November 1997, just after a visit to America by Jiang Zemin in which the Chinese Communist Party leader and head of state held talks with President Clinton. Another prominent dissident, Wang Dan, who had been a leading advocate of democracy in the Tiananmen movement of 1989, was freed from prison at the same time and also deported to the USA.[46]

The most significant change to have occurred in China since the death of Mao, and especially in the years since the Tiananmen Square events of 1989, has not, however, been a product of overt dissent or of the development of civil society. Independent organizations – other than independent

religious groups (which have also been persecuted) – are accorded no legitimacy and remain thin on the ground.[47] As in the Soviet Union in the quarter-
century after the fall of Khrushchev, or (still more) in Czechoslovakia
between 1963 and the spring of 1968, or in Hungary under Kádár, the most
important source of change has been the evolution of the thinking of people
within the official structures.

Institutions set up to advance Communist orthodoxy, such as the Institute
of Marxism-Leninism Mao Zedong Thought and the Central Party School
in Beijing, have been at various times places where highly unorthodox ideas,
political as well as economic, have flourished. The former institute was even
described by the Communist Party's ideology boss, Deng Liqun, in 1983 as
the 'anti-Marxist base camp'. After the crushing of public protest on 4 June
1989, a substantial number of that institute's members were arrested,
temporarily detained, or forced into exile. However, the Central Party School,
in particular, has remained a place where some of the most daringly innovative ideas could be aired. To teach there means that the person is firmly
embedded within the Communist system. Naturally, the institution has its
share of conformists, but their colleagues of reformist disposition have had
the opportunity to influence the thinking of up-and-coming officials who
have studied at the Central Party School and to use their position to stretch
further the limits of the system. The interpenetration of party-state and
society can, in the course of time, work both ways. The influence of
society, as well as of ideas from the world beyond China's borders, can
change the thinking of people within even the most overtly ideologized
organizations. As the Chinese political scientist X.L. Ding has pointed out,
official and semi-official structures can provide both a protective screen
and the material resources which enable unorthodox views to develop and
to be disseminated legally.[48]

An important example of the ambiguous relationship between state and
non-state structures has been the way in which private business has developed in China. State institutions have provided a roof, or what has been
called in China a 'red hat', under which private enterprise can expand under
the protective covering of state authority. Until 1988, the only legal private
economic activity was that conducted by 'individual households' with fewer
than eight employees.[49] But larger businesses were, in fact, created under
the auspices of collective enterprises which had the official imprimatur of
the state. By the time private businesses were permitted to operate – from
1988 – some half a million enterprises were operating 'using the red hat
disguise'.[50] Thus, for example, it was possible even as early as 1983 for an
entrepreneur to employ 500 women in a clothes-making factory in Jingjiang,
Fujian province, under the municipal 'red hat'. This meant that officially it

was a township enterprise, although Mr Hua, the owner, was the sole investor and managed the factory himself. Material benefits, however, accrued to both sides.[51]

Deng Xiaoping's last public foray was a tour of the southern coastal provinces of China in 1992, when he gave his blessing to further economic liberalization.[52] Deng, whose health went into serious decline soon after, died in 1997 at the age of ninety-two. That his authority had declined by the early 1990s as compared with the 1980s was shown by the fact that the mass media, under the control of more conservative Communists, did not print his coastal tour speeches until several months later. This reflected the intense struggle which was going on behind the scenes over the future of economic reform.[53] Nevertheless, Deng's supportive view prevailed, with Jiang Zemin now more fully embracing marketizing change. 'Red hat' concerns continued to exist, but they were no longer a precondition for the success of what were, in all but name, capitalist enterprises. Between 1990 and 2000, private businesses increased in number at a rate of 10 per cent a year. By 2006 over a hundred million people (out of a total population of 1.3 billion) were employed in such enterprises. They contributed almost half of China's GDP and accounted for more than two-thirds of its industrial output.[54] Although these businesses are essentially private, they are still intertwined with and dependent on the state. Their property rights are insecure and depend on the goodwill of the party-state authorities, even though a new law in March 2007 did strengthen the legal foundation of private property.[55]

The business community has shown much greater interest in establishing legal certainty than in democracy. For the sake of good relations with the authorities, they avoid taking contentious political stands, but survey research shows that many are concerned to reduce corruption (and thus avoid having to pay bribes) and to see progress towards a rule of law.[56] However, legal uncertainty can also be of benefit to a significant section of the business community. A good many of those involved in international trade are from the families of party-state officials. For the officials, having both relatives and capital abroad can be seen as part of their 'contingency plans', should the system go the way of its East European counterparts. Many assets which have disappeared from China cease to be wholly – or even mainly – owned by the parent firm. Offshoots are created which are 'geographically and legally distant from the original parent in China', and those companies are 'apt to become the private concerns of their managers'.[57] X.L. Ding, who has made an astute study of informal privatization in China, has noted that 'muddling property relations is a necessary condition for clarifying them later'. When they are 'clarified', this may be by a foreign court several places along the chain of ownership. The loser at that point becomes the Chinese state. Public funds are often used as private capital and invested in risky property, equity and currency markets overseas. As Ding observes, what this means is that 'Communist speculators from China have . . . enjoyed a luxury which may be the envy of their capitalist counterparts: they are guaranteed a big share of the profits while the state is guaranteed all the costs and risks.'[58]

These are among the unintended consequences of the economic reform set in motion by Deng Xiaoping. Corruption, appalling environmental pollution, and greatly increased inequality rank amongst the more dangerous consequences of China's road to a market economy. Nevertheless, China's economic advance over the past three decades has been dramatic. In the last twenty years in particular, growth rates have exceeded 7 per cent per year and have usually been above 10 per cent.[59] Even conservative estimates suggest that China is likely to have overtaken the United States as the world's largest economy well before the middle of this century (although changing demographics add a note of uncertainty).[60] Economic growth has been accompanied by a remarkable reduction of the direst poverty in China over the past quarter of a century. Using the same criteria of measurement, 15 per cent of the population were in 1985 below this near-starvation level. By 2008 it had dropped to 1.6 per cent.[61] A very large-scale transfer of property ownership has taken place in these years, albeit accompanied by numerous abuses, some of which have been noted in this chapter. Small-scale businesses have been entirely privatized and many medium-sized state enterprises have been sold. Housing was privatized in the late 1990s, leading to the upgrading of many properties to enhance their value.[62] Foreign direct investment in China has led to much higher levels of efficiency and productivity. That has not been an unmixed blessing. It is the multinationals, with their global market reach, who have taken advantage of cheap labour in China, and China's indigenous industries have found it difficult to compete with them.[63] Yet the investment from overseas companies has undoubtedly been to China's overall benefit.[64]

Chinese Politics in the Twenty-First Century

When Deng Xiaoping chose Jiang Zemin to be party general secretary, he also, in effect, picked Jiang's successor by 'anointing', as Susan Shirk notes, 'Hu Jintao, another cautious engineer-politician, a decade ahead of time'.[65] From 1992 a member of the Standing Committee of the Politburo and heir apparent to Jiang, Hu Jintao became party general secretary and head of state in 2002. His style of leadership has been more consensual than that of his predecessors. Within the political elite he has built coalitions rather than adopting a 'winner-takes-all' approach. And in policy he has put greater emphasis than before on more balanced regional economic development and on social harmony.[66] A year after Hu became party leader and president, Wen Jiabao, the former aide to the ousted Zhao, became prime minister. Wen, the son of schoolteachers, who made his career working in poor inland regions of China, has shown a capacity to connect emotionally with the rural poor.[67] He has also displayed some awareness of the damaging gulf between the political elite and the mass of the people at a time when China's prosperity has increased impressively but inequalities have become greater. During the severe earthquake which hit China's Sichuan province in May 2008, he visited the most stricken areas and made a good initial impression on the survivors. However, the question on the lips of many of the bereaved – why schools collapsed killing children while local party headquarters in the same area survived almost unscathed – awaited an answer. The most likely cause was that theft and corruption led to skimping on materials and safety considerations on all but the most prestigious party-state buildings. The Sichuan earthquake left at least 87,000 people dead or missing and destroyed the livelihood of almost two million others. Bereaved parents who demanded investigations into the cause of the collapse of schools were subsequently told 'not to make trouble' and to accept cash compensation for each child lost.[68]

At the time of writing, Hu remains general secretary and president and Wen remains premier. New conventions of leadership change have been introduced, whereby party leaders are expected to serve for two terms of five years each in between party congresses. Jiang Zemin duly retired as party leader at the Sixteenth Party Congress in 2002 (although he continued to chair the committee which supervised the armed forces until 2004), and the expectation is that Hu should continue as party general secretary and president of the Chinese state until, but not beyond, 2012. All this depends on continued economic progress being matched by political stability. Stability based on electoral choice and political accountability is likely to be longer-lasting than that based on authoritarian adaptation, but thus far the Chinese leadership has favoured the latter rather than the former. There is wider debate within the Communist Party, but strict controls remain on the dissemination of information. If the 4,000-mile-long Great Wall of China was the old method of keeping the country safe from its enemies, the modern method is the Great Firewall, which selects what can be transmitted by the internet in this increasingly computerized country. Information illustrating the lack of democracy, or human rights abuses, or discussing the prospects for democratization in China is blocked. Yet Premier Wen implicitly recognized in 2007 both that China is not at present a democracy and that it is desirable and possible 'to build a democratic country with the rule of law under socialist conditions'. It would, however, take a long time.[69]

Chinese party intellectuals have devoted much time and effort to examining the causes of the collapse of Communist systems in the Soviet Union and Eastern Europe. While the official and, usually, actual aim is to learn lessons that will prevent China from suffering a similar fate, the discussions can also be an indirect way of criticizing Chinese political realities. In the Soviet Union during the Brezhnev era, as noted in Chapter 20, this method was employed the other way round. Criticism of Mao and Maoism became an esoteric way of criticizing Stalin and Stalinism at a time when overt criticism of the Stalin era was forbidden. Some of the self-criticism in China has, however, gone well beyond what was published in the Soviet Union under Brezhnev, and is more akin to the kind of warning heard during Gorbachev's perestroika. Thus, in 2004, Yu Yunyao, who was at the time deputy head of the Central Party School, said in an interview: 'To the party as a whole, the longer it is in power, the greater the danger of its being divorced from the masses and the grimmer the test of fighting corruption. With regard to leading cadres, the higher his position, the greater his power, and the longer he assumes leadership, the larger the number of seductions and the greater the possibility of his being corrupted.'[70]

Some of the attempts to promote 'democratization' amount to no more than window-dressing. As in a number of other Communist countries, there are several puppet parties in China which have been totally under the thumb of the Communists. In 2007, two people from these minor parties were appointed to ministerial posts. However, in China, as in Eastern Europe, members of the fellow-travelling parties have been less able to promote change than those who are well established within the ruling Communist Party. There have also been experiments with contested elections at the village level. But these are, at most, symptoms of change encouraged from above rather than drivers of reform. Innovation has stemmed from the top of the party hierarchy. In the sixty years of Chinese Communist rule, this has often meant, above all, the top party leader. After the death of Mao, however, the leadership has been more oligarchical than autocratic. That also increases the number of access points available to those in the broader political elite who wish to promote change. It is noteworthy that over the years many of the most important reform ideas, including ones which have been translated into policy, have emanated from the Central Party School in Beijing.[71]

The obverse of ostensible concessions to democracy which have little

substance is that pronouncements which can seem merely banal and propa-
gandistic may turn out to augur real change. One such was the concept of
the 'Three Represents', elaborated by Jiang Zemin in 2001, especially in a
major speech at the Central Party School. The Three Represents were:

1. The party should represent the advanced productive forces in society.
2. The party should represent advanced modern culture.
3. The party should represent the interests of the vast majority of the people.[72]

Especially important was the first item on the list, for what this was intended
to signify, as became increasingly clear, was that the party should embrace
the entrepreneurs in the private sector who represented the most dynamic
element in the economy. To put it more bluntly, with just a little simplifi-
cation, capitalists were now welcome to be Communists! The incentive for
the entrepreneur to join the Chinese Communist Party is, in the words of
a leading specialist on the CCP, that 'the party today represents a de facto
"political protection racket" for those in private business'.[73] That is not, of
course, the language of the party leadership, but Jiang himself placed
greatest emphasis on the first 'advanced productive forces' category. When
he was succeeded as party leader by Hu Jintao, the emphasis changed to
the third point – representation of 'the vast majority of the people'. Hu,
as well as the premier Wen Jiabao, had in mind the great mass of the people
in the interior of China who had not fared nearly so well as a result of
economic reform as those in the coastal areas, the latter being Jiang's major
constituency.[74] The fact that without abandoning any of the three categories of representation Hu could signal a shift of policy by concentrating
on the third is an example of the importance of esoteric discourse within
ruling Communist parties, especially those which are more oligarchical
than autocratic.

Under the rule of the Kims, father and son, in North Korea, or during
the periods when Stalin and Mao were at the peak of their power, the main
concern of high officials in these three countries was to echo faithfully the
language and priorities of *the* leader. The 'Three Represents', however, in
addition to providing scope for a shift of priorities from one top leader to
the next, enabled others to put their own gloss on the concept. Thus, the
Shanghai party theoretician Liu Ji, whom Jiang brought to Beijing when he
became general secretary, and who is credited with coining the notion of
the Three Represents, was by 2006 talking more boldly (albeit in an interview with an American scholar), saying: 'We will first achieve democracy
within the CCP and then extend it to the whole population.'[75] The term
'democracy' has been used increasingly in the Hu Jintao era, with Hu himself

emphasizing intra-party democracy. The principle of 'democratic centralism' is still firmly upheld, but the adjective has become somewhat more
meaningful, with different viewpoints and feedback taken into account, even
though strict discipline in the implementation of decisions is maintained.[76]

China in the twenty-first century remains a highly authoritarian state,
but it has become an increasingly consultative authoritarianism. Rather than
fight economically or socially important groups, the Communist Party has
attempted to co-opt them. The fact that even the wealthiest entrepreneurs
can only survive in China if they maintain the goodwill of the party-state
authorities gives them an incentive to conform politically. Many of the entrepreneurs, indeed, have close family connections with high party and state
officials and were able to embark on privatization thanks to both their formal
and informal links with political power-holders. The private business people
then have some cards to play. Many of them have acquired property overseas, where, often, their children are educated, and to the extent to which
they feel insecure in their property ownership in China, they can, by various
means, transfer capital abroad.[77]

China's rulers have been increasingly unable to mobilize the population
on the basis of Communist ideology, whether Marxism-Leninism or Mao
Zedong Thought, although they have added on 'Deng Xiaoping Theory'
and the 'Three Represents'. They cannot overtly abandon the foundations
of the official ideology without raising fundamental questions about their
right to rule. Yet the watered-down version which has taken the place of
the old rhetoric does not send the pulse racing. That is not necessarily a
matter for regret. When people *were* aroused – during the Great Leap
Forward and the Cultural Revolution – the result was mayhem and tens of
millions of unnecessary deaths. In that context there may even be something to be said for the less than stirring title of president and party leader
Hu's major speech to the Seventeenth Congress of the CCP in 2007: 'Hold
High the Great Banner of Socialism with Chinese Characteristics and Strive
for New Victories in Building a Moderately Prosperous Society in All
Respects'.[78] Yet for many in the party, including those who see marketization, privatization and increasing inequality as a betrayal of the Communist
movement's ideals, the traditional ideology still has some purchase. China's
remarkable economic development into the workshop of the world – on
which the global economy, not least that of the United States, is increasingly dependent – comes at a political price for the Communist leadership.
The interdependence of the Chinese and American economies naturally
cuts both ways. A prolonged recession in the United States could endanger
the economic and social stability of China.[79]

More fundamentally, a more prosperous society, and above all, a better-educated citizenry, develops expectations which are different from those of the overwhelmingly peasant country in which the Communists came to power in 1949. The party has recognized new social realities, but in the process, this changes the character of the party. The CCP is overwhelmingly the largest Communist Party in the world, with over 74 million members at the end of 2007.[80] The 'economically active' population of China at that time was 769 million people.[81] Therefore approximately one in ten adults in employment was a party member. This is, in fact, the norm for a Communist system in which the party's power has been consolidated. In the course of 2007, almost 100,000 students joined the party, and they were the largest single category of new members, accounting for 35.8 per cent of party recruits in that year. This trend is of some significance. Survey research in China has shown that the higher the respondents' education, the more likely the person is to support political reform.[82] About 16,000 of those admitted to the party in 2007 were from what the CCP calls the 'new social stratum', a term used for businessmen, managers in the private sector, citizens working for foreign companies and self-employed professionals. Women remain grossly under-represented, but efforts are being made to alter that. At the end of 2007, they made up just 20.4 per cent of the total party membership, but they constituted 35.7 per cent of the new members admitted that year.[83]

Legitimation of the regime, in a country without a tradition of pluralist democracy, depends not only on continued economic growth but on the mobilization of national (and at times nationalist) sentiment behind the existing order. There has been a conscious revival of national pride in China's great cultural tradition which Mao, in the Cultural Revolution, attempted to stamp out. National self-esteem and the intense desire for China to be recognized internationally as a great and worthy power is a unifying element in the relationship between leaders and people. The Beijing Olympic Games of August 2008, with their spectacular opening ceremony, drawing attention far more to China's achievements over several millennia than to the six decades of Communist rule, were a striking manifestation of this. Whether adaptation to changing economic and social realities will allow China to remain a recognizably Communist system in its political structures and style of rule, or whether underlying tensions in the society and the ruling party will force further systemic change sooner rather than later (for they certainly will at some point) is an open question. National tensions are one source of conflict, although China has an easier task of controlling disaffected national groups than had the rulers of the Soviet Union, where Russians constituted just half of the total Soviet population. China is more comparable to post-Soviet Russia, where 90 per cent of the people are ethnic Russians, as in China 90 per cent are of Han ethnicity. Nevertheless, the violent resistance of Uighur separatists in the province of Xinjiang, which borders Turkmenistan, Kazakhstan and Mongolia, and where the Muslim Uighur constitute a majority of the population, poses a problem for the leadership comparable to that of Tibet.[84] In neither case is there any political grouping in Beijing willing to contemplate allowing secession, but a Chinese government increasingly interconnected with the outside world is less impervious than in the past to international opinion on the way it handles such conflict.

Whereas Mao made a virtue of conflict – class rather than national – the Chinese Communist Party leadership today strives for political and social harmony, under what they sometimes call 'consultative democracy' (comparable to the 'guided democracy' to be found in other authoritarian systems), as distinct from pluralist democracy. Yet social and political tensions remain. In the summer of 2007, a letter signed by many retired party officials was sent to the Central Committee of the party. The signatories complained about a loss of political orientation and went on: 'The reforms now being carried out in China are reforms for turning the public ownership system into the private ownership system and for turning socialism into capitalism.'[85] The party leadership did not, of course, agree, and much depends on how each of the terms is defined. However, there is enough of an element of truth in what the veteran party cadres wrote to raise the question, to which I return in Chapter 30: to what extent does it still make sense to regard China as Communist?

23

The Challenge of the West

The West posed a problem for Communist systems simply by being there. The countries people in Eastern Europe knew most about – those of Western Europe and North America – offered an attractive alternative to Soviet-type rule on many grounds. In the post-Stalin era a majority of citizens in the European Communist states knew that 'the West' enjoyed both a higher material standard of living and far more freedom than they did. The most popular aspect of Communist systems with the population as a whole was the welfare state – free education, largely free health care, and full employment.[1] However, it was not in the Soviet Union or Eastern Europe that the best medical and other social services on the European continent were provided. They were far surpassed by the Scandinavian countries and such major Western European states as the Federal Republic of Germany, France and Great Britain. A well-informed minority of those living under Communist rule were aware of this – a higher proportion of the population in the central European countries than in the Soviet Union.

Another area where the Communist world lagged well behind the West – in this case, behind the United States in particular – was that of high technology. There was nothing remotely equivalent to Silicon Valley in any of the Communist states, including the Soviet Union, although, ironically, much of the assembling of the world's electronic equipment now takes place in China. There were certain areas of technology where the Soviet Union, in particular, achieved a very high level, such as rocketry (whether for space exploration or military purposes), but in most spheres a substantial gap remained between Communist Europe and the West. As a result, the foreign intelligence services of Communist states put a lot of effort into stealing technological blueprints in the West. What they were unable to steal, they sometimes had to buy, although Western countries put restrictions on the export of high technology which could be put to military use. The Russian novelist, philosopher and political essayist Alexander Zinoviev, who had a love–hate relationship both with the Soviet Union and with the West, was an astute observer of the doublethink characteristic of the Brezhnev era.

On the problem of the West, he wrote in his satirical novel, *The Yawning Heights:* 'On top of all that, there's abroad. If only it didn't exist! Then we'd be home and dry. But they're eternally dreaming up something new over there. And we have to compete with them. To show our superiority. No sooner have you pinched one little machine from them than it's time to pinch the next one. By the time we've got it into production, the bastard's obsolete!'[2] It was only in that self-same 'abroad', of course, that such a novel could be published, as it was in 1976. In addition to technological lag, there was a chronic shortage of consumer goods in the unreformed Communist countries. That is not true of China today, with its reformed economy and ample availability of consumer durables, but it was true of the European Communist states whose systems collapsed at the end of the 1980s.

The Helsinki Process and Détente

The 1970s are known as a period of détente. The fundamentals of Communist systems did not change during that time; nor did the essence of the East–West relationship. Nevertheless, three successive American presidents – Richard Nixon, Gerald Ford, and Jimmy Carter – held summit talks with Leonid Brezhnev. A more fundamental, although controversial, part of détente was what became known as the Helsinki process. This turned out to be a more significant challenge from the West than the Soviet leadership had bargained for when they persuaded Western countries to embark on the road which led to Helsinki. The Helsinki process consisted both of the negotiations, which began in 1972 (and took place mainly in Geneva) and led to the signing of the Helsinki Agreement on Security and Co-operation in Europe in 1975, and the follow-up conferences that were held periodically to check that the signatories were complying with the Helsinki principles.

'Détente' meant different things to different people, but could be broadly defined as signifying a relaxation of tension and a reduction of the likelihood of war, which did not, however, preclude struggle in the realm of ideas. Indeed, Soviet leaders made clear that neither their favoured term, 'peaceful co-existence', nor détente (*razryadka*, which also means 'unloading', in its Russian version) meant ideological co-existence. The Soviet Union aimed to triumph ideologically by all means short of world war. Yet they were far from favouring a free contestation of ideas. They devoted vast resources to political censorship and to jamming foreign radio in order to keep unwelcome ideas out of Communist Europe. The Conference on Security and Co-operation in Europe, which resulted in the Helsinki agreement – known officially as the Final Act[3] – was very much a Soviet initiative, but one which backfired. All the European states apart from Albania participated in the talks leading up to the Final Act, and the United States and Canada also took part. The participation of the USA, in particular, was already a concession from the Soviet side and tacit rejection of the view that what went on in Europe was none of America's business.

The United States did not, of course, wish to be excluded from discussions of any significance on security in Europe, and their European allies wanted them to be involved. Yet neither Richard Nixon (who had been succeeded as president by Gerald Ford before the signing of the Final Act) nor Henry Kissinger, in his roles as Nixon's national security adviser and subsequently secretary of state under Presidents Nixon and Ford), were in the least enthusiastic about the Helsinki process as such. Nixon told British officials that the US government 'had never wanted the conference', and Kissinger was impatient with the emphasis of European negotiators on human rights. He tried to persuade his NATO allies to adopt a more 'realistic' stance, which would have meant acceding more readily to the Soviet view.[4] It is hard to avoid the conclusion that Kissinger was uncomfortable with multilateral discussions. He preferred important negotiations with the Soviet Union to be handled in bilateral relations with the United States, preferably by himself. In the several years leading up to the Helsinki Agreement, however, European negotiators played a crucial role. Especially important was the cohesion and determination shown by 'the Nine', the members at that time of the European Economic Community (EEC), which later, with expanded membership, was to become the European Union.

What the Soviet Union sought from the conference was an acknowledgement both by the United States and by the countries of Western Europe of the immutability of the borders established at the end of World War Two. They had some success in portraying the results of the conference in precisely those terms, but in fact, Western negotiators were able to insist on important qualifications on this issue. The borders were declared to be 'inviolable' rather than 'immutable', and this meant that they could be changed consensually, although not by armed force. That was explicitly ruled out. The agreement, however, said plainly that 'frontiers can be changed, in accordance with international law, by peaceful means and by agreement'.[5] Among those who insisted on this were the West German negotiators, and indeed, this Helsinki precept was one of the foundations for the eventual reunification of Germany. In principle, the wording of the Final Act also appeared to rule out the kind of military intervention the Soviet Union had undertaken in Czechoslovakia, stating that 'the participating states . . . will refrain from any manifestation of force for the purpose of inducing another participating State to renounce the full exercise of its sovereign rights'.[6]

The discussions leading up to the Final Act, and the document eventually agreed, were divided into four parts, which became known during the negotiations as Baskets One, Two, Three and Four. Basket One contained security and confidence-building measures and included useful provisions designed to make more difficult surprise attack or war by accident. It also included the strongest commitment to human rights to be found in any part of the document. The participating states were signing up to 'respect human rights and fundamental freedoms, including the freedom of thought, conscience, religion or belief, for all without distinction as to race, sex, language or religion'.[7] Basket Two included economic co-operation, science and technology. Basket Three, the one which caused greatest trouble to the Soviet side both during the negotiations and later, spelled out in greater detail what was entailed by the human rights principle contained already in Basket One. This included 'freer and wider dissemination of information of all kinds'. Basket Four contained what was, in a sense, the first step in implementing Basket Three, since it obliged the signatories to publish and disseminate widely the text of the agreement and to attend follow-up meetings.[8]

The Soviet leader, Leonid Brezhnev, was strongly committed to securing what became the Helsinki agreement, as was the foreign minister, Andrey Gromyko. Having initiated the process, they then staked Soviet prestige on getting what they thought would be a higher level of recognition of the Communist states which had existed since the second half of the 1940s. To achieve this, they had to authorize concessions, especially on the human rights aspect of Basket One and on much of Basket Three, which caused apprehension to some of their colleagues. Indeed, they worried Gromyko himself, who told the leader of the Soviet negotiating team, Anatoly Kovalev, that 'it would be good to cut out the bottom from this Third Basket'.[9] On both the Soviet and Western sides there were internal differences in the lead-up to the signing of the Final Act. However, those in the Soviet Union were kept under wraps, while the disagreements among Western politicians and commentators were very much in the open. Now much more is known about the doubts and dissension on the Soviet side. Yury Andropov, as KGB chairman, could see that the third part of the agreement was likely to bring a basket of troubles to that institution. He observed: 'The principle of inviolability of borders – this is of course good, very good. But I am concerned about something else: the borders will be inviolable in a military sense, but in all other respects, as a result of the expansion of contacts, of the flow of information, they will became transparent . . . So far the game is being played on one side of the field – the Ministry of Foreign Affairs is gaining the points, and the KGB is losing them.'[10] Suslov, behind the scenes, also viewed the agreement with suspicion, but since Brezhnev hailed it as a triumph, and since the Soviet mass media emphasized only those parts of the accords which the leadership wished to see stressed (although they fulfilled their obligation to publish the actual text in full), no one was in a position to dissent publicly.[11]

Many in the West did not observe what Andropov foresaw, and opposed the Helsinki Agreement on the grounds that it was a sell-out to the Soviet Union. Among conservative politicians, Ronald Reagan and Margaret Thatcher were among the most prominent of those opposed to Helsinki. Reagan, still governor of California but a presidential aspirant, declared that 'all Americans should be against it'. Mrs Thatcher in 1990 conceded that she had been mistaken in her scepticism about the Helsinki accords, having underestimated their long-term effects. In fact, she said, they had been 'a tremendous encouragement and inspiration to dissident groups', and 'many people in East and Central Europe today can trace their new freedom to the Helsinki Agreements'.[12] At the time, many Western critics – politicians, journalists and academics – took at face value the Soviet claim that the accords ratified the division of Europe. Both the *New York Times* and the *Wall Street Journal* criticized President Gerald Ford for signing the agreement. In a more balanced assessment, the British ambassador to Moscow at the time of the signing of the Helsinki Final Act, Sir Terence Garvey, discussed the pros and cons of the Conference on Security and Co-operation in Europe (CSCE) in a lengthy dispatch to the foreign secretary, James Callaghan. He saw more pluses than minuses, and advocated moving 'quite soon on points where current Soviet practice is clearly incompatible with the Final Act'. Garvey summed up:

> The CSCE has given the Russians something that they had long wanted very much, perhaps even come to over-value. But the Western Governments have gained also – in limiting and qualifying their endorsement of a situation they do not intend to change, in forcing the Russians to do battle on ground hitherto taboo and, not least, in cohesion and the practice of co-operation . . . And in the longer perspective, the practice of *détente* may foster developments in Soviet policies which ultimately make the USSR a less intractable, even a more reliable, partner.[13]

In fact, dissident groups both within the Soviet Union and in Eastern Europe were soon citing the Helsinki Final Act to legitimize their activities. The groups which set themselves up to monitor their own countries' adherence to the CSCE principles posed particular problems for the authorities. The secret police could, and did, harass such groups. It was, however, more than usually embarrassing for state signatories to the Helsinki accords to arrest and imprison their own citizens when they were exercising their moral right to try to ensure that governments abided by the norms they had signed up to. In the short run, though, it seemed that, so far as the Soviet Union was concerned, the critics of the Helsinki Agreement were right. Embarrassing it may have been, but Yury Orlov, a physics professor who became the leader of what was called the Public Group to Assist the Implementation of the Helsinki Accord in the USSR, was arrested in 1977 and not released from prison camp until 1986. Yet Orlov had seen the potential of the Helsinki Final Act. Meeting his fellow dissident Ludmilla Alexeyeva in 1976, he had said: 'Lyuda, don't you see this is the first international document in which the issue of human rights is discussed as a component of international peace?' Orlov said that the document provided an opportunity 'to involve other countries in monitoring the Soviet performance on human rights'. Alexeyeva agreed, adding in her memoirs: 'Our message wasn't that difficult to understand, but the West had focused its attention on the narrow issue of Jewish emigration. The Soviet democratic movement had not been able to generate such support.'[14]

Now, though, heads of governments and foreign ministers, visiting the Soviet Union and the Eastern European states, had the authority of the Helsinki Final Act to bring up human rights issues. These could no longer be so easily dismissed by their hosts as internal matters on which they had no need to respond.[15] While Helsinki was very far from being the only factor that contributed to the striking enhancement of civil liberties in the Soviet Union after 1985, the desire of Gorbachev and of Gromyko's successor as foreign minister, Eduard Shevardnadze, not to be put on the defensive on the CSCE accords was certainly one of them. Dramatic change in the treatment of dissidents, a widening of the opportunities for foreign travel, and a freer flow of information and ideas began to emerge in 1986. By 1988 they had become qualitatively different from the practices of the Brezhnev era.

Eurocommunism

Western challenges to the Soviet Union and to orthodox Communism came in many different forms. One such challenge was the movement that became known as 'Eurocommunism'. In the West itself, it was greeted with even more scepticism than the Helsinki process. There was legitimate debate on how sincere was this attempt on the part of a significant number of Western

Communists to achieve a reconciliation between the democratic values of their own societies and the ideology they espoused. There should have been no doubt, however, about its deviation in important respects from Soviet orthodoxy. If it was not taken seriously by Western governments, for whom it posed little threat, it was taken seriously enough by the leadership of the Soviet Communist Party, for whom it did appear to be at least potentially dangerous. This change in the thinking and behaviour of important West European Communist parties – most notably the Italian and Spanish parties and, to a much lesser extent, the French – did not prevent their subsequent drastic decline. The development did, though, challenge Soviet assumptions of ideological hegemony. Soviet leaders were especially concerned that it was the Communist parties which at the time had some serious popular support in their own countries (although they had been happy to accept Soviet financial aid) that were no longer willing to see Moscow as the fount of all political wisdom. Also worrying, not just for the CPSU but for a number of ruling Communist parties, was the fact that some of *their* members were attracted by the ideas of their West European comrades.

Among the more important stimuli to Eurocommunism was the Prague Spring, which attracted many members of Western European parties, including the major Italian one and the underground Spanish party (Spain at that time being still under the authoritarian rule of General Franco). The Soviet invasion of Czechoslovakia was a blow to these Communists, for whom the Czech reformers seemed to have much to offer. It led them within a few years to take a more critical look at their Soviet mentors. The atmosphere of détente, including the Helsinki process, was also a factor stimulating the development of more independent thinking among West European Communists in the early and mid-1970s.[16] In the coldest years of the Cold War they offered unconditional support to the Soviet Union.

The term 'Eurocommunism' was coined by a Yugoslav journalist, Frani Barbieri, in an article published on 26 June 1975. There had already been some signs of fresh thinking in several of the European Communist parties, and Barbieri wrote his piece a fortnight *before* the meeting which later was seen as the official launch of the movement – a gathering in Tuscany at which the leaders of the Italian and Spanish parties, Enrico Berlinguer and Santiago Carrillo, both spoke.[17] A joint declaration by these two parties was published on 12 July 1975. It referred to the recent fall of the Portuguese and Greek dictatorships and the forthcoming change in Spain, and declared that in the 'new conditions created by the positive progress of international détente', it was time to find 'new ways of bringing about closer co-operation among all democratic forces for a policy of democratic and socialist renewal of society, and for a positive outcome of the crisis now affecting European capitalist countries'. Emphasizing the importance of 'reflection on the specific historical conditions of each country in the West European context', they claimed that 'in our countries socialism can only be strengthened by the development and full operation of democracy'. In a passage particularly irksome for their Soviet official readers, they observed that 'there must be no official state ideology', but there must be competing political parties, independent trade unions, religious and other freedoms. Setting themselves somewhat apart from the international Communist movement, orchestrated from Moscow, they concluded with the declaration: 'The Italian and Spanish communist parties, which work out their internal and international policies in complete autonomy and independence, are fully aware of their grave national and European responsibilities. From these common viewpoints they will in future develop their fraternal relations sealed by a broad and solid friendship.'[18]

Neither of these parties had embraced social democracy. They remained in the 1970s unremittingly hostile to capitalism, and in their internal organization they preserved the strict discipline and limited rights of debate characteristic of democratic centralism. Yet Berlinguer and Carrillo were making a break with the past, not least in questioning Soviet orthodoxy and elements of Soviet history which had never been disowned by Stalin's heirs. Thus, Carrillo, in a book entitled *'Eurocommunism' and the State* (for the Spanish and Italian parties soon embraced the term 'Eurocommunism', even though they had not invented it), was highly critical of the fact that Moscow had been so slow in embracing a popular front against fascism. He cited the case of the leader of the British Communist Party, Harry Pollitt, who had considered that an anti-fascist war began the day Nazi Germany attacked Poland – and was sacked from his post as general secretary for this deviation from the Soviet line. Later, when the Soviet Union was attacked by Germany, Pollitt was reinstated. Carrillo also criticized the lies that had been told about Trotsky – as an 'agent of fascism', for example – and said it was 'high time that Trotsky's role in the Revolution was presented in an objective way'.[19] There were strict limits to Carrillo's deviation. He had become neither a Trotskyist nor a social democrat, but he was particularly outspoken on the matter of Czechoslovakia. In words which were to bring down the wrath of Moscow on his head, he wrote:

> For us, for the Communist Party of Spain, the culminating point in winning our independence was the occupation of Czechoslovakia in 1968. The preparations for that operation had been carried out with methods similar to those employed in the famous trials of 1936, which had been exposed at the Twentieth Congress of the Communist Party of the Soviet Union, or similar to those used in the denunciation of Yugoslavia in 1946 . . . stories were concocted that

were light-years away from the truth. This was more than we could be expected to swallow. Czechoslovakia was the straw which broke the camel's back and led our parties to say: 'No.' That kind of 'internationalism' had come to an end as far as we were concerned . . . True internationalism must be something else.[20]

The Spanish Communist Party (PCE) even went so far as to drop Leninism from its official ideology, although the party programme continued to describe the PCE as 'Marxist' and 'revolutionary' as well as 'democratic'.[21] Carrillo's most heinous sin of all in the eyes of the Soviet leadership was, as Robert Legvold noted at the time, his justification of 'an independent West European model of socialism as the most powerful means for "democratizing" the regimes in Eastern Europe'.[22] Berlinguer, although serious in his deviation from Soviet ideology, was more tactful in his dealings with Moscow, while the French Communist Party (PCF) was the least convincing in its Eurocommunism of these three significant West European Communist parties.[23] Its leader, Georges Marchais, made what was more of a tactical than a strategic shift, although he too joined Berlinguer in a joint declaration with the PCI, published in November 1975.[24]

Up until the perestroika period, the Soviet leadership and their ideologists made a clear distinction (not always picked up in the West) between what they called 'different roads to socialism' (which at most times they were ready to embrace) and the idea of 'different socialisms', which they denounced as a heresy. Thus, when the Prague Spring reformers spoke of a 'pluralistic socialism' or 'socialism with a human face', they were told firmly that there is only one socialism. Exactly the same response from Moscow greeted Santiago Carrillo. In a highly critical review of his 'Eurocommunism' and the State, the Soviet weekly, New Times, emphasized that the very concept of 'Eurocommunism' was erroneous because it appeared to refer not to specific features of the strategy of particular Communist parties but to 'some specific brand of communism'. However, the review went on: 'there is only one communism – if we speak of true, scientific communism – namely, that whose foundations were laid by Marx, Engels and Lenin, and whose principles are adhered to by the present-day communist movement.'[25]

In Eastern Europe, it was the leadership of the Communist Party of Czechoslovakia which felt most threatened by Eurocommunism. They owed their positions to the Soviet invasion which Berlinguer and Carrillo had deplored. Accordingly, they used the most extreme language in condemning Eurocommunism. The hard-line Slovak Communist, Vasil Bilak, declared that its content was 'tantamount to treason'. The Bulgarian party leader,

Todor Zhivkov, was quick to follow Moscow's lead. He declared that the concept of Eurocommunism reflected the desire of reactionaries to raise a wall between the fraternal parties of the socialist community and those of Western Europe.[26] The East Germans, perhaps surprisingly, were more restrained in their criticism and engaged in dialogue with the Italian Communists, while the Hungarian and Polish parties were reluctant to be drawn into the hostilities. The Romanian party leadership, while being careful not to associate themselves with anything resembling the pluralist democracy to which the Eurocommunist parties now paid tribute, were happy to select from the Western European parties' statements those elements which seemed to shore up their own relative autonomy from Moscow. The Yugoslavs were still more openly sympathetic to Eurocommunism, seeing it as support for their policy of non-alignment.[27]

The impact of Eurocommunism on oppositionists and dissidents in the Soviet Union and Eastern Europe was less than on the party intelligentsia. For many of the opposition, not least in Poland, any kind of Communism was anathema, no matter what prefix was attached to it. However, for those in the Soviet Union whom Roy Medvedev termed the 'party democrats' (although he himself had been expelled from the CPSU in 1969), this critique from West European Communists reinforced their own doubts about such actions as the invasion of Czechoslovakia and added to their concern about many aspects of the Soviet system which they had also imposed on Eastern Europe.[28]

Travel to the West

During the Brezhnev years in the Soviet Union there was a Jewish joke about a rabbi in a provincial Ukrainian town who was asked what he would do if the borders round the country were one day opened. 'I would climb the tallest tree,' he replied. 'But why?' he was asked. 'Very simple,' came the response. 'So I wouldn't be swept away by the crowds rushing to leave.'[29] As noted in Chapter 20, a great many Soviet Jews, in particular, did leave in the 1970s and 1980s, but of greater importance for long-term change in the Soviet Union and east-central Europe was the travel to the West of citizens from the European Communist states who then returned to their own countries. Only a minority were allowed to sample the wares of capitalism. As a percentage of their populations, there were more Poles and Hungarians than Russians or Romanians. For many of them, however, this travel exacerbated their dissatisfaction with what was on offer in their homelands and increased their desire for domestic change.

Those who travelled to the West from the Soviet Union and Eastern Europe had many incentives, in addition to patriotism, for going back to their native countries. Almost invariably, they had been obliged to leave close members of their families, including their spouses, at home. Since the Soviet Union had the last word on the scope and limits of change within most of Communist Europe (Yugoslavia, Albania and, to a lesser extent, Romania were the exceptions), the impact of the West on *Soviet* travellers was of particular significance. The authorities in the USSR quite consciously divided citizens into those considered 'politically mature' enough to be allowed to venture westwards and those who could not be sufficiently relied upon. The great majority of the population were not licensed to visit the West. Those who were on the list of *vyezdnye* (people permitted to travel abroad) belonged also to the category of *solidnye lyudi* – reliable people by Soviet criteria. This meant that most of them would be careful with whom they spoke favourably of what they had seen abroad. However, to the extent that they viewed what they had seen in the West positively, their social status and political standing made that the more potentially consequential. Those allowed to travel as individuals, rather than as part of carefully shepherded and supervised tourist groups, in many cases belonged to the party intelligentsia. They naturally included also some senior party and state officials.

Hundreds of influential travellers to the West, whether from research institutes or even the heart of the party apparatus, plainly preferred the evidence of their own eyes to Soviet stereotypes. No such traveller was more important than Mikhail Gorbachev, who has made clear that his visits to Western Europe in the 1970s were, indeed, eye-openers for him.[30] He has acknowledged that it was this foreign travel which first made him realize the gulf between Soviet propaganda about the West and the reality. Seeing how civil society and West European political systems worked led to a questioning of his 'a priori faith in the advantages of socialist over bourgeois democracy'. Confronted with the reality of higher living standards in Western Europe, he asked himself the question, 'Why do we live worse than in other developed countries?'[31] Most of these visits by Gorbachev were as a member of a small and informal group of tourists or in a Communist Party delegation. They included short stays in Italy (as early as 1971, and again to that country later in the decade), Belgium, France, the Netherlands and West Germany.

When he was not yet general secretary but already one of the most important members of the Politburo, Gorbachev made three foreign visits in the first half of the 1980s which had an especially great impact on him. The first was in 1983 to Canada, where he saw at first hand how far ahead of Russian agriculture was Canadian farming. He also had his earliest opportunity to engage in East–West dialogue in conversations with Canadian officials and politicians. When he met with the Canadian prime minister, Pierre Trudeau, their talks ranged well beyond agriculture to include major foreign policy issues. When he was preparing for this trip, Gorbachev told the Director of the Institute of the United States and Canada in Moscow, Georgy Arbatov, that he would like to see him. As Arbatov later recalled, he prepared a lot of material about Canadian agriculture, only to be told by Gorbachev that he knew all about that. What he wanted was Arbatov's evaluation of Canadian politics and foreign policy and his assessment of Soviet–American relations and the international climate.[32] Having prepared himself well, Gorbachev was able to display flexibility in his discussions with the Canadian prime minister. Later in the same year, Trudeau told Margaret Thatcher that Gorbachev had 'been prepared to argue and make at least verbal concessions'.[33] During his Canadian visit, Gorbachev formed a political friendship with the Soviet ambassador to Ottawa, Alexander Yakovlev. As noted in Chapter 20, he was able to facilitate Yakovlev's desire to return to Moscow after ten years in Canada. Following Gorbachev's intercession with General Secretary Andropov, Yakovlev became director of the major think-tank, IMEMO. For Yakovlev himself, his years in Canada were of exceptional importance. He viewed the Soviet political and economic system much more critically at the end of his decade in a free and prosperous Western country than he had at the beginning of his exile from the Soviet corridors of power.

The second foreign visit by Gorbachev which had a big impact on him was to Italy in June 1984 for the funeral of the Italian Communist leader Enrico Berlinguer. Not only was Berlinguer the most senior of the Eurocommunists, but he had headed a party with genuine mass support. Gorbachev was impressed by the hundreds of thousands of people who spontaneously came out on to the streets of Rome, and by the fact that the farewell to Berlinguer became a national occasion. He was struck particularly by the attendance of the Italian president, Alessandro Pertini, at the funeral of a Communist leader, and by Pertini's bowing his head before the coffin of the leader of such an opposition party. This, Gorbachev wrote later, was an example of 'a different way of thinking and a different political culture'.[34] It could not have deviated more from Soviet ideology and practice, and it was a culture which clearly appealed to him.

The third especially important foreign visit made by Gorbachev in the period before he became Soviet leader was to Great Britain in December 1984. This followed from a decision of Margaret Thatcher, at the start of her second term as British prime minister in 1983, to devote more of her time to foreign policy. East–West relations during the first Reagan administration were particularly tense, and ministers and officials in the British Foreign Office were concerned about the lack of dialogue between Britain (as well as the United States) and the Soviet Union. In the early 1980s, however, they were unable to persuade the prime minister that this was a problem. A decision, which was described by the prime minister's private secretary as 'a change of policy',[35] arose out of a two-day seminar at the prime minister's country residence, Chequers, in September 1983. The meeting brought together ministers and academic specialists on the Soviet Union and Eastern Europe. Both the Foreign Office and the academics advocated increased contact at all levels with the countries of Communist Europe.[36] The foreign policy adviser to the prime minister from 1984 to 1992, Sir Percy Cradock, later noted that this seminar 'inaugurated a more open approach to Eastern Europe and led eventually to the first meeting with Gorbachev'.[37] The Foreign Office suggested that the prime minister might consider making a visit to Hungary. Mrs Thatcher did so in early February 1984, her first visit to a Warsaw Pact country since her arrival in 10 Downing Street. They also proposed that the foreign secretary should attempt to have meetings with all his East European counterparts. In the course of 1985 alone, the holder of that office, Sir Geoffrey Howe, visited Bulgaria, Romania, the GDR, Czechoslovakia and Poland.[38]

The prime minister decreed that the change of policy towards more active engagement with the Soviet Union and Eastern Europe would not be publicly announced.[39] But it was not by chance that Gorbachev came to Britain three months before he was chosen by the Politburo and Central Committee of the CPSU to become general secretary. It was a result of a conscious decision by the prime minister and the Foreign Office that the lack of high-level contact with the Soviet Union and Eastern Europe was unhelpful and conducive to dangerous misunderstanding.[40] The meeting itself was important for both sides. Although Gorbachev and Thatcher disagreed on many issues in their meeting at Chequers, which far exceeded the time originally allotted to it, it engendered mutual respect. Gorbachev also had a fruitful meeting with British parliamentarians, and in his speech to them he used terms which were to gain in significance once he had become Soviet leader, such as the need for 'mutual security', 'new political thinking' and Europe as 'our common home'.[41] At the end of Gorbachev's visit to Britain, Margaret Thatcher famously announced: 'I like Mr Gorbachev. We can do business together.'[42]

The importance of the visit lay not only in Gorbachev's exposure to leading Western politicians but in the good impression he made on his hosts. That was the more significant because of the warmth of the Thatcher–Reagan relationship and the fact that President Reagan trusted the British prime minister's judgement. Thus, when Mrs Thatcher flew to the United States within days of her meeting with Gorbachev and conveyed to Reagan her positive assessment of him, this had some resonance. She told Reagan, his Secretary of State George Shultz, Secretary of Defense Caspar Weinberger and Vice-President George H.W. Bush that Gorbachev was 'much less constrained' than the Soviet Foreign Minister Gromyko. He was 'more charming, open to discussion and debate, and did not stick to prepared notes'.[43] When the British prime minister next met Gorbachev, it was in his capacity as the new leader of the Soviet Union. She was one of many world leaders in Moscow for Chernenko's funeral. In a meeting with Gorbachev, scheduled to last fifteen minutes but which lasted for almost an hour, she told him that his visit to London had been 'one of the most successful ever'.[44] The foreign secretary, Geoffrey Howe, who was present at the conversation, reported that the bonhomie was not quite universally appreciated back home. On reading the note of the meeting, one 'hard-boiled Foreign Office official' said he was 'bothered' that 'the PM seems to go uncharacteristically weak at the knees when she talks to the personable Mr Gorbachev'. In fact, Howe adds, although the two leaders 'relished each other's company', they never completely 'lowered their guard'.[45]

Foreign travel did not automatically broaden the minds of Soviet officials. Few were as well travelled as Andrey Gromyko but he remained set in his ways. Many Soviet politicians and bureaucrats found rationalizations for the extent to which the USSR lagged far behind its Western rivals. Others, for the sake of their careers, engaged in prolonged self-censorship. But the more East–West travel was allowed to take place, the greater was the erosion of Marxist-Leninist ideology. Ideas of liberty and democracy were under no such threat. Communist doctrine, including that purveyed in the official newspaper of each country's Communist Party, was, in any event, legally available in democracies. Western governments had, or should have had, no reason for concern about an increase in the modest numbers of people allowed to travel to their countries from the Soviet and East European states. Pressure groups and politicians who tried to keep out Soviet visitors were slowing, rather than quickening, the process of change in the Communist world. Thus, when the Daughters of the American Revolution, back in 1959, passed a resolution opposing cultural exchanges with Communist countries because the 'underlying purpose [is] the softening of Americans toward communism',[46] they were not only underestimating their fellow citizens. They were displaying also a lack of understanding (shared by some Western intelligence agencies) of which side in these exchanges had more to lose from the contacts by way of impact on their values and beliefs.

It was also the Communist side which suffered the embarrassment of defections. Defections *to* the Soviet Union of writers, artists or dancers were virtually unheard of. Those who did defect in that direction were mainly Westerners who had worked for the KGB, whether out of ideological belief or for mercenary reasons. They included some of the most famous British spies, who had, indeed, served the Soviet Union out of Communist conviction – Kim Philby, Donald Maclean, Guy Burgess and, later, George Blake. There was much more movement in the opposite direction. To take ballet dancers alone, the three most outstanding of those who defected, Rudolf Nureyev (in 1961), Natalia Makarova (in 1970) and Mikhail Baryshnikov (in 1974), came primarily in search of greater artistic freedom. They also resented the kind of surveillance to which they were subjected by their KGB minders when travelling abroad. During the perestroika era, there was a radical change of attitude in Moscow both to those artists who had, on their own initiative, defected and to those who had been forced into exile by the Soviet authorities. Thus, Baryshnikov and Makarova (who, like Nureyev, were graduates of the Leningrad Ballet School and had been members of Leningrad's Kirov Ballet) were invited in 1987 to dance at the Bolshoi Theatre in Moscow.

Foreign Radio

Seeing 'the West' was more important than hearing about it. However, while only thousands, during the Cold War years, were able to travel from Communist states to Western countries and return home again, millions were able to listen to foreign radio. The strict censorship which meant that the domestic mass media provided an almost exclusive diet of good news from the Communist homeland and bad news from the capitalist world was breached mainly by broadcasts from the west. The most popular were those given by fellow nationals in the languages of the countries concerned. Thus, the American taxpayer funded Radio Liberty (RL), which broadcast to the Soviet Union, and Radio Free Europe (RFE), which broadcast in the languages of all the East European states. Both radio stations were situated in Munich. West Germany itself was a major broadcaster. A particularly influential one was the British Broadcasting Corporation (BBC), which operated in all the major languages of the Communist world. All these transmissions were, however, subjected to severe jamming. In the Soviet Union it was almost impossible to hear them in the cities above the screeching interference that had been superimposed on the voices from abroad. In the countryside it was often easier. Thus, many of the intellectually and politically curious could pick up the broadcasts at their dachas even when the jamming defeated them in the city.

People did not necessarily accept, still less agree with, everything they heard, but in central Europe in particular these broadcasts from fellow nationals abroad were trusted more than the domestic mass media, especially on the major political issues of the day. Jamming was occasionally relaxed. Thus, the foreign-language broadcasts of the major national broadcasters, such as the BBC, were no longer jammed for a period leading up to and beyond the Helsinki Agreement of 1975. Even then, there was no let-up in the jamming of RL and RFE, which were seen by the Communist authorities as forms of psychological warfare. The jamming of all broadcasts in the languages of the European Communist states, including Russian, was resumed with a vengeance, however, when worker opposition in Poland got under way later in the decade. The last thing the authorities wanted was objective news about the rise of an independent trade union movement in a Communist state. In terms of information from 'abroad', East Germany was a special case, since people could not only listen to radio broadcasts from West Germany but also watch television emanating from there.

For the rest of Communist Europe, it is of some significance that broadcasts in English – by, most notably, the Voice of America and the BBC – were not jammed. That was partly because only a highly educated minority in the population could follow them, and also because their news was not specially focused on the Communist world (in the way RL and RFE broadcasts were) or towards contradicting the precepts of the Department of Propaganda of the Central Committee. These radio stations were tuned into especially at times of international crisis, when they provided a very different perspective from that of the official Communist media. While it is difficult to measure the degree of influence of foreign broadcasts, their importance lies in the fact that they deprived Communist regimes of the complete monopoly over the sources of information to which they aspired. They were listened to more, proportionately, in Poland than in the Soviet Union, but I took part in quite a number of conversations in Russia in which the starting point was something someone had heard on foreign radio. There were those who preferred the BBC to other broadcasters because they said it was the 'most objective', and others who preferred Radio Liberty because it provided more political information relating to the Soviet Union.

The party leadership needed these outside voices, as sources of information, less than did ordinary mortals, since they had summaries of what the foreign mass media were saying prepared for them. There were also books published in very small editions which were available only to Central Committee members – such as translations of Western politicians' memoirs and some of the works of the Eurocommunists – and were not on sale to the broader public. Even so, it was far from uncommon for senior party and state officials to listen to foreign radio. Zinoviev, in *The Yawning Heights*, in which the Soviet Union is given the name Ibansk, has a section on 'History yet to come', in which Communism has prevailed worldwide and so there were 'no fashions to imitate, nowhere to seek refuge from the stresses of Ibanskian life or to acquire a few foreign goodies, no one to blame all your troubles on, no one to brag about your amazing successes to'.[47] The 'beloved enemy' who 'had given life at least some degree of interest and meaning' was no more. Zinoviev portrays the country's leader searching in vain for some enlightenment from abroad: 'On one occasion His Leadership spent an entire evening twiddling the knobs of his radio hoping to find some slanderous voice, no matter how faint and far away, and to hear some mite of truth about Ibansk. But alas there were no voices left at all.'[48]

In the real world, 'abroad' continued to exist and to be strikingly different. Broadcasts went in both directions – not only from West to East but, of course, also from the Communist states to Western countries. The latter were not jammed, but they were very little listened to. In the war of words, democratic countries had the advantage that broadcasts from Communist states were not forbidden fruit but boring propaganda, whose main thrust could be read quite freely (and more interestingly) in parts of the Western media.

Ronald Reagan and Pope John Paul II

When former president Ronald Reagan died in 2004, he was widely credited with having overthrown Communism. One year later, Pope John Paul II died and the same claim was made for him.[49] In reality, both president and pope played a part in the demise of Communism, but far from the most decisive. Moreover, Reagan's role has been much misunderstood. It was not his rhetoric – as when he described the Soviet Union as an 'evil empire' in 1983, or when, speaking at the Brandenburg Gate in Berlin in June 1987, he said, 'Mr Gorbachev, open this gate! Mr Gorbachev, tear down this wall!'[50] – that produced fundamental change in Communist systems. Nor was it primarily the United States arms build-up, including Reagan's Strategic Defense Initiative, better known as SDI or 'Star Wars'. Most of these things strengthened the hard-liners within the Soviet political elite more than the reformers. It made more difficult the task of those who were seeking a qualitative improvement in East–West relations. Politicians emphasizing success they attribute to Reagan's support for military build-up generally overlook a very different aspect of his outlook. Reagan had a hatred of nuclear weapons and was ready to believe that SDI, the anti-missile system that would supposedly destroy incoming rockets armed with nuclear warheads, would make them obsolete. Those with more knowledge of the practicalities, such as the head of Soviet space research, thought the idea was absurd. What worried the Russians was the technological spin-offs which would come from the vast investment Reagan was proposing to devote to SDI, not a belief that the system would actually work.[51]

But alongside increased spending on military build-up and the hard-line rhetoric (which worried also some of America's allies), there was a Reagan who saw himself as a peacemaker, not a warmonger, and who was ready to negotiate with the Soviet Union if he could find a negotiating partner. Even during his first term as president, he made overtures to Moscow that were rebuffed. On 24 April 1981 he wrote a personal letter to Brezhnev which was intended to thaw some of the frost between the two 'superpowers', but, in Reagan's own words, he got 'an icy reply from Brezhnev'.[52] Moreover, it was no part of Reagan's policy to aim to break up the Soviet Union. Jack Matlock, who was the senior Soviet specialist on the National Security Council in Washington in Reagan's first term, and the United States ambassador to Moscow from 1987 to 1991, has stressed that 'President Reagan was in favour of bringing pressure to bear on the Soviet Union, but his objective was to induce the Soviet leaders to negotiate reasonable agreements, not to break up the country.'[53] An important internal American government document (which remained classified until long after the Soviet Union had ceased to exist), entitled 'U.S. Relations with the USSR', was issued on 17 January 1983. In Matlock's words, it 'contained no suggestion of a desire to destroy the Soviet Union, to establish U.S. military superiority, or to force the Soviet Union to jeopardize its own security'. It endorsed negotiations with the Soviet Union 'consistent with the principle of strict reciprocity and *mutual interest* [italics added]'. The only respect in which this document for internal consumption of US policy-makers went beyond the public statements was in its intention 'to promote, within the narrow limits available to us, the process of change in the Soviet Union toward a more pluralistic political and economic system in which the power of the privileged ruling elite is gradually reduced'.[54]

Secretary of State George Shultz subsequently instituted a series of Saturday breakfasts for senior officials to try to iron out the disagreements among the various government agencies. Although those present included Defense Secretary Caspar Weinberger and CIA chief William Casey, as well as Shultz, National Security Adviser Robert McFarlane, and Vice-President George H.W. Bush, no one present argued that the United States 'should try to bring the Soviet Union down'. They understood that American attempts to exploit Soviet problems 'would strengthen Soviet resistance to change rather than diminish it'.[55]

These assumptions underlying American policy are far removed from what has been said by many of those who served in the Reagan administration. After the Soviet system and the Soviet Union itself ceased to exist, it was claimed that achieving those ends had been Reagan's policy objectives all along. What is indisputable is that the president himself sent out mixed signals, especially in his first term. Some of his rhetoric indeed suggested that it was a policy aim to dispatch the Soviet system to the dustbin of history. Yet Reagan was aware that it was one thing to wish to see an end to Communism and another to take active measures to bring it about. That might have unintended consequences and would certainly get in the way of his desire for dialogue. Within the Reagan administration as a whole there were clear divisions – most notably between Shultz, after he succeeded Al Haig as secretary of state, and Weinberger, the secretary for defense. The divisions were, if anything, even sharper a rung or two lower in these departments.

If Reagan, as the evidence presented by Shultz, Matlock and others strongly suggests, wished to pursue a dual-track approach – anti-Communist values combined with military strength on the one hand, and a desire for dialogue and wish to reach concrete agreements on the other – the Soviet leadership in the first half of the 1980s thought Reagan sincerely believed only in the first of these tracks. As a result, nothing changed for the better in the US–Soviet relationship during Reagan's first term. The Cold War got colder and there were even moments when nuclear war could have broken out by accident, as in 1983, when there was concern in Moscow that the United States was preparing a first strike against the Soviet Union. A NATO exercise was altered to make it abundantly clear that this was, indeed, only an exercise and not the lead-up to a surprise attack.[56] Ronald Reagan's presidency overlapped with four Soviet leaders – Leonid Brezhnev, Yury Andropov, Konstantin Chernenko, and Mikhail Gorbachev. No lessening of tension or amelioration of the Cold War took place until some months after the fourth and last of these became general secretary in March 1985. No liberalization occurred in Soviet policy towards Eastern Europe during Reagan's first term. Nor did the countries of Eastern Europe become freer or more democratic.

The end of the Cold War is not the same phenomenon as the end of Communism in Europe, but there is an interconnection. The Cold War almost certainly did more to keep Communist systems going than to bring them down. The ever-present threat of an external enemy was used as a justification for highly authoritarian (at times totalitarian) rule. Political dissent was portrayed as a betrayal of the 'socialist motherland' and the external threat was used to justify censorship and restrictions on foreign travel. What Communist systems were far less equipped to survive was closer contact with more prosperous democratic countries and a marked relaxation of international tension. Thus, insofar as President Reagan contributed to the demise of Communism, it was not so much (as is widely believed) by his perceived contribution to making the Cold War colder between 1980 and 1984, but by helping, in partnership with Gorbachev, to ensure that it came to a peaceful end. This happened just a year after Reagan left office, when one by one the countries of Eastern Europe became independent and non-Communist. George Bush the elder and his secretary of state James Baker played their part in this, but the breakthrough to qualitatively better East–West relations had occurred on the watch of Reagan and Shultz.[57]

The contribution of Pope John Paul II has been discussed in the previous chapter. For Catholics in Eastern Europe, a formidable pope emerging from a state under Communist rule provided not only spiritual solace but also political inspiration. This was especially so in the Pope's native Poland, where the remarkable growth of the Solidarity movement owed much to the galvanization of the nation brought about by John Paul II's triumphal return to his homeland in 1979. Within the Soviet Union, the republic in which the Pope's influence was felt most strongly was Lithuania, with its large Catholic population. Nevertheless, even in Poland, where the state appeared to be much weaker vis-à-vis society than elsewhere in Eastern Europe (and where autonomous organizations were stronger than elsewhere in the Communist world), that state was able to reassert itself. It was powerful enough to turn the mass movement of Solidarity (which had engaged in dialogue with the state authorities and been accepted almost as a legitimate partner in 1980–81) into the weakened, underground organization of 1982–87. Poles had a strong sense that behind their own Communist party and government stood a powerful Soviet state, unwilling to see Poland break with Communism and what was called (of all things) the Warsaw Pact. That perception undoubtedly helped the Polish party-state authorities to reimpose Communist 'order', using their own resources. Since the Soviet Union was the ultimate guarantor of that order, a vote by the Communist 'cardinals' in the Soviet Politburo in March 1985 turned out to be even more important than the vote of the cardinals in Rome in 1978. Although nothing could have been further from the intention of Politburo members when they cast their votes in the Kremlin, this was to open the way to the peaceful dismantling of Communism.

PART FIVE

INTERPRETING THE FALL
OF COMMUNISM

24

Gorbachev, Perestroika, and the Attempt to Reform Communism, 1985–87

On 11 March 1985, Mikhail Gorbachev became the fourth person to lead the Soviet Union in the space of less than two and a half years. Leonid Brezhnev, after eighteen years as General Secretary of the CPSU, died on 10 November 1982. He was succeeded by Yury Andropov, who, on the death of Suslov at the beginning of 1982, had replaced him as the second secretary in the Communist Party. Important though the KGB was, for Andropov (who had headed that organization for fifteen years) this was a definite promotion. It made him the front-runner to succeed Brezhnev, although most of Brezhnev's entourage would have preferred Konstantin Chernenko. Within a few months of becoming Soviet leader, Andropov's health went into serious decline and he survived just fifteen months in the highest political office. He died in February 1984 and was succeeded by Chernenko, already aged seventy-two. He, in turn, lasted a mere thirteen months, dying on the evening of 10 March 1985. Within less than twenty-four hours – an unprecedentedly short time – the Soviet Union had a new leader, the fifty-four-year-old Mikhail Gorbachev.[1]

The fact that a gerontocracy had been running the Soviet Union was underlined by the deaths of these leaders in such quick succession. When the already ailing Chernenko was elected general secretary in February 1984, it was joked in the Soviet Union that 'the Central Committee had unanimously elected Comrade Konstantin Ustinovich Chernenko as General Secretary and agreed that his ashes would be buried in the Kremlin wall'. In similar vein, it was said that Margaret Thatcher, who went to the Soviet Union for the first time since she became prime minister to attend Andropov's funeral, had telephoned President Reagan and said: 'You should have come for the funeral, Ron. They did it very well. I'm definitely coming back next year.' And so she did – for Chernenko's obsequies, but with the added incentive of resuming her acquaintanceship, made just three months earlier, with the Soviet Union's new leader, Mikhail Gorbachev.

Prologue

The rigor mortis of a succession of Soviet leaders was matched by the slow-down to a halt in the rate of the country's economic growth. That so many members of the Politburo and Secretariat of the Central Committee had been allowed to grow old together symbolized a stagnating system. Andropov had tried to inject some dynamism into the economy by tightening work discipline. A lot of police time was spent making sure that people were not visiting hairdressers during working hours. Researchers in the social sciences and humanities, who normally worked in libraries or at home, were obliged to turn up on the same days at their institutes. Sometimes this meant they were crowded into a small space in which there was practically standing room only.[2] Needless to say, the economic dynamism imparted by such measures was modest. Andropov also set Gorbachev and a former factory manager from the Urals, Nikolay Ryzhkov, who had been promoted to a secretaryship of the Central Committee, the task of examining what needed to be done to make the economic system work more efficiently. When, however, they asked to see the detailed state budget, Andropov refused permission. It was, evidently, a state secret even from members of the top leadership team, most of whom, in any event, would have been unable to make head or tail of it.[3] Andropov had been a supporter over many years of the policy Kádár had pursued in Hungary, and given time, he might have backed a measure of economic reform in the Soviet Union. He was, though, a reformer only within narrow limits. He remained an implacable opponent of overt dissent and of any development in the direction of political pluralism.

The most important contribution to reform Andropov made in his fifteen months as general secretary was in extending the responsibilities and enhancing the authority of Gorbachev, whom he wished to elevate above Chernenko, so that Gorbachev would be his direct successor. This was not because Andropov imagined for a moment that Gorbachev would pursue the policies he subsequently did, but because he valued his intelligence and energy. Andropov's physical weakness, however, undermined his political strength. He made a handwritten addition of a final paragraph to a speech to a plenary session of the Central Committee in December 1984 that, confined to a hospital bed, he was too ill to deliver in person. In that additional paragraph he proposed that Gorbachev (rather than Chernenko) should, in his absence, chair the Politburo and secretariat. This was a clear, but unsuccessful, attempt to designate his successor. Chernenko, together with the chairman of the Council of Ministers, Nikolay Tikhonov, and the minister of defence, Dmitry Ustinov, took the decision that Andropov's addendum would *not* be read out. Andropov's aide Arkady Volsky tried to approach Gorbachev to tell him what had occurred, but found his way barred. Volsky later told the American journalist David Remnick what happened when he then spoke to the head of the General Department of the Central Committee, Klavdy Bogolyubov. Volsky told him he would have to call Andropov to tell him what had happened. Bogolyubov replied: 'Then that will be your last phone call.'[4] (Bogolyubov was a reactionary and corrupt party official who had hitherto literally stood to attention when he received a telephone call from Andropov. He grovelled before the power of a general secretary and bullied those of a lower rank. Not long after Gorbachev came to power, Bogolyubov was expelled not only from the Central Committee apparatus but also from the Communist Party.)[5] Andropov was incandescently angry at this failure to obey his instructions, but it was clear that power was slipping from his grasp.[6] His intention to change the pecking order for the succession in favour of Gorbachev remained unknown to all but a handful of people.

The Soviet Union had been somewhat revitalized during Andropov's brief tenure as leader – at least, in comparison with the later Brezhnev years. Chernenko's thirteen months were more like a throwback to the latter, even though Gorbachev had become the second secretary of the CPSU. Following Andropov's death, there were renewed attempts – by Tikhonov and others – to stop Gorbachev's further progress. However, thanks to Andropov's earlier support, Gorbachev had been supervising large swathes of the Central Committee apparatus, and was in a strong enough position to inherit the number two slot when Chernenko vacated it on his becoming number one in the party. However, the dead hand of Chernenko (and his conservative Communist entourage) prevented any significant change of policy during this interregnum. Apart from a major speech in December 1984 (delivered against Chernenko's wishes), in which he voiced his boldest critique thus far of stereotypical thinking in the Soviet Union,[7] Gorbachev was careful not to rock the boat and thus to provide ammunition for his political enemies. Some of the older members of the top leadership team took advantage of Chernenko's particularly uninspiring leadership to manifest their nostalgia for Stalin. For several of them the mass killing of people in the 1930s for crimes they did not commit appeared to be a minor offence. The major offence had been committed by Khrushchev – telling the world about it. At a Politburo meeting on 12 July 1984, Minister of Defence Dmitry Ustinov said of Khrushchev: 'Just think of what he did with our history, with Stalin.' When Gromyko responded by saying that Khrushchev had delivered an 'irreparable blow to the positive image of the Soviet Union in the eyes of the whole world', Ustinov added that Khrushchev had put into the hands of Westerners 'such arguments, such material, as to discredit us for long years'. Not to be outdone, Gromyko chipped in: 'In fact, it was thanks to this that so-called "Eurocommunism" was born!'[8]

The nostalgia for Stalin and the impulse to kick Khrushchev, who had been dead and buried for thirteen years, got under way when Chernenko told the Politburo that he had met with Vyacheslav Molotov, for many years Stalin's right-hand man, who had been overjoyed at their recent decision to readmit him to party membership.* The ninety-three-year-old Molotov told Chernenko that this decision meant a 'second birth' for him. Welcoming Molotov back into the party was, given his age, a symbolic gesture, but a symbol of a further retreat, compared even with the Brezhnev years, from Khrushchev's anti-Stalinism. It had led, Chernenko told the Politburo, to letters from Malenkov and Kaganovich requesting their readmission also to the party. There was broad support for that, but no final decision was taken at the meeting. Ustinov raised an issue which would have amounted virtually to a public rehabilitation of Stalin by proposing that the city of Volgograd be restored to the name which had made it famous during the war: Stalingrad. This was something they should consider doing as part of the celebration of 'the fortieth anniversary of the victory over fascism' the following year. However, by May 1985, Ustinov was dead and Gorbachev was general secretary, and no such name-change took place. In 1984, Gorbachev, who had to be careful not to alienate senior members of the Politburo if he were to be Chernenko's successor, contented himself by saying in response to Ustinov's Stalingrad suggestion: 'That proposal has both positive and negative aspects.'[9] As Alexander Yakovlev later observed: 'In the circumstances that existed towards the middle of the 1980s, a future leader, if he wished for serious changes, had to begin with "great craftiness" – to set a great goal but not speak publicly about it.' Such a leader, added Yakovlev, had to be well aware that the system was replete with punitive organs of power. He had, therefore, to exercise caution and be 'a master of precisely calculated compromise'.[10]

---

* In an unpublished book, which he wrote mainly in 1988 and completed in March 1989, Gorbachev observed that even though he was a member of the Politburo – and, he might have added, a very senior one – he knew nothing about the fact that Molotov was all set to return to the party. This manuscript, provisionally entitled 'Perestroika Tested by Life. Diary Notes', is in the archives of the Gorbachev Foundation, to whom I am grateful for access to it ('Perestroyka – ispytanie zhizn'yu. Dnevnikovye zapisi', p. 58). The book was not published because Gorbachev felt it had been overtaken by events and by the evolution of his own thinking.

Gorbachev, caution in Chernenko's Politburo notwithstanding, was a thoroughgoing anti-Stalinist.[11] Both his grandfathers, who were peasant farmers, had been arrested at different times in the 1930s. His wife Raisa's maternal grandfather was arrested, accused of Trotskyism (although he knew nothing of Trotsky), and, in his granddaughter's words, 'disappeared without trace'. Raisa Gorbachev added: 'My grandmother died of grief and hunger as the wife of an "enemy of the people". And the four children she left behind were left to the mercy of fate.'[12] At the time, most people who had members of their family arrested did not connect this with the person of Stalin, still less with the fundamentals of the system. Mikhail Gorbachev was no exception in that respect. But he was one of those whose eyes were opened to the immense guilt of Stalin by Khrushchev's Secret Speech in 1956. He himself went on, when he had the power and opportunity, not just to reorganize the system Stalin had developed on foundations laid by Lenin (as Khrushchev had done), but to introduce transformative change. The point at which radical reform turned into systemic transformation was in the summer of 1988, as we shall see in the next chapter. Much changed, however, already in the years 1986–87. In his speech on the eve of the seventieth anniversary of the Bolshevik revolution, Gorbachev in November 1987 authoritatively broke the taboo on criticism of Stalin and Stalinism which had been in place since the early Brezhnev years when he declared: 'It is sometimes asserted that Stalin did not know the facts about the lawlessness. Documents we have at our disposal speak to the fact that this is not so. The guilt of Stalin and of his closest associates before the party and people for indulging in mass repression and lawlessness is enormous and unforgivable. This is a lesson for all generations.'[13]

How the Change Began

There are those who, in hindsight, think that transformative change was bound to occur in the Soviet Union in the second half of the 1980s. Yet it would be hard to find anyone who at the time predicted change remotely comparable to that which took place. Even though the Soviet system was both inefficient and oppressive, and the economy had virtually stopped growing, that did not mean that there was no alternative to radical change. To the extent that the system was liberalized and democratized, however, economic failure became a more critical issue, and some of the perestroika-era economic policies exacerbated the problems. The views of every member of the Politburo at the time of Chernenko's death are known. It is, accordingly, safe to say that if anyone from their ranks other than Gorbachev had

been chosen as general secretary, the Soviet Union would have neither liberalized nor democratized. Highly authoritarian (or totalitarian) regimes, by
definition, can suppress opposition and provide a multitude of reasons for
belt-tightening. If Andropov had enjoyed better health, minor reform, stopping far short of what occurred under Gorbachev, might well have proceeded.
If Chernenko had lived longer, nothing much would have changed while
he was general secretary.

Whether one calls the Soviet system on the eve of perestroika highly
authoritarian or totalitarian, the difference between such systems and a
democracy is that their governments can survive – not indefinitely, but over
a number of decades – deteriorating economic performance. Many Third
World dictators, with far less sophisticated levers of propaganda and coercion than those available to the Soviet leadership, have survived with
economies which were in far worse shape than that of the Soviet Union in
the 1980s. If the Soviet economy was suffering from what was close to a
crisis in 1985, it was a 'crisis' perceived only by a minority of people within
the political elite – those acutely conscious of the long-term decline in the
rate of Soviet economic growth and of the technological lag between the
Soviet Union and the West (with the newly industrialized nations of Asia
also making faster progress than the USSR). But this was not a crisis in the
sense that there was significant public unrest; still less were the foundations
of the system being threatened. By 1990–91, the Soviet Union was in a real
crisis, but it was reform which produced that crisis rather than crisis automatically instigating reform. Highly authoritarian regimes have ways other
than liberalizing of maintaining control and hence of postponing the kind
of crisis which threatens the very existence of the regime. Indeed, as de
Tocqueville observed, the social order immediately before a revolution, and
destroyed by it, is almost invariably less oppressive than what was there
before. The moment of greatest danger for an authoritarian regime is when
it undertakes reform.

THE CHOICE OF GORBACHEV

Chernenko's death on 10 March 1985 was a necessary but far from sufficient
condition for the momentous change in the Soviet system that was to follow.
Gorbachev, as second secretary, was the first person in the Soviet leadership
to be told by the top Kremlin doctor of the general secretary's demise.
Summoning Politburo members to a meeting later the same evening,
Gorbachev took the chair. (He had already been presiding at Politburo as
well as secretariat meetings at times when Chernenko was too ill to attend.)
There were some sitting at the table who would have liked to prevent him

becoming general secretary, but they had neither the numbers to stop him nor a plausible alternative candidate. Since they had nothing to gain from voting against the certain winner, within twenty-four hours Gorbachev had been unanimously chosen as the party's – and hence the country's – leader by both the Politburo and the Central Committee. No one in the top leadership at that time had any inkling of how far he would be prepared to go in domestic reform or in changing foreign policy. Indeed, Gorbachev himself, though he had made up his mind about the need for reform and a fresh approach to international relations, certainly did not have in mind such far-reaching change in the Soviet system as was to occur. Still less did he envisage the disintegration of the Soviet Union. He was chosen not because he was a reformer or because he was thought to be a 'soft-liner', but because he was in the strongest position politically to advance his claim and was recognized by the 'selectorate' as someone who combined intelligence and dynamism.[14] His relative youth (though prior to the Brezhnev era, fifty-four would not have been considered young for a Soviet politician) had also become an advantage, since state funerals for aged leaders had been embarrassingly frequent.

To help ensure that his translation to the post of greatest political power in the Soviet Union would proceed smoothly, Gorbachev had done a deal with Andrey Gromyko. It involved an understanding that Gromyko would become Chairman of the Presidium of the Supreme Soviet, which meant that he would be the formal head of state. Gorbachev was content to hold off from taking that position for another three years, even though in their brief periods as general secretary both Andropov and Chernenko had followed Brezhnev's example and added the headship of state to their party leadership. The advantage of this concession was twofold. First of all, it meant that Gorbachev had the influential Gromyko's active support in the leadership succession stakes. It was Gromyko who spoke first to recommend him, at the Politburo meeting of 11 March. Later in the same afternoon, he made the speech proposing him to the Central Committee. The second advantage was still more important, for even without Gromyko's active support, Gorbachev would probably have become general secretary. The deal meant that Gromyko, who had been foreign minister for almost thirty years – since 1957 – would no longer be in charge of foreign policy. Less than three months after Gorbachev became Soviet leader, Gromyko, indeed, moved to the more honorific position of head of state. On Gorbachev's proposal, the party first secretary in Georgia, Eduard Shevardnadze, was appointed foreign minister. Unlike other long-serving Soviet leaders, Gorbachev did not advance to the top leadership team (of Politburo members or secretaries of the Central Committee) anyone who had been his subordinate in his native region. But in Shevardnadze, he was promoting someone with whom he had good relations and who was without experience in foreign policy. For Gorbachev, this both facilitated a fresh approach and meant that he himself would be the dominant figure in the making of foreign policy. That would have been more difficult if Gromyko, with his personal experience and excellent memory of almost every major international event since the Second World War, had still been in post. (Gromyko had even headed the Soviet delegation at the Dumbarton Oaks conference on the foundation of the United Nations, and he participated in the 1945 Yalta and Potsdam conferences.)

New People and New Concepts

The immediate stimulus to change in the mid-1980s was economic. Gorbachev was alone in the Politburo in March 1985 in being serious about reform, but he had no preconceived plan. His first and most important step was to encourage discussion and debate and to replace almost all of the aides he inherited from his predecessor as general secretary. He consulted widely among specialists. Among those who wielded influence in the earliest years of perestroika were two reformist scholars who were brought from the Siberian branch of the Academy of Sciences to Moscow – the economist Abel Aganbegyan and the sociologist Tatyana Zaslavskaya. As closer advisers he brought in two of the most enlightened Central Committee officials – Anatoly Chernyaev, a deputy head of the International Department, and Georgy Shakhnazarov, deputy head of the Socialist Countries Department. Both were consulted informally almost from the outset. Chernyaev became a full-time aide – and Gorbachev's principal foreign policy adviser – from February 1986. Shakhnazarov became a comparably influential full-time aide, advising both on Eastern Europe and on political reform of the Soviet system, from February 1988. By turning to different and more open-minded people for advice from very early in his general secretaryship, Gorbachev thus changed 'the balance of influence' among advisers even before he was in a position to change the 'balance of power'.

He began to do the latter, however, by pensioning off some of the most conservative members of the Politburo, such as Nikolay Tikhonov, Grigory Romanov and Viktor Grishin, all of whom went into forced retirement before the end of 1985. It was in September of that year that Gorbachev replaced Tikhonov with Ryzhkov as chairman of the Council of Ministers. For the next five years it was Ryzhkov who had primary responsibility for the management and reform of the Soviet economy. Gorbachev, while very concerned about the economy, took the view that it was the primary responsibility of the Council of Ministers. He was also concerned to put an end to the practice of party organs partially duplicating as well as overseeing the work of economic ministries. (In 1988 he abolished all the branch economic departments of the Central Committee of the CPSU, except that which supervised agriculture.) Gorbachev himself was more preoccupied with political reform and with foreign policy. The new second secretary of the party, Yegor Ligachev, had, though, a large say in party appointments. It was on his recommendation to Gorbachev that Boris Yeltsin moved from the first secretaryship of the industrial Sverdlovsk region to head a Central Committee department in Moscow. At the end of 1985 Yeltsin, who for the past half-year had been a secretary of the Central Committee, was appointed head of the Moscow party organization, in succession to Grishin. The appointment, which seemed significant at the time, was, in retrospect, momentous. Yeltsin rapidly fell out with his would-be patron Ligachev and, later, with Gorbachev.

In this first phase of Gorbachev's leadership, policy innovation and personnel change were very much instigated from the top. The Soviet system was so hierarchical and authoritarian that major change could come from nowhere else. By the later 1980s, that was no longer the case, for the system itself by then had been radically changed. However, in the mid-1980s it remained not only strictly hierarchical but also highly ideologized. Thus, to introduce new concepts was of far greater import than a politician adopting fresh terminology within a Western democracy. Three words which Gorbachev had already uttered in his December 1984 speech, prior to becoming general secretary, reappeared and were much stressed in the 1985–87 period with which this chapter is concerned. They were: *uskorenie* (acceleration), perestroika (literally reconstruction, but with very different meanings over time), and glasnost (openness or transparency). The first of these terms was much used in the very earliest period of Gorbachev's leadership. The message was that it was 'time to get the country moving again', especially economically. This was not a return simply to the old Soviet emphasis on quantity of production. It was meant to signify qualitative improvement, based on new technology. In fact, though, there was little economic improvement and the economy was hard hit by a drastic drop in energy prices.[15] High oil prices might have cushioned quicker movement in the direction of a market economy (had such a policy been adopted earlier), but their depressed level had at least the advantage of illustrating the weaknesses of the Soviet economy. It underlined how great was the economy's dependence on high foreign currency earnings from the sale of natural resources, and how much therefore it stood in need of systemic change. When it became all too clear that economic growth was *not* accelerating, *uskorenie* was used less and less in Soviet political discourse.

The overarching term for what occurred in the Gorbachev era was pere-stroika. When Gorbachev succeeded Chernenko, the word 'reform' was still taboo in Soviet politics, as it had been ever since the Prague Spring. Thus, the term 'perestroika', which did not (at that time) have such pejorative connotations for the conservative majority of party and state officials, served as camouflage for reform. During the first three years of his period in power – up to, and a few months beyond, the end of 1987 – Gorbachev believed that the Soviet system was reformable. The political system, he thought, could be significantly liberalized, and economic decision-making could be considerably decentralized. Some concessions would be made to market principles, but the market would play an ancillary role. A strong element of central planning would remain, as would state ownership. Gorbachev, however, favoured the development of small co-operatives, especially in the service sector, seeing this also as a contribution to democratization of the workplace.[16] (In 1988, a far-reaching Law on Co-operatives was introduced. In practice, many of the co-operatives were to become thinly disguised private enterprises.)

Before long, Gorbachev rehabilitated the word 'reform', and at the Twenty-Seventh Party Congress in early 1986 he said that 'radical reform' was needed. It was, however, at two plenary sessions of the Central Committee in 1987 that reform actually began to take on a more radical hue, much more effectively in the political than in the economic sphere. It was telling also that the plenum on political reform came first. That was held in January 1987, and the session on economic reform only in June of the same year. Political change was coming to be the higher priority for Gorbachev, partly because he believed that without it, economic reform would not be achievable, but also because he was increasingly attracted to political liberalization and democratization for their own sakes. In his speech to the January 1987 Central Committee plenum, Gorbachev complained that thinking about socialism had remained at the level of the 1930s and 1940s in many respects. As one small sign of change, he offered encouragement to more co-operative and individual house-building. Much of the language had a different tone from that of even a year earlier. Linking perestroika and democracy, he added: 'Only thus is it possible to open up space for the mightiest creative force of socialism – free labour and free thought in a free country.' Supporting in the meantime more intra-party democracy, with genuine elections of party officials (although not at the highest level), he proposed a special party conference to be held in 1988 to consider the questions of 'the further democratization of the life of the party and society as a whole'.[17] That conference, discussed in the next chapter, was to mark the turning point at which Gorbachev moved beyond being a reformer of the Soviet system to become a systemic transformer.

By 1987, perestroika had already come to mean radical reform. Later it changed its meaning again, at least so far as Gorbachev was concerned. It came to signify a dismantling of the Soviet political system as it had existed for seven decades. But for others in the leadership, it meant no more than some restructuring or modernization of the existing system. Perestroika, in other words, meant different things to different people and to the same people at different times. In the later stages of the Gorbachev era its imprecision could be a disadvantage, but the concept had served its purpose. Under its banner a serious reform process was launched, and the concept's lack of ideological baggage helped, initially at least, to lull the suspicions of the enemies of change.

The other concept to be emphasized, glasnost, also changed its meaning over time. At first the greater openness was marginal compared with what had gone before, but Gorbachev appointed Alexander Yakovlev as head of the Department of Propaganda of the Central Committee, elevating him to a secretaryship of the Central Committee at the Twenty-Seventh Congress in 1986. With Yakovlev's active support, and Gorbachev's approval, there was, as early as 1986–87, a great expansion of the limits of the possible in terms of what could be published, what films could be screened, and which plays staged. The leadership of all the artistic unions was changed, for the old leaderships, no less than the censorship, had been an integral part of the system which stultified creative talent and looked askance at any innovative ideas. At the Twenty-Seventh Congress of the CPSU in February 1986, Gorbachev devoted a section of his long report to 'The further democratization of the society and the deepening of the socialist self-government of the people'. In that part of his speech he said: 'The *widening of glasnost* is a principle for us. This is a political question. Without glasnost there is not and cannot be democratism, political creativity of the masses, and their participation in administration.'[18]

One stimulus to greater openness soon after that congress was the catastrophe at the Chernobyl nuclear power station in 1986. The accident occurred on 26 April, and only on the evening of the 28th did Soviet television make a minimally informative announcement about it. In the meantime, the radioactive contamination had been reported abroad. However, this glaring absence of glasnost was used to good effect by journalists and scholars, who pushed for greater freedom of information. They argued that the failure to provide accurate and timely news of the nature and scale of the disaster showed the need for more genuine glasnost.* They linked this with a demand for greater public accountability of officialdom. Georgy Shakhnazarov, who became one of Gorbachev's most influential aides, observed that Chernobyl 'inflicted a decisive blow against the mania for secrecy, inducing the country to open itself up to the world'.[19]

Much of what began to be published had been written years before but was unacceptable in the pre-perestroika Soviet Union. By 1987 the limits were being pressed wider by the week, testing the scepticism of Western observers. Early in 1987, when I tried to persuade the historian of ideas Isaiah Berlin that really serious political change was under way, he replied: 'I'll believe things are changing in the Soviet Union when they publish Akhmatova's Requiem.' This poem, written in the late 1930s, at a time when Anna Akhmatova's son was incarcerated in Stalin's camps, is dedicated to the victims of the Stalinist repression. A few weeks after that conversation, I was able to write to Berlin to say that Requiem had just been published for the first time in Moscow in an edition of 175,000 copies.[20] There were further changes also in the language of politics, with the lead again coming from the top. The term 'pluralism' had long been taboo in the Soviet Union. If it appeared in print, it was only in the form of an attack on the concept, which was associated with 'bourgeois democracy' and with Prague Spring and Eurocommunist heresy. However, in different contexts in 1987 Gorbachev made positive use of the term when he spoke of an emerging 'socialist pluralism' and about a 'pluralism of opinion'.[21] This gave a green light to others, many of whom began to write in praise of pluralism and often did not bother to insert the 'socialist' qualifier.

The change did not go unnoticed or unchallenged by conservative voices within the party leadership. At a Politburo meeting on 15 October 1987 – just

---

* Accidents in nuclear power plants have led authorities even in democracies to attempt to play down their scale and significance. Thus, when there was a major fire which affected the nuclear reactor at Windscale, Cumbria, in October 1957, the British prime minister Harold Macmillan took extraordinary steps to ensure that the detailed report by a leading nuclear scientist, Sir William Penney, on the causes and consequences of the accident would be known to only a small group of people within the government. Macmillan instructed the Atomic Energy Authority not to permit any leakage of the report. Not only were all their printed copies destroyed, so was the type used by the printers. See Alistair Horne, Macmillan 1957–1986, the second volume of his official biography (Macmillan, London, 1989), pp. 54–5. Yet, Horne adds, the danger to life from the Windscale disaster was much greater than from the accident at Three Mile Island in the United States in 1979, which got far more worldwide publicity.

one of several occasions at which detailed consideration was given to the report Gorbachev was to make at the celebration of the seventieth anniversary of the October Revolution – there were objections to the appearance in the document of the concept of 'socialist pluralism'. Both the First Secretary of the Communist Party of Azerbaijan, Heidar Aliev, and Anatoly Lukyanov (at that time the secretary of the Central Committee who was supervising, among other bodies, the military and the KGB) expressed their disquiet. Aliev said that the term should be changed to *samoupravlenie* (self-government), for 'that is our word, and Marx spoke of it. But pluralism . . . arose in the West as an ideological term.'[22] In fact, *samoupravlenie* was an idea that had been much deployed already by Gorbachev, including in his speech in December 1984 several months before he became party leader. 'Pluralism' went somewhat beyond this. It had the additional implication of a variety of autonomous and alternative sources of ideas and perhaps even of power. It was the latter heresy which drew Lukyanov's attention. He was prepared to accept 'a socialist pluralism of opinion within society' but not a commitment to 'socialist pluralism' with a full stop after it, as it appeared in the draft speech. In the West, he said, this meant a pluralism of power. He added: 'But we – Communists, the party – will not divide power with anyone.'[23]

In similar vein, the chairman of the KGB, Viktor Chebrikov, objected to Gorbachev's draft report saying that an 'authoritarian-bureaucratic model of socialism' had been constructed in the Soviet Union. This was a Western formula and they needed to find their own. Gorbachev responded that Bukharin had used these words in the early years after the revolution, but he conceded that they would have to change the word 'model', substituting 'methods' or 'means'.[24] The amount of time Politburo members spent agonising over words underlines the importance of ideational change within the Soviet Union. New concepts which offered new ways of looking at Soviet reality began to dissolve the ideological cement holding the political system together. Aliev, Chebrikov, Lukyanov and others in the Soviet leadership were not mistaken when they viewed this undermining of orthodox Marxism-Leninism as a danger for the Communist political order. Their temporary victories, however, did not stem the tide of new concepts entering Soviet political discourse during the second half of the 1980s. Although Gorbachev's speech for the celebration of the seventieth anniversary of the Bolshevik revolution had been diluted by the criticism of the conservative majority in the Politburo, it provided a stimulus to a re-examination of Stalinism. Not only did he emphasize Stalin's guilt. He also announced that, since the rehabilitation of the victims of the repression had virtually ceased in the mid-1960s, a new commission would be set up to examine the still unresolved cases of those who had been imprisoned or killed during the

Stalin years.[25] The person Gorbachev appointed to head that commission was Yakovlev, who went on not only to rehabilitate vast numbers of the unjustly repressed (all too often posthumously), but, later, to publish much new documentary material on the state terror.

Athough glasnost and a fresh vocabulary of politics were first introduced from above, it was of decisive importance that there was a constituency for reform within the society. Many of the more talented writers, scientists and scholars who added their voices to the discussion were a product of what was in many respects a strong system of higher education in the Soviet Union. Previously, they had talked in one way round the kitchen table and in a much more circumspect manner when writing or in public speech. A private glasnost had developed ever since Khrushchev's time. Now it became a public glasnost. Before the end of 1989, glasnost had become virtually indistinguishable from freedom of speech. That was not yet so in 1987, but it was already qualitatively different from 1977, not to speak of 1937. It was in 1987 that the lines of the division between overt dissidents and reformers who stayed (sometimes by the skin of their teeth) within the parameters of the system began to disappear. In December 1986 Gorbachev telephoned Andrei Sakharov in his home in Gorky, where he had lived in exile from Moscow already for seven years, and told him he was free to return to Moscow and resume his 'patriotic work'. (The Sakharovs had not hitherto been allowed a telephone in Gorky, so they knew that something was up when one was suddenly installed.) Gorbachev probably had in mind primarily Sakharov's work as a scientist. However, as a physicist Sakharov was part of an international community of scholars, and from the moment of his release from exile – indeed, in the telephone conversation with Gorbachev which announced it – he campaigned on behalf of people who had been imprisoned for the spreading of dissident ideas. This was his most strictly patriotic work, attempting to bring Soviet observance of human rights up to morally acceptable standards.

Reform Dilemmas

In many ways it took greater *boldness* to liberalize (and later to significantly democratize) the Soviet system, for this threatened to turn it into something different in kind, than to attempt economic reform. The Chinese Communist Party leadership has survived a substantial marketization of the economy, but has not taken many risks with its monopoly of political power. In the Soviet Union the existing economic system was much more thoroughly entrenched than in China. Organizationally, it was very much the system that had been consolidated since the 1930s. To change it successfully was even more *difficult* than political reform. Moreover, the political changes meant that people were no longer afraid to voice their discontent. That made marketization, which for many essential foodstuffs and services could only mean far higher prices, all the harder. A political liberalization produced an immediate improvement in the quality of life, whereas a halfway house in economic reform made things worse rather than better. A more comprehensive economic reform would still produce a deterioration in most people's living standards *before* they got better.

The Soviet planned economy never worked well, although it could produce impressive results in certain targeted sectors, including weaponry, aircraft production and space-related technology. It did, however, work after a fashion and on an entirely different set of operating principles from a market economy. That is notwithstanding the fact that there was never a total absence of market relations in the Soviet Union. Peasants sold the produce from their private plots locally and teachers gave private tuition, even at times when neither activity was officially sanctioned. The corollary of this is that no country with an essentially market economy allows the market to determine everything. The state intervenes to regulate the market even in normal times. It affects prices through heavier taxation on certain products (such as alcohol or scarce energy resources). It also makes illegal the sale of products and substances – for example, heroin – even when there is effective demand, in an economic sense, for them. And in times of financial crisis, as in 2008, even American free-market ideologues found themselves begging the federal government to rescue them and their banks.

Nevertheless, an economic system must be primarily a command economy or primarily a market economy. All attempts to find a 'third way' have ended in failure, although a 'mixed economy' (embracing public as well as private ownership) was prematurely written off by fickle political and intellectual fashion. A totally unregulated market economy would be no less disastrous than a command economy. However, the basic principles governing the operation of command and market economies are different. The most heralded measure of economic reform in the early Gorbachev era was the Law on the State Enterprise of 1987. It was a genuine attempt to devolve more power to factory level, enhance the autonomy of enterprise managers, and reduce the central control of ministries. Since, however, these enterprises were not operating with market prices, the reform had unintended consequences. In the absence of a market, profit was a poor guide to efficiency. The factories had more power to determine prices themselves and often raised them for their own short-term benefit and with inflationary consequences. Later, this greater

enterprise autonomy facilitated a process of privatization by the 'red directors' – the factory managers who succeeded, as the Soviet Union came to
an end, in turning themselves into the new owners.

One attempted reform which seemed to be socially justified but turned
out to be economically and politically harmful was a Central Committee
resolution of May 1985 concerned with tackling the Soviet Union's severe
problem of drunkenness and alcoholism. The teetotal second secretary,
Ligachev, a man of enormous energy who at that time enjoyed good personal
relations with Gorbachev, was the prime mover in the anti-alcohol policy.
The campaign went beyond rhetoric and involved the shutting-down of
many retail outlets for the sale of alcohol, leading to long queues at those
which remained. It also involved the destruction of quite a number of vineyards, not least in Georgia, although vodka rather than wine was the problem.
Public opinion polls showed that for quite some time the anti-alcohol measures were approved by a majority of women and disapproved by a majority
of men. While they reduced the number of accidents both on the roads
and at work, they did serious damage to the country's finances. Since the
state had long had a monopoly on the production and sale of alcohol, the
mark-up on each bottle was a very important source of revenue. The new
scarcity of legally produced alcohol led hardened drinkers to turn to moon-
shine – often at a high cost to their health as well as the exchequer. The
more radical anti-alcohol measures were phased out in 1988, at the same
time as Ligachev lost ground within the highest echelons of the party.[26]
Gorbachev, though, had publicly backed the measures, which caused incon-
venience not only to alcoholics but to moderate drinkers, and most of the
anecdotal blame was attached to him.

YELTSIN BREAKS RANKS

Reform produced tensions within the Soviet leadership. It was not difficult
in the early years of perestroika, by reading between the lines, to discern
from their public utterances sharp differences between, for example, Ligachev
and Yakovlev. Nevertheless, Politburo discussions remained (until after the
Soviet Union had ceased to exist) top secret and a surface unity was maintained in public. The façade of collective solidarity was, however, broken
on 21 October 1987 by one member of the top leadership team, Boris Yeltsin.
Gorbachev, having already had his draft report for the celebration of the
anniversary of the revolution approved in its watered-down version by the
Politburo, presented it to the Central Committee on that date. Endorsement
by this stage was a formality and the occasion was already something of a
celebration. Until, that is, Yeltsin rose to speak. Ligachev was chairing the

proceedings at that time and did not wish to give him the floor, but Gorbachev intervened to let Yeltsin have his say. Gorbachev may have had some inkling of what was coming, for Yeltsin had written to him on 12 September, while he was on holiday in the Crimea, outlining several complaints and saying that he wished to resign from his official posts.[27]

Yeltsin devoted much of that letter to criticism of party second secretary Ligachev, who chaired the Politburo in Gorbachev's absence and invariably rubbed Yeltsin the wrong way. The political style of both men had a strong authoritarian streak, but whereas the conservative Communist inclinations of Ligachev were fairly clear, Yeltsin's political convictions at the time were a curious mixture. At the Politburo meeting at which Gorbachev's use of 'socialist pluralism' had been criticized, one of Yeltsin's criticisms of the draft report for the seventieth anniversary of the Bolshevik revolution was that not enough attention had been paid precisely to that revolution, and too much to the earlier February revolution, even though that was 'bourgeois democratic', which, Yeltsin added, the draft had failed to point out.[28] When Gorbachev received Yeltsin's letter offering his resignation, he phoned him and proposed that they meet to talk about his concerns after the seventieth anniversary celebrations. He thought that he had secured Yeltsin's agreement on that matter.

Yeltsin was taking a huge political risk in suggesting resignation. The system was still such that it was far from an obvious long-term career move. However, as a result of the relatively modest changes already introduced, public opinion was just beginning to be a political factor, and Yeltsin was popular in Moscow. His dismissal of many of his predecessor's appointees for corruption or inefficiency and his blunt speaking went down well, as did his well-publicized occasional journeys on the Moscow metro or trolleybus. After Yeltsin made his speech to the Central Committee plenum, he became still more popular with many Muscovites. Inaccurate copies of what he had said were circulated. They reflected popular prejudices and made the speech more radical than it actually had been. It was said that he had attacked the excessively high profile of Gorbachev's wife, Raisa. Many Russians took a very traditional view of the place of the spouse of a politician, and resented Raisa Gorbachev's public presence and what they suspected was her excessive influence over her husband. (Later the same year Gorbachev told Tom Brokaw, in an interview for American television, that he discussed 'everything' with his wife.[29]) Yeltsin angered Gorbachev by questioning, in face-to-face conversation, the role of Raisa.[30]

Yeltsin's criticisms when he addressed the Central Committee on 21 October were mild compared with some of those he made later, but to make an unscheduled and critical speech at a meeting whose purpose was to give the stamp of approval to an important party document was a striking violation of Soviet norms. Among Yeltsin's main charges were that decisions that had been taken over the past two years had not been implemented, that there had been no economic improvement, and that there had been a growth in the glorification of the general secretary by a number of full members of the Politburo. An additional grievance, which he did not mention in the speech, was that he was still a candidate, or non-voting, member of the Politburo, rather than a full member.[31] One Central Committee speaker after another denounced Yeltsin for his outburst and what they regarded as his self-aggrandizement. Some did so more crudely than others. Even the most liberal member of the Politburo, Alexander Yakovlev, criticized him. In an interview three years later Yakovlev said: 'I was not convinced that Yeltsin had adopted a democratic position at that time. I was under the impression that his position was conservative.'[32]

Yeltsin later had second thoughts about resigning his Moscow party first secretaryship. Less than three weeks after the Central Committee session Yeltsin, who suffered from periodic depression, made what seemed like a half-hearted suicide attempt, cutting himself on the stomach and side with a pair of office scissors. Having been detained in hospital as much on account of his mental state as his physical condition, Yeltsin was taken from his hospital bed in order to be verbally attacked, and dismissed from his position as city boss, by the municipal party committee. He returned to his sick bed immediately after that meeting and remained hospitalized for three months.[33] Although no longer in the inner party leadership, he was still a member of the Central Committee and was appointed First Deputy Chairman of the State Committee for Construction. By past standards, that was getting off lightly, but the manner of his removal from higher office was a humiliation Yeltsin never forgave. Precedent would have suggested that his political disgrace meant that Yeltsin's hopes of ever regaining high office were over. He had deliberately broken the rules of the game of Soviet politics. However, over the next three years those very rules were to change in ways he could scarcely have foreseen but, as an instinctive politician, may have fleetingly felt. To be the subject of concerted attack from the party leadership was no longer a blow from which recovery was impossible. It had become by the end of the 1980s a political commendation, a badge to be worn with pride.

The Beginning of the End of the Cold War

Within the various international and social science institutes people with radical ideas felt free to express them openly for the first time. Indeed, from the reformist wing of the party leadership there was even encouragement 'to think the unthinkable', especially concerning new approaches in foreign policy. For Gorbachev, ending the Cold War was a prime policy objective. He was concerned about the dangers of war by accident during times of high tension. He also regarded a peaceful external environment as a necessary condition for reform at home. A particular concern was to reduce the excessive budgetary demands of the military-industrial complex. Neither Gorbachev nor anyone else knew precisely how large a part of Soviet expenditure was military-related, but he was in no doubt that it was far higher than it should be. As the radical economic reformer Yegor Gaidar later observed, there could be no clarity on the extent to which Soviet prices for military technology reflected economic reality.[34] But as he went on to emphasize: 'If a country with an economy about one-fourth the size of the United States manages to support military parity with the United States and its allies and at the same time can finance forty divisions on the Chinese border, common sense tells us that the military was expensive.'[35]

Such expenditure had obvious implications for the rest of the Soviet economy. The shortage of consumer goods and the low technological level of most Soviet enterprises, other than in military industry, was due not only to the absence of a market economy. With a higher share of national investment, the inadequacies of the civilian sector would have been less severe than they were. Yet the consequences of this imbalance were a price successive Soviet leaderships had been prepared to pay for military might and 'superpower' status. Gorbachev was alone in the Politburo he inherited in being willing to challenge the automatic priority accorded military expenditure. Politicians whom he promoted, especially Eduard Shevardnadze and Alexander Yakovlev but including also Vadim Medvedev and Nikolay Ryzhkov, shared his assessment, while other Politburo members avoided getting into open confrontation with the general secretary, whose authority within the system in the early years of perestroika was still immense.

Gorbachev also used both his power of appointment and his power of persuasion to keep the military chiefs sufficiently on side until late in the perestroika era. Anatoly Dobrynin is but one of a number of high-ranking Soviet officials to have noted the unhappiness of the Soviet military at the foreign and defence policy Gorbachev was pursuing.[36] Although, however, the armed forces and military industry constituted the most influential of institutional interests in the Soviet system, they remained under the control of the party leadership. Gorbachev was able to make skilful use of the unscheduled flight of a young West German into Soviet airspace to effect change at the top of the military hierarchy. In May 1987, Matthias Rust succeeded in flying into the Soviet Union in his single-engine light plane, landing it on the edge of Red Square, just a stone's throw from the Kremlin. Although most Russians I knew were amused by this, neither the political nor the military leadership found it funny. Summoned to a Politburo meeting, the Chief of the Air Defences, General Alexander Koldunov, admitted that he had learned about the intrusion only after the aircraft had landed. Gorbachev asked sarcastically whether he got the information from the Moscow traffic police.[37] Koldunov was relieved of his post. More significantly, Gorbachev used the opportunity to replace the minister of defence, Sergey Sokolov, by the more obedient (until he took part in the attempted coup against Gorbachev in August 1991) Dmitry Yazov. Dobrynin notes:

> Opposition by the military became more moderate. Sokolov was followed into retirement by about one hundred generals and colonels, conservative military leaders who also opposed Gorbachev's reforms and his concessions to the Americans. But the military establishment by and large remained discontented with Gorbachev, and this would show time and again.[38]

Gorbachev's 'New Thinking' on foreign policy had come as a considerable shock not only to the military but also to party ideologists. The ideas, which drew both on the thinking going on in research institutes such as IMEMO and the Institute of the United States and Canada and on Gorbachev's own wide reading, were dramatically new in the Soviet context. Within the higher echelons of the party, Yakovlev, Chernyaev and Shakhnazarov played significant roles also in their formulation. Gorbachev abandoned a 'winner-takes-all' view of the world and radically downgraded class conflict as the supposed determinant of international relations. He became the first (and only) Soviet topmost leader to subordinate a theoretical commitment to class considerations to universal values. The New Thinking included the common-sense proposition that nuclear war would destroy not only one or another social class but humankind. (Indeed, 'common sense' became an expression approvingly used in Soviet political discourse in one of many departures from Marxism-Leninism.) What, therefore, was required was mutual security and recognition of all-human interests, which transcended those of any particular nation or class.[39]

Given this change of outlook at the top of the Soviet political system, any American president would have been likely to respond favourably and would have come under some pressure both from domestic public opinion and from European governments to do so. Ronald Reagan had the advantage, however, that his anti-Communist credentials were very well established. He was thus reasonably immune to criticism from more extreme hard-liners (who were to be found not only outside the administration but also in the highest echelons of the Department of Defense and the CIA). Yet Reagan's interest in peace-making, as noted in the previous chapter, was much greater than has been popularly believed. What made possible far-reaching agreements on arms reductions between the United States and the Soviet Union was the signifi-cance he attached to his personal assessment of people. There had been no summit meetings between an American president and a Soviet leader in the 1980s until Reagan and Gorbachev met at Geneva in mid-November 1985. When they did meet, it was important that the American president found himself liking Gorbachev. That was in spite of the fact that they disagreed on most of the issues, especially SDI, to which Reagan was wholly committed and Gorbachev no less opposed. Reagan called both in private and public for the Soviet Union to get out of Afghanistan. He did not then know that Gorbachev was even keener than he was to bring Soviet troops home, although the process took longer than he wished. It was February 1988 before Gorbachev announced publicly that all Soviet troops would leave Afghanistan within a year. The last Soviet soldier duly left in February 1989. As was the case with the United States in Vietnam, the Soviet Union wished to extricate itself from Afghanistan without too much loss of face. They also wanted to avoid handing the country over to extreme Islamists. The United States, however, continued to back many of the latter in their effort to dislodge from power the pro-Soviet Afghan leader Najibullah.[40]

There were to be three more summit meetings between Reagan and Gorbachev after Geneva – one, indeed, in every year of Reagan's second term as president. The two leaders met in Reykjavik in October 1986 and in Washington in December 1987. Their last full-scale summit – in Moscow – will be touched on in the next chapter. Reykjavik was an apparent failure when it ended. A grim Reagan left after the two leaders had come very close to a far-reaching agreement but failed because of SDI. Both had agreed to make deep cuts in their nuclear arsenals and to move towards their complete elimination. Gorbachev, however, made the agreement conditional on Reagan remaining within the limits of the Soviet understanding of the Anti-Ballistic Missile Treaty of 1972, which would have prevented Reagan proceeding as he wished with his favourite project. Among those present, Dobrynin thought it was odd that Gorbachev had been 'as stubborn on SDI as Reagan'.[41] Nevertheless, before the impasse was reached, Gorbachev had accepted Reagan's 'zero option' on the removal of Soviet SS20s from Europe in return for the removal of American Pershing and Cruise missiles from the European continent. In 1981, when Reagan first proposed that all intermediate-range nuclear weapons be removed from Europe, this zero option was dismissed out of hand by the Soviet leadership. The Soviet weapons had already been deployed and the American weapons were still not in place. There was also the possibility that opposition from European public opinion would prevent their deployment. That, however, had subsequently gone ahead.

The agreement on intermediate-range nuclear missiles that would have been reached in Reykjavik, had SDI not proved a stumbling block, was in fact signed at the successful Washington summit the following year. Both Reagan and Gorbachev recovered from their initial disappointment over the 1986 meeting to reflect on how close they had come to a far-reaching understanding and on how they had established a good working relationship. Neo-conservatives in Washington, as well as former secretaries of state Alexander Haig and Henry Kissinger and the Senate Republican leader, Senator Bob Dole, vigorously opposed the signing of the INF treaty that eliminated the intermediate-range nuclear forces. The American ambassador to Moscow (and former National Security Council expert on the Soviet Union), Jack Matlock, later remarked: 'It was a striking irony that many of the persons objecting to the INF Treaty had been original supporters of the zero option. Apparently, in their eyes, the zero option was useful only so long as the Soviet Union rejected it.'[42] In fact, Gorbachev conceded more than Reagan. The Soviet Union committed itself to destroying more nuclear weapons and to permitting for the first time intrusive on-site inspections. But Gorbachev got what he wanted – a constructive relationship with the Western world, the possibility of reducing the arms burden on the Soviet economy, and the way clear, it seemed, to get on with the task of reform.

25

The Dismantling of
Soviet Communism, 1988–89

Many people believe that Communism came to an end in the Soviet Union in 1991, either just after the failed August coup or when the Soviet state itself ceased to exist in December. But it does not make much sense to call the Soviet system Communist after the end of 1989. The years 1988–89 saw both the dismantling of the principal defining features of Communism and the simultaneous and interconnected ending of the Cold War. The break-up of the Soviet Union at the end of 1991 into fifteen successor states was an unintended consequence of the new freedoms and partial democratization of the Soviet political system. It also owed much to the peaceful transformation of Eastern Europe, itself the most important manifestation of the Cold War's ending.

While Chapter 27 is concerned with the disintegration of the Soviet state, in the present chapter we shall see how the *system* was transformed. In the course of 1988–89 there was a huge increase in the number of independent organizations on Soviet territory. In what was an even more remarkable break with the past, contested elections took place for a new legislature with real power. And the most sensitive issues were being publicly debated both within the Communist Party and in the broader society. By the end of 1989, a raft of new freedoms had been introduced. As Alexander Solzhenitsyn (after criticizing Gorbachev for what he termed his 'thoughtless renunciation of power') observed: 'Let us be clear that it was Gorbachev, and not Yeltsin, as is now widely being claimed, who first gave freedom of speech and movement to the citizens of our country.'[1]

By the end of 1989, not only had Solzhenitsyn's novels *Cancer Ward* and *The First Circle*, previously deemed unsuitable for publication in the Soviet Union, appeared in Moscow, so had his more devastating indictment of the Soviet experience, *The Gulag Archipelago*. A leading historian of Russia, writing in 2008, said that 'it is hard to imagine any circumstances in which *The Gulag Archipelago*, which Solzhenitsyn was secretly writing throughout the 1960s, could have been published in the Soviet Union'.[2] This was certainly unimaginable in the Soviet *system*. Yet devastating as it was for Communist ideology and the official version of Soviet history, this work *was* legally published in the Soviet Union in 1989. The Soviet state still had more than two years of existence ahead of it, but the fact that such a work as Solzhenitsyn's *Gulag* could appear in print was a sure sign that the system had become something different in kind. By that time, other works that had previously been condemned as anti-Communist and anti-Soviet slanders, such as George Orwell's *Animal Farm* and *Nineteen Eighty-Four* and Arthur Koestler's *Darkness at Noon*, had also appeared. For the small minority of Soviet citizens who had surreptitiously read these works in foreign editions, this was, indeed, unimaginable as recently as the beginning of 1985. Passing on a contraband copy of such a book was then a criminal offence. This transformation did not occur without a struggle. In early 1988 it reached a new phase, with an attempt to turn the political clock back.

Struggle and Breakthrough

What became known as the 'Nina Andreyeva affair' began with the publication of an article in the newspaper *Sovetskaya Rossiya* which, while not attacking perestroika directly, was a neo-Stalinist rejection of the essence of the changes. The article had a significance that did not lie in the person of the author, a chemistry lecturer in a Leningrad technological institute named Nina Andreyeva. Her own draft was worked on by officials of the Central Committee, with the knowledge and support of Ligachev, and published just as Gorbachev was leaving on a foreign trip, as was Yakovlev. The fact that it went unanswered for three weeks led many people to believe that the article represented a new official line. It would have done so had Ligachev and those in the Politburo who thought like him prevailed. The Andreyeva article complained about a new and unhealthy emphasis on terror and repression in discussion of Soviet history. In passages which her Central Committee co-authors doubtless supplied, Andreyeva cited positive statements about Stalin by Winston Churchill and from the memoirs of Charles de Gaulle. The article deplored the new tendency to describe the class struggle and the leading role of the proletariat as obsolete. There was a distinct anti-semitic tinge to the piece. A number of people of Jewish origin are mentioned in it, and the only one who escapes unscathed is Karl Marx. Moreover, Andreyeva revived the concept of 'cosmopolitanism', in the name of which Stalin conducted an anti-semitic purge at the end of the 1940s and beginning of the 1950s. Lest anyone should be in doubt what she meant by the term, she linked it with 'refusenikism'. The term 'refuseniks' had been applied to Soviet Jews who, in the 1970s, wished to emigrate but had been refused permission.[3] The Andreyeva article used it differently. It meant 'refusing socialism'. It inveighed also against 'a pluralism that is far from socialist'. With more foundation than most of its assertions, the article held that the cardinal question had become 'recognizing or not recognizing the leading role of the party'.[4]

The significance of the article was threefold. First, it had powerful backing from within the Central Committee of the CPSU. Second, it was treated as authoritative, with Ligachev recommending it to party organizations. Third, more than half the members of the Politburo initially agreed with it, as Gorbachev was to discover. In an informal discussion among Politburo members on 23 March 1988 (which Yakovlev recounted to Chernyaev), Ligachev raised the subject of the article in *Sovetskaya Rossiya*. 'A very good article. Our party line,' he said. Vitaly Vorotnikov said it had been an absolutely correct and necessary article. Andrey Gromyko and another veteran conservative Communist, Mikhail Solomentsev, added their agreement with those sentiments. The KGB chairman Viktor Chebrikov had his mouth open to join in the praise, but was interrupted before he could do so. The happy mood was disturbed when Gorbachev said: 'And I have a different opinion.'[5] He said that he never objected to someone expressing their views and that they could publish them anywhere they liked, but he had found out that this article was written by directive and was recommended to party organizations.* That was another matter. Gorbachev added that they would need to talk about it in the Politburo.[6] In fact, many local newspapers in the Soviet Union, with encouragement from the part of the Central Committee apparatus controlled by Ligachev, had republished the Andreyeva article. So, in East Germany, had *Neues Deutschland*. The article was music to the ears of Erich Honecker.

After the regular Politburo business had been dealt with the following day, Gorbachev returned to the article. Those who had praised it the previous evening began a retreat to the other side of the fence or perched uneasily on it. Some who had not spoken earlier now had the opportunity to join the discussion on Gorbachev's side. His allies, Shevardnadze and Vadim Medvedev, did so sincerely and robustly, as did Ryzhkov. But the most telling contribution was a detailed analysis of the text by Yakovlev. He showed how

---

* In his unpublished book manuscript, mentioned on page 484, Gorbachev noted that many regional party officials received telephone calls from the Central Committee telling them to republish the Nina Andreyeva article and to 'propagandize it'. When a response to the article appeared in *Pravda*, they concluded that a struggle was going on in the leadership and they understood that 'behind "Nina Andreyeva" stand certain forces' (M.S. Gorbachev, 'Perestroyka – ispytanie zhizn'yu', pp. 46–7).

at every point the article had opposed the policies of perestroika which the CPSU had approved, most recently at the previous month's Central Committee plenum. Since it was clear that Yakovlev was speaking not only for himself but for Gorbachev, others round the table fell into line. Thus, for example, Oleg Baklanov, the secretary of the Central Committee who supervised military industry – and who in August 1991 was a leading member of the group which mounted a coup against Gorbachev – said that he had found the article 'interesting', but now, after listening to Yakovlev and Medvedev, he saw it 'through different eyes'.[7] Yakovlev's contribution to the discussion is not fully recorded in the records of that Politburo meeting, but it was the basis of the authoritative, unsigned article which, at Gorbachev's behest (and with his participation), was published in *Pravda* on 5 April. It rebutted point by point the 'anti-perestroika manifesto' which a majority of the Politburo, left to themselves, had supported.

This curious episode was important in several different ways. It indicated how much resistance there was to Gorbachev and to the reformist wing of the leadership within the party apparatus. Indeed, one of Gorbachev's supporters in the Politburo later said that it was only 'the tip of the iceberg' of growing conservative opposition to Gorbachev and his policies.[8] It had also, however, been an attempt to produce a radical change of course that achieved precisely the opposite effect. Since Ligachev was implicated in the approval of the article and Yakovlev had led the attack on it, with the conservative majority of the Politburo shamefacedly falling into line once Gorbachev had made clear where he stood, it shifted the balance of forces within the leadership in the direction of those who favoured radical change. That was all the more important because the Communist Party was about to start preparing the documents to be presented to the Nineteenth Party Conference, which had been trailed more than a year earlier. Its main purpose, as noted in the previous chapter, was to consider 'further democratization of the party and society'.

What the Nina Andreyeva affair also abundantly demonstrated was that the power of the general secretary could still be decisive. In 1988, although this was not to be true for much longer, a determined party leader could get his way in Soviet politics, especially in the ideological sphere. The Andreyeva episode was revealing in another respect. Several weeks of uncertainty had seen a return to self-censorship on the part of a great many Soviet intellectuals. They included not a few who just a couple of years later were to criticize Gorbachev for what they called his 'half-measures' or 'indecisiveness'. However, in 1988 they heavily relied on him to turn the tables on conservative and reactionary forces within the political establishment. In March–April 1988, the direction in which the Soviet state was to move was determined, ultimately, by the general secretary, while the overwhelming majority of the intelligentsia preserved a discreet silence throughout the time when it looked as if party policy was going into reverse.*

There was to be more real discussion and clash of opinion at the Nineteenth Party Conference, convened at the end of June 1988, than at any party congress or conference since the 1920s. Yet, as in the past, the policy documents presented to the conference were prepared over a period of several months in advance of the event. It was during this time that Gorbachev, having seen the strength of the opposition to reform of the system, became convinced of the need for more fundamental change. From the spring of 1988 onwards, albeit with some subsequent zig-zags and tactical retreats, he moved from being a within-system reformer to becoming a systemic transformer. Faced by foot-dragging and opposition from a majority within the party apparatus – even more at the regional and local level than in the central organs in Moscow – as well as from within the ministries, the KGB, and the military, Gorbachev and his supporters drew support from public opinion, which was beginning to matter more than in the past.

In particular, 1988 was the year in which pressure groups of various kinds began to spread. Known as the 'informals', they became an element of de facto pluralism within the Soviet political system. Their membership was still small, but they included articulate advocates of more radical reform. In many cities, what were called 'Popular Fronts in support of Perestroika' were set up, and it was the more radical variant of perestroika they supported. One of the most serious of the independent organizations to become firmly established in 1988 was Memorial, an association set up to honour the victims of Stalin. It became a significant pressure group vis-à-vis the authorities and an influence on public opinion. Most notable among its leading figures was Andrei Sakharov, but the organization united many of the Soviet Union's prominent reformers, bringing together both party members and non-members. A more specifically anti-Communist but less influential organization, called the Democratic Union, was among other associations to hold a founding conference in 1988.[9]

---

* One of the leading 'New Thinkers' on foreign policy within Gorbachev's team, Andrey Grachev, tried in vain to find an editor of a daily newspaper willing to publish a rebuttal of the Andreyeva article. Only Yegor Yakovlev, editor of the weekly *Moskovskie novosti*, was ready for battle. When Grachev attempted to persuade the editor of *Izvestiya*, Ivan Laptev, who had a liberal reputation, to publish a reply to the Andreyeva assault on the reform process, Laptev responded: 'No, we are powerless against Ligachev.' See Andrey Grachev, *Kremlevskaya khronika* (Eksmo, Moscow, 1994), p. 126.

Although these independent bodies constituted a breakthrough inasmuch as they were organized from below, their small memberships at this stage meant that their impact on a broader public was much less than that of the more adventurous of the official publications. Mass-circulation weeklies, such as *Ogonek* (Little Light) and *Moskovskie novosti* (Moscow News), and the monthly journals, among which *Novy mir* (New World) was now far from alone in publishing essays and creative literature of a kind unthinkable in the past, had an impact on millions of Soviet citizens. The editors who had been appointed to the two most radical weeklies, under the benevolent eye of Alexander Yakovlev when he was supervising the media, remained in post throughout the perestroika era. It was in the summer of 1986 that the Ukrainian poet and journalist Vitaly Korotich became editor of *Ogonek* and an anti-Stalinist Russian journalist, Yegor Yakovlev, took over the editorship of *Moskovskie novosti*. Yakovlev, who was to be protected by Gorbachev as well as his namesake, Alexander Yakovlev, in the Politburo, had been fired from more than one position in the Brezhnev era because of his nonconformism.

HISTORY SPEEDING UP

The boldest of the weeklies and monthlies saw their circulation soar.[10] Book publishing also broke down old barriers. Works long banned in the Soviet Union but which had found fame in the West, notably Pasternak's *Doctor Zhivago* and a more devastating indictment of the Soviet past, Vasily Grossman's *Life and Fate*, had been published by the time of the Nineteenth Party Conference in the summer of 1988. This was a remarkable turnaround. Pasternak had been reviled by Soviet politicians and literary bureaucrats for his novel, and not allowed to accept the award of the Nobel Prize for Literature. Grossman, for his part, had been told by Mikhail Suslov, when he was the guardian of Soviet ideology, that his book would not be published in two hundred years.[11] History speeded up during perestroika. New books as well as hitherto unpublishable old ones had an undoubted impact on political opinion.

On the eve of the Nineteenth Conference, a collective volume appeared, called *There's No Other Way*. It was a rallying cry for perestroika in the radical understanding of the concept.[12] A majority of the authors were members of the Communist Party, among them the book's editor, the historian Yury Afanasiev. They included political analysts such as Yevgeny Ambartsumov and Fedor Burlatsky, who had long advocated reform in the pre-perestroika Soviet Union, sometimes in Aesopian language, while testing the limits of tolerance of the party authorities. The sociologist Tatiana Zaslavskaya, who had earlier in the 1980s received a party reprimand for her gloomy (and leaked) report on the condition of Soviet society, but who had already been consulted by Gorbachev on several occasions, was also one of the contributors. There were several non-party members among the authors. The most distinguished of them was Sakharov. Typically, he did not pull his punches. He wrote, for example, that 'the Afghanistan adventure embodies in itself all the danger and irrationality of a closed totalitarian society'.[13] And this in a book published in 100,000 copies by an official Moscow publishing house in June 1988.

Against these voices calling for faster liberalization and democratization, there were increasingly open demands from a very different part of the political spectrum to put an end to perestroika and to return to 'traditional values'. In the Brezhnev era, Russian nationalist deviation from Marxist-Leninist norms had been the closest thing to a form of permitted dissent. In a number of editorial boards of journals, especially those which came under the jurisdiction of the Writers' Union of the Russian republic (RSFSR), a rearguard action was fought against perestroika. Some liberal Russian nationalists, among them a much-respected literary scholar, Dmitry Likhachev, and Sergey Zalygin, a non-party member who was appointed editor of Novy mir in 1986, gave their support to Gorbachev and perestroika. However, a majority of the nationalists were horrified by the developing pluralism which gave their ideological enemies – Westernizers – a platform they had not enjoyed in the past. What was worse, the latter were evidently enjoying support from the highest reaches of the party hierarchy – from Gorbachev himself and from Yakovlev. Accordingly, even some of the nationalist writers who had in the past been critical of the CPSU now looked for allies among Communist Party officials who were alarmed by perestroika. They looked also to the military.

As time went on, especially by 1990–91, there was a real convergence of view between nationalist writers on the one hand, and party bureaucrats and the Ministry of Defence's Main Political Administration for the Armed Forces on the other. They were in agreement in discarding most Marxist-Leninist ideology and on emphasizing the idea of a strong Russian state and the dangers of democratization. But as glasnost had developed into an ever-greater freedom of speech and publication, open criticism of the party bureaucracy had made officialdom as a social stratum increasingly unpopular. What the nationalist intellectuals gained, therefore, from that alliance, in the form of support from people who still held some institutional power, they lost in their appeal to a wider public.[14] Nevertheless, in the last two years of the Soviet Union's existence, the abandonment of Marxism-Leninism by many of the party conservatives was to come close to matching its abandonment by the radical party reformers. It was what each wanted to put in its place that differed. The central argument of the Russian nationalists, and even many of the party conservatives, became that the world was divided not into antagonistic social classes but into individualistic and collectivist civilizations. They held that to introduce Western-style political and economic institutions into such a collectivist civilization as that of Russia would destroy traditional values, including those preserved by the Orthodox Church, and bring about the destruction of the Russian state. Not surprisingly, this argument has had still more resonance in post-Soviet Russia.[15]

It was not views such as these which were attacked at virtually every Politburo meeting from 1987 onwards, but the writings of those deemed the common enemies of Russian nationalists and party conservatives alike. Those targeted were the outspoken critics of the Soviet past and of fundamental features of the Soviet political and economic system – people who, in many cases, had been influenced by Western liberal and democratic thought and by what they knew of Western political practice. The waywardness of the mass media was deplored and the attention of Politburo members was drawn to particular articles which for Yakovlev were audacious and welcome but for Ligachev were slanderous and deplorable. The fact that Ligachev was until September 1988 the second secretary of the party, with some responsibility for ideology, which, however, he shared with Yakovlev, meant that mixed signals were being sent out from the highest echelons of the CPSU. In contrast with pre-perestroika times, editors could, according to their dispositions, take their cue from Ligachev or from Yakovlev.

Gorbachev was put under constant pressure from a majority in the Politburo to restore 'order' in the mass media, and sometimes responded with criticism of particular publications. Nevertheless, his position remained close to Yakovlev's and far from that of Ligachev. Indeed, whereas Ligachev had been brought into the top leadership team by Andropov, Yakovlev had moved from being, formally, outside the top five hundred of the Soviet political elite in 1985 (he was not even a candidate member of the Central Committee) to being in the top five (a full member of the Politburo and also a secretary of the Central Committee) from the summer of 1987. That extraordinarily accelerated promotion he owed entirely to Gorbachev. In September 1988, however, Gorbachev attempted to end the mixed signals emanating from the party leadership by removing both Ligachev and Yakovlev from dealing directly with ideology. For Ligachev it was a definite demotion. He became the secretary of the Central Committee overseeing agriculture. For Yakovlev it was more of a sideways move. He became the overseer of international policy. Vadim Medvedev was put in charge of ideology.

Medvedev was a loyal Gorbachev supporter and his views were more like Yakovlev's than Ligachev's, but he was much more cautious than Yakovlev and did not always spot an impending radicalization of Gorbachev's position. Glasnost had increased the appetite of a highly educated Soviet public for important literary and political works they had hitherto been denied, and those monthly journals with pro-perestroika editorial boards competed with one another for the most notable writers. *Novy mir*, having published the early Solzhenitsyn in Tvardovsky's time, got in touch with him at his exile in Vermont by telephone and telegram. They believed, not without reason, that they were in pole position to resume where they had left off more than two decades earlier. Solzhenitsyn, though, drove a hard bargain. *Novy mir* wanted to begin by publishing his novels, *The Cancer Ward* and *The First Circle*, but Solzhenitsyn said that *The Gulag Archipelago* had to be published first. Since that work made clear the culpability not only of Stalin but also of Lenin for the repressive labour camp system, it was a high hurdle for a Soviet literary journal to clear.

In June, the editor of *Novy mir*, Sergey Zalygin, had an unpleasant meeting with Medvedev which left him thinking that there was no prospect of publishing Solzhenitsyn. Yet the very next day at a Politburo meeting Gorbachev proposed that the Soviet Writers' Union should decide this matter for themselves. That was a dramatic change of policy. It did not automatically ensure publication, since the Writers' Union of the USSR was not exactly a hotbed of radicalism (although less conservative than the Writers' Union of the Russian Republic). However, they clearly sensed the way the political wind was blowing, and the direction in which Gorbachev was leaning, and gave the go-ahead. In July 1989, the text of Solzhenitsyn's Nobel Prize lecture was published in *Novy mir* and the journal was able to announce that the first instalment of *The Gulag Archipelago* would appear in the August issue.[16]

Throughout the perestroika period, Mikhail Gorbachev was on the radical wing of the Communist Party leadership. When the broader political elite became more openly divided, he sometimes took one step back before moving two steps forward. However, the extent to which the fundamental direction of policy marked a sharp break with the past depended up until the spring of 1989 almost entirely on Gorbachev. What was of decisive importance was a combination of the institutional power and authority of the *Gensek* (as the general secretary was known) and the reformist disposition, self-assurance and persuasiveness of the particular holder of that office.[17] In the spring of 1988, Gorbachev had a series of meetings with different groups of regional party secretaries in order to prepare them for the Nineteenth Conference and the changes ahead. A majority of those who took part viewed with concern radical reform of a political system in which they had possessed unchallenged authority within their own domain. In these meetings Gorbachev emphasized, above all, the need for democratization, by which, though, he did not yet mean a multi-party system. Those who attended the meeting on 11 April 1988 were told that 'the process of democratization must include separating state and party functions' and that 'we need to eliminate the gulf between form and content in our political institutions'.[18] Meeting with another group of regional party officials a week later, Gorbachev raised a still thornier issue, saying: 'You know, it's not only in the West that the question is posed: on what basis do twenty million [members of the CPSU] rule 200 million? We conferred on ourselves the right to rule the people!'[19] He went on to tell the regional officials that the party had not completed the process conceived in 1917: 'On the contrary, there arose a command-administrative system that contradicted it.'[20]

In the lead-up to the Nineteenth Conference, Gorbachev had even more important meetings, often late in the evening or at weekends, with a small group of advisers, at which ideas were freely debated, as well as the more formal meetings of the Politburo which had to approve the documents to be presented to the conference. However, the 'theses' published in advance of that major party event largely reflected the evolution of Gorbachev's views, although some of the things he wanted to do, such as bring fresh blood into the Central Committee by co-opting new members at the conference, were vetoed by the Politburo.[21] Whereas, when he came to power Gorbachev wished to reform the Soviet system, he now wanted to change its political essence. He told his aides that when he had discussed the 'theses' for the Nineteenth Conference with Hans-Jochen Vogel, the leader of the German Social Democrats, Vogel had found in them 'a social-democratic element'. Gorbachev added: 'I made no objection.'[22]

REAGAN IN MOSCOW

The American ambassador to the Soviet Union, Jack Matlock, was in Helsinki to brief President Reagan on the eve of his visit to Moscow when the Russian text of the 'theses' for the Nineteenth Party Conference was faxed to him. He was astonished to find an entirely new commitment to such principles as the separation of powers, a variety of freedoms, and independence of the judiciary. 'What the "theses" described', he concluded, 'was something closer to European social democracy' than to Soviet Communism. Matlock summarized the document for the president and told him that 'if they turned out to be real, the Soviet Union could never again be what it had been in the past'.[23]

Ronald Reagan, who was visiting Russia for the first time, arrived in Moscow on 29 May 1988 and stayed in the Soviet Union until 2 June. His fourth summit meeting in as many years with Gorbachev had fewer matters of substance to settle than had the Washington summit of the previous year, but it made up for that with its symbolic significance. For Soviet citizens, the sight of an American president, who just a few years ago was perceived as the arch-enemy and a menace to their very existence, strolling amicably in Red Square with the general secretary of the Soviet Communist Party, Mikhail Gorbachev, was both remarkable and reassuring. They concluded that the threat of nuclear war had been definitively removed. When Reagan was asked by a reporter inside the grounds of the Kremlin whether he still thought the Soviet Union was an 'evil empire' – the term he had used in 1983 – the president responded: 'No, I was talking about another time, another era.'[24] Reagan gave a speech at Moscow State University – in front of a bust of Lenin – in which he spoke about 'the technological and information revolution', about 'how important it is to institutionalize change – to put guarantees on reform', and on the need 'to remove the barriers that keep people apart', with a specific reference to the Berlin Wall. However, he also told the Moscow students: 'Your generation is living in one of the most exciting, hopeful times in Soviet history.'[25]

On 6 June, Gorbachev reported favourably to the Politburo on Reagan's visit. He said that it showed that a principled and constructive policy, based on realism, could produce a result. (He was talking about Soviet policy, although Reagan and Shultz were, understandably enough, to make quite similar judgements about the policy they had pursued.) Gorbachev noted that television coverage in the United States had enabled the average American to see the ordinary Russian and to witness the friendly reception Reagan received. Furthermore: 'The President, with all his prejudices, was able to see things realistically and spoke honestly about his impressions. And he was not embarrassed to correct his former odious evaluation.'[26] The visit further strengthened Gorbachev at a time when he was about to move to transformative change of the Soviet political system. His foreign policy had led to a dramatic reduction in East–West tension and had enhanced his own popularity both at home and abroad.

Although Gorbachev's popularity was later to decline rapidly in the Soviet Union, while remaining high in the West, he still had very strong domestic support during 1988–89. As late as December 1989, 81 per cent of citizens of Russia, and 84 per cent of respondents in the Soviet Union as a whole, fully or partly approved of Gorbachev's activity.[27] His ratings were to reach comparable levels in the United States. In mid-1986, 51 per cent of Americans had 'a favourable impression of Gorbachev'. That rose substantially over the next two years, and after Reagan's Moscow visit, the figure was as high as 83 per cent.[28] Perceptions in the USA of the Soviet Union had also changed (as they had in Europe). At the beginning of Reagan's second presidential term in 1984, 54 per cent of Americans regarded the Soviet Union as 'an enemy', whereas in May 1988 – even before Reagan's Moscow visit – only 30 per cent still held that view.[29]

From Liberalization to Democratization

The Nineteenth Party Conference was the point at which change in the Soviet political system became much more fundamental, even though a majority of the delegates were far from radical reformers. The Russian nationalist writer Yury Bondarev attacked the policies that had been pursued over the previous three years and compared perestroika to an aeroplane taking off without knowing where it was going to land.[30]

Gorbachev later remarked that when Bondarev used this analogy, it aroused a feeling of protest in him, 'but I did not openly show my feeling at the time'. Perestroika was a process that evolved over time. Gorbachev's own views, in particular, became more radical, not least because of the opposition he faced from conservative forces. Thus, the criticism that there should have been a blueprint at the outset was misplaced. In retrospective reflections of his own, Gorbachev wrote that 'we strove to be finished with the old Bolshevik tradition: to create an ideological construct and afterwards to strive to introduce it in the society, not taking into consideration the means, not considering the opinions of the citizens'.[31] Bondarev, nevertheless, got a more sympathetic reception from the conference delegates than did the liberal editor of *Znamya*, Georgy Baklanov, who, in a later speech, attacked him. Gorbachev had to intervene several times to insist that Baklanov be allowed to continue with his speech when delegates tried to drown him out, telling them that they were free to agree or disagree with the speaker but that this had to be done democratically.[32]

Boris Yeltsin also addressed the conference and called for the resignation of members of the Politburo who had spent many years in Brezhnev's Politburo and were thus responsible for the condition that the party and the country was in. Yeltsin brought into the open his conflict with Ligachev, who responded with a vigorous attack on him. Yeltsin, however, concluded his speech by appealing for his 'political rehabilitation', saying that he would rather have it in his lifetime than fifty years after he was dead. This was in spite of the fact that he was still a nominal, though entirely marginalized, member of the party's Central Committee. He appeared, therefore, to be pleading for a return to the top leadership team. He wanted, he said, to be rehabilitated in the eyes of Communists, adding that such a decision would be 'in the spirit of perestroika'. As late as the summer of 1988, even Yeltsin could not envisage exercising power other than from and through the higher echelons of the Communist Party of the Soviet Union.[33]

Ligachev was not the only Politburo member to be criticized by name in conference speeches. The Politburo veterans Gromyko and Solomentsev were also singled out for attack in speeches that were reported at length on Soviet television. Gorbachev was not yet criticized explicitly – the authority of the general secretaryship still protected him – but in a number of speeches, not least that of the writer Bondarev, he was implicitly blamed. A number of notable speeches notwithstanding, the key breakthrough measures had been decided in advance by Gorbachev and his advisers – and then some-what watered down by the Politburo. The conference accepted without overt opposition the principle of greater democratization, including contested elections for a new legislature, and also a reduction in the size of the party apparatus. The expectation was that all this would take at least a decade, if ever, to be put into effect. But at the end of his closing speech to the conference, Gorbachev pulled a surprise. He said that there was one more resolution which he admitted had been 'formulated quickly': this was that the new legislature, to be chosen by contested elections, should be up and running by April of the following year, and that the radical reduction in the size of the party apparatus should be carried out before the end of 1988. Having told his audience that it was 'vitally necessary' to adopt the resolution, he put it to a vote and got the result he had bounced the dele-gates into agreeing. Afterwards a Central Committee member, Ivan Laptev (chief editor of the newspaper *Izvestiya*), heard 'major party workers', espe-cially from the regions, saying 'What have we done?'[34]

The unreformed Supreme Soviet typically met twice a year for a total of three or four days. There was just one candidate for 'election' in each constituency and the deputies were essentially chosen by the party appa-ratus. Central Committee officials were thus able to decide in advance on the social composition of the legislature – how many women, how many workers, how many military personnel, for example. Membership was very much a part-time occupation, one which conferred honour and some degree of privilege rather than power. It was, therefore, an exceptionally import-ant act of democratization to institute contested elections for a legislature which would be meeting for eight months of the year – four months at a time. The electorate were to choose deputies for a larger outer body called the Congress of People's Deputies of the USSR that itself would meet for far longer periods than the old Supreme Soviet. It would, however, elect an inner body, called the Supreme Soviet (though bearing no resemblance to its predecessor), and that would be the legislative organ in session for the greater part of the year. Of the 2,250 members of the Congress of People's Deputies, 750 were to be elected from constituencies based on population size and 750 from national-territorial units. On that latter slate, Estonia, with its population of a million, gained the same number of seats as Russia with approximately 150 million inhabitants. Controversially, the remaining third of the deputies was to be chosen by 'public organizations', ranging from the Communist Party and the Komsomol, through the Writers', Film-Makers' and Theatre Workers' Unions, to the Academy of Sciences.

This was by no means fully fledged democracy, but even in post-Soviet Russia that has not at any point been achieved. It was, however, moving beyond liberalization to democratization, for democratization is a *process*. In a country with as long an authoritarian tradition as that of Russia, it was intrinsically unlikely that it would become a thoroughgoing democracy in a single leap. But the electoral contest this time was real. There was vigorous debate in meetings and on television. This was not a multi-party election. More than 85 per cent of candidates nominated and over 87 per cent of those elected were members of the Communist Party. The fact, however, that these party members were competing against one another, and advocating very different policies, was of immense significance. It shot to pieces the principle of democratic centralism. In a minority of constituencies a powerful local personality succeeded in becoming the single candidate. That did not ensure election. He (and in such cases it was invariably a he) still had to get more than 50 per cent of the votes cast. That proved to be an obstacle too many for the first secretary of the Leningrad regional party organization and candidate member of the Politburo, Yury Soloviev, who was rejected by more than half of his electorate. This led to his forced retirement in the same year from his party posts. In effect, the electorate as a whole now had a democratic device not only for choosing deputies but also for making untenable the position of unpopular party officials. As many as thirty-eight party first secretaries – at various levels of the hierarchy – were defeated in the elections, as were the prime ministers of Latvia and Lithuania.[35]

The most dramatic elections, and those of greatest long-term significance, were of a number of deputies determined to defend the national interests of their particular republics (they were not yet demanding outright independence), especially the Baltic states and Georgia, together with Boris Yeltsin's runaway success. Yeltsin had chosen to stand for a seat which embraced the whole of Moscow, since the capital counted as one of the national-territorial units of the USSR. He was still a member of the Communist Party, but his opponent, the manager of a large car factory in Moscow, was strongly favoured by the party apparatus. However, Yeltsin campaigned vigorously and in his speeches attacked party privileges. He drew huge crowds at his rallies and won the seat with a remarkable 89 per cent of the popular vote.[36] What made his election so important was that this was the first time in Soviet history that a prominent politician who had been expelled from the ruling circles was able to make a comeback thanks to public opinion. Thanks, too – although ironically, since Yeltsin was to be his nemesis – to Gorbachev. It was only Gorbachev's innovation of competitive elections which made such a comeback possible. The American ambassador Jack Matlock aptly observed: 'I found Yeltsin's victory less astonishing than the fact that *the votes had been counted honestly* . . . An important milestone on the road to Russian democracy had been passed.'[37]

When the new legislature met, another giant step of democratization was taken. The proceedings were broadcast live on television. Day after day viewers saw deputies criticizing party leaders, the KGB and the military and many other Soviet sacred cows. A majority of the deputies were not radical reformers, but enough of them were to make this the first legislature in Soviet history which would attempt to call its leaders to account. Indeed, it did so a good deal more vigorously than the Russian parliament was to be doing a decade or two later. Nikolay Ryzhkov had to present his ministerial team to the new legislature for approval. So exacting was the confirmation process that Ryzhkov thought he had got off quite lightly when just nine out of his sixty-nine nominations were 'killed off' by the legislature.[38] That this legislature was going to be very different from its predecessor, which had belonged entirely to the decorative part of the Soviet constitution, became clear on its very first day. Gorbachev was proposed as chairman of the Supreme Soviet – in effect, the speakership, which turned out to be far too onerous an addition to his other duties and which he later gave up. The nomination of Gorbachev alone was immediately challenged by, among others, Andrei Sakharov, who had been elected to the legislature from the most prestigious of the public organizations, the Academy of Sciences. Sakharov said he did 'not see anyone else who could lead our country', but his support for Gorbachev was conditional and, as a matter of principle, there should be a competitive election.[39] A Leningrad deputy, Alexander Obolensky, who was not a member of the Communist Party, proposed himself, and in a vote as to whether his name should appear on the ballot, as many as 689 voted in favour of that – a significant minority, although 1,415 supported the single name of Gorbachev and in the subsequent vote over 95 per cent of the deputies endorsed him.

The first session of the congress began on 25 May 1989 and lasted until

9 June. In late May some 80 per cent of the Soviet urban population were watching or listening to the congress proceedings, whether at home or at work. Later in the year television stopped live broadcasting of the legislature, screening instead edited highlights in the evening. The reason was that too many working hours were being lost to the novelty of televised political debate. The parliamentary sessions had an estimated audience of between ninety and a hundred million people.[40]

Was the Soviet System Communist in December 1989?

The dismantling of Soviet Communism was still incomplete at the end of 1989, but enough had changed for the USSR to be no longer a Communist system in the sense outlined in Chapter 6 of this book. Of the three pairs of defining features of Communism discussed there, the two relating to the *political* system are the most important – the interlinked *monopoly of power* of the Communist Party and *democratic centralism* within it. In place of the strict hierarchy and severe discipline connoted by democratic centralism, the party was riven by groups and factions, with a different line being taken by the party organizations of particular republics and with vastly different political orientations to be found within the primary party organizations in the workplace. Thus, not only had democratic centralism ceased to operate, but the 'leading role' of the Communist Party was already seriously undermined, even at a time when it remained part of Article 6 of the Soviet constitution.

The constitution had never been an accurate guide to political reality in the years of totalitarianism and post-totalitarian authoritarianism. In the first sixty years of Communist rule in Russia, there was no mention of the party's 'leading role' in the Soviet constitution. That entered the constitution only in 1977. Thus, its presence or absence in the constitution could hardly be a criterion for judging when the system was or was not Communist. It was not only in the unreformed Soviet system that the constitution was remarkably unrevealing about the realities of political life. It was also a poor guide to politics on the ground at a time when that very ground was shifting in 1988–89. The elections themselves signified the end of democratic centralism. Conservative Communists found themselves competing against Communists who were, in essence, social democrats. Stalinists found themselves opposed by liberals, even though both were members of the Communist Party. They also pitted deputies from some republics against the central party-state authorities. This nationalities dimension of political change is a theme to be taken up in Chapter 27.

Within the Congress of People's Deputies of the USSR in 1989, a new political force called the Inter-Regional Group of Deputies rapidly came into existence. This was an organization of radical democrats who soon acquired renown.[41] It brought together such major but disparate figures as Yeltsin and Sakharov. Although almost all its leading members – among them Yeltsin, the historian Yury Afanasiev, and the economist Gavriil Popov – belonged to the CPSU (with Sakharov the major exception in that respect), the Inter-Regional Group became an organization opposing the leadership of the Communist Party. It was not only foot-dragging conservative Communists they attacked, but also Gorbachev, whom Afanasiev, in particular, and Yeltsin castigated for not being willing to make fundamental change in the system. The attacks missed the points that Gorbachev's own authority within the Communist Party was now declining as a result of attacks from both ends of the political spectrum, and that he could not unilaterally declare an official end to the monopoly of power of the party (which de facto was already well under way). Gorbachev, in fact, raised the issue of removing the 'leading role of the party' from the Soviet constitution at a Politburo meeting in June 1989, but only Yakovlev, Shevardnadze and Medvedev supported such a move, and a decision was shelved. Earlier, he had wanted the issue to be addressed in the context of authorizing work on an entirely new Soviet constitution, but a very clear Politburo majority took the view that work on a new constitution should not be initiated at such a time of flux.[42]

For the Inter-Regional Group of Deputies, removing the constitutionally guaranteed 'leading role' of the Communist Party became an increasingly salient issue, affected (as we shall see in the next chapter) by events in Eastern Europe. Although the group was not numerically strong enough in the legislature to win votes there, the deputies who belonged to it constituted a liberal-democratic opposition, one which was very effective in gaining publicity and substantial support in the country. On 12 December 1989, the opening day of a new session of the Congress of People's Deputies, Sakharov pressed again for the party's leading role to be removed from the constitution. Although Gorbachev by this time was in agreement with him, he could not concede the point on the floor of the congress without the prior assent of the Central Committee. Two days later, after addressing a 'stormy caucus' of the Inter-Regional Group, Sakharov went home to prepare his speech for the next day of the Congress – and died of a heart attack that evening.[43] His death added to the emotional impact of the drive for constitutional change.

In February 1990, Gorbachev secured the agreement of the Central Committee to take the Communist Party's 'leading role' out of Article 6, and the following month that constitutional change was formally enacted by the Congress of People's Deputies. What the whole process revealed, however, was that the party was deeply divided, and that since the creation of the new legislature, the central party organs were now following, not leading, informed opinion within the society. The monopoly of power of the Communist Party was challenged not only by the diversity of the mass media but by organized groups such as the Inter-Regional Group of Deputies in the legislature. Moreover, quite a number of the new political parties which came into formal existence in 1990–91 had their origins in political clubs formed in 1988–89. In a few cases, such as that of the small Democratic Party, they began describing themselves as political parties before the end of 1989.

The two *economic* criteria of a Communist system – command rather than market economy, and state ownership rather than private or mixed ownership – survived longer than democratic centralism and the leading role of the party. But they did not survive unscathed. By the end of 1989, the command economy was ceasing to work. The Law on the State Enterprise of 1987 had devolved power to factory managers, and the State Planning Committee (Gosplan), the Ministry of Finance and the branch industrial ministries were losing their ability to control economic enterprises. Furthermore, Gorbachev had in September 1988 abolished most of the economic departments of the Central Committee, so that the party had essentially lost its 'leading role' in the economy. The changes seriously weakened the top tier of command from what Western economists named a 'command economy', what in the Soviet Union had been called a 'planned economy', and which Gorbachev himself had, since 1988, pejoratively labelled a 'command-administrative system'.

Ministries and party officials also found themselves facing workers' strikes in 1989. Strikes were legalized in that same year. Apart from posing a major challenge to the party authorities, the strikes played havoc with what was left of 'the plan'.[44] State ownership was also reduced in scope by the important Law on Co-operatives of 1988. Indeed, many of the co-operatives quite quickly became thinly disguised private enterprises. Nevertheless, the most that could be claimed for economic transition in the Soviet Union by the end of 1989 – indeed, by the end of 1991 – was that it had ceased to be a functioning command economy without becoming a market economy. As an increasingly dysfunctional hybrid, it added a new pressure from below for change to the Communist system. Soviet citizens, thanks to the new freedoms, were better aware than ever of the higher standards of living in Western democracies. Both the market and democracy began to be linked in people's minds with the promise – perhaps panacea – of rapidly rising living standards.

The two *ideological* defining features of Communism discussed in Chapter 6 – the sense of belonging to an international Communist movement and the aspiration to build communism – had disappeared totally by the end of 1989. As is well known, and as the next chapter discusses, Communist systems throughout Eastern Europe came to an end in the course of that year. There was thus no longer an international Communist movement worthy of the name, although a small number of Communist countries survived, including one as important as China. The member states of the Warsaw Pact were no longer Communist, and though as an organization the Warsaw Pact was not wound up until 1 July 1991, it had from December 1989 onwards neither ideology nor a hegemonic power to hold it together. When the East Europeans dispensed with Communist rule, this had a devastating effect also on Western Communist parties. The leadership of the Soviet Communist Party were more concerned with the survival of their own state than with the fate of Western Communist parties, none of which, other than at a local level, had ever come to power in their own countries.

They had also given up even the pretence of being interested in building 'communism'. Far from wanting the state to wither away, they were desperately trying to prevent it from disintegrating. Most of the defining features of a Communist system had, then, disappeared not only in east-central Europe but in the Soviet Union by the end of 1989. For a substantial part of the Soviet leadership, the task before them appeared to involve revival of the Communist system, as they had understood it, as a way of saving Soviet statehood. Gorbachev took a different view. Since the evolution of his own views had led him to a social democratic conception of socialism,[45] he had no wish to put together again the Communist system he had played the leading part in dismantling. He was, however, desperately concerned with preserving Soviet statehood. Later Gorbachev came to accept that since the USSR was a 'party-state' – with party and state institutions inextricably intertwined – a weakening of the party automatically led to a weakening of the state.[46] The disintegration of the state is, however, a subject for the chapter after next.

26

The End of Communism in Europe

Once Communist regimes had collapsed in Europe in 1989, their demise was widely pronounced to have been inevitable – often by the same people who just months before had assumed that no Soviet leadership would ever tolerate the transition from Communist to non-Communist rule of any Warsaw Pact country. The varied reasons why the regimes survived for as long as they did are explored in Chapter 28, and the long-term reasons for Communism's failure and collapse are the theme of Chapter 29. This chapter is more concerned with the issue of why and how European Communist states ceased to be Communist at the time they did – in 1989–90.

The place to start is with the single most important reason why the east-central European Communist states, in particular, had not collapsed *earlier*. That was successive Soviet leaderships' willingness to use, in the last resort, as much force as was necessary to preserve Communist systems in the countries that mattered most to them. Albania and Yugoslavia had been allowed to become independent of the Soviet Union, although they too were still, in their different ways, Communist. But the Soviet Union had, up until the mid-1980s, given every indication that the preservation of what they called 'socialism' in Poland, Hungary, Czechoslovakia, East Germany, Bulgaria and, to a somewhat lesser extent, Romania was non-negotiable.

The second major, and connected, reason why Communism lasted so long in east-central Europe was that the populations of those countries, like governments in the capitals of Western Europe and in Washington, *believed* in the Soviet Union's determination to uphold Communist rule throughout what had long been known as 'the Soviet bloc'. Perceptions are crucial in politics, and East Europeans firmly believed that to take on their own rulers meant taking on the Soviet Union as well. Even in Poland, the country which had seen the growth of by far the largest and most impressive opposition movement in any Communist state, Solidarity had been reduced to an underground organization that was a shadow of its former self by the mid-1980s. If the Polish population could have been sure that there was no chance of a Soviet intervention, thus making a bad situation worse, it would have been harder for the internal forces of coercion in Poland to succeed in subduing Solidarity. *Armed* resistance in any of these countries was out of the question, not only because of the disproportionately greater strength of the Soviet army but because of the extent to which the armed forces of the east-central European states were integrated into the Soviet-dominated Warsaw Pact structure.

It followed that if the Soviet leadership were to abandon what had been known since 1968 as the 'Brezhnev doctrine' – the claim that they had 'the right and duty' to intervene in any 'fraternal country' in order to preserve 'socialism', as defined in Moscow – the way would be open for speedy and dramatic change throughout the continent. A majority of Soviet-type states in Eastern Europe would have ceased to be Communist long before 1989 but for the determination in Moscow to maintain the status quo. That fixation with control had been shown in Hungary in 1956, in Czechoslovakia in 1968, and in the sustained pressure on the Polish leadership to restore 'order' in 1981. Moreover, Western countries had accepted the division of Europe even in the early post-war years when the United States, in particular, was far stronger vis-à-vis the Soviet Union than it was in the mid-1980s. The USA may have been marginally stronger than its Soviet rival in 1985, but since each side had enough nuclear weapons to destroy the other many times over, the military (as distinct from economic) advantage was meaningless.

The situation was utterly different from that of the late 1940s. The acronym MAD, standing for Mutually Assured Destruction, reflected the fact that deterrence was a two-way street. Neither NATO nor the Warsaw Pact would or could consider the deliberate use of force to change the political map of Europe. Even the periodic sharp tensions over Berlin had not been allowed to reach the point of military conflict, since it was all too evident that this could rapidly escalate into devastating nuclear war. If a war had started, and it was by no means impossible, it would most likely have been as a result of an accident or misperception – technical failure or human error. The potential consequences were sufficiently horrendous that, quite apart from the waste of human and material resources entailed by the arms race, MAD was indeed mad in the long run.

The facilitating condition for the transition from Communism in east-central Europe in the course of 1989 was the transformation of Soviet foreign policy under Gorbachev. The radical changes in the domestic political system of the Soviet Union, especially in the period between the Nineteenth Party Conference in June 1988 and the contested elections of March 1989 for the Congress of People's Deputies of the USSR, played a scarcely less significant part. But the issue of intervention or non-intervention by the Soviet Union was of decisive importance. Gorbachev had already told the East European Communist leaders that there would be no more Soviet military incursions to keep them in office. It was up to them to retain or win the support of their own people. He began conveying that message as early as his meetings with them when they came to the Soviet Union for Chernenko's funeral in 1985. Gorbachev observed later that it seemed as if his interlocutors 'did not understand me very well and even didn't believe me'. They had heard the story about being treated as equal partners before and probably thought: 'We'll see.'[1] Gorbachev made the same points still more clearly at subsequent meetings with his Warsaw Pact counterparts. Even if, however, the East European Communist Party leaders could bring themselves to believe that in all circumstances the Soviet Union would refrain from intervening militarily, they had no wish to pass on such non-interventionist declarations to their own people. It was in the Communist party leaderships' interests for the people to believe that behind their domestic rulers stood the might of the Soviet army.

It was, therefore, of momentous significance when Gorbachev in 1988 made plainer than ever, and *in public*, his opposition to military intervention. He did this first of all when addressing the Nineteenth Party Conference. In his main report to the conference, delivered on 28 June, he said:

> A key place in the new thinking is occupied by the concept of freedom of choice. We are convinced of the universality of this principle for international relations, when the main and general world-wide problem has become the very survival of civilization . . . In this situation the imposition from outside – by any means, not to speak of military means – of a social structure, way of life, or policy is from the dangerous armoury of past years. Sovereignty and independence, equal rights and non-interference are becoming the generally recognized norms of international relations . . . To oppose freedom of choice means placing oneself against the objective movement of history itself. That is why the policy of force in all its forms has historically outlived itself.[2]

Faced by this idealistic formulation, even a cynic should have recognized that these were not the words of a leader contemplating intervention in Eastern Europe. By stating so plainly the principle of non-intervention (with no special 'privilege' of intervention offered to fraternal 'socialist' states), Gorbachev was making it much harder to justify any repeat of 1956 or 1968. It amounted to an open renunciation of the 'Brezhnev doctrine'. Since much of the attention devoted to the speech focused, understandably, on Gorbachev's plans for reconstructing the Soviet political system, the ideological breakthrough represented by the passage quoted did not receive as

much attention as it deserved. It received more attention – most importantly in Eastern Europe – when Gorbachev made essentially the same points
in a major speech at the United Nations in December 1988.

Even then, in the Western mass media, those general but highly significant points were almost entirely overlooked. In his memoirs, Pavel
Palazchenko – Gorbachev's brilliant English-language interpreter (and with
his large moustache and bald head, an easily recognizable figure at summit
meetings) – notes a remark of George Shultz about Gorbachev's UN speech.
The press, he said, had been captivated by the 'hard news' of Soviet unilateral troop reductions. Gorbachev had announced that over the next two
years the Soviet Union would reduce the strength of its armed forces by
half a million men. It would also remove 10,000 tanks, 8,500 artillery systems
and 800 military aircraft from Eastern Europe.[3] (The Soviet leader had
succeeded in obtaining the approval of the Politburo on 24 November 1988
for the troop reductions.)[4] But the media had ignored, said the former US
secretary of state, the 'philosophical' first half of Gorbachev's speech. And
Shultz added: 'if anybody declared the end of the Cold War, he did in that
speech. It was over. And the press walked by that.' Palazchenko remarks
that it was not only the press but 'almost the entire US foreign policy establishment' which missed the significance of what Gorbachev was saying.[5]

The import of Gorbachev's words was especially great for Eastern Europe,
although far from everyone, even among the politically attentive, in those
countries took what he said at face value. Some, however, were prepared
to put those words to the test. In that United Nations speech, Gorbachev
stressed the 'binding nature of the principle of freedom of choice'. This,
he added, was a 'universal principle', applying both to socialist and capitalist
countries, and allowing no exceptions.[6] His remarks were directed at both
Western countries and at hard-liners in the Soviet bloc. Neither side, said
Gorbachev, should be trying to export its own brand of democracy, which
in any event, when implemented as an 'export order', was often quickly
cheapened.[7] The first draft of the speech had been written by Gorbachev's
aide Anatoly Chernyaev. Others contributed, and then Gorbachev rewrote
the text himself. He had intended the speech to be an 'anti-Fulton – Fulton
in reverse' – to bring to a definitive end the division of the world which
had been dramatized by Winston Churchill in his 'iron curtain' speech at
Fulton, Missouri, in March 1946.[8]

Just a few weeks earlier, and not coincidentally, Gorbachev had proposed
to Andrey Gromyko, who had been involved in the making of Soviet foreign
policy throughout the entire post-Second World War period, that he resign
from his position as formal head of the Soviet state – Chairman of the Presidium
of the Supreme Soviet – and from the Politburo. Gromyko obediently complied.

Gorbachev added the headship of state to his party general secretaryship, having waited much longer to do so than did his two immediate predecessors. The United Nations speech did not inaugurate, as Gorbachev had idealistically and perhaps naïvely hoped, a more peaceful and rational epoch of international co-operation and acknowledged interdependence. It did, however, raise expectations in Eastern Europe. When those were acted upon, the repercussions in the Soviet Union itself were profound. In the process, Gorbachev's own political position was fatally undermined. The reverse influence of Eastern Europe on the Soviet Union is, however, one of the themes of the next chapter.

Soviet foreign policy by the end of 1988 was in the hands of three people who were adamantly opposed to any future Soviet military intervention in Eastern Europe. Gorbachev was the dominant policy-maker, but Alexander Yakovlev was now the senior secretary supervising the International Department of the Central Committee, and Eduard Shevardnadze remained foreign minister. Gorbachev's most influential aides, Anatoly Chernyaev and Georgy Shakhnazarov, were also very much in favour of allowing the East Europeans to determine their own destinies. Shakhnazarov, as a specialist on Eastern Europe, was particularly influential. As early as October 1988, in a memorandum to Gorbachev, he said that the problems of the 'socialist commonwealth' were a result of the 'economic and political model of socialism' which had taken shape in the Soviet Union and had then been foisted on the East Europeans in the post-war period.[9] In the same memorandum, he questioned whether the presence of Soviet troops in any Eastern European country apart from the GDR served Soviet interests.

Gorbachev was receptive to Shakhnazarov's advice. Neither he nor Yakovlev and Shevardnadze needed any persuading that military intervention in Eastern Europe should never be undertaken again. There were, however, many in the Soviet political establishment – still more in the military and KGB – who, over the next two years, were to become extremely critical of renunciation of the use of force when the price of this was 'the loss', as they saw it, of Eastern Europe. That Soviet troops stayed in their barracks as one East European country after another became independent in the course of 1989 was not because there was a consensus in Soviet political and military circles in favour of such a policy. Yegor Ligachev, who from 1985 until 1988 had been the second secretary within the party, Oleg Baklanov, the secretary of the Central Committee in charge of military industry, and Vladimir Kryuchkov, the chairman of the KGB, were opposed to letting Eastern Europe go its own way. A number of very senior military figures also spoke out against this, focusing their anger on Yakovlev and Shevardnadze rather than Gorbachev. They were no less disapproving of Gorbachev, but the very fact that in 1989, and for the most part even in 1990, they hesitated to attack him directly and publicly illustrated the extent to which, in the hierarchically organized Communist Party, the authority and power of the general secretaryship aided Gorbachev in pushing through policies to which a substantial section of the Communist elite were opposed. If Gorbachev had been deposed as general secretary in early 1989, the balance of forces within the Soviet political elite would have changed dramatically. Within the Soviet military, in particular, there were many senior figures who were still ready to use all the force they could command to prevent the loss of dependent regimes which they regarded as their legitimate gains from the Second World War.[10]

Gorbachev did not envisage that the East European countries would wish to break all ties with the Soviet Union. His hope was that they would follow his example and introduce a Soviet-style perestroika or revive the 'socialism with a human face' of the Prague Spring. That moment, however, had already passed. Even though the citizens of Eastern Europe did not make the choices Gorbachev would have preferred, he showed himself ready to allow that 'freedom of choice' of which he had spoken in his 1988 Nineteenth Conference and United Nations speeches. Gorbachev, Yakovlev and Shevardnadze were well aware, too, that any Soviet intervention would not only do great damage to East-West relations, which had already improved dramatically, but would also strengthen conservative forces within the Soviet Union. The precedents were clear. Both the crushing of the Hungarian revolution and, still more, the military intervention to put an end to the Czechoslovak reform movement in 1968 had weakened would-be reformers in the USSR as well as throughout Eastern Europe.

The reverse side of the coin also applied. Soviet acceptance of radical change within any one Eastern European country was bound to have far-reaching consequences. It was always likely, and it was something of which Soviet leaders from Stalin to Andropov were acutely conscious, that once the Soviet leadership condoned fundamental change in any particular Warsaw Pact country, the example would be followed in other East European states. So it proved in 1989. The dismantling of a Communist system, which was going ahead in a more unobtrusive way in the Soviet Union itself, proceeded at breakneck speed in east-central Europe. Political freedoms and national independence were highly contagious. The Soviet Union was the hegemonic power in the eastern half of the European continent, and its reaction – or inaction – remained of decisive importance. As early as 13 April 1989, at a meeting of the Politburo, Gorbachev spoke surprisingly warmly about a remark which the leader of the German Social Democratic Party, Hans-Jochen Vogel, had made to Alexander Yakovlev during Vogel's recent visit to Moscow, namely that 'the international Communist movement has already to all intents and purposes ceased to exist, but the socialist idea continues to live in social democracy'.[11] The evolution of Gorbachev's own ideas enabled him to accept calmly the dramatic changes in Eastern Europe during the remainder of that year.

Hungary

The movement for sweeping change began in the two countries which had most consistently shown reformist tendencies over the years – Hungary and Poland. Ever since the Prague Spring was crushed, they had been the two Warsaw Pact countries most likely to embrace change. Poland did so dramatically during 1980–81, and the rise of Solidarity to challenge directly the power of the party-state was unique in the history of Communist systems. However, after the imposition of martial law in Poland, Hungary emerged as the most relaxed country in the region from the early to the mid-1980s.

Kádár, from the most inauspicious of starts in 1956, when he was charged by the Soviet leadership with the task of restoring order in Hungary, presided over a gradual liberalization and appeared to be the East European leader who, in the Brezhnev era, best understood the limits of Soviet tolerance. More importantly, he was prepared to see Hungary press to those limits. This applied especially to economic reform, but could be seen also in the arts and in intellectual life more generally. A leading Hungarian sociologist and intellectual, Elemér Hankiss, could get away with describing the regime in a book as 'neo-feudal', although, as he told me in 1981, 'I couldn't say it on TV.' I recall a discussion in that same year in the Institute of Sociology of the Hungarian Academy of Sciences in which Hankiss said, in the company of a large group of his colleagues, 'There are no Marxists in the Institute of Sociology.' That struck me as surprising, not just because Hungary was a self-proclaimed 'socialist state' but because at that time there were very few sociology departments in European or North American universities without Marxists. What was also striking about the remark was that it was made in a crowded room rather than in one-to-one conversation. A discussion ensued as to whether one of their colleagues might be a Marxist, and was finally settled when Hankiss declared: 'No, she's not *really* a Marxist!' (Hankiss, who spent some months in prison in the aftermath of the 1956 Hungarian revolution, went on to head Hungarian Public Television in the early post-Communist years, and later became Director of the Institute of Sociology.) If we take the period from the beginning of the 1970s to the mid-1980s, only in Poland did such semi-public discussions range as freely as they did in Hungary.

That Hungary had developed from a harsh dictatorship to a relatively mild authoritarian regime was recognized by the Carter administration when in early 1978 they returned the medieval symbol of Hungarian statehood, the Crown of St Stephen, to Hungary. It had been taken out of the country in 1945 and in the intervening years was safely deposited by the American government in Fort Knox.[12] A number of prominent Western politicians who visited Hungary in the first half of the 1980s were rather impressed by Kádár, among them the speaker of the US House of Representatives 'Tip' O'Neill, and British Prime Minister Margaret Thatcher. More to the point, he earned at least grudging respect, and often more than that, in Hungary. Kádár's major biographer captures well both the relative popularity and its context when he observes:

> Western commentators' frequent (and unverifiable) claim that Kádár could have won a free election missed the point: much of his popularity rested on his seeming the best option under any *realistic* circumstances. Compared with Hungary's recent past, and with figures such as Brezhnev, Husák and Ceauşescu, he did seem benign . . . He seemed to be the best guarantor of a modest but bearable existence.[13]

When Kádár died in July 1989, more than 100,000 people attended his funeral. Ten years later he emerged, surprisingly, as the 'greatest Hungarian' of the twentieth century in a survey of Hungarian opinion.[14] By 1999, there was some nostalgia for the relative stability of the Kádár era, though few desired a return to Communist rule. It was remembered that Kádár had been genuinely devoted to raising people's living standards and that, after the early years of post-1956 repression, he had followed the maxim of 'who is not against us is with us'. Few leaders in the Communist world were further removed both politically and temperamentally from the zealots of the Chinese Cultural Revolution or the fanaticism of the Khmer Rouge. The lugubrious Kádár remained a believer in the Communist party's right to rule, but he was content to seek 'passive obedience from a de-politicised population, not mobilization in pursuit of grand political ambitions'.[15]

If Kádár's style of restrained authoritarian rule was as good as it got – which was, of course, far from good – during the years in which Brezhnev presided in the Kremlin, it was ill suited to a time of ever more radical reform in the Soviet Union. Hungary's partially reformed economy performed badly in the 1980s. By the spring of 1988 the country also lagged well behind the Soviet Union in political reform and the extension of freedom. In this new, more permissive international context, the cautious and ageing Kádár had become a liability. He was ousted from power in May 1988 and replaced by Károly Grósz, who moved from the prime minis-tership to become First Secretary of the Hungarian Socialist Workers' Party. By this time there was some genuine dialogue between party reformers and civil society activists in Hungary, but Grósz himself was no advocate of radical change. The most serious political reformer in the party leadership was Imre Pozsgay, who along with Rezsö Nyers (the main architect of Hungary's economic reform) entered the Politburo when Kádár left. Pozsgay favoured dialogue with organizations enjoying real autonomy from the party-state, and in the course of 1988 such organizations emerged – the Hungarian Democratic Forum in September and the Alliance of Free Democrats two months later.[16] Pozsgay's radicalism was to make him the most popular of Hungarian Communists with the population as a whole. Change was also more circumspectly embraced by Grósz's successor as prime minister, the young, non-ideological, and well-educated economist Miklós Németh.

Pozsgay was willing to put his head above the parapet before it was neces-sarily safe to do so, and at a time when the opposition to the Communists in Hungary was still too weak for them to mount a serious attempt to attain state power. His contribution to quickening the pace of change was, there-fore, important. While Grósz was attending the business community's annual economic conference in Davos in January 1989, Pozsgay took advantage of his absence to make two startling statements on a popular Hungarian radio programme. He announced – as a preliminary result of an examination of Hungarian history since 1956 authorized by the ruling party – that what had happened in 1956 should be considered a 'popular uprising'.[17] This may have been blindingly obvious in the Western world, but in official Hungarian circles, in the Soviet Union, and throughout Communist Europe, the Hungarian events of 1956 had been definitively characterized as a 'counter-revolution'.[18] The Hungarian Communist party Politburo had, however, established a committee to analyze political, economic and social develop-ments over the previous three decades. Its historical sub-committee, one of four working groups, was chaired by Ivan Berend, an eminent economic historian who since 1985 had been President of the Hungarian Academy of Sciences. In 1988–89 he was also a member of the party's Central Committee. A longstanding reformer within the system, he, together with his committee, had now come up with an evaluation which called into question whatever remote claim on legitimacy the system might have. As Berend put it, writing some years later: 'If the suppressed people's uprising fought for genuine democratic and national demands, then the Kádár regime was a conserva-tive "counter-revolution".'[19]

Pozsgay's other bombshell was to answer in the affirmative a question as to whether the Communists might learn to co-exist with another party. He said that they had to learn to do so not just with one other party but with two or more.[20] The Hungarian legislature, in fact, passed laws in February permitting the development of a multi-party system, having over the previous two months already legalized rights of association and assembly. And on 20 February the Central Committee of the Hungarian Communist party voted to give up the party's 'leading role'. By May the party was recognizing that the government should be responsible not primarily to it but to a revived parliament. In the same month the party leadership agreed to open round-table talks with the democratic opposition. A mixture of reform from above and pressure from below accelerated the rate of change. Imre Nagy and four others who had been executed in the wake of the Hungarian revolution were reburied in June 1989 in ceremonies which brought 300,000 Hungarians on to the streets, while many more watched this symbolic reappraisal of modern Hungarian history on television. By October Hungary was no longer a Communist state. In that month, following a party congress, a majority of the Communist party (the Hungarian Socialist Workers' Party) split off from the HSWP to form the Hungarian Socialist Party and embraced social democracy. The round-table discussions produced an agreement to move to free elections for a new and powerful legislature. The principle of direct election of a president was also agreed. On 23 October 1989, the existing parliament, which had swum with the tide of public opinion, authorized the country's change of official name from Hungarian People's Republic to the Hungarian Republic.[21]

Poland

Poland's trajectory in reforming, and then ending, Communist rule was much less gradualist than that of Hungary from the early 1960s to the late 1980s. With the rise of Solidarity in 1980–81, Polish society had presented a frontal challenge to the party-state which was not matched in Hungary until 1989, and not fully even then, for systemic change in Hungary owed at least as much to the evolution of the views of Communist party reformers into Communist party dismantlers as it did to the numerically small opposition groups. In Poland, however, with the imposition of martial law in December 1981, the Polish Communist party (the PUWP) had been able to imprison leading figures in Solidarity, make the organization illegal, and use the military as an instrument of their rule. They had little chance of winning hearts and minds, but they had resumed their hold on the levers of state power. Jaruzelski, however, aspired to follow a path similar to that which had been taken by Kádár. He, too, hoped to preside over a gradual liberalization, and in the meantime followed the Kádár line that those who were not actively in opposition to the Communist state would be considered to be 'with us'. Even reformers, though, within the Polish Communist party had far less credibility within the broader society than their Hungarian equivalents at the time when the latter embarked on talks with the opposition movement in Hungary. Accordingly, Jaruzelski and his colleagues long hesitated before reopening a dialogue with Solidarity. Although still an underground movement, Solidarity had begun flexing its muscles once more from early 1988. In January it called for protests against price rises and throughout the year there were numerous work stoppages. Following a coal miners' strike in August, the government lost a vote of confidence even in the unreformed Polish parliament (the Sejm), and a new government was appointed, headed by a relatively reformist Communist, Mieczysław Rakowski.

The Polish party-state authorities were acutely conscious that Poland's economic situation was worsening and that this was exacerbating popular dissatisfaction. Already heavily indebted to Western banks, they were also aware that they were unlikely to get Western governments to lend a hand so long as Solidarity was being suppressed. With the domestic political and economic climate deteriorating from the standpoint of the authorities, Solidarity was in a strong position to make a comeback. The international context was now propitious, with radical Soviet reforms under way and much-improved relations established between the Soviet Union and Western countries. The Polish opposition remained cautious, however, about attempting to deprive the country's Communists of all power. They could not be certain that the Soviet leadership would tolerate that, or whether, indeed, in those circumstances Gorbachev would still be in the Kremlin. Round table talks began between the Polish government and independent social organizations, the latter led by Lech Wałesa and Solidarity, in February 1989. The institution of round tables – a procedure whereby the monopoly of power of Communist parties was surrendered in the course of discussion and agreement – was pioneered in Poland and spread to other east-central European countries.

The strength of support in Polish society for the opposition forces – including the backing of the Catholic Church and the moral authority of the Pope and, to a lesser extent, of the Polish primate, Cardinal Glemp[22] – helped to ensure that the party-state authorities yielded by far the most ground. Solidarity compromised also for the sake of agreement, but when the outcome of the talks was made public in early April 1989, it seemed clear that the Polish political system would never be the same again. Solidarity was legalized, the Catholic Church was accorded full legal status (lack of which had not prevented church attendance in Poland being the highest in Europe, East or West) and the first stage of constitutional reform was agreed. There were to be parliamentary elections in which half the seats would be freely contested. In the seats for which they were allowed to compete, Solidarity swept the board in the June elections. They won ninety-nine out of a hundred seats in the less powerful upper chamber, the Senate, and they had 161 out of 460 members of the Sejm. Those elected under the Solidarity banner were of different political dispositions – some conservatives, some liberals, some social democrats – but the aura of Solidarity and the immense popularity of Lech Wałesa swept them into parliament. Scarcely less striking was the fact that of pro-government candidates in thirty-five *uncontested* seats, only two were elected. In the other thirty-three cases, more than half the electors had scored out the name of the candidate, who had thus not secured the necessary 50 per cent of the vote.[23]

In October of 1989 a Polish actress, Joanna Szczepkowska, announced on television that 'on 4 June 1989 communism in Poland ended'. One of the leading figures in Solidarity, the historian (later to become foreign minister) Bronisław Geremek observed that 'it's the plain truth, and I entirely agree with her'.[24] While the Polish democratization process had not yet run its full course, a free election in which Solidarity had been the most successful quasi-party, the Polish United Workers' Party had been humiliated, *and* the Communists had *accepted* that outcome meant that Poland was, indeed, no longer a Communist state. It had been part of the tacit understanding between Solidarity and the party-state authorities that General Jaruzelski would remain head of state. In the post-election political climate, and in the new Sejm, it was far from certain that he would be chosen by that body. Solidarity deputies, against the wishes of many of their rank and file, had to connive in his election – by one vote. Accepting the end of the party-state, Jaruzelski simultaneously resigned from the leadership of the PUWP and from the Politburo and Central Committee, although he continued to be commander-in-chief of the armed forces.[25]

In Solidarity's strategic thinking, this particular measure of continuity had seemed desirable by way of reassurance to the Soviet Union. It made sense, for of all the Eastern European leaders, Jaruzelski was the one with whom Gorbachev's relations were best. (They were worst with Ceauşescu and Honecker.) The new prime minister, however, was a leading Solidarity activist whom Wałesa had chosen for the role, Tadeusz Mazowiecki. He became the first non-Communist head of government in Eastern Europe since Communist rule was established in the region.* Adam Michnik, a veteran of the Polish opposition movement and a leading figure in Solidarity, noted that in this period of transition, Jaruzelski as president had been 'completely loyal to the democratic process'. However, he added that in 1989 'it was not the communists who legitimized Solidarity, but it was Solidarity who legitimized the communists'.[26] That 'legitimation', if it could be termed such, was short-lived. Mazowiecki's government set about dismantling what was left of the Communist system. The task was completed by the end of 1989, by which time constitutional amendments had removed the Communist party's 'leading role' (which in political practice had been conspicuously absent for more than half a year) and had renamed the state the Republic of Poland. The government and parliament also endorsed the radical economic reforms proposed by the new minister of finance, a neo-liberal economist, Leszek Balcerowicz. The process of transition was complete when Jaruzelski resigned the presidency in 1991 and Lech Wałesa was elected President of Poland. In October of that year, in the first fully free elections in Poland during the post-Second World War period, the parties which belonged to the Solidarity coalition won a majority in both chambers of parliament.

East Germany

Both the Helsinki Agreement and, still more, the West German government's *Ostpolitik*, by reducing the isolation of East Germany following the building of the Berlin Wall in 1961, contributed to the hopes of the people for change within the GDR. Yet in both German states most citizens assumed, up to and including the mid-1980s, that for the foreseeable future this would,

---

* A four-man ad hoc committee of the CPSU Politburo was appointed to assess the situation in Poland. It was politically balanced, with the KGB chief Vladimir Kryuchkov and Defence Minister Dmitry Yazov acting as counterweights to the reformists Alexander Yakovlev and Eduard Shevardnadze. They reported that events in Poland were having 'a negative influence on the European socialist states, strengthening concern about the fate of socialism'. Nevertheless, the tone of the report, dated 20 September 1989, was fairly calm, as was the response of the Politburo meeting, over which Gorbachev presided, that considered the report on 28 September. The resolutions of the Politburo and the report of the committee are available in the Hoover Institution Archives: 'Vypiska iz protokola No. 166 Zasedaniya Politbyuro TsK KPSS ot 28 sentyabrya 1989 goda', HIA, Fond 89, 1.991, opis 9, file 33.

at best, take the form of liberalization within East Germany and of closer contacts between the two states rather than their unification.[27] Robert Havemann, a natural scientist and an idealistic Communist who had been imprisoned during World War Two by the Nazis, but for whom the crushing of the Prague Spring was the last straw, was untypical in perceiving in the 1970s how fragile was the GDR's apparent stability. He wrote in 1978: 'I have no thought of leaving the GDR, where one can really observe how step by step the regime is losing, or has already lost, all credibility, and how it would take only a few external impulses or events to send the Politburo to the devil.'[28] It was, however, generally assumed that not only was the Soviet Union committed to supporting Communist rule throughout Eastern Europe but that, for historical reasons, this applied doubly to the GDR.

While political reform in the Soviet Union and, still more, the new thinking on foreign policy were of decisive importance in facilitating both the peaceful dismantling not only of the Berlin Wall but also of the Communist system in the GDR and the subsequent unification of the two German states, domestic change in East Germany was far from inconsequential. From the late 1970s until the mid-1980s, the one form of dissent which the party-state authorities in the GDR even partially permitted was within the Christian Church. It was extremely circumscribed dissent, with the rules of the game monitored by the omnipresent State Security Police – the Stasi. The party-state authorities looked to the Church to lend its support to the official peace movement – in particular, to speak up against the placing of NATO missiles in Europe.[29] Protestant Church activists were, however, much more in tune with international Christian opposition to the arms race than with the demands of the authorities, and their unhappiness with the militarization of their own society led to tensions with the East German state.[30] The opportunity to take part in somewhat freer discussion than was possible elsewhere attracted significant numbers of young people to the Church groups, but these were invariably infiltrated by the Stasi. Dissent was, as a result, kept well under control until 1989, when both the Stasi and the more cautious of the Church leaders lost control of the movement.[31]

While reunification was to show how inefficient the GDR economy had been – it had looked respectable only by comparison with some of its Communist neighbours – there is little doubt about the effectiveness of the state's repressive organs. The numbers of the security police – and of Stasi informers – were higher in proportion to the population as a whole than were the security police in the Soviet Union or elsewhere in Eastern Europe, apart from Romania. The omnipresence of the Stasi was not the only reason why most people accommodated themselves to the regime, but it was certainly a major one. Havemann, however, had been quite right to forecast that 'a few external impulses or events' would be enough 'to send the Politburo to the devil'. Especially since these 'external impulses and events' turned out to be on a momentous scale – the radical changes in the Soviet Union and the still more overt process of dismantling the Communist system which was under way in Poland and Hungary during the first half of 1989. It was understandable, therefore, that it was precisely in the late summer of 1989 that 'increasing numbers of East Germans began to change from being passive subjects to active citizens'.[32]

The scale of the change in Germany went far beyond the intentions of the person who had done most to set it in motion, although he was prepared to live with it. Gorbachev had, on the one hand, wished to see reform in the GDR and was implicitly critical in public (and openly so in his circle of advisers) of Honecker. On the other, he made clear time and again that the Soviet Union would not resort to force in Eastern Europe. For those who had missed, or discounted, Gorbachev's major statements in 1988, the abandonment of the 'Brezhnev doctrine' was reiterated at least twice in July 1989 – at a Warsaw Pact summit meeting in Bucharest and, still more clearly, in an address to the Council of Europe. The fact that he repeated his commitment to non-intervention at a time when regime change in Hungary and Poland was already under way was a very encouraging sign for the populations of the four countries whose leaderships up to that point had been highly resistant to change: East Germany, Czechoslovakia, Bulgaria and Romania.[33] Addressing the Council of Europe in Strasbourg on 6 July, Gorbachev noted that the political and social orders of European countries had changed in the past and might change again in the future. He went on: 'However, this is exclusively a matter for the peoples themselves to decide; it is their choice. Any interference in internal affairs, or any attempts to limit the sovereignty of states – *including friends and allies, or anyone else* – are impermissible.'[34]

The crisis for the GDR regime began in May 1989, when the Hungarians opened their border to Austria and thousands of East Germans made their way to the Federal Republic of Germany via Hungary and Austria. Hungarians themselves had for years been free to travel abroad and return home again, but East German travel had been tightly restricted ever since the Berlin Wall went up. Before long, citizens of the GDR were besieging the West German embassies in Prague and Warsaw, seeking permission to travel to the Federal Republic. The mass exodus further undermined the authority of the East German regime, and their attempt to stem the flow led to mass demonstrations in October, especially in Leipzig. A visit by Gorbachev for the fortieth anniversary of the foundation of the GDR on 7 October did Honecker no good whatsoever. The East Berlin crowd chanted

'Gorbi, Gorbi!' and made very clear their preference for Gorbachev and his policies over Honecker and his. Gorbachev offered no words of support for Honecker but, in a restrained warning, said that 'Life itself punishes those who delay.'[35] Honecker, along with several of his allies, was replaced in a Politburo palace coup carried out on 17 and 18 October, but his successor, Egon Krenz, inspired little support. He presented himself to Gorbachev as someone who, unlike Honecker, was all for perestroika. He also sought to take credit for the fact that force had not been used against the demonstrators in Leipzig on 9 October. That, however, doubtless owed more to Gorbachev's visit two days before and his known preference for dealing with protests non-violently than to the predispositions of either Honecker or Krenz. Indeed, Krenz had approved of the brutal suppression of the Tiananmen Square demonstrators in Beijing earlier in the year.[36]

Responding to the pressure of public opinion, the new East German leadership decided to relax the regulations on travel abroad, but it was far from their intention to open the borders completely. It was a careless answer on the evening of 9 November by Politburo member and party spokesman Günter Schabowski to Tom Brokaw, the news presenter of the American TV station NBC, which gave the impression that East German citizens were from that moment entirely free to leave the GDR. This interpretation was immediately picked up by West German television (which was, of course, watched in East Germany). One Federal Republic television station prematurely announced that 'the gates in the Berlin Wall stand wide open'.[37] At that moment they remained firmly closed. However, perceptions, even misperceptions, can change reality. Since tens of thousands of people believed that the wall was being opened, they arrived at the borders in such numbers that those who guarded them – in the absence of clear instructions one way or the other – decided they had no option but to allow them through. All controls on people leaving the GDR (and returning again) were lifted at 11.30 p.m. on 9 November. It was two hours later in Moscow than Berlin, and so Gorbachev got the news only the next morning. As one commentator put it, 'when East Germans were dancing on the wall, the Soviet leadership was sound asleep'. Nevertheless, when Gorbachev received a report from the East German ambassador the following morning and was informed that they had opened all border crossings along the wall, he told him that they had 'taken the proper action' and asked him to inform the GDR leadership of that.[38]

Between 10 November and the end of 1989, over 120,000 people left the GDR. In the whole of 1989, during most of which people had to take a more circuitous route, almost 350,000 left. The Communist party disintegrated in the face of the new realities, but was reconstituted as the

Party of Democratic Socialism. This was not enough to save a separate East German state. In the light of the huge gulf in living standards between East and West Germany, not to speak of the qualitative difference in terms of human rights and freedoms, 'a GDR with open borders – a prerequisite for any form of truly democratic socialism – could scarcely hope to survive'.[39] In January 1990 it was already clear that the East German state was doomed. By the following month, movement to unification had been approved – ultimately in a 10 February meeting between Gorbachev and West German chancellor Helmut Kohl. In elections in the GDR in March 1990, the Christian Democrat-led 'Alliance for Germany' emerged as the most successful coalition of parties, with just over 48 per cent of the votes.[40]

This was not what some of the most committed opponents of the regime in East Germany, including those who led the demonstrations in October 1989, had wanted. As Timothy Garton Ash wrote in 1990: 'This turn of events – or rather of popular aspirations – left the Church and opposition activists who had led the October revolution curiously disconcerted. For their starting-point had always been that they did not want reunification. Rather, they wanted to work for a better, a genuinely democratic German Democratic Republic.'[41] By this time, however, neither the official elite of the GDR nor the counter-elite of the opposition had any control over the flow of developments. Demonstrators in their tens of thousands had shouted in October 'We are the people!' After 9 November this became 'We are one people.' The aspiration for a united Germany became unstoppable – other than through the use of massive force. However, the 12,000 men of the Berlin border regiments were not mobilized, although as recently as February of the same year they had shot dead a twenty-year-old East Berliner, Chris Gueffroy, as he attempted to cross the border to West Berlin.[42] Still more importantly, the 350,000 Soviet soldiers in the GDR stayed in their barracks. During the mass protests of October and November, one major worry for Gorbachev was that there might be attacks on Soviet troops in East Germany, for that would have made his policy of non-intervention difficult to sustain. This did not happen, and he and his key allies in the Soviet leadership accepted both the fall of the wall and, subsequently, German unification.[43]

Czechoslovakia

Czechs and Slovaks, like East Germans (especially in 1953), had their own experience of Soviet crackdowns. After 1968, a majority of the population felt they had no option but to accommodate themselves to the post-invasion regime. Indeed, Dubček's successor, Gustáv Husák, even attained a measure of popularity in Slovakia. A Slovak himself, he was particularly attentive to Slovak economic interests. But the leadership of the Czechoslovak Communist Party remained acutely conscious that they owed their power to the Soviet military intervention. They feared and eschewed political and economic reform, and kept under tight surveillance the small dissident movement. That became more organized from 1977 with the formation of what was called Charter 77.[44] Operating as an underground organization, producing and distributing *samizdat*, and keeping alive the aspiration to democracy, it brought together former Communists (who had been expelled from the party for their active role in the Prague Spring) and non-Communist activists. The most notable, and subsequently the most renowned, of the latter was the playwright Václav Havel. A number of the Chartists, including Havel, served several terms of imprisonment. Opposing the Husák regime was a hazardous activity, and a majority of the population steered clear of it. Superficial compliance, however, was not to be confused with internal acceptance of the post-1968 Communist order. After the crushing of the Prague Spring, a smaller proportion of the population of Czechoslovakia than at any time since the Second World War actually believed in the merits of a Communist system or in the possibility of significantly improving it. But once bitten, twice shy. One of the 1968 activists who had been expelled from the Communist Party in 1970 gloomily told me in Prague in 1976: 'Nothing will change here until things change in the Soviet Union.'

In essence, he turned out to be absolutely right. It was, however, important that when things did change in the Soviet Union there were people available, notably the Chartists, who had continued to challenge the authority of the Communist state and to think independently and seriously about democratic alternatives. It was from their ranks, modest in numbers but rich in talent, that many of the most important positions in post-Communist Czechoslovakia were filled. Czechs had a reputation in Eastern Europe, especially among Poles and Hungarians, for being cautious, but they had surprised their neighbours in 1968. After Husák succeeded Dubček as leader of the Communist Party of Czechoslovakia in April 1969, Czechoslovakia was returned to a political order akin to that of the late 1950s – not the savagery of the early 1950s or the beginnings of intellectual ferment in the mid-1960s, but a drearily oppressive conservative Communism.[45] For the next twenty years there was an outward calm, but once a majority of the people could be sure that by demanding their democratic rights they were not paving the way for a repeat entry by Soviet tanks, they acted.

The action came from outside the Communist Party, which was left belatedly reacting to events it could not control. Since the several hundred thousand most active reformers had either left the party or had been expelled from it in the aftermath of the Soviet invasion of 1968, few ruling parties had less of a reformist current within them than that of Czechoslovakia on the eve of the regime's overthrow. Husák, while retaining the presidency of the country, had resigned from the party leadership in December 1987. He had been replaced by Miloš Jakeš, one of the Czech politicians who had been in favour of Soviet military intervention in 1968, so hardly an improvement on his predecessor. There were signs of stirring within the Czech population already in 1988, when as many as 400,000 people signed a petition calling for more religious freedom and less state intervention in Church affairs. Indeed, throughout the first half of the 1980s, the Roman Catholic Church (including the aged Cardinal Tomášek), inspired by the Polish pope in the Vatican, displayed a greater independence from the state authorities than hitherto and attracted more worshippers, even though Catholicism was traditionally less strong in the Czech lands than in Slovakia.[46]

Although Gorbachev wished to see reform in Czechoslovakia, he stuck to his policy of non-interference. His old friend Zdeněk Mlynář later reproached him for this, saying that with a Communist Party leadership entrenched in Czechoslovakia thanks to the earlier intervention of Soviet tanks, to tell the Czechs and Slovaks now that they were free to do as they wished, and the Soviet Union would not interfere, was 'like telling a person whose legs have been broken: "Well, come on now, you can go where you want."'[47] One response to a similar complaint was given by Vadim Medvedev, who had been one of Gorbachev's strongest supporters in the Politburo. Interviewed in 1994, he said: 'The memory of our intervention . . . gave rise to such a level of distrust toward us that if we had pronounced ourselves heavily in favour of a given leader, that would have been enough to ensure his failure.'[48] In fact, the Soviet Union did 'interfere' constructively in two respects. At the end of 1988 Yakovlev told the Czechoslovak leaders that they had to stop jamming Radio Free Europe to comply with the Helsinki Final Act. The Communist authorities in Prague were very reluctant to agree. Gorbachev had to weigh in to reinforce this demand. From the beginning of 1989 the jamming ceased, and Havel was among those whose words could henceforth be heard by Czech listeners. The other interference was a strong 'recommendation' from Moscow to the Czechoslovak leadership that they should not use force to quell protests and opposition.[49]

This followed the brutal suppression of a demonstration by students on 17 November 1989. The student protest, and especially the way the authorities had responded to it, set in motion the speedy and peaceful ending of the Communist system. The Civic Forum, in which Havel became the acknowledged leader, was created on 19 November. It represented a broadening of the composition of those who had been active in Charter 77. Among those who joined was Alexander Dubček, who was given a rapturous reception by around a quarter of a million people in Prague's Wenceslas Square when, along with Havel and prime minister Ladislav Adamec (the member of the Communist leadership who was first to realize the way the wind was blowing), he addressed the crowd. Government changes followed thick and fast after this, but the rug was pulled from under the feet of even the more moderate members of the Communist leadership when a Warsaw Pact summit meeting in Moscow in early December declared the invasion of Czechoslovakia in 1968 to have been wrong and illegal.[50] Since every member of the government ultimately owed his position to that intervention, it was no surprise when Adamec resigned as prime minister on 7 December and Husák resigned from the presidency on the 9th. In the same month a predominantly non-Communist government was formed, in which several leading Chartists made dramatic transitions from manual work to high office, none more so than Jiří Dienstbier, who moved from being a stoker to foreign minister. On 28 December Dubček was co opted as Chairman of the Federal Assembly (Speaker of the Parliament), which proceeded the following day to elect Václav Havel President of Czechoslovakia.

In the space of six weeks Czechoslovakia had gone from being an orthodox Communist regime to a democracy. This owed a great deal to the precedents which had already been set elsewhere in Eastern Europe and which emboldened the population to act in a way they had not done since 1968. It clearly owed even more to the changes that had occurred in Moscow. Nevertheless, it was important that citizens had informal leaders they could trust who were able to negotiate with the government – now from a position of strength – and ensure that power passed entirely peacefully from a Communist oligarchy to accountable democrats. Václav Havel famously described the events as a 'velvet revolution'. Rita Klímová, who, interpreting for her friend Havel, was the person who put those words into the English language, had earlier in the year been refused permission by the authorities to come to Britain for a holiday. Havel had just time, before the year ended, to appoint her as Czechoslovak ambassador to the United States.

Bulgaria

The transition from Communist rule began a little earlier in Bulgaria than in Czechoslovakia but was not completed so quickly and dramatically. Repression of the Turkish minority in Bulgaria was one of the triggers of opposition. That opposition was not particularly widespread. It was confined mainly to a small section of the intelligentsia, while the majority of the population kept their distance. An Independent Association for the Defence of Human Rights in Bulgaria was formed in early 1988, just one of a number of civil society associations which began to emerge. The changes, however, got seriously under way with a palace coup. The long-serving Communist leader Todor Zhivkov was deposed on 10 November 1989, one day after the fall of the Berlin Wall. His successor, and the Politburo member who led the revolt against Zhivkov, was Petûr Mladenov. He appeared by the following month to have embraced political pluralism, but in July 1990 he was forced to resign when a video-recording showed him in the previous December advocating the use of tanks against demonstrators.[51] Mladenov was replaced as president by Zheliu Zhelev, an academic philosopher who in mid-November 1989 had emerged as the leader of a grouping of independent organizations which called itself the Union of Democratic Forces (UDF).[52]

The Communist party's leading role was removed from the Bulgarian constitution in early 1990, and in April of that year the party changed its name to Bulgarian Socialist Party (BSP). It was an important moment in transition to democracy when the UDF, very narrowly, defeated the BSP in multi-party parliamentary elections in October 1991. It is hard to pinpoint a precise month when Communism ended in Bulgaria. Moreover, a system ceasing to be Communist is not identical to it becoming a democracy. In the case of the fifteen former republics of the Soviet Union, in particular, a variety of non-Communist authoritarian regimes, some hybrid systems, and only a few democracies emerged. Bulgaria, at any rate, ceased to be Communist in the first half of 1990. In the early months of that year the leading role of the Communist Party disappeared in practice, as well as from the constitution.

Romania

Among the Warsaw Pact countries, only in Romania did Communism end with serious bloodshed. It was not coincidental that this was the state over which the Soviet Union had the least influence. Nicolae Ceauşescu had, over the years, become an increasingly despotic ruler. For a time he was given a lot more credit in Western capitals than he deserved because of the semi-detached position he occupied within the Warsaw Pact and his willingness to take an independent line from Moscow. His standing was highest in the West when Romanian troops did not join the other Warsaw Pact forces in the invasion of Czechoslovakia. In contrast, however, having long argued for the non-interference of one Communist country in the affairs of another (meaning the Soviet Union should not dictate to Romania), he changed his tune in 1989 and at a Warsaw Pact meeting in July 1989 urged intervention in Poland.

Romania in the 1980s was undoubtedly the most internally oppressive of all Warsaw Pact countries. Communist states came in many different forms. Ceauşescu's Romania carried nepotism and personalistic rule to an extreme. Next to him, the most important political figures in the country were his wife, Elena, and his son, Nicu, who was being groomed to succeed him. Relatives occupied key positions in the security police, the Ministry of Defence, the State Planning Commission, and many other major institutions. Ceauşescu remained to his death an admirer of Stalin. The Soviet dictator, however, had never used members of his family as his principal political partners and executants of policy. Ceauşescu's nepotism went so far that, as distinct from Stalin's 'socialism in one country', he was said to have created 'socialism in one family'. It has been aptly observed that while the regime, so long as Ceauşescu headed the party and state, was never less than totalitarian, from the mid-1970s until his death it also became 'increasingly sultanistic'.[53]

Mikhail Gorbachev, in his memoirs, remarks that he had met many ambitious people in his life and that it would be hard to find a major politician who was without ambition and self-belief. However, Ceauşescu's vanity was in a class by itself.[54] His style of rule was such that defiance of the regime was especially difficult and dangerous, but Ceauşescu paid for his isolation from any criticism and for his vain delusions by not seeing the end coming. The sequence of events which led to his overthrow and execution was sparked by the resistance of a highly respected Protestant pastor, Laszlo Tőkés, a member of the Hungarian minority in Romania, who had suffered constant harassment by the *Securitate*. When the secret police tried to evict him from his parish and home in Timişoara on 15 December 1989, thousands of people – ethnic Romanians as well as Hungarians – surrounded his house, defying the security police and triggering a huge anti-Ceauşescu and anti-Communist demonstration. The rebellion continued on 16 and 17 December and was then bloodily put down. The resistance and the ruthless use of force which ended it became known to Romanians from foreign radio. But Ceauşescu fully identified himself with the repression in a televised broadcast on 20 December. He even praised the army and the security police for their 'utmost forbearance' before they took action – which had resulted in a massacre.[55]

Ceauşescu's supreme confidence that he still had all the levers of power in his hands led him to call for a massive demonstration of support on the Palace Square of the Romanian capital, Bucharest, the following day. Although there were many party and state security officials shepherding the crowd, the event – which was shown on television news throughout the world later that day – turned out wholly unexpectedly for Ceauşescu. While he addressed the crowd, cheers turned to boos and the approved chants of 'Ceauşescu and the People' changed to 'Ceauşescu the Dictator'. As Vladimir Tismaneanu observed, power had 'slipped from the balcony of the Central Committee building to the street'.[56] In what was the only violent revolution in Europe of 1989, hundreds of thousands of people took part in anti-Ceauşescu demonstrations on 22 December. The *Securitate* fired on the demonstrators but the army changed sides and helped them to seize the television station. When the Central Committee building was attacked, Nicolae and Elena Ceauşescu took off by helicopter from its roof. They were later caught by the army and accused of 'genocide', based on the false information that around 60,000 people had been killed over the previous few days when the actual figure was around 600.[57] There were enough real crimes for which they could have been convicted without resort to that gross exaggeration, but there was an evident desire by Romania's new aspirant rulers to do away with the Ceauşescus as quickly as possible. In fact, Nicolae and Elena Ceauşescu were executed by firing squad on Christmas Day 1989. Ghoulish though the event was, for many Romanians it seemed like a Christmas present.

It was not so clear whether the speedy end of the Ceauşescus also meant the instant end of Communism in Romania. Power was seized by a self-appointed body, the National Salvation Front (NSF). Whereas the Civic Forum in Czechoslovakia had its deep roots in the opposition movement and especially Charter 77, the NSF came from nowhere. It included some genuine democrats as well as leading Communists, and it seemed that it was the latter who were orchestrating the new politics. Nevertheless, the overthrow of the dictator had changed the entire context of Romanian politics, and from early 1990 there was a plurality of political parties and pressure groups, with students, intellectuals, and the Hungarian ethnic minority especially active.[58] This, then, was hardly a Communist system any longer, although it was not until September 1992 that free elections took place.

Albania

Since the Albanians and Yugoslavs had made their own revolutions independently of the Soviet Union, and since neither country had any reason to worry about possible Soviet military intervention, they were in a different category of Communist state from those which belonged to the Warsaw Pact. They were also very different from each other. Albania had been an extreme example of totalitarian rule under Enver Hoxha, who, however, had died in 1985. His successor, Ramiz Alia, showed no sign of softening Albania's criticism of the Soviet Union, but the country did become slightly less isolated. The end of Communism in most of Eastern Europe could not but, however, have an effect on the populations of both Albania and Yugoslavia, especially Yugoslavia, since it was so much more open to the world. Significant reform had already been carried out in Yugoslavia, and information on developments in the rest of Europe, East and West, was readily available.

Yet the 'domino effect', whereby the United States had feared that one country after another would become Communist in Asia if South Vietnam did, seemed to be much more of a reality in the fall of Communism. Even Albania was not immune to contagion (to change the metaphor) from the rest of Eastern Europe. As so often happens in totalitarian or authoritarian regimes, liberalization led to more radical demands for change rather than dampening down dissent. Several ameliorative measures, including the release of some political prisoners and the beginnings of economic reform, between December 1989 and the summer of 1990 merely stimulated a series of demonstrations and some rioting. There was also pressure on the authorities for citizens to be allowed to leave the country. As had happened with East Germans, foreign embassies were inundated by would-be emigrants, and in late 1990 and early 1991 15,000 people left Albania for Greece and 20,000, often by seizing ships, made their way to Italy.[59] Albania, with its population of only some three million people, was the poorest country in Europe and much of the discontent was economic. Between 1989 and 1992 the country was in acute economic crisis, and this, combined with the example shown by the rest of Eastern Europe, spelled the end of Communism.[60]

Demands for an end to food shortages developed into political demands for an end to the monopoly of power of the Communists and for abolition of the secret police. On 11 December 1990 a party plenum agreed to the legalization of opposition parties, and the very next day a party calling itself the Democratic Party of Albania (DPA) was founded.[61] In the course of 1991, amidst severe social and economic problems, political pluralism developed and the country ceased to be Communist. That was very far from being the end of Albania's problems, but evidence that it had at least left Communist rule behind came with competitive elections held in March 1991. These were, however, held too soon for the new political parties. The successor party to the Communists, the Socialist Party of Albania, gained over 67 per cent of the vote as compared with the Democratic Party's 30 per cent. One year later, in fairer elections, these results were virtually reversed. The DPA won almost 63 per cent of the votes and the Socialist Party just over 25 per cent.[62]

Yugoslavia

Unlike Albania, Yugoslavia had enjoyed elements of political pluralism for some years. Moreover, Yugoslavia had been more open to the world and more decentralized than any other Communist state over a period of several decades. Yet its transition from a watered-down Communist rule became the most catastrophic in Europe. The disintegration of the federal state was accompanied by a succession of civil wars and 'ethnic cleansing'. The calamity-strewn post-Communist experience of a majority of Yugoslavia's successor states is beyond the scope of this volume. I am concerned here only with the end of Communism. It is enough to note that whereas Czechoslovakia's 'velvet revolution' was followed by 'velvet divorce' between the Czech Republic and Slovakia, in Yugoslavia a staggered and uneven transition from Communism was followed by a whole series of conspicuously bloody divorces.

Yet Yugoslavia in the late 1980s in some ways seemed better prepared for life after Communism than countries which had been under the tightest of central controls. A genuinely federal system, combined with the 'socialist market economy', devolved significant power from the centre. Even though in Yugoslavia the Communists were the one legal party (called the League of Communists from 1952), it was sometimes remarked in the 1970s and 1980s that the state had a multi-party system, one for each republic plus the federal party organization.[63] Republican parties, which corresponded broadly with the territories of the major ethnic groups, strove to serve the interests of their own republic. The advantages of political diversity were more than counterbalanced, however, by the disadvantages of extreme inter-republican economic inequalities. There was always latent tension, kept under control so long as Tito was alive, over the distribution of resources among the republics. The richest, Slovenia and Croatia, resented being levelled down to help the poorest, Macedonia and Montenegro, not to mention Kosovo, which had autonomous status within the Serbian republic. No country in Europe had such vast differences in the standard of living between one region and another as had Yugoslavia. This, in conjunction with ethnic tensions, was a time-bomb under the reformed Communist system and the unity of the state. Slovenia had a per capita income six times higher than that of Kosovo. Indeed, the Slovenian income level was three times closer to that of Germany and France than it was to Kosovo's.[64]

By the end of the 1980s, Yugoslavia was bound together neither by ideology (Marxism-Leninism had long lost any appeal) nor by a united Communist party, and ever since Tito's death it had lacked a charismatic leader sufficiently respected to be able to keep inter-republican rivalries and inter-ethnic tensions in check. The most obvious – and most dangerous – alternative source of ideological legitimation was nationalism. That was the path chosen by the Serbian Communist leader Slobodan Milošević. Once he realized that Yugoslavia was highly unlikely to survive in the form of Tito's federation, Milošević set his sights on creating (or recreating) a Greater Serbia. He had become the leader of the Serbian League of Communists in 1987 and had instantly played the nationalist card. He had also encouraged a cult of his own personality, so that when provincial Serbian towns offered him honorary citizenship, this was judged by the official press to be more newsworthy than the fall of the Berlin Wall.[65] Milošević held mass rallies of Serbs in Kosovo and attempted to intimidate the Kosovar (Albanian) majority in that province. His policies were seen elsewhere in Yugoslavia as presaging an attempt to create a Greater Serbia, and this led the most economically advanced of the republics, Slovenia, to be the first to decide to secede. As an initial move in that direction, the reformist Slovene Communists left the federal League of Communists in early 1990.[66] Not only was democratic centralism within the Yugoslav party a dead letter, the party itself was disintegrating, presaging the disintegration of the state.

The transition from Communism took place unevenly throughout the country, but was largely completed in the course of 1990. Only in Slovenia did this mean an almost instant attainment of democracy. Elsewhere the post-Communist regimes were, initially, hybrids at best. Milošević himself fought a competitive election in late 1989 and won almost 90 per cent support in a poll with a high turnout.[67] He used to the full the advantages bestowed by his control of party and state resources, but his combination of nationalist rhetoric and lip-service to socialist ideals garnered broad support in Serbia at that time. The fact that the ballot was genuinely secret and the election contested was in itself a departure from Communist rule. Soon after the election victory the Communists renamed themselves the Socialist Party of Serbia. More conspicuously non-Communist parties were successful in keenly contested elections in Slovenia and Croatia in April and May 1990. In Croatia they brought to power a former Communist who had spent some years in prison for nationalist deviation, Franjo Tudman, who had more in common with Milošević than either man would have liked to think. During his presidency, the Serbs in the part of Croatia known as Krajina were 'ethnically cleansed' in a civil war in which Milošević was not the only national leader to condone atrocities. In authoritarian style of government and self-aggrandizement, there was, moreover, little to choose between Milošević and Tudman.[68] By 1990 Croatia was no longer Communist, but it was only following Tudman's death in 1999 that it was able to complete a transition to democracy. By the end of 1991, all six Yugoslav republics – Serbia, Slovenia, Croatia, Bosnia, Macedonia and Montenegro – had held competitive elections. By December 1991 the whole of Yugoslavia was no longer Communist. It was also no longer Yugoslavia. The federal president (the holder of a post which, after Tito's death, rotated among representatives of the different republics) resigned on the grounds that the state over which he formally presided no longer existed.[69]

The events of 1989 saw the international Communist movement give way to an international de-Communizing movement. The former had been tightly organized, the latter was not, but the transnational influences were no less great. Awareness of the differences between political and economic conditions in Western and Eastern Europe played its part, but that knowledge had been around for some time. What was new in 1989 was the example of democratizing change in the Soviet Union and Soviet tolerance of still more rapid democratization in the Warsaw Pact states. When Spain and Portugal and other conservative authoritarian regimes became democratic in the 1970s, that process had little impact on Eastern Europe. It seemed too remote from the realm of possibility for countries under Communist rule and Soviet hegemony. Each of the eight Communist states (in addition to the Soviet Union) discussed in this chapter had its own distinctive history and culture, but their systems had vital components in common. Once one or two countries had demonstrated that the Communist power-holders were far from invincible, they served as a point of reference for the others. Geographical proximity, the power of example, and a Soviet leadership which, remarkably, had embraced 'freedom to choose' did the rest.

27

The Break-up of the Soviet State

A 'nationalities problem' existed in the Soviet Union long before the 1980s. And it was one taken very seriously by the pre-Gorbachev Soviet leadership. Nationalism was a different way of looking at the world from official Marxism-Leninism, and was a potential threat to the stability of the multi-national Soviet state in the long run. Partly because of this concern, the Communist Party leadership devoted vast resources to promoting a supra-national Soviet identity. Moreover, they encouraged the political police to be ruthless in dealing with any overt manifestations of nationalism. So long as the Soviet party-state remained unreformed, nationalism presented a problem, but it was a containable one.

The mass terror of the 1940s, in which whole nations – among them the Chechens and the Crimean Tatars – as well as tens of thousands of people from the Baltic states were deported from their native lands, showed just how far Stalin was prepared to go. After that, more selective reprisals for any manifestation of nationalist sentiment were sufficient to maintain Soviet-style order. Of the fifteen nations accorded the status of union republics within the USSR, the most disaffected were Estonia, Lithuania and Latvia. Yet after the killings, mass arrests and deportations in these Baltic states in the 1940s, a similar level of extreme punishment was not necessary to secure superficially compliant behaviour even there. As one Estonian post-Communist parliamentarian put it, most people did not think that 'the best way of approaching a wall is to run against it with your head'.[1] Estonians preferred to manoeuvre around the system by, for example, publishing works in Brezhnev's time which could not get past the censorship in Russia. It helped that the Russian censors did not read Estonian and that the Estonian censors were more tolerant than their Russian counterparts. It was, though, in the Baltic republics that overt dissent also flourished more than elsewhere in the Soviet Union, involving a larger proportion of the population. During the Brezhnev era, a Lithuanian underground publication acquired the widest readership of any *samizdat* work in the USSR. This was the *Chronicle of the Lithuanian Catholic Church*, which brought together both religious and nationalist dissent.

Yet even in the Baltic republics, nationalists were, before the advent of perestroika, fighting a defensive battle to preserve as much as possible of distinctively national cultures, and were in no position to pursue dreams of separate statehood. It was the liberalization and partial democratization of the Soviet system which brought independence within the realm of the thinkable by 1989. By 1991 it was unstoppable – other than through a return to a level of coercion which Gorbachev was not prepared to countenance. Perestroika had already by 1988 produced a rise in the general level of political and economic expectations in the Soviet Union. And when the Balts were able to watch on television one East European state after another achieving independence peacefully in the course of 1989, this had a huge impact. It strengthened the hopes and radicalized the aims of those seeking the maximum practicable degree of national autonomy.

If this applied most strongly to Lithuanians, Estonians and Latvians, it encompassed Georgians, Armenians and a substantial minority of the population of Ukraine and Moldova as well. The Soviet republics least interested in independence were those of Central Asia. In all the movements for greater autonomy or outright independence in the perestroika era, national elites, including a section of the political elite, played an important part. In Central Asian republics such as Kazakhstan and Uzbekistan, the elites owed their positions entirely to Soviet power and they were highly secularized. It was not difficult for the party-state authorities to guess that if their republics became independent countries, the official doctrine which would take the place of Marxism-Leninism would be Islam. Central Asian party bosses viewed that prospect with apprehension. As it turned out, most republican first secretaries were able to make quite a seamless transition to becoming rulers of the post-Soviet Central Asian states, but they had no way of knowing in advance that this would be so. Communist rule gave way to an authoritarian post-Communism, in which the rulers paid lip-service to Islam but, especially in Uzbekistan, dealt extremely harshly with radical Islamic elements.

Although the Soviet authorities over the decades took pains – and inflicted pain – in order to prevent nationalism getting out of hand, they also contributed to the strengthening of national consciousness in unintended ways. Illiterate or barely literate peasants, whose focus was on their extended family, immediate community or village, had very little sense of national identity in the earliest years of the Soviet Union. However, a combination of changing social structure, which saw many peasants move into the cities to become urban workers, and an educational system which produced near-universal literacy, altered that. In particular, the rise of a native intelligentsia was important, for intellectuals tend to be the bearers of nationalist ideology.

In Central Asia, where nationalism was weakest, it was the emergent intelligentsia which began to create the kind of national histories and myths which provided its cultural foundation.

Moreover, one of the ways in which the Soviet state had assuaged nationalism was by making national territories the administrative units by which the country was governed. The fifteen nations with union republican status had more institutional resources than the others, but there was a hierarchy of national territories, including so-called autonomous republics (among them Tatarstan and Bashkortostan within the Russian republic) and 'autonomous regions'. None of these administrative units in reality was autonomous, but all accorded some privileges to the nationality after which they were named. The union republics, in particular, provided a number of benefits for the titular nationality. The political recognition and structural supports also raised the national consciousness of many peoples who had very little sense of nationhood prior to the creation of the Soviet Union. That was generally true of the Central Asian republics and of Belarus (Belorussia). It was also largely true of Ukraine.[2] The USSR had, however, peoples with a longer national lineage, the Georgians and Armenians being particular cases in point.[3] In the Soviet period, union republican institutions probably did less to reinforce a Russian sense of nationhood, associated with the territory of the Russian republic, than was the case with the titular nationalities of other republics. On the one hand, Russia had fewer separate institutions than the other union republics. On the other, Russians played such a dominant role in the all-Union structures that they were tempted to see the USSR as a whole as a greater Russia. It was, after all, the successor state to the Russian Empire.[4]

Although the union republics were subordinate to the central authorities in Moscow, their status was envied by nationalities not among the fifteen accorded that level of institutional recognition. *Some* decision-making was devolved to the republican level. And at least as important, the republican institutions provided prestigious *jobs* for those who belonged to the titular nationality. Care, however, was taken by the central organs of the Communist Party, prior to the Gorbachev era, to make sure that these concessions to national sentiment did not lead down a slippery slope to national autonomy. In the post-Stalin period it was usual for the first secretary of the republican party organization to be a national of that republic. But to ensure that the person did not pursue any kind of nationalist agenda, the second secretary, who kept an eye on him (they *were* all men), would be a Russian or Ukrainian. In addition to the republican Central Committee, each union republic had a Council of Ministers, a Supreme Soviet, its own branch of the Academy of Sciences, and support for teaching in the language of the nation in its schools and universities. Russian was the lingua franca of the USSR, so the aim in most republics was bilingualism.

Political institutions, including those of the republics, were crucially important for sustaining the Soviet system and preserving the Soviet state. So long, however, as the most important institution of all was the centralized and strictly disciplined Communist Party, only limited decision-making power was devolved to the republican Councils of Ministers and none of any substance to the rubber-stamp Supreme Soviets in each union republic. Real power within the republic was wielded by the party first secretary, and he in turn was dependent on the support of the all-Union party leadership in Moscow. However, in the course of 1989–90, power at the centre was incrementally moved from the party to state institutions. And at varying speeds this shift in the locus of the preponderance of power occurred also in the republics. Competitive elections in 1989 for the new legislature at the federal level – the Congress of People's Deputies – gave opportunities to citizens in the republics to send to Moscow deputies they thought would advance the interests of their nation. Two major institutional innovations in 1990 – the creation of a Soviet presidency and contested elections for parliaments in the republics of the USSR – were part of the democratization process, but they had the huge unintended consequence of strengthening fissiparous tendencies within the Soviet Union.

The first of these innovations saw Gorbachev chosen in March as President of the Soviet Union. He was elected to that post by the Congress of People's Deputies of the USSR. If he had taken the risk of holding a general election to choose a president, this would have strengthened the chances of preserving at least the greater part of the Soviet Union. Whoever won would then have had the legitimacy conferred through direct election by the country as a whole.[5] The winner would probably have been Gorbachev, whose popularity was in decline but was still in March 1990 ahead of that of the fast-rising Boris Yeltsin, according to the most reliable surveys.[6] The idea of a presidency was, however, copied by the republics. Both Boris Yeltsin in Russia and the first secretary of the Communist Party in Kazakhstan, Nursultan Nazarbaev, cited the creation of a Soviet presidency as a reason for having presidents also in their republics.[7] Without such a precedent, it is doubtful if they would have been able to invent such an office – a major innovation in the part of the world occupied by the Soviet Union. Thus, Yeltsin and the other presidents-to-be indirectly owed those offices to Gorbachev's advisers, among whom Georgy Shakhnazarov was an especially persuasive advocate of a French-style presidency.[8] It was the creation of republican presidencies while the Soviet Union was still in existence which enabled a number of republican first secretaries to survive with comparative ease the

Union's collapse. Their party posts disappeared with the demise of the CPSU, but their presidencies continued.

The second major institutional change that further undermined the unity of the Soviet state was the parliamentary elections in the republics which took place at various times in 1990. When the citizens of the Baltic states went to the polls in February and March, pro-independence candidates were overwhelmingly successful. Lithuania was in the vanguard of this movement. In the election for its new parliament, the nationalist movement, Sajūdis, won 106 out of 114 seats.[9] It proceeded to form a government that actually declared Lithuania to be independent, although that was not recognized at the time either by the Soviet leadership or by most of the outside world. In Georgia, too, elections held as late as October 1990 brought nationalists to power, headed by a former dissident, Zviad Gamsakhurdia, who campaigned on a pro-independence platform and who, once in power, showed scant regard for Georgia's minorities, especially in Abkhazia and South Ossetia. The coming to power of the anti-Communist, anti-Russian Gamsakhurdia, with the backing of other extreme nationalists, led to a sharp reduction in the democratic rights which non-Georgians had begun to enjoy within the republic, thanks to the changes in Moscow.

Russia – Keystone of the Union

Of greatest importance for the future was what happened in Russia. Boris Yeltsin, in a direct election in June 1991, won more votes than his five opponents put together, thus obviating the need for a second round in the presidential election. As President of Russia, he was enormously strengthened in his power struggle with Gorbachev, since the latter had not been elected by the people as a whole. As problems accumulated in the Soviet Union, with no sign of economic improvement, Yeltsin had become increasingly popular as an authoritative figure who had broken with the Communist Party leadership. Within what by 1990–91 was called the democratic opposition, he stood out because he had been a party boss. But that, paradoxically, was part of his attraction for many voters. He had the aura of one who was used to wielding power, and conveyed the image of a strong leader as well as that of a bold critic.

In 1990 a loose organization which called itself Democratic Russia was set up.[10] The specific goals of Democratic Russia as of the first half of 1990 included challenging the authority of the Communist Party, subjecting the KGB to parliamentary scrutiny, creating what at that time they called a 'regulated market economy' (although later, free market ideologues in their ranks were to ridicule Gorbachev for qualifying his support for a market economy with the adjective *regulated*), and, especially important in the present context, achieving the sovereignty of the Russian republic.[11] This movement was partly inspired by the example of Andrei Sakharov, who had died in December 1989. Sakharov, however, had sought the radical reform of the entire Soviet Union and had never thought of separating Russia from developments elsewhere in the USSR. Indeed, few among those who spoke about sovereignty for Russia realized initially that this implied, and was liable to lead to, the dissolution of the Soviet state.[12]

Yet the keystone of the Soviet Union was the Russian republic. Russians made up approximately half the Soviet population (some millions of them living in other republics) and the Russian republic occupied three-quarters of Soviet territory. Thus *a* Union could have survived the loss of the Baltic states and even some others, but the Soviet Union was the successor state to the pre-revolutionary Russian Empire, and the idea of a Union without Russia was too absurd to merit a moment's consideration. Given that the Soviet Union was, in a sense, a greater Russia, and that parts of the Union, such as Crimea (handed over to Ukraine by Khrushchev in a gesture which at the time made little practical difference to anyone), were historically Russian, it could be assumed that a Russian leader would be the last person to wish to break it up. Yet Democratic Russia became the movement which provided organizational support for Boris Yeltsin, and Yeltsin himself became the most influential advocate first of an ill-defined Russian sovereignty, and ultimately of full independence.

The more power Yeltsin attained in Russia, the more he played the Russian card against the all-Union authorities in general and against Gorbachev in particular. While he paid lip-service up to the summer of 1991 to preservation of the Union, his actions played a decisive role in the break-up of the Soviet state. As early as May 1990, Yeltsin asserted the supremacy of Russian law over Soviet law.[13] Both for him and for his ambitious entourage, this was primarily a weapon in the struggle for power with Gorbachev, but it was a significant step on the way to the destruction of the USSR. Whereas Gorbachev was the key initiator and guardian of the liberalization and democratization of the Soviet state, Yeltsin was the politician who did more than any other to bring about that state's disintegration. In post-Soviet Russia, surveys have consistently shown that a majority of Russians regret the break-up of the Soviet Union (though not the demise of Communism), and Gorbachev, as well as Yeltsin, is held responsible for that. It is true that if there had been no liberalization of the Soviet Union, the authorities, as in the past, could have ruthlessly crushed any nationalist demonstration. If there had been no democratization, pro-independence deputies would not have come within a million miles of the corridors of power. In those respects Gorbachev provided the facilitating conditions for the fragmentation of the Soviet Union. Prior to perestroika, any Lithuanian or Georgian who campaigned for independence would have been arrested. And Yeltsin would neither have dreamt of seeking to separate Russia from the USSR nor have been able to take a single step in that direction, had he so wished.

In the 1990 elections for the new Russian parliament – a year before he became Russian president – Yeltsin won an overwhelming victory, just as he had done in the elections for the all-Union legislature in 1989. Standing in 1990 in his native Sverdlovsk rather than Moscow, he received 84 per cent of the votes. Subsequently, he was elected Chairman (Speaker) of the Russian Supreme Soviet at the end of May. From this time on, even before the presidential election of the following year, Yeltsin made himself the principal spokesman for Russia, whose interests he posited against those of the Union. Ever since the electoral campaign of 1989, if not earlier, people had felt a new freedom to voice their grievances in public. By 1990 these had a strong anti-Communist component that was not there before. Most Soviet citizens outside the Baltic states had simply taken the rule of the Communist Party for granted. It had been there all their lives. Their aspirations for change were for a different style of rule, different leaders or different policies rather than a different party. And indeed, even Yeltsin did not offer them an alternative party. He caught the new mood of growing criticism of the CPSU as an institution when he theatrically resigned from the party at the end of a speech to the Twenty-Eighth Congress on 12 July 1990.[14] However, neither then nor later did he join any other party – and political parties were to remain weak organizations in Russia even in the post-Communist period. Yeltsin's support for pro-independence movements in other republics was congenial to many Russian liberals, but for the mass of Russian voters it was his attack on party privilege and economic shortages which had broader appeal.

For conservative Communists in Russia – and they were a majority within the party apparatus at all levels, as well as among party members in the military, the KGB and most of the ministries – the rise of Yeltsin and of the Democratic Russia movement added to the extreme alarm they already felt about the transformation of the political system over which Gorbachev presided. Many of them were more conscious than was Gorbachev of the extent to which the preservation of a Soviet *state* of fifteen republics depended on the controls and coercion which were integral parts of the Communist *system*. They were able to slow down some of the changes which Gorbachev wished to introduce,[15] but not to change the political direction in which he was moving either in domestic or foreign policy. Thus, the conservative opponents of Gorbachev pressed for the creation of a Russian Communist Party, pointing to the fact that Russia was the only one of the fifteen union republics without its republican party organization. Since it was clear that this could become a conservative counterweight to the radical reformists within the all-Union party upper echelons (themselves a minority there, but having the inestimable advantage of the general secretary on their side), Gorbachev resisted the creation of such a Russian party for as long as he could. Yeltsin's becoming Chairman of the Russian Supreme Soviet in May 1990 was for the conservative Communists the last straw. In June a founding conference (which they later termed the First Congress) created a Russian Communist Party. A backward-looking regional party secretary, Ivan Polozkov, was elected its first secretary.

From the summer of 1990 onwards, more openly than before, Gorbachev was under constant attack from two flanks – the conservatives on the one side, and pro-independence nationalists and radical democrats on the other. Dissatisfaction with him and with the all-Union authorities became more widespread because of the state of the economy, in which shortages had become worse rather than better and prices were rising (although nothing like so dramatically as they rose, and were bound to rise, when the state fixing of prices was ended at the beginning of 1992 as the first act of Yeltsin's acting prime minister, Yegor Gaidar). A Gorbachev supporter in the Politburo, and an economist by original profession, Vadim Medvedev, later observed that 1988 was 'the last more-or-less successful year' economically.[16] By 1989–90, the range of basic consumer items in short supply included soap, razor blades, schoolbooks, television sets, refrigerators and washing machines.[17] The hybrid Soviet economy – no longer a functioning command economy, but not yet a market economy – clearly required urgent action. For a brief period, in the summer of 1990, it brought co-operation between the Gorbachev and Yeltsin teams. Economists, equally divided between those linked to Gorbachev and those associated with Yeltsin, but all convinced of the Soviet Union's need to move from a command to a market economy, met together to work out a programme for this transition. The Gorbachev part of the team was headed by Stanislav Shatalin, a long-term advocate of the need for a market mechanism and one of the first members of the CPSU publicly to declare himself to be a social democrat. It included also Nikolay Petrakov, who at the beginning of 1990 had become the first profes- sional economist in Gorbachev's entourage. In the course of that year he persuaded Gorbachev that the Chairman of the Council of Ministers, Nikolay Ryzhkov, was part of the problem rather than of the solution. An econo- mist who was later (as leader of the political party Yabloko) to become a serious critic of Yeltsin and the economic policy of post-Soviet Russia,

Grigory Yavlinsky headed the Yeltsin group in these talks. His team included Russia's future acting prime minister, Gaidar.

The group as a whole achieved a high level of consensus. After working intensively over several weeks in a dacha near Moscow, they produced in August a 239-page document called 'Transition to the Market', plus an accompanying volume of draft legislation which they believed would be required for this process. The main document began by stressing that the group had been established on the joint initiative of Gorbachev and Yeltsin and that its existence was dependent on their 'joint support'. It stated baldly that Soviet society, as a result of many years of the 'dominion of a totalitarian social and political system' was in 'deep crisis'.[18] The document showed not the slightest deference to traditional Soviet ideology and did not once mention the word 'socialism'. It proposed the speedy construction of market institutions, large-scale privatization, and a very substantial devolution of power to the republics. The authors set out a time-scale of 500 days to achieve the breakthrough, and their proposals became known variously as the 'Five Hundred Days Programme', 'the Shatalin–Yavlinsky Plan' or the 'Shatalin Plan' (using the name of the more senior of these economists). Gorbachev read the document several times, interrogated its authors on various points, and was initially extremely enthusiastic. Yeltsin, as even his sympathetic major biographer concedes, did not read as much as a page of the document but, relying (as he often did) on political instinct, endorsed it unreservedly.[19]

Gorbachev's retreat from support for this joint programme put an end to any prospect of collaboration with Yeltsin, although that, in any case, would doubtless have been short-lived. It also sharpened the differences between the all-Union and Russian legislatures. The crucial sticking point for Gorbachev was that he was persuaded that so much power was being devolved to the republics that this would lead to the dissolution of the Soviet Union. To say that he wished to avoid that outcome at *all* costs would be wrong, for he was not prepared to pay the price of systematic coercion and massive bloodshed, which could have crushed separatist movements. Prevention had been easier than cure, and the normal levers of control of the Soviet system had been sufficient before expectations were raised. Now much more violence would have been required, and Gorbachev was not prepared to countenance this. But he was determined, by all means short of that, to preserve the Union.

The Five Hundred Days Programme acquired great political significance, leading to still more polarization. Its economic merits were overstated. The Director of the Institute of Economics of the Academy of Sciences, Leonid Abalkin, was at the time an adviser to Ryzhkov and a leading sceptic about the document his fellow economists had produced. He said that if the Shatalin–Yavlinsky team really could bring the country out of deep economic crisis in five hundred days, he would put up a monument to them and regularly lay flowers at it.[20] One of the members of the team, Yevgeny Yasin, commented some years later on the programme's 'early, loud success with the public and its quiet death on a dusty bookshelf'. He said that such documents had always 'been a tool of politics first and foremost', only later serving the needs of economic reform. 'This', he notes, 'was doubly true of the "500 Days".'[21] Yasin added: 'Gorbachev was put under intense pressure, which he could not resist. Yeltsin did not seem to be very upset by the end of his alliance with Gorbachev, which had raised such high expectations. He clearly saw new political opportunities in Gorbachev's being guilty for the failure of their joint program.'[22]

Flashpoints

If the position of Russia was central to the survival or collapse of the Soviet Union, the flashpoints until 1990–91 were elsewhere. One of the first instances of unrest, partly related to national resentments, was in Kazakhstan in December 1986. Gorbachev had removed the long-serving Brezhnevite first secretary of that republic, Dinmukhamed Kunaev, who had recommended – partly to make mischief, but mainly to prevent his younger rival, Nursultan Nazarbaev, from succeeding him – that a non-Kazakh be appointed to the post. As there was also a desire on the part of the Gorbachev leadership to break up cosy and corrupt networks in Kazakhstan, a Russian, Gennady Kolbin, who had been second secretary in Georgia, was chosen. Those in the Kazakh elite who felt threatened by this could count on the support of young people outraged by the appointment of a non-Kazakh. A demonstration against the choice of Kolbin was forcibly put down, in the manner of the past, with several hundred demonstrators injured and at least two killed. Kolbin, however, held the first secretaryship of Kazakhstan for two and a half years, being replaced by Nazarbaev in June 1989.

Other nationality-related protests occurred in every year of perestroika but with increasing intensity in 1990–91. In 1987, Crimean Tatars who had been exiled from their homeland by Stalin demonstrated in large numbers in Red Square. The Soviet police acted with a restraint never seen in the past, and a nine-person commission under the chairmanship of Gromyko (at that time still Chairman of the Presidium of the Supreme Soviet) was set up to investigate their complaints. A more intractable problem was the disputed land of Nagorno-Karabakh, which was part of the republic of

Azerbaijan but whose population was overwhelmingly Armenian. Both in Nagorno-Karabakh and in the Armenian capital of Yerevan there were insistent demands that the territory be transferred to the jurisdiction of Armenia. This was not, as was the case with the Baltic republics, a dispute between the republics and the centre, but between two neighbouring republics. Gorbachev, a consensus-seeker in such situations, found that no consensus was possible here. Indeed, both Azeris and Armenians before long were blaming the all-Union authorities for being on the side of their opponents. Azeris muttered about the influence of people of Armenian origin in Gorbachev's entourage (among them Shakhnazarov and the economist Aganbegyan, although the latter was only an ad hoc adviser, and not much consulted after 1987). In 1988 a number of Armenians, long-term residents in Azerbaijan, were killed by Azeris, and in response, members of the Azeri minority in Nagorno-Karabakh were killed by Armenians. On Gorbachev's suggestion Yegor Ligachev was dispatched to the Azeri capital, Baku, and Alexander Yakovlev to Yerevan to attempt to pour oil on the troubled waters. The outcome was that the Azeris were left feeling that Ligachev was on their side while the Armenians felt they had Yakovlev's backing. This was one of the issues which had been simmering for decades, but the unreformed Soviet system simply put a lid on it. When the lid was removed by perestroika, everything boiled over.

After the parallel missions of Ligachev and Yakovlev had failed to resolve the dispute, Gorbachev took the more drastic step of putting Nagorno-Karabakh under the direct rule of an official sent from Moscow. The person chosen was Arkady Volsky, a former aide to Andropov who had headed one of the economic departments of the Central Committee. Arriving in Nagorno-Karabakh in July 1988, Volsky spent almost a year and a half there as head of a Committee of Special Administration. He did much to address the grievances of the Armenian population, providing them with access for the first time to Armenian television, facilitating the acquisition of Armenian textbooks and the opening of a theatre presenting Armenian plays, as well as allowing the teaching of Armenian history in schools (which had been disallowed by the Azeri administration). However, when Volsky returned to Moscow in November 1989, the territory reverted to rule by Azerbaijan and continued to be a source of extreme tension between Armenians and Azeris with periodic bloodshed.

The worst violence was in January 1990, when a pogrom of Armenians in Baku caused at least sixty deaths. This led to an exodus of Armenians from the Azeri capital in which they had long constituted a significant minority of the population. (Gorbachev's aide Shakhnazarov – born in Baku in 1924 – was from that community.) The emissary to Azerbaijan chosen on this occasion was Yevgeny Primakov, one of Gorbachev's advisers (who in post-Soviet Russia was to serve as foreign minister and, more briefly, as prime minister). Primakov urged that firm action be taken against the Popular Front of Azerbaijan, a nationalist organization blamed for the murder of the Armenians. The retaliatory measures undertaken by Soviet troops were so harsh that even the official death count was eighty-three, and some Azeri sources claimed that several hundred people had been killed. Of the various occasions when nationalists were suppressed violently, this was the only time when the use of force was explicitly authorized by Gorbachev. He believed that the introduction of troops had been necessary to prevent still more attacks on Armenians, but regretted the extent of the bloodshed.[23] Unfortunately, there is little reason to suppose that those killed by Soviet troops were the same people who had killed the Armenians, and the indiscriminate response turned out to be a stimulus to pro-independence sentiments in Azerbaijan.

A particularly outrageous use of force was applied against peaceful Georgian demonstrators in April 1989. The protesters were overwhelmingly young people who were both supporters of Georgian independence from the Soviet Union and opponents of the secession of Abkhazia. They occupied a central square in the Georgian capital, Tbilisi, over several days, but on the night of 8/9 April they were attacked by Soviet troops and nineteen of the demonstrators (mainly young women) were brutally killed and several hundred others injured.[24] The nature of the crackdown was not only morally repugnant but entirely counterproductive from the standpoint of the central authorities. It gave a huge stimulus to the movement within Georgia for complete independence from the USSR. When the demonstration began, Gorbachev, Shevardnadze and Yakovlev were on a lengthy foreign trip – to Cuba, with a stopover in Britain on the way back. They were met on their return at the airport by a group of Politburo members led by Ligachev. The KGB chairman, Viktor Chebrikov, told them about the prolonged protest in Tbilisi. Gorbachev's response was to say that it must be settled by political means, without violence. He proposed that Shevardnadze, as the former Georgian first secretary and the only Georgian in the Politburo, fly to Tbilisi – along with another Politburo member, Georgy Razumovsky – in order to ensure a peaceful resolution. Shevardnadze, however, after speaking by telephone to his successor as Georgian first secretary, was persuaded that everything was under control and he did not need to come at once. The killings took place that night.[25] Anatoly Sobchak, a prominent democratic deputy in the new Russian legislature, headed a committee of inquiry into what had happened in Tbilisi. Reflecting later on the tragedy, he wrote: 'If Shevardnadze had on 7 April been in Moscow and not in London and if at

night on the 8th he had flown to Georgia, as Gorbachev proposed, the
slaughter in front of the Government building evidently could have been
avoided.'[26]

While Gorbachev, Shevardnadze and Yakovlev were still in London,
Ligachev, standing in for Gorbachev in the Politburo, had authorized the
sending of army and Ministry of Interior units to the Georgian capital. The
decision to use force to disperse the demonstrators was taken by the military commanders on the spot, with the approval of the minister of defence,
Dmitry Yazov. Gorbachev and Shevardnadze were both shocked by the
outcome. Shevardnadze now flew to Tbilisi – but too late. The damage had
been done, not least to the prospect of Georgians being content to remain
part of the Soviet Union. Gorbachev, at a Politburo meeting on 13 April,
said that the Georgian tragedy underlined the need to 'learn to work in
conditions of democracy'. But this was still not understood by Soviet officialdom. 'Our cadres', he said, 'regard political methods as a display of weakness. Force – that's the thing!'[27]

This was borne out in early 1991 in the Baltic states. In the winter
of 1990–91, Gorbachev, having been deserted by many pro-democracy
party intellectuals following the breakdown of his short-lived vicarious co-
operation with Yeltsin in the shape of the Five Hundred Days team of economists, retreated to what he thought was the centre ground. The only time
that he was in the centre of the Soviet political spectrum during the perestroika era was between October 1990 and March 1991. Hitherto he had been
in the vanguard of reform, and he was to attempt to seize the initiative again
in April 1991. But in that winter, weakened on one flank, he depended more
on the other, and made a tactical retreat which left him more vulnerable to
the pressure of the conservative majority within the party-state leadership.
Although it is conceivable that only such a temporary retreat staved off his
overthrow by hard-liners that winter, it was almost certainly a strategic error.

At the time, the Western mass media paid much attention to the criticism of Gorbachev from radical Russian democrats who had broken with
him and become supporters of Yeltsin. They were somewhat less aware
of the intensity of the pressures to which he was being subjected from
the other side. Wearing several hats – President of the USSR, General
Secretary of the Central Committee of the CPSU, and Commander-in-
Chief of the Armed Forces – Gorbachev had, nevertheless, switched his
operating base from the party leadership to the state presidency. The
problem was that this was an office without institutional supports, whereas
the party organization permeated every level of society. Gorbachev now
convened Politburo meetings only once a month instead of weekly, as had
been Soviet practice. At a meeting of the Politburo on 16 November 1990,

he was attacked in a way which showed that the old deference to a general secretary was no longer something he could rely on.[28] There was unanimity that the Presidential Council, an advisory body which Gorbachev had set up and which the Politburo viewed as a rival, should be abolished. In fact, the Presidential Council could not give orders to anyone, but neither now – to their immense chagrin – could the Politburo. Gorbachev rejected most of their demands, but he did wind up the largely ineffective Presidential Council. The Politburo member who now supervised the party organization (and who was to be part of the plot to overthrow Gorbachev less than a year later), Oleg Shenin, said the key question was: 'Are we a ruling party or are we not?'[29] For Shenin the answer was still very clearly in the affirmative. Ivan Polozkov, the First Secretary of the Russian Communist Party, formed earlier that year, told Gorbachev bluntly: 'Your guilt lies in the fact that you do not operate through the party.'[30] Gorbachev agreed that he did not, but far from promising a return to party rule, said the problem was that he did not yet have the presidential structures that would take the place previously occupied by the party.[31]

Several of the Politburo members called for the declaration of a state of emergency. Having failed to persuade Gorbachev to do this in November 1990, they resorted to other means. The actions taken in the Baltic states in January 1991 were aimed at producing that outcome. Sixteen demonstrators were killed by KGB special forces on 13 January in Lithuania, and a week later four people were killed in Latvia. These crackdowns were intended by the KGB, the military, and the conservative majority within the upper echelons of the Communist Party to be just the beginning of a more general crackdown which would put a stop to separatist tendencies and reinstate the leading role of the party. They would have welcomed a violent response from citizens in the Baltic states, since this would have made it easier to press their demand for a state of emergency akin to martial law.[32] The fact, however, that the Lithuanians, Latvians and Estonians resolutely stuck to peaceful means in their pursuit of national independence enabled Gorbachev to put a stop to the use of state violence the day after it occurred in each case.

The countervailing influences – against those of the hard-liners – included liberal opinion in Russia and other Soviet republics. Yeltsin took a strong and courageous line against the use of force in the Baltic states (although several years later he sanctioned the prolonged bombardment of the Chechen capital, Grozny, leaving it looking like Dresden or Stalingrad at the end of World War Two). The United States and other Western countries, which had never recognized the incorporation of the Baltic states in the USSR in the first place, made clear their opposition to the use of force against peaceful

Lithuanian and Latvian demonstrators.[33] Most decisive, though, was Gorbachev's aversion to bloodshed and his political belief that resort to violent repression merely made the task of preserving the Union more intractable. Gorbachev's reluctance to shed blood is emphasized by Alexander Yakovlev, whose portrait of him, in the last book he wrote before his death, is nuanced but far from uncritical.[34] That same trait is deplored by one of the most influential of contemporary hard-line Russian nationalists, Alexander Dugin, who has written that Gorbachev should have been ready 'to kill', continuing: 'The morality of an ordinary person is different from the morality of a ruler . . . Gorbachev did not have the historic right to put an end to the activity of the Warsaw Pact, and he should have exterminated Yeltsin for the breakup of the Soviet Union (if not earlier).'[35] While Dugin expresses the point more extremely, it is a common criticism of Gorbachev in Russia today that he failed to sanction the use of force to prevent the Soviet Union from breaking up.

The Circular Flow of Influence

The amount of force required to impose Communist or any imperial rule is not static. As already noted, it varies according to whether expectations have been aroused or remain low. Even a leadership willing to use all the physical coercion at their command would have found it harder to deal with a concerted effort by many nations to become independent than with one nation at a time. In Eastern Europe in pre-perestroika times I heard people bemoan the fact that the challenges to Soviet hegemony had been mounted singly (whether Hungary in 1956, Czechoslovakia in 1968, or Poland in 1980–81). Co-ordination was, however, impossible. Even if a handful of dissidents, closely monitored by the secret police when they were not in prison, managed to meet, they had little chance of mobilizing populations as a whole. They did not in the pre-perestroika years have access to media of communication that could have provided the possibility of co-ordinating simultaneous defiance of Soviet-imposed rulers.

What happened in the Soviet Union, however, profoundly influenced all the East European countries. Between 1985 and 1988, the growing liberalization in the Soviet Union raised expectations. When the Gorbachev leadership began to implement measures of democratization as well – announced in 1988 and put into effect in the the first half of 1989 with contested elections for the new legislature – this gave new hope to Poles and Hungarians and spread optimism about the prospects for change throughout the continent. With one country after another in the course of the year becoming independent and non-Communist, the flow of influence which had begun in the Soviet Union turned full circle. What was happening in east-central Europe, especially Poland (with the elections in the summer of 1989 which saw the victory of Solidarity), had a huge impact on the Baltic republics of the USSR in particular. While a majority of Estonians, Latvians and Lithuanians had longed for full independence, even the most optimistic of Balts did not dare imagine in 1985 that all three states would be no longer part of the Soviet Union, and no longer Communist, by the end of 1991.

It was of particular significance for the Baltic states that their Scandinavian neighbours had long enjoyed freedom and democracy, combined with an enviably high standard of living. What was happening with *those* neighbours was, however, not new. What *was* new from 1989 onwards was the knowledge that the Soviet armed forces had not been deployed to prevent the Eastern European countries from becoming independent. This raised the distinct possibility that similar restraint might be applied in the cases of Lithuania, Estonia and Latvia. That circular flow of influence – from the Soviet Union to Eastern Europe and back again – was crucially important. If force had been used to quell anti-Communist and pro-independence movements, people within even the most restive of Soviet republics would have drawn the conclusion that it would be applied all the more quickly and decisively in their case. But since Soviet troops had been kept in their barracks, the opposite conclusion was drawn. Two KGB colonels reported to their superiors in Moscow from Vilnius in May 1990 that 'separatist elements have gained the upper hand' and people are saying, 'if the Soviet government could do nothing to prevent the downfall of its socialist allies [in Eastern Europe], why do we have anything to fear?'[36]

Ukraine, the second largest Soviet republic after Russia in population (Kazakhstan was the second largest territorially), was also radicalized by the developments in Eastern Europe. An early stimulus to a more critical attitude to the authorities had been the disaster at the Ukrainian nuclear power station of Chernobyl in 1986. It was, however, only in September 1989, with the dramatic changes in Eastern Europe (especially Ukraine's western neighbour, Poland) well under way, that the People's Movement in Support of Perestroika – Rukh – was formed. *Rukh* means 'movement' in Ukrainian, and later it developed into a movement in support of independent statehood, rather than perestroika. The Polish influence on Rukh was quite direct. A delegation from Solidarity, which a few months earlier had won a parliamentary election in Poland, attended the movement's founding conference. Early in the proceedings Adam Michnik, the most prominent of the Polish delegates, received a rapturous reception for a speech which ended with a resounding 'Long live a free, democratic, and

just Ukraine!' Earlier he had praised perestroika as 'the key to democratization throughout the region' but said it was too soon to rule out a revival
of 'great Russian chauvinism'.[37] At the time, most of the Ukrainian speakers
at the conference opted for 'independence' while attempting to square the
circle by saying that this would be 'within a Soviet federation'. By the
autumn of 1990, when Rukh had become a movement of several hundred
thousand people, its goal was more unambiguously that of independent
statehood. Polish influence was important, although Rukh did not achieve
a comparable level of mass support to that which had been accorded
Solidarity in Poland.[38]

What happened in Eastern Europe in 1989–90 had another effect. It shattered the confidence of many within the Soviet political elite – Russians as
well as officials belonging to other nationalities. The great majority of these
officials had taken for granted that what they called 'socialism' was one of
the two great economic and political systems in the world, and that it was
indestructible. By the mid-1980s, few of them any longer believed that it
would spread into Western Europe, but they were totally unprepared for
its disappearance in Eastern Europe. For many, the response was a backlash against Gorbachev and perestroika. For a few, it led to deathbed conversion to the apparently still more radical alternative being offered in Russia
by Yeltsin. And for a majority, it led to a loss of whatever faith – which had,
in most cases, been an unreflective habit of mind rather than thought-
through conviction – in Marxism-Leninism they had hitherto retained. When
Gorbachev's conservative and hard-line enemies finally took drastic action
against him, their rhetoric spoke of saving Soviet statehood, not the legacy
of Marx and Lenin.

The Coup and the End of the USSR

Gorbachev's tactical retreat in the winter of 1990–91 did not achieve the
result he wanted of strengthening the process of 'revolutionary change by
evolutionary means'. It lost him former friends among the radical reformers
and increased the animosity of conservative Communists and hard-liners in
the military and the KGB. Every attempt the latter had made to undertake
a sustained crackdown on anti-Communist and separatist movements was
stymied within twenty-four hours by Gorbachev's unwillingness to go along
with such plans. The 'opponents of perestroika', Gorbachev later told his
friend Zdeněk Mlynář, had 'wanted to establish a blood bond with me, to
subordinate me to a kind of gangsters' mutual protection society, a situation in which a person is left with nowhere to turn'.[39] In fact, he sought a

way out, first through holding a referendum on whether people wanted a renewed and reformed federation, and second by opening talks with the leaders of whichever republics were willing to attend to discuss the distribution of power. It was aimed at reaching agreement on the kind of federal system the Soviet Union should have in the future, to be formalized in a new, voluntary Union Treaty.

During the winter of 1990–91, however, a number of personnel changes temporarily strengthened the hard-liners. Disturbed by the way things were going domestically, and under severe attack from the Soviet military, Shevardnadze resigned from the post of foreign minister in December 1990, although his replacement Alexander Bessmertnykh, a career diplomat, did not significantly differ in his views from his predecessor. But under pressure from within the state and party structures, Gorbachev replaced the distinctly liberal minister of the interior, Vadim Bakatin, with Boris Pugo, who in August 1991 was to be one of those who mounted the coup against Gorbachev. He also appointed the colourless apparatchik Gennady Yanaev to the new post of vice-president – another poor choice. Gorbachev had assumed that Yanaev, whom he did not know well, would do his bidding, but he too joined the attempted coup against him less than a year later. During this time, Alexander Yakovlev, while retaining his office in the Kremlin, was largely sidelined. He had chosen not to remain on the Politburo, and the advisory Presidential Council, of which he was a member, had been abolished in November 1990.

Gorbachev's zig-zags in 1990–91 have to be understood not only in the context of the polarization of Soviet society but also in the light of his intense desire to preserve the Union. While by this time he had consciously rejected and substantially replaced the Soviet *system* he inherited, the last thing he wanted was to see the disappearance of the Soviet *state*. Accepting that it would be both wrong and counterproductive to attempt to hold it together by force, he began with the March 1991 referendum in which the question posed was: 'Do you believe it essential to preserve the USSR as a renewed federation of equal sovereign republics in which the rights and freedoms of a person of any nationality will be fully guaranteed?' Six republics – Estonia, Latvia, Lithuania, Armenia, Georgia and Moldova – refused to hold the referendum. By going ahead with the vote without them, Gorbachev was implicitly accepting the possibility that some republics might secede. The right of secession was actually incorporated in the Soviet constitution and had been there since Stalin's time. Until the perestroika era, however, any attempt to exercise it would have been a short step towards execution or, at best, long years in the Gulag. The percentage answering 'yes' in the referendum did not fall below 70 per cent in any of the republics, including Ukraine, which posed the question. Over 80 per cent of the total adult population of the Soviet Union voted. It still seemed possible, therefore, that a union, smaller than before and with far more power devolved to the republics, might be preserved.

When in April 1991 Gorbachev launched what became known as the Novo-Ogarevo process, named after the country residence in which the talks took place, to hammer out a new and voluntary Union Treaty, the same nine republics, including Russia and Ukraine, took part. The negotiations left the Communist Party, including the Politburo, out in the cold. Gorbachev's latest zig-zag alienated still further those who viewed with growing alarm the future of the Soviet Union, the more so because many hitherto federal powers were being ceded to the republics. These were demanded by Yeltsin, in particular, but also by the Ukrainian leader Leonid Kravchuk, a former party ideologue who, very late in the day, but with some success, was busy reinventing himself as a champion of the Ukrainian national cause. Yeltsin's overwhelming victory in the June 1991 presidential election in Russia strengthened his hand immensely in the negotiations. If this Union Treaty had been signed and implemented, Gorbachev's position would have been more akin to that of the president of the European Union than to the presidency of a unified state. In the draft treaty, the initials of the state, which was becoming a loose federation, were to remain USSR, but instead of standing for Union of Soviet Socialist Republics, it now stood for the Union of Soviet Sovereign Republics.[40]

Gorbachev – who believed that as a result of patient negotiation he had achieved a modus vivendi with the leaders of the republics and sidelined his hard-line critics – went on vacation to his presidential holiday home in Foros on the Crimean coast in early August. The plan was that he would return to Moscow in time for the signing of the Union Treaty on 20 August. Although most of the essentials of the Soviet system had changed since 1985, one thing which had not changed was that it was dangerous to be away from Moscow at a time when highly placed enemies wished to remove you. Gorbachev was not aware of the extent to which hostility to the whole turn perestroika had taken – democratization and its unintended consequences – was shared by people in high positions, many of whom were in those offices because he had appointed them.

On 18 August, Gorbachev's residence and those immediately adjacent were surrounded and he and his family were put under house arrest. Along with Gorbachev were his wife Raisa, daughter Irina, his son-in-law, and his two young granddaughters. A number of members of his staff were also forbidden to leave the complex, among them Chernyaev, who had been assisting Gorbachev with an article he was to publish imminently and with the speech he would deliver at the initialling of the Union Treaty on 20 August. In the article, which was a ringing defence of democratization, political pluralism, and also movement to a market economy, Gorbachev wrote:

> The introduction of a state of emergency, in which even some supporters of perestroika, not to mention those who preach the ideology of dictatorship, see a way out of the crisis, would be a fatal move and the way to civil war. Frankly speaking, behind the appeals for a state of emergency it is not difficult sometimes to detect a search for a return to the political system that existed in the pre-perestroika period.[41]

The timing of the attempted coup was determined by the need to prevent the Union Treaty being signed. Those who set out to reimpose a pre-perestroika 'order' believed that the treaty so weakened the central government that this was their last chance to prevent a slide into disintegration of the Union. They were later to accuse Gorbachev of having been at best indecisive and at worst a traitor. However, their own indecisiveness and general incompetence led to their putsch collapsing within three days. Moreover, in their folly they greatly hastened the outcome – the collapse of the Soviet Union – which they wished, above all, to avoid. In one sense this was not a 'putsch', for those who attempted to take over the reins of state power were already holding all the crucial offices of state – except one, the presidency. Those involved in the conspiracy against Gorbachev included Vice-President Gennady Yanaev (who, with trembling hands, announced at a news conference that he was now the acting president), Prime Minister Valentin Pavlov (who had succeeded Ryzhkov at the beginning of that year), KGB Chairman Vladimir Kryuchkov, Minister of Defence Dmitry Yazov, Minister of the Interior Boris Pugo, Politburo member and secretary of the Central Committee in charge of the party organization Oleg Shenin, and the Deputy Chairman (to Gorbachev) of the Defence Council Oleg Baklanov. What the affiliations show is that this was not simply a group of individual malcontents, but people representing the most powerful institutional interests in the country. They had, nevertheless, not been able through persuasion and normal political processes to bend Gorbachev to their will. They now hoped that when they presented him with a fait accompli, they would be able to persuade him – 'temporarily', as they dishonestly suggested – to hand over power to a self-appointed State Committee for the State of Emergency.

Among those who were intimately involved in their plans was Anatoly Lukyanov, who had succeeded Gorbachev as Chairman of the Supreme Soviet of the USSR when Gorbachev became president. Lukyanov and

Gorbachev were not friends, but they had known each other ever since they overlapped as students in the law faculty of Moscow University. An even worse betrayal from Gorbachev's point of view was that of his chief-of-staff, Valery Boldin, who had become one of his aides a decade earlier. The first Gorbachev knew of the plot was when he was told by his head bodyguard that a group of people had arrived and had demanded to see him. He asked how they had been allowed to gain entry, and was told that General Plekhanov was with them. Yury Plekhanov was the head of the Ninth Department of the KGB with overall responsibility for the security of the Soviet leadership. He, of course, was a party to the coup.

The group which Plekhanov led into Gorbachev's office at Foros – in the hope of persuading, or intimidating, him to hand over his powers – consisted of Shenin, Baklanov, Boldin and army general Valentin Varennikov, the hard-line commander of Soviet ground forces who had been in charge of the troops in Vilnius when the January killings occurred. It was he who, of all Gorbachev's uninvited guests, adopted the most aggressive tone and demanded his resignation as president. 'At the end of the conversation,' Gorbachev related shortly afterwards, 'using the strongest language that the Russians always use in such circumstances, I told them where to go.'[42] Indeed, Varennikov, when he was being interrogated by the legal investigator of his case, following his arrest and that of his co-conspirators after the coup had failed, saw fit to complain that Gorbachev had used 'unparliamentary expressions' when addressing him and the other members of the delegation.[43]

Baklanov told Gorbachev that Yeltsin had already been arrested, and then amended that by saying he would be arrested before long. However, Lukyanov, who had promised to provide legal cover for the coup at a meeting of the USSR Supreme Soviet on 26 August, persuaded Kryuchkov to revoke the order for Yeltsin's arrest and adopt a 'wait-and-see position' so far as the Russian president was concerned.[44] That was just one example of the plotters' indecision. It was also a monumental error from their point of view. Apart from Gorbachev and those under house arrest along with him at Foros, the rest of the country, including Yeltsin, woke up only the next morning to the news that a State Committee for the State of Emergency had taken control of the country. Kryuchkov telephoned Yeltsin at his dacha and, doubtless hoping that his animosity to Gorbachev would count for something, tried to persuade him to co-operate, but to no avail. Yeltsin was allowed to make his way unhindered to the Moscow White House, the home at that time of the Russian parliament.[45]

Yeltsin immediately became the focal point of resistance to the coup. With neither the Commander-in-Chief of the Armed Forces, Gorbachev, nor the elected President of Russia endorsing the sudden change of government, senior army officers were themselves divided, as was, to a lesser extent, the KGB. Yeltsin's political instincts served him well when he strode out of the White House, mounted one of the tanks beside the building, and presented a picture of defiance to the putschists which went round the world. He urged 'the unity of the Soviet Union and the unity of Russia', and said that the illegal and immoral action by the self-appointed State Committee would 'return us to the epoch of the Cold War and the isolation of the Soviet Union from the world community'.[46] The plotters had failed to cut off all the White House's communications with the outside world, and those inside the building were able to give interviews to foreign journalists (although the Soviet media had been promptly censored). Yeltsin was able to speak by telephone to leaders of Western countries, including President George H.W. Bush. The first head of government to call him was the British prime minister John Major.[47]

Some Western leaders assumed that the 'new government' would be there to stay. With the military, KGB and Ministry of Interior chiefs on board, they reckoned that the game was up for those who had tried to transform the Soviet political system. Almost all Soviet ambassadors made the same assumption, as did the heads of a majority of the Soviet republics. In Ukraine, Kravchuk, who received a visit from General Varennikov, promptly caved in – and in the aftermath of the failed coup had to work harder than ever in his reinvention of himself as a national liberator and democrat. It may have been just as well for Yeltsin that Varennikov had been sent first to Foros and then to Kiev, for had he been in Moscow, it is likely that he would not have hesitated to give orders to troops to use their weapons. In the course of the few days the coup lasted, several hundred thousand Moscow citizens surrounded the White House, thus raising the political stakes of any storming of the building. Nevertheless, they could not, in any sense, defend it, and if the leaders of the coup had followed the logic of their initial action, Yeltsin and those who stood with him in the White House could have been arrested.

The coup lasted only three days. Ironically, since one of the main objections to Gorbachev had been his unwillingness to use force to bring recalcitrant separatists into line, the putschists lost because they too hesitated to use the weaponry they commanded. Three young people were killed by the military in Moscow during the short-lived putsch, but accidentally. Tanks left the Moscow streets on 21 August, and that same day a delegation from the Russian parliament, together with two Gorbachev allies, Primakov and Bakatin, flew to Foros to see the Soviet president. The coup plotters had announced to the world that Gorbachev was too ill to continue to perform his duties. In fact he was in robust health, but the strain had a severe effect on his wife, Raisa. When she heard by radio that the coup leaders were also flying to Foros to meet with Gorbachev, she feared that their intention was to do something that would reduce her husband's health to the state they had claimed it was in. She herself suffered a partial stroke, and over the next two years her health was impaired.

Since Gorbachev's resistance to the putsch had been hidden from the world, and Yeltsin's had been broadcast worldwide, including latterly in the Soviet Union itself, he was the major victor of the botched coup. He was quick to seize the advantage. In Gorbachev's presence, at the Russian parliament on 23 August, Yeltsin suspended the activity of the Communist Party in the Russian republic. Before the end of the month the CPSU, with Gorbachev's acquiescence, had been disbanded. That the party which Lenin founded no longer existed was a dramatic turn of events. The very fact, however, that senior party officials had to involve themselves in an attempt to seize state power by force underlined the point that the party's 'leading role' had already been taken away from it. Gorbachev, more politically weakened than he realized immediately after his return to Moscow, was soon increasingly willing to co-operate with Yeltsin in order to secure a Union Treaty, but Yeltsin had lost interest in sharing power with him for any longer than he could help. That their relationship deteriorated was partly due to personal factors. The way Shakhnazarov put it was to say that 'magnanimity is not in the character of Yeltsin and humility is not in the character of Gorbachev'.[48] The whole political context had, however, changed. Leaders of the most pro-independence republics, conscious of how close things had come to reversal to an extremely authoritarian regime – which in order to *reimpose* a pre-perestroika order would have had to be harsher than Brezhnev's rule – seized the opportunity to declare independence. This time it was recognized both in Moscow and internationally. The independence of the three Baltic states was accepted on 6 September and that of Armenia four days later. Georgia and Moldova insisted that they already were independent.

Gorbachev – with Bakatin back in the government as Chairman of the KGB, tasked with cutting it down to size, with Shevardnadze returning as late as November 1991 as foreign minister, and with the leading putschists in prison – succeeded in getting the Novo-Ogarevo process reinstated. However, he ran up against maximalist demands from Yeltsin and now Kravchuk, the latter compensating for his pusillanimity at the time of the coup. Gorbachev and those who, along with him, strove to preserve – or rather create – a union on the lines of the European Union seemed to make some headway, but through massive concessions. The USSR was now to become the USS – the Union of Sovereign States – and was to be a confederation rather than even a loose federation, with the member states calling the shots. A major blow against even that kind of union was struck when

Ukraine held a referendum on independence on 1 December. Whereas three-quarters of the Ukrainian electorate had voted for a 'renewed federation' in March 1991, 90 per cent now opted for independence.

The ultimate nail in the coffin of the Soviet Union was hammered home by the leaders of the three Slavic republics – Yeltsin, Kravchuk and their Belorussian counterpart Stanislav Shushkevich. Meeting in Belarus on 8 December, they announced that the Soviet Union was ceasing to exist and that they were going to create in its place a Commonwealth of Independent States. (Such a body was established but it was not destined to attain much institutional substance or political significance.) In the months following the coup, Gorbachev and Yeltsin had been sharing the Kremlin, and, like 'dual power' in 1917, this 'dual tenancy' was to be short-lived. For Yeltsin, the fact that no union meant no Gorbachev in the Kremlin was not the least of the advantages of winding up a state which in one form or another had existed for centuries.

Most Western countries had not favoured the break-up of the Soviet Union, making an exception only for the independence of the Baltic states. There was much apprehension that the dissolution of the USSR would be followed by civil wars and possibly a loss of control over nuclear weapons. Moreover, Gorbachev had earned a lot of goodwill with his Western counterparts for his role in ending the Cold War and facilitating the independence of the countries of Eastern Europe. For him there was a clear distinction between those states discarding Soviet tutelage and the disintegration of the state into which he had been born. Brezhnev, as we have seen in an earlier chapter, feared that he might be ousted if one Warsaw Pact country, Czechoslovakia, were to get away with pursuing a more democratic course (while not even threatening to leave the Warsaw Pact). Gorbachev had, in the eyes of his conservative Soviet critics, 'lost' the whole of Eastern Europe. It is hardly surprising that he doubted whether he could politically survive losing parts of the Soviet state. He was guided, however, by conviction and emotion as well as expediency. For him, the way ahead lay in the voluntary association of peoples and acknowledgement of their interdependence. The European Union came to appear an increasingly pertinent example. Emotionally, like many Russians (and not a few Ukrainians), he found it hard to envisage the separation of Russia and Ukraine. He himself was of partly Ukrainian descent and his wife was half-Ukrainian. He had to bow, however, to what was now the inevitable. At a meeting in the Kazakhstan capital, Almaty, on 21 December 1991, to which Gorbachev was not invited, the heads of the Soviet republics willing to join the Commonwealth of Independent States declared that the Soviet Union would cease to exist at the end of that month. In a televised farewell broadcast from the Kremlin on 25 December, Gorbachev said that although he favoured 'sovereignty' of the republics, he could not support the complete dismemberment of the Soviet Union – actions which had not been ratified either constitutionally or by popular vote (in Russia at least).

In fact, at that time – and only then – the most reliable surveys showed a majority of Russians in favour of Russian 'independence'. If a union, smaller than before, could have been held together by consent, there was no reason why that should be considered a less democratic outcome than the emergence of fifteen separate states. (And indeed, at least half of them were before very long less democratic than they had been in the final years of the Soviet Union.) To treat as absolute the right of every nation to self-determination is an inadequate formula, for within virtually every 'nation-state', and certainly within the Soviet successor states, there were national minorities which could make such a claim on their own behalf. In a number of cases, such as the Abkhaz and South Ossetians in Georgia, they did.

While deeply regretting the loss of the Union, Gorbachev was able, on the positive side, in his farewell broadcast to claim that the society 'had been freed politically and spiritually', that the Cold War had been ended and the 'threat of world war removed'. He added: 'We opened ourselves up to the rest of the world, renounced interference in the affairs of others, and the use of troops beyond our borders. In response, we have gained trust, solidarity and respect.'[49] That renunciation of the use of force both in Eastern Europe and within the Soviet borders also, however, contributed greatly to the dissolution of the Soviet state. The break-up of the USSR was further hastened by Yeltsin's ultimate unwillingness to share power in any kind of union. Russia, for better or worse, had been at the heart of the Soviet Union and Russians had been the dominant nationality within the political system both pre-perestroika (though Stalin, of course, was a Georgian) and during it. As the Soviet Union's principal successor state, the Russian Federation was granted the permanent seat on the UN Security Council which had been occupied by the USSR. Russia was now a smaller state than it had been since the eighteenth century, although it remained the largest country on earth.

28

Why Did Communism Last so Long?

The main, though not exclusive, answer to the question of why Communism lasted so long in most European countries lay in the political resolve and military power of the USSR. Soviet leaders, until the late 1980s, were determined to sustain the Communist systems they had created or helped to create. Even in Albania and Yugoslavia, where Communism was not Soviet-imposed, the example of the party-state, developed in the USSR, was hugely influential. And every other European Communist state would have broken with Communism earlier had it not been for Soviet overlordship. Stark reminders of this reality were issued from time to time, whether in East Germany in 1953, Hungary in 1956 or Czechoslovakia in 1968. That is not to imply there were no internal sources of stability within the East European Communist states. Although, however, policies and institutions which kept the Soviet Union itself quiescent operated in Eastern Europe too, on their own they were not enough. To the extent that the regimes were deemed a foreign imposition, they were not sustainable without Soviet support. That leads naturally to the question: why did Communism survive in the Soviet Union itself for over seventy years?

In the first place there was the effectiveness of Communist institutions as instruments of social and political control. The Communist party had a presence in every substantial workplace, as did the security police, although the latter were less identifiable. In normal times the party was strictly disciplined and had a clearly defined hierarchy, with vast power concentrated in the apparatus of the Central Committee and its inner leadership – the party leader, the Politburo and the secretariat. The Department of Propaganda of the Central Committee oversaw television and radio, newspapers, journals and the book trade, and the propaganda work of both party and state institutions. There was a system of censorship with many layers. At its crudest it involved the jamming of foreign radio. Domestic television and radio were especially carefully controlled. A British television newsreader complained some years ago about having to read out too much gloomy news on the TV bulletins. That was not a problem for his Soviet and East

European counterparts, other than when they were reporting the latest calamities in the West. Domestically, until the era of glasnost, they were able to record one success after another, often accompanied by pictures of cheerful factory workers or smiling milkmaids. Newspapers, journals and books were subject to an official censorship, called Glavlit in the Soviet Union (although even to mention in print the existence of the censorship was in itself an offence – divulging a state secret). But most of the censorship was done by editors and authors themselves. They knew the limits of the possible – somewhat broader in small-circulation specialist books than they were in mass-circulation newspapers – and self-censored their work accordingly. Some writers were skilful at stretching the limits of the possible, but for the most part the system worked to keep ideas dangerous to the system from being expressed – or, if expressed, done so in such an Aesopian way that normally only someone who already shared such unorthodox ideas would spot the allusion.

In Stalin's time, and even after it, the censorship ensured that people could become 'unpersoned'. Thus, for example, a volume of the Great Soviet Encyclopedia including the letter 'Z' (which comes quite early in the Cyrillic alphabet) was already in the press when the distinguished medical scientist Vladimir Zelenin was arrested as part of the fabricated 'doctors' plot' in 1952. With time at a premium, he was replaced by a short entry on the zelenaya lyagushka (the green frog) – thus, as Alec Nove observed, 'providing the only known instance of a professor actually turning into a frog'.[1] (Along with the other doctors, Zelenin was released from prison after Stalin's death, and appeared in the 1972 volume of the third edition of the Great Soviet Encyclopedia at the expense of the frog.) When Beria was arrested in 1953, his entry was already in print in the second edition of this major Soviet encyclopedia. Accordingly, all its subscribers were sent a replacement entry on the Bering Straits and instructed to cut out the Beria biography and replace it with a lengthy disquisition on that sea.[2] While such exclusion of people who had played an important part, for better or worse, in Soviet history was, naturally, a source of dissatisfaction for those who thought for themselves in the USSR, the censorship remained one of the pillars on which Communist states rested.

The system had a sophisticated array of rewards and punishments. In the early stages of Communist rule – and, of course, at the time of high Stalinism – arrests on a massive scale, accompanied by executions, produced a reign of terror. However, in 'normal' Communist times, most citizens did not have to worry about a knock on the door in the middle of the night. They understood the rules of the game and adjusted their behaviour accordingly. Everyone's employment prospects depended on not falling foul of the party-state. One of the most brilliant scholars I knew worked in a difficult speciality whose research was incomprehensible to the party-state authorities and did not impinge on ideology. In the mid-1970s, however, he found himself demoted from being a lecturer with a salary of 280 roubles a month to junior scientific worker with a monthly salary of 185 roubles. (The rouble at that time was worth slightly more than a dollar, according to the official exchange rate – very much less than a dollar on the black market.) The demotion was for political reasons. The scholar did not hide from his friends his view that everything that was wrong about the Soviet Union began not with Stalin, but with Lenin. Although he did not seek to broadcast his arguments, even in *samizdat*, not only his friends but also the KGB – which had, of course, a presence in his workplace – were well aware of what he thought. He also had foreign friends, and they included people whom he had no particular professional reason (or excuse) to meet. This was Brezhnev's time, so for critical views expressed in a circle of friends, both Soviet and foreign, you did not – as in the Stalin era – enter the Gulag. But control over careers was an effective enough sanction. The risk of losing your job was a bigger disincentive to nonconformity than the threat of a warning from the KGB (although that was also not to be taken lightly). There were, however, people – my friend among them – who accepted career setbacks as a price worth paying for their intellectual autonomy. Naturally, he never joined the Communist Party.

Among those who did join the party, there were some who went a step further than speaking critically in private and wrote letters to the party leader or to the Central Committee to complain about decisions already taken, such as, to take a concrete example, the exile of Academician Sakharov from Moscow in 1980. If, as was often the case, someone had a job in a research institute and also a teaching post at a university, he or she would keep the first post but lose the second. Since such people should clearly not be allowed to influence the young, their university job would come to an abrupt end, thereby depriving them of half their income. Such a person would also find it difficult, if not impossible, to have his or her writings accepted for publication. There was a long ladder of recognition and retribution. The next rung down was expulsion from the Communist Party (and it was much better never to have joined the party than to carry the stigma of having been expelled), followed by dismissal from the one remaining job.

For overt dissidents, people who persistently challenged the authorities, the penalties could be much more severe, ranging from imprisonment to the incarceration of perfectly sane people in psychiatric hospitals.[3] But open dissidents, in the Soviet Union at least, were a tiny proportion of the population. Most people in the post-Stalin era had no need to fear such drastic punishment. Under Stalin, you could find yourself in the Gulag by accident or through anonymous denunciation. In later years it was necessary actually to do something to incur the wrath of the authorities, even if that something were the kind of opposition or dissent which would be perfectly legal in a democracy. The more successful people were within a Communist state, the more, naturally, they had to lose. Those on the *nomenklatura* would, for example, lose their access to the special stores which sold goods and foodstuffs in short supply in the ordinary shops, and have to start queuing along with everyone else at the woefully inadequate retail outlets. Yet almost everyone could be made worse off than they already were, even without being brought before the courts. Should matters go *that* far, there was no such thing as an independent court of law, especially in political cases. The verdict was determined not by the judiciary but by the executive – the party-state authorities.

The censorship in the Soviet Union was sufficiently effective for most of the seven decades that a majority of people were unaware of just how much better provisioned than their own were the welfare states of Scandinavia and Western Europe. They noticed, however, improvements over time in Soviet housing, the health service, working conditions, and educational levels. And comparisons over time were more conducive to support for the system than comparisons with 'abroad'. Education was one area in which Communist states, and the Soviet Union quite notably, did not have to fear comparison with the rest of the world. That education had its limitations, especially the ideological constraints which operated in the social sciences and humanities and prevented the dissemination of knowledge familiar in the West, but most of the European Communist countries had highly literate and numerate societies. The Soviet Union shone, in particular, in mathematics, the natural sciences and engineering.

Many talented people who would have been equally at home in a variety of disciplines deliberately chose the 'hard sciences' because in those fields there were few constraints on their intellectual freedom. They might only exceptionally be able to travel abroad to meet their Western counterparts, but they had access to the most advanced thought in their fields, no matter where it came from. In the major Soviet libraries in the post-Stalin era, a variety of Western scientific journals were on open shelves, but their social science or modern history equivalents were in closed sections, especially if they carried articles on the Soviet Union. A very good reason for gaining access to them would be for work on a book delineating the offences of 'so-called "Sovietologists"' or of 'bourgeois falsificators', whether of the Soviet political system or of the October Revolution. Some of those who read these Western works were doubtless filled with righteous indignation.

Others found more to agree than to disagree with in the writings of some of the 'bourgeois falsificators' and contrived to provide interesting quotations from them in their published critiques. Yet the lack of access in the Soviet Union, other than by trusted specialists, to the vast literature which exposed the limitations of Marxism-Leninism and of the Soviet system (including, not least, that written by Russians but published only abroad) helped to prolong the Soviet system. It followed that when that dam was breached in the second half of the 1980s, the resulting torrent helped to sweep away what perestroika had left of the system's foundations.

The Language of Politics

A major source of stability of the Communist system lay in its control over the language of politics. In every country there is a difference between official discourse and the way people speak in everyday conversation. The gap was especially great in Communist states. Yet the way concepts had been defined, and hammered home, by the party authorities often affected people's thinking more than they realized. This was especially so in the Soviet Union, where a long-established Communist system had developed indigenously. It was far less true of Poland, where the society had retained more autonomy from the state, and, informally, the Catholic Church possessed much more authority than the Communist party. However, most people in most Communist states accepted the word of their rulers that they were living under 'socialism', even though West European socialist parties – which, in contrast with the East European Communist parties, had extensive experience of winning popular elections – viewed such a claim on behalf of one-party police states as absurd. No Western creative writer was more devastating in his portrayal of Communism than George Orwell.[4] Yet Orwell to the end of his life regarded himself as a 'democratic Socialist', even to the extent of habitually using the capital 'S'.*

* Bernard Crick cites Orwell writing, shortly before his death in 1950, about his book *Nineteen Eighty-Four*: 'My recent novel is NOT intended as an attack on Socialism or on the British Labour Party (of which I am a supporter) but as a show-up of the perversions to which a centralized economy is liable and which have already been partly realized in Communism and Fascism . . . I believe also that totalitarian ideas have taken root in the minds of intellectuals everywhere, and I have tried to draw these ideas out to their logical consequences' (Crick, *George Orwell: A Life*, p. 569).

An example of the skilful use of language in defence of the system was the way the term 'anti-Soviet' was employed in the Soviet Union. Criticism of the system was equated with disloyalty to the motherland. While it would seem to be perfectly obvious that a Russian should not be judged unpatriotic for wishing to see his or her country enjoy more democracy, a different and more efficient type of economy, or a more honest examination of its history, any such demand in the unreformed Soviet system was more often than not deemed 'anti-Soviet'. Thus, for example, Sakharov and Solzhenitsyn – whose ways of looking at the world differed greatly from each other as well as from the official Soviet worldview, but who were each Russian patriots – were both in the 1970s and the first half of the 1980s denounced as 'anti-Soviet'. In the sense of being opposed to many fundamental features of the Soviet system, they *were* anti-Soviet, but the term was turned by the authorities into something akin to treason. The equation of criticism of the existing political order with disloyalty to one's country is a stratagem that has been employed by the powers-that-be in many states, but it was used especially effectively in Communist systems. Given that the term 'anti-Soviet' had the connotation of betrayal of one's country, it is hardly surprising that most Soviet citizens, not least Russians, had psychological as well as political reasons for wishing to avoid the epithet being applied to them.

The official vocabulary of politics permeated the thinking even of people who had in many respects liberated themselves from it. I recall, by way of example, a conversation from Moscow of the Brezhnev era. It took place in the late 1960s when several people were discussing a spat between the Soviet authorities and the British newspaper *The Observer*. The subject arose because it was in the apartment of Nelya Yevdokimova, who had translated Michael Frayn's novel *The Tin Men*, and Frayn wrote for *The Observer* at the time. A former husband of the translator, a *Pravda* journalist, was present. Somewhat puzzled by the stand-off between the authorities and this particular paper, Yevdokimova said: 'But I thought *The Observer* was a progressive newspaper?' 'Yes,' the *Pravda* man replied, 'progressive and anti-Soviet.' Nelya laughed and said she had never heard the expression 'progressive and anti-Soviet' before. Even she, who had read Solzhenitsyn and many other authors in *samizdat*, and who told me that she regarded Britain and the Scandinavian countries as the most democratic in the world, had a mental association of the Soviet Union with progressive forces. The juxtaposition of 'progressive' and 'anti-Soviet' was funny in both senses – strange and amusing. (Her parents must have been true Bolshevik believers. 'Nelya' was the diminutive of her first name, 'Ninel', and the latter was Lenin written backwards – one of a number of new names for the new times invented in the first decades of Communist rule.)[5]

Informal Rules of the Game

Communist institutions, of huge importance as they were in maintaining
control over the society, were supplemented by informal rules of the game
which enabled the polity, society and the economy to function in ways which
the formal rules alone could not achieve. To take the most obvious political example, the *nomenklatura* meant that an appointment of political consequence required the approval of the appropriate party committee, whether
city, regional or Central Committee, but this formal requirement was modified in practice by the existence of patron–client relations. Thus, as a party
official rose in the hierarchy, he tended to bring with him, or to promote
in other ways, loyal subordinates from his previous posting. Even Stalin,
whose purges spared no republic, had more people from the Caucasus in
high positions in Moscow than were there by Andropov's time. Khrushchev
advanced people who had been his clients in Ukraine, and Brezhnev, who
had served in Ukraine, Kazakhstan and Moldova, promoted men who had
served him in all three of those Soviet republics. Cronyism was frequently
condemned in Soviet writing, and it could easily – and often did – lead to
corruption. Nevertheless, personal and group loyalties softened the rigid-
ities of the system, while also in the long run undermining the ideology.

To make a non-market economy work and to obtain goods and services
in conditions of perennial shortage required further informal rules of the
game. Three key Russian words for understanding what oiled the wheels
of the Soviet economy and society were *svyazi* (connections), *blat* (pull) and
the less widely used term, *tolkach* (pusher or fixer).[6] 'Connections' were
important for everything from obtaining theatre tickets to getting a good
job. Such contacts could be inherited from parents who had already acquired
a comfortable niche in the Soviet system, and they were much more useful
than money. In the post-Communist world, connections still matter, but in
the acquisition of goods and services they count for far less than wealth.
'Connections' were a privilege mainly of the new Soviet middle class – and,
it goes without saying, of the elite. *Blat* had a more pejorative ring to it
than 'connections'. To get things through 'pull' still more clearly contradicted the ostensible principles of the Soviet system. Whereas someone with
whom one was 'connected' might render a favour without expecting
anything, even indirectly, in return, *blat* involved a reciprocal exchange of
favours. Although ubiquitous in Soviet society, it was not quite respectable.

Thus, even when giving an example of *blat*, one Soviet interviewee
denied that anything other than an act of friendship was involved: 'It is

not that I want something in return when providing a pass to the theatre, but as I have no time my friend may arrange a hospital appointment for me.'[7] The phenomenon of *blat* was not incompatible with friendship, but it was by no means totally disinterested. There was not necessarily a direct exchange of favours between two people. There could be a long and complex chain of favours which provided such various services as access to a good hospital consultant, a nursery or school with a high reputation, consumer goods unavailable in normal state shops, spare parts for a car, scarce books, or a place in a tourist group travelling abroad.[8] Essentially, *blat* was a way of getting around the system. Since the command economy was one of chronic shortage, 'pull' and informal relations were far more important than roubles. How much 'pull' a person had depended, obviously, on that individual's position within the society, but at all social levels in the Soviet Union, there were unofficial networks which, to a certain extent, bypassed the official structures and eased some of the difficulties and frustrations of everyday life.[9]

The command economy would scarcely have worked at all if informal practices had not oiled its wheels. An important role was played by the 'fixer' (*tolkach*), a person who when supplies failed to arrive at a factory could find ways round the problem. The *tolkach* was a pusher and expediter 'who nags, begs, borrows, bribes, to ensure that the needed supplies actually arrive'.[10] While there was some official disapproval of their activities, the pushers were none the less tolerated, for meeting production targets was the top priority for factory managers and their ministerial superiors. In the command economy if one factory fell behind schedule in its supplies to another, the knock-on effect could be huge in the absence of alternative suppliers to which other factories could turn. The semi-legal fixers, who often engaged in barter to ensure a resumption of supplies, were part of the solution. In the unreformed Soviet economy, however, regional party secretaries also played a role in easing economic shortages and snarl-ups which, in principle, should have been the business of Gosplan and the ministries. When something was in short supply in one region and the problem could not be resolved through the state's economic agencies, a telephone call from a regional party secretary to his counterpart in another region could be the answer. Barter had a part to play there, too. The initial contact, for example, in the 1970s between Mikhail Gorbachev, the first secretary of the agricultural area of Stavropol, and Boris Yeltsin, first secretary of the industrial region of Sverdlovsk in the Urals, is described by Yeltsin in his first volume of memoirs thus: 'Our first encounter was by telephone. Quite often we needed to extend each other a helping hand: metal and timber from the Urals, food products from Stavropol. As a rule he never gave us anything over and above the limits imposed by Gosplan, but he did help us to build up our stocks of poultry and meat.'[11]

Was the End of Soviet Communism Economically Determined?

Although the Soviet Union was the richest country in the world in terms of natural resources – and that remains true of post-Soviet Russia – economic performance failed to match this potential. Indeed, there was a long-term decline in the rate of economic growth from the 1950s to the 1980s. The fall in the price of oil in the second half of the eighties hit the Soviet economy especially hard. However, accounts of the end of Communism and of the Soviet Union which rely on economic determinism, as in essence does that of the former Russian acting prime minister, Yegor Gaidar, are ultimately unconvincing.[12] Gaidar is willing to believe that Mikhail Gorbachev gave up the whole of Eastern Europe and made large unilateral reductions of armaments purely for economic reasons, and that also for economic reasons he did not use the force that would be required to put a stop to restive Soviet republics' quest for independence.[13] With the Soviet Union, rather than Eastern Europe, in mind at this point, Gaidar writes: 'Preserving the empire without using force was impossible; holding on to power without preserving it was impossible as well. Using mass repression would obviate the possibility of getting large, long-term, politically motivated credits that would at least postpone the looming state bankruptcy.'[14]

There are several problems with an explanation of political actions in such economic-determinist terms. Without political liberalization and democratization, massive use of force would not have been required to keep the Soviet republics quiescent. Gaidar suggests that Gorbachev was willing to risk the extreme wrath of the armed forces by 'losing' Eastern Europe. He was prepared, by not resorting to forcible repression, to risk losing also large parts of the Soviet Union and, concomitantly, the support of virtually all of the party-state organs. And he holds that Gorbachev pursued such extremely dangerous policies for economic reasons. Yet if Gorbachev had been as obsessed with the economy as Gaidar imagines he was, that was a very strange and roundabout way to deal with it. He took risks which, in Gaidar's own terms, made it impossible for him to hold on to power. Yet he was unwilling to risk moving to market prices, which, as Gaidar insists, was the key to beginning to resolve the issue of shortages and growing economic calamity. That seems very paradoxical, but it is a paradox which is easily resolved, simply because the premise – that all Gorbachev's most important decisions, and non-decisions, were motivated by economic considerations – is wrong. As we have seen in earlier chapters, Gorbachev was far more actively concerned with political than economic reform, although that removed many traditional levers of power. Chinese Communist leaders have been much more fearful of that kind of reform than of marketizing measures, which, so far, they have survived quite comfortably.

The idea that the Soviet Union was doomed to collapse when it did because of poor economic performance is misleading at a more general level. Prolonged economic failure does not by itself lead to the downfall of a highly authoritarian regime. Given the extent to which, for reasons substantially independent of the condition of the economy, liberalization and democratization occurred in the second half of the 1980s, the severe economic problems were a very important contributory factor to the break-up of the Soviet Union. However, an unreformed Soviet Union would have dealt with dissatisfaction – the manifestations of which would have been on a much more modest scale – in the traditional way. Authoritarian rulers of Third World countries, such as Sese Seko Mobuto in the Congo (then Zaire), misgoverned for decades, presiding over corrupt and inefficient regimes which were economic basket cases. An economically inefficient and socially unjust system is not doomed to imminent extinction merely on those accounts. The link between economic failure and turning out a government which exists in democracies (although even there it is not an iron law) does not apply in the same way to authoritarian or totalitarian regimes. The Soviet Union, furthermore, as should be clear, had a far more sophisticated system of controls than any Third World country.

A Communist system could not have continued in the Soviet Union for ever – no system lasts for ever – but it could have continued for significantly longer than it did if fundamental reform had *not* been undertaken. On the eve of perestroika the dissident movement in the USSR had been effectively crushed. The Soviet state was confronted by a vast range of problems, although hardly as great a threat to its survival as the years of the Second World War or the task of rebuilding a devastated country in the immediate post-war years. After muddling through the remaining years of the twentieth century, a Soviet Union which had not changed the fundamentals of the political system would have benefited from the huge increase in energy prices which did so much to bolster the economy of post-Soviet Russia and the popularity of Vladimir Putin, its president between 2000 and 2008.

The Soviet Union had also a number of non-economic sources of support. The fact that it was regarded in the outside world as a superpower – which it owed to its military strength, size, and natural resources rather than economic efficiency – was a source of pride for a majority of citizens of the USSR. The same was true of various successes, ranging from the conquest of space to its world chess champions and tally of Olympic Games medals. The survival of the Communist system and of the Soviet Union for over seventy years owed a good deal also to the services offered by the state – and not only the secret services. Free universal education and health care, together with full employment, were valued by a majority of the population. Here, too, the censorship played its part – the Soviet regime's success over many decades in reducing to a minimum knowledge that far higher standards of welfare were enjoyed in Western Europe (minus the political oppression and secret police surveillance).

The conventional wisdom about the Soviet Union in early 1985 was expressed by the chair (a retired British ambassador) of a conference attended by American, British and European politicians, officials, academics and journalists when he summed up the proceedings by saying: 'There's one thing we all know. The Soviet Union isn't going to change'. There were murmurs of agreement all round the table.[15] By 1992 the collapse of Communism was regarded as 'over-determined' and axiomatic by many of the same people. A wiser voice in 1992 was that of the Stanford University scholar Alexander Dallin, who wrote:

> To claim that the Soviet system was bound to crash amounts to committing what Reinhard Bendix . . . called 'the fallacy of retrospective determinism' – denying the choices (however constrained) that the actors had available before acting . . . We must take care not to introduce retrospectively a clarity, let alone inevitability, where there was contingency and complexity.[16]

Eastern European and Asian Communism

Since the Soviet Union's longevity was the key to the length of Communist rule in Eastern Europe, this chapter has focused on the reasons why Communism lasted as long as it did on Soviet soil. However, many – though not all – of the supports for the system applied also in Eastern Europe. That is true of the highly effective institutional controls, including the party presence in every sizeable workplace, the censorship, and the role of the secret police. It applies, albeit to a lesser extent, to some of the achievements of the Communist system in the realms of education, health provision and full employment. The extent to which these services were a source of support for the regime varied according to people's expectations and comparative knowledge of the non-Communist world. In east-central Europe – East Germany,

Czechoslovakia, Hungary and Poland – there was a greater awareness of conditions in Western Europe than there was in most parts of the Soviet Union. There were other factors which did *not* apply to Eastern Europe. Whereas the international importance of the Soviet Union was a matter of pride not only for Russians but for most Soviet citizens, of different nationalities, it was regarded very differently in Eastern Europe. Only in Bulgaria and, to a considerable extent, in Czechoslovakia before (but not after) 1968 was there quite broad pro-Russian and pro-Soviet sentiment.

The ways of getting round the system and the shortage economy discussed in the Soviet context applied also in other Communist states. They were engendered more by the system, and its intrinsic failures, than by cultural tradition. Nevertheless, the response to the problems had its culturally specific features. The phenomenon of *blat* in the Soviet Union has been compared with that of *guanxi* in China (although, as the Chinese term literally translates as 'connections', it could also be compared with the Russian *svyazi*).[17] Both terms refer to 'the use of personal networks for getting things done'. The Chinese practice of *guanxi* has its specific features, with the exchange of gifts and favours, including banquets. It is more related to kinship than was *blat* in Russia, and the moral obligation to reciprocate a gift is stronger. Not to return a favour would be not only imprudent (as in the case of *blat*) but an unthinkable breach of loyalty and rejection of emotional ties.[18] Nevertheless, cultural differences notwithstanding, in both countries these practices flourished and became socially important in conditions of a shortage economy and of the failure of official channels of distribution to meet people's needs.[19] Since in China as well as Russia it is now possible to purchase many formerly scarce goods and services for hard cash, in some respects *guanxi* is less significant in society than it was. (In both countries, however, the market economy is of a type in which officials can make or break a business. Thus, in Communist China, as with *svyazi* and *blat* in post-Soviet Russia, *guanxi* remains important for business purposes. It flourishes especially in the relationship between entrepreneurs and local officials and, more generally, smooths access to influential people, state contracts, bank loans, favourable tax incentives and 'exemptions from troublesome laws and regulations'.)[20]

Finally, when considering why Communist regimes lasted so long, it is important to mention nationalism, even though that counts also as a major contributory factor to the regimes' dissolution. National sentiment worked for or against Communism at different times and, especially, in different places. In the Soviet Union there was a significant element of Russian nationalism in what the regime preferred to call Soviet patriotism. That, naturally, worked best for the Russian 50 per cent of the Soviet population, but some of the other nationalities in the USSR, as we have seen in earlier chapters, also had their nationhood advanced (even if inadvertently) by social change and institutional structures in the Soviet period. Throughout most of Eastern Europe, where Communism was seen as an alien system emanating from the Soviet Union, nationalist feelings were, of course, in conflict with Communism, no matter how hard the regimes tried to produce a narrative which linked the system with the 'most progressive' part of that particular nation's past.

Outside Europe, though, Communists were able to draw on the theme of national liberation and anti-colonialism to attract broader support than could be achieved by an appeal to Communist ideology alone. In China, even though the Communists fought a bitter civil war with the Nationalists, the Communist Party itself made a powerful appeal to those who wished to see China reassert itself as a nation after a century and a half of humiliation at the hands of foreigners. In Vietnam and Cuba, anti-imperialist sentiments and national pride were also of great importance both in the foundation of the regimes and for their persistence. These three Third World countries all had indigenous revolutions, and while that has been no guarantee of survival (as the cases of Russia, Yugoslavia and Albania demonstrated), it can at least safely be said that indigenous revolution is a better predictor of Communist survival than non-indigenous founding of the regime.

29

What Caused the Collapse of Communism?

Communist systems had, as we have seen, many ways of surviving, even though their command economies performed less efficiently than market economies, their societies were unfree, and their polities lacked democratic accountability. Lack of freedom and lack of accountability in the short run assisted survival by obscuring and outweighing the relative economic failure. In the long run, they were at least as likely as economic stagnation to be the undoing of Communism. However, as Keynes remarked, in the long run we are all dead. Why the system ended *when* it did in the various European Communist states is a topic already addressed in Chapter 26. In this chapter, the main focus is on the Soviet Union. The reason for that is straightforward. The Soviet state held the key which could unlock doors throughout Eastern Europe. If *it* ceased to be Communist, it was clear that the survival hopes for Communism in all other Warsaw Pact countries were minimal. In contrast, Communism in Asia has been more resilient. While that has owed much to lack of information about – or opportunities to explore – possible alternatives, it is also related to transition from predominantly agricultural to industrialized economies. Although that was true also of a number of European Communist states, it was more comprehensively true of their Asian counterparts. The massive social mobility which resulted was in the short and medium term a support for the regimes which had overseen such sweeping change.

On a long time-scale, social and economic factors are of fundamental importance in explaining how Communism came to be *rejected* in the Soviet Union and, as a consequence, collapsed in Eastern Europe. The more immediate reasons for the dramatic changes of the late 1980s were, however, the result of particular political choices. The choices that were made owed a lot initially to the *stimulus* of relative economic failure, but the radical political changes which were introduced in the Soviet Union after 1985 were by no means economically *determined*. Since, however, everyone by the mid-1980s could agree that the Soviet economy was not performing well, that weakened the conservative opposition to reform proposals. Moreover, it was initially easier to put forward ideas for political reform by arguing (rightly or wrongly) that they were essential for economic progress. Before long, though, political change was advocated for its own sake.

Nationalism contributed greatly to the collapse of Communism in Eastern Europe, but in the Soviet Union it became a powerful force leading to the break-up of the USSR only *after* fundamental changes had already taken place in the political system. Ultimately, it was the combination of new ideas, institutional power (the commanding heights of the political system having fallen into the hands of radical reformers), and political choices (when other options *could* have been chosen) which led to the end of Communist rule in Europe.

Social Change

Over time, the successes of Communism as well as the failures increased the system's vulnerability. In the Soviet Union of 1939, only 11 per cent of the population had received more than an elementary education. By 1984 the percentage who had attended at least secondary school had risen to 87 per cent. The more educated the population became, the more they were inclined to seek information denied to them by the party-state authorities. Those who knew foreign languages could do so more readily, since broadcasts other than in the languages of the particular Communist state were not, as a rule, jammed. By the mid-1980s the Soviet Union had quite a large, educated middle class.* The proportion of people with higher education had grown substantially in the post-Stalin years. In 1954 just a little over 1 per cent of the population had completed higher education. By 1984 there were well over five million students currently in higher education and eighteen and a half million people who had completed such an education, the latter making up almost 7 per cent of the total population of the USSR.[1]

This meant that the percentage of the *adult* population with a higher education was in double figures – and particularly high in Moscow and Leningrad. By nurturing a highly educated population, Communism

---

* The term 'middle class' was not used in the Soviet Union with reference to Soviet society until the perestroika era. Even then, it was defined in very different ways – as was the more common term, 'intelligentsia', which could refer to all who had received a higher education or, more narrowly and normatively, to people of critical and independent minds. The notion of middle class in the late Soviet period is discussed briefly in G.G. Diligenskiy, *Lyudi srednego klassa* (Obshchestvennoe mnenie, Moscow, 2002), pp. 102–10.

contained the seeds of its own destruction. It became harder to treat adults like Victorian children who should be seen but not heard and who should simply accept that those in authority knew what was good for them. It became, for example, increasingly anomalous that educated Soviet citizens could not travel just as freely as did the Westerners they saw visiting their own country. It was no less frustrating that they should be denied access to books or films of their own choice as distinct from those that party-state officials decided were suitable for them.* For open-minded members of the Soviet political elite who *had* been given the opportunity to travel abroad, that experience was important. Seeing for themselves countries that were both more democratic and more prosperous than the Soviet Union significantly influenced the outlook of Mikhail Gorbachev and that of the second most important reformer of the perestroika years, Alexander Yakovlev.[2]

Demographically, Communist parties became more representative of

---

* Notwithstanding the difficulties, many intellectuals within the Soviet Union as well as in Eastern Europe read far more widely in foreign literature than did their Western counterparts. The very fact that something was difficult to obtain added to its attraction. It is also the case that, even in Russia (where, as already noted, there were works considered taboo that were, nevertheless, published in Estonia), the Brezhnev era saw the publication of far more English-language novels translated into Russian than there were contemporary Russian novels translated into English. Graham Greene and Evelyn Waugh were among the most popular English translated authors. Among British novelists who began to publish only in the post-Second World War period, those whose work appeared in Russian during the Brezhnev years included Melvyn Bragg, Basil Davidson, Margaret Drabble, Michael Frayn, William Golding, Susan Hill, Iris Murdoch, Piers Paul Read, Alan Sillitoe, John Wain, Raymond Williams and John Wyndham. It goes without saying that works which cast the Communist system in an unfavourable light were not translated into the languages of Communist states until the perestroika era, but much mainstream English-language fiction did appear. One unclassifiable work which was extremely popular in Communist Europe was C. Northcote Parkinson's *Parkinson's Law* (John Murray, London, 1957). Among the appreciative readers of the Russian translation of *Parkinson's Law*, published in Moscow in 100,000 copies in the mid-1970s, was the first secretary of the Communist Party in the Stavropol region, Mikhail Gorbachev (as he revealed during his first visit to London in 1984). I remember a Hungarian sociologist, who visited Glasgow University in the late 1960s, saying that he did not understand why *Parkinson's Law* was regarded as a satirical and humorous work. It was deadly serious! Since the bureaucratic empire-building within Communist systems outdid Western bureaucracy, many of Parkinson's 'laws' brought instant recognition.

their societies over time. All major social groups were represented, although some much more than others. The highly educated and city dwellers had a disproportionately large presence in the party. In all Communist parties the full-time officials wielded more power than any other group, although at certain times and places (especially China during the Cultural Revolution) officialdom was attacked in the name of revolutionary renewal. In the major ruling parties well-educated specialists became over time a larger component of the party membership. Where liberalization took place from above, as in Hungary, their reformist influence was important. In Poland, the outstanding example of democratization from below, a larger proportion of social scientists than in other European Communist states were able to pursue their careers without joining the Communist party. But Poland was in a more significant way unique, being the only country in which organized workers were in the vanguard of a movement against Communist rule. Together with their supporters within the intelligentsia, they would probably have brought about systemic change in Poland at the beginning, rather than the end, of the 1980s but for their consciousness of Poland's geopolitical position and their taking into account the possibility of Soviet intervention.

Economic Problems

If the *successes* of the Communist era, including educational advances, were part of the explanation of the transformative change of the second half of the eighties, it was an accumulation of serious *problems* that was the initial trigger for radical reform. Even though economic reform was to become a lower priority for Gorbachev than political reform, and less of a preoccupation than ending the Cold War, the most important initial stimuli to perestroika were economic. The slowdown over time in the rate of economic growth, the fact that technological innovation was occurring faster in the newly industrialized countries of Asia than in the Soviet Union, and the excessive burden placed by the military-industrial complex on the Soviet exchequer were major concerns for Gorbachev and his supporters. This relative economic failure was accompanied by a host of social problems which had accumulated during the Brezhnev era – a declining birth rate, an increase in the infant mortality rate, an increased death rate among middle-aged men and (linked to the last point) a major problem of alcoholism.

One of the greatest failures of Communist economic systems was in creating new technology. As the Hungarian economist János Kornai noted, the economies of the Communist world compared very unfavourably in this respect with market economies.[3] Among the reasons for the poor performance were the meagreness of the rewards for success and the weakness of the penalties for failure. High efficiency and speedy technological development did not bring any special advantages; continuing to produce the same old product did not count as failure. Shortfalls and waste, arising in part from technological inertia, were 'automatically excused in retrospect by the soft budget constraint'.[4] Kornai's concept of 'soft budget constraint' highlights important defects of the command economy, in which 'soft' credit can be obtained, the budget is not controlled by the need to make a profit (as it is in a market economy), and prices are determined bureaucratically. When extra costs were incurred, prices were allowed to rise, either openly or in a disguised form through a lowering of the quality of the product (which was not usually high to begin with).[5] And purchasers, whether of consumer goods or producer goods, did not have the option of taking their custom elsewhere.

In the Brezhnev era, countless books and articles were published in the Soviet Union on the 'scientific and technical revolution'. Yet this was not where that revolution was happening. Conservative Soviet Communists placed a lot of faith in computers as the ultimate panacea for solving the problems of economic planning, believing that they would show that those calling for movement towards a market economy were misguided. Yet computerization did not turn out to be a substitute for the market. A cartoon – in Hungary – captured this when it showed a group of serious-looking men standing beside a massive bank of computers, waiting for the answer to all the country's economic problems. One of them reads out the verdict the computer has come up with: 'It says that supply should be adjusted to meet demand.' In spite of the enthusiasm of Soviet technocrats for computers, the USSR was particularly backward in information technology. Making that point, the head of the Soviet section of the British Foreign Office, Nigel Broomfield, in an internal government document in 1983, accurately predicted that 'the Soviet system will change from within' and 'whether it will collapse or evolve is perhaps the key question'. What would be decisive, he maintained, was 'economic failure and the inability to understand and control the technological communications revolution which is now sweeping the developed world'.[6]

The Soviet Union's inability to participate in the information revolution meant that it was, indeed, ill equipped to benefit from economic globalization. So long, however, as the rulers of the Soviet state were more concerned with maintaining their sovereign, and highly authoritarian, control over domestic developments, being laggards in information technology was not a wholly negative factor for them. As became very clear in 2008, to be part of the global economy had its down side. Among the countries to suffer serious economic difficulties as a result of the global financial crisis were post-Soviet Russia – and, still more, Ukraine. Standing aside from the revolution in information technology certainly prevented the Soviet Union from maximizing its economic potential. Even if it had continued to stand apart, however, and had eschewed political changes of the kind introduced during perestroika, this would not necessarily have led to economic or political collapse. The rest of Europe would still have bought Soviet oil and gas. Moreover, China's Communist rulers in the twenty-first century have found a halfway house of participation in information technology, whereby parts of the internet (containing politically awkward information) are closed off to Chinese citizens, while those parts which are economically useful remain open.

Nationalism

There was no uniform path from Communism to post-Communism (and the latter term, rather than democracy, is used advisedly, for post-Communist states include many authoritarian and hybrid regimes). Communist parties changed over time. All, sooner or later, diluted or even abandoned their original revolutionary ideology. Some, more than others, began to reflect values more broadly held within their own societies. The party, in some places more than others, embraced distinctively national sentiments. Thus, for example, after becoming First Secretary of the Communist Party of Lithuania in October 1988, Algirdas-Mikolas Brazauskas cautiously, but increasingly, espoused the Lithuanian national cause and got into arguments not only with conservative Communists but also with the reformist wing of the Soviet leadership in Moscow, while being attacked at home by his anti-Communist domestic rival, Vytautas Landsbergis.[7] When, however, a party leader in a multinational state became aggressively nationalist, as did Milošević in Serbia, the result could be disastrous.

Nationalism was always a potential threat to Communist rule, though some liberalization of the system was needed before that potential became reality. Its potency was especially great in multinational Communist states. In particular, nationalism was never far below the surface of Yugoslav or Soviet life. There were those both within Communist states and outside who dismissed it as a serious threat to the systems with the argument that – as distinct from hard economic facts – nationality is a slippery and subjective concept and difficult to delineate with any precision. However, if enough people share a subjective perception – even if it is based on myth, as is all national identity to a greater or lesser degree – this becomes part of the objective reality with which politicians have to deal. The two main ways in which Communist rulers responded to that reality were through severe repression of any demonstration of nationalism and by manipulation of symbols of national identity to steal some of the clothes of anti-Communist nationalists. Even the East German Communist authorities got in on the act. Martin Luther, Frederick the Great and Bismarck were among the major figures from a Prussian past who were co-opted as part of the GDR's supposedly distinctive inheritance.[8] During the Stalinist era of the Soviet Union, Peter the Great and even Ivan the Terrible were viewed as 'progressive for their time', creators of a greater Russia, and precursors of the great Stalin.

The more ethnically heterogeneous the society, the more difficult a trick this was, however, to pull off. Russian nationalism or Serbian nationalism could be used to rally Russians or Serbs, but was liable to alienate other nationalities within the Soviet and Yugoslav states. Moreover, with federal structures based on national boundary lines, regional differences and grievances became bound up with national sentiment. Even so, nationalism did not lead to the demise of Communist rule in any country until the radical reforms of the Soviet perestroika had made their mark. And in the case of the USSR, nationalism's role in the dismantling of the Soviet *state* was substantially more important than the part it played in the transformation of the Communist *system*. The strength and political significance of nationalism in the last years of the Soviet Union were unintended consequences of the far-reaching changes introduced from above by Gorbachev in 1987–88.

Critical Thinking within the Party

The closest precursor to perestroika was the Prague Spring.[9] Quite early in the Gorbachev era, the new spokesman of the Soviet Ministry of Foreign Affairs, Gennady Gerasimov, himself a within-system reformer of longstanding, was asked what the difference was between the Prague Spring and perestroika. His droll reply was 'Twenty years.' In both instances the movement for change came from within the Communist Party and reached fruition when the coming to power of a new party leader altered the balance of forces within the political elite. There were, of course, some fundamental differences between the two cases. Dubček, unlike Gorbachev, was the facilitator rather than the driver of reform within the party leadership. A decent and fairly open-minded man, Dubček leaned more in the direction of his reformist colleagues than in that of the conservatives within a deeply divided

Central Committee and Politburo. Another major difference was that far-reaching reform in Czechoslovakia was interrupted after only eight months, whereas its Soviet equivalent lasted for almost seven years. Moreover, influential as the Prague Spring was within the international Communist movement – especially on the West European 'Eurocommunists' – it was incomparably less important than liberalizing and democratizing change within the Soviet Union. That paved the way for the demise of Communism in Eastern Europe.

The development of critical thinking within the party intelligentsia in the years leading up to the Czechoslovak reforms and those in the Soviet Union between 1985 and 1989 (discussed in Chapters 19 and 20) is crucial to understanding both the Prague Spring and perestroika. For many observers such spectacular change came out of the blue, but its preconditions were established in both countries well in advance of actual measures of liberalization and democratization. In Communist states generally, and in the Soviet Union specifically, the vast majority of leading specialists in the social sciences – academic lawyers as well as economists, sociologists and political analysts – were members of the Communist Party. It was from their ranks that the most influential ideas for change emanated. The availability of fresh and critical thinking on the political and economic system, and from within the ruling party itself, was of decisive importance when chance, rather more than conscious choice, produced party leaders open to fresh ideas and innovative policy. However, the system was such that, barring revolution – an undertaking so hazardous in Communist states that it was rarely attempted – only change at the apex of the political hierarchy could determine whether fresh and critical thinking would remain a mere intellectual diversion or whether it would influence the real world of politics.

Reform-minded intellectuals who remained in the ruling parties throughout decades in which only minimal reform occurred were often regarded as time-servers by those of a critical turn of mind who chose to stay outside the party's ranks. They could be accused of self-deception in believing that only from within the official structures could they hope to bring about radical reform or (for their aims were generally more modest) at least influence the direction of state policy. There is no uniform answer across the whole Communist world to the question of whether 'within-system reformers' (or 'intrastructural dissenters') were right or wrong in their assessment that the most realistic way of bringing about change for the better was from inside the party.[10] In more than half the Communist states, in so far as there was such a presence of reformist intellectuals within the ruling party, there was very little to show for it. However, in Hungary to a considerable extent, in Czechoslovakia until the reform movement was snuffed out by Soviet tanks, and in the crucially important cases of the Soviet Union and China, intra-party reform was more decisive than pressures from outside the party ranks in changing the system in highly significant ways.[11]

It is clear that only a minority of people joined the party with the idea of reforming it from within. One who can be believed when she says she did join with that aim in view is Ludmilla Alexeyeva, who later became a prominent Soviet dissident, having decided that 'my belief that the party could be reformed from within was nothing but an illusion'.[12] Yet though the Communist Party was not successfully reformed in the Soviet Union – most of its leading officials supported the August coup of 1991, which was intended to turn the clock back to pre-perestroika times – it *was* from inside the party that the changes to the entire political system were introduced and promoted. Initiated by Gorbachev, listening to the advice of 'intrastructural dissenters' who had endured a long wait for a reformer in the Kremlin, the changes were pushed through in the face of foot-dragging and opposition from the party conservatives, some of whom were eventually sufficiently desperate to put the general secretary (who was also president) under house arrest.

If only a minority of radical reformers within the CPSU joined the party with the express intention of changing the *system*, that raises the question of what changed the *minds* of the party reformers. I have already quoted, in Chapter 19, the remark of a Czech economist that 'the greatest stimulus to change is failure'. To recognize an unsatisfactory economic performance or lack of freedom as failure, however, requires some standard of comparison. Even then, the policy implications of failure have to be determined – more discipline and tighter controls, or more market and a new respect for civil liberties? Some of the influence on party reformers, as we have seen in Chapter 23, came directly from the West. People within the political elite and leading specialists in various fields, who were also party members, had much more chance of travelling to Western countries than had the average citizen in Communist countries, and what they saw and heard had an impact.

Nevertheless, the initial stimulus to think differently often came from people who were, in some sense, writing from 'within the ideology', rather than as opponents of it. As Kornai put it, referring to a time when he was 'still half or three-quarters a Communist': 'The works that affect a person most strongly in the state of mind I was then in are not ones diametrically opposed to the views held hitherto by the doubter – that is, not those attacking the Communist Party from without.'[13] He himself was influenced at that early period of his intellectual evolution by the Yugoslav Communist theorist Edvard Kardelj and by Isaac Deutscher's biography of Stalin (which he read in German). Many

reformers within the ranks of ruling parties broke with Communist orthodoxy in stages. First of all they came to reject the cruelty of Stalinism, while
continuing to believe that the Communist Party should retain a monopoly
of power and that all would be well if only there were a return to Leninist
norms. For many, a more fundamental stage was eventually reached, at which,
as Kornai puts it, 'former believers understood that the *real* system that had
developed in the Soviet Union and the other Communist countries embodied
not only Stalin's but Lenin's and even some of Marx's basic ideas'.[14]

This did not usually lead reformers within the ruling parties to mount
direct attacks on Lenin. Rather, in a war of quotations, they used whatever
in Lenin's voluminous writings suited their purpose. In the Soviet Union,
in particular, Lenin remained a source of legitimation of political views at
least until the end of the 1980s. Even Alexander Yakovlev, who in post-Soviet
Russia came to regard Lenin with abhorrence, was citing him respectfully
as late as 1989.[15] Gorbachev retained an esteem for Lenin not only up to the
end of his time in power but also beyond it. However, he broke with *Leninism*
on one fundamental principle after another.[16] He abandoned democratic
centralism in favour of what in 1987 he called 'socialist pluralism'. By early
1990 he had endorsed 'political pluralism'. He accepted the need for checks
and balances and emphasized the importance of the rule of law. His political beliefs evolved to the point at which they were virtually indistinguishable from those of the social democrats of Western Europe. Even while he
remained General Secretary of the Central Committee of the CPSU,
Gorbachev told his aides he felt close to social democracy. The major
programmatic documents of the CPSU in 1990 and 1991 reflected this political evolution. Above all, Gorbachev broke with Lenin by recognizing that
means in politics are no less important than ends, and that utopian goals,
which are always likely to be illusory, will be all the more of a chimera if
pursued by violent and undemocratic means.

Transformational Leadership and Institutional Power

What made possible largely peaceful change away from Communism in the
Soviet Union was a similar evolution in the views of a small minority of
party officials and a larger minority of party intellectuals *while they were
already in positions of responsibility*. No one who thought as Gorbachev did
in 1988, not to speak of 1990–91, could have become general secretary in
1985 unless he had been an actor of Oscar-winning talents who kept all his
real opinions to himself. Gorbachev was already, when he became party
leader, much more of a reformer than his Politburo colleagues realized, but

it was, precisely, *reform* of the system, not transformative change, he had in mind at that point. The further development of his thinking was of exceptional importance because he already occupied the post of supreme institutional power within the Soviet system and became thereby the single most influential person in the Communist world.

Lech Wałesa in 1980–81 was a rare case of a leader from outside the Communist party having a major impact on the policy of a ruling party, forcing a series of retreats – up to the point at which the party-state authorities returned to the offensive and imposed martial law. Even within the ruling party it was uncommon for supreme authority to belong to anyone other than the party leader, whether he was called general secretary, first secretary or chairman. But in his later years such authority did accrue to Deng Xiaoping in China, even after he had given up his major party offices. Nevertheless, he had attained that status as a result of his long and respected service to the party. Boris Yeltsin also was a hugely influential leader between 1989 and 1991, at a time when he held no high party office, other than nominal membership of the Central Committee up to the point at which he resigned from the CPSU in July 1990. However, by that time the system had been transformed to such an extent that election to state offices – first, the all-Union legislature, then the Russian legislature, and finally the Russian presidency – provided an alternative and, by this time, superior source of authority and legitimacy to that offered by the party.

Had there not, however, been an evolution in the views of a number of people a rung or two lower in the party hierarchy, even such a reform-minded leader of the CPSU as Gorbachev would have been hamstrung. But there were such people. Yakovlev had been brought back into the party apparatus by Gorbachev, who subsequently promoted him with exceptional rapidity. Shevardnadze had been a relatively enlightened first secretary of the Communist Party in Georgia and was to become Gorbachev's surprise choice to succeed Gromyko as foreign minister. Deputy heads of Central Committee departments, Chernyaev (from the International Department) and Shakhnazarov (from the Socialist Countries Department), were to become especially important aides to Gorbachev. They, and other enlightened officials who were brought into Gorbachev's circle of advisers, were highly supportive of his innovative foreign policy and reform of the political system. They also themselves made important contributions to what was called the 'New Political Thinking', especially on foreign policy. These were people whose contacts with the intelligentsia within their own country and experience of the outside world had led to gradual, but fundamental, change in their way of looking at the world. (Shevardnadze was the exception. He had extensive contact with the Georgian intelligentsia, but practically none with 'abroad' until *after* he became foreign minister.) Like Gorbachev, these various officials had in their youth taken most of the official doctrine in Stalin's USSR for granted. By the second half of the 1980s, their political evolution had brought them close to social democracy.

Which Came First – Crisis or Reform?

In the long run, it was often argued before 1985, the Communist system could not survive *without* being reformed. That was doubtless true, and China is an example of a state which has introduced radical economic reform and has – thus far – preserved many of the essential features of a Communist polity. What perestroika demonstrated, however, was that Communism could not survive *with* radical reform of its political system. By the time political pluralism had been introduced, it was, quite simply, no longer meaningful to describe the state as Communist. The introduction of such reform produced fissures within the ruling party itself. What had been the most powerful institutions in the country – the Politburo and secretariat of the Central Committee – began to send mixed signals to the society, as their members visibly pulled in different directions. Once democratization had affected the ruling party, it could not be confined to it. There turned out to be a logical link between the two principal political characteristics of a Communist system. The party's monopoly of power depended on the preservation of democratic centralism. In the absence of strict limitation on political debate and of tight central control over the flow of information, the Communist Party's grip on the levers of power was seriously weakened. Even before other political parties were legalized, democratizing reform of the Soviet political system led to the speedy erosion of the CPSU's 'leading role'.

In the Soviet Union reform produced crisis more than crisis forced reform. The fate of the Soviet system and of the Soviet state did not hang in the balance in 1985. By 1989 the fate of both did. A majority within the party-state apparatus of the USSR fervently wanted to preserve both the system and the state, believing that the destiny of one was linked to that of the other. But by the end of the 1980s Gorbachev and the reformist wing of the party leadership had already introduced change that made the political system different in kind. From 1988 they consciously pursued systemic change, but they wanted speedy evolution rather than sudden collapse. As distinct from their intention of dismantling the Communist system, Gorbachev and most of his advisers were strongly opposed to the break-up of the Soviet state. They recognized, however, the intimate relationship between means and ends, and they were not prepared to sacrifice the liberalized and democratizing political system on the altar of violent suppression of national separatism. The views of Gorbachev and like-minded supporters such as Yakovlev, Chernyaev and Shakhnazarov had evolved, at varying speeds and under different constraints, from wishing to reform the system to seeking a 'third way' – a new model of 'socialism with a human face'. Gorbachev in 1989 used approvingly that phrase from the Prague Spring which had so infuriated Brezhnev, since it seemed to cast aspersions on *his* face and that of the system he represented.

Yet Gorbachev (the evolution of whose views mattered so much because of his institutional power – as general secretary and, from March 1990, also as president) moved beyond that. By 1990–91, he no longer aspired to build something which had not yet been seen on earth, but a society which had produced a tangible enhancement of the quality of political life and which would, he hoped, produce comparable improvements in the standard of living. In other words, the model had become that of the European social democracies or the kind of social market economy which existed in West Germany. Gorbachev and his associates did not, of course, come remotely close to attaining such an economic goal. Whether it could eventually have been reached if there had been no August 1991 attempted coup, and if the break-up of the Soviet Union had been partial rather than so complete, remain unanswered, and unanswerable, questions. But perestroika had achieved a great deal. Along the way, fear of the state authorities was removed, liberty was introduced, competitive elections took place, and democratic accountability emerged in the USSR. It was not simply coincidental that these things happened shortly before the Soviet state itself ceased to exist. The task of holding together a democratized multinational state, in which each nation could point to a long list of grievances, was far harder than preserving the Union as a highly authoritarian state. Until the mid-1980s it had been taken for granted that every manifestation of nationalism would be stamped out ruthlessly. It was when that ceased to be the case that expectations were raised and Soviet statehood was called into question.

The Free Flow of Information

'It's a sociological law that the more information you give people, the more government policy becomes dependent on public opinion.' Those were the words of Rafael Safarov, an Armenian political sociologist and a senior researcher in the Institute of State and Law in Moscow, in a conversation I had with him in the mid-1970s. Perhaps sociological law was pitching it a bit high, but it was a good generalization. What is more, Safarov made essentially the same point, in somewhat more convoluted language, in a book, *Public Opinion and State Administration*, published in an edition of 6,000 copies in Moscow in 1975.[17] Although the Helsinki agreement later in the same year declared that the participating states must '*Make it their aim* to facilitate the freer and wider dissemination of information of all kinds',[18] this certainly did not become an aim of any of the Communist states. It was only some three years into Gorbachev's perestroika that a free flow of information became a political reality in the Soviet Union. Only then, indeed, did public opinion, as understood in Western countries, became a serious factor in the political equation. It transpired that a better-informed public did become much more critical of the party and state authorities. Even the reformist wing of the leadership, which had been in the vanguard of change in the first four years of perestroika, was often responding to public opinion more than it was leading it in the last two years or so of the Soviet state.

Although it is difficult to *over*estimate the significance of the institutional changes that were agreed at the Nineteenth Party Conference in 1988 – especially competitive elections for a working legislature – the earlier introduction of glasnost, not only as a concept but as a developing reality, should never be *under*estimated. Glasnost and institutional innovation worked in tandem. Contested elections and publication in the mass media of the results of opinion polls on sensitive political issues became concrete ways in which popular opinion could exert influence.[19] By the late 1980s, glasnost had become almost identical to freedom of speech, and the flow of information had reached unprecedented levels for the Soviet Union. The jamming of foreign broadcasts had stopped, but the Soviet domestic mass media had changed so much that even highly critical Soviet citizens turned first to their own newspapers, and especially to the most radical of the home-grown and officially published weeklies and journals. It is not surprising that conservative Communists complained at virtually every meeting of the Politburo about the press being out of control. A free flow of information and a Communist system were mutually incompatible. Highly authoritarian regimes need state censorship and give rise to self-censorship. During perestroika, the first withered away before being formally replaced by an enlightened press law, and the latter was abandoned in the new atmosphere of tolerance. Freedom of speech and of publication became the most important manifestations of the new pluralism, and a bulwark against a return to the past.

The International Context

Finally, the collapse of Communism must be seen in international context. Since the Soviet Union was the hegemonic power in Eastern Europe, the transformation of both its political system and its foreign policy is explanation enough of the collapse of Communism in all the regimes which had either at their foundation or later been placed in power by Soviet force of arms. Changes within the international Communist movement had already made an impact on the thinking of members of Communist parties, going back to the Soviet–Yugoslav split. The changes in China after the death of Mao Zedong were even more important. Whereas ruling Communist parties, not least the CPSU, found themselves in the 1960s and the first half of the 1970s defending themselves against accusations of 'revisionism' emanating from China, by the middle of the 1980s economic reform had proceeded further in China than in the Soviet Union or Eastern Europe, with only Hungary coming close to Chinese economic reform (while surpassing China in terms of political relaxation).

The improvement in East–West relations was even more important than the continuing diversity (but decline in antagonism) within the international Communist movement. One cannot say that Communism ended in Europe as a result of the end of the Cold War, for the dismantling of a Communist system in the Soviet Union and a qualitative enhancement of Soviet relations with both the United States and Western Europe went hand in hand. However, Cold War tensions invariably worked to the advantage of hardliners within the Soviet Union and Eastern Europe. In the immediate aftermath of the Second World War, Western powers (including the one which mattered most, the United States) had been prepared to see East Europe as a region in which the Soviet Union had considerable influence. When, however, Stalin imposed Soviet-type systems on these states, that was the single most important cause of the development of the Cold War. The hostility was intensified at various times by the actions of both sides, including the Soviet military interventions in Hungary in 1956 and Afghanistan in 1979. The 1968 invasion of Czechoslovakia made a greater impact in Western Europe than in the United States, although in Europe, as well as the USA, it was quite soon followed by improved relations with Brezhnev's Soviet Union – the détente of the early 1970s.

A central paradox, however, is that the Cold War, which was seen on the Western side as a struggle to keep Communism at bay and to restrain the Soviet Union, also helped to sustain the Soviet system. It is true that the arms race was proportionately a much heavier burden on the Soviet than on the American economy, although it was not negligible even in the latter case.[20] But, as Alec Nove put it: 'The centralized economy, Party control, censorship, and the KGB were justified in the eyes of the leaders, and of many of the led, by the need to combat enemies, internal and external.'[21] On the one hand, excessive military expenditure overstrained and distorted the Soviet economy. On the other, it was the Cold War which helped the party leadership to maintain control, and even loyalty, and to accord the military-industrial complex and the security forces their major roles within the system. Throughout the post-war period, the icier the Cold War became, the stronger was the position of hard-liners inside the Soviet Union. One corollary of Gorbachev's efforts to end the Cold War, in which he found a much readier partner in Ronald Reagan than many on either side of the Atlantic had expected, was a weakening of the Ministry of Defence and the KGB as institutional interests within the Soviet system, and a rapid decline in the influence of conservative Communist opponents of domestic reform.

Before perestroika, the most that could be achieved in US–Soviet relations was an agreement on the rules of the game and enough prudent interaction to avoid getting on a slippery slope to nuclear war. Lessons were learned from the extreme danger in which the world was placed by the Cuban missile crisis. But only with the coming to power of Gorbachev, his appointment of a new foreign policy team, and his willingness to look afresh at the fundamental issues of East–West relations did a qualitative change in the relationship become possible. Ronald Reagan, George Shultz and Margaret Thatcher were among those who declared that the Cold War was over by the end of 1988. If the visit of President Reagan to Moscow in the summer of 1988 signalled the psychological end of the Cold War, Gorbachev's speech to the United Nations in December of the same year brought it to an end ideologically. It was, however, the acquisition of national independence, together with the rejection of Communist systems, in Eastern Europe in the course of 1989 which put the seal on the Cold War's ending. Gerasimov, the adroit press spokesman of the Ministry of Foreign Affairs, produced the best sound-bite (and speaking in English rather than his native Russian). At the end of the harmonious summit meeting between Gorbachev and President George H.W. Bush in Malta in December 1989, he said: 'We buried the Cold War at the bottom of the Mediterranean Sea.' Earlier that year, confirming that the 'Brezhnev doctrine' was dead, Gerasimov quipped that it had been replaced by the 'Sinatra doctrine' – letting the East Europeans do it *their* way.

30

What's Left of Communism?

Very little is left of Communism in Europe where the movement began. As recently as the mid-1980s, half of Europe was controlled by Marxist-Leninist parties. Today, no state in that continent is ruled by Communists, nor are they remotely close to coming to power. In both Eastern and Western Europe, Communist parties are but a shadow of their former selves. Even in Russia, where throughout the 1990s the Communist Party of the Russian Federation provided the main opposition to the Yeltsin administration, the CPRF appears enfeebled. In the autumn of 2008 they were presented with what would have seemed at one time a political gift – a global crisis of capitalism! Russia was far from immune to it. By the end of October, the Moscow stock market had lost 70 per cent of its value at the beginning of the year.[1] Not only did the CPRF fail to exploit the economic difficulties; they were deliberately restrained, not wishing to exacerbate the financial turmoil. A secretary of the Communist Party Central Committee, Oleg Kulikov, announced that they would be making no public criticism of the government, since to do so 'would only harm the market and the anti-crisis programme'.[2] All very patriotic, but a far cry from the revolutionary doctrine enunciated by Marx, Engels and Lenin. Long before that, of course, there were many, and very different, deeds and statements of Communist parties, not least in Russia, that would hardly have been recognized by Marx and Engels as deriving from their doctrine. Yet the influence of the ideas of the founding fathers was huge, especially in the earlier years of the development of Communist parties. When the worldwide financial crisis came to a head in the second half of 2008, it did at least lead to an increase in sales of *Das Kapital* in Germany, but neither there nor anywhere else in Europe did it lead to a revival of Marxist-Leninist parties.

Outside Europe, the current which has swept away ruling Communist parties has very occasionally been reversed. By far the most notable fresh success for such a party in the twenty-first century has been in the continent where Communism has retained its most substantial presence, Asia. In Nepal, a landlocked country of just under thirty million inhabitants, situated between China and India, a party which deemed itself to be Maoist emerged victorious in genuinely competitive elections in April 2008. The Communist Party of Nepal (United Marxist-Leninist) became the dominant partner in a coalition government. One month after the election, the Nepalese monarchy – which had lasted for some 240 years – was abolished. A non-Communist, Ram Baran Yadav, was chosen to occupy a largely cere-monial presidency, and the much more powerful position of prime minister went to the leader of the Communist Party, Pushpa Kamal Dahal, who prefers to be known by his *nom de guerre*, Prachanda (which means 'The Fierce One').

This followed years of civil war (ended only in 2006), in which more than 12,000 people were killed. While the party followed the Maoist path of waging war in the countryside, it eventually came to power legally. With Nepal's huge neighbour, China, now pursuing a policy remote from Maoism, it is far from clear that Nepal will become a fully fledged Communist state, still less one which will seek to emulate the turmoil of Mao's Cultural Revolution. Economically, the country is dependent on trade with India, and Prachanda has said that Nepal will retain multi-party competition, foreign investment, and a private sector. The country is desperately poor – one of the secrets of the Maoists' success – and although the Communist Party is the dominant partner in the government, it would be premature to conclude that Nepal has increased the number of existing Communist states from five to six. Time will tell, but so far not only Nepal's political system but also the ruling party's ideology appears to be in transition. It is adapting to a very different international environment from that in which Asian Communist parties came to power in the twentieth century.[3]

There is, after all, no longer an international Communist movement. Of the six defining characteristics of a Communist system elaborated in Chapter 6 of this book, it is the last two ideological features which have most completely disappeared. One of those was the sense of belonging to such an international Communist movement. It had its headquarters in Moscow, although Mao's China offered an alternative pole of attraction. That trans-national movement has gone, and so has the aspiration to build a commu-nist society. In spite of lip-service to the goal of communism, no ruling Communist Party any longer places emphasis even in theory on movement towards that stateless society, the culminating and 'inevitable' stage of human development, as envisaged by Marx.

Insofar as it is still meaningful to describe as Communist the largest and most important of the states still governed by a Communist party, it is because China fully retains the monopoly of power of the party and the strictly hierarchical organization and discipline associated with democratic centralism. In many ways, however, China today is a hybrid system. So far removed from Communist orthodoxy has its economy become that it has even been described as an example of 'party-state capitalism'.[4] Yet the party's 'leading role' and democratic centralism not only define it politically, they also remain pillars of the country's still highly authoritarian (but less than totalitarian) system. There has, though, been significant ideological adaptation to a changing world, as well as bold innovation in economic policy. Reflecting as well as promoting an increasing pragmatism, Deng Xiaoping said that many generations would be required to build the first stage of socialism. This implied several hundred years, and raises the further hypothetical question for students of Communism: how long, then, after that would it take to construct the second stage – communism? In fact, the aspiration to build communism has been put so far ahead into the unknowable future that it is perfectly obvious that this task is not even on the long-term agenda of the CCP leadership. Indeed, in China there is very little contemporary interest in building socialism, never mind communism. Or, as Chris Patten – Britain's last governor of Hong Kong and an astute observer of China – put it, exaggerating only slightly: 'There is no Marxism left in China, though there are bits of Leninism.'[5]

Of the six defining features of a Communist system, China, then, meets only the two important political aspects. Since Mao's death it has moved substantially away from the economic criteria. Its concessions to the market have been on such a scale that it cannot now be considered a command economy. So far as ownership is concerned, there is still a large state sector, but by 2006 private enterprise in China accounted for almost half of the country's GDP and more than two-thirds of its industrial output.[6] In a related development, inequality has greatly increased, especially the urban–rural divide. That inequality is substantially higher than the European average and marginally higher than in the United States.[7] There is, in fact, increasing concern in China about the size of the gap between rich and poor. If China has become the workshop of the world, it is a workshop in which many are paying a high price. Accidents at work killed 101,480 people in China in 2007. In the same year there were 229 people killed at work in Great Britain.[8] The difference in the size of the two country's populations – China's is approximately twenty-two times higher than that of Britain – does not come even remotely close to explaining such a remarkable disparity. It has a lot to do with the nature of the work in which most people are employed in the two countries, but is related still more to the absence of democratic and legal accountability in China. Unsafe practices as well as corruption (a major problem in the Asian Communist states, not least in China) flourish in the absence of democratically elected politicians and an

independent judiciary who can hold both economic and political execu-
tives to account.

While China's Communist leaders have shown little or no inclination to
move towards democracy in a Western sense, they have thought seriously
about changing their political terminology as well as their Maoist inheritance. It is a little-known fact that the Chinese Communist leadership, having
sidelined the notion of 'communism' in the utopian sense, came close even
to jettisoning the name 'Communist'. In the earliest years of this century,
serious consideration was given by the top leadership of the CCP to changing
the name of their party, removing the word 'Communist' because it did not
go down well in the rest of the world. In the end, a name-change was
rejected. The argument against the change which carried most weight was
not based either on ideology or on tradition – fealty to the doctrine developed by Marx, Engels, Lenin and Mao. It was the practical argument that
some (perhaps many) members would say that this was not the party they
had joined. The fear was that they would, therefore, set about establishing
an alternative Communist Party. Thus, inadvertently, a competitive party
system would have been created. The need for political control by a single
party was the paramount consideration. The CCP leadership had no intention of embracing political pluralism, and the party's name remained the
same.[9] The contours of democratic centralism, though, are less tightly
restrictive in contemporary China than they have often been in the past.
There is discussion of what kind of reform China needs, and a lot of attention has been devoted to the lessons to be drawn from the collapse of
Communism in the Soviet Union and Eastern Europe. The former head of
the CCP propaganda department, Wang Renzhi, was by no means the only
contributor to the intra-party debate to conclude that to follow 'the path
of European democratic socialism' would be a step down 'the slippery slope
to political extinction for the CCP'.[10]

In all the established Communist states left standing – China, Cuba,
Laos, North Korea and Vietnam – the leading role of the party and democratic centralism remain intact. Indeed, that is the chief justification for
calling them Communist. However, they differ greatly in the extent to
which they still possess the defining features of a Communist system
economically – state ownership of the means of production and a command,
rather than market, economy. As we have seen, China, so far as ownership
is concerned, is already a mixed economy, and it has become in the main
a market economy. Vietnam has followed in China's post-Mao footsteps.
From 1986 onwards it, too, embraced marketizing reform. Indeed, there
are analysts who, while acknowledging the strength of the party-state institutions in both countries, have classified both China and Vietnam as 'post-

communist'.[11] Clearly, which category one puts these countries into depends on how much weight is accorded to the political as distinct from the economic criteria of Communism. Their political institutions are Communist, and they are still paying homage, however unconvincingly, to the writings of Marx, Engels and Lenin (and in China to both Mao Zedong and Deng Xiaoping, very different though these former leaders were). In Vietnam, Ho Chi Minh is added to the ideological pantheon, though within two decades of Saigon being renamed Ho Chi Minh City, its inhabitants were calling it once again Saigon.[12]

In Laos and in Cuba there has been modest movement away from the classical command economy, which, in Stalinist form, is now to be found only in North Korea. Yet neither Laos nor Cuba has gone anything like as far down the road to the market as have China and Vietnam. The population of Laos is only eight million, and a majority of the people are subsistence rice farmers. Reporting from Laos in the year 2000, a BBC correspondent noted that the traffic was so light in the capital city, Vientiane, that hens lived around one of the main roundabouts. Politically and economically, the regime is a severe one, but Buddhism is now tolerated, as, advertently or inadvertently, are drugs. Indeed, as Owen Bennett-Jones observed, whereas for Marx religion was the opium of the people, in Laos, 'opium is the opium of the people'.[13] Cuba, with its population of eleven million, was under Fidel Castro one of the most egalitarian of Communist states and the most resistant to any kind of 'market socialism'. It remains relatively egalitarian, but since Castro, as a result of severe illness, was officially succeeded as leader by his brother Raúl in February 2008 (the younger Castro having been in charge de facto since August 2006), some modest steps towards widening pay differentials have been taken. The party newspaper *Granma* justified these in June 2008 by saying, 'If it's harmful to give a worker less than he deserves, it's also harmful to give him what he doesn't deserve.'[14] While Cuba remains a poor country, and preserves the essentials both of a Communist political and economic system, it has survived the collapse of the Soviet Union, its main economic benefactor, and more than forty years of sanctions imposed by the United States with the purpose of toppling the regime.

Explaining Communist Longevity

This raises the question of why four Communist states in Asia and one in the Caribbean have survived for so long. It goes without saying that they have had the same supports which worked effectively for seven decades in the Soviet Union – powerful institutions, starting with a disciplined ruling party, an omnipresent secret police, and a rigorous censorship. Moreover, although two of the five states (China and Vietnam) have undertaken radical economic reform, they have not taken the risk of embarking on fundamental political reform, even though a modest liberalization of the two regimes has taken place gradually since the 1980s. What all five states have succeeded in doing, however, is linking Communism and nationalism, making the development of a strong state part of their appeal to national pride. In this they have been blessed by having enemies to be invoked, whenever needed, as a potent external threat. That has aided the effort to rally patriotic support behind the system.

Cuba is an especially interesting case from this point of view. Its survival, after the collapse of Soviet and East European Communism, was regarded by many observers as improbable. However, United States policy towards Cuba, from the time of Castro's takeover up to the time of writing (late 2008), has played an enormous part in preserving the Cuban Communist system in aspic. Uncle Sam was already a bogeyman in Cuba *before* the island became Communist. Since then, the American economic embargo, including a ban on US passport-holders from visiting the island, has achieved precisely the opposite effect from that intended. It has increased anti-Americanism, strengthened the standing of the Castro leadership, bolstered the Communist system, and kept the great majority of the Cuban people poorer than they otherwise would have been. American engagement with Cuba, if it had begun several decades ago, would undoubtedly have led to liberalization – and, in all probability, substantial democratization – of the regime. A policy of 'doing nothing to help Castro' has had the wholly unintended consequence of sustaining him and the regime as the David who successfully defied Goliath.

All the Asian Communist states have, to varying degrees, likewise viewed the United States as a major enemy. Three of the four – North Korea, Vietnam and Laos – were at various times subjected to American military attack. Almost 60,000 American servicemen lost their lives in the Vietnam War, but by the time that war ended in 1975, some three million Vietnamese soldiers and civilians had been killed. Vietnam's economy was destroyed in the course of the conflict, and untold ecological damage was inflicted. The toxic substances, including Agent Orange, used to defoliate the forests (and thereby reveal the hiding places of enemy soldiers) were still causing unusually large numbers of cancers and birth defects in Vietnam years after the war ended.[15] Thus, in spite of the harshness of the regime imposed by the Communists, it has not been difficult to project the enemy image of the United States or to evoke terrible memories of the war and a measure of gratitude to Vietnam's peacetime rulers for rebuilding the country.

The Indochina War left Communists in charge of Laos also, and gave them the possibility of making anti-Americanism a rallying cry. When the Pathet Lao seized control of the whole of Laos in the mid-1970s, they took revenge on the minority ethnic group the Hmong, who, equipped by the United States, had attacked the Ho Chi Minh Trail through Laos to Vietnam. About 100,000 of the Hmong were killed by the Communists and another 100,000 succeeded in making their way gradually to the United States.[16] The reputation of the United States in Laos was damaged not only by its bombing of the infiltration trails in Laos but by its apparent abandonment of the anti-Communist insurgents once a peace settlement of the Indochina War had been reached.

North Korea is a case apart. It remains the most totalitarian of Communist states. It, too, has the United States as a past and prospective enemy. But it has a deadly rival much closer to home than the USA – South Korea. To have on its borders a Korean state which is much more prosperous and incomparably more democratic is a clear threat to the future existence of North Korea. Moreover, there are still almost 30,000 American troops stationed on the Korean peninsula as of 2008, a number which has been gradually reduced. Thus, the Kims, father and son, have had no difficulty in maintaining a siege mentality in their highly militarized state. Because of the manifest failure of the hard-line regime in North Korea to provide a decent standard of living for its citizens, control over information about the outside world is tighter than in any other Communist country. Although it would appear, on the face of it, to be more difficult for the North Korean leadership than for Communist leaders elsewhere to play the patriotic card, since (like their old East German counterparts) they are part of a divided nation, they have, nevertheless, had some success in this endeavour. Kim Il-sung has been portrayed as the person who liberated Korea from Japanese rule and who then successfully defied the United States. The leadership also nails its nationalist colours to the mast of an eventually united Korea under Communist rule. (Korea will surely be united at some future date, but, no less surely, as a non-Communist state.)

Even though the establishment of a Communist system in the northern part of the Korean peninsula was mainly the work of the Soviet Union, North Korea went on to establish a foreign policy independent of both the USSR and China. In this respect, as in others, it can be compared with Romania, where for several decades the nationalist card was played with a measure of success. Without the Soviet Union, there would have been no Communist regime, but under Ceauşescu, a somewhat independent line on foreign policy was taken – *against*, for example, military intervention in Czechoslovakia in 1968, and (again, in contradistinction to Soviet policy) *for* intervention in Poland in 1989.[17] Both North Korea and Romania also went further than any other Communist regime in a personalist politics that had sultanistic and dynastic elements. In North Korea, Kim Jong-il did, indeed, succeed his father as the supreme ruler of the country, and in Romania, Nicolae Ceauşescu was grooming his son, Nicu, for the succession.[18]

Broad comparative studies of authoritarian regimes (embracing not only Communist systems) have shown that personalistic rule tends to last longer when it is linked to a ruling party. The party organization can help keep in line potential rivals to the supreme leader and prevent them from endangering his power.[19] In a party as disciplined as that of the Communists, this works especially effectively. Nevertheless, in Communist states which have moved beyond both totalitarianism and the extreme 'personality cult' characteristic of North Korea, institutions are both enabling and constraining. They enable the party leader and the Politburo to get decisions implemented throughout the country. The hierarchical nature of the party does, indeed, make it difficult for anyone to challenge the top leader, and it gives him an undoubted advantage in the determination of policy. However, the high degree of institutionalization also means that *if* the leader wishes to break with the past, and embark on a *radically new course*, political subtlety is required. The leader has to use his powers of persuasion as well as power of appointment to get radical reform accepted by the highest party organs. That clearly applied to Gorbachev and the Soviet perestroika. It was scarcely less true of Deng Xiaoping and the move to marketization and a substantial private sector in the Chinese economy.

Apart from the appeal of nationalism and the utility of having an enemy to denounce and hold responsible for current difficulties, it is clearly to the advantage of Communist systems if they can deliver adequate social services and fast economic growth. Cuban success in training doctors and providing a reasonable standard of health care, in spite of the country's economic backwardness, has already been noted (in Chapter 16) as one of the supports of the regime. Moreover, a Communist leadership may find that concessions can be made to some sections of society which help to dampen down dissent without involving potentially dangerous political reform. Thus, Cuba and even Laos have over the years become more tolerant of religious believers, with Cuba going so far as to make religious observance compatible with membership of the Communist Party. In Vietnam, too, many of the restrictions on religious groups have been lifted.[20] Religious observance has also increased in China, with some revival of Buddhism. There is, though, extreme suspicion of religious and quasi-religious organizations which are not under the control of the state. When a Buddhist group known as Falun Gong began to attract many adherents in China in the late 1990s, mass arrests accompanied its denunciation as a dangerous cult.[21]

China and Vietnam have the advantage over the other remaining Communist states of relative economic success. With China leading the way, both countries have become important participants in the global marketplace. With a population of more than eighty-two million people, Vietnam is by a wide margin the second most populous remaining Communist state (albeit a long way behind China's over 1.3 billion). As noted in an earlier chapter, capitalists have been allowed to become Communists in China – i.e. to join the CCP. In Vietnam, Communist Party members were given full permission from 2006 onwards to engage in commercial activities.[22] As a result of Vietnam's economic reform, which has earned it membership of the World Trade Organization, the country's relations even with the United States have improved. If it has thus lost some of the political 'advantage' of a potential external threat, its relative economic success has helped to compensate. The same thing has happened in China, which for years was seen as a dangerous potential enemy by both the United States and the Soviet Union. Now China has a mutually beneficial, and highly interdependent, economic relationship with the USA. And it is on far better terms politically with non-Communist Russia than it was with the Soviet leadership throughout most of the post-Stalin era.

Its qualitatively new economic intertwining with the United States means that China, even more than Vietnam, is substantially deprived of the convenient enemy which could bolster support for the system. (NATO's accidental bombing of the Chinese embassy in Belgrade in 1999 was, however, almost too effective in resuscitating the enemy image. It led to nationalist demonstrations in China which came close to getting out of the control of the authorities.) China's extraordinarily fast rate of economic growth in recent decades is also a double-edged sword for the Communist system. If the growth continues unabated, there will be a very large class of relatively prosperous people, increasingly well informed about the outside world. China may then join the ranks of the Communist systems whose successes, and not only their failures, have sown the seeds of their own destruction. Already in the year 2005, over 250 million Chinese had mobile phones, and more than seventy million of them had regular access to the internet, albeit with increasingly rigorous censorship of information deemed dangerous for the regime.[23] As Chris Patten has observed: 'Even blocking some of the most politically sensitive websites cannot give the government the total control over access to information that it once enjoyed. The handling of the SARS virus epidemic was one indicator of the incapacity of even an authoritarian state to write its own story and to cope with modern menaces without greater transparency.'[24]

China, however, has some way to go before it reaches the levels of education – with the threat they pose to authoritarian rule – of east-central Europe and the former Soviet Union. In the year 2000, the average number of years of schooling of those aged twenty-five and over in China was only 5.74, four years less than the average in countries classified by economists as 'advanced' and, indeed, than the average in 'transitional economies'. It is estimated, though, that by 2020 there will be a hundred million people in China who have completed higher education, and that by 2025 the average person over twenty-five will have had eight years of schooling.[25] Studies of values in China have shown that the higher the education of respondents, the more likely they are to support political reform.[26] Nevertheless, those who belong to the educated elite, as well as the political leadership, value China's social stability and recoil with horror at the memory of Mao's Cultural Revolution. To the extent that democratization is seen as a development which could get out of control and give rise to instability, it is by no means automatic that a majority of those with higher education will take the risk of pressing for political democracy. If, however, there is no social upheaval over the next decade, the Cultural Revolution will become a less salient factor in their consciousness and the prospects for democratic reform may correspondingly improve.[27]

One of the weaker reasons sometimes given for the persistence of Communist and other authoritarian regimes in Asia is that 'culture is destiny'.[28] That is not to say that political culture does not matter, but rather to emphasize that political cultures change, although this rarely happens overnight. The argument that countries of Confucian tradition are ill suited to the development of democracy was effectively rebutted by Kim Dae Jung four years before he became president of South Korea.[29] Kim played a major role in the democratization of South Korea, first as an opposition leader who was imprisoned (and at one point sentenced to death), and ultimately, from 1998 to 2003, as South Korean president. The example of his own country – as well as that of Japan and Taiwan – has illustrated the point that neither Confucianism nor what are sometimes called 'Asian values' impose an insuperable barrier to democracy. More generally, it can be said that a state's political culture inheritance makes democratization a much more uphill task in some countries than others. It was, indeed, readily predictable that the Baltic states would make a rapid transition from Communist government to democracy, and no surprise that the former Central Asian republics of the Soviet Union have exchanged one form of authoritarian rule for another (and with considerable continuity of practices as well as of leading personnel). However, cultures are not immutable. Every country in the world today which is regarded as democratic was at one time authoritarian, whether under the rule of a local monarch or chieftain or that of a foreign imperial power.[30]

China is an exceptionally significant case, not only because of its own size and economic importance, but for the future – or non-future – of a form of Communism in Asia. Should China lose the two most salient characteristics of a Communist system it still retains, the collapse of Communist regimes elsewhere is likely to follow. It will be less automatic than was the case in Eastern Europe after the pillars of a Communist system were dismantled in the Soviet Union. China is not the regional hegemon in the sense in which the USSR was. However, if it continues to combine fast economic development with relative social stability, while avoiding democratization of its political system, the chances are that Communism will survive longer also in other Asian countries – longer certainly than if China were to match its abandonment of the economic characteristics of Communism with a similar departure from its political norms.[31] In the absence of social crisis, it is likely that the direction China takes will be determined by the political elite or a reformist section of it, as was the case with the Soviet perestroika with its profound consequences.

However, economic recession in the wake of the global financial crisis which began in 2008 raises other possibilities. Falling demand for Chinese products has invoked the spectre of scores of millions of Chinese workers becoming newly unemployed. None other than China's prime minister, Wen Jiabao, has warned that unless a fast pace of economic development can be sustained, 'factors damaging social stability will grow'.[32] Democracies have the great advantage that when things go wrong, the incumbent government can be blamed and voted out. The political system itself is preserved as a result of the exercise of democratic accountability. An authoritarian regime which is driven to relying on economic performance for legitimacy faces special difficulties when that performance weakens. As we have seen elsewhere, that does not automatically lead to systemic change, but in conditions in which Communist ideology has lost whatever attraction it once had – and in the absence of the mobilizing possibilities engendered by Cold (or hot) War – social unrest becomes dangerous. In China's case it could present political leaders with a stark choice – either a return to still more severe repression or accepting the risks involved in serious democratization of the political system.

Epitaph for an Illusion

The idea of building communism, a society in which the state would have withered away, turned out to be a dangerous illusion. What was built instead was Communism, an oppressive party-state which was authoritarian at best and ruthlessly totalitarian at worst. Although it had some common features, it changed over time and differed hugely from one part of the world to another. The Soviet Union was a far less fearful place to inhabit in the Brezhnev era than it was in the late 1930s. Poland and Hungary throughout the Communist period were manifestly undemocratic, but life *there* was qualitatively less oppressive and thuggish than it was in China during the years in which the Cultural Revolution was wreaking havoc. Communism in east-central Europe, more generally, was bad enough, especially during the years when Stalin was still alive, but it never came close to being as murderous as Pol Pot's Cambodia/Kampuchea.

Yet even more diverse than these regimes were the people who joined Communist parties. In non-Communist states – especially fascist, right-wing authoritarian, or racist regimes – those who joined the party often did so for the best of motives. The American writer Howard Fast, who joined the Communist Party in 1943, did so believing that the destination was 'the total brotherhood of man, a world-wide unity of love and creativity in which life is neither wasted nor despised'.[33] The last straw for Fast, who left the CPUSA in 1956, was what Eastern European Communist diplomats told him about the persecution, including anti-semitic purges, which had been conducted under Communist rule in their homelands.[34] He argued, in the book he wrote to explain his break with the party, that if anything could save Communism, it would be Western bellicosity. What would defeat it was the power of ideas. Communism was an idea, and an idea could not be dealt with by force. 'It must', he wrote in 1958, 'be bent over the anvil of truth to test its strength. I do not believe that this particular idea if put to the test can survive.'[35]

In Western countries, the obvious course for people who had joined the Communist Party for idealistic reasons was to leave it once they had found how wide was the gap between their ideals and the practice of power within even their own non-ruling party, not to speak of the crimes authorized by ruling parties and committed by the secret police in Communist states. This was easier said than done, for those who left the party were made to feel the stigma of betrayers of a sacred cause. Since the Communist movement tended to envelop the whole of their lives, to break with the party was also to break with almost all their friends. It was, therefore, easier to renounce their membership at a time when others were doing so, as many did following Khrushchev's Secret Speech in 1956, with still more following after Soviet tanks crushed the Hungarian revolution later in the same year.

Within Communist states themselves, a different logic operated from that which made sense under conditions of political pluralism. Deng Xiaoping (who should not be idealized, for he was ruthless in suppressing the

Tiananmen Square protesters in 1989) played a decisively important part in putting the madness of the Cultural Revolution into reverse and in introducing radical economic reform which led to rapidly improving living standards in China. It goes without saying that Deng could achieve this only as a result of his standing within the highest echelons of the Communist Party. In the Soviet Union, it was people who had been born some years after the Bolshevik revolution, who had taken the Soviet system as a given and had in their youth joined the CPSU, who played far and away the most decisive role in transforming the Communist system into something different in kind. Mikhail Gorbachev was first and foremost among them. Others, whose importance has been discussed in earlier chapters, included Alexander Yakovlev and, in an advisory capacity, Anatoly Chernyaev and Georgy Shakhnazarov.

In Eastern Europe, as distinct from the Soviet Union, most of those who worked to change the system from the inside had already joined the party before the Communists came to power. Once a Communist party did seize power, people of the most diverse views and personalities joined for a wide variety of reasons, but most commonly to further (or, at least, not retard) their careers. But in Czechoslovakia, for example, it was not those who shifted their allegiance from democratic parties and joined the victorious Communist Party in furtherance of their careers who subsequently bent their efforts radically to reform the system. The most active participants in the Czechoslovak reform movement, and in the Prague Spring of 1968 which was its culmination (and a forerunner of the Soviet perestroika), were party members who as young men and women in the immediate post-war years had joined the Communist Party full of revolutionary zeal for 'building socialism'. In Yugoslavia, Milovan Djilas had been a dedicated revolutionary and one of Tito's closest comrades-in-arms during the Partisan war against Nazi occupation during World War Two. He became a bold critic of the system that had been established (and was imprisoned by Tito for his pains), arguing that idealization of the revolution had become a cover for 'the egotism and love of power of the new revolutionary masters'.[36] Having evolved into a democratic socialist (his 1962 book, *Conversations with Stalin*, was dedicated to the memory of the British Labour Party hero, Aneurin Bevan), Djilas ended up hoping that 'monolithic ideological revolutions will cease, even though they have roots in idealism and idealists'.[37]

If those whose names are associated with amelioration or reform of the Communist system (in a few decisive cases amounting to transformative change) were, more often than not, leading members of the party, that was because the system was such that in normal times change could come from nowhere else. Poland was the great exception, although even there, as we have seen, Solidarity was effectively crushed as a mass movement at the end of 1981 and re-emerged as a force in political life only after change had been instituted at the top of the Soviet political hierarchy. It was the liberalization and subsequent partial democratization of the Soviet political system, together with the transformation of Soviet foreign policy under Gorbachev, which changed the whole political climate in Eastern Europe.

The part played by Western democracies in producing change in the Communist world did not lie primarily in their military alliance. Important though that was for discouraging further Communist expansion, it also helped Communist leaders to maintain their power and, in some countries, to win quite broad popular acceptance. Great stress was placed on the threat posed by external enemies, and the regime's domestic critics were portrayed as being in thrall to the malign West. It was through simply being there as a better alternative to Communist rule that democracies prevailed in the battle of ideas. The example of greater tolerance, of free elections, accountable government, and respect for human rights, plus substantially higher living standards, had a profound effect not only on the minority of citizens from Communist states who had the opportunity to visit Western countries but on the more open-minded Communist officials themselves. Change in the ideas of leaders who already occupied positions of institutional power was of exceptional importance. Thus, Gorbachev came to believe that the kind of order which existed in the democracies of Western Europe was order of a qualitatively higher kind than that imposed by the KGB in the Soviet Union, and that what had been called 'socialism' in the Soviet Union was a perversion of socialist ideals.[38]

As an alternative way of organizing human society, Communism turned out to be a ghastly failure. Partly because, however, its ideology included some genuinely humanistic aspirations, trampled on though they were by the party-state authorities, reformers were able to begin to make changes by arguing from within the ideology, choosing their quotations carefully. If, though, the change was to be as thoroughgoing as that of the Soviet perestroika, the ideational innovation had to move well beyond the boundaries of the thought of Marx and Lenin. Although many of the ideas which were influential – as Communist systems ceased to exist in Europe and parts of Asia, including former Soviet Central Asia – were of universal validity, it is not surprising that they have been reflected convincingly in the political life of only a minority of post-Communist states. As Robert Dahl has pointed out, although democracy has been debated off and on for some 2,500 years, its practice has been rare in human experience.[39] There can be many false starts. Former Communist states are not alone in retreating, in many cases, from democratization before they have advanced very far along the road to democracy. That form of government comes, of course, in different institutional forms, but in essence must include the real, and not merely nominal, possibility for a people to hold their rulers accountable and to turn them out of office in free and fair elections. The good news, as Dahl also emphasizes, is that democracies, once firmly established, are remarkably resilient.[40] Consolidated democracies are hardly ever exchanged for a form of authoritarian rule, and however imperfectly they function, they have shown themselves more capable of delivering justice as well as freedom than any state built on the foundations laid by Marx and Lenin.

Acknowledgements

This book has taken over two years to write, but it is the product of some forty-five years of study of Communism. That has included numerous study visits to many Communist countries, beginning more than four decades ago. In the course of those visits I learned much from so many different people that it would be invidious even to begin naming those who influenced my thinking on the subject. Where remarks made to me in Communist countries have been included in the book itself, I have generally identified the person who made the statement, although I have not done so in the case of a country still under Communist rule.

Before I mention those who have been of direct help by commenting on parts of *The Rise and Fall of Communism*, I should like to record two important longer-standing debts, although the people concerned are no longer alive. That I have written this book at all (as well as much else on related themes) is due to Leonard Schapiro, who died a quarter of a century ago but in his day was the leading specialist in Britain on Soviet politics. He taught at the London School of Economics and Political Science where I was a student at the end of the 1950s and in the early 1960s. It was Schapiro who, on the strength of an essay I had written in my final year as an undergraduate, encouraged me to apply for a graduate studentship in Russian and Communist studies. My own tentative ideas about graduate work had concerned different fields entirely. That I wound up being interviewed for such an award by a committee chaired by Michael Oakeshott, and including Schapiro, set the direction of my subsequent career – and was entirely due to Schapiro's persuasion. The other early mentor to whom I still feel indebted is Alec Nove (who was also on the LSE committee which interviewed me). I began my university teaching career in Glasgow University in 1964. Nove had moved to Scotland from the LSE the previous year to head Glasgow's Institute of Soviet and East European Studies. My appointment was in the Department of Politics, but I learned a lot in conversations and seminars with such a stimulating and perceptive colleague as Nove. Although the family roots of both Schapiro and Nove lay in the Russian Empire, they

differed significantly from one another in their analyses of Soviet and
Communist systems. Each of them, however, made a major contribution
to that broad field, providing complementary insights.

I have also many more recent debts to record. A number of friends and
colleagues read at least one chapter of this book (several chapters in some
cases) and gave me their comments. In general, these led me to add to, rather
than subtract from, what I had written, although I remain conscious of what
I have had to leave out. In a book of this scope, not only each chapter but
most of the sections within any particular chapter could have become books
in themselves. The colleagues who read chapters in their areas of expertise
also saved me from making a number of errors. I am enormously grateful
for their help and advice. In alphabetical order, those to whom I am thus
indebted are: Professor David Anderson of St Cross College, Oxford; Alan
Angell, St Antony's College, Oxford; Owen Bennett-Jones of the BBC; Sir
Rodric Braithwaite, former British ambassador to the Soviet Union; Dr Paul
Chaisty, St Antony's College; Professor Richard Crampton, St Edmund Hall,
Oxford; Richard Davy, formerly of *The Times* and *The Independent*; Professor
Rosemary Foot, St Antony's College; Dr Nandini Gooptu, St Antony's College;
Professor Yoram Gorlizki, Manchester University; Dr Sudhir Hazareesingh
of Balliol College, Oxford; Professor Charles King, Georgetown University;
Dr Mark Kramer of Harvard University; Professor Rana Mitter, St Cross
College, Oxford; Kenneth (Lord) Morgan, Queen's College, Oxford; Dr Julie
Newton, St Antony's College; Dr Alex Pravda, St Antony's College; Professor
Alfred Stepan, Columbia University; Professor Arthur Stockwin, St Antony's
College; Professor William Taubman of Amherst College; and Dr Steve Tsang,
St Antony's College. On particular points I have consulted, and had very
helpful responses from, Dr Roy Allison of LSE, Martin Dewhirst of Glasgow
University, Dr David Johnson of St Antony's College, Dr Tomila Lankina of
De Montfort University, Leicester, Dr John Maddicott, Exeter College, Oxford,
John Miller, La Trobe University, Professor Ronald Suny, University of
Michigan, Dr Zachary Shore of the Naval Postgraduate School in California
and Dr William Tompson of OECD. For specific items of research assistance, I am grateful to graduate students Nina Kozlova of St Antony's College
and Stéphane Reissfelder of Lincoln College, Oxford.

The main archival sources I have used have been located in the National
Security Archive in Washington DC (where Svetlana Savranskaya was a
particularly helpful guide to their resources), the Hoover Institution Archive
at Stanford University (where I had valuable help from Martina Podsklanova),
and the Gorbachev Foundation in Moscow (with access to important materials facilitated by Anatoly Chernyaev, Olga Zdravomyslova and Sergey
Kuznetsov). Among the other archival documents used are some British

ACKNOWLEDGEMENTS 621

government papers which I was able to get declassified under the UK Freedom of Information Act. Archival references, books and articles are cited in full on their first mention in the endnotes to each chapter of the book – subsequently in abbreviated form.

I am very grateful to the British Academy for the award of a Small Research Grant which greatly facilitated my research. In particular, it funded fruitful visits to both Washington and Moscow for archival research. My greatest long-term institutional debt – as may be discerned from the affiliation of quite a number of the colleagues mentioned earlier in these acknowledgements – is to St Antony's College, Oxford. I have benefited greatly from my membership of the Department of Politics and International Relations of the University of Oxford, and from interaction with colleagues there. The Oxford system is such, however, that, in the humanities and social sciences, most Fellows spend the greater part of their time in their college. The fact that St Antony's is a graduate college specializing in the social sciences and modern history has in itself been a big advantage. Even more helpful has been the fact that the college is devoted to study of problems of the real world, housing a range of regional centres, each containing first-rate specialists on different countries. The libraries I have most used have also been at St Antony's – the Russian and Eurasian Studies Centre Library, which Jackie Willcox ran with great efficiency and helpfulness for a quarter of a century before being succeeded by the no less admirable Richard Ramage, and the main college library, where my thanks are due to its long-serving librarian Rosamund Campbell. The electronic resources of the University of Oxford library system have also been a boon.

I am immensely grateful to my literary agent, Felicity Bryan, for the expertise, enthusiasm and support she has provided, along with her highly efficient colleagues in the Felicity Bryan Agency in Oxford. I am greatly indebted also to George Lucas in New York for negotiating the American edition of this book. I have also had the pleasure of working with editors who have offered me much valuable advice and have been courteously patient. For this I warmly thank Will Sulkin and Jörg Hensgen in London, Virginia (Ginny) Smith in New York, and Tim Rostron in Toronto. I have benefited especially from Jörg's and Ginny's close reading of the manuscript and helpful comments.

Finally, I must thank my wife Pat, not only for carefully reading the manuscript chapter by chapter, but also for putting up with the long hours I spent working on this book. Delightful grandchildren, happily, provided much compensation. They have a special place in the dedication of this book. Perhaps one day they may even read it.

Notes and Sources

Introduction

1. Confirmed in a personal communication of 31 August 2007 by Professor Viktor Kuvaldin, who in March 1989 entered the International Department of the Central Committee of the Communist Party of the Soviet Union as a member of a group of consultants on foreign policy.

1 The Idea of Communism

1. Andrzej Walicki, *Marxism and the Leap to the Kingdom of Freedom: The Rise and Fall of the Communist Utopia* (Stanford University Press, Stanford, 1995, p. 71). See also Karl Popper, *The Open Society and its Enemies, Vol. II, The High Tide of Prophecy: Hegel and Marx* (Routledge & Kegan Paul, London, 3rd ed., 1957); and Popper, *The Poverty of Historicism* (Routledge & Kegan Paul, London, 2nd ed., 1960). • **2**. Popper, *The Open Society and its Enemies, Vol. II*, p. 122. • **3** Max Beer, *A History of British Socialism* (Allen & Unwin, London, 1953), Vol. 1, p. 6. See also Alexander Gray, *The Socialist Tradition: Moses to Lenin* (Longmans, London, 1947), p. 38. • **4**. Acts, Chapter 4, Verse 32, *The Bible* (King James Authorised Version). • **5**. Norman Cohn, *The Pursuit of the Millennium: Revolutionary Millenarians and Mystical Anarchists of the Middle Ages* (Pimlico, London, 2004), p. 193. (Cohn's pioneering study was first published in 1957.) • **6**. Beer, *A History of British Socialism*, p. 23. • **7**. Cohn, *The Pursuit of the Millennium*, p. 200. • **8**. Ibid. • **9**. Ibid., p. 198. • **10**. Beer, *A History of British Socialism*, p. 27. • **11**. Ibid., p. 28. • **12**. This is the usual rendering of the verse, although there are a number of variants. The version I have quoted is that used by the nineteenth-century socialist William Morris, in his account of an imaginary conversation with the fourteenth-century priest. See Morris, *A Dream of John Ball* (Seven Seas Publishers, Berlin, 1958), p. 24. It involves already a modernization of Ball's language. In an earlier rendering it is: 'When Adam dalf and Eve span, Who was then a gentilman?' (Beer, *A History of British Socialism*, Vol. 1, p. 27). At one time the earliest use of it was attributed (wrongly, it now appears) to Richard Rolle of Hampole, who was born in the late thirteenth century and died in 1349. The origins of the verse remain unknown. According to Norman Cohn, at the time John Ball preached a sermon, taking that verse as his text, it was already 'a traditional

proverb' (*The Pursuit of the Millennium*, p. 199). • **13**. Cohn, *The Pursuit of the Millennium*, p. 207. • **14**. Ibid., p. 216. • **15**. Ibid., p. 217. • **16**. Ibid., pp. 119–226. • **17**. Friedrich Engels, *Anti-Dühring* (Foreign Languages Publishing House, Moscow, 2nd ed., 1959), p. 217. This is a translation of the 3rd German edition of that work by Engels, published in 1894. • **18**. Cohn, *The Pursuit of the Millennium*, pp. 247–8. • **19**. It was written in Latin. For an excellent edition, with a modern translation by Paul Turner, see Thomas More, *Utopia* (Penguin, London, revised edition, 2003). • **20**. Ibid., Introduction by Turner, p. xx. • **21**. Ibid. • **22**. More, *Utopia*, p. 45. • **23**. Ibid., p. 111. • **24**. Ibid., p. 113. • **25**. Gray, *The Socialist Tradition*, pp. 70–2. • **26**. See, for example, Norman Hampson, *The Enlightenment* (Penguin, Harmondsworth, 1968); and Roy Porter, *Enlightenment: Britain and the Creation of the Modern World* (Penguin, London, 2000). • **27**. See, in particular, Baron de Montesquieu, *The Spirit of the Laws*, translated by Thomas Nugent with an Introduction by Franz Neumann (Hafner, New York, 1949; first published in Paris in 1748 as *Des l'esprit des loix*); Adam Smith, *Lectures on Jurisprudence*, edited by R.L. Meek, D.D. Raphael and P.G. Stein (Clarendon Press, Oxford, 1978) (Smith's lectures were delivered at Glasgow University in the 1750s and early 1760s; this edition is mainly of student notes of his lectures in the 1762–63 academic year); and John Millar, *Observations Concerning the Distinction of Ranks in Society* (John Murray, London, 1771). See also Anand Chitnis, *The Scottish Enlightenment: A Social History* (Croom Helm, London, 1976); Ronald L. Meek, 'Smith, Turgot, and the "Four Stages" Theory', in Meek, *Smith, Marx, and After: Ten Essays in the Development of Economic Thought* (Chapman and Hall, London, 1979), pp. 18–32; and A.H. (Archie) Brown, 'Adam Smith's First Russian Followers', in Andrew S. Skinner and Thomas Wilson (eds.), *Essays on Adam Smith* (Clarendon Press, Oxford, 1975), pp. 247–73, esp. pp. 270–2. • **28**. Biancamaria Fontana, 'Democracy and the French Revolution', in John Dunn (ed.), *Democracy: The Unfinished Journey 508 BC to AD 1993* (Oxford University Press, Oxford, 1992), p. 107. • **29**. Leszek Kołakowski, *Main Currents of Marxism. Its Rise, Growth, and Dissolution*, translated from the Polish by P.S. Falla (Clarendon Press, Oxford, 1978), Vol. 1, *The Founders*, p. 186. For a much fuller discussion of Babouvism, see J.L. Talmon, *The Origins of Totalitarian Democracy* (Secker and Warburg, London, 1952), Part III, 'The Babouvist Crystallization'. • **30**. Kołakowski, *Main Currents of Marxism*, Vol. 1, p. 187. • **31**. Ibid., pp. 187–92; and Robert Nisbet, *History of the Idea of Progress* (Heinemann, London, 1980), pp. 246–51. • **32**. See Gareth Stedman Jones, in Karl Marx and Friedrich Engels, *The Communist Manifesto* (Penguin, London, 2002), p. 173; and David McLellan, *Karl Marx: His Life and Thought* (Macmillan, London, 1973; Paladin paperback ed., 1976), pp. 186–7. • **33**. Kołakowski, *Main Currents of Marxism*, Vol. 1, pp. 198–203. • **34**. Ibid., pp. 203–11, esp. p. 209. • **35**. Ibid., pp. 213–14. • **36**. G.D.H. Cole, Introduction to Robert Owen, *A New View of Society and other Writings* (Dent, London, 1927), pp. x–xi. See also Margaret Cole, *Robert Owen of New Lanark* (Batchworth Press, London, 1953); and Beer, *A History of British Socialism*, Vol. 1, pp. 160–81. • **37**. Margaret Cole, *Robert Owen of New Lanark*, p. 151. • **38**. Ibid., p. 152. • **39**. Ibid., p. 156. • **40**. Ibid., p. 159. Although New Harmony did not live up to Owen's expectations as a shining example of a new form of community, it left some useful legacies. Owen's son, David Dale Owen, remained in New Harmony, and

the laboratory he established there was the headquarters of what became the United States Geological Survey. William Maclure – a Scots immigrant to the United States who became a successful businessman and philanthropist and had helped Owen finance New Harmony – also stayed on to preserve the enlightened Education Society and School of Industry he had set up. (All four of Robert Owen's sons and one of his daughters eventually settled in the United States. Apart from the successful David Dale Owen, another son, Robert Dale Owen, became a US Congressman.)
• 41. The literature on Marx and Marxism is voluminous. For particularly good biographical studies of Marx, which naturally discuss also his ideas, see Isaiah Berlin, *Karl Marx* (Oxford University Press, 2nd ed., 1948); McLellan, *Karl Marx: His Life and Thought*; and Francis Wheen, *Karl Marx* (Fourth Estate, London, 1999). On Engels, see David McLellan, *Engels* (Fontana, Glasgow, 1977); and Terrell Carver, *Friedrich Engels: His Life and Thought* (Macmillan, London, 1989). On Marxism as a doctrine, apart from the books by Popper, Walicki and Kołakowski already cited, important studies include John Plamenatz, *German Marxism and Russian Communism* (Longman, London, 1954); George Lichtheim, *Marxism* (Routledge and Kegan Paul, 1961); Shlomo Avineri, *The Social and Political Thought of Karl Marx* (Cambridge University Press, Cambridge, 1968); David McLellan, *Marx before Marxism* (Macmillan, London, 1970; rev. ed., Pelican, London, 1972); Angus Walker, *Marx: His Theory and its Context. Politics as Economics* (Longman, London, 1978); and David McLellan, *Marxism after Marx* (Macmillan, London, 1979). • 42. Wheen, *Karl Marx*, p. 18. • 43. Berlin, *Karl Marx*, p. 215. • 44. Wheen notes that Jenny's mother's wedding present 'was a collection of jewellery and silver plate embellished with the Argyll family crest, a legacy from the von Westphalens' Scottish ancestors' and that during the next few years 'the Argyll family silver spent more time in the hands of pawnbrokers than in the kitchen cupboard' (Wheen, *Karl Marx*, p. 52). The help provided by Engels was much more substantial. Although Marx was close to destitution during his first fifteen years in London, from the late 1860s 'Engels was able to settle a generous annual income on him' which in the monetary values of a century later meant that 'Engels subsidized Marx and his family to the extent of over £100,000' (McLellan, *Engels*, p. 67). • 45. McLellan, *Karl Marx: His Life and Thought*, p. 46. • 46. McLellan, *Engels*, p. 15. • 47. Ibid., pp. 15–16. • 48. Wheen, *Karl Marx*, pp. 261–5; and McLellan, *Engels*, pp. 20–1. • 49. McLellan, *Engels*, pp. 21–2. • 50. Volume 1 of *Capital* was published first in German (*Das Kapital*) in 1867. The first English edition was published only twenty years later – after Marx's death, edited by Engels. • 51. Karl Marx and Friedrich Engels, *The Communist Manifesto*, first published 1848, cited here in the scholarly edition of Gareth Stedman Jones (Penguin, London, 2002), p. 219.
• 52. Cited in Berlin, *Karl Marx*, p. 193. • 53. For a discussion of the Gotha Programme and Marx's criticism of it, see McLellan, *Karl Marx: His Life and Thought*, pp. 431–5.
• 54. Karl Marx, *Critique of the Gotha Programme* (Foreign Languages Publishing House, Moscow, 1959), p. 22. (Marx's critique of the 'Gotha Unity Congress' programme of the German Social Democrats was written in London in 1875. It was first published by Engels in 1891.) • 55. Ibid. • 56. Robert C. Tucker, *The Marxian Revolutionary Idea* (Allen & Unwin, London, 1970), p. 15. • 57. Marx, 'Preface to *A Critique of Political Economy*', in David McLellan (ed.), *Karl Marx: Selected Writings*

(Oxford University Press, Oxford, 2nd ed., 2000), p. 426. • 58. Ibid., p. 202. • 59. Engels, 'Preface to the English Edition of 1888' of Marx and Engels, *The Communist Manifesto* (ed. Gareth Stedman Jones), op.cit., pp. 202–3. • 60. Karl Marx, *Capital*, Vol. 1 (Progress Publishers, Moscow, 1965), pp. 794–6. • 61. Ibid., p. 9. • 62. See, for example, G.Kh. Shakhnazarov and F.M. Burlatsky, 'O razvitii marksistsko-leninskoy politicheskoy nauki', in *Voprosy filosofii*, Vol. 12, 1980, pp. 10–22, at p. 12. • 63. Plamenatz, *German Marxism and Russian Communism*, p. 9. • 64. Ibid. • 65. David McLellan, in McLellan, *Karl Marx: Selected Writings*, p. 377. • 66. Ibid. • 67. 'Letter to Vera Sassoulitch' in McLellan, *Karl Marx: Selected Writings*, pp. 623–7. • 68. Ibid., p. 623. • 69. Marx and Engels, 'Preface to the Russian Edition of 1882' of the *Communist Manifesto* (ed. Gareth Stedman Jones), p. 196. • 70. Stedman Jones points to evidence indicating that Marx was willing to go further than Engels and to allow that 'a transition from village commune to advanced communism might be possible without a proletarian revolution in the West' (Stedman Jones, in Marx and Engels, *The Communist Manifesto*, p. 261). Engels may have been a restraining and more cautious voice in the composition of the Preface of 1882. • 71. Karl Marx, *The Eighteenth Brumaire of Louis Bonaparte* (Progress, Moscow, 1967), p. 10. This work of Marx was first published – in New York – in 1852.

2 *Communism and Socialism – the Early Years*

1. Edmund Wilson, *To the Finland Station: A Study in the Writing and Acting of History* (Fontana, London, 1960), pp. 271–3. • 2. Isaiah Berlin, *Russian Thinkers* (Hogarth Press, London, 1978), pp. 110 and 192. • 3. Leszek Kołakowski, *Main Currents of Marxism*, Vol. 1, *The Founders* (Clarendon Press, Oxford, 1978), pp. 248–9. • 4. Ibid., pp. 250–1. • 5. Ibid., pp. 255–6. • 6. Mikhail Bakunin, *Statehood and Anarchy*, quoted by Kołakowski, ibid., p. 252. • 7. Kenneth O. Morgan, *Keir Hardie: Radical and Socialist* (Weidenfeld & Nicolson, London, 1975), p. 40. • 8. Ibid. • 9. Ibid., p. 289. • 10. Ibid., p. 216. • 11. James Farr, 'Understanding conceptual change politically', in Terence Ball, James Farr and Russell L. Hanson, *Political Innovation and Conceptual Change* (Cambridge University Press, Cambridge, 1989), pp. 24–49, at p. 30. • 12. Donald Sassoon, *One Hundred Years of Socialism: The West European Left in the Twentieth Century* (Fontana, London, 1997), p. 7. • 13. Dmitri Volkogonov, *Lenin: A New Biography*, translated by Harold Shukman (The Free Press, New York, 1994), p. 8. • 14. Ibid., pp. 8–9. • 15. Ibid., p. 8. • 16. Robert Service, *Lenin: A Biography* (Macmillan, London, 2000), p. 42. • 17. Cited by Nina Tumarkin, *Lenin Lives! The Lenin Cult in Soviet Russia* (Harvard University Press, Cambridge, Mass., enlarged ed., 1997), pp. 257–8. • 18. The prestige of the Lenin anniversary speech was such that, strangely enough, even as important a reformer in the last years of the Soviet Union as Alexander Yakovlev continued late in life to resent the fact that Mikhail Gorbachev had never invited him to be the Lenin orator. This was rather an odd grievance, for before the Soviet Union ceased to exist, Yakovlev had turned against Lenin, and in the post-Soviet years he came to the conclusion that Lenin was 'the initiator and organizer of mass terror in Russia' and 'eternally indictable for crimes against humanity'. See Yakovlev, *Sumerki* (Materik, Moscow, 2003), pp. 26

and 495–6. • **19.** Neil Harding, *Leninism* (Macmillan, London, 1996), p. 18. As Harding observes: 'The trauma of Alexander's execution may well have had a profound psychological effect on Lenin's whole career but we shall never be able to assess it, not only because the impact of such personal tragedies is inherently difficult to gauge, but also because Lenin himself was extraordinarily reticent about the matter' (ibid.). • **20.** Ibid., pp. 20–1; and Nikolay Valentinov, *Encounters with Lenin* (Oxford University Press, London, 1968), p. 176. • **21.** Orlando Figes, *A People's Tragedy: The Russian Revolution 1891–1924* (Jonathan Cape, London, 1996), pp. 146–7. • **22.** Neil Harding (ed.), with translations by Richard Taylor, *Marxism in Russia: Key Documents 1879–1906* (Cambridge University Press, Cambridge, 1983), pp. 29–30. • **23.** Andrzej Walicki, *A History of Russian Thought From the Enlightenment to Marxism* (Clarendon Press, Oxford, 1980), p. 251. • **24.** Valentinov, *Encounters with Lenin*, p. 203. • **25.** G.V. Plekhanov, 'Propaganda Among the Workers', in Harding (ed.), *Marxism in Russia: Key Documents 1879–1906*, pp. 59–67, at p. 65. • **26.** Louis Fischer, *The Life of Lenin* (Weidenfeld and Nicolson, London, 1964), pp. 20–1. • **27.** Ibid. • **28.** Berlin, *Russian Thinkers*, p. 228. • **29.** Ibid., pp. 229–30. • **30.** Ibid., p. 230. • **31.** Valentinov, *Encounters with Lenin*, p. 63. • **32.** Ibid. • **33.** Valentinov, *Encounters with Lenin*, p. 64. • **34.** V.I. Lenin's *What is to be Done?*, edited with an introduction by S.V. Utechin (Clarendon Press, Oxford, 1963), p. 117. • **35.** Service, *Lenin: A Biography*, p. 152. • **36.** Leonard Schapiro, *The Communist Party of the Soviet Union* (Methuen, London, 2nd ed., 1970), pp. 49–50. • **37.** Leon Trotsky, *My Life: An Attempt at Autobiography* (Penguin, Harmondsworth, 1975). Trotsky wrote this book in 1929. • **38.** Ibid., pp. 50–1; and Figes, *A People's Tragedy*, pp. 195–6 and 198 • **39.** Bertram D. Wolfe, *Three Who Made a Revolution: A Biographical History* (Beacon Press, Boston, 1948), pp. 243–4. • **40.** Ibid., p. 244. • **41.** Marc D. Steinberg, 'Russia's *fin de siècle*, 1900–1914', in Ronald G. Suny (ed.), *The Cambridge History of Russia. Volume III: The Twentieth Century* (Cambridge University Press, Cambridge, 2006), pp. 67–93, at p. 75. • **42.** V.I. Lenin, *One Step Forward, Two Steps Back* (Progress, Moscow, 1969), p. 211. • **43.** Ibid., p. 210. • **44.** See the Preface to the English edition (first published in 1909) of Eduard Bernstein, *Evolutionary Socialism: A Criticism and Affirmation* (Schocken Books, New York, 1961), p. xxii. • **45.** David McLellan, *Karl Marx: His Life and Thought* (Macmillan, London, 1973; Paladin paperback ed., 1976), p. 424. • **46.** Bernstein, *Evolutionary Socialism*, p. 203. • **47.** Ibid. • **48.** Ibid., pp. 203–4. • **49.** Ibid., p. 219. • **50.** Ibid., pp. xxviii–xxix. • **51.** Ibid., p. 146. • **52.** Cited by Sassoon, *One Hundred Years of Socialism*, p. 19.

3 The Russian Revolutions and Civil War

1. Baruch Knei-Paz, *The Social and Political Thought of Leon Trotsky* (Clarendon Press, Oxford, 1978), p. 15. • **2.** Trotsky, *Nashi politicheskie zadachi* (1904), cited by Isaac Deutscher, *The Prophet Armed. Trotsky: 1879–1921* (Oxford University Press, Oxford, 1970), p. 90. • **3.** Sheila Fitzpatrick, *The Russian Revolution* (Oxford University Press, Oxford, 1982), p. 25. • **4.** For an account of Russian history which takes such an interpretation to an extreme, see Tibor Szamuely, *The Russian Tradition* (Secker & Warburg, London, 1974). • **5.** Fitzpatrick, *The Russian Revolution*, p. 25. • **6.** Volsky (Valentinov) contrasted the respectful and reasoned way in which the Menshevik leader, Martov, listened to those same views of his, with which Martov also disagreed, with Lenin's stream of abuse. See Nikolay Valentinov, *Encounters with Lenin* (Oxford University Press, London, 1968), esp. pp. 205–43. • 7. Moshe Lewin, *Lenin's Last Struggle* (Pluto Press, London, 1975). • 8. See Terence Emmons, *The Russian Landed Gentry and the Peasant Emancipation of 1861* (Cambridge University Press, Cambridge, 1968); and Daniel Field, *The End of Serfdom: Nobility and Bureaucracy in Russia, 1855–1861* (Harvard University Press, Cambridge, Mass., 1976). • 9. Hugh Seton-Watson, *The Russian Empire 1801–1917* (Oxford University Press, London, 1967), pp. 563–4. • 10. Dominic Lieven, *Nicholas II: Emperor of All the Russias* (John Murray, London, 1993), pp. 144–5. • 11. Orlando Figes, *A People's Tragedy: The Russian Revolution 1891–1924* (Jonathan Cape, London, 1996), p. 175. • 12. Ibid., p. 178. • 13. Leon Trotsky, *My Life: An Attempt at Autobiography* (Penguin, Hardmondsworth, 1975), p. 184. See also Leon Trotsky, *1905* (Penguin, Harmondsworth, 1973). • 14. Trotsky, *My Life*, p. 184. • 15. Ibid., pp. 185–6. • 16. For a vivid account of one such bank raid, see Simon Sebag Montefiore, *The Young Stalin* (Weidenfeld & Nicolson, London, 2007), pp. 1–11. • 17. Dmitri Volkogonov, *Lenin: A New Biography*, translated by Harold Shukman (The Free Press, New York, 1994), pp. 54–5. For a fuller account of the financing of the Bolsheviks prior to the 1917 revolution, see ibid., pp. 49–63. • 18. Figes, *A People's Tragedy*, p. 223. • 19. Geoffrey Hosking, *The Russian Constitutional Experiment: Government and Duma, 1907–1914* (Cambridge University Press, Cambridge, 1973), p. 148. See also Figes, *A People's Tragedy*, pp. 221–32. • 20. Figes, *A People's Tragedy*, p. 196. • 21. Ibid., pp. 196–7. • 22. Fitzpatrick, *The Russian Revolution*, p. 32. • 23. Ibid., pp. 332–3. • 24. See Figes, *A People's Tragedy*, pp. 289–91. • 25. Seton-Watson, *The Russian Empire 1801–1917*, pp. 721–2. • 26. Figes, *A People's Tragedy*, p. 291. • 27. Volkogonov, *Lenin*, p. 104. • 28. Donald Treadgold, *Twentieth Century Russia* (Rand McNally, Chicago, 2nd ed., 1964), p. 119. • 29. Lieven, *Nicholas II*, p. 231. • 30. Volkogonov, *Lenin*, pp. 208–12; Lieven, *Nicholas II*, pp. 241–5. • 31. Fitzpatrick, *The Russian Revolution*, p. 34. • 32. Robert Service, *Lenin: A Biography* (Pan Macmillan, London, 2002), pp. 255–9; Volkogonov, *Lenin*, pp. 110–11 and 120–1. • 33. Service, *Lenin*, pp. 261–3. • 34. See Robert Service, *The Bolshevik Party in Revolution: A Study in Organisational Change 1917–1923* (Macmillan, London, 1979); and Fitzpatrick, *The Russian Revolution*, pp. 36–7. • 35. Fitzpatrick, *The Russian Revolution*, pp. 36–7. • 36. Volkogonov, *Lenin*, p. 173. • 37. Ibid., p. 176. • 38. Karl Kautsky, *The Dictatorship of the Proletariat* (University of Michigan Press, Ann Arbor, 1964 – first published 1919), p. 140. • 39. Ibid., pp. 19–20. • 40. Ibid., p. 74. • 41. Figes, *A People's Tragedy*, p. 574. • 42. George Leggett, *The Cheka: Lenin's Political Police* (Clarendon Press, Oxford, 1981), p. 359.

4 'Building Socialism': Russia and the Soviet Union, 1917–40

1. V.I. Lenin, *The State and Revolution* (Foreign Languages Publishing House, Moscow, 1962; first published 1917), p. 192. • 2. Ibid., p. 145. • 3. Ibid. • 4. Ibid., p. 157. • 5. Ibid., p. 152. • 6. A.J. Polan, *Lenin and the End of Politics* (Methuen, London, 1984), p. 11. • 7. Neil Harding, *Lenin's Political Thought: Volume 2. Theory and Practice in the*

Socialist Revolution (Macmillan, London, 1981), p. 140. • **8.** John Plamenatz, *German Marxism and Russian Communism* (Longman, London, 1954), p. 248. • **9.** Polan, *Lenin and the End of Politics*, p. 129. • **10.** See Leonard Schapiro, '"Putting the Lid on Leninism": Opposition and dissent in the communist one-party states', in Schapiro (ed.), *Political Opposition in One-Party States* (Macmillan, London, 1972), pp. 33–57, esp. 35–41. • **11.** Leonard Schapiro, *The Origin of the Communist Autocracy. Political Opposition in the Soviet State: First Phase 1917–1922* (Bell, London, 1955), p. 301. • **12.** Ibid., p. 303. • **13.** Ibid., pp. 318–19. • **14.** Schapiro, '"Putting the lid on Leninism"', p. 43. • **15.** Alec Nove, *An Economic History of the U.S.S.R.* (Pelican, Harmondsworth, 1972), pp. 85–6. • **16.** T.H. Rigby, *Lenin's Government: Sovnarkom 1917–1922* (Cambridge University Press, Cambridge, 1979), p. 178. • **17.** Sheila Fitzpatrick, *The Russian Revolution* (Oxford University Press, Oxford, 1982), p. 101. • **18.** See James Harris, 'Stalin as General Secretary: the appointments process and the nature of Stalin's power', in Sarah Davies and James Harris (eds.), *Stalin: A New History* (Cambridge University Press, Cambridge, 2005), pp. 63–82, esp. 74–80. • **19.** See Terry Martin, *The Affirmative Action Empire: Nations and Nationalism in the Soviet Union, 1923–1939* (Cornell University Press, Ithaca, 2001). • **20.** Bohdan Krawchenko, *Social Change and National Consciousness in Twentieth Century Ukraine* (Macmillan, London, 1985), p. 86. • **21.** Ibid., p. 89. • **22.** Martin, *The Affirmative Action Empire*, pp. 12–13. • **23.** Nikita Khrushchev, *Khrushchev Remembers: The Last Testament*, translated and edited by Strobe Talbott (André Deutsch, London, 1974), p. 278. • **24.** David R. Shearer, 'Stalinism, 1928–1940', in Ronald G. Suny (ed.), *The Cambridge History of Russia, Volume III, The Twentieth Century* (Cambridge University Press, Cambridge, 2006); and Michael Lessnoff, 'Capitalism, Socialism and Democracy', *Political Studies*, Vol. XXVII, No. 4, 1979, pp. 584–602, at pp. 599–600. • **25.** Robert Service, *Stalin: A Biography* (Macmillan, London, 2004), p. 245. • **26.** Lewis Siegelbaum, 'Workers and Industrialization', in Suny (ed.), *The Cambridge History of Russia: The Twentieth Century*, pp. 440–67, at p. 446. • **27.** Ronald G. Suny, *The Soviet Experiment: Russia, the USSR, and the Successor States* (Oxford University Press, New York, 1998), p. 224. • **28.** Ibid., pp. 223–4. • **29.** Ibid., p. 226. • **30.** Ibid., p. 228; Sheila Fitzpatrick, *Everyday Stalinism. Ordinary Life in Extraordinary Times: Soviet Russia in the 1930s* (Oxford University Press, New York, 1999), p. 169; and Michael Ellman, 'Stalin and the Soviet Famine of 1932–33 Revisited', *Europe-Asia Studies*, Vol. 59, No. 4, June 2007, pp. 663–93. • **31.** Leon Trotsky, *The Revolution Betrayed: What is the Soviet Union and Where is it Going?* (Pathfinder Press, New York, 5th ed., 1972; first published 1937), and Trotsky, *The Stalin School of Falsification* (Pathfinder Press, New York, 3rd ed., 1972; first published 1937). • **32.** Sheila Fitzpatrick (ed.), *Cultural Revolution in Russia, 1928–1931* (Indiana University Press, Bloomington, 1978). • **33.** See Stephen F. Cohen, *Bukharin and the Bolshevik Revolution: A Political Biography 1888–1938* (Wildwood House, London, 1974). A Russian translation of this book (banned in the Soviet Union prior to the Gorbachev era) was read by Mikhail Gorbachev in the summer of 1987. Bukharin was fully rehabilitated in 1988, the centenary of his birth and the fiftieth anniversary of his execution. • **34.** Fitzpatrick, *The Russian Revolution*, pp. 118–19. • **35.** Sheila Fitzpatrick, *Education and Social Mobility in the Soviet Union 1921–1934* (Cambridge University Press, Cambridge, 1979), p. 169. • **36.** Ibid., p. 176. • **37.** Martin, *The*

Affirmative Action Empire, pp. 126–7. • **38.** Some would include Georgy Malenkov in the list of Soviet leaders, for immediately after Stalin's death, in the period 1953–54, he was no less important than Khrushchev. This was, however, essentially a period of oligarchic rule, and when one man emerged on top, that man was the Communist Party's General (or First) Secretary, Khrushchev. • **39.** Interview with Alexander Zinoviev, 'Why the Soviet system is here to stay', in G.R. Urban (ed.), *Can the Soviet System Survive Reform?* (Pinter, London, 1989), pp. 44–107, at p. 74. This interview was first published in the journal *Encounter* in April and May 1984. It caused an outcry and Zinoviev did not at that time take responsibility for the authenticity of the text because he was not given the opportunity to check it. See Charles Janson, 'Alexander Zinoviev: Experiences of a Soviet Methodologist', in Philip Hanson and Michael Kirkwood (eds.), *Alexander Zinoviev as Writer and Thinker* (Macmillan, Basingstoke, 1988), pp. 22–3. However, when the interview was republished in Urban's book, it appeared with a postscript by Zinoviev written in 1988. He does not retract what he said in the interview, but observes that his critics failed to distinguish sociological analysis from moral judgement. He emphasizes that he did not consider 'that collectivization was a blessing; it was an appalling tragedy'. But, he adds, 'those who survived the tragedy had no desire to go back' (in Urban, *Can the Soviet System Survive Reform?*, p. 106). • **40.** George Leggett, *The Cheka: Lenin's Political Police* (Clarendon Press, Oxford, 1981), pp. 15–27. • **41.** *Izvestiya TsK KPSS*, No. 4, 1990, pp 190–3, at p. 193. • **42.** Shearer, 'Stalinism, 1928–1940', in Suny (ed.), *The Cambridge History of Russia: The Twentieth Century*, p. 214. • **43.** Roy Medvedev, *Let History Judge: The Origins and Consequences of Stalinism*, revised and expanded edition (Oxford University Press, Oxford, 1989), pp. 258–60, esp. p. 258; and David Holloway, 'Science, Technology, and Modernity', in Suny (ed.), *The Cambridge History of Russia: The Twentieth Century*, pp. 549–78, at p. 560. • **44.** Rose L. Glickman, 'The Russian Factory Woman, 1880–1914', in Dorothy Atkinson, Alexander Dallin and Gail Warshofsky Lapidus (eds.), *Women in Russia* (Harvester Press, Hassocks, 1978), pp. 63–83, at p. 63. • **45.** Ibid., pp. 62–3. • **46.** Gail Warshofsky Lapidus, *Women in Soviet Society: Equality, Development, and Social Change* (University of California Press, Berkeley, 1978), pp. 60–1; and Peter H. Juviler, 'Family Reforms on the Road to Communsm', in Juviler and Henry W. Morton, *Soviet Policy-Making: Studies of Communism in Transition* (Pall Mall Press, London, 1967), pp. 29–55, at pp. 31–2. • **47.** Lapidus, *Women in Soviet Society*, pp. 5–6. • **48.** David L. Hoffmann, *Stalinist Values: The Cultural Norms of Soviet Modernity, 1917–1941* (Cornell University Press, Ithaca, 2003), pp. 100–2. • **49.** Ibid., p. 106. • **50.** Ibid., p. 112. • **51.** Ibid., pp. 111–12. • **52.** Richard Stites, *Russian Popular Culture: Entertainment and Society since 1900* (Cambridge University Press, Cambridge, 1992), pp. 72–8. • **53.** Ibid., p. 72. • **54.** Richard Taylor, *The Politics of the Soviet Cinema 1917–1929* (Cambridge University Press, Cambridge, 1979), p. 98. • **55.** John Gooding, *Socialism in Russia: Lenin and his Legacy, 1890–1991* (Palgrave, Basingstoke, 2002), p. 136. • **56.** Ibid. • **57.** Ibid. • **58.** Oleg V. Khlevniuk, 'Stalin as dictator: the personalization of power', in Davies and Harris (eds.), *Stalin: A New History*, pp. 108–20, at p. 110. See also the same author's more detailed recent study: Khlevniuk, *Master of the House: Stalin and his Inner Circle* (Yale University Press, New Haven, 2009). • **59.** Service, *Stalin*, p. 317.

• 60. I. Stalin, 'Rech' na pervom vsesoyuznom soveshchanii stakhanovtsev', in *Voprosy Leninizma* (11th ed., Politizdat, Moscow, 1952), pp. 531–44, at p. 531. • 61. Fitzpatrick, *Everyday Stalinism*, p. 185. • 62. I. Stalin, 'O proekte Konstitutsii Soyuza SSR', in *Voprosy Leninizma*, pp. 545–73, at p. 556. • 63. Ibid., p. 553. • 64. Cited in Suny, *The Soviet Experiment*, p. 263. • 65. N.S. Khrushchev, *The Secret Speech delivered to the closed session of the Twentieth Congress of the Communist Party of the Soviet Union*, with an introduction by Zhores and Roy Medvedev (Spokesman Books, Nottingham, 1976), p. 33. • 66. Ibid., pp. 33–4. • 67. Ibid., p. 34. • 68. Suny (ed.), *The Cambridge History of Russia: The Twentieth Century*, p. 40. • 69. Anne Applebaum, *Gulag: A History* (Penguin, Harmondsworth, 2004), pp. 515–22. • 70. Associated Press report from Moscow of 26 September 2007, in Johnson's Russia List, 2007, No. 2003, 27 September 2007, p. 43.

5 *International Communism between the Two World Wars*

1. Donald Sassoon, *One Hundred Years of Socialism: The West European Left in the Twentieth Century* (Fontana, London, 1997), p. 32. • 2. E.H. Carr, *The Bolshevik Revolution 1917–1923, Vol. 3* (Penguin, Harmondsworth, 1966), pp. 507–9, 512–16 and 522–4; and Milan Hauner, *What is Asia to Us? Russia's Asian Heartland Yesterday and Today* (Unwin Hyman, London, 1990), p. 7. • 3. Mary Fulbrook, *History of Germany 1918–2000: The Divided Nation* (Blackwell, Oxford, 2nd ed., 2002), p. 20; and Sassoon, *One Hundred Years of Socialism*, p. 31. • 4. Eric D. Weitz, *Creating German Communism, 1890–1990: From Popular Protests to Socialist State* (Princeton University Press, Princeton, 1997), p. 92. • 5. Ibid., p. 89; and Fulbrook, *History of Germany 1918–2000*, pp. 20–4. • 6. Zara Steiner, *The Lights that Failed: European International History 1919–1933* (Oxford University Press, Oxford, 2005), p. 10. • 7. Joseph Rothschild, *East Central Europe between the Two World Wars* (University of Washington Press, Seattle, 1974), pp. 139–45. • 8. Ibid., p. 143. • 9. Ibid., p. 148. • 10. Hugh Seton-Watson, *Eastern Europe between the Wars 1918–1941* (Harper & Row, New York, 3rd ed., 1967), pp. 186–7; and George Schöpflin, *Politics in Eastern Europe* (Blackwell, Oxford, 1993), pp. 43–5. • 11. Rothschild, *East Central Europe between the Two World Wars*, p. 148. • 12. Ibid., p. 150. • 13. Ibid., p. 151. • 14. Norman Davies, *A History of Poland. Volume II: 1795 to the Present* (Clarendon Press, Oxford, 1981), p. 396. • 15. Ibid., p. 399. • 16. Jonathan Haslam, 'Comintern and Soviet Foreign Policy, 1919–1941', in Ronald G. Suny (ed.), *The Cambridge History of Russia, Vol. III: The Twentieth Century* (Cambridge University Press, Cambridge, 2006), pp. 636–61, at p. 639. • 17. Adam Westoby, *The Evolution of Communism* (Polity, Oxford and Cambridge, 1989), p. 38. • 18. See Haslam, 'Comintern and Soviet Foreign Policy, 1919–1941', pp. 636–7. • 19. Ibid., p. 640. • 20. Sassoon, *One Hundred Years of Socialism*, pp. 32–3. • 21. Westoby, *The Evolution of Communism*, p. 47; and Haslam, 'Comintern and Soviet Foreign Policy, 1919–1941', p. 644. • 22. Stephen F. Cohen, *Bukharin and the Bolshevik Revolution: A Political Biography 1888–1938* (Wildwood House, London, 1974), p. 294; Bertram Wolfe, *A Life in Two Centuries* (Stein and Day, New York, 1981), p. 496; and Sassoon, *One Hundred Years of Socialism*, p. 76. • 23. Carole Fink, 'The NEP in Foreign Policy: The Genoa Conference and the Treaty of Rapallo',

in Gabriel Gorodetsky (ed.), *Soviet Foreign Policy 1917–1991: A Retrospective* (Frank Cass, London, 1994), pp. 11–20, esp. p. 15; and Robert Service, *Lenin: A Biography* (Macmillan, London, 2000), pp. 440–1. • **24.** Fink, 'The NEP in Foreign Policy', p. 19. • **25.** Steiner, *The Lights that Failed*, pp. 174–5. • **26.** Introduction by Ivo Banac to Banac (ed.), *The Diary of Georgi Dimitrov 1933–1949* (Yale University Press, New Haven, 2003), pp. xxv–xxvi. • **27.** Raphael Samuel, *The Lost World of British Communism* (Verso, London, 2006), pp. 41–2. • **28.** See John McIlroy, 'The Establishment of Intellectual Orthodoxy and the Stalinization of British Communism 1928–1933', *Past and Present*, No. 192, August 2006, pp. 187–226, esp. p. 189. • **29.** '"Politsekretariat IKKI trebuet": Dokumenty Kominterna i Kompartii Germanii, 1930–1934', *Istoricheskiy arkhiv*, No. 1, 1994, pp. 148–74. • **30.** F.W. Deakin, H. Shukman and H.T. Willetts, *A History of World Communism* (Weidenfeld & Nicolson, London, 1975), p. 77. • **31.** Ibid., p. 76; and Branco Lazitch and Milorad M. Drachkovitch, *Biographical Dictionary of the Comintern*, revised and expanded edition (Hoover Institution Press, Stanford, 1986), pp. 465–7. • **32.** '"Sobytiya zastali partiyu vrasplokh": Pis'mo aktivista Kompartii Germanii K. Fridberga I.V. Stalinu, 1933 g.', *Istoricheskiy arkhiv*, No. 3, 1996, pp. 211–15. • **33.** The Russian archive-based journal (cited above), which provides the full text of Friedberg's letter, states, incorrectly, that 'Friedberg' was arrested in 1937 by the NKVD and 'shared the bloody fate of hundreds of thousands of political emigrants from Germany and many other countries at that time in the USSR' (ibid., p. 213). However, Karl Gröhl – who was better known under one of his other pseudonyms, Karl Retzlaw, than as either Gröhl or Friedberg – lived on until 1979, dying in Frankfurt on 20 June at the age of eighty-three. He published memoirs eight years earlier in which he mentioned, briefly, his letter to Stalin. See Karl Retzlaw (Karl Gröhl), *Spartakus – Aufstieg und Niedergang. Erinnerungen eines Parteiarbeiters* (Neue Kritik, Frankfurt am Main, 1971), p. 361. Gröhl wrote at the same time as his letter to Stalin, and along similar lines, to Comintern Secretariat member Iosif Pyatnitsky whose own fate was to be less fortunate than Gröhl's. He was arrested by the NKVD in 1937 and executed in 1939. • **34.** Banac (ed.), *The Diary of Georgi Dimitrov 1933–1949*, p. xvi. • **35.** Ibid., pp. xvi–xvii and xxv. • **36.** Ibid., pp. xxvi–xxvii. • **37.** Weitz, *Creating German Communism*, p. 280. • **38.** Ibid. • **39.** Stanley G. Payne, *The Spanish Civil War, the Soviet Union, and Communism* (Yale University Press, New Haven, 2004), p. 122. • **40.** Ibid., pp. 186–7. • **41.** Ibid., pp. 157–8. • **42.** Ibid., pp. 164–6. • **43.** Ibid., p. 166. • **44.** Ibid., pp. 167–70. • **45.** Ibid., p. 261. • **46.** Ibid., pp. 207–8. • **47.** Ibid., p. 153. • **48.** Ibid., p. 316. • **49.** Haslam, 'Comintern and Soviet Foreign Policy', p. 656. • **50.** Keith Feiling, *The Life of Neville Chamberlain* (Macmillan, London, 1946), p. 378. • **51.** Sassoon, *One Hundred Years of Socialism*, p. 84. • **52.** Banac (ed.), *The Diary of Georgi Dimitrov 1933–1949*. Dimitrov is citing Klement Voroshilov's report to a plenary session of the Central Committee of the Soviet Communist Party on 27 March 1940. • **53.** Nikita Khrushchev, in his memoirs, has much to say about the war with Finland that 'cost us so dearly' and adds: 'I'd say we lost as many as a million lives.' See Khrushchev, *Khrushchev Remembers*, translated and edited by Strobe Talbott (Little, Brown, Boston, 1970), p. 155. For an account of Finnish losses based on the official documentation in Finland, see Osmo Jussila, Seppa Hentila, Jukka Nevakiki, *A Political History of Finland since 1809: from Grand Duchy to Modern State* (Hurst, London, 1995),

p. 191. These authors cite Soviet sources claiming that 49,000 were killed on the Soviet side, but add that the Finns have estimated the Red Army's losses to be at least four times the figure they admitted to. Widely different figures for the Soviet death toll in this short but ferocious war continue to be given by different authors. Citing a post-Communist Russian source on Soviet losses in armed conflicts, Catherine Merridale gives a figure of over 126,000 for Soviet dead in the Winter War with Finland and puts the number of Finns killed at just over 48,000. See Merridale, *Ivan's War: The Red Army 1939–45* (Faber & Faber, London, 2005), p. 44. Other Western accounts have put the figure for Soviet losses either dramatically higher or markedly lower. Ronald Suny suggests that around a quarter of a million Soviet troops lost their lives, compared with 25,000 Finns, a ratio of ten to one. See Suny, *The Soviet Experiment: Russia, the USSR, and the Successor States* (Oxford University Press, Oxford and New York, 1998), p. 304. That is close to what is suggested by Finnish scholars. A more recent book accepts a figure adjacent to the official Soviet one, giving the number of Soviet troops killed in the Winter War as 'at least 49,000'. See Bernard Wasserstein, *Barbarism and Civilization: A History of Europe in Our Time* (Oxford University Press, Oxford, 2007), p. 293. • **54**. Suny, *The Soviet Experiment*, pp. 303–4. • **55**. Sassoon, *One Hundred Years of Socialism*, p. 85. • **56**. Geoffrey Nowell Smith and Quintin Hoare, Introduction to Antonio Gramsci, *Prison Notebooks*, edited and translated by Hoare and Nowell Smith (Lawrence and Wishart, London, 1971), p. xciv. • **57**. Ibid. • **58**. David McLellan, 'Western Marxism', in Terence Ball and Richard Bellamy (eds.), *The Cambridge History of Twentieth Century Political Thought* (Cambridge University Press, Cambridge, 2003), p. 286. • **59**. Gramsci, *Prison Notebooks*, pp. 332–3. • **60**. McLellan, 'Western Marxism', p. 288. • **61**. Annie Kriegel, *The French Communists: Profile of a People* (University of Chicago Press, Chicago, 1972), p. 108. • **62**. Ibid., p. 369. • **63**. Ibid. • **64**. Stéphane Courtois and Marc Lazar, *Histoire du Parti Communiste Français* (Presses Universitaires de France, Paris, 2nd ed., 2000), p. 143. • **65**. Kriegel, *The French Communists*, pp. 214–23. • **66**. Lazitch and Drachkovitch (eds.), *Biographical Dictionary of the Comintern*, p. 125; and Kriegel, *The French Communists*, pp. 217–18 and 277–8. • **67**. Edward Taborsky, *Communism in Czechoslovakia 1948–1960* (Princeton University Press, Princeton, NJ, 1961), pp. 6–7. • **68**. Ibid. • **69**. Guenter Lewy, *The Cause that Failed: Communism in American Political Life* (Oxford University Press, New York, 1990), p. 7. • **70**. Bertram D. Wolfe, *A Life in Two Centuries: An Autobiography*, with an Introduction by Leonard Schapiro (Stein and Day, New York, 1981), esp. pp. 442–551. • **71**. Ibid., p. 441. • **72**. Witold S. Sworakowski (ed.), *World Communism – A Handbook 1918–1965* (Hoover Institution Press, Stanford, 1973), pp. 462–72. • **73**. Lerry Keplair and Stephen Englund, *The Inquisition in Hollywood: Politics in the Film Community 1930–60* (University of Illinois Press, Urbana and Chicago, 2003). • **74**. Kevin Morgan, Gidon Cohen and Andrew Flinn, *Communists and British Society 1920–1991* (Rivers Oram Press, London, 2007), p. 169. • **75**. Henry Pelling, *The British Communist Party: A Historical Profile* (Adam and Charles Black, London, 1958), p. 192. • **76**. Morgan, Cohen and Flinn, *Communists and British Society 1920–1991*, p. 26. • **77**. Ibid., pp. 188–96 and 240. • **78**. Westoby, *The Evolution of Communism*, p. 72. • **79**. Rana Mitter, *A Bitter Revolution: China's Struggle with the Modern World* (Oxford University Press, Oxford, 2004), pp. 36–7. • **80**. Ibid., p. 37. • **81**. Jonathan D. Spence, *The Search for Modern China* (Norton,

New York, 2nd ed., 1999), pp. 310–11. • **82.** Ibid., p. 312. • **83.** Ibid., p. 319. • **84.** Ibid., p. 320. • **85.** Ibid., p. 321. • **86.** Ibid., pp. 319–20. • **87.** Mitter, *A Bitter Revolution*, p. 159. • **88.** Ibid., pp. 159–61. • **89.** The most unremittingly hostile account of Mao's activities, which casts doubt on his authority among party members in the inter-war years, is by Jung Chang and Jon Halliday, *Mao: The Unknown Story* (Jonathan Cape, London, 2005). This influential book has, however, been more critically received by specialists on China – including many who are far from being admirers of Mao – than by non-specialist reviewers. The book has been challenged not only in reviews but in review articles in the specialist journals on China. See, for example, Gregor Benton and Steve Tsang, 'The Portrayal of Opportunism, Betrayal, and Manipulation in Mao's Rise to Power', *The China Journal*, No. 55, January 2006, pp. 95–109; Timothy Cheek, 'The New Number One Counter-Revolutionary Inside the Party: Academic Biography as Mass Criticism', ibid., pp. 109–18; Lowell Dittmer, 'Pitfalls of Charisma', ibid., pp. 119–28; and Geremie R. Barmé, 'I'm So Ronree', ibid., pp. 128–39.

6 *What Do We Mean by a Communist System?*

1. See, for example, the posthumously published book by the former Soviet Communist Party Central Committee official and Gorbachev aide Georgiy Shakhnazarov, *Sovremennaya tsivilizatsiya i Rossiya* (Voskresen'e, Moscow, 2003), pp. 179–80; and former Polish Communist prime minister Mieczysław Rakowski, in Andrei Grachev, Chiara Blengino and Rossella Stievano (eds.), *1985–2005: Twenty Years that Changed the World* (World Political Forum and Editoria Laterza, Turin, 2005), p. 35. • **2.** See Andrew Roberts, 'The State of Socialism: A Note on Terminology', *Slavic Review*, Vol. 63, No. 2, Summer 2004, pp. 349–66. • **3.** The Swedish social democrats were the first major, and successful, political party to go beyond the 'revisionism' of Eduard Bernstein. See Sheri Berman, *The Primacy of Politics: Social Democracy and the Making of Europe's Twentieth Century* (Cambridge University Press, New York, 2006). • **4.** See Evan Luard, *Socialism without the State* (Macmillan, London, 1979), David Miller, *Market, State and Community: Theoretical Foundations of Market Socialism* (Clarendon Press, Oxford, 1990), Herbert Kitschelt, *The Transformation of European Social Democracy* (Cambridge University Press, Cambridge, 1994), Julian Le Grand and Saul Estrin (eds.), *Market Socialism* (Clarendon Press, Oxford, 1989), Thomas Meyer with Lewis Hinchman, *The Theory of Social Democracy* (Polity, Cambridge, 2007), Alec Nove, *The Economics of Feasible Socialism* (Allen & Unwin, London, 1983), Stephen Padgett and William E. Paterson, *A History of Social Democracy in Postwar Europe* (Longman, London, 1991) and Donald Sassoon, *One Hundred Years of Socialism* (Fontana, London, 1997). • **5.** Michael Lessnoff, 'Capitalism, Socialism and Democracy', *Political Studies*, Vol. XXVII, No. 4, December 1979, pp. 594–602, esp. p. 601. • **6.** Alan Bullock, *Ernest Bevin: Foreign Secretary* (Oxford University Press, Oxford, 1985), pp. 105–6. • **7.** Ibid., p. 848. • **8.** See Archie Brown, 'The Study of Totalitarianism and Authoritarianism', in Jack Hayward, Brian Barry and Archie Brown (eds.), *The British Study of Politics in the Twentieth Century* (Oxford University Press, for the British Academy, Oxford, 1999), pp. 345–94, at pp. 345–7; and Gabriel

A. Almond, *The Appeals of Communism* (Princeton University Press, Princeton, NJ, 1954), pp. 74 and 133. • **9**. Gale Stokes, *The Walls Came Tumbling Down: The Collapse of Communism in Eastern Europe* (Oxford University Press, New York, 1993), p. 133. • **10**. John H. Kautsky, *Communism and the Politics of Development: Persistent Myths and Changing Behavior* (Wiley, New York, 1968), p. 216. • **11**. See Alan Angell, 'The Left in Latin America Since c. 1920', in Leslie Bethell (ed.), *The Cambridge History of Latin America*, Vol. VI, Part 2, Politics and Society (Cambridge University Press, Cambridge, 1994), pp. 163–232. • **12**. Jasper Becker, *Rogue State: Kim Jong Il and the Looming Threat of North Korea* (Oxford University Press, New York, 2005), p. 77. • **13**. Philip Hanson, *The Rise and Fall of the Soviet Economy: An Economic History of the USSR from 1945* (Longman, London, 2003), p. 9. • **14**. Alec Nove, *The Soviet System in Retrospect: An Obituary Notice*, The Fourth Annual Averell Harriman Lecture, 17 February, 1993, Columbia University, New York, p. 22. • **15**. Alec Nove, *Glasnost' in Action: Cultural Renaissance in Russia* (Unwin Hyman, London, 1989), p. 236. • **16**. Michael Oakeshott, 'Political Education', in Oakeshott, *Rationalism in Politics and Other Essays* (Methuen, London, 1962), p. 127. • **17**. T.I I. Rigby, *The Changing Soviet System: Mono-organisational Socialism from its Origins to Gorbachev's Restructuring* (Edward Elgar, Aldershot, 1990), p. 166. The quotation is from a chapter entitled 'Political Legitimacy under Mono-organisational Socialism' which Rigby first published in 1983. • **18**. Mikhail Gorbachev and Zdeněk Mlynář, *Conversations with Gorbachev: On Perestroika, the Prague Spring, and the Crossroads of Socialism* (Columbia University, New York, 2002), p. 37. • **19**. Rudolf L. Tőkés, *Hungary's Negotiated Revolution: Economic reform, social change, and political succession, 1957–1990* (Cambridge University Press, Cambridge, 1996), p. 428. • **20**. Republished in Eric Hobsbawm, *Revolutionaries* (Abacus, London, 1999), pp. 5–6. • **21**. See Michael Kenny, *The First New Left: British Intellectuals after Stalin* (Lawrence & Wishart, London, 1995). • **22**. Raphael Samuel, *The Lost World of British Communism* (Verso, London, 2006), pp. 47–8. • **23**. Hobsbawm, *Revolutionaries*, p. 6.

7 The Appeals of Communism

1. Donald Sassoon, *One Hundred Years of Socialism: The West European Left in the Twentieth Century* (Fontana, London, 1997), p. 95. • **2**. Ibid., pp. 95–6. • **3**. Gabriel A. Almond, *The Appeals of Communism* (Princeton University Press, Princeton, NJ, 1954), pp. 104–5. • **4**. Stéphane Courtois and Marc Lazar, *Histoire du Parti Communiste Français* (Presses Universitaires de France, Paris, 2nd ed., 2000), pp. 145–6 and 296. • **5**. Ibid., p. 32. • **6**. Almond, *The Appeals of Communism*, p. 104. • **7**. Bernard Shaw, *The Intelligent Woman's Guide to Socialism and Capitalism* (Constable, London, 1928). • **8**. Howard Fast, *The Naked God: The Writer and the Communist Party* (Bodley Head, London, 1958), pp. 14–15. • **9**. Shaw, *The Intelligent Woman's Guide to Socialism and Capitalism*, p. 441. • **10**. Ibid., p. 443. • **11**. Hugh McDiarmid, *First Hymn to Lenin and Other Poems* (Unicorn Press, London, 1931), pp. 11–13. • **12**. Sidney and Beatrice Webb, *Soviet Communism: A New Civilization* (Longmans, Green & Co., London, 1937); quoted from 3rd edition, Longmans, 1944, p. 971. • **13**. Ibid., p. xi. • **14**. Ibid., p. 970. • **15**. Ibid. • **16**. Ibid., p. 973. • **17**. André Gide in Richard Crossman (ed.), *The God that Failed*, new edition with an introduction by David C. Engerman (Columbia University Press, New York, 2001), p. 173. • **18**. Ibid., pp. 173 and 184. • **19**. Ibid., p. 181. • **20**. Arthur Koestler, *Darkness at Noon* (Jonathan Cape, London, 1940); cited from Penguin Classics edition, Harmondsworth, 1964, p. 190. • **21**. Eric Hobsbawm, *Revolutionaries* (Abacus, London, 1979), p. 13. • **22**. Fast, *The Naked God*, p. 30. • **23**. Ibid., pp. 30–1 • **24**. Guenter Lewy, *The Cause that Failed: Communism in American Political Life* (Oxford University Press, New York, 1990), p. 61. • **25**. Kevin Morgan, Gidon Cohen and Andrew Flinn, *Communists and British Society 1920–1991* (Rivers Oram, London, 2007), p. 83. • **26**. Douglas Hyde, *I Believed. The Autobiography of a former British Communist* (Heinemann, London, 1951), p. 290. • **27**. Raphael Samuel, *The Lost World of British Communism* (Verso, London, 2006), p. 53. • **28**. Robert D. Putnam, 'The Italian Communist Politician', in Donald L.M. Blackmer and Sidney Tarrow (eds.), *Communism in Italy and France* (Princeton University Press, Princeton, 1975), p. 177. • **29**. Ibid., pp. 177–8. • **30**. Samuel, *The Lost World of British Communism*, pp. 53–6. • **31**. Ibid., p. 58. • **32**. Almond, *The Appeals of Communism*, pp. 162–3. • **33**. Sudhir Hazareesingh, *Intellectuals and the French Communist Party: Disillusion and Decline* (Clarendon Press, Oxford, 1991), p. 15. • **34**. Ibid., p. 101. See also Courtois and Lazar, *Histoire du Parti Communiste Français*, pp. 279 and 285–7. • **35**. Sidney Tarrow, 'Party Activists in Public Office: Comparisons at the Local Level in Italy and France', in Blackmer and Tarrow (eds.), *Communism in Italy and France*, pp. 150–1. • **36**. Almond, *The Appeals of Communism*, p. 173. • **37**. As noted also by Almond, ibid., p. 105. • **38**. Dan Diner and Jonathan Frankel, 'Introduction. Jews and Communism: The Utopian Temptation', in Frankel (ed.), *Dark Times, Dire Decisions: Jews and Communism*, p. 3. • **39**. George Schöpflin, *Politics in Eastern Europe 1945–1992* (Blackwell, Oxford, 1993), pp. 42–3. • **40**. Alec Nove, *The Soviet System in Retrospect: An Obituary Notice* (The Fourth Averell Harriman Lecture, Columbia University, New York, 1993), pp. 14–15. • **41**. Jaff Schatz, 'Jews and the Communist Movement in Interwar Poland', in Frankel (ed.), *Dark Times, Dire Decisions*, p. 20. • **42**. Ibid., p. 32. • **43**. Ibid., p. 30. • **44**. Ibid., p. 32. • **45**. Theodore Draper, *The Roots of American Communism* (Elephant paperback ed., Chicago, 1989), p. 79. • **46**. Ezra Mendelsohn, 'Jews, Communism, and Art in Inter-war America', in Frankel (ed.), *Dark Times, Dire Decisions*, p. 101. • **47**. Lewy, *The Cause that Failed*, pp. 6–7. • **48**. Ibid., p. 295. • **49**. Ibid. • **50**. Samuel, *The Lost World of British Communism*, p., 67. • **51**. Jason L. Heppell, 'Party Recruitment: Jews and Communism in Britain', in Frankel (ed.), *Dark Times, Dire Decisions*, p. 163. • **52**. Ibid. • **53**. Ibid. • **54**. Hobsbawm, *Revolutionaries*, p. 300. • **55**. Ibid. • **56**. Heppell, 'Party Recruitment', p. 165. • **57**. For a good brief discussion of what the *nomenklatura* does, and does not, mean, see John H. Miller, 'The Communist Party: Trends and Problems', in Archie Brown and Michael Kaser (eds.), *Soviet Policy for the 1980s* (Macmillan, London, 1982), pp. 20–3.

8 *Communism and the Second World War*

1. Winston S. Churchill, *The Second World War, Volume IV, The Hinge of Fate* (Cassell, London, 1951), p. 443. • **2**. On the plethora of warnings Stalin received, see John Erickson, *The Road to Stalingrad: Stalin's War with Germany* (Weidenfeld & Nicolson,

London, 1975), pp. 87–98; and Christopher Andrew and Vasili Mitrokhin, *The Mitrokhin Archive: The KGB in Europe and the West* (Allen Lane Penguin Press, London, 1999), pp. 122–5. • **3**. Robin Edmonds, 'Churchill and Stalin', in Robert Blake and Wm Roger Louis (eds.), *Churchill* (Oxford University Press, Oxford, 1993), p. 311. • **4**. Ibid., p. 313. • **5**. Andrew and Mitrokhin, *The Mitrokhin Archive*, p. 123. • **6**. Ibid. • **7**. Ibid., pp. 123–4. • **8**. Christopher Andrew and Oleg Gordievsky, *KGB: The Inside Story of its Operations from Lenin to Gorbachev* (Hodder and Stoughton, London, 1990), pp. 195–6, 202–4 and 212. • **9**. William Taubman, *Khrushchev: The Man and his Era* (The Free Press, New York, 2003), pp. 256–7. • **10**. Andrew and Gordievsky, *KGB*, p. 351. • **11**. Erickson, *The Road to Stalingrad*, pp. 4–5. For detailed figures on the proportion of the senior officer corps arrested during Stalin's purge of the army, see A.A. Kokoshin, *Armiya i politika: Sovetskaya voenno-politicheskaya i voenno-strate-gicheskaya mysl', 1918–1991 gody* (Mezhdunarodnye otnosheniya, Moscow, 1995), pp. 40–51. On Tukhachevsky, see ibid., pp. 49 and 104–5. • **12**. Erickson, *The Road to Stalingrad*, p. 15. • **13**. Catherine Merridale, *Ivan's War: The Red Army 1939–45* (Faber & Faber, London, 2005), pp. 76 7. • **14**. Rodric Braithwaite, *Moscow 1941: A City and its People at War* (Profile Books, London, 2006), pp. 216–17, 223 and 225. • **15**. Ibid., p. 152. • **16**. Antony Beevor, *Stalingrad* (Penguin, London, 2007), p. 428. • **17**. Omer Bartov, *The Eastern Front, 1941–1945, German Troops and the Barbarisation of Warfare* (Macmillan, London, 1985), p. 120. • **18**. Norman Davies, *Europe at War 1939–1945: No Simple Victory* (Macmillan, London, 2006), p. 312. • **19**. Bartov, *The Eastern Front, 1941–1945*, pp. 107 8. • **20**. Ibid., p. 156. • **21**. For long the accepted figure was twenty million. A recent study by two British historians of the Soviet Union and the Second World War puts the total at 'roughly 25 million'. See John Barber and Mark Harrison, 'Patriotic War, 1941–1945', in Ronald G. Suny (ed.), *The Cambridge History of Russia, Vol. III: The Twentieth Century* (Cambridge University Press, Cambridge, 2006), pp. 217–42, at p. 225. • **22**. Ibid. • **23**. Braithwaite, *Moscow 1941*, pp. 303 5. • **24**. Ibid., p. 7. • **25**. Barber and Harrison, 'Patriotic War, 1941–1945', pp. 224–5. • **26**. Beevor, *Stalingrad*, p. 48. • **27**. Ibid., p. xiv. • **28**. Ibid., p. 419. • **29**. Davies, *Europe at War 1939–1945*, p. 312. • **30**. Hoover Institution Archives, Fond 89, Reel 1.1993, opis 14. Beria's three-and-a-half-page letter to Stalin is in Fond 89 of the Russian state archive, RGANI, in Moscow. It is now available in microfilm in a number of major Western libraries, including that of the Hoover Institution, which catalogued the contents of Fond 89. Until 1989, when the head of the International Department of the Central Committee of the Communist Party of the Soviet Union, Valentin Falin (Volkogonov Papers, National Security Archive, R 6522, memorandum of 6 March 1989), informed the party leadership that the Polish officers had been killed by the NKVD on the orders of Stalin and Beria, the Soviet authorities had pretended even among them-selves, as well as to the outside world, that this had been another German atrocity. A Politburo meeting of 15 April 1971 approved Foreign Minister Andrey Gromyko's protest to the British Foreign Office about a BBC film 'hostile to the Soviet Union ... about the so-called "Katyn affair"' (Volkogonov Collection, National Security Archive). At a Politburo meeting on 5 April 1976 there was discussion of how to combat Western propaganda alleging Soviet responsibility for the killings in Katyn forest (Volkogonov Collection, NSA, R8966). It was as late as 13 April 1990 that it was decided that the Polish President Jaruzelski should be informed that there was now sufficiently convincing proof that the Polish officers had been killed at Katyn on the instructions of the leadership of the NKVD at that time (HIA, Fond 89, Reel 1.1991, opis 9, file 115, p. 2). • **31.** See Robert Conquest, *The Nation Killers* (Sphere Books, London, 1972). • **32.** Bernard Wasserstein, *Barbarism and Civilization: A History of Europe in Our Time* (Oxford University Press, Oxford, 2007), p. 401. • **33.** Braithwaite, *Moscow 1941*, p. 305. • **34.** See Timothy Snyder, '"To Resolve the Ukrainian Problem Once and for All": The Ethnic Cleansing of Ukrainians in Poland', *Journal of Cold War Studies*, Vol. 1, No. 2, Spring 1999, pp. 86–120, esp. 91–4; and Bohdan Krawchenko, *Social Change and National Consciousness in Twentieth Century Ukraine* (Macmillan, London, 1985), esp. pp. 154–64. • **35.** Krawchenko, *Social Change and National Consciousness in Twentieth Century Ukraine*, pp. 153 and 166. • **36.** Ibid., p. 166. • **37.** Ibid. • **38.** See, for example, Winston S. Churchill, *The Second World War, Volume V: Closing the Ring* (Cassell, London, 1952), pp. 272–84. • **39.** Donald Sassoon, *One Hundred Years of Socialism: The West European Left in the Twentieth Century* (Fontana, London, 1997), p. 92. • **40.** D. George Kasoulous, 'The Greek Communists Tried Three Times – and Failed', in Thomas T. Hammond (ed.), *The Anatomy of Communist Takeovers* (Yale University Press, New Haven, 1975), pp. 293–309. • **41.** Ibid., p. 305. • **42.** Paul Shoup, *Communism and the Yugoslav National Question* (Columbia University Press, New York, 1968), p. 59. • **43.** Dennison Rusinow, *The Yugoslav Experiment 1948–1974* (University of California Press, Berkeley, 1977), p. 5. • **44.** Milovan Djilas, *Wartime* (Harcourt Brace Jovanovich, New York, 1977), p. 253. For Deakin's assessment of Djilas, see F.W.D. Deakin, *The Embattled Mountain* (Oxford University Press, Oxford, 1971), esp. pp. 84–5. • **45.** Ibid., p. 369. • **46.** Churchill, *The Second World War: Volume V*, p. 423. • **47.** Ibid. • **48.** Stephen Peters, 'Ingredients of the Communist Takeover in Albania', in Hammond (ed.), *The Anatomy of Communist Takeovers*, pp. 273–93. • **49.** Ibid., pp. 291–2. • **50.** Rana Mitter, *A Bitter Revolution: China's Struggle with the Modern World* (Oxford University Press, Oxford, 2004), pp. 121 and 138. • **51.** Jürgen Domes, 'The Model for Revolutionary People's War: The Communist Takeover of China', in Hammond (ed.), *The Anatomy of Communist Takeovers*, p. 520. • **52.** Mitter, *A Bitter Revolution*, pp. 170 and 175. • **53.** Domes, 'The Model for Revolutionary People's War', p. 520. • **54.** Mitter, *A Bitter Revolution*, pp. 183–4.

9 *The Communist Takeovers in Europe – Indigenous Paths*

1. Jung Chang and Jon Halliday, *Mao: The Unknown Story* (Vintage Books, London, 2006), p. 52. • **2.** Donald Sassoon, *One Hundred Years of Socialism: The West European Left in the Twentieth Century* (Fontana, London, 1997), p. 93. • **3.** Stephen Peters, 'Ingredients of the Communist Takeover in Albania', in Thomas T. Hammond (ed.), *The Anatomy of Communist Takeovers* (Yale University Press, New Haven, 1975), p. 276. • **4.** See Jon Halliday in *The Artful Albanian: The Memoirs of Enver Hoxha*, edited and introduced by Jon Halliday (Chatto & Windus, London, 1986), p. 2. • **5.** Ibid., pp. 2–3. • **6.** Ibid., pp. 273–92, at 280. • **7.** Ibid., pp. 32–3. • **8.** Peters, 'Ingredients of the Communist Takeover in Albania', pp. 290–2. • **9.** Dennison Rusinow, *The*

Yugoslav Experiment 1948–1974 (University of California Press, Berkeley and Los Angeles, 1978), pp. 2–3. • **10**. Ibid., p. 12. • **11**. Phyllis Auty, *Tito: A Biography* (Longman, London, 1970), p. 265. • **12**. Ibid., p. 266. • **13**. Ibid., pp. 268–9. • **14**. David Dyker, 'Yugoslavia: Unity out of Diversity?', in Archie Brown and Jack Gray (eds.), *Political Culture and Political Change in Communist States* (Macmillan, London, 1977), pp. 66–100, at p. 76. • **15**. Those who had been called 'Ethnic Muslims' became known as Bosniaks. They are also, of course, Bosnians, but that is a broader term, embracing all the citizens of contemporary Bosnia, whatever their ethnic origin or religious affiliation. • **16**. Gordon Wightman and Archie Brown, 'Changes in the Levels of Membership and Social Composition of the Communist Party of Czechoslovakia, 1945–73', *Soviet Studies*, Vol. XXVII, No. 2, July 1975, pp. 396–417, at pp. 396–7. • **17**. Archie Brown and Gordon Wightman, 'Czechoslovakia: Revival and Retreat', in Brown and Gray (eds.), *Political Culture and Political Change in Communist States*, pp. 159–96, at p. 163. • **18**. Jacques Rupnik, *Histoire du Parti Communiste Tchécoslovaque: Des origines à la prise du pouvoir* (Presses de la Fondation Nationale des Sciences Politiques, Paris, 1981), pp. 188–9. • **19**. Edward Taborsky, *Communism in Czechoslovakia 1948–1960* (Princeton University Press, Princeton, 1961), pp. 19–21 and 100–2. • **20**. Ibid., p. 20. • **21**. Wightman and Brown, 'Changes in the Levels of Membership and Social Composition of the Communist Party of Czechoslovakia', pp. 397 and 401. • **22**. Taborsky, *Communism in Czechoslovakia*, p. 21. • **23**. Melvin P. Leffler, *For the Soul of Mankind: The United States, the Soviet Union, and the Cold War* (Hill and Wang, New York, 2007), p. 62. • **24**. Pavel Tigrid, 'The Prague Coup of 1948: The Elegant Takeover', in Hammond (ed.), *The Anatomy of Communist Takeovers*, pp. 399–432, at pp. 406–7. • **25**. Ibid., p. 409. • **26**. Ibid., p. 417. • **27**. Ibid., pp. 419–20. • **28**. Ibid., p. 427. • **29**. His former aide – a committed democrat – Lubomír Soukup was convinced this was suicide, but his explanation of it, when he had access for the first time to the mass media in Czechoslovakia in 1968, brought no comfort to those who wished to present a rosy account of the events of February 1948. It was, said Soukup (and I heard this directly from him on more than one occasion when we were colleagues teaching in Glasgow University during the 1960s), Masaryk's last protest against the destruction of democracy in Czechoslovakia by the Communists. • **30**. Vladimir V. Kusin, *The Intellectual Origins of the Prague Spring: The Development of Reformist Ideas in Czechoslovakia 1956–1967* (Cambridge University Press, Cambridge, 1971), p. 7.

10 *The Communist Takeovers in Europe – Soviet Impositions*

1. Robin Edmonds, 'Churchill and Stalin', in Robert Blake and Wm Roger Louis (eds.), *Churchill* (Oxford University Press, Oxford, 1993), pp. 320–1; Winston S. Churchill, *The Second World War, Volume VI: Triumph and Tragedy* (Cassell, London, 1954), pp. 198–9; Geoffrey Best, *Churchill: A Study in Greatness* (Penguin, London, 2002), p. 258; and Vladislav M. Zubok, *A Failed Empire: The Soviet Union in the Cold War from Stalin to Gorbachev* (University of North Carolina Press, Chapel Hill, 2007), pp. 20–1. • **2**. Churchill, *The Second World War, Volume VI*, pp. 201–2. • **3**. Best, *Churchill*, pp. 259–60. • **4**. Churchill, *The Second World War, Volume VI*, p. 200. • **5**. Geoffrey Roberts,

'Stalin at the Tehran, Yalta, and Potsdam Conferences', *Journal of Cold War Studies*, Vol. 9, No. 4, Fall 2007, p. 30. • **6**. Norman Davies, *God's Playground: A History of Poland, Vol. II: 1795 to the Present* (Clarendon Press, Oxford, 1981), pp. 399–403. • **7**. Timothy Snyder, '"To Resolve the Ukrainian Question Once and for All"', *Journal of Cold War Studies*, Vol. 1, No. 2, Spring 1999, pp. 86–120, at p. 101. • **8**. Ibid. • **9**. Roberts, 'Stalin at the Tehran, Yalta, and Potsdam Conferences', p. 34. This statement is from the official Soviet record of the conference in the Russian Ministry of Foreign Affairs Archives. It is among those excluded from the documents which were published in the Soviet Union. • **10**. Roy Jenkins, *Churchill* (Pan Books, London, 2002), p. 762. • **11**. Ibid. • **12**. Bernard Wasserstein, *Barbarism and Civilization: A History of Europe in Our Time* (Oxford University Press, Oxford, 2007), pp. 414–15. • **13**. Edmonds, 'Churchill and Stalin', p. 326. • **14**. Ibid. • **15**. *Off the Record: The Private Papers of Harry S. Truman*, edited by Robert H. Ferrell (Harper & Row, New York, 1980), pp. 21–2. • **16**. Truman's diary entry for 15 July 1945 at Potsdam, ibid., p. 53. • **17**. George F. Kennan, *Memoirs 1925–1950* (Pantheon, New York, 1967), p. 279. • **18**. Truman, *Off the Record*, pp. 58–9. • **19**. Ibid., p.. 349. • **20**. Jan M. Ciechanowski, *The Warsaw Rising of 1944* (Cambridge University Press, Cambridge, 1974); and Norman Davies, *God's Playground, Vol. II*, pp. 472–80. • **21**. Joseph Rothschild, *Return to Diversity: A Political History of East Central Europe since World War Two* (Oxford University Press, New York and Oxford, 1989), p. 79. • **22**. Hugh Seton-Watson, *The Imperialist Revolutionaries: World Communism in the 1960s and 1970s* (Hutchinson, London, 1980), p. 14. • **23**. R.J. Crampton, *Eastern Europe in the Twentieth Century – and After* (Routledge, Abingdon, 2nd ed., 1997), p. 221. • **24**. Susanne S. Lotarski, 'The Communist Takeover in Poland', in Thomas T. Hammond (ed.), *The Anatomy of Communist Takeovers* (Yale University Press, New Haven, 1975), pp. 339–67, at p. 353. • **25**. Crampton, *Eastern Europe in the Twentieth Century*, p. 221. • **26**. Ibid., pp. 220–1. • **27**. Bennett Kovrig, *Communism in Hungary: From Kun to Kádár* (Hoover Institution Press, Stanford, 1979), p. 128. • **28**. Ibid., pp. 138–40. • **29**. Ibid., pp. 224–8. • **30**. Ibid., pp. 227–8. • **31**. Peter A. Toma and Ivan Volgyes, *Politics in Hungary* (Freedman, San Francisco, 1977), pp. 6–9. • **32**. Rudolf L. Tőkés, 'Hungary', in Witold S. Sworakowski (ed.), *World Communism: A Handbook* (Hoover Institution Press, Stanford, 1973), pp. 184–91. • **33**. Ibid., p.. 188. • **34**. Crampton, *Eastern Europe in the Twentieth Century*, p. 225. • **35**. Ghiţa Ionescu, *Communism in Rumania 1944–1962* (Oxford University Press and Royal Institute of International Affairs, London, 1964), pp. 61–2. • **36**. Ibid., pp. 83–6. • **37**. Ibid., pp. 90–2. • **38**. As is clear from his diary entries. See Ivo Banac (ed.), *The Diary of Georgi Dimitrov 1933–1949* (Yale University Press, New Haven, 2003), pp. 351–83. • **39**. R.J. Crampton, *A Concise History of Bulgaria* (Cambridge University Press, Cambridge, 2nd ed., 2005), p. 183. • **40**. Ibid., p. 228. • **41**. Ibid., pp. 183–8. • **42**. Hans W. Schoenberg, 'The Partition of Germany and the Neutralization of Austria', in Hammond, *The Anatomy of Communist Takeovers*, p. 374. • **43**. Wolfgang Leonhard, *Child of the Revolution* (Ink Links paperback ed., London, 1979), pp. 329–30. This important book was first published in German in 1955 as *Die Revolution entlässt ihre Kinder*. • **44**. Zubok, *A Failed Empire*, pp. 62–3. • **45**. Leonhard, *Child of the Revolution*. Leonhard escaped from East Germany in 1949 to Yugoslavia, where he spent two years. He has lived subsequently in the United States and in the united

Germany. • **46.** Ibid., pp. 359–65. • **47.** Mary Fulbrook, *History of Germany 1918–2000: The Divided Nation* (Blackwell, Oxford, 2nd ed., 2002), p. 129. • **48.** Ibid., pp. 133–4. • **49.** Eric D. Weitz, *Creating German Communism, 1890–1990: From Popular Protests to Socialist State* (Princeton University Press, Princeton, 1997), p. 352. • **50.** Gary Bruce, 'The Prelude to Nationwide Surveillance in East Germany: Stasi Operations and Threat Perceptions, 1945–1953', *Journal of Cold War Studies*, Vol. 5, No. 2, Spring 2003, pp. 3–31. • **51.** Kennan, *Memoirs 1925–1950*, pp. 547–59. • **52.** Ibid., pp. 294–5. • **53.** Ibid., p. 294. • **54.** Ibid., p. 295. • **55.** Ibid. • **56.** Roy Jenkins, *Churchill* (Pan Macmillan, London, 2002), p. 812. • **57.** Patrick Wright, *Iron Curtain: From Stage to Cold War* (Oxford University Press, Oxford, 2007), pp. 82–4. • **58.** Ibid., p. 152.

11 *The Communists Take Power in China*

1. Jürgen Domes, 'The Model for Revolutionary People's War: The Communist Takeover of China', in Thomas T. Hammond (ed.), *The Anatomy of Communist Takeovers* (Yale University Press, New Haven, 1975), pp. 516–33, at pp. 520–1. • **2.** V.S. Myasnikov, 'SSSR i Kitay vo vtoroy mirovoy voine', *Novaya i noveyshaya istoriya*, No. 4, 2005, pp. 3–29, at p. 21. • **3.** The Russian historian Academician Myasnikov cites Mao as saying that it was the entry of Soviet troops into Manchuria which played a greater part in ending the Japanese occupation of China than the dropping of two atomic bombs on Japanese cities by the United States – ibid., p. 24. • **4.** Jonathan Spence, 'China', in Michael Howard and William Roger Louis (eds.), *The Oxford History of the Twentieth Century* (Oxford University Press, Oxford, 1998), pp. 216–26, at pp. 221–2. • **5.** Craig Dietrich, *People's China: A Brief History* (Oxford University Press, New York and Oxford, 3rd ed., 1998), p. 48. • **6.** John King Fairbank and Merle Goldman, *China: A New History* (Harvard University Press, Cambridge, Mass., 2nd enlarged edition, 2006), p. 311. • **7.** Roderick MacFarquhar (ed.), *The Politics of China: The Eras of Mao and Deng* (Cambridge University Press, Cambridge, 2nd ed., 1997), p. 1. • **8.** Fairbank and Goldman, *China: (A New History*, p. 302. • **9.** Rana Mitter, *A Bitter Revolution: China's Struggle with the Modern World* (Oxford University Press, Oxford, 2004), p. 183. • **10.** Domes, 'The Model for Revolutionary People's War', p. 521. • **11.** Jung Chang and Jon Halliday, *Mao: The Unknown Story* (Vintage Books, London, 2006), pp. 296–7; and Domes, 'The Model for Revolutionary People's War', pp. 522–3. • **12.** Jacques Guillermaz, 'The Soldier', in Dick Wilson (ed.), *Mao Tse-Tung in the Scales of History* (Cambridge University Press, Cambridge, 1977), pp. 117–43, at pp. 117 and 124–5. • **13.** Domes, 'The Model for Revolutionary People's War', p. 526. • **14.** Dietrich, *People's China*, p. 31. • **15.** Milovan Djilas, *Conversations with Stalin* (Rupert Hart-Davis, London, 1962), pp. 164–5. • **16.** Domes, 'The Model for Revolutionary People's War', pp. 525–6. See also Dietrich, *People's China*, p. 31. • **17.** A.V. Pantsov, 'Kak Stalin pomog Mao Tszedunu stat' vozhdem', *Voprosy istorii*, No. 2, 2006, pp. 75–87, at p. 78. • **18.** Chang and Halliday, *Mao: The Unknown Story*, pp. 264 and 279. • **19.** Ivo Banac (ed.), *The Diary of Georgi Dimitrov 1933–1949* (Yale University Press, New Haven, 2003), pp. xxxvii–xxxviii. • **20.** A Russian historian who has studied the Comintern documents suggests that Stalin may have been deliberately misinformed. Dimitrov knew nothing of this telegram proposal, no evidence of it has emerged, and it is likely, in the view of A.V. Pantsov, that it never existed. See Pantsov, 'Kak Stalin pomog Mao Tszedunu stat' vozhdem', p. 81. • **21.** Banac (ed.), *The Diary of Georgi Dimitrov*, p. 42 (italics in original). • **22.** According to Jung Chang and Jon Halliday, Wang Ming's life was endangered not by Stalin but by Mao Zedong. They suggest that Mao orchestrated more than one attempt to poison Wang when he was back in China, and the attempts succeeded to the extent of permanently undermining Wang's health. See Chang and Halliday, *Mao: The Unknown Story*, pp. 262–6, 271 and 649. • **23.** Pantsov, 'Kak Stalin pomog Mao Tszedunu stat' vozhdem'. • **24.** Ibid., p. 79. • **25.** Odd Arne Westad, *The Global Cold War: Third World Interventions and the Making of Our Times* (Cambridge University Press, Cambridge, 2005), p. 65. • **26.** Dietrich, *People's China*, p. 32. • **27.** Pantsov, 'Kak Stalin pomog Mao Tszedunu stat' vozhdem', p. 85. • **28.** Chang and Halliday, *Mao: The Unknown Story*, pp. 225–6. • **29.** Frederick C. Teiwes, 'The Establishment and Consolidation of the New Regime, 1949–57', in MacFarquhar (ed.), *The Politics of China*, pp. 5–86, at p. 13. • **30.** Lowell Dittmer, 'Pitfalls of Charisma', *The China Journal*, No. 55, January 2006, pp. 119–28, at p. 126. • **31.** Teiwes. 'The Establishment and Consolidation of the New Regime, 1949–57', p. 17. • **32.** Ibid., p. 18. • **33.** Ibid., p. 70. • **34.** Ibid., p. 18. • **35.** Ibid., p. 29. • **36.** Ibid., p. 22. • **37.** Fairbank and Goldman, *China: A New History*, p. 348. • **38.** Fairbank, in ibid., pp. 348–9. • **39.** Chang and Halliday, *Mao: The Unknown Story*, p. 394. For the number of 400,000, the authors cite Deng Xiaoping, speaking to Japanese Communists. For the figure of a million they refer to a Russian-language source – Sergo Beria's 1994 biography of his father, the NKVD chief Lavrenti Beria (ibid., pp. 394 and 719). An American figure which conflates those killed or missing with those wounded lists 900,000 Chinese casualties. See Dietrich, *People's China*, p. 67. • **40.** Chang and Halliday, *Mao: The Unknown Story*, p. 394. • **41.** Yoram Gorlizki and Oleg Khlevniuk, *Cold Peace: Stalin and the Soviet Ruling Circle, 1945–1953* (Oxford University Press, Oxford, 2004), p. 97. • **42.** Introduction by James G. Hershberg to a collection of correspondence between Stalin and Mao Zedong and between Stalin and the Soviet ambassadors in China and North Korea, *Cold War International History Project Bulletin*, No. 14/15, Winter 2003–Spring 2004, pp. 369–72. • **43.** Chang and Halliday, *Mao: The Unknown Story*, p. 377. There are, however, still some unanswered questions about the Sino-Soviet relationship on the eve of Chinese participation in the Korean War, including discrepancies between the Chinese and Russian versions of Mao's letter to Stalin of 2 October 1950. A Chinese scholar, Shen Zhihua, has recently argued that 'the main reason for Mao's decision to send troops to Korea was to avert Soviet entry into north-east China in the wake of North Korea's defeat and the extension of the war to Manchuria'. See Yafeng Xia, 'The Study of Cold War International History in China: A Review of the Last Twenty Years', in *Journal of Cold War Studies*, Vol. 10, No. 1, Winter 2008, pp. 81–115, at p. 108. • **44.** Letter of Stalin to Mao, dated 4 October 1950, sent via Soviet Ambassador to Beijing, 5 October 1950, *Cold War International History Project Bulletin*, No. 14/15, pp. 375–6. • **45.** 'Russian Documents on the Korean War 1950–1953', ibid., pp. 370 and 376. • **46.** Dietrich, *People's China*, p. 671; and Julia C. Strauss, 'Paternalist Terror: The Campaign to Suppress Counterrevolutionaries and

Regime Consolidation in the People's Republic of China, 1950–1953', *Comparative Studies in Society and History*, Vol. 44, No. 1, January 2002, pp. 80–105, at pp. 87–9. • **47.** Ibid., p. 69. • **48.** Strauss, 'Paternalist Terror', pp. 80–1. • **49.** Ibid., pp. 94–6. • **50.** Ibid., p. 72; and Fairbank, in Fairbank and Goldman, *China: A New History*, pp. 360–4. • **51.** Arguably, such a view of the world was also to be found in Confucianism. • **52.** Dietrich, *People's China*, pp. 72–6. • **53.** Ibid., pp. 77–8. • **54.** Teiwes, 'The Establishment and Consolidation of the New Regime, 1949–1957', pp. 38–9. • **55.** Ibid., p. 42.

12 Post-War Stalinism and the Break with Yugoslavia

1. Alex Inkeles and Raymond A. Bauer, *The Soviet Citizen: Daily Life in a Totalitarian Society* (Harvard University Press, 1961), esp. pp. 233–80. • **2.** Cited in D.G. Nadzhafov and Z.S. Belousova (eds.), *Stalin i kosmopolitizm: Dokumenty Agitpropa TsK KPSS 1945–1953* (Materik, Moscow, 2005), p. 18. • **3.** Catherine Merridale, *Ivan's War: The Red Army 1939 1945* (Faber & Faber, London, 2005), p. 293. • **4.** Ibid., p. 198. • **5.** David Brandenberger, 'Stalin as symbol: a case study of the personality cult and its construction', in Sarah Davies and James Harris (eds.), *Stalin: A New History* (Cambridge University Press, Cambridge, 2005), pp. 249–70, at p. 270. • **6.** 'Sekretaryu TsK. Tovarishchu N.S. Khrushchevu, 14.2.1956', Vokogonov Papers, National Security Archive, R1217. This is one of the numerous papers from the Russian archives, photocopies of which were supplied to the Library of Congress by General Dmitriy Volkogonov. Copies of them are also in other libraries. I used them in the National Security Archive in Washington. Chagin, who welcomed Khrushchev's speech to the 1956 Party Congress, was at the time of his meeting with Stalin in 1926 the editor of a newspaper, *Krasnaya gazeta*. • **7.** Brandenberger, 'Stalin as Symbol', p. 250. • **8.** Robert C. Tucker, *The Soviet Political Mind: Studies in Stalinism and Post-Stalin Change* (Praeger, New York, 1963), pp. 16–19. • **9.** Yoram Gorlizki and Oleg Khlevniuk, *Cold Peace: Stalin and the Soviet Ruling Circle, 1945–1953* (Oxford University Press, Oxford, 2004), pp. 60–1. • **10.** Ibid. • **11.** This was less important than his control of the unified organs of repression, for the title notwithstanding, he was not the only first deputy chairman of the Council of Ministers. Molotov and Bulganin were also given that title. See Robert Service, *Stalin: A Biography* (Macmillan, London, 2004), p. 587. • **12.** Gorlizki and Khlevniuk, *Cold Peace*, pp. 52–3. • **13.** Much of the documentary evidence for this is to be found in Nadzhafov and Belousova (eds.), *Stalin i kosmopolitizm*. • **14.** Sergo Mikoyan, 'Stalinism as I saw it', in Alec Nove (ed.), *The Stalin Phenomenon* (Weidenfeld & Nicolson, London, 1993), pp. 152–96, at p. 157. • **15.** T.H. Rigby, 'Was Stalin a Disloyal Patron?', in Rigby, *Political Elites in the USSR: Central Leaders and Local Cadres from Lenin to Gorbachev* (Edward Elgar, Aldershot, 1990), pp. 127–46. • **16.** Oleg V. Khlevniuk, 'Stalin as Dictator: The personalization of power', in Davies and Harris (eds.), *Stalin: A New History*, pp. 108–20, at p. 115. • **17.** Rigby, 'Was Stalin a Disloyal Patron?', p. 143. • **18.** Ibid. • **19.** Nadzhafov and Belousova (eds.), *Stalin i kosmopolitizm*, pp. 31–2; and Gorlizki and Khlevniuk, *Cold Peace*, pp. 20–1 and 75–7. • **20.** Nadzhafov and Belousova (eds.), *Stalin i kosmopolitizm*, p. 31. • **21.** Gorlizki and Khlevniuk, *Cold Peace*, pp. 75–6. • **22.** Joshua

Rubenstein, *Tangled Loyalties: The Life and Times of Ilya Ehrenburg* (Tauris, London, 1996), p. 262. • **23**. Ibid. • **24**. Gorlizki and Khlevniuk, *Cold Peace*, p. 75. • **25**. Ibid., p. 25. • **26**. In the words of two scholars whose work is based on close scrutiny of the relevant Soviet documents: 'Rather than initiating these campaigns [against the slightest unorthodoxy on the part of the intelligentsia], as some earlier scholars have surmised, the archives show that Zhdanov was Stalin's compliant, hard-pressed, and ultimately rather bewildered agent.' See ibid., p. 31. • **27**. Vera Dunham, *In Stalin's Time: Middleclass Values in Soviet Fiction* (Cambridge University Press, Cambridge, 1976), p. 13. • **28**. Dennison Rusinow, *The Yugoslav Experiment 1948–1974* (University of California Press, Berkeley and Los Angeles, and Royal Institute of International Affairs, London, 1977), pp. 19–21. • **29**. Ibid., p. 25. • **30**. Milovan Djilas, *Conversations with Stalin* (Rupert Hart-Davis, London, 1962), pp. 155–7. • **31**. Ibid., p. 162. • **32**. Ibid., p. 164. A Russian scholar who has studied the relevant Soviet archives argues that it was the Yugoslav attitude to the Greek civil war, much more than any infringement of Albanian sovereignty, which enraged Stalin. He began to suspect Tito of 'pursuing hegemonic aims in the Balkans'. See N.D. Smirnova, 'Stalin i Balkany v 1948 g.: Problemy natsional'noy bezopasnosti SSSR', in A.O. Chubaryan, I.V. Gayduk and N.I. Egorova (eds.), *Stalinskoe desyatiletie kholodnoy voyny: fakty i gipotezy* (Nauka, Moscow, 1999), pp. 36–44, at p. 42. • **33**. T.V. Volokitina, 'Stalin i smena strategicheskogo kursa Kremlya v kontse 40-kh godov: ot kompromissov k konfrontatsii', in Chubaryan, Gayduk and Egorova (eds.), *Stalinskoe desyatiletie kholodnoy voyny*, pp. 10–22, esp. p. 19. • **34**. Djilas, *Conversations with Stalin*, p. 161. • **35**. Ibid., p. 159. Djilas wrote a report for the Central Committee of the Communist Party of Yugoslavia on the Moscow meeting, to which he did not have access (since by that time he had become a political dissident in Yugoslavia), while writing his *Conversations with Stalin*. It was retained in Tito's personal archive and has now been translated, published in a journal of archival materials, and compared with information from other national archives, including the Soviet and Bulgarian. In essence, the passages I have cited from Djilas's book correspond with his more official report at the time, but they are expressed more colourfully in the book. One point which is somewhat at odds with his book account of the Stalin–Dimitrov encounter is that in his 1948 report for the Central Committee he says that 'the criticism of Dimitrov by Stalin, although rough in form, was expressed in friendly tones'. Perhaps this was an example of wishful thinking at a time when Djilas, like other Yugoslav leaders, did not yet want to think ill of Stalin and the Soviet Union. See 'Report of Milovan Djilas about a secret Soviet-Bulgarian-Yugoslav meeting 10 February 1948', translated by Vladislav Zubok, *Cold War International History Project Bulletin* (Woodrow Wilson Center, Washington DC), No. 10, March 1998, pp. 128–34, esp. p. 132. • **36**. Rusinow, *The Yugoslav Experiment*, p. 28. • **37**. Milovan Djilas, *Tito: The Story from Inside* (Weidenfeld & Nicolson, London, 1981), p. 32. • **38**. Milorad M. Drachkovitch, 'Yugoslavia', in Witold S. Sworakowski (ed.), *World Communism: A Handbook 1918–1965* (Hoover Institution, Stanford, 1973), pp. 503–13, at p. 509. • **39**. Zhores A. Medvedev and Roy A. Medvedev, *The Unknown Stalin*, translated by Ellen Dahrendorf (Tauris, London, 2003), pp. 61–2. The Medvedevs say their information came directly from Aleksei Snegov, a former Khrushchev aide, who said that this was one of five notes or letters found under a pile of newspapers in one of the drawers of Stalin's desk when it was being moved from the dead leader's former study. • 40. 'Stalin's Plan to Assassinate 'Tito', *Cold War International History Project Bulletin*, No. 10, March 1998, p. 137. • 41. Rusinow, *The Yugoslav Experiment*, p. 29. • 42. N.S. Khrushchev, *The 'Secret' Speech*, with an Introduction by Zhores and Roy Medvedev (Spokesman Books, Nottingham, 1976), pp. 61–2. • 43. R.J. Crampton, *Eastern Europe in the Twentieth Century – and After* (Routledge, London, 2nd ed., 1997), p. 260. • 44. Rusinow, *The Yugoslav Experiment*, p. 30. • 45. Ibid. • 46. Ibid., p. 36. • 47. Ibid., p. 39. • 48. John Lewis Gaddis, *Strategies of Containment: A Critical Appraisal of American National Security Policy during the Cold War*, revised and expanded edition (Oxford University Press, Oxford and New York, 2005), p. 66. • 49. Cited in Rusinow, *The Yugoslav Experiment*, pp. 44–5. • 50. Ibid., p. 61. • 51. Fred Singleton, *Twentieth Century Yugoslavia* (Macmillan, London, 1976), pp. 134–42. • 52. Rusinow, *The Yugoslav Experiment*, pp. 62–80; and Sharon Zukin, *Beyond Marx and Tito: Theory and Practice in Yugoslav Socialism* (Cambridge University Press, Cambridge, 1975), pp. 21–5. • 53. Smirnova, 'Stalin i Balkany v 1948 g.', p. 43. • 54. Volokitina, 'Stalin i smena strategicheskogo kursa Kremlya v kontse 40-kh godov', p. 21. • 55. Crampton, *Eastern Europe in the Twentieth Century*, pp. 261–2. • 56. G.P. Murashko and A.F. Noskova, 'Sovetskoe rukovodstvo i politicheskie protsessy T. Kostova i L. Rayka (po materialam rossiyskikh arkhivov)', in Chubaryan, Gayduk and Egorova (eds.), *Stalinskoe desya-tiletie kholodnoy voyny*, pp. 23–35, esp. pp. 24–7. • 57. Roger Gough, *A Good Comrade: János Kádár, Communism and Hungary* (Tauris, London, 2006), p. 45. • 58. Ibid., p. 53. • 59. Ibid., p. 60. • 60. Murashko and Noskova, 'Sovetskoe rukovodstvo i politicheskie protsessy T. Kostova i L. Rayka', p. 31. • 61. Ibid. • 62. For a discussion of Gomułka's arrest and imprisonment and for the range of possible reasons why he was neither tortured nor killed, see Nicholas Bethell, *Gomułka: His Poland and His Communism* (Pelican, Harmondsworth, rev. ed., 1972), pp. 171–93. • 63. Ibid., pp. 184–5. • 64. Eric D. Weitz, *Creating German Communism, 1890–1990: From Popular Protests to Socialist State* (Princeton University Press, Princeton, 1997), pp. 360–1. • 65. Crampton, *Eastern Europe in the Twentieth Century*, p. 263. • 66. There is much evidence for this in Chubaryan, Gayduk and Egorova (eds.), *Stalinskoe desyatiletie kholodnoy voyny*. See, for example, the chapter by Murashko and Noskova, p. 33. • 67. Edward Taborsky, *Communism in Czechoslovakia 1948–1960* (Princeton University Press, 1961), pp. 102–3. • 68. Jiří Pelikán (ed.), *The Czechoslovak Political Trials, 1950–1954: The Suppressed Report of the Dubček Government's Commission of Inquiry, 1968* (Macdonald, London, 1971), p. 104. • 69. Ibid., p. 106. • 70. Ibid., p. 110. • 71. See Crampton, *Eastern Europe in the Twentieth Century*, pp. 262–4; Taborsky, *Communism in Czechoslovakia*, pp. 75–6; and Karel Bartošek, 'Central and Southeastern Europe', in Stéphane Courtois, Nicolas Werth, Jean-Louis Panné, Andrzej Paczkowski, Karel Bartošek and Jean-Louis Margolin, *The Black Book of Communism: Crimes, Terror, Repression* (Harvard University Press, Cambridge, Mass., 1999), pp. 394–456, at pp. 433–6. • 72. Crampton, *Eastern Europe in the Twentieth Century*, p. 265. • 73. Christopher Cviic, 'The Church', in Abraham Brumberg (ed.), *Poland: Genesis of a Revolution* (Vintage Books, New York, 1983), pp. 92–108, at p. 96. • 74. Crampton, *Eastern Europe in the Twentieth Century*, p. 267; and Bartošek, 'Central and Southeastern Europe', pp. 407–37.

• **75**. Khrushchev, *The 'Secret' Speech*, p. 59. • **76**. Ibid. • **77**. Dmitrii Shepilov, *The Kremlin's Scholar: A Memoir of Soviet Politics under Stalin and Khrushchev*, ed. Stephen V. Bittner and trans. Anthony Austin (Yale University Press, New Haven, 2007), pp. 132–54, at p. 135. • **78**. Roy Medvedev, *Let History Judge: The Origins and Consequences of Stalinism*, revised and expanded edition (Oxford University Press, Oxford, 1989), pp. 783–5. • **79**. *Khrushchev Remembers*, ed. and trans. Strobe Talbott (Little, Brown, Boston, 1970), pp. 248–9. • **80**. Gorlizki and Khlevniuk, *Cold Peace*, p. 91. • **81**. Ibid., pp. 91–2. • **82**. *Khrushchev Remembers*, pp. 250–8. Characteristically for the Brezhnev era, the last edition of the Great Soviet Encyclopedia – *Bol'shaya Sovetskaya Entsiklopediya*, Vol. 5, 1971, p. 268; and Vol. 13, 1973, p. 560 – published entries on Kuznetsov and Voznesensky without a word about how their lives ended. • **83**. *Khrushchev Remembers*, p. 257. A post-Soviet biography of Kosygin, based on family and archival sources, comes no closer to explaining how he survived, though it makes plain that for many months he believed that he was liable to be arrested at any moment: V.I. Andriyanov, *Kosygin* (Molodaya gvardiya, Moscow, 2003), pp. 118–25. • **84**. Geoffrey Hosking, *Rulers and Victims: The Russians in the Soviet Union* (Harvard University Press, Cambridge, Mass., 2006), p. 264. The fullest documentary account of the planning and execution of the campaign from within the Central Committee of the party is to be found in Nadzhafov and Belousova (eds.), *Stalin i kosmopolitizm*, op. cit. • **85**. Nadzhafov and Belousova (eds.), *Stalin i kosmopolitizm*, p. 15; and Josephine Woll, 'The Politics of Culture, 1945–2000', in Ronald G. Suny (ed.), *The Cambridge History of Russia. Volume III: The Twentieth Century* (Cambridge University Press, Cambridge, 2006), pp. 605–35, at pp. 608–9. • **86**. Nadzhafov and Belousova (eds.), *Stalin i kosmopolitizm*, pp. 221 and 667. • **87**. Gorlizki and Khlevniuk, *Cold Peace*, pp. 156 and 217. • **88**. Ibid. • **89**. Nadzhafov and Belousova (eds.), *Stalin i kosmopolitizm*, pp. 651–2. • **90**. Gorlizki and Khlevniuk, *Cold Peace*, pp. 158–9. • **91**. David Holloway, *Stalin and the Bomb: The Soviet Union and Atomic Energy 1939–1956* (Yale University Press, New Haven, 1994), pp. 213–16. • **92**. Ibid., pp. 203 and 216. • **93**. Shepilov, *The Kremlin's Scholar*, p. 118. • **94**. Holloway, *Stalin and the Bomb*, pp. 207–8. See also Loren R. Graham, *Science in Russia and the Soviet Union: A Short History* (Cambridge University Press, Cambridge, 1993); Zhores Medvedev, 'Stalin and Lysenko', in Medvedev and Medvedev, *The Unknown Stalin*, pp. 181–99; and Shepilov, *The Kremlin's Scholar*, pp. 115–28. • **95**. Max Hayward, *Writers in Russia: 1917–1978*, edited with an introduction by Patricia Blake (Harvill, London, 1983), p. 158. • **96**. Gorlizki and Khlevniuk, *Cold Peace*, pp. 162 and 222; and Service, *Stalin*, pp. 581–90. • **97**. In Khrushchev's words: 'When Stalin died, 109 people were killed. 109 people died because everyone moved like a mob and smothered them.' See 'Khrushchev's Second Secret Speech', *Cold War International History Project Bulletin*, No. 10, March 1998, pp. 44–9, at p. 47. • **98**. See the account of one of those who was in that crowd: Zdeněk Mlynář, *Nightfrost in Prague: The End of Humane Socialism* (Hurst, London, 1980), pp. 24–6; and also Shepilov, *The Kremlin's Scholar*, p. 31. • **99**. John Gooding, *Socialism in Russia: Lenin and his Legacy, 1890–1991* (Palgrave, Basingstoke, 2002), pp. 140–1. • **100** Shepilov, *The Kremlin's Scholar*, pp. 1, 5 and 19–21.

13 Khrushchev and the Twentieth Party Congress

1. William J. Tompson, *Khrushchev: A Political Life* (Macmillan, London, 1995), pp. 114–15; and William Taubman, *Khrushchev: The Man and His Era* (Free Press, New York, 2003), p. 240. • 2. Tompson, *Khrushchev*, p. 118. • 3. See V. Naumov and Yu. Sigachev (eds.), *Lavrentiy Beriya 1953. Stenogramma iyul'skogo plenuma TsK KPSS i drugie dokumenty* (Mezhdunarodnyy fond 'Demokratiya', Moscow, 1999), esp. p. 111. • 4. Taubman, *Khrushchev*, pp. 244–9. Nikita Khrushchev has provided his own colourful account of the post-Stalin power struggles in *Khrushchev Remembers* (Little, Brown, Boston, 1970), pp. 306–41. An account which partly confirms and partly contradicts Khrushchev is that of Dmitrii Shepilov, *The Kremlin's Scholar: A Memoir of Soviet Politics under Stalin and Khrushchev* (Yale University Press, New Haven, 2007), pp. 244–76. Some of the struggle emerges in a large collection of Soviet archival documents, in which Presidium of the Central Committee sessions are reported, sometimes in note form, at other times with verbatim speech: A.A. Fursenko (ed.), *Prezidium TsK KPSS 1954–1964: Chernovye protokol'nye zapisi zasedaniy. Stenogrammy* (Rosspen, Moscow, 2004). • 5. Khrushchev's son provides both a memoir of his father and a discussion of the progress and fate of his father's memoirs in Sergei Khrushchev, *Khrushchev on Khrushchev: An Inside Account of the Man and His Era*, edited and translated by William Taubman (Little, Brown, Boston, 1990). Digitized versions of the tapes and complete printed transcripts are kept in the John Hay Library of Brown University in the United States. Sergei Khrushchev, who is now an American citizen, is associated with that university. • 6. *Khrushchev Remembers*, p. 301. • 7. Ibid., p. 303. • 8. Ibid., p. 276. • 9. Fursenko (ed.), *Prezidium TsK KPSS 1954–1964*, p. 5. • 10. Yoram Gorlizki and Oleg Khlevniuk, *Cold Peace: Stalin and the Soviet Ruling Circle 1945–1953* (Oxford University Press, Oxford, 2004), p. 222. • 11. Ibid., p. 166. • 12. Fursenko (ed.), *Prezidium TsK KPSS 1954–1964*, p. 883. • 13. Khrushchev's conversation on the arrest of Beria (one of his favourite topics) with Shepilov: Shepilov, *The Kremlin's Scholar*, p. 264. • 14. Ibid., pp. 266–7. • 15. Ibid., p. 267. • 16. Taubman, *Khrushchev*, p. 253. • 17. Ibid., pp. 254–5. See also Timothy K. Blauvelt, 'Patronage and Betrayal in the post-Stalin succession: The case of Kruglov and Serov', *Communist and Post-Communist Studies*, Vol. 41, No. 1, March 2008, pp. 105–20. • 18. Ibid., p. 256. • 19. Shepilov, *The Kremlin's Scholar*, pp. 269–70; and Taubman, *Khrushchev: The Man and His Era*, p. 256. • 20. Fursenko, *Prezidium TsK KPSS 1954–1964*, p. 1195. • 21. Naumov and Sigachev (eds.), *Lavrentiy Beriya 1953*, p. 88. • 22. Taubman, *Khrushchev*, pp. 256–7. • 23. Shepilov, *The Kremlin's Scholar*, p. 275. • 24. Khrushchev's major biographer, William Taubman, notes: 'Khrushchev and Malenkov each claimed he led the coup against Beria. Molotov, who hated them both, and Mikoyan, who got along with both, confirmed Khrushchev's account' (*Khrushchev*, p. 250). • 25. T.H. Rigby, *Political Elites in the USSR: Central leaders and local cadres from Lenin to Gorbachev* (Edward Elgar, Aldershot, 1990), pp. 150–1. • 26. Ibid., pp. 154–5. • 27. Key documents from the Soviet archives on this are translated and published in *Cold War International History Project Bulletin*, No. 10, March 1998, pp. 72–98. • 28. Fursenko (ed.), *Prezidium TsK KPSS 1954–1964*, p. 42. • 29. Ibid., p. 45. • 30. Ibid., p. 893. • 31. Joshua Rubenstein, *Tangled Loyalties: The Life and Times*

of Ilya Ehrenburg (Tauris, London, 1996), pp. 278–82. • **32**. Ludmilla Alexeyeva and Paul Goldberg, *The Thaw Generation: Coming of Age in the Post-Stalin Era* (Little, Brown, Boston, 1990), p. 74. • **33**. Ibid., p. 71. • **34**. A. Artizov, Yu. Sigachev, I. Shevchuk and V. Khlopov (eds.), *Reabilitatsiya: kak eto bylo. Fevral' 1956–nachalo 80-kh godov* (Materik, Moscow, 2003), p. 71. • **35**. N.S. Khrushchev, *The Secret Speech* (Spokesman Books, Nottingham, 1976), p. 45. • **36**. Artizov et al., *Reabilitatsiya: kak eto bylo*, pp. 192–3. I am grateful to Yoram Gorlizki for drawing my attention to this work and to the great disparity in the numbers of people who were released from the Gulag as compared with the minority who were formally rehabilitated. Cf. Anne Applebaum, *Gulag: A History* (Penguin, London, 2003), pp. 456–7. • **37**. *Khrushchev Remembers: The Last Testament*, trans. and ed. Strobe Talbott (André Deutsch, London, 1974), pp. 78–9. • **38**. Ibid., p. 81. • **39**. Fursenko, *Prezidium TsK KPSS 1954–1964*, pp. 879–80. • **40**. Shepilov, *The Kremlin's Scholar*, pp. 276 and 304–5. • **41**. Fursenko, *Prezidium TsK KPSS 1954–1964*, pp. 19–24. • **42**. Ibid., pp. 35–40 and 886–7. • **43**. Aleksandr Fursenko and Timothy Naftali, *Khrushchev's Cold War: The Inside Story of an American Adversary* (Norton, New York, 2006), p. 21. • **44**. Fursenko, *Prezidium TsK KPSS 1954–1964*, pp. 35–6. • **45**. The evidence is to be found in the reports of the meetings of the Presidium of the Central Committee, published for the first time in Russia comparatively recently. See Fursenko (ed.), *Prezidium TsK KPSS 1954–1964*, pp. 88–106. • **46**. Anastas Ivanovich Mikoyan, *Tak bylo: Razmyshleniya o minuvshem* (Vagrius, Moscow, 1999), pp. 597–8. • **47**. Fursenko (ed.), *Prezidium TsK KPSS 1954–1964*, p. 96. • **48**. Mikoyan, *Tak bylo*, p. 594. • **49**. Shepilov, *The Kremlin's Scholar*, p. 392; and Mikoyan, *Tak bylo*, p. 592. • **50**. Shepilov, *The Kremlin's Scholar*, pp. 391–2; and Taubman, *Khrushchev*, pp. 274–83. • **51**. Mikoyan, *Tak bylo*, p. 594. In the first volume of his memoirs, Khrushchev says that he raised the issue of a speech criticizing Stalin with the party Presidium only after the Twentieth Congress was under way. The documentary evidence (note 52) shows that it was agreed in the Presidium on 13 February 1956, the day before the congress opened, that such a speech would be made and that the speaker would be Khrushchev. However, Khrushchev had no access to documents when he was dictating his memoirs and his memory (which, in general, was remarkably good) let him down at times. He would appear to be unreliable also when he states there that he had wanted Pospelov to deliver the speech but was prevailed upon by his colleagues to make it himself. Mikoyan's account is more convincing. Where Khrushchev's memory coincides perfectly with that of Mikoyan (ibid.) is in his observation that Molotov, Kaganovich and Voroshilov were opposed to such a speech being made at all. See *Khrushchev Remembers*, pp. 347–53. • **52**. Fursenko (ed.), *Prezidium TsK KPSS 1954–1964*, p. 106. • **53**. Taubman, *Khrushchev*, p. 271. • **54**. Ibid. • **55**. Tompson, *Khrushchev*, p. 156. Tompson says that if Mikoyan spoke after the Presidium had taken a decision in favour of Khrushchev delivering his speech to the final closed session, 'then he may have been testing the waters for Khrushchev himself'. He may, indeed, for we now know that the Presidium gave its approval to Khrushchev delivering his Secret Speech three days before Mikoyan's intervention. • **56**. Mikoyan, *Tak bylo*, pp. 594–5. • **57**. Taubman, *Khrushchev*, pp. 283–4. • **58**. The report was published in a journal of the Central Committee of the CPSU which existed in the last three years of the Soviet Union's existence: 'O kul'te lichnosti i ego posledstviyakh. Doklad Pervogo sekretarya TsK KPSS N.S. Khrushcheva XX s"ezdu KPSS 25 fevralya 1956 g.', *Izvestiya TsK KPSS*, No. 3, 1989, pp. 128–70. Among several English-language editions of the speech is that edited by Roy and Zhores Medvedev and published on the twentieth anniversary of the speech – already cited in note 37. • **59**. Khrushchev, *The Secret Speech*, pp. 40–1. • **60**. Ibid., pp. 41–2. • **61**. Ibid., p. 67.

14 Zig-zags on the Road to 'communism'

1. Apart from his political journalism, Orwell, of course, provided profound insight into, and scathing condemnation of, the Soviet system as it had developed under Stalin in his most famous novels, *Animal Farm*, first published in 1945, and *Nineteen Eighty-Four*, completed in 1948 (and the title chosen by reversing the last two numbers) and first published in 1949. • **2**. Merle Fainsod, *How Russia is Ruled* (Harvard University Press, Cambridge, Mass., 1953); and Fainsod, *Smolensk under Soviet Rule* (Macmillan, London, 1958). • **3**. William Taubman, *Khrushchev: The Man and His Era* (Norton, New York, 2003), pp. 285–7. • **4**. Ibid, pp 316–17. • **5**. See Anastas Ivanovich Mikoyan, *Tak bylo: razmyshleniya o minuvshem* (Vagrius, Moscow, 1999), p. 597. • **6**. Dmitrii Shepilov, *The Kremlin's Scholar: A Memoir of Soviet Politics under Stalin and Khrushchev* (Yale University Press, New Haven, 2007), p. 397. • **7**. Taubman, *Khrushchev*, pp. 310 and 319. • **8**. Mikoyan, *Tak bylo*, p. 600. • **9**. Ibid., p. 599 • **10**. Taubman, *Khrushchev*, p. 314. • **11**. The plenum lasted from 22 to 29 June. A transcript of the proceedings was published in post-Soviet Russia. See N. Kovaleva, A. Korotkov, S. Mel'chin, Yu. Sigachev and A. Stepanov (eds.), *Molotov, Malenkov, Kaganovich 1957. Stenogramma iyun'skogo plenuma TsK KPSS i drugie dokumenty* (Mezhdunarodnyy fond 'Demokratiya', Moscow, 1998). • **12**. William J. Tompson, *Khrushchev: A Political Life* (Macmillan, London, 1995), p. 181. • **13**. Ibid., p. 182. • **14**. Shepilov, *The Kremlin's Scholar*, esp. pp. 277–314 and 387–400. • **15**. Taubman, *Khrushchev*, pp. 310–11. • **16**. See Robert V. Daniels, 'Stalin's Rise to Dictatorship, 1922–29', in Alexander Dallin and Alan F. Westin (eds.), *Politics in the Soviet Union: 7 Cases* (Harcourt, Brace & World, New York, 1966), pp. 4–5; and Daniels, *Is Russia Reformable? Change and Resistance from Stalin to Gorbachev* (Westview, Boulder, 1988), pp. 88–93. • **17**. A.A. Fursenko (ed.), *Prezidium TsK KPSS 1954–1964: Tom 1. Chernovye protolkol'nye zapisi zasedaniy. Stenogrammy* (Rosspen, Moscow, 2004), pp. 269–73 and 1015–17. • **18**. Ibid., pp. 271 and 278. • **19**. Ibid., p. 277. • **20**. 'Vystuplenie Marshala Sovetskogo Soyuza G.Kh. Zhukova na sobranii partiynogo aktiva Ministerstva oborony i Moskovskogo garnizona 2 iyulya 1957 g.', Volkogonov Papers, R 9191, National Security Archive, Washington DC., esp. p. 21. • **21**. Ibid., p. 20. • **22**. Fursenko (ed.), *Prezidium TsK KPSS 1954–1964*, p. 279. • **23**. Taubman, *Khrushchev*, pp. 362–3. • **24**. Ibid., p. 363. • **25**. *Khrushchev Remembers: The Last Testament*, trans. and ed. Strobe Talbott (André Deutsch, London, 1974), pp. 17–18. • **26**. Mikoyan, *Tak bylo*, p. 608–11. • **27**. Taubman, *Khrushchev*, pp. 285 and 301. • **28**. Veljko Mićunović, *Moscow Diary* (Chatto and Windus, London, 1980), p. 187. • **29**. Ibid., p. 188. • **30**. *Khrushchev Remembers: The Last Testament*, p. 67. • **31**. Ibid., pp. 530–1 (italics in original). • 32. Robert C. Tucker has an illuminating discussion of this in his 'The Image of Dual Russia', in Tucker, *The Soviet Political Mind* (Praeger, New York, 1963), pp. 69–90, esp. pp. 87–9. • 33. As Khrushchev put it: 'In connection with *Doctor Zhivago*, some might say it's too late for me to express regret that the book wasn't published. Yes, maybe it is too late. But better late than never' (*Khrushchev Remembers: The Last Testament*, p. 77). Khrushchev gives a fuller account of the Pasternak affair in the third volume of his memoirs: *Khrushchev Remembers: The Glasnost Tapes* (Little, Brown, Boston, 1990), pp. 195–201. • 34. Taubman, *Khrushchev*, pp. 384–8. • 35. See Priscilla Johnson and Leopold Labedz (eds.), *Khrushchev and the Arts: The Politics of Soviet Culture, 1962–1964* (MIT Press, Cambridge, Mass., 1965), esp. pp. 120–2 and 186–210. • 36. *Programme of the Communist Party of the Soviet Union* (Foreign Languages Publishing House, Moscow, 1961), p. 128. • 37. Ibid., p. 62 (italics in original). • 38. Ibid., p. 123 (italics in original). • 39. Ibid., p. 127. • 40. Ibid., pp. 62 and 85. • 41. Taubman, *Khrushchev*, pp. 514–15. • 42. On the Moscow housing boom of the Khrushchev era, see Timothy J. Colton, *Moscow: Governing the Socialist Metropolis* (Harvard University Press, Cambridge, Mass., 1995), pp. 367–76. • 43. William Taubman, 'The Khrushchev period, 1953–1964', in Ronald G. Suny, *The Cambridge History of Russia. Volume III: The Twentieth Century* (Cambridge University Press, Cambridge, 2006), pp. 268–91, at p. 280. • 44. See T.H. Rigby, *The Changing Soviet System: Mono-Organisational Socialism from its Origins to Gorbachev's Restructuring* (Edward Elgar, Aldershot, 1990), p. 215. • 45. For a good account, see Robert J. Osborn, *Soviet Social Policies: Welfare, Equality, and Community* (Dorsey Press, Homewood, Ill. 1970), pp. 95–135 ('Equality of Educational Choice'). • 46. Michael Bourdeaux, 'Religion', in Archie Brown and Michael Kaser (eds.), *The Soviet Union since the Fall of Khrushchev* (Macmillan, London, 2nd ed., 1978), pp. 156–80, at p. 156. • 47. Ibid. • 48. Alec Nove, *An Economic History of the U.S.S.R* (Pelican, Harmondsworth, 1972), p. 331. • 49. Ibid., pp. 331–2. • 50. David Holloway, 'Science, Technology, and Modernity', in Suny (ed.), *The Cambridge History of Russia, Volume III: The Twentieth Century*, pp. 549–78, at pp. 562–3. • 51. Loren R. Graham, *Science in Russia and the Soviet Union* (Cambridge University Press, Cambridge, 1993), pp. 257–9. • 52. *Khrushchev Remembers: The Last Testament*, p. 448. • 53. Vladislav M. Zubok, *A Failed Empire: The Soviet Union in the Cold War from Stalin to Gorbachev* (University of North Carolina Press, Chapel Hill, 2007), p. 138. • 54. Ibid., pp. 149–51; and Mikoyan, *Tak bylo*, p. 606. • 55. Zubok, *A Failed Empire*, pp. 151–2. See also Vojtech Mastny, 'The 1963 Nuclear Test Ban Treaty: A Missed Opportunity for Détente?', *Journal of Cold War Studies*, Vol. 10, No. 1, Winter 2008, pp. 3–25. • 56. Solzhenitsyn published a fascinating account of Soviet literary politics, including the campaign to get this, his first published work in the Soviet Union, into print. See Alexander I. Solzhenitsyn, *The Oak and the Calf: Sketches of Literary Life in the Soviet Union*, translated by Harry Willetts (Collins and Harvill Press, London, 1980). He provides in this book an affectionate, but not uncritical, account of Tvardovsky, but is much less generous to Khrushchev's aide Lebedev, who on a number of occasions pushed wider the limits on what could be published in the Soviet Union. • 57. Taubman, *Khrushchev*, pp. 588–602. • 58. Johnson and Labedz (eds.), *Khrushchev and the Arts*, pp. 120–2. • 59. *Khrushchev Remembers: The Last Testament*, p. 80. • 60. Taubman, *Khrushchev*, pp. 519–23; and Mikoyan, *Tak bylo*, pp. 610–11. Mikoyan accompanied Kozlov to Novocherkassk and urged restraint, but Kozlov had no compunction about authorizing the use of armed force in which between twenty and thirty people died. • **61**. Report from Novocherkassk of 7 June 1962 from Deputy Chairman of the KGB, P. Ivashutin, Volkogonov Papers R 3305, National Security Archive. • **62**. Taubman, *Khrushchev*, p. 617. • **63**. Mikoyan, *Tak bylo*, p. 615. • **64**. Taubman, *Khrushchev*, p. 5. • **65**. Ibid., pp. 3–17; and Sergei Khrushchev, *Khrushchev on Khrushchev: An Inside Account of the Man and His Era* (Little, Brown, Boston, 1990), pp. 83–162. • **66**. Tompson, *Khrushchev*, p. 276. Tompson adds (p. 277): 'Khrushchev must also have known that in an earlier time he would undoubtedly have been shot after his removal from office.'

15 *Revisionism and Revolution in Eastern Europe*

1. V. Naumov and Yu. Sigachev (eds.), *Lavrentiy Beriya 1953. Stenogramma iyul'skogo plenuma TsK KPSS i drugie dokumenty* (Mezhdunarodnyy fond 'Demokratiya', Moscow, 1999), p. 111. • **2**. Alexey Filitov, '"Germany Will Be a Bourgeois-Democratic Republic": The New Evidence from the Personal File of Georgiy Malenkov', *Cold War History*, Vol. 6, No. 4, 2006, pp. 549–57, at pp. 550 and 553. • **3**. Ibid., pp. 350–1. • **4**. Ibid., p. 353. • **5**. Ibid., pp. 549–51. See also the discussion of the confused policymaking process in the party Presidium in Moscow at this time, based on archival evidence, in Christian F. Ostermann, '"This is not a Politburo, But a Madhouse": The Post-Stalin Succession Struggle. Soviet *Deutschlandpolitik* and the SED: New Evidence from Russian, German, and Hungarian Archives', *Cold War International History Project Bulletin (CWIHPB)*, No. 10, 1998, pp. 61–72. • **6**. Filitov, '"Germany Will Be a Bourgeois-Democratic Republic"', p. 554. • **7**. 'Memorandum of V. Chuikov, P. Iudin and L. Il'ichev to G.M. Malenkov, 18 May 1953', in *CWIHPB*, No. 10, 1998, pp. 74–8. • **8**. Hope Harrison, *Driving the Soviets Up the Wall: Soviet-East German Relations, 1953–1961* (Princeton University Press, Princeton, 2003), pp. 25–48; Peter Pulzer, *German Politics 1945–1995* (Oxford University Press, Oxford, 1995), pp. 95–7; and Eric D. Weitz, *Creating German Communism 1890–1990: From Popular Protests to Socialist State* (Princeton University Press, Princeton, 1997), p. 360. • **9**. Weitz, *Creating German Communism*, p. 362. • **10**. Otto Ulč, 'Pilsen: The Unknown Revolt', *Problems of Communism*, Vol. XIV, No. 3, May–June 1965, pp. 46–9, at p. 49. Ulč was an assistant judge in Pilsen in the immediate aftermath of the disturbances and attended the trials of those who took part in the revolt. He also had access to the secret documentation, and his account of the event, from which my summary of it is drawn, is well informed. Later Ulč became a professor of political science in the United States and the author of *Politics in Czechoslovakia* (W.H. Freeman, San Francisco, 1974). • **11**. Leszek Kołakowski, *Main Currents of Marxism, Vol. III: The Breakdown* (Clarendon Press, Oxford, 1978), pp. 173–4. • **12**. Ibid., p. 174. • **13**. Victor Sebestyen, *Twelve Days: Revolution in 1956. How the Hungarians tried to topple their Soviet masters* (Phoenix, London, 2007), p. 102. • **14**. Ibid., pp. 102–3. • **15**. Peter Raina, *Political Opposition in Poland 1954–1977* (Poets and Painters Press, London, 1978), pp. 30–1. •

16. János Kornai, *By Force of Thought: Irregular Memoirs of an Intellectual Journey* (MIT Press, Cambridge, Mass., 2006), p. 63. • 17. Ibid. • 18. I remember seeing on my first study visit to Prague in March 1965 a window display of Brus's books, translated into Czech. He was one of the influences on the Czech economic reformers of the second half of the 1960s – not least on their leading spokesman, Ota Šik. • 19. Sebestyen, *Twelve Days*, pp. 77–8. • 20. Kornai, *By Force of Thought*, p. 57. • 21. Sebestyen, *Twelve Days*, p. 27. • 22. Ibid., p. 17. • 23. Phyllis Auty, *Tito: A Biography* (Longman, London, 1970), pp. 258–9. • 24. Tony Kemp-Welch, 'Khrushchev's "Secret Speech" and Polish Politics: The Spring of 1956', *Europe-Asia Studies*, Vol. 48, No. 2, 1996, pp. 181–206, at pp. 186–7; and Norman Davies, *God's Playground. A History of Poland: Volume II: 1979 to the Present* (Clarendon Press, Oxford, 1981), p. 583. • 25. Raina, *Political Opposition in Poland 1954–1977*, pp. 42–3. • 26. Kemp-Welch, 'Khrushchev's "Secret Speech" and Polish Politics', p. 199. • 27. I am indebted to Mark Kramer (personal communication of 6 May 2008) for the figure of 'at least 74' dead. Archival material from Poznań has made clear that the long-accepted figure of fifty-three who lost their lives was significantly understated. See also Mark Kramer, 'New Evidence on Soviet Decision-Making and the 1956 Polish and Hungarian Crises', *CWIHPB*, Nos. 8–9, 1996–97, pp. 358–84; and Kramer, 'The Soviet Union and the 1956 Crises in Hungary and Poland: Reassessments and New Findings', *Journal of Contemporary History*, Vol. 33, No. 2, 1998, pp. 163–214. • 28. Kramer, 'New Evidence on Soviet Decision-Making . . .'. • 29. Ibid., p. 361. • 30. *Khrushchev Remembers: The Last Testament* (André Deutsch, London, 1974), p. 205. • 31. Kołakowski, *Main Currents of Marxism: Vol. III*, p. 454. • 32. Charles Gati, *Failed Illusions: Moscow, Washington, Budapest, and the 1956 Hungarian Revolt* (Stanford University Press, Stanford, 2006), pp. 36–7. • 33. Ibid., pp. 37 and 224–6. • 34. Roger Gough, *A Good Comrade: János Kádár, Communism and Hungary* (Tauris, London, 2006), p. 98. • 35.Gati, *Failed Illusions*, p. 138. • 36. Ibid. • 37. Ibid., pp. 131–2. • 38. Sebestyen, *Twelve Days*, pp. 96–7. • 39. Ibid., p. 99. • 40. Ibid., pp. 303–4. • 41. Ibid., pp. 115–17. • 42. Ibid., pp. 124–5. • 43. Ferenc A. Váli, *Rift and Revolt in Hungary: Nationalism versus Communism* (Harvard University Press, Cambridge, Mass., 1961), pp. 284–305. • 44. Mikoyan and Suslov's Letter to the CC CPSU on Situation in Budapest, 25 October 1956, Volkogonov Papers, R 2476, National Security Archive, Washington DC. • 45. A.S. Stykalin, 'Soviet–Yugoslav Relations and the Case of Imre Nagy', *Cold War History*, Vol. 5, No. 1, 2005, pp. 3–22; and Péter Vámos, 'Evolution and Revolution: Sino-Hungarian Relations and the 1956 Hungarian Revolution', Cold War International History Project Working Paper No. 54, November 2006 (Woodrow Wilson Center, Washington DC). • 46. Csaba Békés, 'The 1956 Hungarian Revolution and the Declaration of Neutrality', *Cold War History*, Vol. 6, No. 4, 2006, pp. 477–500, at p. 482. • 47. A. Stykalin, 'The Hungarian Crisis of 1956: The Soviet Role in the Light of New Archival Documents', *Cold War History*, Vol. 2, No. 1, 2002, pp. 113–44, at pp. 132–3. • 48. Gati, *Failed Illusions*, p. 177; and Stykalin, 'The Hungarian Crisis of 1956', pp. 134–5. • 49. Kramer, 'The Soviet Union and the 1956 Crises in Hungary and Poland', pp. 192–3. • 50. See, for example, the testimony of the Yugoslav ambassador to Moscow, Velko Mićunović, a former Partisan who enjoyed relations of trust with Tito, in Mićunović, *Moscow Diary* (Chatto & Windus,

London, 1980), pp. 134–46. See also Gati, *Failed Illusions*, p. 192. • **51**. Békés, 'The 1956 Hungarian Revolution and the Declaration of Neutrality', p. 483. • **52**. Mićunović, *Moscow Diary*, p. 134. • **53**. Sir Brian Barder, cited by Keith Kyle, 'To Suez with Tears', in Wm Roger Louis (ed.), *More Adventures with Britannia: Personalities, Politics and Culture in Britain* (Tauris, London, 2003), pp. 265–81, at p. 272. • **54**. Stykalin, 'The Hungarian Crisis of 1956', pp. 136–7; Anthony Nutting, *No End of a Lesson: The Story of Suez* (Constable, London, 1967); and Kyle, 'To Suez with Tears'. • **55**. Békés, 'The 1956 Hungarian Revolution and the Declaration of Neutrality', p. 491. • **56**. Gati, *Failed Illusions*, pp. 192–3. • **57**. From the protocol of the meeting of Kádár and Ferenc Münnich with the Soviet leadership in Moscow, 3 November 1956, in A.A. Fursenko (ed.), *Prezidium TsK KPSS 1954–1964, Tom 1* (Rosspen, Moscow, 2004), p. 200. • **58**. Kramer, 'New Evidence', p. 363. • **59**. Gough, *A Good Comrade*, pp. 93–4. • **60**. Ibid., p, 372; Anastas Mikoyan, *Tak bylo: Razmyshleniya o minuvshem* (Vagrius, Moscow, 1999), p. 598; and William Taubman, *Khrushchev: The Man and His Era* (Free Press, New York, 2003), p. 298. • **61**. Kramer, 'New Evidence', pp. 371–2 and 376. • **62**. Fursenko (ed.), *Prezidium TsK KPSS 1954 1964*, pp. 193–201; and Kramer, 'New Evidence', pp. 372–3. • **63**. Gough, *A Good Comrade*, p. 98. • **64**. Ibid. • **65**. Rudolf L. Tőkés, *Hungary's Negotiated Revolution: Economic Reform, Social Change and Political Succession* (Cambridge University Press, Cambridge, 1996), p. 15. • **66**. Fursenko (ed.), *Prezidium TsK KPSS 1954–1964*, pp. 201–2. • **67**. *Khrushchev Remembers* (Little, Brown, Boston, 1970), p. 425. • **68**. Ibid., p. 424. • **69**. Kramer, 'New Evidence', p. 376; and Tőkés, *Hungary's Negotiated Revolution*, pp. 13–14. • **70**. Tőkés, *Hungary's Negotiated Revolution*, p. 13. • **71**. Stykalin, 'Soviet–Yugoslav Relations and the Case of Imre Nagy', p. 14. • **72**. Sebestyen, *Twelve Days*, p. 292. • **73**. Ibid. • **74**. Gati, *Failed Illusions*, p. 3. • **75**. Ibid., pp. 2 and 90. Gati observes (p. 2): 'the more evident goal was to satisfy the far-right wing of the Republican Party led by Senator Joseph McCarthy and roll back the Democrats from Capitol Hill – rather than liberate Central and Eastern Europe from Soviet domination'. • **76**. Ibid., p. 101. For a carefully nuanced discussion of Hungarian RFE broadcasts at the time of the Hungarian revolution, which partly disagrees with Gati's assessment, see A. Ross Johnson, 'Setting the Record Straight: Role of Radio Free Europe in the Hungarian Revolution of 1956', Occasional Paper No. 3, Woodrow Wilson International Center for Scholars, Washington DC, October 2006. • **77**. Gati, *Failed Illusions*, p. 109. For the social composition of the active Hungarian insurgents, see the survey-based data in Bennett Korvig, *Communism in Hungary: From Kun to Kádár* (Hoover Institution Press, Stanford, 1979), p. 310. • **78**. Sebestyen, *Twelve Days*, pp. 34–7 and 258–9. • **79**. Ibid., p. 266. • **80**. Kramer, 'New Evidence', p. 377. • **81**. Ibid. • **82**. J.F. Brown, *Eastern Europe and Communist Rule* (Duke University Press, Durham, NC, 1988), pp. 160–1. • **83**. Gough, *A Good Comrade*, p. 120. • **84**. Ibid., p. 256. • **85**. Ibid., p. xi.

16 *Cuba: A Caribbean Communist State*

1. Along with other revolutionary parties and student groups, Communists were, however, active in urban resistance and played a rather greater part in undermining

the pre-Castro regime than post-revolutionary Cuban historiography acknowledges.
• 2. Volker Skierka, *Fidel Castro: A Biography*, translated by Patrick Camiller (Polity,
Cambridge, 2004), pp. 15–17; and Fidel Castro, *My Life*, ed. Ignacio Ramonet and
trans. Andrew Hurley (revised edition, Allen Lane, London, 2007), pp. 2, 6 and 21–2.
• 3. Alan Angell, 'The Left in Latin America since c. 1920', in Leslie Bethell (ed.),
The Cambridge History of Latin America. Vol. IV, Part 2: Politics and Society (Cambridge
University Press, 1994), pp. 163–232, at p. 176. • 4. Skierka, *Fidel Castro*, pp. 6–7. • 5.
Ibid., pp. 10–20. • 6. Ibid., p. 5. In the letter to the American president, Castro under-
stated his age, saying that he was a twelve-year-old. • 7. Castro, *My Life*, pp. 80–1.
• 8. Skierka, *Fidel Castro*, p. 24. • 9. Ibid., pp. 30 and 32. • 10. There is a slight
discrepancy between the numbers of men with whom Castro mounted the attack
as related in Castro's memoirs and in the account of his recent major biographer.
The discrepancy is greater in their accounts of the number of soldiers in the barracks.
Volker Skierka puts the number of government troops billeted there at 700, whereas
Castro says there were 1,500. Cf. Skierka, *Fidel Castro*, p. 34; and Castro, *My Life*, pp.
121–2. • 11. Skierka, *Fidel Castro*, pp. 34–7; Fidel Castro, *History Will Absolve Me*
(Jonathan Cape, London, 1968); and Castro, *My Life*, pp. 104–34. • 12. Castro, *History
Will Absolve Me*, p. 104. Some accounts of the speech describe it as lasting four hours,
others say five hours. Castro spoke extemporaneously and the speech was not recorded.
He wrote it up in prison and it was smuggled out in matchboxes for publication
(Skierka, *Fidel Castro*, p. 36). • 13. Castro, *History Will Absolve Me*, p. 103. • 14. Skierka,
Fidel Castro, pp. 38–9. • 15. Ibid., pp. 40–1. • 16. Castro, *My Life*, p. 182; and Skierka,
Fidel Castro, pp. 46–7. • 17. Luis E. Aguilar, 'Currents in Latin America: Fragmentation
of the Marxist Left', *Problems of Communism*, Vol. XIX, No. 4, July–August 1970, pp.
1–12, at p. 7. • 18. Skierka, *Fidel Castro*, pp. 56–7. • 19. Robert F. Lamberg, 'Che in
Bolivia: The "Revolution" That Failed', *Problems of Communism*, Vol. XIX, No. 4,
July–August 1970, pp. 25–37, at p. 36. There was also revolutionary activity in the
towns, including general strikes, which were unconnected with Castro's revolutionary group. This, too, helped to undermine the old regime. • 20. Skierka, *Fidel
Castro*, pp. 60–1. • 21. Ibid., p. 61. • 22. Ibid., pp. 68–9. • 23. Castro, *My Life*, p. 203.
• 24. Skierka, *Fidel Castro*, p. 69. • 25. Castro, *My Life*, pp. 146–57. • 26. Ibid., p. 157.
• 27. Karl E. Meyer, 'Cuba's Charismatic Communism', *Problems of Communism*, Vol.
XI, No. 6, November–December 1962, pp. 44–5. • 28. Theodore Draper, quoted in
ibid., p. 45. • 29. Skierka, *Fidel Castro*, p. 72. • 30. Ibid., pp. 72–3. • 31. Ibid., p. 76.
• 32. Ibid., p. 82. • 33. Ibid., pp. 84–5. • 34. Ibid., pp. 87–9. • 35. Ibid., p. 89. • 36.
Kevin Devlin, 'The Permanent Revolutionism of Fidel Castro', *Problems of
Communism*, Vol. XVII, No. 1, 1968, pp. 1–11, at p. 2; and Skierka, *Fidel Castro*, p. 196.
• 37. Castro, *My Life*, p. 272; and Aleksandr Fursenko and Timothy Naftali, *Khrushchev's
Cold War: The Inside Story of an American Adversary* (Norton, New York, 2006), p. 436.
• 38. Aleksandr Fursenko (ed.), *Prezidium TsK KPSS 1954–1964, Tom 1: Chernovye
protokol'nye zapisi zasedaniy. Stenogrammy* (Rosspen, Moscow, 2004), p. 556; Fursenko
and Naftali, *Khrushchev's Cold War*, pp. 426–507; and Anastas Ivanovich Mikoyan, *Tak
bylo: Razmyshleniya o minuvshem* (Vagrius, Moscow, 1999), p. 606. • 39. Castro, *My
Life*, p. 258. • 40. Fursenko and Naftali, *Khrushchev's Cold War*, p. 490. • 41. Mikoyan,
Tak bylo, p. 606. The notes taken of the long discussions on the Cuban crisis in the

Presidium of the Central Committee of the CPSU were far from full. They are reproduced in Fursenko (ed.), *Prezidium TsK KPSS 1954–1964*, pp. 617–25. • **42**. Castro, *My Life*, p. 283–4. • **43**. Melvin P. Leffler, *For the Soul of Mankind: The United States, the Soviet Union, and the Cold War* (Hill and Wang, New York, 2007), p. 166. • **44**. Ibid., pp. 166–7; and Vladislav M. Zubok, *A Failed Empire: The Soviet Union in the Cold War From Stalin to Gorbachev* (University of North Carolina Press, Chapel Hill, 2007), pp. 149–53. • **45**. Castro, *My Life*, pp. 285–6. • **46**. Ibid., p. 288. Castro added that this had to be borne in mind when comparisons were made with Eastern Europe, where at one time there were 'attempts to construct Socialism' but where they 'are now attempting to construct capitalism'. • **47**. Ibid., p. 248. • **48**. Ibid. • **49**. Skierka, *Fidel Castro*, pp. 163–5. • **50**. Ibid., p. 165. • **51**. From *Granma*, 19 March 1967, cited in Devlin, 'The Permanent Revolutionism of Fidel Castro', p. 4. • **52**. Daniela Spenser, 'The Caribbean Crisis: Catalyst for Soviet Projection in Latin America', in Gilbert M. Joseph and Daniela Spenser, *In From the Cold: Latin America's New Encounter with the Cold War* (Duke University Press, Durham NC, 2008), pp. 102–4. • **53**. Castro, *My Life*, p. 580. • **54**. Ibid., pp. 174–6. • **55**. Carlos Acosta, *Carlos Acosta: A Cuban Dancer's Tale* (HarperCollins, London, 2007), p. 32. • **56**. Edward Gonzalez, 'Castro and Cuba's New Orthodoxy', *Problems of Communism*, Vol. XXV, No. 1, January–February 1976, pp. 1–19, at p. 5. • **57**. Ibid., pp. 7–9. • **58**. Skierka, *Fidel Castro*, p. 220. • **59**. Jorge I. Domínguez, 'Cuba in the 1980's', *Problems of Communism*, Vol. XXX, No. 2, March–April 1981, pp. 48–59, at p. 52. • **60**. Angell, 'The Left in Latin America', p. 210. • **61**. Piero Gleijeses, 'The View from Havana: Lessons from Cuba's African Journey, 1959–1976', in Joseph and Spenser (eds.), *In From the Cold*, pp. 112–33, at p. 119. • **62**. Ibid., pp. 120–2. • **63**. Ibid., pp. 123–4. • **64**. Ibid., p. 129. • **65**. Anatoly Dobrynin, *In Confidence: Moscow's Ambassador to America's Six Cold War Presidents (1962–1986)* (Random House, New York, 1995), p. 362. • **66**. Ibid., pp. 362–3. • **67**. Domínguez, 'Cuba in the 1980's', p. 57. • **68**. 'The Cuban Paradox', *Harvard Public Health Review*, Summer 2002: http://www.hsph.harvard.edu/review/review_summer_02/677cuba.html. • **69**. See Gloria Giraldo, 'Cuba Rising in Major UN Indices', *MEDICC Review*, 9 April 2007; Marc Schenker, 'Cuban Public Health: A Model for the US?', from *CIA World Factbook, 2001* and schenker.ucdavis.edu/CubaPublicHealth.ppt; Castro, *My Life*, pp. 585 and 709 (n. 14); and Skierka, *Fidel Castro*, p. 302. • **70**. William Leogrande, 'Republic of Cuba', in Bogdan Szajkowski (ed.), *Marxist Governments: A World Survey*, Vol. 2 (Macmillan, London, 1981), pp. 237–60, at p. 251. • **71**. Domínguez, 'Cuba in the 1980's', p. 57. • **72**. Pascal Fontaine, 'Communism in Latin America', in Stéphane Courtois et al., *The Black Book of Communism* (Harvard University Press, Cambridge, Mass., 1999), pp. 647–82, at pp. 661–2; and Skierka, *Fidel Castro*, pp. 87 and 227. • **73**. Skierka, *Fidel Castro*, p. 87. • **74**. Ibid., p. 245.

17 *China: From the 'Hundred Flowers' to 'Cultural Revolution'*

1. Craig Dietrich, *People's China: A Brief History* (Oxford University Press, Oxford, 3rd ed., 1998), p. 84. • **2**. Ibid., pp. 86–9. • **3**. Frederick C. Teiwes, 'The Establishment and Consolidation of the New Regime, 1949–1957', in Roderick MacFarquhar (ed.),

The Politics of China: The Eras of Mao and Deng (Cambridge University Press, Cambridge, 2nd ed., 1997), p. 67. • **4.** Dietrich, *People's China*, p. 89. • **5.** Ibid., p. 90. • **6.** Ibid., p. 91. • **7.** Teiwes, 'The Establishment and Consolidation of the New Regime', pp. 73–4. • **8.** *Khrushchev Remembers: The Last Testament* (Deutsch, London, 1974), p. 253. • **9.** Ibid., pp. 76–7. • **10.** Rana Mitter, *A Bitter Revolution: China's Struggle with the Modern World* (Oxford University Press, Oxford, 2004), pp. 189–90; John King Fairbank and Merle Goldman, *China: A New History* (Harvard University Press, Cambridge, Mass., 2nd enlarged ed., 2006), p. 364; and Lowell Dittmer, 'Pitfalls of Charisma', in *The China Journal*, No. 55, January 2006, p. 124. • **11.** Lorenz M. Lüthi, *The Sino-Soviet Split: Cold War in the Communist World* (Princeton University Press, Princeton, 2008), p. 71; and Dietrich, *People's China*, p. 113. • **12.** *Khrushchev Remembers: The Last Testament*, pp. 271–2. • **13.** Lüthi, *The Sino-Soviet Split*, p. 72. • **14.** Fairbank and Goldman, *China: A New History*, pp. 80–1. • **15.** Dietrich, *People's China*, p. 118. • **16.** Kenneth Lieberthal, 'The Great Leap Forward and the Split in the Yan'an Leadership 1958–1965', in MacFarquhar (ed.), *The Politics of China*, pp. 87–147, at p. 88; and Dietrich, *People's China*, p. 123. • **17.** Mitter, *A Bitter Revolution*, pp. 196–7; Roderick MacFarquhar and Michael Schoenhals, *Mao's Last Revolution* (Harvard University Press, Cambridge, Mass., 2006), p. 2008; Lüthi, *The Sino-Soviet Split*, pp. 116–18; and Jonathan Fenby, *The Penguin History of Modern China: The Fall and Rise of a Great Power, 1850–2008* (Allen Lane, London, 2008), pp. 415–16. Fenby cites a secret CCP report which puts the death toll from the famine at over forty million. • **18.** Lieberthal, 'The Great Leap Forward', pp. 103–4. • **19.** Ibid., p. 112. • **20.** Lüthi, *The Sino-Soviet Split*, pp. 114–18; and Dietrich, *People's China*, pp. 136–8. • **21.** Lieberthal, 'The Great Leap Forward', pp. 116–22. • **22.** Mao's ambition to take over the leadership of the Communist world doubtless began earlier – shortly after the death of Stalin. See Mercy A. Kuo, *Contending with Contradictions: China's Policy toward Soviet Eastern Europe and the Origins of the Sino-Soviet Split, 1953–1960* (Lexington Books, Lanham and Oxford, 2001). • **23.** Lüthi, *The Sino-Soviet Split*, pp. 73–4. • **24.** Ibid., p. 77. • **25.** *Khrushchev Remembers: The Last Testament*, p. 255. • **26.** MacFarquhar and Schoenhals, *Mao's Last Revolution*, pp. 81–2. • **27.** *Khrushchev Remembers: The Last Testament*, p. 259. See also William Taubman, *Khrushchev: The Man and His Era* (Simon & Schuster, London, 2003), pp. 388–92. • **28.** Lüthi, *The Sino-Soviet Split*, pp. 136–8. • **29.** 'Memorandum of Conversation of N.S. Khrushchev with Mao Zedong, Beijing', 3 October 1959 (Cold War International History Project Virtual Archive, National Security Archive, Washington DC, R 9204), pp. 1–13, at p. 5. • **30.** Ibid., pp. 6 and 9. • **31.** Lüthi, *The Sino-Soviet Split*, pp. 172–3. • **32.** Ibid., pp. 174–5. • **33.** Ibid., p. 177. • **34.** Ibid., p. 244. • **35.** Ibid., p. 264. • **36.** Ibid., p. 285. • **37.** MacFarquhar and Schoenhals, *Mao's Last Revolution*, p. 9. • **38.** Lüthi, *The Sino-Soviet Split*, pp. 289–90. • **39.** At times of crisis in his relations with the United States – as in 1954–55 and 1958 – Mao was careful not to risk provoking an American attack. See Steve Tsang, *The Cold War's Odd Couple: The Unintended Partnership between the Republic of China and the UK, 1950–1958* (Tauris, London, 2006), pp. 115–51. • **40.** MacFarquhar and Schoenhals, *Mao's Last Revolution*, p. 8. • **41.** Dietrich, *People's China*, p. 179. • **42.** Ibid., pp. 179–80. • **43.** MacFarquhar and Schoenhals, *Mao's Last Revolution*, p. 17. On the campaign against Wu Han more generally, ibid., pp. 15–19. • **44.** Ibid., pp. 333–6. • **45.** Harry Harding, 'The Chinese State in Crisis, 1966–1969', in

MacFarquhar (ed.), *The Politics of China*, pp. 148–247, at p. 240. • **46**. Ibid., p. 244. Some authors put the figure much higher. Jamie Morgan, in his article, 'China's Growing Pains: Towards the (Global) Political Economy of Domestic Social Instability', *International Politics*, Vol. 45, No. 4, 2008, pp. 413–38, cites (p. 416) a figure of four million. • **47**. Harding, 'The Chinese State in Crisis, 1966–1969', pp. 242–3. • **48**. MacFarquhar and Schoenfals, *Mao's Last Revolution*, pp. 358–9. • **49**. Ibid., p. 409. • **50**. Ibid., p. 411. • **51**. Ibid., p. 20. • **52**. Harding, 'The Chinese State in Crisis', pp. 241–2. • **53**. Dietrich, *People's China*, p. 187. • **54**. See 'Forum on Mao and the Cultural Revolution in China', in *Journal of Cold War Studies*, Vol. 10, No. 2, Spring 2008, pp. 97–130, esp. Yafeng Xia at pp. 111–12. • **55**. Dietrich, *People's China*, p. 256. • **56**. MacFarquhar and Schoenhals, *Mao's Last Revolution*, p. 3. • **57**. Ibid. • **58**. See, for example, Fedor Burlatskiy, *Mao Tsedun i ego nasledniki* (Mezhdunarodnye otnosheniya, Moscow, 1979). For discussions of literature which used ostensible discussion of China as a way of raising issues in the Soviet context forbidden by censorship, see Gilbert Rozman, *A Mirror for Socialism: Soviet Criticisms of China* (Princeton University Press, Princeton, NJ, 1985); and Alexander Lukin, *The Bear Watches the Dragon: Russia's Perceptions of China and the Evolution of Russian–Chinese Relations Since the Eighteenth Century* (M.E. Sharpe, Armonk, 2003), esp. pp. 75–250. • **59**. For a very readable account of Nixon's visit to China and its implications, see Margaret MacMillan, *Seize the Hour: When Nixon Met Mao* (John Murray, London, 2006).

18 Communism in Asia and Africa

1. Christopher Bluth, *Korea* (Polity, Cambridge, 2008), p. 11. • **2**. Dae-Sook Suh, 'A Preconceived Formula for Sovietization: The Communist Takeover of North Korea', in Thomas T. Hammond (ed.), *The Anatomy of Communist Takeovers* (Yale University Press, New Haven, 1971), pp. 475–89, at pp. 476–7. • **3**. Ibid., pp. 483–4. • **4**. Ibid., pp. 482–3. • **5**. Introduction by James G. Hershberg to 'Russian Documents on the Korean War, 1950–53', in *Cold War International History Project*, No. 14/15, Winter 2003–Spring 2004, pp. 369–73; and Bluth, *Korea*, pp. 15–17. • **6**. Jasper Becker, *Rogue Regime: Kim Jong Il and the Looming Threat of North Korea* (Oxford University Press, New York, 2005), pp. 131–3. • **7**. Bluth, *Korea*, pp. 22–32. • **8**. Ibid., pp. 36–7. • **9**. Niccolò Machiavelli, *The Prince* (Dent, London, 1958), p. 102. Machiavelli wrote *The Prince* in 1513. • **10**. David Hume, 'On the First Principles of Government', in *Essays Moral, Political and Literary* (Oxford University Press, Oxford, 1963), pp. 29–34, at p. 31. These essays were first published in 1741 and 1742. • **11**. William J. Duiker, *Ho Chi Minh* (Hyperion, New York, 2000), p. 64. • **12**. Ibid. • **13**. Ibid., p. 75. • **14**. Ibid., p. 306. • **15**. Ibid., pp. 321–32. • **16**. Dennis J. Duncanson, 'Vietnam: From Bolshevism to People's War', in Hammond (ed.), *The Anatomy of Communist Takeovers*, pp. 490–515, at p. 506. • **17**. Duiker, *Ho Chi Minh*, pp. 397 and 443. • **18**. Ibid., pp. 445–6. • **19**. Ibid., pp. 455–61. • **20**. Ibid., pp. 473, 477–9, 491–2, and 500–1. • **21**. Duncanson, 'Vietnam: From Bolshevism to People's War', p. 51. • **22**. Jeffrey Race, *War Comes to Long An: Revolutionary Conflict in a Vietnamese Province* (University of California Press, Berkeley, 1972), pp. 181 and 197. • **23**. Seth Jacobs, '"No Place to Fight a War":

Laos and the Evolution of U.S. Policy toward Vietnam, 1954–1963', in Mark Philip Bradley and Marilyn B. Young (eds.), *Making Sense of the Vietnam Wars: Local, National, and Transnational Perspectives* (Oxford University Press, New York, 2008), pp. 45–66, at p. 45. • **24**. Ibid., p. 51. • **25**. Ibid., pp. 46–51. • **26**. Henry Kissinger, *Years of Upheaval* (Little, Brown, Boston, 1982), p. 21. • **27**. Jacobs, '"No Place to Fight a War"', p. 59. • **28**. Ibid., p. 49. • **29**. Kissinger, *Years of Upheaval*, pp. 18–23. • **30**. Jean-Louis Margolin, 'Vietnam and Laos: The Impasse of War Communism', in Stéphane Courtois et al., *The Black Book of Communism: Crimes, Terror, Repression* (Harvard University Press, Cambridge, Mass., 1999), pp. 565–76, at pp. 575–6. • **31**. Jacobs, '"No Place to Fight a War"', pp. 45–6 and 59. • **32**. Ibid., p. 62. • **33**. Fredrik Legevall, '"There Ain't No Daylight": Lyndon Johnson and the Politics of Escalation', in Bradley and Young (eds.), *Making Sense of the Vietnam Wars*, pp. 91–108, at p. 93. • **34**. Gareth Porter, 'Explaining the Vietnam War: Dominant and Contending Paradigms', in Bradley and Young (eds.), *Making Sense of the Vietnam Wars*, pp. 67–90, at pp. 76–80. • **35**. Cited by Legevall, '"There Ain't No Daylight"', pp. 100–1. • **36**. Porter, 'Explaining the Vietnam War', pp. 72 and 82. • **37**. Sophie Quinn-Judge, 'Through a Glass Darkly: Reading the History of the Vietnamese Communist Party, 1945–1975', in Bradley and Young (eds.), *Making Sense of the Vietnam Wars*, pp. 111–34, at p. 117. • **38**. Lien-Hang T. Nguyen, 'Cold War Contradictions: Toward an International History of the Second Indochina War, 1969–1973', in Bradley and Young (eds.), *Making Sense of the Vietnam Wars*, pp. 219–49, at pp. 229–30. • **39**. Quinn-Judge, 'Through a Glass Darkly', pp. 127 and 130. • **40**. Nguyen, 'Cold War Contradictions', p. 235. • **41**. Ibid., pp. 234–9. • **42**. David W.P. Elliott, 'Official History, Revisionist History, and Wild History', in Bradley and Young (eds.), *Making Sense of the Vietnam Wars*, pp. 277–304, at p. 281. • **43**. Ibid., p. 288. • **44**. Ibid., p. 297. • **45**. Ibid., p. 295. • **46**. Jean-Louis Margolin, 'Cambodia: The Country of Disconcerting Crimes', in Courtois et al., *The Black Book of Communism*, pp. 577–635, at p. 609. • **47**. Ibid., p. 581. • **48**. Ibid. • **49**. On the doubtful appropriateness of the term 'genocide' for the slaughter which ensued, see the observations of former UN Under-Secretary-General Marrack Goulding, in his book *Peacemonger* (John Murray, London, 2002), pp. 247–8. See also the discussion of 'genocide' in Margolin, 'Cambodia', pp. 633–5. • **50**. Patrick Raszelenberg, 'The Khmers Rouges and the Final Solution', *History and Memory*, Vol. 11, No. 2, 1999, pp. 62–93, at pp. 81–2. • **51**. Margolin, 'Cambodia', p. 582. • **52**. Ibid., p. 620. • **53**. Ibid., pp. 589–90 and 635. • **54**. Ibid., pp. 582–3. • **55**. Ibid., pp. 631–2. • **56**. Goulding, *Peacemonger*, pp. 247–8. • **57**. Ibid., p. 588. • **58**. Jimmy Carter, *Keeping Faith: Memoirs of a President* (Bantam, New York, 1982), p. 254. • **59**. Ibid., p. 256. • **60**. Zbigniew Brzezinski, *Memoirs of the National Security Adviser 1977–1981* (Weidenfeld and Nicolson, London, 1983), pp. 408–14. • **61**. Ibid., p. 409. • **62**. In his memoirs, Marrack Goulding cites this as an example of how the 'world-wide struggle against Soviet-led Communism had distorted the values which the West itself claimed to be defending' (Goulding, *Peacemonger*, p. 248). • **63**. Odd Arne Westad, *The Global Cold War* (Cambridge University Press, Cambridge, 2005), p. 300; Dilip Hiro, *Between Marx and Mohammad: The Changing Face of Central Asia* (HarperCollins, London, paperback ed., 1995), p. 234; and Vladislav M. Zubok, *A Failed Empire: The Soviet Union in the Cold War from Stalin to Gorbachev* (University of North Carolina Press, Chapel Hill, 2007), p. 259. • 64. Hiro, *Between Marx and Mohammad*, p. 234. • 65. Westad, *The Global Cold War*, p. 302. • 66. Ibid., pp. 301–2. • 67. Ibid., p. 303. • 68. 'Zapis' besedy A.N. Kosygina, A.A. Gromyko, D.F. Ustinova, B.N. Ponomareva s N.M. Taraki 20 marta 1979 goda', Hoover Institution Archives (hereafter HIA), Fond 89, 1.1003, opis 42, file 3, pp. 2 and 15. • 69. Ibid., p. 3. • 70. Ibid., p. 8. • 71. Ibid., p. 12. • 72. Ibid., p. 13. • 73. Westad, *The Global Cold War*, p. 316. • 74. Ibid., p. 313. • 75. Ibid., p. 321. • 76. Ibid. • 77. HIA, Fond 89, 1.1003, opis 42, file 10, pp. 1–2. • 78. Ibid., p. 4. • 79. Ibid., p. 5. • 80. Westad, *The Global Cold War*, p. 322. • 81. Ibid., p. 357. • 82. Ibid., p. 356. • 83. Hiro, *Between Marx and Mohammad*, pp. 237–8. • 84. Peter Berton, 'Japanese Eurocommunists: Running in Place', *Problems of Communism*, Vol. XXXV, No. 4, 1986, pp. 1–30, esp. pp. 1–3. • 85. J.A.A. Stockwin, *Governing Japan: Divided Politics in a Resurgent Economy* (Blackwell, Oxford, 4th ed., 2008), pp. 198–9. For a useful short history of the JCP, see also Stockwin, 'Japan Communist Party' in Haruhiro Fukui (ed.), *Political Parties of Asia and the Pacific* (Greenwood Press, Westport, 1985), pp. 500–14; and Berton, 'Japanese Eurocommunists'. • 86. Guy Pauker and Ewa Pauker, 'Indonesia', in Witold S. Sworakowski (ed.), *World Communism: A Handbook 1918–1965* (Hoover Institution Press, Stanford, 1973), pp. 200–5, at p. 203. • 87. Ibid., p. 204. • 88. Adam Westoby, *Communism since World War II* (Harvester Press, Brighton, 1981), pp. 182–5. • 89. Pauker and Pauker, 'Indonesia', p. 204. • 90. Westoby, *Communism since World War II*, p. 191. • 91. Dan Diner and Jonathan Frankel, in their essay on 'Jews and Communism: The Utopian Temptation', mention South Africa as one of the many places where Jews 'were disproportionately represented in the Communist movement (be it in the total membership, the apparatus, or the leadership)'. See Frankel (ed.), *Dark Times, Dire Decisions: Jews and Communism* (Avraham Harman Institute of Contemporary Jewry of the Hebrew University of Jerusalem and Oxford University Press, Oxford, 2004), p. 3. • 92. Martin Meredith, *The State of Africa: A History of Fifty Years of Independence* (Simon & Schuster, London, 2006), pp. 122–3. • 93. Westad, *The Global Cold War*, pp. 215–16. • 94. Ibid., p. 216. • 95. Nelson Mandela, *The Long Walk to Freedom* (Abacus, London, 1995), p. 321. • 96. William Beinart, *Twentieth Century South Africa* (Oxford University Press, Oxford, 2nd ed., 2001), pp. 167–8. • 97. Mandela, *The Long Walk to Freedom*, p. 134. • 98. Ibid., pp. 428–37. • 99. Ibid., p. 436. • 100. See Adrian Guelke, 'The Impact of the End of the Cold War on the South African Transition', *Journal of Contemporary African Studies*, Vol. 14, No. 1, 1996, p. 97. See also Meredith, *The State of Africa*, pp. 434–5. • 101 Meredith, *The State of Africa*, pp. 385–6. • 102. A.N. Yakovlev, *Gor'kaya chasha: Bol'shevizm i Reformatsiya Rossii* (Verkhne-Volzhskoe izdatel'stvo, Yaroslavl', 1994), p. 190. • 103. For discussion of these issues, see, for example, Jerry F. Hough, *The Struggle for the Third World: Soviet Debates and American Options* (Brookings Institution, Washington DC, 1986), esp. pp. 226–57. The argument about societies prematurely striving for socialism applied also in Asia, and such a neo-Marxist critique of Soviet orthodoxy in the Brezhnev era was developed, particularly notably, by Nodari Simonia, first at the Institute of Oriental Studies of the Academy of Sciences of the USSR and later at the Institute of World Economy and International Relations (IMEMO), of which Simonia became director in the post-Soviet era. See, for example,

L.I. Reysner and N.A. Simonia (eds.), *Evolyutsiya vostochnykh obshchestv: sintez tradi-tsionnogo i sovremennogo* (Nauka, Moscow, 1984). • 104. Frederick Cooper remarks that even before Frelimo 'dropped its Marxist-Leninist label', the substance of the ideology 'had long been a mixed bag'. See Cooper, *Africa since 1940: The Past of the Present* (Cambridge University Press, Cambridge, 2002), p. 144. • 105. Westad, *The Global Cold War*, pp. 216–18. • 106. Ibid., pp. 244–5. • 107. Meredith, *The State of Africa*, pp. 311–19. • 108. Fidel Castro, *My Life* (Allen Lane, London, 2007), pp. 329 and 333. • 109. Ibid., p. 322. • 110. Meredith, *The State of Africa*, pp. 243–8. • 111. Ibid., pp. 331–42. • 112. Westad, *The Global Cold War*, pp. 286–7 and 383–4.

19 The 'Prague Spring'

1. I raised the theoretical possibility of a 'Moscow Spring', making the point that 'a movement for democratising change can come from within a ruling Communist Party as well as through societal pressure', in a paper I wrote for a seminar convened by the British prime minister, Margaret Thatcher, at Chequers on 8 September 1983. Under the UK Freedom of Information Act (2000), which became operational in 2005, the Cabinet Office and Foreign Office documents relating to that seminar have been declassified. Extensive use of them is made in Archie Brown, 'The Change to Engagement in Britain's Cold War Policy: The Origins of the Thatcher–Gorbachev Relationship', *Journal of Cold War Studies*, Vol. 10, No. 3, 2008, pp. 3–47. See also Adam Roberts, 'International Relations after the Cold War', *International Affairs*, Vol. 84, No. 2, 2008, pp. 335–50. • 2. Jan Gross, 'War as Revolution', in Norman Naimark and Leonid Gibianskii (eds.), *The Establishment of Communist Regimes in Eastern Europe, 1944–1949* (Westview, Boulder, 1997), pp. 17–40, at p. 38. • 3. Igor Lukes, 'The Czech Road to Communism', in Naimark and Gibianskii, pp. 243–65. • 4. Rita Klímová (née Budínová) was the person who said this to me. She was, in fact, only sixteen in February 1948, but already an enthusiastic young Communist. In 1968 her father, Stanislav Budín, was editor of one of the most reformist journals in Czechoslovakia, *Reportér*. Budínová (as she then was, before a second marriage in 1978) was an economist, teaching at Charles University. She was expelled from her university post and from the Communist Party in 1970. She subsequently became an active dissident. • 5. I quoted this in my tribute to Rita Klímová on her death in 1994. For that, and for Richard Davy's accompanying obituary of Klímová, see *The Independent*, 7 January 1994, p. 14. • 6. In a conversation I had with him in Prague in March 1965. • 7. *XIII. Sjezd Komunistické Strany Československa, Praha 31. V. – 4. VI. 1966* (Svoboda, Prague, 1966), pp. 302–9, esp. p. 309. • 8. Zdeněk Mlynář, *Nightfrost in Prague: The End of Humane Socialism*, trans. Paul Wilson (Hurst, London, 1980), p. 65. • 9. Ibid., p. 66. Mlynář saw the official documents relating to the sale of the effects of those executed when he briefly worked in the procurator-general's office in the mid-1950s. He learned directly about the earlier admiration of the tea service from Clementis's widow in 1956. • 10. Ibid. • 11. Outstanding and politically unorthodox films were made at various times throughout Eastern Europe, not least in Poland and Hungary. On film in the whole area, including the Soviet Union, see

the perceptive survey by Mira Liehm and Antonin J. Liehm, *The Most Important Art: East European Film After 1945* (University of California Press, Berkeley and Los Angeles, 1977). • **12**. Mlynář, *Nightfrost in Prague*, p. 60. • **13**. Ibid., p. 59. • **14**. Ibid., p. 58. • **15**. Dušan Hamšík, *Writers Against Rulers* (Hutchinson, London, 1971), p. 174. • **16**. Ibid., p. 182. • **17**. Jaromír Navrátil (ed.), *The Prague Spring 1968: A National Security Archive Documents Reader* (Central European University Press, Budapest, 1998), pp. 9–10. • **18**. Ibid., p. 11. • **19**. Vojtěch Mencl and František Ouředník, 'Jak to bylo v lednu' (part of a series of articles on the lead-up to the Prague Spring), in *Život strany*, No. 19, September 1968, p. 12. • **20**. Mencl and Ouředník, *Život strany*, No. 17, August 1968, p. 37. • **21**. Ibid., p. 38. Extracts from Dubček's and Novotný's speeches, based on the original transcripts, appeared in English translation in 1998. They confirm the accuracy of the 1968 report cited above. See Navrátil (ed.), *The Prague Spring 1968*, pp. 13–17. • **22**. Hamšík, *Writers Against Rulers*, p. 181. Novomeský's speech, which, in his absence, was read out to the Writers' Congress in 1967, is published in full in ibid., pp. 177–181. • **23**. H. Gordon Skilling, *Czechoslovakia's Interrupted Revolution* (Princeton University Press, Princeton, NJ, 1976), p. 185. • **24**. Mlynář, *Nightfrost in Prague*, p. 71; and Navrátil (ed.), *The Prague Spring 1968*, p. 7. • **25**. Mlynář, *Nightfrost in Prague*, p. 71; and 'Document No. 4: János Kádár's Report to the HSWP Politburo of a Telephone Conversation with Leonid Brezhnev, December 13, 1967', reproduced in Navrátil (ed.), *The Prague Spring 1968*, pp. 20–2. • **26**. *Khrushchev Remembers* (Little, Brown, Boston, 1970), pp. 365–6; and Skilling, *Czechoslovakia's Interrupted Revolution*, pp. 206 and 398. • **27**. See Kieran Williams, *The Prague Spring and its Aftermath: Czechoslovak Politics, 1968–1970* (Cambridge University Press, Cambridge, 1997), pp. 67–9. Williams observes (p. 67): 'To maintain control of the reform course and prevent Soviet displeasure, censorship after the January plenum was absolutely essential. It was also unrealistic given the hunger for information and the appetite for debate.' • **28**. Ibid., p. 69. • **29**. Skilling, *Czechoslovakia's Interrupted Revolution*, pp. 382–7. • **30**. Cited in Archie Brown and Gordon Wightman, 'Czechoslovakia: Revival and Retreat', in Archie Brown and Jack Gray (eds.), *Political Culture and Political Change in Communist States* (Macmillan, London, 1977), pp. 159–96, at p. 177. • **31**. The information in this paragraph comes from my interviews of reformist party officials and party intellectuals in Czechoslovakia in 1968 and 1969. • **32**. These points are drawn from a longer summary of the contents of the Action Programme in my article, 'Political Change in Czechoslovakia', *Government and Opposition*, Vol. 4, No. 2, Spring 1969, pp. 169–94, at pp. 173–7. • **33**. Skilling, *Czechoslovakia's Interrupted Revolution*, p. 275. • **34**. Ludvík Vaculík, 'Two thousand words to workers, farmers, scientists, artists and everyone' (*Literární listy*, 27 June 1968), in Andrew Oxley, Alex Pravda and Andrew Ritchie, *Czechoslovakia: The Party and the People* (Allen Lane Penguin Press, London, 1973), pp. 261–74, at p. 263. • **35**. Williams, *The Prague Spring and its Aftermath*, p. 90. • **36**. Vaculík, 'Two thousand words . . .', pp. 266–7. • **37**. On the emergence of intellectual and political groupings in Czechoslovakia both before and during 1968, see Vladimir V. Kusin, *The Intellectual Origins of the Prague Spring: The Development of Reformist Ideas in Czechoslovakia* (Cambridge University Press, Cambridge, 1971); and Kusin, *Political Grouping in the Czechoslovak Reform Movement* (Macmillan, London, 1972). • **38**. Skilling,

Czechoslovakia's Interrupted Revolution, p. 202. • **39**. Mlynář was born on 22 June 1930, and hence was as young as 37 in early 1968. Already having been co-opted into the Central Committee apparatus, he was formally elected a secretary of the Central Committee on 1 June 1968. He subsequently became a member of the Presidium, but he resigned from all his political offices in November 1968 in protest at the excessive concessions being made to the Soviet leadership. He was among the many expelled from the Communist Party in 1970. • **40**. Jiří Pelikán (ed.), *The Czechoslovak Political Trials, 1950–1954* (Macdonald, London, 1971), p. 12. This book contains a full translation of the Piller Report. • **41**. Kusin, *Political Grouping in the Czechoslovak Reform Movement*, p. 74. • **42**. On rehabilitation in Czechoslovakia more broadly, see Skilling, *Czechoslovakia's Interrupted Revolution*, pp. 373–411. Even before the fall of Communism, and the opening of the Czech archives, Karel Kaplan was able to use some of the products of his research on the political trials in work he published abroad in the 1970s. See, for example, Kaplan, *Dans les Archives du Comité Central: Trente ans de secrets du Bloc soviétique* (Albin Michel, Paris, 1978). • **43**. Williams, *The Prague Spring and its Aftermath*, pp. 48–9. • **44**. 'Document No. 14: Stenographic Account of the Dresden Meeting, March 23, 1968 (Excerpts)', in Navrátil (ed.), *The Prague Spring 1968*, pp. 64–72, at p. 67. • **45**. Ibid., pp. 68–9. • **46**. Ibid., p. 69. • **47**. Ibid., p. 70. • **48**. Ibid., p. 65. • **49**. Ibid., pp. 71–2. • **50**. Mlynář, *Nightfrost in Prague*, p. 164. • **51**. 'Document No. 28: Stenographic Account of the Soviet–Czechoslovak Summit Meeting in Moscow, May 4–5, 1968 (Excerpts)', in Navrátil (ed.), *The Prague Spring 1968*, pp. 114–25, at p. 117. • **52**. Ibid., p. 116. • **53**. Mlynář, *Nightfrost in Prague*, p. 122. • **54**. Ibid., pp. 121–2. • **55**. Ibid., pp. 122–3. • **56**. Navrátil (ed.), *The Prague Spring 1968*, p. 125. • **57**. 'Document No. 31: Minutes of the Secret Meeting of the "Five" in Moscow, May 8, 1968 (Excerpts)', in Navrátil (ed.), *The Prague Spring 1968*, pp. 132–43, at p. 139. • **58**. Soviet reporting of events in Czechoslovakia in 1968 was highly selective and mendacious. Their attempt to control the flow of information meant that even Western European Communist Party newspapers disappeared from Moscow kiosks. During the 1967–68 academic year – including all of the first half of 1968 – I was an exchange scholar at Moscow State University (under the terms of the Cultural Agreement between Great Britain and the USSR). For days on end the Italian Communist Party newspaper *L'Unità* (especially), the PCF paper *L'Humanité*, and even the British CP's *Morning Star* disappeared from the university's newspaper stalls. The concern of the Soviet authorities about the spread and possible influence of ideas emanating from Czechoslovakia reached neurotic proportions. Once, when I was working in Reading Room Number One (*Pervyy zal*) of the Lenin Library, where normally Western – and, naturally, Communist – journals would be delivered on order, I was refused permission to see a copy of the inoffensive British academic quarterly the *Slavonic and East European Review*. It turned out that the person at the library desk believed that it was a Czech journal. It was only when I finally persuaded her that it was a British publication that the librarian relented. • **59**. Navrátil, *The Prague Spring 1968*, p. 141. • **60**. 'Document No. 32: Cable from the Czechoslovak Ambassador to Yugoslavia, May 9, 1968, on Leonid Brezhnev's Recent Discussions with Josip Broz Tito', in ibid., p. 144. • **61**. 'Document No. 51: Message from Alexander Dubček and Oldřich Černík to Leonid

Brezhnev, July 14, 1968', in ibid., p. 210. • **62.** 'Document No. 52: Transcript of the Warsaw Meeting, July 14–15 1968 (Excerpts)', in ibid., pp. 212–33, at p. 213. This is a translation of the Polish transcript of the proceedings. The 91-page Soviet transcript has not been declassified in Moscow. • **63.** Ibid., p. 214. • **64.** Ibid., pp. 215–18. • **65.** Ibid., p. 218. • **66.** R.G. Pikhoya, 'Chekhoslovakiya, 1968 god. Vzglyad iz Moskvy. Po dokumentam TsK KPSS', *Novaya i noveyshaya istoriya*, Vol. 6, 1994, pp. 3–20, at p. 20. • **67.** Navrátil (ed.), *The Prague Spring 1968*, p. 220. • **68.** R.G. Pikhoya, 'Chekhoslovakiya, 1968 god. Vzglyad iz Moskvy po dokumentam TsK KPSS', *Novaya i noveyshaya istoriya*, Vol. 1, 1995, pp. 34–48, at pp. 35–6. • **69.** Shelest, worried about the impact of Czechoslovak developments in Ukraine, was one of the harshest critics of Dubček and the Prague reformers. See, for example, his speech at a plenary session of the Central Committee of the CPSU on 17 July 1968. It is reproduced in full in *Cold War International History Project Bulletin*, No. 14/15, Winter 2003–Spring 2004, pp. 318–20. • **70.** 'Document No. 65: Speeches by Leonid Brezhnev, Alexander Dubček, and Aleksei Kosygin at the Cierna nad Tisou Negotiations, July 29, 1968 (Excerpts)', in Navrátil (ed.), *The Prague Spring 1968*, pp. 284–97, at pp. 292–3. • **71.** Ibid., pp. 294–5. • **72.** Skilling, *Czechoslovakia's Interrupted Revolution*, pp. 305–6. • **73.** 'Document No. 73: The Bratislava Declaration, August 3, 1968', in Navrátil (ed.), *The Prague Spring 1968*, pp. 326–9, at p. 327. • **74.** 'Document No. 72: The "Letter of Invitation" from the Anti-Reformist Faction of the CPCz Leadership, August 1968', in ibid., pp. 324–5. • **75.** Ibid., p. 324. • **76.** That this was an important consideration for the Soviet leadership was confirmed by Brezhnev when he – together with Kosygin and Politburo member and Chairman of the Presidium of the Supreme Soviet Nikolay Podgorny – met with Czechoslovak president Ludvík Svoboda in the Kremlin on 23 August 1968. See HIA, Fond 89, 1.1002, opis 38, file 57, p. 3. • **77.** 'Document No. 98: Invasion Warning from Czechoslovak Ambassador to Hungary Jozef Púčik, August 20, 1968', in Navrátil (ed.), *The Prague Spring 1968*, p. 410. • **78.** Williams, *The Prague Spring and its Aftermath*, pp. 126–7. • **79.** 'Document No. 92: Leonid Brezhnev's Speech at a Meeting of the "Warsaw Five" in Moscow, August 18, 1968 (Excerpts)', in Navrátil (ed.), *The Prague Spring 1968*, pp. 395–9, at p. 398. • **80.** *Pravda*, 22 August 1968. • **81.** Mlynář, *Nightfrost in Prague*, p. 146. • **82.** Ibid., pp. 147 and 150; Williams, *The Prague Spring and its Aftermath*, p. 127; and 'Document No. 100: Statement by the CPCz CC Presidium Condemning the Warsaw Pact Invasion, August 21, 1968', in Navrátil (ed.), *The Prague Spring 1968*, p. 414. Two other reformist members of the leadership, Presidium member Čestmír Císař and secretary of the Central Committee Václav Slavík, were also asked by Dubček to participate in the drafting of the resolution, but the document (in which the reference to contravention of international law enraged the Soviet leadership) was essentially that written by Mlynář, an academic lawyer by profession. • **83.** On the resistance, see the near-contemporary account of Adam Roberts in Philip Windsor and Adam Roberts, *Czechoslovakia 1968: Reform, Repression and Resistance* (Chatto and Windus, London, for the Institute of Strategic Studies, London, 1969). See also Skilling, *Czechoslovakia's Interrupted Revolution*, pp. 759–810; and Williams, *The Prague Spring and its Aftermath*, pp. 127–37. • **84.** Jiří Pelikán (ed.), *The Secret Vysočany Congress: Proceedings and Documents of the Extraordinary Fourteenth Congress of the Communist Party of*

Czechoslovakia, 22 August 1968 (Allen Lane Penguin Press, London, 1971). • **85**. HIA,
Fond 89, 1.1002, opis 38, file 57, pp. 1 and 40–1. • **86**. The full text was published in
Windsor and Roberts, *Czechoslovakia 1968*, pp. 178–81. • **87**. Podgorny and Shelest
also espoused that hard line. See Pikhoya, 'Chekhoslovakiya, 1968 god', *Novaya i
noveyshaya istoriya*, No. 1, 1995, p. 47. • **88**. Ibid., p. 46–7. • **89**. HIA, Fond 89, 1.1002,
opis 38, file 57, p. 7. • **90**. 'O deyatel'nosti kontrrevolyutsionnogo podpol'ya v
Chekhoslovakii', HIA, Fond 89, 1.1009, opis 61, file 5. • **91**. Ibid., p. 8. • **92**. Williams,
The Prague Spring and its Aftermath, p. 143.

20 'The Era of Stagnation': The Soviet Union under Brezhnev

1. See, for example, Georgi Arbatov, *The System: An Insider's Life in Soviet Politics*
(Random House, New York, 1992), pp. 124–5. • **2**. Brezhnev's observation to Bohumil
Šimon has been related more than once by Zdeněk Mlynář. The quotation is taken
in this case from an interview in G.R. Urban (ed.), *Communist Reformation:
Nationalism, internationalism and change in the world Communist movement* (Temple
Smith, London, 1979), p. 136. • **3**. Arbatov also cites Brezhnev saying (in conversa-
tion with the Soviet ambassador to Czechoslovakia, Stepan Chervonenko, in July
1968) that the search for a political solution should continue, but that he would be
forced to resign as general secretary if he 'lost Czechoslovakia'. See Arbatov, *The
System*, p. 141. • **4**. Brandt describes the political process in his memoirs. See Willy
Brandt, *My Life in Politics* (Penguin, London, 1993), pp. 138–209. • **5**. Arbatov, *The
System*, p. 126. • **6**. Ibid., p. 130. • **7**. Ibid., pp. 130–2. Although Brezhnev did not
ultimately endorse publicly the rehabilitation of Stalin, his inclinations lay in that
direction. Willy Brandt notes that in the first major conversation he had with the
Soviet leader in 1970, Brezhnev made clear that 'he did not want to be identified
with Khrushchev's anti-Stalinist ideas'. On the contrary: 'Stalin, he said, had achieved
much, and after all the country had finally won the war under his leadership; he
would return to favour' (Brandt, *My Life in Politics*, p. 183). • **8**. Archie Brown and
Michael Kaser (eds.), *The Soviet Union since the Fall of Khrushchev* (Macmillan, London,
2nd ed., 1978), pp. 226–8. • **9**. Ibid., p. 226. • **10**. Mikhail Gorbachev, *Zhizn' i reformy*
(Novosti, Moscow, 1995), Vol. 1, pp. 229–30. • **11**. Henry Kissinger, *White House Years*
(Little, Brown, Boston, 1979), p. 527. • **12**. Philip Hanson, *The Rise and Fall of the
Soviet Economy: An Economic History of the USSR from 1945* (Longman, London, 2003),
pp. 100–12. • **13**. See Alexander Solzhenitsyn, *The Oak and the Calf: Sketches of Literary
Life in the Soviet Union*, trans. Harry Willetts (Collins and Harvill, London, 1980). •
14. Andrei Sakharov, *Memoirs* (Knopf, New York, 1990), p. 23. • **15**. Sakharov's own
account of where he differed from Solzhenitsyn is to be found in ibid., pp. 406–9.
• **16**. Roy Medvedev, *Let History Judge: The Origins and Consequences of Stalinism*
(Knopf, New York, 1971; and Macmillan, London, 1972). A revised and expanded
edition was published in 1989 by Columbia University Press, New York, and Oxford
University Press, Oxford. • **17**. In the Introduction to the 1989 English-language
edition of his book (ibid., p. 19), Medvedev was able to mention for the first time
four people who were working within the Central Committee apparatus in the

1960s who helped him greatly during that decade: Georgiy Shakhnazarov, Yuriy Krasin, Lev Delyusin and Fedor Burlatsky. During the late perestroika period, Medvedev's book was finally published in the Soviet Union with the title *Pered sudom istorii* (Before the Court of History). • **18**. Medvedev's letter to Suslov is in HIA, Fond 89, 1.1994, opis 17, file 49, p. 14. The same file (p. 5) contains a letter by KGB chairman Andropov about Roy Medvedev and his book manuscript on Stalinism and the hostile judgement on Medvedev's work, in a joint statement, dated 11 February 1969, signed by V. Stepakov, head of the Department of Propaganda of the Central Committee, S. Trapeznikov, head of the Department of Science and Education, and V. Shauro, head of the Department of Culture (ibid., pp. 1–3). The excommunication of Medvedev from the CPSU which followed did not stop a steady stream of *samizdat* works (almost invariably published abroad) from his pen and from that of his twin brother, Zhores Medvedev. The latter, a biochemist by profession, was incarcerated in a Soviet mental hospital in 1970 entirely for political reasons, and later, when on a research visit to London in 1973, deprived of his Soviet citizenship. He continued thereafter to live and write in London. Although the works of the Medvedevs were among the best-known of unofficial Soviet writings abroad, they were untypical within the Soviet dissident movement. For scholarly studies of that movement, see Peter Reddaway, *Uncensored Russia: The Human Rights Movement in the Soviet Union* (Jonathan Cape, London, 1972); Sidney Bloch and Peter Reddaway, *Russia's Political Hospitals: The Abuse of Psychiatry in the Soviet Union* (Gollancz, London, 1977); and Peter Reddaway, 'Policy Towards Dissent since Khrushchev', in T.H. Rigby, Archie Brown and Peter Reddaway (eds.), *Authority, Power and Policy in the USSR* (Macmillan, London, 1980). • **19**. Peter Reddaway, 'Dissent in the Soviet Union', *Problems of Communism*, Vol. XXXII, No. 6, November–December 1983, pp. 1–15, at p. 14. • **20**. V. Stanley Vardys, 'Lithuanians', in Graham Smith (ed.), *The Nationality Question in the Soviet Union* (Longman, London, 1990), pp. 72–91, at pp. 78–9; and Vardys, *The Catholic Church, Dissent and Nationality in Soviet Lithuania* (Columbia University Press, New York, 1978). • **21**. Laurie J. Salitan, *Politics and Nationality in Contemporary Soviet-Jewish Emigration, 1968–1989* (Macmillan, London, 1992), pp. 96–7. • **22**. John B. Dunlop. *The Faces of Contemporary Russian Nationalism* (Princeton University Press, Princeton, 1983), pp. 87–92; and for a much fuller account of Russian environmentalism and its struggles, Douglas R. Weiner, *A Little Corner of Freedom: Russian Nature Protection from Stalin to Gorbachev* (University of California Press, Berkeley, 1999). • **23**. Dunlop, *The Faces of Contemporary Russian Nationalism*, p. 57. • **24**. Alexei Yurchak, *Everything Was Forever Until It Was No More: The Last Soviet Generation* (Princeton University Press, Princeton, 2006), pp. 158–237, esp. p. 196. • **25**. See Gerald Stanton Smith, *Songs to Seven Strings: Russian Guitar Poetry and Soviet 'Mass Song'* (Indiana University Press, Bloomington, 1984). • **26**. Shakhnazarov told me, in one of the interviews I had with him (in the Kremlin, shortly before he, along with Gorbachev, was turned out of it by Yeltsin in December 1991), that he had felt himself to be a social democrat ever since the early 1960s. See Archie Brown, *Seven Years that Changed the World: Perestroika in Perspective* (Oxford University Press, Oxford, 2007), p. 173. • **27**. A.S. Chernyaev, *Moya zhizn' i moe vremya* (Mezhdunarodnye otnosheniya, Moscow, 1995), pp. 237–80. • **28**. At the very end of the Brezhnev era, although not on the ailing Brezhnev's initiative, a fierce attack on IMEMO was launched by hard-liners in the leadership whose outlook was strongly influenced by Russian nationalism. IMEMO was accused of being in a state of 'ideological collapse', partly due to the influence of 'zionist elements'. On this, see Robert D. English, *Russia and the Idea of the West: Gorbachev, Intellectuals, and the End of the Cold War* (Columbia University Press, New York, 2000), pp. 169–72. For a more detailed study of the episode, see the important institutional history of IMEMO by Petr Cherkasov, *IMEMO: portret na fone epokhi* (Ves' mir, Moscow, 2004), esp. pp. 451–530. • **29**. On the significance of critical thinking within these and other Soviet institutes in the years before perestroika, see, for much fuller discussions, English, *Russia and the Idea of the West*; Neil Malcolm, *Soviet Political Scientists and American Politics* (Macmillan, London, 1984); Ronald J. Hill, *Soviet Politics, Political Science, and Reform* (Martin Robertson, Oxford, 1980); Jeffrey T. Checkel, *Ideas and International Change: Soviet/Russian Behavior and the End of the Cold War* (Yale University Press, New Haven, 1997); Julie M. Newton, *Russia, France, and the Idea of Europe* (Macmillan, London, 2003); and Brown, *Seven Years that Changed the World*, esp. Ch. 6, 'Institutional Amphibiousness or Civil Society: The Origins and Development of Perestroika', pp. 157–89. • **30**. Brown, *Seven Years that Changed the World*, pp. 174–5. • **31**. X.L. Ding, 'Institutional Amphibiousness and the Transition from Communism: The Case of China', *British Journal of Political Science*, Vol. 24, No. 3, July 1994, pp. 293–318. • **32**. Ludmilla Alexeyeva and Paul Goldberg,, *The Thaw Generation: Coming of Age in the Post-Stalin Era* (Little, Brown, Boston, 1990). On INION and Delyusin, see p. 236. Once when I tried to re-contact in the 1970s an erudite person of distinctly anti-Communist views whom I had met on a previous visit, I called INION, where I knew he worked, and told the telephonist I didn't know his extension number: 'Department of Scientific Communism,' she replied. • **33**. Hanson, *The Rise and Fall of the Soviet Economy*, p. 162. • **34**. The growing economic crisis of the 1980s is well described, with much important documentation and illustration, by Yegor Gaidar in *Collapse of an Empire: Lessons for Modern Russia* (Brookings Institution, Washington DC, 2007), although his account of political change in the Soviet Union leans much too strongly towards economic determinism. • **35**. See for the results of one such professional survey Boris Dubin, 'Litso epokhi: Brezhnevskiy period v stolknovenii razlichnykh otsenok', *Monitoring obshchestvennogo mneniya* (VTsIOM, Moscow), No. 3 (65), 2003, pp. 26–40. See also Archie Brown, 'Cultural Change and Continuity in the Transition from Communism: The Russian Case', in Lawrence E. Harrison and Peter L. Berger (eds.), *Developing Cultures: Case Studies* (Routledge, New York, 2006), pp. 387–405.

21 *The Challenge from Poland: John Paul II, Lech Wałesa, and the Rise of Solidarity*

1. Peter Raina, *Political Opposition in Poland 1954–1977* (Poets and Painters Press, London, 1978), p. 146. • **2**. Ibid., pp. 148–9; Leszek Kołakowski, 'The Intelligentsia', in Abraham Brumberg (ed.), *Poland: Genesis of a Revolution* (Vintage Books, New York, 1983), pp. 54–67, at pp. 61–2; and Tadeusz Szafar, 'Anti-Semitism: A Trusty Weapon', in ibid., pp. 109–22, at pp. 112–13. • 3. Andrzej Paczkowski and Malcolm Byrne (eds.), *From Solidarity to Martial Law: The Polish Crisis of 1980–81. A Documentary History* (Central European Press, Budapest, 2007), p. xxix. Paczkowski, in his chapter, 'Poland, the "Enemy Nation"', in Stéphane Courtois et al., *The Black Book of Communism* (Harvard University Press, Cambridge, Mass., 1999), pp. 363–93, at p. 387, gives a figure of 45 killed throughout Poland in the December 1970 strikes and protests. • 4. Timothy Garton Ash, *The Polish Revolution: Solidarity 1980–81* (Jonathan Cape, London, 1983), pp. 11–13; and Jack Bielasiak, 'The Party: Permanent Crisis', in Brumberg (ed.), *Poland: Genesis of a Revolution*, pp. 10–25, at p. 15. • 5. Garton Ash, *The Polish Revolution*, p. 13. • 6. Alex Pravda, 'Poland 1980: From "Premature Consumerism" to Labour Solidarity', *Soviet Studies*, Vol. XXXIV, No. 2, April 1982, pp. 167–99, at p. 170. • 7. The phrase 'premature consumerism' was coined by Pravda in the article noted above. • 8. Garton Ash, *The Polish Revolution*, p. 16. • 9. Ibid. • 10. Ibid., pp. 16–17; Jan B. de Weydenthal, 'Workers and Party in Poland', *Problems of Communism*, Vol. XXIX, No. 6, November–December 1980, pp. 1–22, at pp. 3–4; and Kołakowski, 'The Intelligentsia', p. 63. • 11. Kołakowski, 'The Intelligentsia', pp. 63–5. • 12. On KOR, in particular, and more generally on the development of civil society in Poland, see Michael H. Bernhard, *The Origins of Democratization in Poland* (Columbia University Press, New York, 1993). Bernhard (p. 3) defines civil society as 'a public space located between official public and private life, which is populated by a range of different autonomous organizations'. • 13. Jan Józef Lipski, 'The Founding of KOR', *Survey*, Vol. 26, No. 3, Summer 1982, pp. 61–79. • 14. Garton Ash, *The Polish Revolution*, p. 19. • 15. Maria Hirszowicz, *Coercion and Control in Communist Society: The Visible Hand of Bureaucracy* (Harvester, Brighton, 1986), pp. 181–3. • 16. Garton Ash, *The Polish Revolution*, p. 20. • 17. Carl Bernstein and Marco Politi, *His Holiness: John Paul II and the Hidden History of Our Time* (Doubleday, New York, 1996), p. 175. • 18. Garton Ash, *The Polish Revolution*, p. 29. • 19. Bernstein and Politi, *His Holiness*, pp. 8–9. • 20. Kołakowski, 'The Intelligentsia', pp. 64–6; and Garton Ash, *The Polish Revolution*, p. 32. • 21. Garton Ash, *The Polish Revolution*, p. 23. • 22. Aleksander Smolar, 'The Rich and the Powerful', in Brumberg (ed.), *Poland: Genesis of a Revolution*, pp. 42–53. • 23. Garton Ash, *The Polish Revolution*, pp. 40–1. • 24. Ibid., pp. 42–4. • 25. On further personnel changes, see de Weydenthal, 'Workers and Party in Poland', pp. 13–15. • 26. 'Document No. 3: Cardinal Wyszyński's Sermon at Jasna Góra Following the Outbreak of Strikes, with Reactions', in Paczkowski and Byrne (eds.), *From Solidarity to Martial Law*, pp. 51–6. • 27. Paczkowski and Byrne (eds.), *From Solidarity to Martial Law*, pp. 10–11. • 28. Ibid., pp. 11–12. It is estimated that a million party members out of a total membership of approximately three million joined Solidarity. • 29. 'Document No. 2: Extract from Protocol No. 210 of CPSU CC Politburo Meeting, August 25, 1980', in ibid., p. 50. • 30. These contingency plans were outlined in a top-secret document in which the name of the country the Politburo members were talking about and the number of troops and tanks that would be involved were written in ink in gaps left in the typed document. As happened with a number of exceptionally sensitive issues, not even a Central Committee typist was to be trusted with the information on what was afoot. The document, which is headed simply 'TsK KPSS', and dated 18 August 1980, was signed by Suslov, Gromyko, Andropov, Ustinov and Chernenko. A photocopy is to be found in the Volkogonov Collection, R 9659, National Security Archive, Washington DC. • **31**. Paczkowski and Byrne (eds.), *From Solidarity to Martial Law*, p. xxxiii. • **32**. As reported by Hungarian sociologists during a study visit I made to Budapest in June 1981. Kádár relayed the kind of criticism to be heard in Hungary to the Soviet and East European leaders in Moscow in December 1980, saying: 'When we first got news about the strikes on the coast, there were certain reactions [in Hungary]. I am speaking now not about party members and the party leadership but about the man on the street, thus *de facto* about the ideologically and politically less qualified masses. The first reaction was as follows: what do the Polish comrades think they are doing? To work less and earn more? Then it was said: . . . they want to strike and we are supposed to do the work?' See 'Document No. 22: Minutes of Warsaw Pact Leadership Meeting in Moscow, December 5 1980', ibid., p. 147. Kádár also stated (ibid.) that 'as far as we are concerned, the Polish events are of little concern to us in terms of domestic politics'. While there was, indeed, no sign of Hungarian workers wishing to copy their Polish counterparts, for some reformist party members in Hungary the crisis of the Polish party was a stimulus to thought about political as well as economic reform. • **33**. Ibid., p. xxxiii. • **34**. 'Document No. 18: Letter from Erich Honecker to Leonid Brezhnev, November 26, 1980' in ibid., pp. 134–5. • **35**. 'Document No. 22: Minutes of Warsaw Pact Leadership Meeting in Moscow, December 5, 1980', in ibid., p. 151. • **36**. Ibid., pp. 154–6. • **37**. Ibid., pp. 160–1. • **38**. Georgi Arbatov observed that the fact that the Soviet Union was 'bogged down in Afghanistan may have helped us avoid an even more dangerous adventure: intervention in Poland during the political crisis in 1980'. See Arbatov, *The System: An Insider's Life in Soviet Politics* (Random House, New York, 1992), p. 200. • **39**. Paczkowski and Byrne (eds.), *From Solidarity to Martial Law*, p. 19. • **40**. At a meeting of the Soviet Politburo on 12 March 1981, Brezhnev described Jaruzelski as 'a good, intelligent comrade who has great authority'. See 'Zasedanie Politbyuro TsK KPSS 12 marta 1981 goda' (READD Collection, National Security Archive), p. 6. • **41**. On the duality in the personality of Jaruzelski, see Garton Ash, *The Polish Revolution*, pp. 143–5. • **42**. 'Document No. 39: Transcript of CPSU CC Politburo Meeting, April 2, 1981', in Paczkowski and Byrne (eds.), *From Solidarity to Martial Law*, pp. 239–44, at p. 239. • **43**. On the self-limiting aspect of Solidarity in 1980–81, see the work of the Polish sociologist (one of the intellectual advisers at the birth of Solidarity) Jadwiga Staniszkis, *Poland's Self-Limiting Revolution*, edited by Jan T. Gross (Princeton University Press, Princeton, 1984); and Alaine Touraine et al., *Solidarity. The Analysis of a Social Movement: Poland 1980–1981* (Cambridge University Press, Cambridge, 1983), esp. pp. 64–79. • **44**. Garton Ash, *The Polish Revolution*, p. 207. • **45**. Ibid., p. 212. • **46**. 'Document No. 61: Transcript of CPSU CC Politburo Meeting, September 10, 1981', in Paczkowski and Byrne (eds.), *From Solidarity to Martial Law*, p. 348. • **47**. 'Document No. 72: Transcript of CPSU CC Politburo Meeting on Rusakov's Trip to Eastern Europe', in ibid., pp. 395–9, at pp. 396–7. • **48**. 'Document No. 81: Transcript of CPSU CC Politburo Meeting, 10 December 1981', in ibid., pp. 446–53, at pp. 449–53. • **49**. Paczkowski and Byrne (eds.), *From Solidarity to Martial Law*, p. 35. • **50**. John O'Sullivan, *The Pope, the President, and the Prime Minister: Three Who Changed the World* (Regnery, Washington DC, 2006), p. 187; and Gale Stokes, *The Walls Came Tumbling Down: The Collapse of Communism in Eastern Europe* (Oxford University Press, New York, 1983), p. 117. • **51**. Stokes, *The Walls Came Tumbling Down*, pp. 112–21. • **52**. Ibid., p. 122.

22 Reform in China: Deng Xiaoping and After

1. See Chapter 17, note 8. • **2**. Quoted in Roderick MacFarquhar and Michael Schoenhals, *Mao's Last Revolution* (Harvard University Press, Cambridge, Mass., 2006), p. 457. • **3**. John Gittings, *The Changing Face of China: From Mao to Market* (Oxford University Press, Oxford, 2006), pp. 170–1. • **4**. Craig Dietrich, *People's China: A Brief History* (Oxford University Press, Oxford, 3rd ed., 1998), pp. 238–9. • **5**. Gittings, *The Changing Face of China*, p. 167. • **6**. Ibid. • **7**. Ibid., p. 168. • **8**. Rana Mitter, *A Bitter Revolution: China's Struggle with the Modern World* (Oxford University Press, Oxford, 2004), p. 222. • **9**. Ibid., p. 223. • **10**. Author's interview with Professor Su Shaozhi, Oxford, June 1988. At a party symposium later in 1988, Su (who had headed the Institute of Marxism-Leninism Mao Zedong Thought, but was dismissed from that post in 1987 for calling for more democracy) spoke out boldly against 'ideological prejudices, bureaucratism, sectarianism, Zhdanovism . . . and cultural autocracy' and complained that in spite of sweeping promises 'a lot of forbidden zones still remain in our academic and theoretical studies' (Gittings, *The Changing Face of China*, p. 227). In January 1989 he got into further trouble by speaking his mind at a symposium addressed by the party leader, Zhao Ziyang. He said that in the natural sciences alone there had been since 1949 34 mass campaigns against defenceless victims. He criticized not only the Cultural Revolution as an extreme example but also the 'anti-Rightist movement of 1987', following the dismissal of Hu Yaobang as party leader. Thus, he was criticizing policies decreed not only by Mao but also by Deng. Su added, for good measure, that 'it is wrong to force scholars to accept Marxism'. His speech was sufficiently unorthodox that the Shanghai newspaper which published it faced reprisals. See Jonathan Mirsky, 'Chinese glasnost savaged by guru', *The Observer*, 29 January 1989, p. 23. • **11**. Author's interview with Su Shaozhi, June 1988. • **12**. Gittings, *The Changing Face of China*, pp. 154–9. • **13**. See David Shambaugh, *China's Communist Party: Atrophy and Adaptation* (University of California Press, Berkeley, 2008). • **14**. Dietrich, *People's China*, pp. 242–3. • **15**. Ibid. • **16**. Vivienne Shue, *The Reach of the State: Sketches of the Chinese Body Politic* (Stanford University Press, Stanford, 1988), p. 148. See also Will Hutton, *The Writing on the Wall: China and the West in the 21st Century* (Little, Brown, London, 2007), p. 103. • **17**. Dietrich, *People's China*, p. 244. • **18**. Archie Brown, *The Gorbachev Factor* (Oxford University Press, Oxford, 1996), p. 143. • **19**. Dietrich, *People's China*, pp. 245–6. • **20**. Ibid., p. 249. • **21**. Tony Saich, *Governance and Politics of China* (Palgrave Macmillan, London, 2nd ed., 2004), pp. 100–3. • **22**. Dietrich, *People's China*, p. 270–2. • **23**. Ibid., pp. 273–6. • **24**. Saich, *Governance and Politics of China*, p. 70. • **25**. When I was in China in September 1988, as one of a small group of Oxford scholars who were guests of the Chinese Academy of Social Sciences, I was asked to speak about the Soviet perestroika in virtually every institute we visited in Beijing and Shanghai. • **26**. Mikhail Gorbachev, *Zhizn' i reformy* (Novosti, Moscow, 1995), Vol. 2, pp. 435–6. • **27**. Ibid., p. 444. • **28**. Ibid., p. 446. • **29**. Cited in Joseph Fewsmith, *China since Tiananmen: From Deng Xiaoping to Ho Jintao* (Cambridge University Press, Cambridge, 2nd ed., 2008), p. 30. • **30**. Dietrich, *People's China*, pp. 287–8. • **31**. As Susan Shirk observes: 'When Zhao Ziyang died in 2005, the current leaders revealed their persistent insecurity by suppressing news of the event and restricting the funeral to a small private gathering'. See Susan L. Shirk, *China: Fragile Superpower* (Oxford University Press, New York, 2007), p. 38. Shirk was the senior Department of State official responsible for US relations with China in the Clinton administration. • **32**. Dietrich, *People's China*, p. 289. • **33**. Richard Baum, 'The Road to Tiananmen: Chinese Politics in the 1980s', in Roderick MacFarquhar (ed.), *The Politics of China: The Eras of Mao and Deng* (Cambridge University Press, Cambridge, 1997), pp. 340–471, at pp. 450–1. • **34**. Dietrich, *People's China*, p. 292. • **35**. Ibid. • **36**. Baum, 'The Road to Tiananmen', p. 456. • **37**. Ibid. • **38**. Ibid. Baum gives a figure of between 600 and 1,200 for those killed. • **39**. Dietrich, *People's China*, pp. 298–300. • **40**. Ibid., p. 301. • **41**. Fewsmith, *China since Tainanmen*, pp. 26–7. • **42**. Dietrich, *People's China*, p. 303. • **43**. Fewsmith, *China since Tiananmen*, pp. 30–1. • **44**. Ibid., p. 39. • **45**. Dietrich, *People's China*, pp. 305–6. • **46**. On the relationship between global attention and human rights in China more generally, see Rosemary Foot, *Rights Beyond Borders: The Global Community and the Struggle over Human Rights in China* (Oxford University Press, Oxford, 2000). • **47**. For some of the reasons why civil society is weakly developed in China, see X.L. Ding, 'Institutional Amphibiousness and the Transition from Communism: The Case of China', *British Journal of Political Science*, Vol. 24, No. 3, July 1994, pp. 293–318; Shu-Yun Ma, 'The Chinese Discourse on Civil Society', *The China Quarterly*, No. 137 (March 1994), pp. 180–93; and Alena Ledeneva, '*Blat* and *Guanxi*: Informal Practices in Russia and China', *Contemporary Studies in Society and History*, Vol. 50, No. 1, 2008, pp. 1–27. • **48**. See the important article by Ding, 'Institutional Amphibiousness and the Transition from Communism'. The Chinese Academy of Social Sciences in Beijing and the Shanghai Academy of Social Sciences have also been home to many thinkers who have broken through the barriers of ideological orthodoxy. This is often done indirectly, as in an article on the fate of democratic thought in China published in 1988. Although the author was writing about the pre-Communist period, it is not difficult to see that he also had the Communist era in mind when he wrote: 'But freedom and equality was [*sic*] in fact forgotten, for they seemed to have nothing to do with the salvation of the nation. There was no systematic effort to deal with the Chinese traditional suppression of freedom, human rights and other features of autocracy. As a result, form was paid more attention than content.' Advocacy of democracy is still clearer in his conclusion: 'Chinese modern history shows that, though it was politically a great achievement and not easy to overthrow autocracy, to establish the Republic of China, to draft the constitution and to set up the legislative assembly, it was even more difficult and important to get rid of the feudal influence ideologically and to establish democratic consciousness. As to the latter, we not only should have a sense of urgency, but also should be mentally prepared to have a protracted struggle.' See Xiong Yuezhi, 'A Summary of the Historical Development of the Chinese Democratic Thought', in *SASS Papers* (Shanghai Academy of Social Sciences, Shanghai, 1988), pp. 268-89, at pp. 285 and 289. • **49**. Kellee S. Tsai, *Capitalism without Democracy: The Private Sector in Contemporary China* (Cornell University Press, Ithaca, 2007), p. 53. • **50**. Ibid., p. 53. • **51**. Ibid., pp. 53-4. • **52**. Ibid., p. 54. • **53**. Andrew J. Nathan, 'China's Path from Communism', *Journal of Democracy*, Vol. 4, No. 2, April 1993, pp. 30-42, at pp. 35-6. • **54**. Tsai, *Capitalism without Democracy*, pp. 54-7. • **55**. X.L. Ding, 'Who Gets What, How? When Chinese State-Owned Enterprises Become Shareholding Companies', *Problems of Post-Communism*, Vol. 46, No. 3, May-June 1999, pp. 32-41; Ding, 'Informal Privatization Through Internalization: The Rise of *Nomenklatura* Capitalism in China's Offshore Businesses', *British Journal of Political Science*, Vol. 30, No. 1, 2000, pp. 121-46; Jonathan Story, *China: The Race to Market* (Prentice-Hall, London, 2003), pp. 230-2; and BBC News, 16 March 2007, http://news.bbc.co.uk/1/hi/world/asia-pacific/6456959.stm. • **56**. Tsai, *Capitalism without Democracy*, pp. 81-2. • **57**. Ding, 'Informal Privatization Through Internationalization', p. 138. • **58**. Ibid., pp. 139 and 142. • **59**. Jamie Morgan, 'China's Growing Pains: Towards the (Global) Political Economy of Domestic Social Instability', *International Politics*, Vol. 45, No. 4, 2008, pp. 413-38, at p. 414. • **60**. Albert Kiedel, 'China's Economic Rise – Fact and Fiction' (Policy Brief 61, Carnegie Endowment for International Peace, Washington DC, July 2008), p. 5. Against Kiedel's confident prediction, it is worth noting that, with an ageing population (because of the one-child policy), and fewer economically active young people, the rate of growth may slow considerably. Putting the remarkable post-Mao growth in the size of the Chinese economy in a much longer historical perspective, Chris Patten – the last British governor of Hong Kong – has observed that, so far as it is possible to ascertain, for eighteen of the last twenty centuries China's economy was the biggest in the world. See Chris Patten, *Not Quite the Diplomat: Home Truths about World Affairs* (Allen Lane, London, 2005), p. 264. • **61**. Ibid., p. 9. • **62**. Ibid., pp. 11-12. • **63**. Jianyong Yue, 'Peaceful Rise of China: Myth or Reality?', *International Politics*, Vol. 45, No. 4, 2008, pp. 439-56, at p. 443. • **64**. Longer-established industrialized economies have had a somewhat analogous experience. There was much gnashing of teeth in Britain over the demise of a domestically owned car industry. However, in the twenty-first century it does not seem to trouble either British car workers or the population as a whole that the factories – in which both labour relations and productivity have been much improved – are owned by companies whose headquarters are in Japan, the United States, Germany and France. • **65**. Shirk, *China: Fragile Superpower*, p. 46. • **66**. Shambaugh, *China's Communist Party*, pp. 156-7. • **67**. Shirk, *Fragile Superpower*, p. 68. • **68**. *Financial Times*, 2 July 2008, p. 1. • **69**. Shambaugh, *China's Communist Party*, p. 123. See also Arthur Kroeber, 'China needs proof of democracy's advantage', *Financial Times*, 4 August 2008, p. 13. • **70**. Cited in Shambaugh, *China's Communist Party*, p. 134. • **71**. The point is made by a leading specialist on the Chinese Communist Party, David Shambaugh. The equivalent institution to Beijing's Central Party School has produced important reformers in several other Communist states. See ibid., pp. 137, 139 and 144; and Chapter 19 of the present volume. • 72. Shambaugh, *China's Communist Party*, pp. 111–14; Saich, *Governance and Politics of China*, pp. 84–5; and Fewsmith, *China since Tiananmen*, pp. 5 and 243. • 73. Shambaugh, *China's Communist Party*, p. 114. • 74. Ibid., pp. 114–15. • 75. Ibid., pp. 111 and 121. • 76. Ibid., pp. 138–9. • 77. X.L. Ding, 'Who Gets What, How?'; Ding, 'Internal Privatization Through Internationalization'; and Ledeneva, '*Blat* and *Guanxi*'. • 78. Lindsey Hilsum, 'The great bore of the people', *New Statesman*, 22 October 2007, p. 26. • 79. Yue, 'Peaceful Rise of China', p. 449. • 80. 'Chinese Communist Party membership exceeds 74 million in 2007', http://www.yndehong.cn/1103/2008/07/03/54@23723.htm. • 81. Morgan, 'China's Growing Pains', p. 427. • 82. Tianjian Shi, 'Cultural Values and Democracy in the People's Republic of China', *China Quarterly*, No. 162 (2000) pp. 540–59, at p. 557. • 83. 'Chinese Communist Party . . .', http://www.yndehong.cn/1103/2008/07/03/ 54@23723.htm. • 84. In August 2008, shortly before the opening of the Olympic Games, sixteen Chinese policemen were killed in an attack in Xinjiang, and there were several explosions in the province during the Games themselves. Uighur separatists have waged an unsuccessful campaign for decades against Chinese rule. See the BBC news report of 10 August 2008, 'Blasts in China's Xinjiang region', http.://news.bbc.co.uk/1/hi/world/asia-pacific/7551954. stm. • 85. Cited in Fewsmith, *China since Tiananmen*, p. 282.

23 *The Challenge of the West*

1. The Harvard Project, based on in-depth interviews with 3,000 former Soviet citizens who had either taken the opportunity of the Second World War to stay abroad or had been 'displaced persons' who chose not to return to the USSR, found that the great majority were very attached to the educational and medical provision of the Soviet Union. Those who were at the time of the interviews living in West Germany preferred the German medical system to the Soviet because it, too, was one of 'socialized medicine' but on a higher level. However, they preferred the medical service they had left behind in the Soviet Union to that of the United States because of the high cost of the latter and the extent to which quality of service depended on ability to pay. See Alex Inkeles and Raymond A. Bauer, *The Soviet Citizen: Daily Life in a Totalitarian Society* (Harvard University Press, Cambridge, Mass., 1961), pp. 236–43. • 2. Cited by Philip Hanson, *The Rise and Fall of the Soviet Economy* (Longman, London, 2003), p. 124. • 3. It was published in all 35 countries which were signatories to it. I have used the British document, *Conference on Security and Co-operation in Europe Final Act* (Cmnd. 6198, HMSO, London, 1975). • 4. G. Bennett et al. (eds.), *Documents on British Policy Overseas: Series III, Volume II: The Conference on Security and Co-operation in Europe, 1972–1975* (HMSO, London, 1997), pp. 56–7 and 323–5. • 5. *Conference on Security and Co-operation in Europe Final Act* – from Part 1, Principle I, p. 3. See also Richard Davy (ed.), *European Détente: A Reappraisal* (Royal Institute of International Affairs and Sage, London, 1992), p. 16. • 6. *Conference on Security and Co-operation in Europe Final Act*, p. 3. This wording is to be found in Part 1, Principle II. • 7. This is the first sentence of the lengthy 'human rights and fundamental freedoms' Principle VII of Basket One. Many authors who

would appear not to have read the Final Act have placed human rights exclusively in the Third Basket. This is just one of a number of common errors on the Helsinki agreement exposed by Richard Davy in a forthcoming article, 'Helsinki myths: setting the record straight on the Final Act of the CSCE, 1975', to be published in *Cold War History*. • **8**. See ibid.; and also Davy (ed.), *European Détente*, pp. 16–19. • **9**. Svetlana Savranskaya, 'Unintended Consequences: Soviet Interests, Expectations, and Reactions to the Helsinki Final Act', in Oliver Bange and Gottfried Niedhart (eds.), *Helsinki 1975 and the Transformation of Europe* (Berghahn, Oxford, 2008), pp. 175–90, at p. 181. • **10**. Ibid. For a Russian study by one of the Helsinki process participants which focuses especially on the post-1975 follow-up to the Final Act, see Yu. V. Kashlev, *Khel'sinskiy protsess 1975–2005: svet i teni glazami uchastnika* (Izvestiya, Moscow, 2005). • **11**. In private it was another matter. During a visit to the Institute of State and Law of the Academy of Sciences in Moscow in 1976, I was told that its former director, Viktor Chkhikvadze, a Stalinist by disposition as well as background, who was not generally given to criticizing higher Soviet authority, had muttered: 'Our leaders made a big mistake when they signed the Helsinki accord.' • **12**. Quoted in Davy (ed.), *European Détente*, p. 251. • **13**. 'Sir T. Garvey (Moscow) to Mr Callaghan' [ENZ 3/303/1]', Document No. 141 in Bennett et al. (eds.), *Documents on British Policy Overseas: Series III, Volume II*, pp. 474–9, at pp. 478–9. • **14**. Ludmilla Alexeyeva and Paul Goldberg, *The Thaw Generation: Coming of Age in the Post-Stalin Era* (Little, Brown, Boston, 1990), pp. 280–1. • **15**. Thus, for example, even twelve years after the Helsinki accord was signed, the British prime minister's private secretary, Charles Powell, discussing a seminar held as part of the preparation for Margaret Thatcher's forthcoming visit to the Soviet Union, noted, as one of the conclusions, that 'the Helsinki agreements gave us legitimate grounds to comment on some aspects of what was going on' and that the 'Prime Minister would want to raise *human rights*' (C.D. Powell, 'Seminar on the Soviet Union', 1 March 1987, Cabinet Office Papers, A 2162, pp. 9 and 10. Emphasis in the original. Document obtained under the UK Freedom of Information Act.) • **16**. On that point, see Rudolf L. Tőkés (ed.), *Eurocommunism and Détente* (Council on Foreign Relations and New York University Press, New York, 1978). Tőkés discusses, inter alia, the different views taken of the Helsinki accord, arguing that 'on balance, the Helsinki agreement has been more beneficial to adherents of liberal democracy and to the peoples of Eastern Europe than to the U.S.S.R. and to Moscow's East European clients' (ibid., p. 453). • **17**. Arrigo Levi, 'Eurocommunism: Myth or Reality?', in Paulo Filo della Torre, Edward Mortimer and Jonathan Story (eds.), *Eurocommunism: Myth or Reality?* (Penguin, Harmondsworth, 1979), pp. 9–23, at pp. 9 and 13. • **18**. 'Appendix One: Joint Declaration of the Italian and Spanish Communist Parties, 12 July 1975', in della Torre, Mortimer and Story (eds.), *Eurocommunism*, pp. 330–3. • **19**. Santiago Carrillo, *'Eurocommunism' and the State* (Lawrence and Wishart, London, 1977), pp. 115–18. • **20**. Ibid., pp. 131–2. • **21**. Eusebio M. Mujal-León, 'The Domestic and International Evolution of the Spanish Communist Party', in Tőkés (ed.), *Eurocommunism and Détente*, pp. 204–70, at pp. 255–6. • **22**. Robert Legvold, 'The Soviet Union and West European Communism', in Tőkés, *Eurocommunism and Détente*, pp. 314–84, at p. 377. • **23**. Paradoxically, one of the most convinced

'Eurocommunist' parties was the Japanese. It came to share many of the critical positions of its West European counterparts and condemned the invasions of both Czechoslovakia and Afghanistan. See Peter Berton, 'Japanese Eurocommunists: Running in Place', in *Problems of Communism*, Vol. XXXV, No. 4, July–August 1986, pp. 1–30. • **24.** 'Appendix Two: Joint Declaration of the French and Italian Communist Parties, 15 November 1975', in della Torre, Mortimer and Story (eds.), *Eurocommunism*, pp. 334–8. • **25.** 'Contrary to the Interests of Peace and Socialism in Europe: Concerning the book *"Eurocommunism" and the State* by Santiago Carrillo, General Secretary of the Communist Party of Spain', *New Times*, No. 26, June 1977, pp. 9–13, at p. 10 (italics added). • **26.** Archie Brown and George Schöpflin, 'The Challenge to Soviet Leadership: Effects in Eastern Europe', in della Torre, Mortimer and Story (eds.), *Eurocommunism*, pp. 249–76, at p. 263. • **27.** Ibid., pp. 266–8. • **28.** In addition to the works already cited on Eurocommunism, see Richard Kindersley (ed.), *In Search of Eurocommunism* (Macmillan, London, 1981); Howard Machin (ed.), *National Communism in Western Europe: A Third Way for Socialism?* (Methuen, London, 1983); Roy Godson and Stephen Haseler, *'Eurocommunism': Implications for East and West* (Methuen, London, 1978); and Vadim Zagladin et al., *Europe and the Communists* (Progress, Moscow, 1977). • **29.** The story was told to the Soviet scientist Roald Sagdeev by the Director of the Institute of Nuclear Physics at Akademgorodok (a city created in Siberia specifically for the advancement of science), Andrey Budker, who was himself of Jewish origin. See Sagdeev, *The Making of a Soviet Scientist: My Adventures in Nuclear Fusion and Space from Stalin to Star Wars* (Wiley, New York, 1994), pp. 134–5. • **30.** Mikhail Gorbachev, *Zhizn' i reformy* (Novosti, Moscow, 1995), Vol. 1, pp. 155–70, esp. pp. 168–70. • **31.** Ibid., p. 169. • **32.** Interview with G.A. Arbatov, 8 February 2000, The Hoover Institution and the Gorbachev Foundation (Moscow) Collection, Hoover Institution Archives, Acc. No. 98067-16. 305, Box 1. • **33.** Margaret Thatcher, *The Downing Street Years* (HarperCollins, London, 1993), p. 321, where Thatcher reports what Trudeau told her about Gorbachev later in 1983. • **34.** Gorbachev, *Zhizn' i reformy*, Vol. 1, p. 255. • **35.** Memorandum from John Coles to Brian Fall, 13 September 1983, Foreign Office Papers, RS013/2 (obtained under the UK Freedom of Information Act). • **36.** The meeting on 8–9 September, in which I took part, is one of the themes of my article, 'The Change to Engagement in Britain's Cold War Policy: The Origins of the Thatcher–Gorbachev Relationship', *Journal of Cold War Studies*, Vol. 10, No. 3, Summer 2008, pp. 3–47. • **37.** Percy Cradock, *In Pursuit of British Interests: Reflections on Foreign Policy under Margaret Thatcher and John Major* (John Murray, London, 1997), p. 18. • **38.** Geoffrey Howe, *Conflict of Loyalty* (Macmillan, London, 1994), pp. 428–35. • **39.** Writing to Brian Fall, who was private secretary to Sir Geoffrey Howe, the prime minister's private secretary noted the aim of building up contacts with the Soviet Union 'at higher levels' over the next few years, adding: 'There will be no public announcement of this change of policy.' See 'Policy on East/West Relations', Memorandum from John Coles to Brian Fall, 12 September 1983, Foreign Office Papers, RS013/2. • **40.** The Foreign Office needed no convincing of this. If they had been the prime movers on East–West relations during Margaret Thatcher's prime ministership, this change of policy would have occurred earlier. Geoffrey Howe's predecessor as foreign secretary, Francis Pym, had tried unsuccessfully to change the tone of the rhetoric and to pursue East–West contacts, but got no response from 10 Downing Street – other than his unceremonious dismissal from office on 10 June 1983. See Pym, *The Politics of Consent* (Hamish Hamilton, London, 1984), p. 56; and Brown, 'The Change to Engagement in Britain's Cold War Policy', esp. pp. 11–12 and 27–31. • **41**. 'Vystuplenie pered chlenami parlamenta Velikobritanii, 18 dekabrya 1984 goda', in M.S. Gorbachev, *Izbrannye rechi i stat'i*, Vol. 2 (Politizdat, Moscow, 1987), pp. 109–16. • **42**. *Financial Times*, 22 December 1984, p. 26. • **43**. The transcript of this meeting at Camp David of 22 December 1984 is in the Reagan Library Archive and available online on the website of the Thatcher Foundation: http://www.margaretthatcher.org/archive. Commenting on Margaret Thatcher's contribution to this Camp David meeting, George Shultz later wrote: 'She was enthusiastic about Gorbachev, as had been clear from her public statements.' See Shultz, *Turmoil and Triumph: My Years as Secretary of State* (Scribner's, New York, 1993), p. 509. • **44**. Howe, *Conflict of Loyalty*, p. 430. • **45**. Ibid. • **46**. David Caute, *The Dancer Defects: The Struggle for Cultural Supremacy During the Cold War* (Oxford University Press, Oxford, 2003), p. 31. • **47**. Alexander Zinoviev, *The Yawning Heights*, trans. Gordon Clough (Penguin, Harmondsworth, 1981), p. 649. • **48**. Ibid. • **49**. The US-based British author John O'Sullivan adds the name of Margaret Thatcher to that of Reagan and the Pope. His book is somewhat more nuanced than its title suggests. See O'Sullivan, *The President, the Pope, and the Prime Minister: Three Who Changed the World* (Regnery, Washington DC, 2006). • **50** Ronald Reagan, *An American Life* (Simon and Schuster, New York, 1990), pp. 570 and 683. • **51**. The former director of the Space Research Institute in the Soviet Union, Roald Sagdeev, who was brought into Gorbachev's consultative circle on SDI, advised strongly against any escalation of Soviet expenditure on an SDI-equivalent. He remarked to an American journalist that 'if Americans oversold SDI, we Russians overbought it'. Sagdeev personally thought the idea that SDI could provide a foolproof defence against incoming nuclear missiles was laughable. He argues that the Soviet side paid more attention to SDI than it was worth, but by becoming all the more conscious of its infeasibility, at least they 'saved the country a few billion rubles'. See Sagdeev, *The Making of a Soviet Scientist*, p. 273. • **52**. Ibid. • **53**. Jack F. Matlock, Jr, *Reagan and Gorbachev: How the Cold War Ended* (Random House, New York, 2004), pp. 75–6. • **54**. Ibid., pp. 53–4. • **55**. Ibid., p. 75. • **56**. Howe, *Conflict of Loyalty*, p. 350. The former CIA director, Robert M. Gates, observes that the CIA 'did not really grasp how alarmed the Soviet leaders might have been until some time after the exercise had been concluded'. He cites the British view, which owed much to the information passed to them by Oleg Gordievsky, that 'the threat of a preemptive strike was taken very seriously in Moscow in mid-1983 and early 1984'. See Gates, *From the Shadows* (Simon & Schuster, New York, 1996), p. 272. • **57**. See Melvin P. Leffler, *For the Soul of Mankind: The United States, the Soviet Union, and the Cold War* (Hill and Wang, New York, 2008), esp. pp. 448–50; Shultz, *Turmoil and Triumph*; and Matlock, *Reagan and Gorbachev*.

24 Gorbachev, Perestroika and the Attempt to Reform Communism, 1985–87

1. Gorbachev had, in a sense, been pre-selected as general secretary already on the evening of 10 March when he was designated as chairman of the funeral commission for Chernenko. Viktor Grishin reminded members of the Politburo of this at their meeting formally to choose the general secretary the next day. He had been the person to propose Gorbachev for the funeral commission chairmanship, hoping thus to improve his chances of political survival. At the 11 March meeting Gromyko was the first member to propose Gorbachev and everyone present added words of praise and said that he was the obvious choice. The transcript of that Politburo meeting, 'Zasedanie Politbyuro TsK KPSS 11 marta 1985 goda', is available in Hoover Institution Archives (hereafter HIA), Fond 89, 1.1001, opis 36, file 16, pp. 1–14. • 2. I observed this myself in the Institute of State and Law of the Academy of Sciences in Moscow. • 3. Mikhail Gorbachev, Zhizn' i reformy (Novosti, Moscow, 1995), Vol. 1, pp. 234–5. • 4. David Remnick, Lenin's Tomb: The Last Days of the Soviet Empire (Random House, New York, 1993), p. 192. • 5. Yegor Ligachev, Inside Gorbachev's Kremlin (Pantheon, New York, 1993), pp. 39–43. • 6. Archie Brown, The Gorbachev Factor (Oxford University Press, Oxford, 1996), pp. 68–9. • 7. M.S. Gorbachev, 'Zhivoe tvorchestvo naroda', 10 December 1984, republished in Gorbachev, Izbrannye rechi i stat'i (Politizdat, Moscow, 1987), Vol. 2, pp. 75–198. I discussed this significant speech at some length in 'Gorbachev: New Man in the Kremlin', Problems of Communism, Vol. 34, No. 3, May–June 1985, pp. 1–23. • 8. 'Zasedanie Politbyuro TsK KPSS 12 iyulya 1984 goda', HIA, Fond 89, 1.001, opis 36, file 15, p. 5. • 9. Ibid. • 10. Aleksandr Yakovlev, Sumerki (Materik, Moscow, 2003), pp. 475–6. • 11. His close friend Zděněk Mlynář described Gorbachev to me in June 1979 (six years before he became Soviet leader) as 'open-minded, intelligent, and anti-Stalinist'. At the time Gorbachev became general secretary, Mlynář wrote an important article for the Italian Communist newspaper L'Unità (9 April 1985, p. 9), in which he said that Gorbachev had 'never been a cynic and he is in character a reformer'. Nevertheless, in the early stages of his general secretaryship, as in the years before he became party leader, Gorbachev could repeat the current party orthodoxy even on the concept of Stalinism. Thus, in an interview with the French Communist Party newspaper L'Humanité on 4 February 1986, he responded to a question in which the interviewer cited Western circles which spoke about 'remnants of Stalinism in the Soviet Union' by saying: '"Stalinism" is a concept thought up by the enemies of communism, and is being widely used in order to blacken the Soviet Union and socialism as a whole' (Gorbachev, Izbrannye rechi i stat'i, Vol. 3, pp. 154–70, at pp. 162–3). He went on to speak about the respects in which the Soviet Union was changing – a widening of glasnost, the further development of intra-party democracy and 'socialist democracy in general' – but his response on the concept of Stalinism was that which any previous Soviet leader would have made and, as he was to go on to demonstrate, did not reflect his inner convictions. • 12. Raisa Gorbacheva, I Hope: Reminiscences and Reflections (HarperCollins, London, 1991), pp. 16–17. • 13. M.S. Gorbachev, 'Oktyabr' i perestroyka: revolyutsiya prodolzhaetsya' (speech of 2 November 1987 to joint session of the Central Committee and the Supreme Soviet, in celebration of the Seventieth

Anniversary of 'Great October'), in *Izbrannye rechi i stat'i*, Vol. 5, pp. 386–436, at p. 402. • **14**. Richard Pipes was wrong in thinking that the Politburo chose a 'soft-liner' in Gorbachev, 'a man committed to perestroika and disarmament', in response to the hard-line policies of President Reagan. Neither the transcript of the Politburo meeting at which Gorbachev was proposed by all as general secretary nor the subsequent interviews and memoirs of Politburo members suggest that they were at all aware that they were electing a radical reformer who would also transform the essence of Soviet foreign policy. See Pipes, 'Misinterpreting the Cold War: The Hardliners Had it Right', *Foreign Affairs*, Vol. 71, No. 1, January–February 1995, pp. 154–60, at p. 158. My own argument is set out at substantially greater length than here in a chapter called 'Ending the Cold War', in Archie Brown, *Seven Years that Changed the World: Perestroika in Perspective* (Oxford University Press, Oxford, 2007), pp. 239–76. • **15**. Yegor Gaidar (who was to become acting prime minister in the first post-Soviet Russian government and was an influential economic reformer for much of the 1990s) lays great stress on the heavy blow to the Soviet economy of the fall of oil prices. He notes: 'In 1986, prices fell to an unprecedented low for the previous decade – less than $10 a barrel in prices at that time.' See Gaidar, *Collapse of an Empire: Lessons for Modern Russia* (Brookings Institution, Washington DC, 2007), p. 61. • **16**. 'O perestroyke i kadrovoy politike partii', speech of 27 January 1987, in Gorbachev, *Izbrannye rechi i stat'i*, Vol. 4 (1987), pp. 299–354, at p. 319. • **17**. Ibid., p. 354 • **18**. Gorbachev, *Izbrannye rechi i stat'i*, Vol. 3, pp. 235–43, at p. 241 (italics in the original). • **19**. Georgiy Shakhnazarov, *Tsena svobody: Reformatsiya Gorbacheva glazami ego pomoshchnika* (Rossika Zevs, Moscow, 1993), p. 53. • **20**. It appeared in the journal *Oktyabr'* (previously a very conservative Soviet journal, but, under new editorship, transformed in the Gorbachev era), No. 3, 1987, pp. 130–5. In a letter of 12 May, Berlin replied: 'If, indeed, it was released for general circulation, I am to some degree shaken, as I promised you I would be; evidently something is happening.' However, he remained, as he put it in the same letter, 'obstinately sceptical about fundamental change or the real belief in peaceful co-existence on the part of the Soviet authorities'. • **21**. *Pravda*, 15 July 1987, p. 2; and *Pravda*, 30 September 1987, p. 1. • **22**. 'Zasedanie Politbyuro TsK KPSS 15 oktyabrya 1987 goda', Volkogonov Papers, R 10012, National Security Archive (hereafter NSA), Washington DC, p. 155. • **23**. Ibid., p. 178. • **24**. Ibid., pp. 149–50. • **25**. Gorbachev, *Izbrannye rechi i stat'i*, Vol. 5 (1988), p. 402. • **26**. In September 1988, Chairman of the Council of Ministers Ryzhkov drew the Politburo's attention to many of 'the negative phenomena in the struggle with drunkenness and alcoholism'. These included thousands of deaths arising from the consumption of dangerous alternative intoxicants, shortages in the shops of a variety of products which were being adapted for these purposes, and the immense loss of revenue to the state. See 'O nekotorykh negativniykh yavleniyakh v bor'be s p'yanstvom i alkogolizmom', in *Isvestiya TsK KPSS*, No. 1, 1989, pp. 48–51. See also Stephen White, *Russia Goes Dry: Alcohol, State and Society* (Cambridge University Press, Cambridge, 1996). • **27**. A.S. Chernyaev, *Shest' let s Gorbachevym* (Kul'tura, Moscow, 1993), pp. 174–5; and Timothy J. Colton, *Yeltsin: A Life* (Basic Books, New York, 2008), pp. 138–40. • **28**. 'Zasedanie Politbyuro TsK KPSS 15 oktyabrya 1987 goda', p. 137. • **29**. Brown, *The Gorbachev Factor*, p. 35. • **30**. Colton, *Yeltsin*, pp. 130–1.

• 31. Ibid., pp. 131–2; and Brown, *The Gorbachev Factor*, p. 110. • 32. Brown, *The Gorbachev Factor*, p. 169. • 33. Colton, *Yeltsin*, pp. 146–53. • 34. Gaidar, *Collapse of an Empire*, pp. 111–12. • 35. Ibid., p. 112. • 36. Anatoly Dobrynin, *In Confidence: Moscow's Ambassador to Six Cold War Presidents (1962–1986)* (Random House, New York, 1995), pp. 622–6. • 37. 'Zasedanie Politbyuro TsK KPSS 30 maya 1987 goda', Volkogonov Papers, NSA, p. 485. • 38. Dobrynin, *In Confidence*, p. 626. • 39. For discussion of the intellectual origins of the 'New Thinking' on foreign policy, see Robert D. English, *Russia and the West: Gorbachev, Intellectuals, and the End of the Cold War* (Columbia University Press, New York, 2000); Matthew Evangelista, *Unarmed Forces: The Transnational Movement to End the Cold War* (Cornell University Press, Ithaca, 1999); Stephen Shenfield, *The Nuclear Predicament: Explorations in Soviet Ideology* (Royal Institute of International Affairs and Routledge, London, 1987); and Silvio Pons and Federic Romero (eds.), *Reinterpreting the End of the Cold War: Issues, Interpretations, Periodizations* (Frank Cass, London, 2005). • 40. See on this Melvin P. Leffler, *For the Soul of Mankind: the United States, the Soviet Union, and the Cold War* (Hill and Wang, New York, 2007), pp. 403–14. • 41. Dobrynin, *In Confidence*, p. 622. • 42. Jack F. Matlock, Jr, *Reagan and Gorbachev: How the Cold War Ended* (Random House, New York, 2004), p. 275.

25 *The Dismantling of Soviet Communism, 1988–89*

1. *Der Spiegel* interview with Alexander Solzhenitsyn, www.nytimes.com/2007/07/23/world/europe/23spiegel.html. Similarly, Solzhenitsyn told David Remnick: 'As for freedom of speech, that's the great achievement of Gorbachev and his policy of glasnost. Yeltsin just did not interfere in this process.' See Remnick, *Reporting: Writings from The New Yorker* (Vintage Books, New York, 2007), p. 206. • 2. Sheila Fitzpatrick, 'Like a Thunderbolt', *London Review of Books*, 11 September 2008, pp. 13–15, at p. 14. • 3. Even though the article which appeared under Nina Andreyeva's name was a collective effort, it reflected views which she expressed still more clearly in private, as she did – not least on the subject of Jews – in a long conversation with David Remnick. See Remnick, *Lenin's Tomb: The Last Days of the Soviet Empire* (Viking, New York, 1993), p. 83. • 4. *Sovetskaya Rossiya*, 13 March 1988, p. 3. • 5. *V Politbyuro TsK KPSS ... Po zapisyam Anatoliya Chernyaeva, Vadima Medvedeva, Georgiya Shakhnazarova (1985–1991)* (Al'pina, Moscow, 2006), p. 307. • 6. Ibid. • 7. Ibid., pp. 302–9. • 8. Vadim Medvedev, *V komande Gorbacheva* (Bylina, Moscow, 1994), p. 71. • 9. For a variety of analyses of the development and significance of the unofficial organizations, see Geoffrey A. Hosking, Jonathan Aves and Peter J.S. Duncan, *The Road to Post-Communism: Independent Political Movements in the Soviet Union 1985–1991* (Pinter, London, 1992); M. Steven Fish, *Democracy from Scratch: Opposition and Regime in the New Russian Revolution* (Princeton University Press, Princeton, 1995); and Alexander Lukin, *The Political Culture of the Russian 'Democrats'* (Oxford University Press, Oxford, 2000). • 10. With circulations already high in 1988–89, the journals of liberal, reformist and pro-perestroika orientation saw them rise still more by 1990, far outstripping the total readership of the Russian nationalist journals, although subscriptions to the latter were not negligible.

Thus in 1990 the journals of nationalist orientation, *Nash sovremennik, Moskva* and *Molodaya gvardiya*, had a total of 1.6 million subscribers, whereas the joint readership of their liberal counterparts, *Novy mir, Znamya* and *Yunost'*, was 6.6 million. See Yitzhak M. Brudny, *Reinventing Russia: Russian Nationalism and the Soviet State, 1953–1991* (Harvard University Press, Cambridge, Mass., 1998), p. 230. • **11.** As mentioned in the speech of Georgiy Baklanov, the chief editor of the journal *Znamya*, to the Nineteenth Party Conference: *XIX Vsesoyuznaya konferentsiya Kommunisticheskoy Partii Sovetskogo Soyuza, 28 iyunya – 1 iyulya 1988 goda: Stenograficheskiy otchet* (Politizdat, Moscow, 1988), Vol. 2, p. 21. • **12.** Yu.N. Afanas'ev (ed.), *Inogo ne dano: Sud'by perestroyki. Vglyadyvayas' v proshloe. Vozvrashchenie k budushchemu* (Progress, Moscow, 1988). • **13.** Ibid., p. 126. • **14.** Brudny, *Reinventing Russia*, p. 193. • **15.** Ibid., pp. 252–3. • **16.** Remnick, *Lenin's Tomb*, pp. 266–8. • **17.** A number of people who worked with Gorbachev, including members of the Politburo who were opposed to the main thrust of perestroika, have testified to Gorbachev's powers of persuasion. Thus, for example, Vitaly Vorotnikov (one of those who initially approved of Nina Andreyeva's article) later wrote that in Politburo meetings he often had doubts about the reforms Gorbachev was advocating, but 'in the end I often yielded to the logic of his conviction', adding: 'In that lies my guilt.' See Vorotnikov, *A bylo eto tak . . . Iz dnevnika chlena Politbyuro TsK KPSS* (Sovet veteranov knigoizdaniya, Moscow, 1995), p. 264. • **18.** 'Vstrecha s pervymi sekretaryami obkomov, 11 aprelya 1988 goda', Gorbachev Foundation Archives. • **19.** 'Vstrecha Gorbacheva s tret'ey gruppoy sekretarey obkomov, 18 aprelya 1988 goda', Gorbachev Foundation Archives. • **20.** Ibid. On the significance of labelling the socio-political order as a 'command-administrative system', see T.H. Rigby, 'Some Concluding Observations', in Archie Brown (ed.), *The Demise of Marxism-Leninism in Russia* (Palgrave Macmillan, Basingstoke, 2004), pp. 207–23, at p. 213; and Archie Brown, *Seven Years that Changed the World: Perestroika in Perspective* (Oxford University Press, Oxford, 2007), pp. 287–8. • **21.** See, for example, the extracts from Anatoliy Chernyaev's notes of the Politburo meeting of 19 May 1988, in *V Politbyuro TsK KPSS . . .*, pp. 361–3. • **22.** 'V kabinete u Gorbacheva na Staroy ploshchadi, iyun' 1988 goda (Zapis' Shakhnazarova)', Gorbachev Foundation Archives. • **23.** Jack F. Matlock, Jr, *Autopsy on an Empire: The American Ambassador's Account of the Collapse of the Soviet Union* (Random House, New York, 1995), pp. 121–2. • **24.** Michael R. Beschloss and Strobe Talbott, *At the Highest Levels: The Inside Story of the End of the Cold War* (Little, Brown, London, 1993), p. 9. • **25.** George P. Shultz, *Turmoil and Triumph: My Years as Secretary of State* (Scribner's, New York, 1993), pp. 1103–4. • **26.** 'Politbyuro, 6 iyunya 1988 goda', notes of Politburo meeting of 6 June 1988 of Anatoliy Chernyaev, Gorbachev Foundation Archives. • **27.** The figures are those of the most reliable survey research organization in the last years of the Soviet Union – the All-Union (later All-Russian) Centre for the Study of Public Opinion. These data on Gorbachev's popularity during his years in office were supplied to me by the late Professor Yuriy Levada, the centre's director, in 1993. • **28.** Don Oberdorfer, *The Turn: How the Cold War came to an end. The United States and the Soviet Union, 1983–1990* (Jonathan Cape, London, 1992), p. 294. • **29.** Ibid. • **30.** *XIX Vsesoyuznaya konferentsiya Kommunisticheskoy partii Sovetskogo Soyuza*, Vol. 1, pp. 223–8, at p. 224. • **31.** Mikhail Gorbachev, *Ponyat' perestroyku . . . pochemu eto vazhno seychas* (Al'pina, Moscow, 2006), p. 27. • **32.** *XIX Vsesoyuznaya konferentsiya Kommunisticheskoy* *partii Sovetskogo Soyuza*, Vol. 2, pp. 20–3. • 33. Ibid., pp. 55–62. • 34. Archie Brown, *The Gorbachev Factor* (Oxford University Press, Oxford, 1996), pp. 183–4 and 360–1. • 35. Stephen White, Richard Rose and Ian McAllister, *How Russia Votes* (Chatham House, Chatham, NJ, 1997), p. 28. • 36. Timothy J. Colton, *Yeltsin: A Life* (Basic Books, New York, 2008), p. 166. • 37. Matlock, *Autopsy on an Empire*, p. 210 (italics in original). • 38. Nikolay Ryzhkov, *Perestroyka: Istoriya predatel'stv* (Novosti, Moscow, 1992), p. 291. • 39. *Izvestiya*, 26 May 1989, p. 4. • 40. Survey data on numbers viewing, and on reaction to the debates, were published in *Izvestiya*, 31 May 1989, p. 7, and the same newspaper on 4 June 1989, p. 1. • 41. On the Inter-Regional Group of Deputies, see Michael Urban, with Vyacheslav Igrunov and Sergei Mitrokhin, *The Rebirth of Politics in Russia* (Cambridge University Press, Cambridge, 1997), pp. 159–69. • 42. For a fuller discussion of Gorbachev's changing attitude to 'the leading role of the party', see Brown, *Seven Years that Changed the World*, pp. 306–9. • 43. Edward Kline, Foreword to Andrei Sakharov, *Moscow and Beyond, 1986 to 1989* (Knopf, New York, 1991), pp. xiv–xvii. • 44. For a good analysis of the breakdown of authority within the command economy, see Stephen Whitefield, *Industrial Power and the Soviet State* (Clarendon Press, Oxford, 1993), esp. pp. 206–51. • 45. Archie Brown, 'Gorbachev, Lenin, and the Break with Leninism', *Demokratizatsiya: The Journal of Post-Soviet Democratization*, Vol. 15, No. 2, 2007, pp. 230–44. • 46. Gorbachev, *Ponyat' perestroyku*, p. 373.

26 The End of Communism in Europe

1. Mikhail Gorbachev, *Ponyat' perestroyku . . . pochemu eto vazhno seychas* (Al'pina, Moscow, 2006), p. 70. • 2. M.S. Gorbachev, in *XIX Vsesoyuznaya konferentsiya Kommunisticheskoy partii Sovetskogo Soyuza: Stenograficheskiy otchet* (Politizdat, Moscow, 1988), pp. 42–3. • 3. M.S. Gorbachev, 'Vystuplenie v Organizatsii Ob''edinennykh Natsiy, 7 dekabrya 1988 goda', in Gorbachev, *Izbrannye rechi i stat'i*, Vol. 7 (Politizdat, Moscow, 1990), pp. 184–202, at pp. 198–9; and Pavel Palazchenko, *My Years with Gorbachev and Shevardnadze: The Memoir of a Soviet Interpreter* (Pennsylvania State University Press, University Park, 1997), p. 370. • 4. 'Politbyuro 24 noyabrya 1988 goda', Chernyaev notes, Gorbachev Foundation Archives, Moscow. • 5. Palazchenko, *My Years with Gorbachev and Shevardnadze*, p. 370. • 6. Gorbachev, *Izbrannye rechi i stat'i*, Vol. 7, p. 188. • 7. Ibid. • 8. Vladislav M. Zubok, 'New Evidence on the "Soviet Factor" in the Peaceful Revolutions of 1989', in *Cold War International History Project Bulletin*, No. 12/13, 2001, pp. 5–14, at p. 9; and Andrei Grachev, *Gorbachev's Gamble: Soviet Foreign Policy and the End of the Cold War* (Polity, Cambridge, 2008), pp. 166–7. • 9. Memorandum from Shakhnazarov to Gorbachev in advance of the Politburo meeting of 6 October 1988. See Georgiy Shakhnazarov, *Tsena svobody: Reformatsiya Gorbacheva glazami ego pomoshchnika* (Rossika Zevs, Moscow, 1993), pp. 367–9. • 10. For numerous examples of Soviet political and especially military calls in 1989 for a hard line to be taken over Eastern Europe, see Mark Kramer, 'The Collapse of East European Communism and the Repercussions within the Soviet Union (Part 3)', *Journal of Cold War Studies*, Vol. 7, No. 1, Winter 2005, pp. 3–96. • 11. 'Politbyuro, 13 aprelya 1989 goda', Chernyaev notes, Gorbachev Foundation Archives. • 12. Roger Gough, *A Good*

Comrade: János Kádár, Communism and Hungary (Tauris, London, 2006), p. 201. • **13**. Ibid., p. 203. • **14**. Ibid., pp. 1 and 254–7. • **15**. Ibid., p. 251. • **16**. David Stark and László Bruszt, *Postsocialist Pathways: Transforming Politics and Property in East Central Europe* (Cambridge University Press, Cambridge, 1998), pp. 20–2; and R.J. Crampton, *Eastern Europe in the Twentieth Century – and After* (Routledge, London, 2nd ed., 1997), pp. 380–1. • **17**. Rudolf L. Tőkés, *Hungary's Negotiated Revolution: Economic reform, social change and political succession* (Cambridge University Press, Cambridge, 1996), p. 299. • **18**. Indeed, Gorbachev, although he did not attempt to interfere with Hungarian developments, expressed his disagreement with Pozsgay's evaluation of 1956 in a conversation in early 1989 with Hungarian prime minister Németh. After Németh had said, 'We should not eradicate everything with one stroke, because what we achieved is worth noting', Gorbachev responded: 'I believe that Pozsgay's statements are quite extremist in this respect. The events of 1956 indeed started with the dissatisfaction of the people. Later, however, the events escalated into a counterrevolution and bloodshed. This cannot be overlooked.' See 'Document No. 2: Record of Conversation between President M.S. Gorbachev and Miklós Németh, Member of the HSWP CC Politburo, Chairman of the Council of Ministers of the People's Republic of Hungary, Moscow, 3 March 1989', in *Cold War International History Project Bulletin*, No. 12/13, 2001, pp. 76–7. • **19**. Ivan T. Berend, *Central and Eastern Europe, 1944–1993: Detour from the periphery to the periphery* (Cambridge University Press, Cambridge, 1996), p. 274. • **20**. Tőkés, *Hungary's Negotiated Revolution*, p. 299. • **21**. Crampton, *Eastern Europe in the Twentieth Century*, pp. 392–3. • **22**. On Glemp, see George Weigel, *The Final Revolution: The Resistance Church and the Collapse of Communism* (Oxford University Press, New York, 1992), p. 147. • **23**. Timothy Garton Ash, *The Magic Lantern: The Revolution of '89 Witnessed in Warsaw, Budapest, Berlin, and Prague* (Random House, New York, 1990), p. 33; and Crampton, *Eastern Europe in the Twentieth Century*, p. 392. • **24**. Garton Ash, *The Magic Lantern*, pp. 45–6. • **25**. Crampton, *Eastern Europe in the Twentieth Century*, p. 392. • **26**. Berend, *Central and Eastern Europe, 1944–1993*, p. 266. • **27**. Mary Fulbrook, *Anatomy of a Dictatorship: Inside the GDR 1949–1989* (Oxford University Press, Oxford, 1995), p. 205. • **28**. Cited by Charles S. Maier, *Dissolution: The Crisis of Communism and the End of East Germany* (Princeton University Press, Princeton, 1997), p. 50. • **29**. Fulbrook, *Anatomy of a Dictatorship*, pp. 206–15. • **30**. Maier, *Dissolution*, pp. 170–2. • **31**. Fulbrook, *Anatomy of a Dictatorship*, p. 206. • **32**. Ibid., pp. 246–7. • **33**. Mark Kramer, 'The Collapse of East European Communism and the Repercussions within the Soviet Union (Part 1)', *Journal of Cold War Studies*, Vol. 5, No. 4, 2003, pp. 178–256, at pp. 185–6; and Hans-Hermann Hertle, 'The Fall of the Wall: The Unintended Self-Dissolution of East Germany's Ruling Regime', *Cold War International History Project Bulletin*, No. 12/13, 2001, pp. 131–40, at p. 133. • **34**. Kramer, 'The Collapse of East European Communism', p. 186 (italics added). • **35**. Garton Ash, *The Magic Lantern*, p. 65. • **36**. Fulbrook, *Anatomy of a Dictatorship*, pp. 257–60. • **37**. Hertle, 'The Fall of the Wall', pp. 136–7. • **38**. Ibid., p. 138. • **39**. Fulbrook, *Anatomy of a Dictatorship*, p. 289. • **40**. Hertle, 'The Fall of the Wall', p. 140. • **41**. Garton Ash, *The Magic Lantern*, p. 73. • **42**. Frederick Taylor, *The Berlin Wall 13 August 1961–9 November 1989* (Bloomsbury, London, 2007), pp. 588–90. • **43**. Hertle, 'The Fall of the Wall', pp. 139–40. In addition to the excellent study by Maier, *Dissolution*, significant books on the end of the GDR and the unification of Germany include Timothy Garton Ash, *In Europe's Name: Germany and the Divided Continent* (Jonathan Cape, London, 1993); and Philip Zelikow and Condoleezza Rice, *Germany Unified and Europe Transformed: A Study in Statecraft* (Harvard University Press, Cambridge, Mass., 1995). • **44**. See H. Gordon Skilling, *Charter 77 and Human Rights in Czechoslovakia* (Allen & Unwin, London, 1981). • **45**. H. Gordon Skilling, *Czechoslovakia's Interrupted Revolution* (Princeton University Press, Princeton, 1976), p. 823. • **46**. Crampton, *Eastern Europe in the Twentieth Century*, pp. 384–5. • **47**. Mikhail Gorbachev and Zdeněk Mlynář, *Conversations with Gorbachev: On Perestroika, the Prague Spring, and the Crossroads of Socialism* (Columbia University Press, New York, 2002), p. 85. • **48**. Jacques Lévesque, *The Enigma of 1989: The USSR and the Liberation of Eastern Europe* (University of California Press, Berkeley, 1997), p. 182. • **49**. Ibid., p. 186. • **50**. Vladimir Tismaneanu, *Reinventing Politics: Eastern Europe from Stalin to Havel* (Free Press, New York, 1992), p. 217. • **51**. Crampton, *Eastern Europe in the Twentieth Century*, pp. 396–7. • **52**. R.J. Crampton, *A Concise History of Bulgaria* (Cambridge University Press, Cambridge, 2nd ed., 2005), pp. 212–15. • **53**. Juan J. Linz and Alfred Stepan, *Problems of Democratic Transition and Consolidation: Southern Europe, South America, and Post-Communist Europe* (Johns Hopkins University Press, Baltimore, 1996), p. 349. • **54**. Mikhail Gorbachev, *Zhizn' i reformy* (Novosti, Moscow, 1995), Vol. 2, p. 392. • **55**. Tismaneanu, *Reinventing Politics*, pp. 232–3. • **56**. Ibid., p. 233. • **57**. Lévesque, *The Enigma of 1989*, p. 198. • **58**. Tismaneanu, *Reinventing Politics*, pp. 235–6. • **59**. Berend, *Central and Eastern Europe, 1944–1993*, p. 287. • **60**. Nesti Gjeluci, 'Albania: A History of Isolation', in Teresa Rakowska-Harmstone and Piotr Dutkiewicz (eds.), *New Europe: The Impact of the First Decade*, Vol. 2 (Collegium Civitas Press, Warsaw, 2006), pp. 13–47, at pp. 26–7. • **61**. Crampton, *Eastern Europe in the Twentieth Century*, p. 404. • **62**. Gjeluci, 'Albania: A History of Isolation', pp. 27–8. • **63**. One could even add the party organizations of the two 'autonomous regions' of Kosovo and Vojvodina, although their status was lower than that of the republics. • **64**. Berend, *Central and Eastern Europe, 1944–1993*, p. 293. • **65**. Robin Okey, *The Demise of Communist East Europe: 1989 in Context* (Hodder Arnold, London, 2004), p. 144. • **66**. Misha Glenny, *The Rebirth of History: Eastern Europe in the Age of Democracy* (Penguin, London, 1990), pp. 121–3. • **67**. Leslie Holmes, *Post-Communism* (Polity, Cambridge, 1997), p. 96. • **68**. Okey, *The Demise of Communist East Europe*, p. 151. • **69**. Holmes, *Post-Communism*, p. 98.

27 The Break-up of the Soviet State

1. Anatol Lieven, *The Baltic Revolution: Estonia, Latvia, Lithuania and the Path to Independence* (Yale University Press, New Haven, 2nd ed., 1994), pp. 82 and 106. • **2**. See Bohdan Krawchenko, *Social Change and National Consciousness in Twentieth Century Ukraine* (Macmillan, London, 1985). • **3**. Charles King, *The Ghost of Freedom: A History of the Caucasus* (Oxford University Press, New York, 2008), pp. 178–9. • **4**. On the large issue of Russian statehood, in historical context, see Vera Tolz, *Inventing the Nation: Russia* (Hodder, London, 2001); Geoffrey Hosking, *Russia: People and Empire 1552–1917* (HarperCollins, London, 1997); and Hosking, *Rulers and Victims: The Russians in the Soviet Union* (Harvard University Press, Cambridge, Mass., 2006). • **5**. I have noted elsewhere the various reasons why Gorbachev chose the path of indirect election to the newly-created presidency in 1990 and also why I consider this to have been a strategic error. See Archie Brown, *The Gorbachev Factor* (Oxford University Press, Oxford, 1996), pp. 198–205; and Brown, *Seven Years that Changed the World: Perestroika in Perspective* (Oxford University Press, Oxford, 2007), pp. 209–10. Gorbachev himself came round some years after the Soviet Union had ceased to exist to the view that he should have taken the risk of calling a general election for the Soviet presidency. The risk was not just of losing the election, but of bringing forward the date of a hard-line coup by conservative Communists against him. For Gorbachev's retrospective views on the issue, see Mikhail Gorbachev, *Ponyat' perestroyku ... pochemu eto vazhno seychas* (Al'pina, Moscow, 2006), p. 374. • **6**. *Reytingi Borisa Yel'tsina i Mikhaila Gorbacheva po 10-bal'noy shkale* (VTsIOM, Moscow, 1993). • **7**. Mark Kramer, 'The Collapse of East European Communism and the Repercussions within the Soviet Union (Part 2)', *Journal of Cold War Studies*, Vol. 6, No. 4, 2004, pp. 3–64, at p. 59. • **8**. The system adopted in the Soviet republics, carried over into the post-Communist states, was not a purely presidential system, but what political scientists call 'semi-presidentialism'. As in Fifth Republic France, there was, and is, a dual executive – a president *und* a prime minister. The distribution of power between these two branches of the executive can vary greatly from one semi-presidential system to another. In post-Soviet Russia and, still more, in the former Central Asian republics of the Soviet Union, what emerged was a highly presidentialized form of semi-presidentialism. See Robert Elgie, 'A Fresh Look at Semipresidentialism: Variations on a Theme', *Journal of Democracy*, Vol. 16, No. 3, July 2005, pp. 98–112, esp. p. 104. • **9**. Kramer, 'The Collapse of East European Communism and the Repercussions within the Soviet Union (Part 2)', p. 58. • **10**. Cf. Hosking, *Rulers and Victims*, p. 377; Timothy J. Colton, *Yeltsin: A Life* (Basic Books, New York, 2008), p. 178; Kramer, 'The Collapse of East European Communism and the Repercussions within the Soviet Union (Part 2)', p. 12; and M. Steven Fish, *Democracy from Scratch: Opposition and Regime in the New Russian Revolution* (Princeton University Press, Princeton, 1995), p. 109. • **11**. Hosking, *Rulers and Victims*, p. 377. • **12**. Ibid., p. 378. • **13**. Leon Aron, *Yeltsin: A Revolutionary Life* (HarperCollins, London, 2000), p. 377. • **14**. Colton, *Yeltsin*, p. 184. • **15**. As Gorbachev later observed: 'The presence of a strong conservative tendency in the Politburo, and in general in the higher echelons of the party, led to the fact that not infrequently we were late in taking urgent decisions' (*Ponyat' perestroyku*, p. 374). • **16**. Cited in Yegor Gaidar, *Collapse of an Empire: Lessons for Modern Russia* (Brookings Institution, Washington DC, 2007), p. 141. • **17**. Ibid. • **18**. *Perekhod k rynku: Kontseptsiya i Programma* (Arkhangel'skoe izdatel'stvo, Moscow, 1990), p. 3. • **19**. Colton, *Yeltsin*, pp. 219–20. • **20**. Brown, *The Gorbachev Factor*, p. 152. • **21**. Yevgeny Yasin, 'The Parade of Market Transformation Programs', in Michael Ellman and Vladimir Kontorovich (eds.), *The Destruction of the Soviet Economic System: An Insiders' History* (M.E. Sharpe, Armonk, 1998), pp. 228–37, at p. 235. • **22**. Ibid., p. 237. • **23**. Gorbachev, *Ponyat' perestroyku*, pp. 209–10. • **24**. 'The Tbilisi Massacre, April 1989: Documents', in *Cold War International History Project Bulletin*, No. 12/13, 2001, pp. 31–48. • **25**. Eduard Shevardnadze, *The Future Belongs to Freedom* (Sinclair-Stevenson, London, 1991), pp. 192–5; Brown, *The Gorbachev Factor*, pp. 264–7; and Kramer, 'The Collapse of East

European Communism and the Repercussions within the Soviet Union (Part 2)', pp. 27–32. • **26**. Anatoliy Sobchak, *Khozhdenie vo vlast': Rasskaz o rozhdenii parlamenta* (Novosti, Moscow, 1991), p. 97. • **27**. 'Politbyuro 13 aprelya 1989 goda', Chernyaev notes, Gorbachev Foundation Archives. • **28**. 'Zasedanie Politbyuro TsK KPSS ot 16 noyabrya 1990 goda', Hoover Institution Archives, Fond 89, 1.003, opis 42, file 30. • **29**. Ibid., p. 11. • **30**. Ibid., p. 25. • **31**. Ibid. • **32**. Kramer, 'The Collapse of East European Communism and the Repercussions within the Soviet Union (Part 2)', pp. 46–8. • **33**. See, for example, George Bush and Brent Scowcroft, *A World Transformed* (Knopf, New York, 1998), pp. 496–7; and Jack F. Matlock, Jr, *Autopsy on an Empire: The American Ambassador's Account of the Collapse of the Soviet Union* (Random House, New York, 1995), pp. 454–60. • **34**. Aleksandr Yakovlev, *Sumerki* (Materik, Moscow, 2003), p. 520. • **35**. Aleksandr Dugin, 'Perestroyka po-evraziyski: upushchennyy shans', in V.I. Tolstykh (ed.), *Perestroyka: Dvadtsat' let spustya* (Russkiy put', Moscow, 2005), pp. 88–97, at p. 96. • **36**. Kramer, 'The Collapse of East European Communism and the Repercussions within the Soviet Union (Part 2)', p. 20. • **37**. Mark Kramer, 'The Collapse of East European Communism and the Repercussions within the Soviet Union (Part 1)', *Journal of Cold War Studies*, Vol. 5, No. 4, 2003, pp. 178–256, at pp. 218–19. • **38**. Ibid., p. 222. • **39**. Mikhail Gorbachev and Zdeněk Mlynář, *Conversations with Gorbachev: On Perestroika, the Prague Spring, and the Crossroads of Socialism* (Columbia University Press, New York, 2002), p. 132. • **40**. For a fuller account of this whole process, see my chapter, 'The National Question, the Coup, and the Collapse of the Soviet Union', in Brown, *The Gorbachev Factor*, pp. 252–305. • **41**. Mikhail Gorbachev, *The August Putsch: The Truth and the Lessons* (HarperCollins, London, 1991), Appendix C, 'The Crimea Article', pp. 97–127, at p. 111. • **42**. Ibid., p. 23. • **43**. V.G. Stepankov and E.K. Lisov, *Kremlevskiy zagovor* (Ogonek, Moscow, 1992), p. 14. The authors were at the time procurator general and deputy procurator general of Russia. They quote from the transcripts of the interrogation of the putschists. Later the coup plotters were to change their story and suggest that Gorbachev was not really under house arrest and could have left Foros at any time. Some of Yeltsin's supporters were happy to spread that calumny and a number of Westerners were gullible enough to believe it. For more detailed analyses of its absurdity, see Anatoly Chernyaev, *My Six Years with Gorbachev* (Pennsylvania State University Press, University Park, 2000), ed. and trans. Robert English and Elizabeth Tucker, 'Afterword to the US Edition', pp. 401–23; and Brown, *Seven Years that Changed the World*, pp. 319–24. • **44**. Colton, *Yeltsin*, p. 198. • **45**. Ibid., pp. 198–9. • **46**. Ibid., pp. 199–200. • **47**. Ibid., p. 201. • **48**. Shakhnazarov, *Tsena svobody: Reformatsiya Gorbacheva glazami ego pomoshchnika* (Rossika Zevs, Moscow, 1993), p. 176. • **49**. The full text of Gorbachev's resignation speech is in Mikhail Gorbachev, *Zhizn' i reformy* (Novosti, Moscow, 1995), Vol. 1, pp. 5–8, and in the abbreviated English-language *Memoirs* (Transworld, London, 1996), pp. xxvi–xxix.

28 Why Did Communism Last so Long?

1. Alec Nove, *Glasnost' In Action: Cultural Renaissance in Russia* (Unwin Hyman, London, 1989), p. 4. • **2**. Ibid. • **3**. Sidney Bloch and Peter Reddaway, *Russia's Political Hospitals:*

The Abuse of Psychiatry in the Soviet Union (Gollancz, London, 1977). • **4.** See Bernard Crick, *George Orwell: A Life* (Penguin, London, 1980); Stephen Ingle, *George Orwell: A Political Life* (Manchester University Press, Manchester, 1993); T.R. Fyvel, *George Orwell: A Personal Memoir* (Hutchinson, London, 1982); and Michael Sheldon, *Orwell: The Authorised Biography* (Heinemann, London, 1991). • **5.** Lenin backwards turned into quite a nice-sounding Russian first name. Stranger personal names emerged in the 1920s, including Barrikada (Barricade) and Iskra, named after Lenin's newspaper (*Iskra* – The Spark). See Sheila Fitzpatrick, *Everyday Stalinism. Ordinary Life in Extraordinary Times: Soviet Russia in the 1930s* (Oxford University Press, New York, 1999), pp. 83–4. (Of these names, Iskra was not really new. It existed both as a first name and as a surname in the Russian Empire, especially Ukraine. One of the associates of the Cossack leader, Ivan Mazepa, was named Iskra. He appears as a character in Tchaikovsky's opera *Mazeppa* (the double 'p' is the conventional English spelling), composed in the early 1880s and set in Ukraine at the beginning of the eighteenth century. However, Iskra was far from being a common name, and its re-emergence in the early Soviet period was in homage to Lenin and the Bolsheviks.) • **6.** Especially illuminating on this topic is Alena Ledeneva, *Russia's Economy of Favours: Blat, Networking and Informal Exchange* (Cambridge University Press, Cambridge, 1998). • **7.** Quoted in ibid., pp. 61–2. • **8.** Ibid., esp. pp. 30–2 and 119–21. • **9.** Alena Ledeneva, '*Blat* and *Guanxi*: Informal Practices in Russia and China', *Contemporary Studies in Society and History*, Vol. 50, No. 1, 2008, pp. 1–27, at p. 6. • **10.** Alec Nove, *The Soviet Economic System* (Unwin Hyman, London, 3rd ed., 1986), p. 95 • **11** Boris Yeltsin, *Against the Grain: An Autobiography* (Jonathan Cape, London, 1990), p. 58. A detailed analysis of the economic role of regional party secretaries was provided by Jerry F. Hough in *The Soviet Prefects: The Local Party Organs in Industrial Decision-Making* (Harvard University Press, Cambridge, Mass., 1969). • **12.** Yegor Gaidar, *Collapse of an Empire: Lessons for Modern Russia* (Brookings Institution, Washington DC, 2007). • **13.** Ibid., esp. pp. 169 and 175–6. • **14.** Ibid., p. 175. • **15.** I disagreed with this fundamentally at the time. See Archie Brown, *Seven Years that Changed the World: Perestroika in Perspective* (Oxford University Press, Oxford, 2007), p. 223. • **16.** Alexander Dallin, 'Causes of the Collapse of the USSR', *Post-Soviet Affairs* (formerly *Soviet Economy*), Vol. 8, No. 4, 1992, pp. 279–302, at pp. 297 and 299. • **17.** Ledeneva, '*Blat* and *Guanxi*: Informal Practices in Russia and China'. • **18.** Ibid., pp. 3 and 9–10. • **19.** Ibid., p. 3. • **20.** Mayfair Mei-hui Yang, 'The Resilience of *Guanxi* and its New Deployments: A Critique of some New *Guanxi* Scholarship', *China Quarterly*, No. 170, 2002, pp. 459–76, at p. 464.

29 What Caused the Collapse of Communism?

1. *Narodnoe khozyaystvo SSSR. Statisticheskiy ezhegodnik* (Gosstatizdat, Moscow, 1956), pp. 193 and 221; and *Narodnoe khozyaystvo SSSR v 1984 godu. Statisticheskiy ezhegodnik* (Finansy i statistiki, Moscow, 1985), pp. 29 and 509. • **2.** The point has been elaborated earlier in this volume, especially in Chapter 23. • **3.** János Kornai, *The Socialist System: The Political Economy of Communism* (Clarendon Press, Oxford, 1992), pp. 292–301. • **4.** Ibid., p. 297. Kornai excludes from his analysis military industry, and that, it should be noted, was the sphere in which Soviet technological innovation was strongest. • 5. Ibid., pp. 140–5. • 6. 'East–West Relations: Papers by Academics', Memorandum from N.H.R.A. Broomfield, 7 September 1983, Foreign Office Papers, RS 013/1 (document obtained under the UK Freedom of Information Act). • 7. For a good account of the Lithuanian independence movement, including the person-alities of Brazauskas and Landsbergis, see Anatol Lieven, *The Baltic Revolution: Estonia, Latvia, Lithuania and the Path to Independence* (Yale University Press, New Haven and London, 2nd ed., 1994). • 8. Eric D. Weitz, *Creating German Communism, 1890–1990: From Popular Protests to Socialist State* (Princeton University Press, Princeton, 1997), pp. 374–5. • 9. As noted, for example, by Adam Roberts, 'International Relations after the Cold War', *International Affairs*, Vol. 84, No. 2, 2008, pp. 335–50. • 10. The terminology 'intrastructural dissent' is used by Alexander Shtromas in *Political Change and Social Development: The Case of the Soviet Union* (Peter Lang, Frankfurt am Main, 1981), pp. 74–82. • 11. As always, it is necessary to make a distinction between the Soviet system and the Soviet state. Notwithstanding the great boost given to national separatism by Boris Yeltsin, a party member for thirty years and a party official for more than two decades, the main drive for national independ-ence, resulting eventually in the break-up of the Soviet state, emanated from the broader society, rather than from within the party, in those republics which most actively pursued separate statehood. • 12. Ludmilla Alexeyeva and Paul Goldberg, *The Thaw Generation: Coming of Age in the Post-Stalin Era* (Little, Brown, Boston, 1990), p. 57. • 13. János Kornai, *By Force of Thought: Irregular Memoirs of an Intellectual Journey* (MIT Press, Cambridge, Mass., 2006), p. 63. • 14. Ibid., p. 64. • 15. See Stephen F. Cohen and Katrina vanden Heuvel, *Voices of Glasnost: Interviews with Gorbachev's Reformers* (Norton, New York, 1989), pp. 39–40. • 16. I have argued else-where that Gorbachev's psychological unwillingness to abandon his lifelong respect for Lenin led him to believe that he was in tune with the thinking of the 'late Lenin' (the Lenin of the NEP period), when in fact he had rejected what was fundamental to Lenin's thinking at any stage of his career as a revolutionary. See Archie Brown, *Seven Years that Changed the World: Perestroika in Perspective* (Oxford University Press, Oxford, 2007), pp. 284–94. • 17. R.A. Safarov, *Obshchestvennoe mnenie i gosudarstvennoe upravlenie* (Yuridicheskaya literatura, Moscow, 1975). Safarov wrote (p. 214): 'The greater the sum of information communicated to the society, the higher is the level of competence of public opinion in matters of control over the government, ministries and executive committees of soviets.' Obviously, he had to exclude the Communist Party, although in the broad sense of government, the party was at the heart of it. • 18. *Conference on Security and Co-operation in Europe Final Act* (HMSO, London, 1975), p. 36 (italics in original). • 19. Safarov was just one of a number of scholars who carried out survey research in the 1960s and 1970s in the Soviet Union, but the most sensitive political questions had to be avoided, and there had to be doubts – which vanished only in the much freer atmosphere of the second half of the 1980s – about how willing citizens were to answer the questions frankly, even though they were promised anonymity. • 20. See Yegor Gaidar, *Collapse of an Empire: Lessons for Modern Russia* (Brookings Institution, Washington DC, 2007), pp. 111–13; and Paul Kennedy, *The Rise and Fall of the Great Powers: Economic Change and Military*

Conflict from 1500 to 2000 (Unwin Hyman, London, 1988), pp. 395–6, 498–500, and 513–14. • **21.** Alec Nove, *The Soviet System in Retrospect: An Obituary Notice* (Fourth Annual W. Averell Harriman Lecture, Columbia University, New York, 1993), p. 31.

30 What's Left of Communism?

1. Robert Skidelsky, 'Crisis-hit Russia must scale down its ambition', *Financial Times*, 31 October 2008, p. 15; and 'Net Capital Outflows at $140 Bln', *Moscow Times*, 1 November 2008, p. 4. • **2.** *Kommersant*, 8 October 2008. • **3.** Although not to be compared with Nepal, another place where the Communist Party retains influence is South Africa, where the CPSA is still a significant element within the increasingly divided ANC. • **4.** Henry S. Rowen, 'When Will the Chinese People be Free?', *Journal of Democracy*, Vol. 18, No. 3, July 2007, pp. 38–52. at p. 42. • **5.** Chris Patten, *What Next? Surviving the Twenty-First Century* (Allen Lane, London, 2008), p. 401. • **6.** Kellee S. Tsai, *Capitalists without Democracy: The Private Sector in Contemporary China* (Cornell University Press, Ithaca, 2007), p. 54. • **7.** Ibid., p. 45. Rowen notes that the 'urban-rural Gini coefficient went from 0.28 in 1991 to 0.46 in 2000'. A higher number means more inequality, and the Chinese figures may be compared with the European average of 0.30 and 0.45 in the USA. • **8.** The figure for China is from an official source and cited in Arch Puddington (ed.), *Freedom in the World 2008: The Annual Survey of Political Rights and Civil Liberties* (Freedom House, New York, 2008), p. 163. The British figure, from the Health and Safety Executive, is reported in the *Financial Times*, 30 October 2008, p. 4. • **9.** My source for the information in this paragraph is a senior and well-connected Chinese Communist Party intellectual. • **10.** David Shambaugh, *China's Communist Party: Atrophy and Adaptation* (Woodrow Wilson Center Press, Washington DC, 2008), p. 81. • **11.** See, for example, Cheng Chen and Rudra Sil, 'Stretching Postcommunism: Diversity, Context, and Comparative Historical Analysis', *Post-Soviet Affairs*, Vol. 23, No. 4, 2007, pp. 275–301. • **12.** Patrick J. Heardon, *The Tragedy of Vietnam* (Pearson Longman, New York, 3rd ed., 2008), p. 194. • **13.** Owen Bennett-Jones, 'Laos: 25 years of communism', 30 December 2000: http://news.bbc.co.uk/1/hi/programmes/from_our_own_correspondent/1092752.stm. • **14.** Reported in Rory Carroll, 'Cuban workers to get bonuses for extra effort', *The Guardian*, 13 June 2008, p. 28. • **15.** Heardon, *The Tragedy of Vietnam*, pp. 178–81. • **16.** Ibid., p. 180. • **17.** Mark Kramer, 'The Collapse of East European Communism and the Repercussions within the Soviet Union (Part 1)', *Journal of Cold War Studies*, Vol. 5, No. 4, 2003, pp. 178–256, at p. 198. • **18.** Cheng Chen and Ji-Yong Lee, 'Making sense of North Korea: "National Stalinism" in comparative-historical perspective', *Communist and Post-Communist Studies*, Vol. 40, No. 4, 2007, pp. 459–75, esp. pp. 461–3. • **19.** Jason Brownlee, *Authoritarianism in an Age of Democratization* (Cambridge University Press, New York, 2007), pp. 204–5. • **20.** Puddington (ed.), *Freedom in the World 2008*, p. 777. • **21.** Rana Mitter, *A Bitter Revolution: China's Struggle with the Modern World* (Oxford University Press, Oxford, 2004), p. 309. • **22.** Chen and Sil, 'Stretching Postcommunism', p. 287. • **23.** Chris Patten, *Not Quite the Diplomat: Home Truths about World Affairs* (Allen Lane, London, 2005), p. 279. • **24.** Ibid. • **25.** Rowen, 'When Will the Chinese People be Free?', p. 41; and Robert J.

Barro and Jong-Whu Lee, 'International data on educational attainment: updates and implications', *Oxford Economic Papers*, 3, 2001, pp. 541–63, at p. 549. The same authors note that in international tests of students in mathematics and science, Asian countries occupy the top three places: Singapore, South Korea and Japan (ibid., p. 555). • **26**. Tianjian Shi, 'Cultural Values and Democracy in the People's Republic of China', *The China Quarterly*, No. 162, 2000, pp. 540–59, at p. 557. • **27**. Dingxin Zhao, 'China's Prolonged Stability and Political Future: same political system, different policies and methods', *Journal of Contemporary China*, Vol. 10 (28), 2001, pp. 427–44. Writing at the beginning of this century, Zhao asked (p. 441): 'What will happen after another 20 years or so when the people who have first-hand experience of the Cultural Revolution have grown old? The people by then may take affluence and stability for granted, and the state will no longer be able to use them to justify its rule.' • **28**. See Lee Kuan Yew and Fareed Zakaria, 'Culture is Destiny: A Conversation with Lee Kuan Yew', *Foreign Affairs*, Vol. 73, No. 2, 1994, pp. 109–26. • **29**. Kim Dae Jung, 'Is Culture Destiny? The Myth of Asia's Anti-Democratic Values', *Foreign Affairs*, Vol. 73, No. 6, November–December, 1994, pp. 189–94. • **30**. See Stephen Whitefield (ed.), *Political Culture and Post-Communism* (Palgrave Macmillan, London, 2005). • **31**. See Yu-tzung Chang, Yun-han Chu and Chong-Min Park, 'Authoritarian Nostalgia in Asia', *Journal of Democracy*, Vol. 18, No. 3, 2007, pp. 66–80. The authors suggest (p. 78) that 'the economic and geopolitical rise of China over the last decade' has made the regional environment 'more hospitable for nondemocracies'. • **32**. *Financial Times*, 4 November 2008, p. 12. • **33**. Howard Fast, *The Naked God: The Writer and the Communist Party* (Bodley Head, London, 1958), p. 24. • **34**. Ibid., pp. 26–8. • **35**. Ibid., p. 26. • **36**. Milovan Djilas, *Wartime* (Harcourt Brace Jovanovich, New York, 1977), p. 450. • **37**. Ibid. • **38**. Mikhail Gorbachev, *Ponyat' perestroyku. Pochemu eto vazhno seychas* (Al'pina, Moscow, 2006), pp. 18 and 25. • **39**. Robert A. Dahl, *On Democracy* (Yale University Press, New Haven, 1998), pp. 3 and 180. • **40**. Ibid., p. 188.

Picture Credits

Index